STUDIES IN RESOURCE ALLOCATION PROCESSES

Studies in

Resource Allocation Processes

EDITED BY

KENNETH J. ARROW
James Bryant Conant University Professor, Harvard University

LEONID HURWICZ
Regents' Professor of Economics, University of Minnesota

CAMBRIDGE UNIVERSITY PRESS
Cambridge
London · New York · Melbourne

Published by the Syndics of the Cambridge University Press
The Pitt Building, Trumpington Street, Cambridge CB2 1RP
Bentley House, 200 Euston Road, London NW1 2DB
32 East 57th Street, New York, NY 10022, USA
296 Beaconsfield Parade, Middle Park, Melbourne 3206, Australia

First published 1977

Printed in the United States of America

Library of Congress Cataloging in Publication Data

Arrow, Kenneth Joseph, 1921-
Studies in resource allocation processes.

Some of the studies prepared in cooperation with other authors.

Includes index.
1. Economics, Mathematical – Addresses, essays, lectures.
2. Mathematical optimization – Addresses, essays, lectures.
I. Hurwicz, Leonid, joint author. II. Title. III. Title: Resource allocation processes.
HB135.A79   330′.01′51   76-9171

ISBN 0 521 21522 6

CONTENTS

PREFACE

This book draws together a long series of papers by the two senior authors, alone and in collaboration with each other and with other friends and colleagues, to whose thinking and stimulation we are grateful. Both of us have had a strong primary concern with the workings of the economic system as a mechanism for achieving the optimal allocation of resources. The theme is of course an old one in economic thought; its importance was especially reinforced to us through our teachers, Harold Hotelling and Oskar Lange, and our colleague, Jacob Marschak. The very concept of optimization with resource constraints links the theory with the classical mathematical theory of constrained optimization and the more modern versions of so-called mathematical programming, where emphasis has been placed on inequality constraints.

The important property of the market as a resource allocation mechanism is its decentralization. It has always been assumed in the mainstream of economic theory, though frequently only implicitly, that the transmission of detailed information about tastes or technology is costly and that there is a virtue to systems in which decisions are made at the point where the information already existed. This desire for decentralization has, however, to be reconciled with the need for balance in the economy as a whole, most especially, in the need to respect limitations on the overall availability of resources. The mathematical characterizations of constrained optima, at least in the Lagrangian formulation and its generalizations, suggests the possibility of decentralization. The optimum position can, with the aid of certain auxiliary variables, be sustained as an equilibrium among separate agents, each having access to a different pool of information.

However, the question arises whether this equilibrium can be approximated by a series of steps each of which requires very limited interchanges of information. It was this question that the two authors began to study in the summer of 1951 at the RAND Corporation. Our interest was stimulated by some results of Paul Samuelson on market-like approximations to the solution of linear programming problems, published much later. (P. A. Samuelson, "Market Mechanisms and Maximization," in J. Stiglitz (ed.), *The Collected Scientific Papers of Paul A. Samuelson*, Vol. 1. Cambridge, Mass., and London: The M.I.T. Press, 1966, pp. 425-92). We showed that gradient methods applied in a natural way to the Kuhn-Tucker saddle-point characterization of constrained optima gave rise to a suitable decentralized system of approximations; this work is summarized in Part II.4 in this volume and was developed at greater length in a book, K. J. Arrow, L. Hurwicz, and H. Uzawa, *Studies in Linear and Nonlinear Programming*. Stanford, Calif.: Stanford Univ. Press, 1958, Chapters 6, 8, and 11. It was further observed that with a suitable modification, a somewhat decentralized system of approximations could be developed even for nonconcave problems (for example, those with increasing returns), although only local stability was demonstrable (see the first article, and, for a later generalization, the second article in Part II.5). A general survey of these results together with a detailed examination of their economic implications appears in Part II.1; a particular reinterpretation with regard to the internal operation of a firm is developed in Part II.3.

Although most of the work was dynamic, that is, the stability theory of approximations to a constrained maximum, the Kuhn–Tucker theorem was extended by the authors and others in two directions (Part II.2); a weaker version of the so-called constraint qualification, a condition on the constraint set needed for the validity of the Kuhn–Tucker–Lagrange criteria, and an extension of the sufficiency theorems from the case where the maximand and constraint functions were concave to that where they are quasi-concave. In a somewhat different direction, the convexity of the constraint sets arising in economies with production was shown to hold approximately when there are many firms even if each has a nonconvex production possibility set (third article in Part II.5).

So far the economic systems discussed here have had a single goal, as embodied in a single maximand. But economic theory and the real world have long been concerned with economies with multiple objectives, specifically, the welfares of each of the consumers. The analogs of the dynamic processes for single-objective economies are precisely the supply-and-demand models familiar from the stability theory of the competitive economy. The stability concept used has traditionally been local. The articles in Part III.4 are extensions of earlier work in that area, particularly dealing with stability criteria that are independent of the speeds of adjustment on each of the separate markets. However, they also deal with supply-and-demand relations in which expectations of future prices as well as present prices are variables and the expectations are formed in one way or another as extrapolations from their previous time path. In Part III.5, traditional supply-and-demand theory is extended to the situation where some of the relations are shifting in time, a problem that arose in the interpretation of a particular "shortage."

The *global* stability of the competitive economy was first studied in the articles appearing in Part III.1. The local theory concerned itself with showing conditions under which, starting in the neighborhood of an equilibrium, the dynamic system would lead to convergence to the equilibrium; global stability asked the same question for any starting point. A number of sufficient conditions for global stability results were obtained at that time. The mathematical techniques were based on a method of Liapunov for establishing stability.

One of the leading sufficient conditions is gross substitutability. A weakened version is shown to be sufficient in the articles of Part III.2; the second of these articles also deals with nonlinear price adjustment and with demand affected by expected prices. It, therefore, provides a global generalization of the local analysis in the second article of Part III.4.

Closely related to these problems is the stability of equilibrium points in *n*-person games (see Part III.3). If each individual player adjusts his strategy according to a gradient method on the assumption that the strategies of all other players remain unchanged, the resulting dynamic process is shown to converge under certain conditions. Stability under conditions of oligopoly is a special case.

The supply-and-demand model takes as axiomatic that the price on any market responds to the difference in supply and demand. Article III.6 is a discursive attempt to provide a deeper foundation for that assumption in the usual terms of economic behavior.

Hurwicz has been especially concerned over the years with a more general formulation of the adjustment dynamics of decentralized systems. He has sought to place the specific approximation systems, such as the foregoing, in a framework in terms of which alternative methods can be developed and some comparisons made. The basic concepts are expressed in Part IV. A setting of most of the work reported in this volume in a wider perspective appears in Hurwicz's Ely lecture appearing here as Part I.

Finally, the Appendix contains a joint paper on the foundations of decision-making under uncertainty; an axiom system is developed that yields different implications than the more usual ones leading to subjective probability.

The senior authors worked, separately and together, on the papers reproduced in this volume at many institutions: the RAND Corporation, the Cowles Commission for Research in Economics at the University of Chicago, Stanford University, the University of Minnesota, the Center for Advanced Study in the Behavioral Sciences, Cornell University, and Harvard University; we are grateful for the hospitality of these institutions. We also wish to thank our collaborators, H. David Block, William M. Capron, Alain C. Enthoven, F. J. Gould, Stephen M. Howe, Maurice McManus, Marc Nerlove, and Hirofumi Uzawa, for the joy of working with them and their gracious permission to reprint articles here.

Kenneth J. Arrow
Leonid Hurwicz

ACKNOWLEDGMENTS FOR REPRINTED ARTICLES

K. J. Arrow. "Toward a theory of price adjustment." In M. Abramovitz et al., *The Allocation of Economic Resources*. Stanford: Stanford University Press, 1959, pp. 41–51.

K. J. Arrow. "Price-quantity adjustments in multiple markets with rising demands." In K. J. Arrow, S. Karlin, and P. Suppes (eds.), *Mathematical Methods in the Social Sciences 1959*. Stanford: Stanford University Press, 1960, pp. 3–16.

K. J. Arrow. "Optimization, decentralization, and internal pricing in business firms." In *Contributions to Scientific Research in Management*. Western Data Processing Center, Graduate School of Business Administration, University of California at Los Angeles, 1960, pp. 9–18.

K. J. Arrow. "Stability independent of adjustment speed." In G. Horwich and P. A. Samuelson (eds.), *Trade, Stability, and Macroeconomics*. New York and London: Academic Press, 1974, pp. 181–202.

K. J. Arrow, H. D. Block, and L. Hurwicz. "On the stability of competitive equilibrium II." *Econometrica*, 27 (1959), 82–109.

K. J. Arrow and W. M. Capron. "Dynamic shortages and price rises: the engineer-scientist case." *Quarterly Journal of Economics*, 63 (1959), 292–308.

K. J. Arrow and A. C. Enthoven. "Quasi-concave programming." *Econometrica*, 29 (1961), 779–800.

K. J. Arrow, F. J. Gould, and S. M. Howe. "A general saddle-point result for constrained optimization." *Mathematical Programming*, 5 (1973), 225–34.

K. J. Arrow and L. Hurwicz. "Reduction of constrained maxima to saddle-point problems." In J. Neyman (ed.), *Proceedings of the Third Berkeley Symposium on Mathematical Statistics and Probability*. Berkeley and Los Angeles: University of California Press, 1956. V, 1–20.

K. J. Arrow and L. Hurwicz. "Gradient methods for constrained maxima." *Operations Research*, 5 (1957), 258–65.

K. J. Arrow and L. Hurwicz. "On the stability of competitive equilibrium I." *Econometrica*, 26 (1958), 522–52.

K. J. Arrow and L. Hurwicz. "Competitive stability under weak gross substitutability: the Euclidean distance approach." *International Economic Review*, (1960); 38–49.

K. J. Arrow and L. Hurwicz. "Decentralization and computation in resource allocation." In R. W. Pfouts (ed.), *Essays in Economics and Econometrics*. Chapel Hill: University of North Carolina Press, 1960, pp. 34–104.

K. J. Arrow and L. Hurwicz. "Some remarks on the equilibria of economic systems." *Econometrica*, 28 (1960); 640–46.

K. J. Arrow and L. Hurwicz. "Stability of the gradient process in n-person games." *Journal of the Society for Industrial and Applied Mathematics*, 8 (1960), 280–94.

K. J. Arrow and L. Hurwicz. "Competitive stability under weak gross substitutability: nonlinear price adjustment and adaptive expectations." *International Economic Review*, 3 (1962); 233–55.

K. J. Arrow and L. Hurwicz. "An optimality criterion for decision-making under ignorance." In C. F. Carter and J. L. Ford (eds.), *Uncertainty and Expectations in Economics*. Oxford: Basil Blackwell, 1972, pp. 1–11.

K. J. Arrow, L. Hurwicz, and H. Uzawa. "Constraint qualifications in maximization problems." *Naval Research Logistics Quarterly*, 8 (1961), 175–91.

K. J. Arrow and M. McManus. "A note on dynamic stability." *Econometrica*, 26 (1958); 448–54.

K. J. Arrow and M. Nerlove. "A note on expectations and stability." *Econometrica*, 26 (1958); 297–305.

A. C. Enthoven and K. J. Arrow. "A theorem on expectations and the stability of equilibrium." *Econometrica*, 24 (1956); 288–93.

L. Hurwicz. "Optimality and informational efficiency in resource allocation processes." In K. J. Arrow, S. Karlin, and P. Suppes (eds.), *Mathematical Methods in the Social Sciences 1959*. Stanford: Stanford University Press, 1960, pp. 27–46.

L. Hurwicz. "On informationally decentralized systems." In C. B. McGuire and R. Radner (eds.), *Decision and Organization*. Amsterdam and London: North-Holland, 1972, pp. 297–336.

L. Hurwicz. "The design of resource allocation mechanisms." *American Economic Review Papers and Proceedings*, 58 (May, 1973), 1–30.

PART I

General introduction

The design of resource allocation mechanisms

Traditionally, economic analysis treats the economic system as one of the givens. The term "design" in the title is meant to stress that the structure of the economic system is to be regarded as an unknown. An unknown in what problem? Typically, that of finding a system that would be, in a sense to be specified, superior to the existing one. The idea of searching for a better system is at least as ancient as Plato's *Republic*, but it is only recently that tools have become available for a systematic, analytical approach to such search procedures. This new approach refuses to accept the institutional status quo of a particular time and place as the only legitimate object of interest and yet recognizes constraints that disqualify naive utopias.

A wealth of ideas, originating in disciplines as diverse as computer theory, public administration, games, and control sciences, has, in my view, opened up an exciting new frontier of economic analysis. It is the purpose of this paper to survey some of the accomplishments and to consider outstanding unsolved problems and desirable directions for future efforts.

It is not by accident that the terms "analytical" and "institutional" were only a few words apart in the preceding statement of scientific goals of our inquiry. In the past, especially in the nineteenth century, cleavage developed between analysts who tended to focus on the competitive and monopolistic market models and institutionalists who, either as historians or as reformers, felt the need for a broader framework, but found the existing analytical tools inadequate for their purposes. It is perhaps symbolic that a lecture named after "the father of institutional economics in the United States" [66] should provide a forum for a step toward synthesis of the two approaches.

I should make clear that I do not regard Richard T. Ely as a hundred percent kindred spirit. One reason for this may be seen from the following quotation of his views [17] on mathematical economics:

> No mention has been made of the younger "mathematical school" of political economists, of whom the chief representatives are Stanley Jevons . . . and Léon Walras . . . , because it is difficult to see in their mathematico-economical works anything more than a not very successful attempt to develop further the older abstract political economy. Any advance of the science due to the mathematical character of their method has certainly not yet become widely known, and the writer is much inclined to believe that the works which have advocated the application of mathematics to economics

form no essential part of the development of economic literature. Certain unreal conceptions and a few definitions are used as bases for mathematical deductions. [p. 60]

Yet I find much to agree with Ely in his broader scientific objectives. However, I shall not go so far as to propose reinstatement into the bylaws of the American Economic Association the platform provisions which he proposed [18] when the Association was being formed:

> 1. We regard the state as an educational and ethical agency whose positive aid is an indispensable condition of human progress. While we recognize the necessity of individual initiative in industrial life, we hold that the doctrine of *laissez-faire* is unsafe in politics and unsound in morals; and that it suggests an inadequate explanation of the relations between the state and the citizens. [pp. 6–7]

What I do sympathize with in Ely's attitude is the desire to view the economic system as a variable and to go beyond analytical frameworks that were unable to cope with this problem. A sharp statement illustrative of the "activist" point of view of that era (quoted by Ely who, however, characterizes it as too narrow) is the following definition, due to the Belgian Emile de Laveleye, dating from 1882: "Political economy may . . . be defined as the science which determines what laws men ought to adopt in order that they may, with the least possible exertion, procure the greatest abundance of things useful for the satisfaction of their wants, may distribute them justly and consume them rationally." I do feel that Ely underestimated the potential of development of theory (and of mathematical theory in particular) to help in this endeavor; but given the lag of a better part of a century in this development, perhaps he can be forgiven.

In what follows I want to focus on developments that are relatively recent, primarily those of the last two decades, and characterized by at least an attempt at rigorous mathematical formulation. First, however, I want to acknowledge the value of work that preceded the recent period.

In spirit, I regard the Utopians, and Utopian socialists in particular, as the initiators of what one might call an "activist" (as well as critical) attitude toward the social system in general, and the economic system in particular. They were, in a sense, the first systems designers in the social sphere. Marx, Engels, and their followers broke with the Utopian socialists. An unfortunate byproduct was the neglect of problems of resource allocation in the ("historically inevitable") socialist economy of the future, with Kautsky something of an exception. In the late nineteenth century there were, however, nonsocialist (and even antisocialist) economists who tackled the problem in a remarkably objective spirit, among them Pareto, Boehm-Bawerk, and von Wieser.[1] Barone's now famous 1908 paper [9] was at least partly stimulated by Pareto's earlier analysis.

A "second round" of discussion was largely provoked by von Mises' skepticism as to even a theoretical feasibility of rational allocation under socialism.

Oskar Lange's contribution to the debate in the 1930's is well known, but there was a remarkable earlier reply by Jacob Marschak in 1924 [45].

While Lange's line was to be that socialism is as capable of playing the perfectly competitive game as is capitalism, Marschak took the opposite view: capitalism is a world not of perfect competition but of monopolies and cartels, which (in a Schumpeterian spirit) has its good points, especially in the realm of dynamics. Marschak expected similar phenomena under the brand of democratic "socialism" he had in mind and was not depressed by the prospect. He felt that the advantages of imperfect competition would carry over into collectivism. The real issues would be not rational economic calculation, but motivation, stimulation of initiative, and intensity of effort — under an egalitarian system where managers would be democratically elected. (Still, he regarded these problems as less severe than those of "centralistic" socialism.)

In the 1930's, two major lines of development are relevant. One line was the work of Lange, Lerner, and others on resource allocation in a socialist economy, the slightly earlier (1929) paper by F. M. Taylor on trial and error methods, Hotelling's contribution on marginal cost pricing and consumer-producer surplus, and the "new welfare economics" of Hicks, Kaldor, Scitovsky, and others. The other line of development, started in the 1940's, was the mathematization of "classical welfare economics" by Lange [37], Allais [1, 2], Debreu [14, 15], Arrow [4], and Koopmans [34], with the Arrow-Hahn book [5] a recent entry in this series.

I have so far been stressing the ideas oriented toward redesigning the economy of a nation or similar collectivity. But with the enormous growth of private enterprises and governmental bodies, similar issues arise in determining the relationships between the headquarters of a firm and its divisions, or a ministry (department) and its components. Most of the proposed mechanisms are highly relevant in such circumstances, but the team theory model may be particularly appropriate.

There is also a close relationship with information theory and with problems of administrative organization. For linking up resource allocation with information processing and organization, major credit must go to J. Marschak's [46] development of economic theory of information and to Herbert Simon [63] for his work on organization and economic behavior.

Also one should not forget a pioneering effort toward an abstract formalization undertaken by J. B. Kruskal, Jr., and Allen Newell in "A Model for Organization Theory" [36], circulated at Rand Corporation in 1950 but, I believe, never published.

It has been said, only half in jest, that the theory of organization is a field rich in definitions, but short on results in the form of theorems. This is no longer true. There are two categories of results. On the one hand, quite a few specific allocation mechanisms have been invented and their properties, such as feasibility, optimality, and convergence, rigorously established. On the other hand, there are also some more general results, dealing with the possibility or impossibility of various types of decentralized mechanisms, depending on the environments with which they must cope. We shall mention a few of these results, following the sampling of the specific mechanisms and the discussion of a framework required for formulating the more general questions.

I. Specific mechanisms whose properties have been investigated

As promised, we shall now sample, although very incompletely, some of the wealth of specific mechanisms that have been formulated in a rigorous way, mostly during the last two decades – but without forgetting the crucial influences of their less formal predecessors.

We shall confine ourselves to procedures that have been formulated with sufficient precision to avoid ambiguity as to which economic agent says what to whom and when. This makes it possible to determine the informational requirements, as well as convergence and optimality properties.

A major impetus was given to the design of such mechanisms by these developments of the 1940's:

1) activity analysis and linear programming (including the simplex method) – Dantzig, Kantorovitch, Koopmans;

2) game theory, including the iterative solution procedures – von Neumann and Morgenstern, George Brown, Julia Robinson;

3) discoveries concerning the relationships connecting programming (linear or nonlinear), two-person zero sum games, and the long known Lagrange multipliers – Gale, Kuhn, Tucker.

While in economics one deals with goal conflicts due to multiplicity of consumers, linear and nonlinear programming models usually presuppose a single well-defined objective function to be, say, maximized, i.e., a situation corresponding to an economy with a single consumer. So it is not surprising that the mechanisms designed under the influence of programming theory dealt to a large extent with one-objective-function problems and thus failed to face the crucial issue of goal conflict. Nevertheless, one should not underrate their usefulness as a necessary step on the road to the harder multi-objective problem, since the difficulties of the simpler situations do not disappear when goal conflicts are introduced.

We can distinguish two strands here: one, a rather close relative of the programming approach; the other, "team theory" [19-21, 46, 47, 55], more closely related to the theory of statistical inference and decision making. We shall concentrate on the former.

We thus have a situation where there is only one consumer (individual, firm, or even nation) and, hence, only a single utility function to be maximized, but a multiplicity of producers and resource holders. The technological relations

(production functions) and limits of resource availability constitute the constraints subject to which maximization must be carried out.

Two difficulties make the problem nontrivial: calculation and information
transfer. First, consider the calculation of the maximizing values for the variables of the problem. Assuming even that all the relevant information concerning the parameters of the problem is in the hands of a computing agency, this
agency needs a well-defined computational procedure (algorithm) to find
solutions.

For linear economies, the simplex method is such an algorithm. For "smooth"
(nonlinear) unconstrained maximization problems resembling the task of groping
one's way in the dark to the top of a hill, the obvious idea of moving uphill is
embodied in the notion of gradient (or "steepest ascent") processes. Equally evident is the fact that a valley between the spot one is at and the peak of the hill
would cause trouble; hence, the success of gradient procedures depends on the
curvature characteristics of the terrain, a natural requirement being that the hill
be dome-like (technically, a strictly concave function).

A natural extension of the gradient process idea was suggested by the famous
Kuhn-Tucker theorem associating with a constrained maximum a saddle point,
i.e., a maximum–minimum point of the so-called Lagrangean expression; thus
the search for a maximum with respect to certain decision variables was con-
verted into a mixture of maximizing and minimizing tasks to each of which one
could apply the gradient idea (groping upward in terms of the decision variables
and downward with respect to certain auxiliary variables – Lagrange multipliers
to the mathematician, shadow prices to the economist). *Statically*, the Kuhn-
Tucker result required little more than the concavity (not necessarily strict) of
the relevant functions and, hence, was applicable to linear problems as well as
the typical smoothly curved pictures of classical economics (Pareto, Hicks).
But we shall see that dynamics was more troublesome.

Even when there is an algorithm suitable for calculations by an agency to
whom all the data are available, it may be that the information-processing capacity of any one such agency is inadequate because of the size of the problem
(the number and complexity of constraints, objectives, and variables). If there
are several potential information-processing agencies (and here every human
brain qualifies to some extent), we may be saved by devising computing procedures which parcel out the work among them; these are called decomposition algorithms. (In recent years, related problems have been studied in connection
with the design of electronic computer utilization under the label of multi-
processing.)

It should be recalled that one of Hayek's [22, p. 212] chief points in sum-
ming up the state of the debate concerning the feasibility of a centralized
socialist solution was that the number of variables and equations would be "at
least in the hundreds of thousands" and the required equation solving "a task
which, with any of the means known at present, could not be carried out in a
lifetime. Any yet these decisions would . . . have to be made continuously . . . ."

The market-simulation procedure developed by Lange and Lerner may be viewed as an early example of a decomposition algorithm.

From the point of view of the economics of information processing, it is clear that a parceling out of the task may be advantageous even if single agency capacity constraints have not been reached; this may well lower the resource cost and cut down the time required for the completion of the computing process.

But another informational consideration, stressed by Hayek [22, 23], has gained special prominence: the difficulty of placing all the relevant information in the hands of a single agency because information is dispersed throughout the economy. A natural assumption is that, initially, each economic unit has information about itself only: consumers about their respective preferences, producers about their technologies, and resource holders about the resources. An attempt to transfer all this information to a single agency before it starts its calculations is regarded as either impossible (in the sense that much information would be lost) or too costly in relation to the existing accuracy requirements. (One reason for this difficulty is that even the individual units have the required information only in potential form, except for situations corresponding to their past experience: e.g., firms know only certain parts of their production functions. It is easier to use "localized" procedures which require an exploration only of the relevant parts of the individual units' maps; but such localization is impossible if whole maps are to be conveyed to the single computing agency at the beginning of the computing process.)

If the economic units which initially are the only ones with information about themselves are also capable of carrying out calculations, it is natural to seek computing procedures that would both minimize the need for information transfers and also parcel out the tasks of calculation. This is what informationally decentralized procedures are meant to accomplish.

In the 1930's it would have been most natural to start with "smooth" strictly concave economies (diminishing marginal utilities and returns), without kinks or corner solutions. But around 1950, linear models were in fashion. Furthermore, the simplex method was available and proved to be convergent. Since the simplex method, applied to the economy as a whole, lacked informational decentralization, a search for an alternative was bound to occur. For the economist, an obvious candidate was a simulated (perfectly competitive) market process à la Lange, Lerner, and (specifically in the context of a linear economy) the Koopmans model with a helmsman representing the consumer, production managers maximizing profits, and resource custodians adjusting prices according to excess demand.

From a static point of view, the equilibrium of such a process would be optimal. But if the initially proposed process and quantities were "wrong," would there be convergence to equilibrium? To make this question meaningful, one must specify the dynamics of the adjustment process, e.g., by how much prices are to be raised per unit of time given the magnitude of excess demand, etc. A pioneering model of this type is due to Samuelson [58] who postulated a system of differential equations in which prices vary proportionately to excess demand, and resource use rises when low resource prices yield positive profits. He immediately noted that this dynamic system would behave like a frictionless pendulum, i.e., would not converge to an equilibrium position. Whether we are thinking of computations or of designing an economy, we must look further.[2]

Samuelson's discovery posed a challenge: can an informationally decentralized convergent allocation process be designed for linear economies? (Of course, there is also the problem of designing such processes for economies with increasing returns. But here the difficulties are bound to be serious, since the competitive mechanism lacks even the usual static properties.)

One line of attack involves the replacement of the fixed (that is, parametric) price idea by that of a price *schedule* and is applicable not only in the linear (constant returns) case, but also under increasing returns. (See the modified Lagrangean Arrow-Hurwicz approach below.) Another approach, to be discussed first, retains the parametric prices; it grew out of linear programming techniques, with the Dantzig-Wolfe decomposition method [13] its earliest example.

The Dantzig-Wolfe economy has special features which provide scope for the decomposition approach. These are the usual features of a resource allocation model without technological externalities, in which the objective function is a sum of the contributions of the individual units and in which certain resources must be utilized by all units. (Both the objective function and the overall constraints are "additively separable.") The mechanism may be viewed as a dialogue between the producing units (who know their technologies and contributions to the objective function) and a "center" which knows the total resources available. One aspect of the dialogue is that the center proposes tentative resource prices and the producing units develop corresponding profit-maximizing production programs (with prices treated parametrically). In the light of these programs, the center revises the proposed prices. Because of the linear character of the economy, both the center and the producing units can use linear-programming (primal and dual) techniques, and an equilibrium is reached in a finite number of steps. So far, we may regard the algorithm as a variety of the market (parametric price) process. But there is a difference. The final allocation will not necessarily correspond to the final production programs of the producing units. Rather, the center will "order" each producing unit to undertake a program which "mixes" (averages) the final proposal with several previous ones.[3]

As pointed out by Baumol and Fabian [10], the procedure can be extended to situations where constraints pertaining to single producing units are nonlinear, while the overall constraints pertaining to resources needed by all units remain linear. In this case, however, the units must have a computational algorithm for their nonlinear problem since the simplex method can no longer be used. For other nonlinear economies, and especially those with increasing returns, different processes had to be sought.

Before we look at those, however, let us examine a mechanism designed specifically to guide a *linear* economy but in a manner that partly reverses the roles played by the "center" and the "periphery" (the producing units), the process due to Kornai and Lipták [35]. The assumption concerning the economy, as in the Dantzig-Wolfe model, is that of "block angularity," i.e., there are subsets of constraints each pertaining to a given sector and also resource constraints affecting the whole economy. In the dialogue, the center proposes allotments of scarce resources to the various sectors; then each sector responds with shadow prices (marginal rates of substitution) minimizing the value of the allotment subject to sectoral dual constraints (nonprofit condition for every sectoral activity). The center's aim, on the other hand, is to maximize the contributions of the sectors to the objective function, i.e., to maximize the value of the allocated resources at the shadow prices received from the sectors, subject to the limitation of available resource totals.

Taking advantage of the equivalence of linear-programming programs and games, Kornai and Lipták, by structuring the dialogue as a fictitious game, are able to establish convergence to an equilibrium with any desired degree of accuracy, though (unlike in the Dantzig-Wolfe procedure) without reaching the equilibrium in a finite number of steps. In addition to the latter disadvantage, it has also been pointed out [30] that the Kornai-Lipták procedure is not completely informationally decentralized, since each sector's resource sectoral allotments must be large enough ("evaluable") to assure the existence of a feasible solution for that sector.

One advantage claimed for the Kornai-Lipták procedure is that it may be computationally manageable where alternative decomposition algorithms are not. I regret that I have not had an opportunity to look into this question. But another feature of this process is of great interest to the economist. This is the fact that the center, instead of simulating the market as does the Taylor-Lange-Lerner mechanism, specifies quantitative input and output targets or restrictions, while the sectors supply the center with productivity information in the form of shadow prices. This appears more in line with many observed planning practices and thus may provide a useful descriptive model.

There are several other mechanisms, in general designed for nonlinear economies, which are also of the "quantity-guided" type (as distinct from the "price-guided" type), that is, where the center sends out messages concerning quantities (e.g., targets) and the periphery (the producing units, sectors) responds with marginal entities or shadow prices. Informationally, since the center is sending different quantity messages to different sectors, its total signals are of higher dimensionality than in price-guided systems where the same message (price vector) goes out to all sectors. (We must bear in mind that each quantity vector has the same dimension as the price vector.) Whether this difference is significant is somewhat controversial; the negative has been strongly expressed by Marglin [44] who has constructed quantity-guided (called by him "command") counterparts of certain price-guided processes. One of Marglin's mechanisms requires the center to allocate the scarce inputs on the basis of information obtained from the producing units concerning their marginal productivities and their excess demands. Adjustment ceases when aggregate excess demand is zero and the marginal productivities of producers are equalized. (A similar process was proposed by Heal [24].)

A process, characterized by a mixture of price- and quantity-guided elements and also due to Heal [25], is particularly interesting because (with some qualifications) it converges to optima even for nonconvex economies, in particular for increasing returns. An essential informational feature is that certain functions of each producing unit's marginal productivities (roughly, its shadow prices for particular resources) must be conveyed to the center. The center can then calculate improved resource allotments, or else it may calculate and send to the units a resource price (the same for all units) and so enable them to determine their respective resource requirements. The latter option is, of course, informationally more decentralized: it requires fewer message transfers from the center to the periphery, and fewer computations are carried out at the center. (Marglin had a similar process for a more restricted class of economies. It is not clear whether his process could be adapted to corner maxima in nonconvex cases.)

Heal's process has the further merit that if the initial allocation is feasible, so are all the later ones, thus satisfying a Malinvaud postulate. (The same seems true of Marglin's process, although, unlike Heal, he does not assume the initial position to be feasible.) The maintenance of feasibility is simple in models without intermediate goods because the procedure always allocates all available resources and producers are required to stay on their efficient frontiers. The matter gets more complicated when intermediate goods are introduced and only special cases appear to have been dealt with so far by this approach.

Processes in which the center specifies quantities and the peripheral units convey their individual marginal rates have also been used in models where public goods are among those to be allocated. I shall mention three treatments of this case, due to Drèze and de la Vallée Poussin [16], Malinvaud [43], and Aoki [3]. In the versions known to me each is somewhat specialized: Malinvaud and Drèze-Poussin have only one producer but many consumers, Aoki only one consumer; also Drèze-Poussin deal primarily with the case of only one private good, although they indicate how the results may be generalized to more. Aoki's economy is closest to those we have been considering so far because it has only one consumer (the center), hence, no income distribution problems; it also has many producers. His mechanism uses price-guidance for private goods and quantity-guidance for public goods. A producer develops production plans that maximize net revenue given the central "guidelines" (prices for the private goods, quantities for the public goods), and conveys to the center his demands for private goods and marginal evaluations, including marginal cost, for public goods. The center, in turn, adjusts the price of each private good according to the difference between its marginal utility and price (as in the Arrow-Hurwicz gradient process); the targets for public goods are increased in proportion to the net aggregate of marginal valuations (users' minus producers'); thus the center combines the functions of the helmsman and resource custodian of the Koopmans model for private goods with target setting for public goods. The other two processes have the same adjustment rule for public goods targets, but differ in other respects. In particular, they specify the rules of income distribution.

All three processes converge (at least locally) under suitable convexity assumptions concerning the environment. Somewhat paradoxically, Malinvaud's process does not seem to satisfy his desiderata of feasibility maintenance and monotonicity, while the other two do.

I shall now go back to the price-guided processes, but more briefly because they came earlier and are better known. Here again, I shall focus on the one consumer case. For a linear economy, Koopmans [33] described the functioning of such a mechanism in the spirit of the Taylor-Lange-Lerner rules by setting up an "allocation game" to be played, in an informationally decentralized manner, by a helmsman (setting the prices of final goods and thus representing consumer preferences), commodity custodians (adjusting the prices of resources according to excess demand), and activity managers who determine the production programs. Koopmans' adjustment rule (similar to Samuelson's) is that managers expand profitable activities and curtail those bringing losses; in a constant returns economy this is equivalent to profit maximization. Koopmans stressed that "the dynamic aspects of these rules have on purpose been left vague." We know that Samuelson's experiment in this direction yielded nonconvergent oscillations.

On the other hand, in an economy where all functions (including the utility indicator) are strictly concave (i.e., we have diminishing returns), similar rules produce a process with the desired stability properties. Utilizing the notion of gradient approach to the saddle point of the Lagrangean expression, Arrow and Hurwicz [8] used the following rules: the helmsman, taking the prices of desired commodities as given, changes each final demand at a rate equal to the difference between its marginal utility and price; each manager, again taking prices as given, changes the scale of his process in proportion to its marginal profitability; each commodity custodian varies the price of his commodity in proportion to excess demand. (I am omitting modifications pertaining to corners and zero prices.) A limiting form of such a process is the price-adjustment method in which prices are varied as before, but both the helmsman and each manager reach (as against merely moving toward) the values of their decision variables which maximize their respective objective functions: for the helmsman, the difference between utility and price; for the manager, the level of profit. The familiar Walrasian competitive process is a variant of such price-adjustment in which the demand for final goods is determined by utility maximization subject to a budget constraint with specified income or wealth.

Although the gradient process is informationally decentralized and converges to an optimum under strict concavity assumptions, it has certain disadvantages. To begin with, it is formulated in continuous time, while realistic mechanisms operate more naturally by iterations, i.e., with a discrete time parameter.

But it is possible to construct a discrete time parameter counterpart of the gradient process. In fact, this was done by Uzawa [67] and further elaborated by Malinvaud [42] who, however, pointed out another undesirable feature of the gradient process: although it converges to a feasible solution, its "interim" proposals are, in general, not feasible. In other words, while the process pushes the participants toward compatibility in their claims on resources, they may be demanding either more or less than the total available while the process is going on. Thus if the gradient process were to be interrupted at a finite time, there might be a problem of reconciling incompatible claims.

Malinvaud then formulated a desideratum, viz., that (discrete time parameter) adjustment processes yield feasible solutions after a finite number of iterations. He then proceeded to construct two processes (for different environments) which satisfied this desideratum. In both cases he assumed that the initial proposal, serving as the point of departure for the iterations, was feasible. In effect, he was paying a "price" for the feasibility of all his interim proposals – namely, he assumed that the center had an additional piece of information: a feasible point of departure; the Arrow-Hurwicz gradient process, on the other hand, was designed for situations where this information was not available to the center.

It is worthwhile to become acquainted with Malinvaud's second procedure. The center proposes prices to the producing units which, in turn, determine production plans maximizing the value of the firm's output in terms of those prices. The center then builds up its picture of each unit's production set (see Fig. 1) by taking all convex mixtures of its previous proposed input-output vectors, together with the initial feasible vector, assumed known to the center. (Since the production sets are assumed convex, this yields an increasing subset of the unit's true production set. But, again, there is an informational price to be paid: the center must accumulate, on a disaggregated basis, all past proposals from the units.) Treating its pictures of the production sets as if they were the actual sets, the center then maximizes its utility function subject to the resource availability constraint and proposes a new set of prices corresponding to the relevant marginal rates of substitution.

It could perhaps happen that, even after several iterations, the only production program compatible with resource constraints is the one originally assumed known to the center; or that, even if new feasible programs are generated, their utility is no higher than that of the original known feasible allocation. But it was shown by Malinvaud that, as the number of iterations goes to infinity, the utility associated with the corresponding plans tends to the upper bound of its feasible values.

Roughly speaking, the center constructs plans which would be nearly optimal for the economy if its images of the individual production sets were sufficiently close to correct. The informational price paid is the need for building up these images; in effect, the information concerning the production functions is being transferred to the center, although on an installment plan. This differs from the usual informationally decentralized procedures where the center does not accumulate such information and never knows more than the structure of the production set in the neighborhood of the current proposal.

Good 2

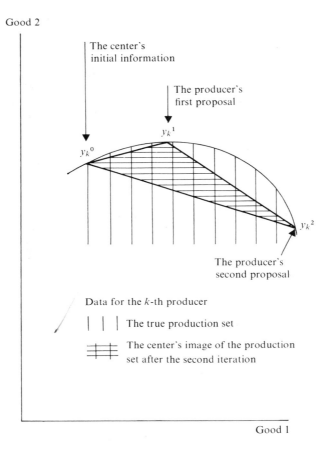

The center's
initial information

The producer's
first proposal

$y_k{}^1$

$y_k{}^0$

$y_k{}^2$

The producer's
second proposal

Data for the k-th producer

| | | The true production set

The center's image of the production
set after the second iteration

Good 1

Figure 1

The process also illustrates another desideratum formulated by Malinvaud: that the utility of successive proposals should not decrease as iterations progress ("monotonicity"). The preceding process obviously satisfies this requirement because earlier proposals are always among the available alternatives during the utility maximization phase of the center's calculations. (Heal's process also has the monotonicity property when the initial proposals are feasible.)

A procedure, which is a sort of dual to that of Malinvaud, has been proposed by Weitzman [68]. While Malinvaud's center is rather timid and only considers plans known to be feasible for the units, Weitzman's central planning agency constructs imaginary production sets it knows to be too ambitious, formulates targets that are, in general, infeasible, and then lets the units scale down the proposals to feasible levels. (See Fig. 2.) Also, the units provide the center with respective marginal rates (shadow prices) as a basis for subsequent central targets. Here, again, the center must accumulate all previous information concern-

Good 2

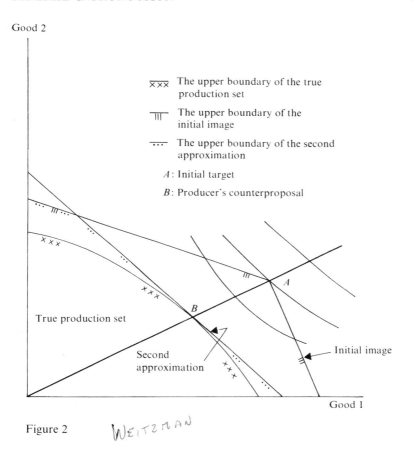

The upper boundary of the true production set

The upper boundary of the initial image

The upper boundary of the second approximation

A: Initial target

B: Producer's counterproposal

True production set

Second approximation

Initial image

Good 1

Figure 2   WEITZMAN

ing the structure of the individual production sets. Convergence is assured (even in a finite number of steps when the production sets are polyhedral). But the center's proposals will, in general, be infeasible for the units, and the units' counterproposals may not be compatible with resource availabilities. Hence, termination after a finite number of iterations may give rise to the same problems of feasibility brought out by Malinvaud with reference to gradient processes.

Perhaps a less ambitious form of the Malinvaud feasibility postulate would be acceptable: that the process should not depart from feasibility once it has encountered a feasible point in the process of iterations and that, in any case, it should converge to optimality, hence, to a feasible point. I have not explored Malinvaud's processes in the light of this modified postulate. It seems, however, that the following procedure would satisfy the modified postulate: use the gradient process when starting from an infeasible set of proposals, but switch to a Malinvaud type mechanism as soon as a feasible point is reached.

We may note that the feasibility problem arises for any Walrasian tâtonnement process which is terminated at a finite time. Typically, supply will not equal demand for all goods and, if actual allocation is to be made at the termination time, one must have a way of resolving conflicts. When demand exceeds supply, one can think of prorating the available goods or using the first come first served principle. However, this will not, in general, yield a feasible solution. Even for a pure exchange economy some individuals might be getting less than subsistence requirements; with production involving intermediate goods the situation would be all the more difficult.

Informational considerations aside, both cumulative procedures (Malinvaud's and Weitzman's) rely on the convexity of production sets. Malinvaud's other price-guided process (related to Taylor's suggestions) assumes a Leontief-Samuelson constant returns economy. What about decentralized resource allocation in *nonconvex* environments?

We have already seen one procedure designed to cope with such situations,

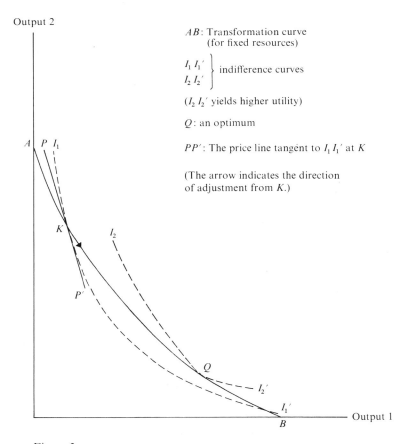

Output 2

AB: Transformation curve
(for fixed resources)

$I_1 I_1'$
$I_2 I_2'$ } indifference curves

($I_2 I_2'$ yields higher utility)

Q: an optimum

PP': The price line tangent to $I_1 I_1'$ at K

(The arrow indicates the direction of adjustment from K.)

Output 1

Figure 3

that of Heal [25]. This process is shown to converge to a "critical point" of the optimization problem, i.e., a point where first-order conditions for maximization are satisfied. Under conditions of convexity, such points will, of course, be (at least local) maxima. But without convexity, they no longer need be even local maxima. Now in Heal's process, if one starts from a feasible point which is not a critical point, the subsequent points will also be feasible and have a rising utility; hence, the point to which the process converges cannot be a local minimum, but it need not be a maximum. (See Figures 3 and 4.) However, if the starting point happened to be a local minimum, it seems that the rules of the process would generate an equilibrium there. It may be that this difficulty could be avoided by some modification of Heal's rules (e.g., by tâtonnement in the neighborhood of any critical point).

An alternative was proposed by Arrow and Hurwicz [6-8]. Mathematically, it amounts to rewriting the nonconcave constraints in such a manner that the *modified Lagrangean* expression becomes locally strictly concave in the activity variables so that a local saddle point is created and the gradient method can be

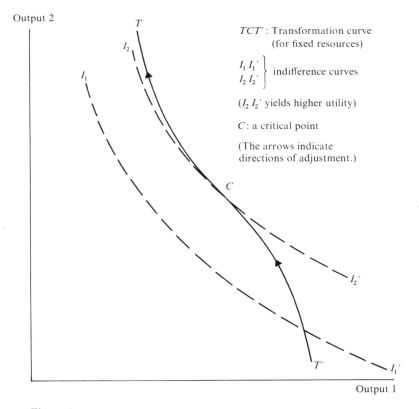

TCT': Transformation curve (for fixed resources)

$\left.\begin{array}{l} I_1 \, I_1' \\ I_2 \, I_2' \end{array}\right\}$ indifference curves

($I_2 \, I_2'$ yields higher utility)

C: a critical point

(The arrows indicate directions of adjustment.)

Figure 4

used, at least locally. (There are many ways of bringing about this modification.) Hence, we then have available to us a gradient process which is guaranteed to converge to a local optimum, not merely to a local critical point. Admittedly, convergence to a global optimum would be preferable. However, in the absence of concavity properties, one cannot hope to guarantee convergence to a global optimum on the basis of local first-order properties only! The modification just described can also be applied to produce *strict* concavity in linear situations. We thus have a solution of the dilemma of nonconvergent oscillations encountered by Samuelson in the linear case.

It should be admitted that computational experiments along these lines [48] did not turn out encouraging. Nevertheless, the economic interpretation of the modified Lagrangean (Arrow-Hurwicz) process seems of interest. Here the Lagrange multipliers are no longer interpreted as prices. In fact, the custodian announces a *price schedule* (of which the Lagrange multiplier is a parameter) with the price depending on the quantity purchased. The helmsman and the managers must perform their marginal calculations on the basis of such schedules. The custodians adjust the schedules by varying the Lagrangean parameters according to supply and demand conditions. Thus optimal allocation is achieved through monopolistic practices and imperfect competition. (Jennergren recently explored the use of price schedules in allocative processes for concave, including linear, environments. Heal made a related suggestion.)

It is not surprising that monopolistic elements should appear in a process that simulates market phenomena, since we know that perfectly competitive equilibrium need not exist in nonconvex situations and even where it exists in linear cases it has certain undesirable indeterminacies. It should be noted that the modified approach just described is informationally less decentralized than was the case in a world of concave functions without the monopolistic modification. It is a major problem of the general theory to what extent such informational losses are unavoidable.

A very different price-guided process was suggested by Radner [55] and developed by Groves [19, 20]. Their framework is that of team theory, with a simple common goal (total output maximization) and randomly fluctuating productivity parameters. The production functions are classical (differentiable and concave, or even quadratic). One of the adjustment processes considered is in the spirit of Lange-Lerner procedures. Others have information structures ranging from complete communication to absence of communication.

The distinguishing feature of the model is that allocative decisions are made without waiting for equilibrium to be reached, hence usually on the basis of only partial information. Also, there is a departure from the Lange-Lerner rules in that the production manager's decisions do not maximize profits, although profit figures are used for informational purposes.

Among the remarkable findings is the fact that the asymptotic value of communication per enterprise (as the number of enterprises increases) is as good under Radner's "One-Stage-Lange-Lerner" process as it would have been under complete communication.

Although the results so far obtained are valid only for rather specialized models, they show how to go beyond traditional equilibrium analysis, while exploiting ideas developed in equilibrium oriented models.

II. Basic concepts

We may think of economists as taking part in a contest to design a "superior" mechanism, with some submitting entries before it has been clarified what would qualify as a mechanism and which mechanisms would be considered superior or even feasible.

It is fortunate that our predecessors did not wait for such definitions. In the process of submitting their entries, they have provided examples of mechanisms, the foremost among them competitive and marginal cost pricing, and, by now, many others which can be used as guides in constructing a definition. Similarly, theorems concerning the efficiency and optimality properties of these mechanisms suggest possible classification criteria.

One could, of course, get by without formalizing what one means by a resource allocation mechanism. But it is then impossible to determine to what extent the various desiderata implicit in the past debates are compatible with one another, or what the "tradeoffs" are among them. Also, in searching for alternatives to known mechanisms for nonclassical situations (indivisibilities, increasing returns, externalities, public goods), it helps to have a rigorous formulation of what a resource allocation mechanism is and which of its features are desirable. Notions of a mechanism different from that given below may well have greater merit. Our picture of a mechanism [26] will in fact sacrifice possible greater generality to gain definiteness and simplicity. Nevertheless, it will be general enough to embrace (as it stands or with minor modifications) most of the economic systems we wish to study.

It is the function of a resource allocation mechanism to guide the economic agents (producers, consumers, bankers, and others) in decisions that determine the flow of resources. Simplifying to the utmost, we may imagine each agent having in front of him a console with one or more dials to set; the selection of dial settings by all agents determines uniquely the flow of goods and services (trade vector) between every pair of agents and also each agent's production (input–output vector), his "trade with nature." Not all dial settings are possible and some are possible only in conjunction with other dial settings. Thus the feasibility of a complex of actions (a specified combination of dial settings for all agents) can be split into individual feasibility and compatibility. (In our standard models, any point on a given agent's production function is individually feasible for this agent, but two individually feasible input–output vectors of two firms may be incompatible if one calls for an input which the other does not propose to supply.)

It is natural to demand that the mechanism should guide the agents toward actions which are at least feasible, and even that can be difficult. Yet in classical welfare economics we require more than feasibility, viz., such attributes as efficiency or optimality. After decades of meanderings, we are fairly clear on our options – from efficiency in production (as defined by Koopmans), through optimality (introduced by Pareto under the label of maximum ophelimity), to the maximization of a social welfare function (as defined by Bergson, Samuelson, or Arrow). From our point of view, these different attributes have an important feature in common: they are defined independently of the mechanism. An optimality criterion which presupposes a particular mechanism cannot serve as a legitimate criterion for comparison with other mechanisms.

Specifically, whether an allocation is or is not optimal depends on its feasibility and on the individual preferences, with feasibility determined by the individual endowments and the technology. The individual endowments, the technology, and preferences, taken together, are referred to as the *environment.* More generally, the environment is defined as the set of circumstances that cannot be changed either by the designer of the mechanism or by the agents (participants).[4]

To simplify matters, we shall confine ourselves to mechanisms analogous to the tâtonnement process where a period of dialogue without action is followed by decisions as to resource flow (production and exchange). Ultimately, we shall need a more general theory in which dialogue, decisions, and actions overlap in time, as in the nontâtonnement processes.

The participants in the dialogue constitute a broader group than the "doers" (consumers, producers, etc.), since they may include governments, planning agencies, central banks, or unions. If we excluded such participants, we should obviously be unable to develop a theory general enough to encompass centrally planned or even mixed economies. The dialogue is an exchange of messages between the participants. The nature and contents of the messages vary from mechanism to mechanism. They may be proposals of actions, bids, offers, plans of resource flow for the whole economy, or they may contain information about the environment (preferences, technology, resource endowments). The totality of messages permissible under a given mechanism constitute its *language.*

The mechanism specifies rules according to which, given the information available to him at a given time, a participant sends messages to others. The information consists of messages previously received, as well as some (direct) knowledge of environment, and are called *response rules* because they govern the message response to messages previously received. (By "direct" is meant knowledge of the environment derived from sources other than messages previously received.) To provide for a transition from dialogue to decisions and actions, the mechanism must also have an *outcome rule* which specifies what actions are to be taken given the course of the dialogue. The rules may be deterministic or probabilistic; mathematically they are expressed as functions.

Both market phenomena and command systems can be fitted into this schema. Thus in the Walrasian tâtonnement process the language consists of prices and quantities demanded or supplied by the various agents. If the model contains an "auctioneer," his response function calls for price changes proportional to aggregate excess demand, while the response functions of others require them to convey their excess demands given the prices called out by the auctioneer. In an extreme version of a "pure command" system, the dialogue starts with the peripheral agents sending to the center messages describing their respective components of the environment (e.g., their resource holdings and production functions), whereupon the center, after suitable data processing and calculations, sends to the peripheral agents the orders for action. In this command system the outcome rule is clear: to carry out the orders received. In the Walrasian tâtonnement process, the matter is a bit more complicated. One must wait until equilibrium is somehow established – i.e., everyone is repeating his previous message. Then the outcome rule is to carry out exchanges according to the equilibrium bids made.

The languages of the two mechanisms are also different. In the Walrasian process, messages are the proposed prices and commodity bundles. Namely, a message can be regarded as an ordered sequence of numbers, as many as there are goods in the system, i.e., as a vector whose dimension is that of the commodity space. In the "pure command" system, a message may contain the description of a production function or of a preference map. Since it may take arbitrarily many parameters to specify a production function, no a priori upper bound can be imposed here on how many numbers might have to be transmitted in such a process. The language of the command process is much larger than that of the Walrasian process. We must remember, however, that the pure command process is finished after only two exchanges of information while the tâtonnement may go on a long time.

The purpose of the two examples has been not to compare their merits, but to illustrate the meaning of the terms used in describing the resource allocation mechanisms we shall be dealing with. We shall call such mechanisms *adjustment processes*.

Thus, an adjustment process is specified by its language, response rules, and the outcome rule. (As we shall see later, "distributional parameter settings" also enter the picture.)

With this formulation, given a class of environments which the designer must cover, there is a well-defined family of adjustment processes that can at all be constructed with any specified language. This is so because, mathematically speaking, the class of environments and the language delimit the domains and ranges of the response and outcome functions (rules), and the class of functions with any given domain and range is well-defined. This opens the door to impossibility or possibility theorems concerning the family of adjustment processes that use specified languages and cover a given class of environments.

(The resemblance to Arrow's social welfare function problem is purely formal: in both cases one is investigating the family of functional relations with specified domains and ranges. However, the functions – rules – defining an adjustment process bear no direct relationship to the social welfare functions.)

We have already mentioned one natural desideratum for adjustment processes – that they yield feasible outcomes. More ambitiously, one may ask that
the outcomes be optimal. A process whose outcomes are optimal for a given
class of environments will be called *nonwasteful over that class.* (For instance, a
competitive process is nonwasteful, in a Pareto optimality sense, over environments that are free of externalities and of locally saturated preferences.) But it is
crucial to realize that nonwastefulness, although appealing, is not enough. After
all, a process lacking any positions of equilibrium would have to be classified as
(vacuously) nonwasteful. So, we would wish to require that the process possess
some equilibrium position for every environment of the class it is designed to
cover.

Yet even this is insufficient. What if the equilibria of the process always tend
to favor one group of participants at the expense of another? The victims would
hardly be comforted by the fact that the outcomes are always Pareto optimal.

Here again the experience of classical welfare economics points the way.
Whether we study Arrow, Debreu, or Koopmans, we find not one but two basic
theorems. One establishes nonwastefulness. The other asserts that any Pareto
optimum can be attained as a competitive equilibrium. A precise statement of
the latter property turns out to be complicated, however. For we know that,
given the option – always available to resource owners – of not trading and not
producing, ordinary competitive equilibrium cannot yield levels of satisfaction
below the original ones. Hence, inferior optima could never be reached and the
second theorem might seem false. But the theorem refers not merely to a market
process. When interpreted within the framework of a private ownership system,
it envisages a market process preceded by transfers of resource holdings and (in
a production economy) of claims to profits [1, 2, 4, 5, 15]. It is these transfers
that can lead to optima that are inferior for some of the participants.

Perhaps the most important point here is that the mechanism can no longer
be viewed as accepting as given the distributional aspects of the system. Rather,
it consists of two parts: a setting of what we may call the *distributional parameters* (resource holdings, profit shares), followed by a tâtonnement procedure.
The property of the competitive mechanism expressed by the second classical
welfare economics theorem, which we shall call *unbiasedness*, amounts to this:
given any conceivable Pareto optimal position of the economy, there exists a
setting of the distributional parameters which would make that position an
equilibrium of the process. (Again this property holds *over some* specified *class
of environments.*) Thus if there is an optimal allocation that cannot be made
into equilibrium by any setting of the distributional parameters, the process fails
the test of unbiasedness.

In a pure exchange economy there is no difficulty in interpreting the meaning
of setting distributional parameters: it is merely a matter of reshuffling the
initial endowment. But in the presence of production, the matter is more complicated. In a private ownership economy, profit shares can be shifted. But in
searching for alternative systems of different institutional nature, we do not

want to commit ourselves to considering profits or incomes as well-defined concepts, since both involve prices, and prices may not be defined in certain institutional structures. (This, incidentally, shows some of the difficulties of even formulating the problem without implicitly presupposing marketlike conditions.) Yet it is possible to provide a definition free of institutional limitations by interpreting the distributional parameters as guaranteeing to each participant a minimum level of satisfaction corresponding to a particular resource allocation. The manner in which this guarantee is implemented does involve institutional arrangements.

One more requirement. Ideally, we might demand that the rules of the process send the economy to a uniquely determined allocation. But this turns out to be difficult to accomplish and even the competitive mechanism may yield multiple equilibrium allocations compatible with a *particular* equilibrium price. Since, however, all these allocations happen to have the same utility for all participants, the indeterminacy is acceptable. We shall call a process *essentially single-valued* if any equilibrium indeterminacies are of this trivial nature. (Note that this does not require that allocations corresponding to *different* equilibrium prices, when there are multiple equilibria, yield the same satisfactions to all participants. Ruled out is only a situation in which, corresponding to a particular equilibrium price, there would be alternative allocations yielding different levels of satisfaction.)

We are now ready to formulate the basic set of performance requirements for processes to be considered: that they be nonwasteful, unbiased, and essentially single-valued. This trio of requirements will be, for short, referred to as *(Pareto-) satisfactoriness*. Whether the requirements are or are not met by a given process depends on the environments in which it is asked to operate. The environments which have the properties stated in the classical welfare economics theorems are, naturally, called classical. Thus *classical environments* are free from externalities or indivisibilities, their sets are convex, etc. In particular, increasing returns are not classical!

With this long introduction, the two great welfare economics propositions may briefly be stated thus: the competitive process is Pareto-satisfactory over classical environments.

This statement immediately provokes the question: what about the nonclassical environments? Can we find Pareto-satisfactory processes for them too? For all environments, or just some?

These questions would be meaningless if some restrictions were not imposed on the information (or incentive) structure of the processes to be considered. The explicit recognition of the role played by the information structure is one of the major accomplishments of Jacob Marschak and Roy Radner [47] in their work on the theory of teams. An analysis of informational issues, with emphasis on feasibility, timing, and costs, with particular reference to the issue of decentralization, is due to Thomas Marschak [49]. Oniki [51] has pioneered in comparisons of numbers of messages that flow in different processes.

The formulation I have adopted here is conceptually much less satisfactory. I consider certain specific restrictions on the informational aspects of the process and then, as a first step, I ask whether for a given class of environments (wider than classical) one can design Pareto-satisfactory processes. (These restrictions are satisfied by the competitive process, so there is no problem with regard to classical environments. But it is proper to ask whether there could be processes that are informationally "even better" than the competitive process. In terms of certain criteria of dimensionality of messages, the answer obtained independently by Hurwicz [28], by Mount and Reiter [50], and – from a somewhat different point of view – by Sonnenschein [64] is in the negative: in a specified sense, one cannot do "better.")

As a second step, adjustment processes can be compared with respect to the required "size" of the language (e.g., the cardinality or dimensionality of the message space), or according to the fineness of the perceptions they call for (informational efficiency), and other aspects of information processing effort or expense. These concepts and their relationships have been studied by Kanemitsu [31] and by Reiter [56, 57].

But back to the "first step," the formulation of requirements. To express them, it is necessary to distinguish between information obtained directly (say, by one's own observation) and through messages received. My first postulate is that participants have direct information only about themselves, not about others. I have never found a good term for this property, but currently I refer to it as *privacy* (of the adjustment process).

It is clear that the restriction on direct information would be virtually meaningless if arbitrary messages were permitted, for then "in one move" any information not available directly could be obtained through a message. Thus the *language* (the set of permissible messages) must somehow be restricted. It turns out from mathematical considerations (something I had not been fully aware of in my original work) that restrictions on the language may also turn out to be ineffective unless certain conditions (akin to but stronger than continuity) are imposed on the response and outcome functions.

The totality of these and certain other conditions (including some pertaining to the language) I have labeled *informational decentralization.* There is, of course, some arbitrariness in such a definition, but it enables us to formulate a simple "yes or no" question: how broad is the class of environments for which Pareto-satisfactory, informationally decentralized processes can be designed? In particular, can informationally decentralized processes be designed for the class of all environments free of externalities (*decomposable environments*)?

III. Some results

With all this machinery, we have finally managed to ask a question. Are there answers? Indeed there are, some positive, some negative.

To begin with, it is possible to construct processes that are informationally decentralized for all decomposable environments. As for nondecomposable environments, it seems that one would have to say "no," but this has not as yet been rigorously established. It can be shown that informational requirements increase when nondecomposability (externalities) enters. While this is hardly surprising, the fact that informational decentralization *is* possible for the class of all decomposable environments, was, to me at least, a surprise, particularly because of the well-known difficulties that arise in the presence of indivisibilities. Indivisibilities do make trouble, but not to the point of making informational decentralization impossible.

To show this, it is sufficient to exhibit an informationally decentralized process which is Pareto-satisfactory for all decomposable environments. In fact, there exists at least one, although with certain limitations and defects. The process works roughly as follows. A message is a listing (or description) of trades (with others or with nature) that a participant is prepared to engage in. The response is a counterproposal listing all those trades that are better, or at least as good, from the respondent's point of view. (You can see why this has been called the *greed process*.) The process does qualify as informationally decentralized because the privacy requirement is satisfied, since the participant needs to know only his own characteristics; and the language, that of trade sets, also fits the definition. (There is no denying, of course, that the messages used are very "heavy" and complex.)

Furthermore, it is simple to show that this process (which is only defined for decomposable environments) yields optimal equilibria and any optimum can be reached by it. It is Pareto-satisfactory. But this is only a static property. Dynamically, the greed process is terrible. Unless we start it from an optimal position, it oscillates indefinitely with constant amplitude. So we get more and look for a *convergent* Pareto-satisfactory process.

It is possible to "fix up" the greed process by building into it a certain amount of "inertia," i.e., dependence on earlier values. Kanemitsu [32] showed that such a greed-inertia combination does result in convergence in *continuous* decomposable environments. This is quite a broad class (including increasing returns and other nonconvexities), but it rules out indivisibilities. Whether one can generalize this to discrete (indivisible) economies is, I believe, an open question.

So, we have not yet exhibited a *convergent* informationally decentralized process that is Pareto-satisfactory for *all* decomposable environments!

At this point, the idea of randomness, not a stranger to search procedures, comes to the rescue. By introducing an element of randomness, we can obtain convergence (although, I must admit, in a probabilistic sense only) and also simplify the structure of messages. This process, developed by Hurwicz, Radner, and Reiter [29], is particularly simple when all goods are *indivisible*. Let me describe it for the two-trader Edgeworth Box case.

At each time point, each participant picks at random (but according to a fixed probability distribution) a trade that will leave him at least as well off as he is at present. If the two trade proposals happen to be compatible, the bargain is sealed, and the traders start all over again from the newly reached point. It is clear that the process has the privacy property: one needs to know only one's preferences and subsistence requirements; in fact, the process, even in the more general situations (with any number of traders and production) is informationally decentralized. Unbiasedness is also intuitively clear: one can pick any optimal allocation as a point of departure and the rules make it impossible to get away; thus there is a (probabilistic) equilibrium. It is not obvious that the traders won't "get stuck" at some nonoptimal position, in which case the process would be wasteful. But a certain amount of mathematics leads to the conclusion that we are protected from such a fate with probability 1.

And note that in the indivisible goods case the messages here are not sets but single trade proposals. Definitely very superior to the greed process.

So, the indivisible case turns out to be relatively simple, although one cannot make any practical claims until the speed of convergence has been investigated. But the usually well-behaved, continuous, *divisible* environment makes trouble here, since under the just-stated rules the probability of encounter would be zero: the proverbial needle in the proverbial haystack. So there has to be a modification: when commodities are perfectly divisible, a proposal will consist of not only the point picked at random but also a certain neighborhood of it (say, a square or a cube), with the further unattractive proviso that any part of the neighborhood whose utility is below that of the original endowment is cut off by the participant before the proposal is sent out. Now if the two (neighborhood) proposals fail to meet, one must try again; if they do meet, a point is chosen at random from the intersection area and the game goes on. Under rather mild assumptions of topological nature, probabilistic convergence can again be proved and the process is Pareto-satisfactory. It also qualifies as informationally decentralized, but it is clear that the informational burden is much greater than in the indivisible case, since the cutoff neighborhoods might be very irregular in shape.

Facing such complexities of the process, it is natural to ask whether these are merely due to lack of cleverness on our part. Can we hope to design a process with all the nice properties of this one but with a smaller informational burden? A. P. Lerner raised this point in his *Economics of Control* [41] after he proposed dealing with indivisibilities by a consumer–producer surplus type of criterion. His answer was that "the necessity of making unreliable estimates is in the nature of the problem and not in the method of solving it. . . . The same estimates and guesses must be made in *any* economy where knowledge is imperfect and where large decisions have to be made" (p. 198).

I believe that Lerner was right, but even now, almost thirty years later, we do not have a rigorous proof of this contention. The main difficulty is conceptual. We must define precisely what would be considered informationally less burdensome. Namely, we need a concept of informational efficiency, somewhat similar to production efficiency – a partial ordering criterion. Once the informational-efficiency ordering is available, we can interpret Lerner's question (although he stated it as an assertion) as follows: is a given proposed process (e.g., that embodying his criterion) informationally *maximally* efficient among, say, informationally decentralized processes that are Pareto-satisfactory for all decomposable environments? Although some informational-efficiency criteria have been suggested, we do not as yet have a definitive answer to Lerner's question.

But there are partial answers based on the criterion of message space size which is related to informational efficiency [57]. In particular, it has been shown that, in the absence of convexity or monotonicity restrictions on the environment, there is no upper bound to the number of auxiliary parameters that must be used in a privacy-preserving Pareto-satisfactory process [28]. This comes close to confirming Lerner's view. Note the contrast with classical environments where the number of auxiliary parameters need only be as high as the number of commodities – as when prices are such parameters. (As already mentioned, fewer auxiliary parameters would not work; the competitive mechanism is "dimensionally efficient.")

When the assumption of decomposability of the environment is abandoned (i.e., externalities are permitted), the preceding processes are not even defined. But when they are redefined so as to cover nondecomposabilities [39], they may lose their informationally decentralized character.

For a particular class of nondecomposable situations, however, an interesting possibility emerges. It is well known that it may be possible formally to eliminate externalities by enlarging the commodity space (although this is based on implicit observability assumptions). Now Starrett [65] has pointed out that such enlargement may introduce nonconvexities in a previously convex world. Namely, we have either fewer goods and convexity but with externalities, or more goods and no externalities, but no convexity. Thus the competitive mechanism fails either way, because of externalities or because of nonconvexities. Still, not all is lost. If continuity is not impaired, a probabilistic process such as that outlined above might provide a decentralized Pareto-satisfactory and convergent solution.

IV. Incentive compatibility

So far we have been asking whether it is possible to design process rules which, if followed, would have certain desirable consequences. Where the answer is in the negative, we at least know our limitations. But if a process with the desired properties is found, the question arises whether one could expect the participants to follow the rules, since there is a possibility of collusions or of individual departures from the prescribed norms. We shall consider only the latter.

Whether a certain configuration of behavior patterns is compatible with the participant's "natural inclinations" is a problem in the theory of games, in this case noncooperative games without side payments. There are differences of opinion as to what constitutes a reasonable concept of solution for such games. For the sake of definiteness we shall adopt that of a Nash equilibrium which seems to be a good formalization of many intuitive ideas prevailing among economists. A configuration of behavior patterns constituting a Nash equilibrium will be referred to as (individual-) *incentive-compatible.* Such a configuration is present if no participant finds it advantageous to depart from his behavior pattern so long as the others do not. For instance, in a bilateral monopoly situation, competitive behavior is not (usually) incentive-compatible because when one participant is a price-taker it would be to the other's advantage to be a price-setter (monopolist) rather than a price-taker.

One might, however, assume that there exists an enforcement system (carrots or sticks) which makes it unattractive for the participants openly to defy the prescribed rules. But suppose that the enforcing agency has no knowledge of the characteristics of the individual participants (their preferences, technologies, or endowments). It is then conceivable that the participants would "cheat" without openly violating the rules. A participant could try to cheat by doing what the rules would have required him to do had his characteristics been different from what they are – i.e., he could "pretend" to be poorer than he is, or less efficient, or less eager for certain goods. (It is important to understand that he would not be doing this directly by uttering false statements, but indirectly by behaving inappropriately according to the rules for his true characteristics.)

Economists have long been alerted to this issue by Samuelson [59] in the context of the allocation problem for public goods. But, in fact, a similar problem arises in a "nonatomistic" world of pure exchange of exclusively private goods. Consider, for instance, an economy consisting of two traders, as conventionally represented by an Edgeworth Box, with classical strictly convex indifference curves and a positive nonoptimal endowment of both goods for both traders. We already noted that if they were both told to behave as price-takers it would pay one of them to violate this rule if he could get away with it. Now we assume that he cannot violate the rule openly, but he can pretend to have preferences different from his true ones. The question is whether he could think up for himself a false (but convex and monotone) preference map which would be more advantageous for him than his true one, assuming that he will follow the rules of price-taking according to the false map while the other trader plays the game honestly. It is easily shown that the answer in the affirmative. Thus, in such a situation, the rules of perfect competition are not incentive-compatible.

It follows that the enforcing authority could not hope to maintain competitive (price-taking) behavior without directly checking up on the participant's characteristics, thus transgressing the requirements of informational decentralization. Perfect competition is not incentive-compatible.

But might there not exist some other set of rules to generate a process avoiding this difficulty? We have so far seen only that the conventional parametric price mechanism will not do the job, and there are many alternative mechanisms one could experiment with. But the same trouble will be present in *any* process yielding Pareto-optimal outcomes and giving the participants the option of remaining at their initial endowments if they so desire (the "no-trade option").

For it turns out that, given any such process, the non-law-abiding trader can profit by behaving in a way that successfully misrepresents his true characteristics [27]. Thus, in a nonatomistic exchange economy, there can be no incentive-compatible mechanism with optimal equilibria and the no-trade option – even though there are no public goods! (See also Ledyard [40].)

These results show that the difficulty is due not to our lack of inventiveness, but to a fundamental conflict among such mechanism attributes as the optimality of equilibria, incentive-compatibility of the rules, and the requirements of informational decentralization. Concessions must be made in at least one of these directions.

The possibility of successful false revelation of individual characteristics is particularly important in an economy with production. The issue has come up in many contexts. It has been raised as an objection to the Lange-Lerner mechanism. It has also been recognized in connection with situations where targets and norms are set, whether for enterprise managers in a Soviet type economy or for workers on a piece rate under capitalism. In all of these cases there is a "superior" and a "subordinate," and the latter has an incentive to depress the norms when the penalty for failure to reach a target is severe.

In analyzing the situation, one should distinguish cases in which the subordinate's reward depends only on activities observed by the superior from those where, as in Leibenstein's X-efficiency model, the subordinate's satisfaction is affected by factors under his control which cannot be observed by the superior. More realistically, one may assume that the superior can observe more or less, but only at a cost. Furthermore, if we think of the superior as a central authority and the subordinate as a manager of a plant, it is reasonable to suppose that the subordinate possesses technological knowledge while the superior knows the (social) objective function and, perhaps, resource availabilities.

Under such circumstances the superior faces a dilemma. If he gives his subordinate a great deal of autonomy and does not make an effort at observation, the subordinate will maximize his own rather than the superior's objective function. If the superior makes the costly effort at observation and deprives the subordinate of autonomy, he is likely to give wrong orders because of his technological ignorance. A possible solution is a reward structure which brings the objectives of the two parties closer together (e.g., output sharing); this may give the subordinate a motivation consonant with the superior's and would make him use his technological knowledge to maximize the superior's objective function if he were given sufficient freedom to select the correct actions. The loss to the superior from sharing may in some cases exceed the gains in efficiency. But we can see that it is meaningful to seek an optimum combination of observation effort, delegation of authority (grant of autonomy), and reward structure.

The example is instructive because it shows the difference in the conceptual structure needed for the investigation of the interplay of authority, incentive, information, and performance issues. Where only performance and information were being investigated, the object of study was the mechanism or adjustment process. But from the viewpoint of incentive and authority structure, it is helpful to note (as does Camacho [12]) that the actual responses of the participants may be regarded as the resultant of two factors: the official rules ("the régime") and the behavorial characteristics of the participants. In general, the rules limit the responses of the participants, but do not prescribe them uniquely. Given the rules, together with the punishment and reward structure for transgressions, the actual responses are determined by the participants' behavioral characteristics. *Laissez-faire* may be defined as a régime granting the participants maximal leeway; at the other extreme (and equally unrealistic) would be an economy in which the rules make all participants into preprogrammed automata.

Aside from value judgments and preferences for freedom of decision making, one can regard the degree of restrictiveness of the régime, together with the reward structure and informational activities (insofar as these can be varied by the designer) as unknowns of the problem. The objective is to obtain optimal performance. The behavioral characteristics of the participants and the class of environments for which the system is being designed are the givens. (Examples of this type, but with information structure regarded as given, were worked out by Camacho.)

Let us go back to consider the incentive-compatibility issue in a production economy, assuming complete observability of all activities (but not necessarily of all characteristics!). A very simple example involves two persons: a farmer producing wheat and a laborer. The farmer wants to maximize the amount of wheat after paying off the laborer (in wheat); the laborer's net satisfaction is measured by the difference between the amount of wheat received and an index of disutility of labor. If the production function and the disutility curve have their classical shapes, there will be a unique Pareto-optimum at a point where the marginal disutility of labor equals its marginal productivity. Perfect competition would produce this resource allocation. But it will be found that the farmer can get more wheat by misrepresenting his production function, namely, by underestimating the marginal productivity at a point below the optimum output level. (It is assumed that the laborer remains a wagetaker.)

Thus again perfect competition is not incentive-compatible. However, unlike under pure exchange, it *is* possible here to devise a reward scheme that would eliminate the incentive toward misrepresentation on the part of one participant. For in this simple farmer–laborer example it so happens that Pareto optimality is equivalent to the maximization of the difference between the total output and the total disutility of labor. (This disutility, under the assumptions made, can be considered cardinally measurable). Thus if the two participants, the farmer and the laborer, are promised fixed shares of this difference (say, one-third for the farmer, two-thirds for the laborer), with the laborer in addition getting an amount of wheat just sufficient to compensate him for the disutility of labor, the farmer will have an interest in reaching the Pareto-optimum. Thus one could ask them to play the market game, but only for the purpose of determining the proper labor input level, following which a noncompetitive "surplus-sharing" rule would be implemented.

Here the manager (farmer) would have an incentive to be truthful. Thus we have a situation where perfect competition is not incentive-compatible for either party but for the manager another process, departing from perfect competition in its distributive aspects, is. However, I rather doubt that this is typical. In more elaborate situations, with the managers' utilities depending on the product mix of the economy, informationally decentralized mechanisms that are incentive-compatible on management side may well fail to exist. But in "team" type situations (with scalar additive outputs) sharing formulas will be safe against misrepresentation, while competitive price mechanisms in general will not. (Related questions of incentive-compatibility were examined by Groves [19].)

The incentives for truthful revelation of incentives when public goods are being allocated were examined by Drèze and de la Vallée Poussin [16]. Unfortunately, their conclusions are not directly comparable with those we have reached for the world of private goods. They do find that, in terms of their criterion, at an equilibrium of the process, all consumers have an incentive to reveal their preferences correctly. However, their criterion is an *instantaneous* change in utility, while the criterion used here (and, it seems, that implicit in Samuelson's argument) refers to the utility of the *final* outcome.[5]

Heal [25] points out that an incentive-compatible reward structure (on the output side) can be obtained for his process in the case of one producer when the center's utility function is positively homogeneous. The producer would not pay for the centrally allocated resources, but would get paid for the outputs, with prices equal to the marginal utilities of the outputs. In this case the utility is a strictly increasing function of the value of output; hence, if the producer were rewarded, say, by a fixed share of the value of output, he would find it to his advantage to maximize the center's utility. Unfortunately, where there are several firms, the one-to-one relationship is between utility and the value of outputs *aggregated* over all producing units; this does not imply *individual* incentive-compatibility.

Jennergren [30] shows the incentive for misrepresentation in the Dantzig-Wolfe decomposition procedure, specifically an incentive to "hide," a part of the (feasible) production set. Both Marglin [44] and Jennergren stress the incentive toward "cheating" under the (parametric) price mechanism in the case of small numbers of producing units. For the "atomistic case," Marglin suggests a combination of a "command" (quantity-guided) system in the search for an optimum with a profit-maximization motive to provide suitable incentives. This is, in a sense, the reverse of the system considered above for the farmer–laborer example.

From the preceding discussion it is evident that the incentive structure is largely determined by what the participants can achieve for themselves by their free actions; this in turn depends on such institutional phenomena as private property, rules for the distribution of profits, or the freedom not to trade. A tool appropriate for the analysis of such phenomena is the characteristic function of a game defined by von Neumann and Morgenstern. Shapley and Shubik [61] carried out a study of different institutional property arrangements, including feudalism, sharecropping, and the village commune, by constructing the corresponding characteristic functions and exploring the different versions of game solutions (von Neumann-Morgenstern solutions, the core, the Shapley value). Thus a significant step is taken toward a formalization of the distributional aspects of the economic system.[6] (The distributional parameters introduced above, as well as the no-trade option, may be regarded as special cases of a similar approach.)

In the context of distributional issues, the conflict between informational decentralization and incentival considerations is illustrated by a model due to Pazner and Schmeidler [54]. Their objective is to show that preassigned income distribution can be attained without sacrificing either Pareto optimality or informational decentralization. To accomplish this, they postulate a central agency distributing money (purchasing power) to individuals in accordance with the desired income distribution. Also, there are central agencies in charge of allocation of manpower. These custodians of labor operate as if they owned it. The workers can buy their leisure back from the manpower agency, but they have no freedom of choice where to work. The total supply of labor is assumed fixed and independent of the rewards. In the absence of individual checking procedures and given ordinary human motivations, such an assumption may be difficult to maintain.

V. Conclusion

The proper integration of the information and incentive aspects of resource allocation models is perhaps the major unsolved problem in the theory of mechanism design. Many other questions also remain unanswered. Nevertheless, I think this survey shows that economic analysis has broken out of its traditional limits in at least two important ways: (1) devising specific new mechanisms; and (2) exploring the constraints and tradeoffs to which the design of mechanisms is subject.

The new mechanisms are somewhat like synthetic chemicals: even if not usable for practical purposes, they can be studied in a pure form and so contribute to our understanding of the difficulties and potentialities of design. The design point of view enlarges our field of vision and helps economics avoid a narrow focus on the status quo, whether East or West.

We have made significant progress in understanding the problems of designing resource allocation mechanisms. But the field is still in its infancy because these are hard problems.

Notes

1   It is striking that Pareto [52, p. 58], in addition to pointing out the theoretical feasibility of rational allocation in what he called a collectivist régime (it would have the same coefficients of production as free competition), also dealt with costs of operating the system: "A second approximation will take account of the expense of putting the mechanism of free competition in full play, and will compare this expense with that necessary for establishing some other new mechanism which society may wish to test." Similarly, in the *Manuel* [53, p. 364], Pareto points out the need to compare the expense on the entrepreneurs and proprietors under the system of private property with that of state employees under collectivism. But, he says, "pure economics does not give us a truly decisive basis for choosing between organization based on private property and a socialist organization."

2   Samuelson himself suggested "a little intelligent speculation or foresight." (Interestingly enough, a contribution by Groves [20] to dynamic team theory exploits a similar idea to increase the average performance of a "truncated" Lange-Lerner process.) In addition to this dynamic defect of the competitive mechanism in a linear economy, several recent papers have also studied what is perceived to be a static defect: even when the prices are correct (i.e., at their competitive equilibrium values), the producer will typically be indifferent between "socially correct" and "incorrect" actions because both types of actions may be on the same iso-profit line. Bessière and Sautter [11] speak of absence of "separability" and Jennergren [30] makes a similar finding. However, with "incorrect" individual actions there would not be equilibrium; this would become evident to the price-setters, because excess demand would be different from zero. Since excess demand must be checked to know whether the price is "correct," the requirement of "separability" in the above sense seems too strong. Nevertheless, it is of some interest to note that where individual profit optima are unique (e.g., with strictly concave production functions), "separability" is present.

3   The need for such averaging is due to the fact that a firm's final program in the Dantzig-Wolfe procedure can be a profit-maximizing "corner," while "social optimality" may require the utilization of a "non-corner" profit-maximizing production program. In effect, by considering the various averages of the producing unit's programs, the center determines the whole set of profit-maximizing programs and, from among those, picks out the socially optimal one. (See Baumol and Fabian [10].)

4   For instance, in a multiperiod model, where inventive activity is a controllable factor of production, the environment is given not by the existing technology, but rather by the relationship between inventive activity and the resulting production function in later periods. This interpretation fits the more general definition of environment if the latter relationship cannot be altered by the decision makers. Similarly, the existing preferences do not constitute the environment in its generalized sense when tastes are malleable, e.g., on grounds adduced by Galbraith. But if the responsiveness of tastes to influences such as advertising cannot be influenced by decision

makers, it should be regarded as part of the environment. (To make meaningful welfare judgments possible, some underlying values or "true preferences" would have to be postulated.)

5 For the case of one private good, Drèze-Poussin find correct revelation the only good strategy in the minimax (as distinct from Nash) sense.

6 See also Shubik [62] and Shapley [60].

References

[1] M. Allais, *A la Recherche d'une discipline économique, I*, Paris 1943.

[2] M. Allais, *Economie pure et rendement social*, Paris 1945.

[3] Masahiko Aoki, "Two Planning Processes for an Economy with Production Externalities," Discussion Paper 157, *Harvard Inst. of Econ. Res.*, Cambridge, Mass., 1970.

[4] K. J. Arrow, "An Extension of the Basic Theorems of Welfare Economics," in J. Neyman, ed., *Proc. of the Second Berkeley Symposium*, Berkeley 1951, 507–532.

[5] K. J. Arrow and F. Hahn, *General Competitive Analysis*, San Francisco 1971.

[6] K. J. Arrow and L. Hurwicz, "Reduction of Constrained Maxima to Saddlepoint Problems," this volume, II.5, pp. 154–177.

[7] K. J. Arrow and L. Hurwicz, "Gradient Method for Concave Programming," in K. J. Arrow, L. Hurwicz, and H. Uzawa, eds., *Studies in Linear and Non-Linear Programming*, Stanford 1958, chs. 6, 8.

[8] K. J. Arrow and L. Hurwicz, "Decentralization and Computation in Resource Allocation," this volume, II.1, pp. 41–95.

[9] E. Barone, "The Ministry of Production in the Collectivist State," in F. A. von Hayek, ed., *Collectivist Economic Planning*, London 1935, 245–290. (Reprinted from *Giornale degli Economisti*, 1908.)

[10] W. J. Baumol and T. Fabian, "Decomposition, Pricing for Decentralization and External Economies," *Management Science*, 1964, *11*, 1–32.

[11] F. Bessière and E. A. Sautter, "Optimization and Suboptimization: the Method of Extended Models in the Non-Linear Case," *Management Science*, 1968, *15*, 1–11.

[12] A. Camacho, "Centralization and Decentralization of Decision Making Mechanisms: A General Model," *Jahrbuch der Wirtschaft Osteuropas*, 1972, *3*, 45–66.

[13] G. B. Dantzig and P. Wolfe, "The Decomposition Algorithm for Linear Programs," *Econometrica*, 1961, *29*, 767–778.

[14] G. Debreu, "Coefficient of Resource Utilization," *Econometrica*, 1951, *19*, 273–292.

[15] G. Debreu, *Theory of Value*, New York 1959.

[16] J. H. Drèze and D. de la Vallée Poussin, "A Tâtonnement Process for Guiding and Financing an Efficient Production of Public Goods," Discussion Paper 6922, *CORE*, Univ. Cath. de Louvain, Belgium 1969.

[17]   R. T. Ely, "The Past and the Present of Political Economy," Johns Hopkins Univ. Studies, Second Series, *III*, 1884.

[18]   R. T. Ely, *Publications of the American Economic Association*, *I*, Baltimore 1887.

[19]   T. Groves, "The Allocation of Resources under Uncertainty: The Informational and Incentive Roles of Prices and Demands in a Team," Berkeley 1969.

[20]   T. Groves, "Market Information and the Allocation of Resources in a Dynamic Team Model," *Joint Autom. Control Conf. of the AACC*, Stanford 1972, 8–17.

[21]   T. Groves and R. Radner, "Allocation of Resources in a Team," *J. of Econ. Theory*, 1972, *4*, 415–441.

[22]   F. A. von Hayek, "The Present State of the Debate," in F. A. von Hayek, ed., *Collectivist Economic Planning*, London 1935, 201–243.

[23]   F. A. von Hayek, "The Use of Knowledge in Society," *Amer. Econ. Rev.*, 1945, *35*, 519–530.

[24]   G. M. Heal, "Planning Without Prices," *Rev. of Econ. Stud.*, 1969, *36*, 346–362.

[25]   G. M. Heal, "Planning, Prices, and Increasing Returns," *Rev. of Econ. Stud.*, 1971, *38*, 281–294.

[26]   L. Hurwicz, "Optimality and Informational Efficiency in Resource Allocation Processes," this volume, IV, pp. 395–412.

[27]   L. Hurwicz, "On Informationally Decentralized Systems," this volume, IV, pp. 425–459.

[28]   L. Hurwicz, "On the Dimensional Requirements of Informationally Decentralized Pareto-Satisfactory Processes," this volume, IV, pp. 413–424.

[29]   L. Hurwicz, R. Radner, and S. Reiter, "A Stochastic Decentralized Resource Allocation Process" (accepted for publication), 1970.

[30]   L. O. Jennergren, *Studies in the Mathematical Theory of Decentralized Resource-Allocation*, Ph.D. dissertation, Stanford Univ. 1971.

[31]   H. Kanemitsu, "Informational Efficiency and Decentralization in Optimal Resource Allocation," *The Econ. Stud. Quart.*, 1966, *16*, 22–40.

[32]   H. Kanemitsu, "On the Stability of an Adjustment Process in Non-Convex Environments – a Case of the Commodity Space (Strong) Inertia-Greed Process," presented at the Second World Congress of the Econometric Society, Cambridge, England, 1970.

[33]   T. C. Koopmans, "Analysis of Production as an Efficient Combination of Activities," in Cowles Commission Monograph 13, T. C. Koopmans, ed., *Activity Analysis of Production and Allocation*, New York 1951, 33–97.

[34]   T. C. Koopmans, *Three Essays on the State of Economic Science*, New York 1957.

[35]   J. Kornai and T. Lipták, "Two-level Planning," *Econometrica*, 1965, *33*, 141–169.

[36]   J. B. Kruskal, Jr. and Allen Newell, "A Model for Organization Theory," Working Paper, *LOGS* 103, Rand Corp., Santa Monica 1950.

[37]   O. Lange, "The Foundations of Welfare Economics," *Econometrica*, 1942, *10*, 215–228.

[38]   O. Lange and F. M. Taylor, in B. E. Lippincott, ed., *On the Economic Theory of Socialism*, New York 1938.

[39]   J. O. Ledyard, "Resource Allocation in Unselfish Environments," *Amer. Econ. Rev.*, 1968, *58*, 227–237.

[40]   J. O. Ledyard, "A Characterization of Organizations and Environments which are Consistent with Preference Revelation," Discussion Paper 5, Center for Math. Studies in Econ. and Mgt. Sc., Northwestern Univ. 1972.

[41]   A. P. Lerner, *The Economics of Control*, New York 1944.

[42]   E. Malinvaud, "Decentralized Procedures for Planning," in Bacharach and Malinvaud, eds., *Activity Analysis in the Theory of Growth and Planning*, London 1967, 170–208.

[43]   E. Malinvaud, "The Theory of Planning for Individual and Collective Consumption," presented at the Symposium on the Problem of the National Economy Modeling, Novosibirsk 1970.

[44]   S. A Marglin, "Information in Price and Command Systems of Planning," in J. Margolis and H. Guitton, eds., *Public Economics*, London 1969, 54–77.

[45]   J. Marschak, "Wirtschaftsrechnung und Gemeinwirtschaft," *Archiv fuer Sozialwissenschaft und Sozialpolitik*, Tuebingen 1924, *51*, 501–520.

[46]   J. Marschak, "Elements for a Theory of Teams," *Management Science*, 1955, *1*, 127–137.

[47]   J. Marschak and R. Radner, *Economic Theory of Teams*, New Haven 1972.

[48]   T. Marschak, "An Example of a Modified Gradient Method for Linear Programming," in K. J. Arrow, L. Hurwicz, and H. Uzawa, eds., *Studies in Linear and Non-Linear Programming*, Stanford 1958, ch. 9.

[49]   T. Marschak, "Centralization and Decentralization in Economic Organizations," *Econometrica*, 1959, *27*, 399–430.

[50]   K. Mount and S. Reiter, "Informational Size of Message Spaces," Discussion Paper 3, Center for Math. Studies in Econ. and Mgt. Sc., Northwestern Univ. 1972.

[51]   H. Oniki, "Communication Costs of Operating Economic Organizations," private circulation 1971.

[52]   V. Pareto, "The New Theories of Economics," *J. of Pol. Ec.*, 1896–97, *5*, 485–502. (Reprinted in *Landmarks in Political Economy*, *1*, Hamilton, Rees, and Johnson, eds., Chicago 1962, 45–60).

[53]   V. Pareto, *Manuel d'économie politique*, *II*, Paris 1963.

[54]   E. A. Pazner and D. Schmeidler, "Decentralization, Income Distribution, and the Role of Money in Socialist Economies," private circulation 1972.

[55]   R. Radner, "Teams," and "Allocation of a Scarce Resource Under Uncertainty: An Example of a Team," in C. B. McGuire and R. Radner, eds., *Decision and Organization*, Amsterdam 1972, chs. 10, 11.

[56]   S. Reiter, "The Knowledge Revealed by an Allocation Process and the Informational Size of the Message Space," Discussion Paper 6, Center for Math. Studies in Econ. and Mgt. Sc., Northwestern Univ. 1972.

[57] S. Reiter, "Informational Efficiency of Iterative Processes and the Size of Message Spaces," Discussion Paper 11, Center for Math. Studies in Econ. and Mgt. Sc., Northwestern Univ. 1972.

[58] P. A. Samuelson, "Market Mechanisms and Maximization," The Rand Corp., Santa Monica 1949. (Reprinted in *Collected Scientific Papers of Paul A. Samuelson, I*, J. E. Stiglitz, ed., Cambridge, Mass. 1966. 425–492.)

[59] P. A. Samuelson, "The Pure Theory of Public Expenditure," *Rev. of Ec. and Stat.*, 1954, *36*, 387–389.

[60] L. S. Shapley, "Simple Games: Application to Organization Theory," presented at the Second World Congress of the Econometric Society, Cambridge, England, 1970.

[61] L. S. Shapley and M. Shubik, "Ownership and the Production Function," *Quart. J. of Econ.*, 1967, *81*, 88–111.

[62] M. Shubik, "Incentives, Decentralized Control, the Assignment of Joint Costs, and Internal Pricing," *Management Science*, 1962, *8*, 325–343.

[63] H. A. Simon, "A Formal Theory of the Employment Relationship," *Econometrica*, 1951, *19*, 293–305.

[64] H. Sonnenschein, "An Axiomatic Characterization of the Competitive Mechanism," presented at the Conference Seminar on Decentralization, Northwestern Univ., Feb. 1972.

[65] D. Starrett, "Fundamental Nonconvexities in the Theory of Externalities," *J. of Econ. Theory*, 1972, *4*, 180–199.

[66] H. C. Taylor, "Obituary: Richard Theodore Ely," *Econ. J.*, 1944, *54*, 132–138.

[67] H. Uzawa, "Iterative Methods for Concave Programming," in K. J. Arrow, L. Hurwicz, and H. Uzawa, eds., *Studies in Linear and Non-Linear Programming*, Stanford 1968, ch. 10.

[68] M. Weitzman, "Iterative Multi-level Planning with Production Targets," *Econometrica*, 1970, *38*, 50–65.

PART II

Economies with a single maximand

1
GENERAL SURVEY

Decentralization and computation in resource allocation

KENNETH J. ARROW
LEONID HURWICZ[1]

I. Formulation of the problem

A. Introduction

In this paper, we wish to discuss the bearing of some recent developments in mathematical economics on the problem of the optimal allocation of resources. We will confine attention here to an economy whose aims are well defined. That is, we assume that the preferences of the economic system can be embodied in a utility function which depends upon the outputs of commodities. For a given technology, the possibilities of different output combinations are restricted by the availabilities of primary resources. The problem of optimal resource allocation is to choose among all the feasible combinations of production processes that combination which maximizes the utility achieved by the economy.

Since the discussion is at a fairly high level of abstraction, the economy being studied may be a nation or some smaller economic system, including a single firm. The assumption that a single utility function represents the objectives of the economy fits best the case of a firm. For a nation, the assumption is less justified, but it provides an introduction, at least, to the more complex problem raised by the presence of many individuals, each of whom judges the workings of the economic system in light of his own utility function. We also avoid the subtle problems involved in defining optimality in the more general case.

The problem of choosing the allocation of primary resources among different productive processes so as to maximize a prescribed utility function is a mathematical one, and its solution in any concrete case can be regarded as a matter of computation. Now any computation, beyond the very simplest, involves a process of successive approximations, that is, a process carried out in several steps, where the calculations in each step make use of the results of the preceding steps and one of the results of each step is an approximation to the desired answer. (The ordinary process of long division is an example of a process of successive approximations; the results of each trial division step are another digit to be added to the quotient and a new dividend to be used in the next trial division.)

That the market place solves the economic problem of equating supply and demand by successive approximations to the equilibrating price or prices is a concept familiar from elementary economics textbooks. In a single market, each approximation results in naming a price and calculating the difference between demand and supply at that price; the next approximation involves adjusting the previous trial price in a manner governed by this difference, with the idea of ultimately wiping it out. The notion of this kind of dynamics in the movement of prices has its roots in the English classical economists, perhaps particularly John Stuart Mill, but it received its first explicit recognition, particularly with reference to simultaneous successive approximations to all prices, in the concept of *tâtonnements* of Léon Walras.[2]

Since welfare economics assures us that under certain assumptions as to the utility function and the productive process (see Section III A below for a more explicit discussion of these assumptions) a competitive equilibrium can be identified with an economic optimum, we may conclude that the method of successive approximations which solves the problem of market equilibrium is also a computational method for solving the problem of optimal resource allocation. Indeed, it was seen in precisely this light by Pareto[3], who compared the market to a computing machine. Of course, as soon as the problem of optimal resource allocation is formulated as the solution of a system of simultaneous equations (namely, the equations defining competitive equilibrium), the possibility arises of solving them by some centralized procedure involving the use of computing machines rather than the market. Pareto objected that the enormous number of equations made such a procedure impossible. A completely centralized organization would require a capacity for storage and processing of technological and other information that exceeds anything likely to be available. The competitive process, on the contrary, achieves *decentralization.*[4] At each stage in the market's process of successive approximations, any individual firm adjusts its tentative production plans making use of information only about the current tentative prices and its own technology. The adjustments of tentative prices, at the same time, depend only on the aggregate demands and supplies. These are simply a sum of the tentative production plans of the individual firms (and consumption plans of consumers) plus the originally existing supplies of basic resources.

Thus the information needed by firms and consumers consists solely of their technologies or utility functions plus prices, while the adjustment of prices is based only on the aggregate of individuals' decisions. It is the minimization of information requirements for each participant in the economy which constitutes the virtue of decentralization.

Our aim here is to state more precisely than hitherto the dynamic system which is implied by the market mechanism, to give conditions under which the resource allocation determined by it converges to the optimal, where optimality is defined in terms of a single utility function for the economy, and to suggest modifications of the market mechanism which still preserve some degree of decentralization for cases where the conditions in question are not satisfied. The conditions for convergence of the unmodified market mechanism are basically those of diminishing or constant returns in production and diminishing marginal utility (in a generalized sense) for the consumption of final demands. To study these dynamic problems, we will make use of a variety of mathematical tools, some of which have arisen in the theory of games and of linear and nonlinear programming and some of which are more classical applications of differential equations to maximization problems.

In Section I, B, we will review the history of the problem of dynamic adjustment to a social optimum from its initial formulation by Walras. In Section I, C, we will state more precisely our resource allocation model. In Section II, the mathematical tools that will be used are reviewed; they are primarily the gradient method (or method of steepest ascent), which is a system of differential equations for solving a maximization problem, and the relation between constrained maxima and saddle points. In Section III, we study the case of production under diminishing or constant returns with a strictly concave utility function (see Definition 1 below; the condition is a generalized form of diminishing marginal utility). In this case two dynamic systems which formalize the intuitive notion of a market mechanism have been shown to converge. In Section IV, we consider the cases where unmodified market processes do not converge, in particular, that of increasing returns. Here three modified market mechanisms are proposed and shown to have some desirable properties. One such mechanism is closely related to imperfect competition, another to speculation. It is also shown that the purely linear case (linear utility function and constant returns to scale), for which the unmodified market mechanisms do not converge, can be completely solved by some of the modified mechanisms.

B. Historical remarks

Most of the discussions in the economic literature on the achievement of a social optimum through the market, whether in a socialist or a capitalist economy, have contented themselves with a static characterization.[5] The main contributors to a dynamic formulation of the market mechanism have been Walras, Pareto, Taylor,[6] Lange,[7] and Samuelson.[8]

In the present study, we are concerned with a single consumer in whose interests the whole economy is run. Walras, Pareto, Taylor, and Samuelson are all concerned with a multiplicity of consumers; Lange deals with both cases. In the many-consumer case, it is assumed that the consumer maximizes his utility instantaneously, so that his demand for commodities is a given function of prices.

Walras was not explicitly concerned with a socialist economy, but he did regard the competitive system as a computing device for achieving a maximum of satisfaction to society. On the production side, he assumed that all production processes were linear-homogeneous.[9] In this case, the profit is proportional to the scale, at any given set of prices, and the marginal profitability is simply a constant. Walras' rule for adjustment when the economic system is in an initial state of disequilibrium is that (a) the price change has the same sign as the excess demand, and (b) the change in the scale of each process has the same sign as the marginal profitability.[10]

Walras' adjustment rule for firms is an inevitable consequence of his assumption of constant returns to scale. We cannot postulate that a firm will instantaneously maximize its profits at any given level of prices; under constant returns, the profit-maximizing scale may be infinite if positive profits are possible at some level, or it may be that there are zero profits at all scales, in which case profit-maximization does not define the behavior of the firm, or, if profits are negative at all positive scales, the optimal scale is zero. Walras correctly saw that under these circumstances he could not prescribe instantaneous profit-maximization in the way he did require instantaneous utility-maximization by the consumer. Despite the necessary character of lagged adjustment, Walras' successors were usually not so careful, and a clearer understanding of the special adjustment problems connected with constant returns to scales was not achieved until the development of game theory and linear programming brought them to the fore.

Pareto explicitly noted that a socialist system would have to mimic the process of competition to achieve an optimal allocation[11] and, following Walras, laid great emphasis on the market as a computing device to solve the system of equations of general economic equilibrium. However, his description of the dynamics of adjustment is considerably less precise than Walras'. In the *Cours* (published in 1896) he indicated rather sketchily his agreement with Walras' description of the competitive process[12] and, while agreeing with Edgeworth that computationally there are many ways of achieving an economic optimum, contends that Walras' way is the natural economic way.[13]

The description in the later *Manuel* is more extensive but more obscure. The discussion of stability implies a dynamic system in which price responds to a difference of supply and demand.[14] However, the meaning of the supply functions for firms is never clearly defined. For those operating under diminishing returns, it is the ordinary profit-maximization rule; for others, it appears rather to be the rule that price equals average cost.[15] The justification for the latter however is based on free entry, which is itself a dynamic process akin to Walras', and should have been introduced explicitly.

Taylor distinguished between primary factors and produced commodities. For any given set of prices of the former, the price of the latter are set so that price equals cost of production.[16] The demand by consumers at these prices indirectly generates a demand for primary factors. The prices of these are then increased if demand exceeds supply, decreased in the opposite case.[17]

Taylor's rule for price-setting by producers is anything but clear. In the special case where constant returns to scale prevail, there is no joint production, and each firm produces a final product directly from primary factors, Taylor's rule is unequivocal. However, in the absence of constant returns, average costs will depend upon a system of simultaneous equations involving the demand functions among others. Even with constant returns, the setting of prices by Taylor's rule require solution of a system of simultaneous equations if products of some firms are used by others. If there are alternative processes for producing the same commodity, there would also be a minimization problem to solve.[18] No indication is given as to the solution of these problems; certainly there would have to be some degree of centralization, in the sense that a central productive agency would have to have access to all the technical coefficients, at least, in order to determine prices.

Lange has been the strongest defender of the proposition that a socialist economy can achieve both an optimal allocation of resources and the computational and informational virtues of decentralization. He presents two adjustment models, according as there is or is not consumers' sovereignty. In both cases, the behavior of firms is defined by the principle of marginal-cost pricing. That is, at given prices, the firm is supposed first to find for any given output the minimum cost of producing it. The output is then determined so as to equate marginal cost, so calculated, to price. The demand functions for factors are determined by the cost-minimization criterion.

This formulation is clearly designed to encompass the cases of both increasing and decreasing returns. In the latter case, it corresponds in general to the single rule of choosing inputs and outputs so as to maximize profits. As we shall see below,[19] the rule is inadequate and strictly speaking incorrect for the case of increasing returns. Further, the rule clearly does not meet the problems raised by the case of constant returns, as sketched above.

The firm's behavior defines the supply and demand functions of firms. In Lange's first model, the demand functions of consumers are defined by utility maximization. The supply and demand functions for the whole market now being defined, the state is to vary prices in accordance with supply and demand. Lange recognized that it had not been proved that this dynamic process would necessarily converge to the equilibrium which corresponded to optimal resource allocation; the process might not converge to anything at all but instead oscillate indefinitely or even diverge explosively.[20] He suggests that the price-adjustment rules of the state might have to be modified in some way to avoid oscillations, as by taking account of the anticipated effects of price changes on quantities, a point which is illustrated below for the case of increasing returns.[21]

Lange's discussion of the second model, where there is only one utility function, that of a Central Planning Board, does not clearly define the dynamic process.[22] The meaning seems to be that the Central Planning Board determines its demand functions from its utility function as if it were a consumer and then prices respond to supply and demand, as before. It is not clear whether the Board is subjected to a budget limitation or it simply equates marginal utility to price.

Samuelson's well-known restatement of the Walrasian dynamic system assumes that supply and demand functions are well-defined. His simultaneous dynamic system is then simply the statement that the rate of change of each price is proportional to the difference between demand and supply. Though the essentials of the system are found in Walras and Lange, it is Samuelson who has first made it explicit, and doubtless our reading of the first two is done through the spectacles supplied by Samuleson.

The development of linear programming put renewed emphasis on the problems raised by constant returns in production. In a purely linear economy, where each process operates under constant returns and the utility function of the economic system is linear, the system of computations analogous to the market led to indefinite oscillations, as was shown by Samuelson.[23] Indeed, this problem was the starting point of the present investigation for the authors.

C. Formal statement of the resource allocation model

Let there be s commodities and m processes for carrying on production of commodities. Each process may be carried on at different scales, and it is not supposed in general that there are constant returns to scale. Let x_j be the scale of the jth process; for most purposes, x_j may most conveniently be thought of as the amount of output of the jth process, or an index of outputs if the process has more than one. Let $g_{ij}(x_j)$ be the amount of commodity i produced by the jth process when the latter is conducted at scale x_j; a negative value for $g_{ij}(x_j)$ refers to an input.

Among the s commodities we will distinguish a sub-class of n *desired* commodities which enter into final uses. The remaining or *primary* commodities are useful only because they enter into the production of the desired commodities directly or indirectly. Let y_i be the amount of desired commodity i used by the economy for final demands – that is, not used up in one of the productive processes. The economy is assumed to possess a single utility function which has as variables the final demands for the desired commodities – that is, a function,

(1) $U(y_1, \ldots, y_n)$.

The total output of commodity i by the productive processes is $\sum_{j=1}^{m} g_{ij}(x_j)$. In addition, some commodities (particularly natural resources and labor) are available in positive quantities without production. Let ξ_i be the amount of commodity i available initially; ξ_i will, of course, be zero for most commodities. A primary commodity for which $\xi_i = 0$ is usually referred to as an *intermediate* commodity, but we shall not need to make a distinction between primary and intermediate commodities. In order for a given set of final demands $y_1, \ldots, y_n$ to be feasible, it is necessary that they do not exceed the total available from the productive sector plus the initial availabilities; it is also necessary that the total output of the primary commodities plus that initially available be at least zero. Hence,

(2.1) $y_i \leq \sum_{j=1}^{m} g_{ij}(x_j) + \xi_i \quad (i = 1, \ldots, n)$,

(2.2) $0 \leq \sum_{j=1}^{m} g_{ij}(x_j) + \xi_i \quad (i = n+1, \ldots, s)$.

Here we designate the desired commodities as $1, \ldots, n$ and the primary commodities as $n + 1, \ldots, s$. The resource allocation problem is then to choose $y_1, \ldots, y_n$ and $x_1, \ldots, x_m$ so as to maximize $U(y_1, \ldots, y_n)$ among all sets of variables which satisfy the feasibility conditions (2).

It is to be noted that we have assumed the absence of external economies and diseconomies (as between processes), since the inputs and outputs g_{ij} do not depend upon the scale of any other process than the jth.

We have presented the production sector of the resource allocation model in the form of processes rather than the more usual production functions. In this, we follow Koopmans[24] who argues persuasively that the latter is a derived concept which already implies some elements of optimization. The formulation in terms of processes is also preferable if the model is interpreted as referring to optimization within a large firm. However, we generalize Koopmans' model by admitting nonlinear functions g_{ij}, so that the effects of nonconstant returns to scale can be studied.

For future reference, note that the variables $y_1, \ldots, y_n, x_1, \ldots, x_m$ are necessarily non-negative from their very definition.

II. Mathematical background

A. *Some notes on unconstrained maxima*

1. Necessary conditions. The numbers $\bar{z}_1, \ldots, \bar{z}_p$ form the *(unconstrained) maximum* of the (real valued) function $f(z_1, \ldots, z_p)$ if $f(\bar{z}_1, \ldots, \bar{z}_p) \geq f(z_1, \ldots, z_p)$ for all possible combinations of values of $z_1, \ldots, z_p$. It is permissible to think of the z_i's as being restricted to non-negative values, if appropriate.

For an economic example of unconstrained maximization in the present model, consider the manager of a single process, say the jth, who buys and sells the commodities at prices $p_1, \ldots, p_n$ which are given to him. His profit, then, is

(3) $\pi_j(x_j) = \Sigma_{i=1}^n p_i g_{ij}(x_j).$

In a competitive world, the manager seeks to choose x_j to maximize (3). Of course, this is an example where there is only one variable.

We are not primarily interested in unconstrained maxima as such, but a brief discussion of some points connected with them will serve to illustrate developments in the more complicated case of constrained maxima with which we are more concerned.

It should first be noted that an arbitrary function need not have a maximum. For example, in (3), if each of the functions $g_{ij}(x_j)$ is linear, then so is $\pi_j(x_j)$ (recall that the prices p_i are taken as given numbers, not variables as far as the process manager is concerned). If the linear function $\pi_j(x_j)$ has a positive slope, then π_j can be made as large as desired by making x_j sufficiently large, so that no finite value can be designated as the maximum. Even a nonlinear function need not have a maximum.

Second, it should be noted that a function may have more than one maximum. An extreme case is a constant, for which all points are maxima; thus if the profit function $\pi_j(x_j)$ is everywhere zero, a situation which arises in linear programming, all values of x_j maximize it.

Third, we have defined a maximum with respect to all permissible variations in the variables, sometimes referred to as a *global maximum*. It is frequently useful to use the weaker concept of a *local maximum,* a set of numbers $\bar{z}_1$, $\ldots, \bar{z}_p$ such that $f(\bar{z}_1, \ldots, \bar{z}_p) \geqq f(z_1, \ldots, z_p)$ for possible values of the z_i's in a small neighborhood of $\bar{z}_1, \ldots, \bar{z}_p$. A global maximum is clearly a local maximum but not, in general, conversely. In this work the term, "maximum," when unqualified, will refer to a global maximum.

If the function f is differentiable and has a local maximum and the variables z_i are unrestricted as to sign, then, as is well known, the partial derivatives $\partial f/\partial z_i = 0$ for all $i = 1, \ldots, p$ when evaluated at the maximum. We shall use the notation f_{z_i} for $\partial f/\partial z_i$ in general and $\bar{f}_{z_i}$ for f_{z_i} evaluated at $\bar{z}_1, \ldots, \bar{z}_p$. Then a necessary condition for a local (and hence for a global) maximum when the z_i's are not restricted as to sign is that $\bar{f}_{z_i} = 0$ $(i = 1, \ldots, p)$.

This last condition is, of course, not sufficient even for a local maximum, let alone a global one. The condition also holds at minima and indeed at some points which are neither maxima nor minima.

2. Concave functions and sufficient conditions.   The condition that the derivatives be zero does become a sufficient condition for a global maximum if the function $f(z_1, \ldots, z_p)$ is restricted to a special class, known as *concave functions.* If there is only one variable, a concave function is one in which the slope is never increasing as the variable increases. A function of one variable is said to be *strictly concave* if the slope is decreasing; such a function is illustrated in Figure 1. A concave function which is not strictly concave differs only in that the graph might have linear segments. It is easy to see graphically that the point $\bar{z}$ at which the derivative is zero is indeed the maximum.

In Figure 1 it can be seen that if we take two points, such as z and z', the part of the graph between the two points lies above the line segment joining them. This property can serve to yield definitions of concavity and strict concavity for functions of any number of variables.

Definition 1.   The (real-valued) function $f(z_1, \ldots, z_p)$ is said to be *concave* if for any two points $(z_1, \ldots, z_p)$ and $(z_1', \ldots, z_p')$ and any third point $(z_1'', \ldots, z_p'')$ such that $z_i'' = \theta z_i + (1 - \theta)z_i$ $(i = 1, \ldots, p)$, where θ is a real number between 0 and 1, $f(z_1'', \ldots, z_p'') \geqq \theta f(z_1, \ldots, z_p) + (1 - \theta)/(z_1', \ldots, z_p')$. The function $f(z_1, \ldots, z_p)$ is said to be *strictly concave* if the strict inequality holds in the last statement.

Note that a linear function is concave but not strictly concave.

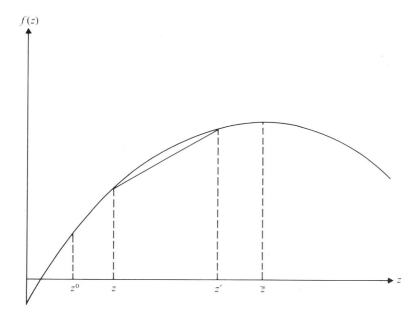

Figure 1

In the case of a single process in a competitive world, where the function (3) is to be maximized, then the condition $d\pi_i/dx_j = 0$ is both necessary and sufficient for maximization if the function $\pi_j(x_j)$ is concave and differentiable. That is, the point of maximum profit is that for which the *marginal profitability* is zero. [If the function $\pi_j(x_j)$ is not concave, then this need not be true; in that case, the point where the marginal profitability is zero might conceivably be a point of minimum profit.] Suppose now that each of the functions $g_{ij}(x_j)$ is concave; then it is easy to see that, since the prices p_i are presumably nonnegative, the function $\pi_j(x_j)$ is also concave. Thus the concavity of the functions $g_{ij}(x_j)$ insures that the condition of zero marginal profitability (price equals marginal cost) is equivalent to profit maximization.

What is the meaning of the condition that the functions $g_{ij}(x_j)$ are concave? For simplicity, assume that the process has only one output, say commodity 1, and that the scale of the process is measured by that output so that $g_{1j}(x_j) = x_j$ (note that this function, being linear, is certainly concave). Since the other commodities are inputs, $g_{ij}(x_j)$ is the negative of the input of commodity i for $i > 1$. Since also $g_{ij}(0) = 0$ (for zero output, zero inputs suffice), it is easy to see that concavity of the function $g_{ij}(x_j)$ means that the input of the ith commodity increases at least as rapidly as the output, which is the same as nonincreasing returns. Strict concavity would imply diminishing returns, while the requirement of concavity alone permits constant returns.

3. The gradient method.   Now consider the problem of finding an uncon-strained maximum by a process of successive approximations, starting from some given first approximation, say $z_1{}^0, \ldots, z_p{}^0$. One possible procedure is to vary each coordinate separately in such a way as to increase the function $f(z_1, \ldots, z_p)$. Thus, suppose $\partial f/\partial z_i > 0$ at the initial point. Then it is reasonable to increase z_i somewhat; the contrary would be true if $\partial f/\partial z_i < 0$. The same reasoning applies to each coordinate. Thus a reasonable process would call for picking a new point $z_1{}^1, \ldots, z_p{}^1$ in such a way that

(4) $z_i{}^1 - z_i{}^0$ has the same sign as $f_{z_i}(z_1{}^0, \ldots, z_p{}^0)$ for each $i = 1, \ldots, p$.

The same procedure can be applied again starting with $z_1{}^1, \ldots, z_p{}^1$; indeed, such repetition is the essence of an iterative procedure. Thus, at the tth step,

(5) $z_i{}^{t+1} - z_i{}^t$ has the same sign as $f_{z_i}(z_1{}^t, \ldots, z_p{}^t)$ for each $i = 1, \ldots, p$.

The method specified by (5) is a method of finite differences; mathematically, it is simpler to assume that the process of adjustment takes place continuously rather than in the small steps implied in (5). To effect this, the finite difference $z_i{}^{t+1} - z_i{}^t$ should be replaced by the corresponding derivative dz_i/dt, that is, the rate of change of the ith coordinate with respect to (computational) time. The requirement in (5) is then replaced by the condition

(6) dz_i/dt has the same sign as $f_{z_i}(z_1, \ldots, z_p)$.

Finally, the simplest way to insure that (6) holds is to require[25]

(7) $dz_i/dt = k_i(\partial f/\partial z_i)$ $(i = 1, \ldots, p)$,

where k_i is a positive constant. Relation (7) defines a system of differential equa-tions; the solution of this system defines each coordinate as a function of time, and this is a description of the adjustment process. We shall refer to (7) as the *gradient method.*[26] The constant k_i is the *adjustment speed.*

It is easy to see that we can assume $k_i = 1$ without loss of generality simply by changing the units in which z_i is measured. For let $z_i{}' = a_i z_i$; then $dz_i{}'/dt = a_i dz_i/dt$, while $\partial f/\partial z_i{}' = (1/a_i)(\partial f/\partial z_i)$, so that (7) becomes

$dz_i{}'/dt = a_i{}^2 k_i(\partial f/\partial z_i{}')$.

We can choose a_i so that $a_i{}^2 k_i = 1$. In this form, with which we shall be mostly concerned, the gradient method becomes

(8) $dz_i/dt = \partial f/\partial z_i$.

For this method to be acceptable, it is necessary that the solution of (8) con-verge to the maximum values $\bar{z}_1, \ldots, \bar{z}_p$. If we look again at Figure 1, it is intu-itively obvious that the process (8) will indeed converge to $\bar{z}$; for if the starting point z^0 is below $\bar{z}$, the rule (8) calls for increasing z up to the point $\bar{z}$ where the derivative is zero but not going beyond. In general, we can make the following statement:

(9)   If $f(z_1, \ldots, z_p)$ is a strictly concave function, then the gradient process
(8) converges to the maximum point $(\overline{z}_1, \ldots, \overline{z}_p)$.

[The requirement of strict concavity instead of concavity is not basic, but the
statement of (9) would have to be more complicated otherwise.]

If $f(z_1, \ldots, z_p)$ is not concave, we might have the situation of Figure 2;
there, if the starting point z^0 is below z^* or between z^* and $\widetilde{z}$, the process will
converge to the local maximum z^* rather than to the global maximum.[27]

4. A limiting form of the gradient method.   We can imagine in equation (7)
that some of the adjustment speeds k_i approach infinity. This is equivalent to
saying that some of the variables, say $z_1, \ldots, z_r$, are adjusted instantaneously
to values which maximize f for given values of the remaining variables $z_{r+1}, \ldots,$
z_p. This may be meaningful in situations where the function $f(z_1, \ldots, z_p)$ is
of such a simple form with respect to $z_1, \ldots, z_r$ that it is computationally
practical to find the maximum with respect to those variables by some fairly
direct method. The other variables $z_{r+1}, \ldots, z_p$ are varied in accordance with
equations (7), which, by a suitable choice of unit, can be written in the form (8),
as has already been explained. The adjustment process then has the form,

(10) $z_1, \ldots, z_r$ maximize $f(z_1, \ldots, z_r, z_{r+1}, \ldots, z_p)$ for given $z_{r+1}, \ldots, z_p$;

(11) $dz_i/dt = \partial f/\partial z_i$ $(i = r + 1, \ldots, p)$.

As the variables $z_{r+1}, \ldots, z_p$ change, the values of $z_1, \ldots, z_r$ which maximize
$f(z_1, \ldots, z_p)$ will usually change too,[28] so that all the variables are actually
changing in the process. If we assume that the function $f(z_1, \ldots, z_p)$ is concave

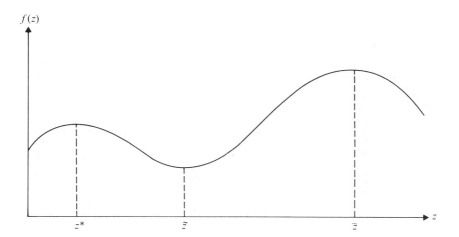

Figure 2

in all the variables, it is necessarily concave in $z_1, \ldots, z_r$, so that (10) is equivalent to

(12) $\partial f / \partial z_i = 0$ $(i = 1, \ldots, r)$.

The adjustment process defined by (11) and either (10) or (12) sounds very reasonable, at least if the equations (12) are computationally practical to solve. The assumption that in a dynamic system some variables adjust slowly while other variables adjust virtually immediately to the first set is a not uncommon one in economics; we shall see its economic interpretation in a resource allocation context later.

This process has one difficulty which has some implications for the structure of the adjustment process in optimal resource allocation. It is possible that for some values of $z_{r+1}, \ldots, z_p$, the function $f(z_1, \ldots, z_p)$ might not have a maximum with respect to $z_1, \ldots, z_r$; that is, $f(z_1, \ldots, z_r, \ldots, z_p)$ might increase indefinitely as one or more of the z_i's $(i = 1, \ldots, r)$ increase to infinity. This is true even if the function $f(z_1, \ldots, z_p)$ is strictly concave. To be sure, if $z_{r+1}, \ldots, z_p$ have the values[29] $\bar{z}_{r+1}, \ldots, \bar{z}_p$, then the function $f(z_1, \ldots, z_p)$ has its maximum value when $z_i = \bar{z}_i$ $(i = 1, \ldots, r)$, so the maximization process is well-defined there. In general, the problem does not arise if $z_{r+1}, \ldots, z_p$ are sufficiently close to the maximizing values $\bar{z}_{r+1}, \ldots, \bar{z}_p$, but it might arise otherwise.

We are also implicitly assuming that the maximum, when it exists, is unique.

Subject to these qualifications, however, the limiting form of the gradient process defined by (11) and either (10) or its equivalent (12) has the same satisfactory convergence properties as those of the gradient process (8). Parallel to (9), we can assert,

(13)   if $f(z_1, \ldots, z_p)$ is strictly concave, then in a region sufficiently close to the maximum so that equations (12) are solvable throughout, the process defined by (11) and (12) converges to the maximum point $(\bar{z}_1, \ldots, \bar{z}_p)$.

5. Non-negative variables.   The preceding discussion has assumed that the variables $z_1, \ldots, z_p$ are unrestricted in range. However, as noted in Section I, C, in our resource allocation problem, we are primarily interested in the case where all variables are required to be non-negative. Consider, for example, the maximization of (3). If the maximizing value of x_j is positive, then, indeed, the derivative has to be zero. Suppose, however, $\pi_j(x_j)$ has its maximum at zero; that is, operating the process at any positive level involves a smaller profit (or greater loss) than not operating at all. This implies that at zero, the marginal profitability cannot be positive, but it might be negative, as illustrated in Figure 3. The same considerations hold when there are several variables. We may thus conclude,

(14) $\bar{f}_{z_i} \leqq 0$ for $i = 1, \ldots, p$; if $\bar{f}_{z_i} < 0$ for some i, then $\bar{z}_i = 0$.

Relations (14) are in general only necessary conditions for a local maximum in general. If the strict inequality never holds, then, as we have seen in Section II, A, 1, the point may be a local minimum. Even if the strict inequality does

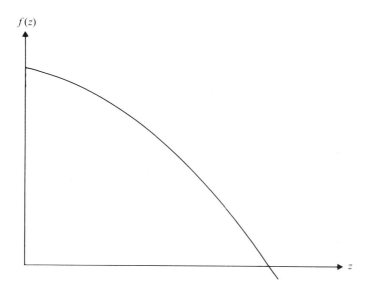

Figure 3

hold for some components but not for others, a point satisfying (14) may be neither a maximum nor a minimum. Even if it is a local maximum, it need not, of course, be a global one.

However, as in Section II, A, 2, relations (14) are a sufficient condition for a global maximum if the function $f(z_1, \ldots, z_p)$ is concave, as illustrated for one variable in Figures 1 and 3.

The gradient method described in (8) also requires some modification when we deal with non-negative variables. If, at some point in the process, one of the variables z_i is zero and if at the same point $\partial f/\partial z_i < 0$, the unmodified gradient method (8) would require z_i to decrease further, that is become negative, which would make no sense if the variable is intrinsically non-negative. This would happen, for example, in Figure 3, if the process has reached the point $z = 0$. To prevent this, we must add to (8) the rule that in this case the variable remains at zero, so that its value does not change, i.e., $dz_i/dt = 0$.

The gradient method then takes the following form:

$$(15) \quad dz_i/dt = \begin{cases} 0 \text{ if } z_i = 0 \text{ and } \partial f/\partial z_i < 0, \\ \partial f/\partial z_i \text{ otherwise.} \end{cases}$$

It is easy to see that in order for the process (15) to stop, that is, for dz_i/dt to equal zero for all i, it is necessary and sufficient that the conditions (14) hold. In other words, the maximum $\bar{z}_1, \ldots, \bar{z}_p$ is the *equilibrium point* of the system of differential equations (15).

In the limiting form of the gradient method, (14) is applicable to the variables $z_1, \ldots, z_r$, in view of (10) applied to the case of non-negative variables. Similarly, for variables $z_{r+1}, \ldots, z_p$, (11) is replaced by (15). The method becomes, then,

(16) $\partial f/\partial z_i \leq 0$, with $\partial f/\partial z_i < 0$ only if $z_i = 0$, for $i = 1, \ldots, r$;

(17) $dz_i/dt = \begin{cases} 0 \text{ if } z_i = 0 \text{ and } \partial f/\partial z_i < 0, \\ \partial f/\partial z_i \text{ otherwise,} \end{cases}$

for $i = r + 1, \ldots, p$.

In both forms of the gradient method, convergence is assured under the same circumstances as in the case of variables unrestricted as to sign.

Finally, for future reference, note that minimization calls for the same rules as maximization, with appropriate changes of sign. Thus, instead of (14), we have for the minimum $\bar{z}$,

(18) $\bar{f}_{z_i} \geq 0$ for $i = 1, \ldots, p$; if $\bar{f}_{z_i} > 0$ for some i, then $\bar{z}_i = 0$.

Again, (18) is a necessary condition for a minimum in general and a sufficient condition if $f(z_1, \ldots, z_p)$ is convex.[30] The gradient method (15) applied to a minimum becomes,

(19) $dz_i/dt = \begin{cases} 0 \text{ if } z_i = 0 \text{ and } \partial f/\partial z_i > 0, \\ -\partial f/\partial z_i \text{ otherwise.} \end{cases}$

B. Constrained maxima and saddle-points

The numbers $\bar{z}_1, \ldots, \bar{z}_p$ form the *constrained maximum* of $f(z_1, \ldots, z_p)$ subject to the constraints

(20) $g_j(z_1, \ldots, z_p) \geq 0$ $(j = 1, \ldots, s)$,

if $f(\bar{z}_1, \ldots, \bar{z}_p) \geq f(z_1, \ldots, z_p)$ for all combinations of values of $z_1, \ldots, z_p$ which satisfy (20). Again, we may and will restrict ourselves to non-negative values. The resource allocation problem of Section I, C deals with such a constrained maximum; here the z's are interpreted to include the x's and the y's $f(z_1, \ldots, z_p)$ is identified with $U(y_1, \ldots, y_n)$ (the fact that U does not depend upon all the z's does not create any difficulty), and

(21) $g_j(z_1, \ldots, z_p) = \begin{cases} \sum_{j=1}^m g_{ij}(x_j) + \xi_i - y_i & (i = 1, \ldots, n) \\ \sum_{j=1}^m g_{ij}(x_i) + \xi_i & (i = n + 1, \ldots, s). \end{cases}$

When the constraints (20) are in the form of equalities rather than inequalities and the variables are not restricted to be non-negative, the classical method of Lagrange multipliers supplies a necessary condition for a constrained maximum. That is, in order that $\bar{z}_1, \ldots, \bar{z}_p$ maximize $f(z_1, \ldots, z_p)$ subject to $g_j(z_1, \ldots, z_p) = 0$ $(j = 1, \ldots, s)$, it is necessary that there exist $\bar{p}_1, \ldots, \bar{p}_s$ such that

$$\overline{f}_{z_i} + \Sigma_{j=1}^s \overline{p}_j \overline{g}_{j,z_i} = 0 \quad (i = 1, \ldots, p),$$
$$(22)$$
$$g_j(\overline{z}_1, \ldots, \overline{z}_p) = 0 \quad (j = 1, \ldots, s).$$

Here, $g_{j,z_i} = \partial g_j / \partial z_i$. This condition has been much used in economics.[31] Thus, the theory of consumer's behavior makes use of a special case of (22), where z_i's are the amounts of different commodities purchased, $f(z_1, \ldots, z_p)$ is the utility derived from a given bundle of commodities, and there is just one constraint, the budgetary constraint, which can be written in the form

$$M - \Sigma_{i=1}^p q_i z_i = 0,$$

where q_i is the price of commodity i and M is total income. In this case, $g_{j,z_i} = -q_i$; the Lagrange multiplier $\overline{p}_1$ is interpreted as the marginal utility of income.

Another application of (22), this time using more than one constant, occurs in Lange's development of the theory of welfare economics.[32]

Equations (22) can be rewritten in an interesting way if we introduce the *Lagrangian L*, defined as

$$(23) \quad L(z_1, \ldots, z_p; p_1, \ldots, p_n) = f(z_1, \ldots, z_p) + \Sigma_{j=1}^s p_j g_j(z_1, \ldots, z_p).$$

It is easy to see that

$$(24) \quad \partial L/\partial z_i = f_{z_i} + \Sigma_{j=1}^s p_j g_{j,z_i}, \quad \partial L/\partial p_j = g_j(z_1, \ldots, z_p).$$

In view of (24), the condition (22) which is necessary for a maximum is that

$$(25) \quad \overline{L}_{z_i} = 0, \quad \overline{L}_{p_j} = 0, \quad i = 1, \ldots, p, \quad j = 1, \ldots, s.$$

This form is rather suggestive. If we take, for example, the p_j's as given numbers, with $p_j = \overline{p}_j$ for each j, then (25) shows that the $\overline{z}_i$'s satisfy at least a necessary condition for a maximum or minimum. Before following up this hint, let us reconsider the constrained maximum problem in the form first proposed.

We want to change the problem which leads to (25) in two ways: the z_i's are to be restricted to be non-negative, and the constraints are to be inequalities, as given in (20). Our presentation here is based on the important study by Harold W. Kuhn and Albert W. Tucker.[33] Analogous to (14), it can be shown that the requirement that the z_i's be non-negative requires modifying the first half of (25) to

$$(26) \quad \overline{L}_{z_i} \leqq 0 \quad (i = 1, \ldots, p); \text{ if } \overline{L}_{z_i} < 0, \text{ then } \overline{z}_i = 0.$$

Considering the constraints as inequalities requires two modifications. First, suppose that, for some j, $g_j(\overline{z}_1, \ldots, \overline{z}_p) > 0$. Then this particular constraint is ineffective, in that the choices of the z's could have been slightly modified without violating the constraints, but it was not found profitable to do so. Since the solution to the constrained maximization problem should be the same if an ineffective constraint is dropped from the problem completely, we would expect (correctly) that

(27)   if $g_j(\bar{z}_1, \dots, \bar{z}_p) > 0$, then $\bar{p}_j = 0$.

The second point is that the $\bar{p}_j$'s must be non-negative. The point of this can be seen by considering a single restraint and giving an economic interpretation to the problem. Let $z_1, \dots, z_p$ be some economic variables (perhaps outputs), $f(z_1, \dots, z_p)$ the return from them in utility or money, and $g(z_1, \dots, z_p)$ the excess supply of some resource, that is, the initial amount available of that resource less the amount needed for the choice of variables $z_1, \dots, z_p$. The condition that $g(z_1, \dots, z_p) \geq 0$ simply amounts to saying that more cannot be used of the resource than is available. Assume, for simplicity, that the $\bar{z}_i$'s are all positive, and that the constraint is effective; then,

(28) $\bar{f}_{z_i} + \bar{p}\bar{g}_{z_i} = 0, \qquad g(\bar{z}_1, \dots, \bar{z}_p) = 0.$

Consider any movement of the z_i's which will increase the return $f(z_1, \dots, z_p)$ as compared with the return when the variables take on the values $\bar{z}_1, \dots, \bar{z}_p$. For example, suppose a small increase in z_1 will increase $f(z_1, \dots, z_p)$. It must be, then, that such an increase is ruled out as being infeasible in that it violates the constraint $g(z_1, \dots, z_p) \geq 0$, for if it were feasible, the $\bar{z}_i$'s could not be the constrained maximum. That is, an increase in z_1 will increase $f(z_1, \dots, z_p)$ but must decrease $g(z_1, \dots, z_p)$ below zero. This requires that

(29) $\bar{f}_{z_1} > 0, \qquad g_{z_i} < 0;$

in view of the first part of (28), we must have $\bar{p} > 0$.

In economic terms, we can imagine that instead of explicitly restraining an economic unit to undertake only feasible policies, we permit any decisions (whether feasible or not) on the z_i's but require it to pay a price p on the amount of the limited resource used. We also let it use any part of the initial supply of the resource or sell any part at the price p. Then the unit's net return can be thought of as $f(z_1, \dots, z_p) + p g(z_1, \dots, z_p)$, which is the Lagrangian. Then the above asserts that, by choosing p to have the non-negative value $\bar{p}$, the unit will be constrained not to violate the feasibility condition.

If we combine (26), (27), and the preceding discussion, with the aid of (20) and the second half of (24), we have the following theorem, due to Kuhn and Tucker:

Theorem 1.   A necessary condition[34] that $\bar{z}_1, \dots, \bar{z}_p$ be a constrained local maximum of $f(z_1, \dots, z_p)$ subject to the constraints $g_j(z_1, \dots, z_p) \geq 0$ ($j = 1, \dots, s$), with all variables non-negative, is that

(a) $\bar{z}_i \geq 0; \bar{L}_{z_i} \leq 0$; if $\bar{L}_{z_i} < 0$, then $\bar{z}_i = 0$ ($i = 1, \dots, p$);

(b) $\bar{p}_j \geq 0; \bar{L}_{p_j} \geq 0$; if $\bar{L}_{p_j} > 0$, then $\bar{p}_j = 0$ ($j = 1, \dots, s$).

Remark.   It is to be stressed that Theorem 1 yields only a *necessary* condition for a *local* maximum. The point is precisely analogous to that which has already been made for unconstrained maxima. Except for the strict inequalities in condition (1), a constrained local minimum would satisfy Theorem 1; even with the inequalities, a point satisfying conditions (a) and (b) might be neither a maximum nor a minimum locally. Further, even if we have a local maximum satisfying the conditions of Theorem 1, there is, in general, no assurance that it will be a global maximum.

Additional conditions on the functions involved are needed to insure that the conditions of Theorem 1 suffice for a global maximum. In view of the corresponding results for unconstrained maxima, it is not surprising to find that conditions (a) and (b) are sufficient for a global maximum if the functions $f(z_1, \ldots, z_p)$ and $g_j(z_1, \ldots, z_p)$ $(j = 1, \ldots, s)$ are all concave functions.

Closely related to this problem is that suggested by the economic interpretation given in the discussion leading up to Theorem 1, namely whether or not the economic unit can be thought of as choosing $z_1, \ldots, z_p$ so as to *maximize* the Lagrangian when the p_j's are set equal to $\bar{p}_1, \ldots, \bar{p}_s$. Condition (a) shows that a *necessary* condition for a maximum must be satisfied [recall condition (14)]. It is certainly not always true that the $\bar{z}_i$'s maximize the Lagrangian given the $\bar{p}_j$'s; in economic terms, it is not always true that the optimal allocation of resources will be achieved by maximizing profits even when the prices of resources are properly set.[35] But there is an important class of cases when in fact we can think of maximizing the Lagrangian with respect to the z_i's. Indeed, we know from earlier discussion (Section II, A, 2) that condition (a) of Theorem 1 is sufficient for a maximum if the Lagrangian is a concave function of the z_i's (taking the p_j's as given at $\bar{p}_1, \ldots, \bar{p}_s$). In turn, we can say that this condition is satisfied if $f(z_1, \ldots, z_p)$ and $g_j(z_1, \ldots, z_p)$ $(j = 1, \ldots, s)$ are all concave functions, for then $L(z_1, \ldots, z_p; \bar{p}_1, \ldots, \bar{p}_s)$ is a combination of concave functions with non-negative coefficients, and any such combination is again concave.

(30)   If the functions $f(z_1, \ldots, z_p)$ and $g_j(z_1, \ldots, z_p)$ are concave, then the maximum of $L(z_1, \ldots, z_p; \bar{p}_1, \ldots, \bar{p}_n)$ is achieved by setting $z_i = \bar{z}_i$ $(i = 1, \ldots, p)$.

In view of the parallelism between conditions (a) and (b) of Theorem 1, it is natural to ask if the $\bar{p}_j$'s *minimize* the Lagrangian given that $z_i = \bar{z}_i$ for all i. Here, this is clearly true, because the Lagrangian is a linear function of the $\bar{p}_j$'s and all linear functions are convex (as well as concave), so the result follows from (18).

(31)   The minimum of $L(\bar{z}_1, \ldots, \bar{z}_p; p_1, \ldots, p_s)$ is achieved by setting $p_j = \bar{p}_j$ $(j = 1, \ldots, s)$.

Statements (30) and (31) suggest the convenience of the following definition as applied to any function depending upon two sets of variables (which we will here regard as non-negative).

Definition 2.   The function $\Phi(z_1, \ldots, z_p; p_1, \ldots, p_s)$ is said to have a *saddle-point* at $(\bar{z}_1, \ldots, \bar{z}_p; \bar{p}_1, \ldots, \bar{p}_s)$ if $\Phi(z_1, \ldots, z_p; \bar{p}_1, \ldots, \bar{p}_s)$ has its maximum in $z_1, \ldots, z_p$ at $\bar{z}_1, \ldots, \bar{z}_p$ and $\Phi(\bar{z}_1, \ldots, \bar{z}_p; p_1, \ldots, p_s)$ has its minimum in $p_1, \ldots, p_s$ at $\bar{p}_1, \ldots, \bar{p}_s$.

The concept of a saddle-point was used by von Neumann and Morgenstern in connection with the theory of zero-sum two-person games.[36] The definition just given is not the most general possible, but it is sufficient for the present purposes. It is useful to think of a game in which player I chooses p real numbers, $z_1, \ldots, z_p$, player II chooses s real numbers, $p_1, \ldots, p_s$, the two choices being made independently, and the amount paid by player II to player I is given by the function $\Phi(z_1, \ldots, z_p; p_1, \ldots, p_s)$. (A negative value means that player I pays player II.) Clearly player I wishes to maximize the function $\Phi(z_1, \ldots, z_p; p_1, \ldots, p_s)$ with respect to the variables $z_1, \ldots, z_p$ at his control for any given choice of player II's variables, while player II wishes to minimize with respect to his variables.

The discussion can be summarized in the following theorem due to Kuhn and Tucker:

   Theorem 2.   If $f(z_1, \ldots, z_p)$ and $g_j(z_1, \ldots, z_p)$ ($j = 1, \ldots, n$) are concave functions of the non-negative variables $z_1, \ldots, z_p$, then a necessary and sufficient condition that $\bar{z}_1, \ldots, \bar{z}_p$ maximize $f(z_1, \ldots, z_p)$ subject to the constraints $g_j(z_1, \ldots, z_p) \geqq 0$ ($j = 1, \ldots, s$) is that there exist numbers $\bar{p}_1, \ldots, \bar{p}_s$ such that the Lagrangian

$$L(z_1, \ldots, z_p; p_1, \ldots, p_s) = f(z_1, \ldots, z_p) + \Sigma_{j=1}^s p_j g_j(z_1, \ldots, z_p),$$

has $(\bar{z}_1, \ldots, \bar{z}_p; \bar{p}_1, \ldots, \bar{p}_s)$ as a saddle-point with all variables being regarded as non-negative.[37, 38]

Theorem 2 has considerable economic interest from a static point of view, i.e., as a characterization of the optimal resource allocation. However, we are here more interested in its implications for a process of successive approximations. In the saddle-point problem, the variables are unconstrained (except that they must be non-negative); hence, it appears possible that a gradient method will make some sense. The equivalence of the saddle-point and constrained maximum problems can then be used to apply the resulting process to the latter problem.

C. Local saddle-point conditions for constrained maxima

Before discussing the gradient method for saddle-points, we will present some local theorems analogous to Theorem 2. If the concavity conditions are not satisfied, we cannot expect to be able to state simple conditions which could characterize a global maximum or distinguish it from a local maximum. However, it would at least be worthwhile to find necessary and sufficient conditions for a local maximum. Theorem 1 does not satisfy this requirement: it only states necessary conditions.

Theorem 2 suggests that a local constrained maximum might be characterized by the local saddle-points of a Lagrangian. This is not true if we take the Lagrangian in the form in which it has been used, but it is true for modifications of the original Lagrangian, of which we present two. First, we will show by an example that a local constrained maximum is not in general a local saddle-point of the Lagrangian. Let the maximand be $f(z_1, z_2) = z_1^2 + z_2^2$ and the constraint $g(z_1, z_2) = 1 - z_1 - z_2 \geq 0$. It is easy to see that the maximum, for non-negative variables, is attained at two points, $(0, 1)$ and $(1, 0)$. Let us consider the second. The Lagrangian is

$$(32) \quad L(z_1, z_2; p) = z_1^2 + z_2^2 + p(1 - z_1 - z_2).$$

By Theorem 1, at the maximum, $L_{z_1} = 0$ (since $\overline{z}_1 = 1 > 0$), so that $\overline{p} = 2$. If the optimal solution were a local saddle-point, the point $(1, 0)$ would be a local maximum of

$$(33) \quad L(z_1, z_2; \overline{p}) = z_1^2 + z_2^2 + 2(1 - z_1 - z_2) = (z_1 - 1)^2 + (z_2 - 1)^2.$$

But clearly any change in z_1 would increase (33), so that the point cannot be a local maximum of (33) and therefore not a local saddle-point.

Our program, then, is to search for a modification of the Lagrangian so that a constrained maximum will correspond to a saddle-point. First we remark that no difficulty occurs with respect to the minimization part of Definition 2, as we have already seen in equation (31); that is, the $\overline{p}_j$'s minimize the Lagrangian $L(\overline{z}_1, \ldots, \overline{z}_p; p_1, \ldots, p_s)$ with respect to the p_j's regardless of assumptions about the functions $f(z_1, \ldots, z_p), g_j(z_1, \ldots, z_p)$. This is because the Lagrangian is linear in the p_j's. Our concern therefore is to modify the Lagrangian so that it be locally concave in the z_i's when the p_j's are set equal to their equilibrium values. More precisely, we shall seek to make the Lagrangian *strictly* concave locally in the z_i's; the strict concavity will be important in the applications of the gradient method to be discussed in the next section. We will refer to Lagrangians modified so as to have the desired concavity properties as *concavified Lagrangians*.

Our first method for concavifying Lagrangian is based on the remark that the constraints in a given maximization problem can be described in different ways. This is analogous to the well-known proposition in consumers' demand theory that monotone transformations of the utility function leave the demands unchanged, the point being that the set of variables which maximizes a function also maximizes any increasing function of it. In the same way, it is possible to transform the constraints without changing the set of values of the variables which satisfy them. Let $\rho_j(u_j)$ be any (real-valued) function of one variable which preserves signs, that is, $\rho_j(u_j)$ is positive, negative or zero according as u_j is positive, negative, or zero, respectively. Let one of the constraints in a maximization problem be that $g_j(z_1, \ldots, z_p) \geq 0$. Define a new function of the variables $z_1, \ldots, z_p$,

$$(34) \quad g_j^*(z_1, \ldots, z_p/\rho_j) = \rho_j[g_j(z_1, \ldots, z_p)].$$

In other words, for any given set of values of the variables z_i, the corresponding value of g_j^* is obtained by first computing $g_j(z_1, \ldots, z_p)$, and then computing the value of $\rho_j(u_j)$ when u_j is set equal to the value of $g_j(z_1, \ldots, z_p)$. Since the function $\rho_j(u_j)$ preserves signs, it follows from (34) that

(35) $g_j{}^*(z_1, \ldots, z_p/\rho_j) \geq 0$ if and only if $g_j(z_1, \ldots, z_p) \geq 0$.

The constraints then are unchanged by the transformation. For any sign-preserving functions $\rho_j(u_j)$, any values of the variables $z_1, \ldots, z_p$ which satisfy the original constraints $g_j(z_1, \ldots, z_p) \geq 0$ also satisfy the transformed constraints $g_j{}^*(z_1, \ldots, z_p/\rho_j) \geq 0$, and conversely, therefore, in particular the values $\bar{z}_1, \ldots, \bar{z}_p$ which maximize $f(z_1, \ldots, z_p)$ under the original constraints are the same as those which maximize it under the transformed constraints. For the transformed problem, the Lagrangian becomes

(36) $L^*(z_1, \ldots, z_p; p_1, \ldots, p_s/\rho)$

$$= f(z_1, \ldots, z_p) + \Sigma_{j=1}^{s} p_j g_j{}^*(z_1, \ldots, z_p/\rho_j).$$

The necessary conditions of Theorem 1 must hold for all the Lagrangians formed by transforming the constraints.

The problem of concavification thus becomes one of choosing among the Lagrangians with transformed constraints a class of Lagrangians for which the concavity property holds. We want however a class which can be defined rather broadly in advance of solving the problem; there is no point in merely showing the existence of a set of functions $\rho_j(u_j)$ for which the Lagrangian (36) is locally strictly concave in the z_i's when $p_j = \bar{p}_j$ for all j if the determination of that set is as hard as the original maximization problem. Fortunately, it is possible to specify a whole class of transforming functions $\rho_j(u_j)$ which depend only on a very general knowledge of the functions involved.

We will present the result in terms of a very specific type of transforming function. Note that since $\rho_j(u_j)$ is negative for u_j negative and positive for u_j positive, it must be increasing at $u_j = 0$. Let us consider the class of functions,

(37) $\rho_j(u_j) = 1 - (1 - u_j)^{1+\eta_i}$,

with η_i an even integer which has this property. The following theorem can be demonstrated:

Theorem 3.   Under certain regularity conditions, for all even η_j's sufficiently large, a necessary and sufficient condition that $\bar{z}_1, \ldots, \bar{z}_p$ be a local maximum of $f(z_1, \ldots, z_p)$ subject to the constraints $g_j(z_1, \ldots, z_p) \geq 0$ is that there exist numbers $\bar{p}_1, \ldots, \bar{p}_s$ such that the Lagrangian,

$L^*(z_1, \ldots, z_p; p_1, \ldots, p_s/\eta)$

$$= f(z_1, \ldots, z_p) + \Sigma_{j=1}^{s} p_j(1 - [1 - g_j(z_1, \ldots, z_p)]^{1+\eta_i}),$$

has $(\bar{z}_1, \ldots, \bar{z}_p; \bar{p}_1, \ldots, \bar{p}_s)$ as a local saddle-point, all variables being considered as non-negative. In particular, the function $L^*(z_1, \ldots, z_p; \bar{p}_1, \ldots, \bar{p}_s/\eta)$ is locally strictly concave in $z_1, \ldots, z_p$.[39]

Notice that the transformation can be chosen from among a wide class since all η_j's sufficiently large will suffice. The particular choice of transformation function (37) is not essential; the basic condition is that the ratio,

$$\rho_j''(0)/\rho_j'(0),$$

be sufficiently large. Another example is $\rho_j(u_j) = 1 - e^{-\eta_j u_j}$.

We will refer to the Lagrangian of Theorem 3 as the *concavified Lagrangian with transformed constraints*. It is in fact a Lagrangian in the ordinary sense applied to a problem which is identical with the original but has the constraints restated.

Before leaving this method of concavification, we note that it can be applied to the situation where the maximand $f(z_1, \ldots, z_p)$ and the constraints $g_j(z_1, \ldots, z_p)$ are linear. In this case, Theorem 2 is applicable, but the Lagrangian is linear in the z_i's, not strictly concave. The latter property, as we have remarked, is desirable in applications of the gradient method to be discussed in the next section. The class of transformation functions which will insure something close to strict concavity of the Lagrangian is very wide indeed, including all strictly increasing strictly concave functions. An application to the resource allocation problem in the linear ease will be made in Section IV, G.

We now proceed to an alternative method of achieving a concave Lagrangian, based on a lemma due to Debreu.[40] In this case, the Lagrangian is modified by subtracting a quadratic function of the constraints; we will therefore refer to it as the *concavified Lagrangian with quadratic modification*. First, consider the case in which the constraints are equalities rather than inequalities, that is, the problem is to maximize $f(z_1, \ldots, z_p)$ subject to the constraints $g_j(z_1, \ldots, z_p) = 0$. Then consider the expression,

(38) $L^\dagger(z_1, \ldots, z_p; p_1, \ldots, p_s/\lambda)$

$$= f(z_1, \ldots, z_p) + \Sigma_{j=1}^s p_j g_j(z_1, \ldots, z_p) - \lambda \Sigma_{j=1}^s [g_j(z_1, \ldots, z_p)]^2,$$

which differs from the usual Lagrangian only in its last term. It is easy to see that the first-order conditions for a constrained maximum are the same for the Lagrangian with quadratic modification as for the usual Lagrangian. But it can also be shown, that[41]

(39) $L^\dagger(z_1, \ldots, z_p; \bar{p}_1, \ldots, \bar{p}_s/\lambda)$ is locally strictly concave in $x_1, \ldots, z_p$
for all λ sufficiently large.

The case of constraints which are inequalities can now be covered by introducing new non-negative variables $w_1, \ldots, w_s$, and observing that the condition $g_j(z_1, \ldots, z_p) \geq 0$ is equivalent to the condition $g_j(z_1, \ldots, z_p) - w_j = 0$. The constraints now being written in the form of equalities, we can apply (39), provided it is observed that the set of variables with respect to which maximization is carried out has been enlarged by the addition of the w_j's.

Theorem 4.   Under certain regularity conditions, for all λ sufficiently large, a necessary and sufficient condition that $\overline{z}_1, \ldots, \overline{z}_p$ be a local maximum of $f(z_1, \ldots, z_p)$ subject to the constraints $g_j(z_1, \ldots, z_p) \geq 0$ is that there exist $\overline{p}_1, \ldots, \overline{p}_s$ and $\overline{w}_1, \ldots, \overline{w}_s$ (these numbers are the same for all λ), such that the Lagrangian with quadratic modification,

$$L^{\dagger}(z_1, \ldots, z_p, w_1, \ldots, w_s; p_1, \ldots, p_s/\lambda)$$

$$= L(z_1, \ldots, z_p; p_1, \ldots, p_s) - \Sigma_{j=1}^{s} p_j w_j - \lambda \Sigma_{j=1}^{s} [g_j(z_1, \ldots, z_p) - w_j]^2,$$

have $(\overline{z}_1, \ldots, \overline{z}_p, \overline{w}_1, \ldots, \overline{w}_s; \overline{p}_1, \ldots, \overline{p}_s)$ as a local saddle-point, all variables being considered as non-negative. In particular the function $L^{\dagger}(z_1, \ldots, z_p, w_1, \ldots, w_s; \overline{p}_1, \ldots, \overline{p}_s/\lambda)$ is locally strictly concave in $z_1, \ldots, z_p, w_1, \ldots, w_s$.

Remark.   When the constraints are equalities, the equilibrium values of the Lagrange multipliers $\overline{p}_j$ may be positive or negative, and the condition $g_j(\overline{p}_1, \ldots, \overline{p}_s) = 0$ is the same as the condition that $\overline{L}_{p_j} = 0$. Since the Lagrangian is linear in the p_j's, this means that for equilibrium values of the z_i's, it is a constant with respect to the p_j's. In particular, one can speak of it as taking a minimum with respect to the p_j's when $p_j = \overline{p}_j$; here the range of variation of the p_j's is unrestricted as to sign. The same statements hold for the Lagrangian with quadratic modification, since the p_j's do not enter the additional quadratic term. It follows that in the saddle-point statement of Theorem 4, one could properly say that the p_j's should be unrestricted as to sign, instead of being non-negative. However, it can be proved that when the constraints are introduced in the special form used there, with a slack variable w_i to transform inequalities to equalities, a saddle-point with respect to non-negative values of the p_j's is also a saddle-point with respect to unrestricted variations.

D. The gradient method for saddle-points

Let us imagine that a game with a saddle-point is played frequently, in fact continuously. At any given trial, player I knows what player II has chosen the previous time. Suppose player I assumes that player II will make the same choice of his variable $p_1, \ldots, p_s$ on the given trial. Then from his point of view, the problem is one of unconstrained maximization. He may then be thought of as starting a gradient process to achieve this maximum, so that this behavior is described by applying (15) to the function $\Phi(z_1, \ldots, z_p; p_1, \ldots, p_s)$, with the variables $p_1, \ldots, p_s$ regarded as given. Thus,

$$(40) \quad dz_i/dt = \begin{cases} 0 \text{ if } z_i = 0 \text{ and } \partial\Phi/\partial z_i < 0, \\ \partial\Phi/\partial z_i \text{ otherwise.} \end{cases}$$

Actually, however, the p_j's are also varying. If player II is thinking along the same lines as player I, he will seek to minimize the payoff function with respect to $p_1, \ldots, p_s$, taking $z_1, \ldots, z_p$ as given. Equation (19) is applicable here, so that

(41) $\quad dp_j/dt = \begin{cases} 0 \text{ if } p_j = 0 \text{ and } \partial\Phi/\partial p_j > 0, \\ -\partial\Phi/\partial p_j \text{ otherwise.} \end{cases}$

We wish to state conditions for the convergence of the gradient method defined by equations (40) and (41). We cannot simply apply the earlier statements about the convergence of the gradient process for an unconstrained maximum. Indeed, if $\Phi(z_1, \ldots, z_p; p_1, \ldots, p_s)$ is strictly concave in the variables $z_1, \ldots, z_p$, taking $p_1, \ldots, p_s$ as given, then the process (40) would converge if the p_j's remained constant. But in fact the latter variables are simultaneously changing as a result of (41). We may think of an anti-aircraft gun shooting at an airplane. After each shot, the gunner may move the gun so as to correct for the observed error, but meanwhile the airplane is moving away from its previous position and in such a way as to make the error as big as possible. Despite the complexity of the problem, it is possible to show the following result[42, 43]:

(42) $\quad$ if $\Phi(z_1, \ldots, z_p; p_1, \ldots, p_s)$ is *strictly* concave in $z_1, \ldots, z_p$ for each set of values of $p_1, \ldots, p_s$ and convex in $p_1, \ldots, p_s$ for each set of values of $z_1, \ldots, z_p$, then the gradient process described by equations (40) and (41) converges to a saddle-point $(\bar{z}_1, \ldots, \bar{z}_p; \bar{p}_1, \ldots, \bar{p}_s)$ of $\Phi(z_1, \ldots, z_p; p_1, \ldots, p_s)$.

That somewhat stronger conditions than the simple concavity assumptions of Theorem 2 are needed for convergence of the gradient method can be seen from the following example.[44] Suppose there is just one z and one p, and

$\Phi(z; p) = z + p - pz.$

It is easy to verify that the unique saddle-point is $z = 1, p = 1$. If we disregard for the moment the non-negativity conditions, the gradient method becomes

$dz/dt = 1 - p, \quad dp/dt = z - 1.$

The solution of this system of differential equations is

$z = 1 + (z_0 - 1) \cos t + (1 - p_0) \sin t,$

$p = 1 + (p_0 - 1) \cos t + (z_0 - 1) \sin t, x$

where (z_0, p_0) is the initial point of the adjustment path. It is easy to see that if z_0 and p_0 are sufficiently close to 1, the solution never becomes negative, so that the above is in fact the solution to the gradient method of (40) and (41) with non-negativity conditions satisfied. Also it is clear that the solution is a periodic function and so never converges to the saddle-point. Instead it cycles endlessly, neither diverging explosively nor converging.[45]

E. The gradient method for constrained maxima

We are now in a position to combine the results of Sections II, B and D. In B, it was stated that a constrained maximum problem was equivalent to a suitable saddle-point problem. In D, it was remarked that, under certain conditions, a saddle-point could be determined by a gradient process. We have merely to apply (42) to the Lagrangian of Theorem 2.

First, when are the hypotheses of (42) satisfied by the Lagrangian? The Lagrangian $L(z_1, \ldots, z_p; p_1, \ldots, p_s)$ is linear in $p_1, \ldots, p_s$ for any given set of z's and hence certainly convex. Suppose that $f(z_1, \ldots, z_p)$ is strictly concave and the g_j's all concave. Then for any given set of non-negative p_j's, the Lagrangian is a sum of concave functions, one of which is strictly concave; hence the Lagrangian is strictly concave. Thus, the Lagrangian satisfies the hypotheses of (42) if $f(z_1, \ldots, z_p)$ is strictly concave and $g_j(z_1, \ldots, z_p)$ is concave for each j.

To describe the gradient method, we must substitute the Lagrangian $L(z_1, \ldots, z_p; p_1, \ldots, p_s)$ for $\Phi(z_1, \ldots, z_p; p_1, \ldots, p_s)$ in (40) and (41). We can then assert:

Theorem 5. If $f(z_1, \ldots, z_p)$ is strictly concave and $g_j(z_1, \ldots, z_p)$ is concave for each j, then the gradient process defined by

$$(43) \quad dz_i/dt = \begin{cases} 0 \text{ if } z_i = 0 \text{ and } f_{z_i} + \Sigma_{j=1}^s p_j g_{j,z_i} < 0 \\ f_{z_i} + \Sigma_{j=1}^s p_j g_{j,z_i} \text{ otherwise,} \end{cases}$$

$$(44) \quad dp_j/dt = \begin{cases} 0 \text{ if } p_j = 0 \text{ and } g_j(z_1, \ldots, z_p) > 0, \\ -g_j(z_1, \ldots, z_p) \text{ otherwise,} \end{cases}$$

converges to a limit $(\bar{z}_1, \ldots, \bar{z}_p; \bar{p}_1, \ldots, \bar{p}_s)$, where $(\bar{z}_1, \ldots, \bar{z}_p)$ is the constrained maximum of $f(z_1, \ldots, z_p)$ subject to the restraints $g_j(z_1, \ldots, z_p) \geqq 0$, where the variables z_j are non-negative.

The gradient method of Theorem 5 can be given an economic interpretation along the lines used in Section II, B. If $f(z_1, \ldots, z_p)$ is considered to be the utility derived from setting some variables at levels $z_1, \ldots, z_p$, and $g_j(z_1, \ldots, z_p)$ is the excess supply of resource j, then p_j can be regarded as the price of resource j. Since g_{j,z_i} is the increase in excess supply (decrease in excess demand) due to a unit increase in z_i, we can interpret

$$-\Sigma_{j=1}^n p_j g_{j,z_i},$$

as the marginal cost attributable to a unit increase in z_i. Hence, the expression,

$$f_{s_i} + \Sigma_{j=1}^n p_j g_{j,z_i},$$

can be interpreted as the difference between marginal utility and marginal cost attributable to a unit increase in z_i. Hence (43) is an instruction to increase z_i if the marginal utility exceeds the marginal cost and decrease it otherwise, with the proviso that the activity level z_i cannot be decreased below zero. Equation (44) has even a simpler interpretation, to increase price if the excess supply is negative (i.e., if demand exceeds supply) and decrease it otherwise, but not below zero. The theorem then asserts that the process just described will eventually converge to the activity levels which yield the highest utility subject to the conditions that demand never exceed supply for any commodity. The process will also define a corresponding set of equilibrium prices.

Theorem 5 is not in present form applicable to the resource allocation model of Section I, C even under the strongest reasonable concavity assumptions. Somewhat stronger theorems are presented in Section III, D.

The proposition contained in (42) can be applied locally to the concavified Lagrangians introduced in Section II, C. Theorems 3 and 4 then yield the following corresponding results.

Theorem 6. If $\bar{z}_1, \ldots, \bar{z}_p$ is a local maximum of $f(z_1, \ldots, z_p)$ subject to the constraints $g_j(z_1, \ldots, z_p) \geq 0$ and certain regularity conditions are satisfied, then the gradient method applied to the concavified Lagrangian with transformed constraints $L^*(z_1, \ldots, z_p; p_1, \ldots, p_s/\eta)$ with η_j's sufficiently large, converges to a saddle-point $(\bar{z}_1, \ldots, \bar{z}_p; \bar{p}_1, \ldots, \bar{p}_s)$ if the initial approximation is sufficiently close.

Theorem 7. If $\bar{z}_1, \ldots, \bar{z}_p$ is a local maximum of $f(z_1, \ldots, z_p)$ subject to the constraints $g_j(z_1, \ldots, z_p) \geq 0$ and certain regularity conditions are satisfied, then the gradient method applied to the concavified Lagrangian with quadratic modification, $L^\dagger(z_1, \ldots, z_p, w_1, \ldots, w_s; p_1, \ldots, p_s/\lambda)$ with λ sufficiently large, converges to a saddle-point $(\bar{z}_1, \ldots, \bar{z}_p, \bar{w}_1, \ldots, \bar{w}_s; \bar{p}_1, \ldots, \bar{p}_s)$ if the initial approximation is sufficiently close.

F. The price-adjustment method

As in Section II, A,.4, we may consider a modification of the gradient method of the previous section in which some of the variables are assumed to adjust infinitely rapidly, or, in other words, to be at all points in the adjustment process at an optimal position given the values of the other variables. For the gradient method described by (43–44), we consider the variant where the z_i's are supposed to maximize the Lagrangian for any given set of p_j's, while the p_j's continue to be adjusted in accordance with (44). In symbols, (43) is replaced by

$$(45) \quad z_1, \ldots, z_p \text{ maximize } f(z_1, \ldots, z_p) + \Sigma_{j=1}^s p_j g_j(z_1, \ldots, z_p)$$

for given $p_1, \ldots, p_s$.

Expressions (44) and (45) together constitute a dynamic system. This system is closer to the usual supply-and-demand model than the system of the preceding section. In the present system, for any given set of prices, the activity levels optimal for that set of prices are determined. These determine, in turn, the supply and demand of each commodity, and the prices then move in a direction determined by the difference of supply and demand. In the system of the last section, the activity levels were not at an optimal level but only being varied so as to increase the difference between utility and costs.

As noted in Section II, A, 4, any system which depends upon instantaneous optimization with respect to some variables runs the risk of being undefined. At any point in the adjustment process where the prices still differ from equilibrium, some of the optimal activity levels might be infinite. With this qualification, however, the *price-adjustment process* defined by (44) and (45) converges satisfactorily.

Theorem 8.   If $f(z_1, \ldots, z_p)$ is strictly concave and $g_j(z_1, \ldots, z_p)$ is concave for each j, then the price-adjustment process defined by (44) and (45) converges in a region sufficiently close to equilibrium so that (45) is always well-defined.

III. Conditions for validity of the natural market mechanisms

In this section, we will state the assumptions about the resource allocation model of Section I, C, for which the global static and dynamic characterizations of an optimum given in Theorems 2, 5, and 8 of Section II can be applied in a straightforward fashion. The resulting criteria have natural economic interpretations. For the static characterization, the assumptions needed are that all the functions involved are concave; for the determination of dynamic processes which converge to an optimum, somewhat stronger conditions are needed.

A. Static characterization of the optimal allocation

We will first make the following two assumptions about the utility sector, respectively, in the resource allocation model of Section I, C:

$(U - C)$ The utility function $U(y_1, \ldots, y_n)$ is a concave function.
$(P - C)$ The functions $g_{ij}(x_j)$ are concave functions.

Assumption $(P - C)$ is a straightforward statement of nonincreasing returns to scale. The status of assumption $(U - C)$ is slightly more complicated. The ordinal point of view would deny meaning to any statement about a utility function which is not invariant under monotonic transformation. Concavity is not a property with the desired invariance; indeed, it implies diminishing (more strictly, nonincreasing) marginal utility for each commodity, a well-known shibboleth for distinguishing the cardinalists from the ordinalists.

The usual ordinalist assumption is that the indifference surfaces are convex to the origin. An alternative formulation can be made in terms of the following definitions:

Definition 3.   A function $f(z_1, \ldots, z_p)$ is said to be *quasi-concave* if for any distinct points $(z_1, \ldots, z_p)$ and $(z_1', \ldots, z_p')$ and any third point $(z_1'', \ldots, z_p'')$ such that $z_i'' = \theta z_i + (1 - \theta) z_i'$ $(i = 1, \ldots, p)$, where $0 < \theta < 1, f(z_1'', \ldots,$

z_p'') is at least as great as the smaller of the two numbers $f(z_1, \ldots, z_p)$ and $f(z_1', \ldots, z_p')$. The function is said to be *strictly quasi-concave* if the strict inequality holds in the last statement.

For the moment, we will not use the last part of the definition. It is easy to see geometrically that an indifference map which possesses a quasi-concave utility indicator indeed satisfies the usual convexity assumptions.[46] This property further is invariant under monotone transformations of f.

Now it has been shown that under certain weak regularity conditions, there exists for any quasi-concave function a monotone transform which is concave.[47] Such a function can, of course, equally well serve as a utility indicator. The significance of $(U - C)$, then, is that among the infinitely many utility functions which represent the indifference map of the economic unit, we can choose (at least) one which is concave.

The problem is to characterize the maximization of the utility function, subject, to the constraints (2), with respect to the variables $y_1, \ldots, y_n, x_1, \ldots, x_m$. It is easy to verify from Definition 1 that a function which is concave with respect to some members of a set of variables and where the other variables do not enter at all is concave with respect to all of them. From $(U - C)$, then, $U(y_1, \ldots, y_n)$ can be regarded as a concave function of all the variables $y_1, \ldots, y_n, x_1, \ldots, x_m$. Similarly, $g_{ij}(x_j)$ are concave functions of the same variables. The function $-y_i$, is a linear and therefore concave function of all these variables. If we let

(46) $\quad g_i(y_1, \ldots, y_n, x_1, \ldots, x_m) = \sum_{j=1}^{m} g_{ij}(x_j) - y_i + \xi_i \quad (i = 1, \ldots, n)$,

(47) $\quad g_i(y_1, \ldots, y_n, x_1, \ldots, x_m) = \sum_{j=1}^{m} g_{ij}(x_j) + \xi_i \quad (i = n + 1, \ldots, s)$

then each of the functions g_i is a sum of concave functions and therefore itself concave. (Note that we write g_i as a function of all the y-variables, though in fact g_i depends only on y_i if $1 \leq i \leq n$ and does not depend on any of the y-variables if $i > n$.)

With the aid of (46) and (47), (2.1) and (2.2) can be rewritten

(48) $\quad g_i(y_1, \ldots, y_n, x_1, \ldots, x_m) \geq 0 \quad (i = 1, \ldots, s)$.

The function g_i is the excess of supply (both produced and natural) over demand (both final and interindustry). It will be referred to as the *excess supply*.

The problem of maximizing $U(y_1, \ldots, y_n)$ subject to the constraints (48) now satisfies the conditions of Theorem 1; the variables $y_1, \ldots, y_n, x_1, \ldots, x_m$ correspond to $z_1, \ldots, z_p$, the function $U(y_1, \ldots, y_n)$ to $f(z_1, \ldots, z_p)$, and the functions g_i to the functions g_j. It can therefore be asserted that

(49) $\quad$ a necessary and sufficient condition that $\bar{y}_1, \ldots, \bar{y}_n, \bar{x}_1, \ldots, \bar{x}_m$ maximize $U(y_1, \ldots, y_n)$ subject to the constraints (48) is that there exist numbers $\bar{p}_1, \ldots, \bar{p}_s$ such that the Lagrangian

$\quad L(y_1, \ldots, y_n, x_1, \ldots, x_m; p_1, \ldots, p_s)$

$\qquad\qquad = U(y_1, \ldots, y_n) + \sum_{i=1}^{s} p_i g_i(y_1, \ldots, y_n, x_1, \ldots, x_m)$, has $(\bar{y}_1, \ldots, \bar{y}_n, \bar{x}_1, \ldots, \bar{x}_m; \bar{p}_1, \ldots, \bar{p}_s)$ as a saddle-point. (Here, p_i is the Lagrange multiplier associated with the constraint $g_j \geq 0$.)

To simplify notation, we shall write y for $(y_1, \ldots, y_n)$ and similarly with the other sets of variables.

From its definition, the saddle-point criterion contains two statements[48]:

(50.1)   the function $L(y, x; \bar{p})$ (i.e., the Lagrangian with the multipliers replaced by their saddle-point values) attains its maximum as a function of y and x when $y = \bar{y}$ and $x = \bar{x}$;

(50.2)   the function $L(\bar{y}, \bar{x}; p)$ attains its minimum at $p = \bar{p}$.

We will now give some economic interpretation to the statements (50) by considering them in more detail. First, consider (50.2); the interpretation has already appeared in the discussion leading up to Theorem 2. The function $L(\bar{y}, \bar{x}; p)$ is linear in p. A mechanical application of (18) in Section II, A, 5, leads to the following results:

(51) $g_i(\bar{y}, \bar{x}) \geq 0$

(52)   if $g_i(\bar{y}, \bar{x}) > 0$, then $\bar{p}_i = 0$.

Expression (51) is a repetition of the feasibility conditions (48) or (2); (52) adds the condition that for any commodity for which supply exceeds demand at the optimum the associated Lagrange multiplier is zero.

To draw the implications of (50.1), we will replace in the Lagrangian g_i by its definition as given in (46) and (47).

(53) $L(y, x; \bar{p}) = U(y_1, \ldots, y_n) + \sum_{i=1}^{n} \bar{p}_i [\sum_{j=1}^{m} g_{ij}(x_j) - y_i + \xi_i]$

$+ \sum_{i=n+1}^{s} \bar{p}_i [\sum_{j=1}^{m} g_{ij}(x_j) + \xi_i]$

$= [U(y_1, \ldots, y_n) - \sum_{i=1}^{n} \bar{p}_i y_i]$

$+ \sum_{j=1}^{m} [\sum_{i=1}^{s} \bar{p}_i g_{ij}(x_j)] + \sum_{i=1}^{s} \bar{p}_i \xi_i.$

The Lagrangian has now been expressed as the sum of $(m + 2)$ terms. The first depends on $y_1, \ldots, y_n$, but not on any of the x_j's. Each of the next m is of the form,

$\sum_{i=1}^{s} \bar{p}_i g_{ij}(x_j) = \bar{\pi}_j(x_j),$

say, and depends only on one variable, the scale x_j of the jth process. Finally, the last term is a constant. To maximize a sum of functions each depending on a different set of variables involves only maximizing each of them separately. Condition (50.1) can then be written,

(54.1)   the function $U(y_1, \ldots, y_n) - \sum_{i=1}^{n} \bar{p}_i y_i$ attains its maximum with respect to $y_1, \ldots, y_n$ at $y_i = \bar{y}_i$ $(i = 1, \ldots, n)$;

(54.2)   for each j, the function $\bar{\pi}_j(x_j)$ attains its maximum at $x_j = \bar{x}_j$.

The economic and institutional interpretation of the above criteria, particularly (52) and (54), as is by now familiar, requires identifying the Lagrange multiplier associated with a commodity restraint as the price of that commodity. Thus p_i may be thought of as the price of commodity i. Condition (52) then states that the equilibrium price is zero for any commodity for which there is an excess of supply over demand at equilibrium. Condition (54.1) says that the final demands are to be chosen so as to maximize the difference between their utility and their cost (at equilibrium prices).

In discussing (54.2), first note that, by definition, $\bar{\pi}_j(x_j)$ is the profit (calculated at equilibrium prices) obtained by running the jth process at scale x_j. Then (54.2) states that each process should be run at a scale which will yield maximum profit.

Conditions (54), particularly, bring out the possibility of decentralization through the price system. Given the set of equilibrium prices, the choice of the final demands can be made separately from the choices of the process scales, and, further, the latter can be made separately from each other. Let us imagine that a *manager* is appointed for each process and that a *helmsman* is charged with choosing final demands.[49] For any given set of prices, each manager is instructed to choose that scale which will lead to a maximum of the profits,

$$(55) \quad \Sigma_{i=1}^n p_i g_{ij}(x_j) = \pi_j(x;p).$$

At the same time, the helmsman is instructed to determine the level of the final demands so as to maximize the difference between utility and costs, $U(y_1, \ldots, y_n) - \Sigma_{i=1}^n p_i y_i$. For each desired commodity i, the choice of x_j by each manager determines an output (possibly negative) $g_{ij}(x_j)$ by the jth process, while the helmsman's decision includes one for y_i. Thus net demand for the desired commodity i for final and intermediate use is

$$y_i - \Sigma_{j=1}^m g_{ij}(x_j);$$

for the equilibrium prices, conditions (51) and (52) require that this net demand does not exceed the initial supply ξ_i and that, if the two are unequal, the price $\bar{p}_i$ must be zero (if the optimum can be reached without using the full initial supply, then the commodity is a free good). Similarly, for a primary commodity i, the net demand,

$$-\Sigma_{j=1}^m g_{ij}(x_j),$$

must be compared with the initial supply ξ_i; at equilibrium, the net demand must not exceed the initial supply, and the price $\bar{p}_i$ must be zero if there is an excess supply.

The elements of decentralization here are clear. For a given set of prices, a process manager need know only the prices and the technology of his own process in order to arrive at the optimal level for his process. The helmsman need only know the prices of the desired commodities and the utility function. Finally, the equilibrium on each market may be checked separately; for any given market, the test requires knowing only the net demand, which is an aggregate of many individual decisions, the initial supply, and the price.

Theorem 9.   If $(U - C)$ and $(P - C)$ hold, then $\bar{y}_1, \ldots, \bar{y}_n$, and $\bar{x}_1, \ldots, \bar{x}_m$ are final demands $y_1, \ldots, y_n$ and process levels $x_1, \ldots, x_n$ which maximize the utility function $U(y_1, \ldots, y_n)$ subject to the feasibility constraints if there exist prices $\bar{p}_1, \ldots, \bar{p}_s$ such that the following conditions are satisfied:

(a) $\bar{y}_1, \ldots, \bar{y}_n$ maximize the difference, $U(y_1, \ldots, y_n) - \sum_{i=1}^{n} \bar{p}_i y_i$, between utility and costs;

(b)   for each process j, $\bar{x}_j$ maximizes the profit, $\sum_{i=1}^{s} \bar{p}_i g_{ij}(x_j)$;

(c)   for each desired commodity i, the aggregate excess of supply over demand, $\sum_{j=1}^{m} g_{ij}(\bar{x}_j) + \xi_i - y_i$, is non-negative; if positive, then the price $\bar{p}_i$ is zero.

(d)   similarly, for each primary commodity i, the aggregate excess of supply over demand, $\sum_{j=1}^{m} g_{ij}(\bar{x}_j) + \xi_i$, is non-negative; if positive, then the price $\bar{p}_i$ is zero.

It may be noted that there may be more than one maximum in (a) or (b). This will usually be the case in (b) if the functions g_{ij} are linear, as in the linear programming case. In general, in this case, a process manager will find a range of scales, each of which achieves the possible profit, but only some scales will in fact be optimal for the economy. The choice by the manager of a scale which is not optimal for the economy as a whole will be revealed by a violation of one of the conditions (c) or (d). The validity of Theorem 9 is not affected by this remark, but the force of the decentralization argument is somewhat weakened under these conditions.

B. An alternative static characterization of the optimal allocation

Theorem 9 as a characterization of an optimal allocation is, of course, closely related to the criteria of welfare economics, as given by Hotelling, Lange, Koopmans, Allais, Lerner, and Bergson.[50] However, condition (a) is somewhat different from the analogous characterization of Pareto optima when there are many consumers. In the latter case, each consumer is faced with a constrained maximization problem, that of maximizing the utility function subject to a budget restraint. Since we are here treating the special case where there is only one consumer, there should be and is an analogous theorem, with (a) replaced by a constrained maximization.

Let $\bar{M} = \sum_{i=1}^{n} \bar{p}_i \bar{y}_i$, the total expenditure of the helmsman at equilibrium. Suppose he is now told to maximize utility subject to the constraint that his expenditures be $\bar{M}$, i.e.,

(56) $\sum_{i=1}^{n} \bar{p}_i y_i = \bar{M}$.

Since the result of a maximization is not affected by changing the maximand by a constant, the problem is equivalent to maximizing $U(y_1, \ldots, y_n) - \bar{M} = U(y_1, \ldots, y_n) - \sum_{i=1}^{n} \bar{p}_i y_i$ subject to the constraint (56). But we already know that the unconditional maximum for the last maximization is $y_i = \bar{y}_i$ $(i = 1,$ $\ldots, n)$. Since this solution satisfies the constraint (56), it must also be the constrained maximum. Hence (a) is equivalent to

(57) $\bar{y}_1, \ldots, \bar{y}_n$ maximize $U(y_1, \ldots, y_n)$ subject to the constraint (56).

So far, this is not very interesting since the condition (57) requires a knowledge of $\bar{M}$. Now let us recall the homogeneity properties of demand and supply functions derived from utility – and profit – maximization. The behavior described in (57) is that of the consumer in the usual theory of demand. If $\bar{M}$ is changed to any value M and the prices changed in the same proportion, the choice of the y_i's is unaffected. At the same time, the choice of x_j is unaffected by a change of all prices in the same proportion. Hence, if $\bar{M}$ is replaced by any number M, we can choose the price $\bar{p}_i$ so that (57) and (b) of Theorem 9 are satisfied. In (c) and (d), the prices enter directly only in the form of conditions for zero prices; but a change of all prices in the same proportion leaves the zero prices unaltered. We can state:

Theorem 9'.   Theorem 9 remains valid if (a) is replaced by (a') $\bar{y}_1, \ldots, \bar{y}_n$ maximize $U(y_1, \ldots, y_n)$ subject to the budget restraint, $\sum_{i=1}^{n} \bar{p}_i y_i = M$, where M can be chosen arbitrarily.

The constrained maximum (a') is, as usual in consumers' demand theory, invariant under monotonic transformations of the utility function. It can thus be shown that Theorem 9', unlike Theorem 9, remains valid if the utility function is to be merely quasi-concave, rather than concave.

C. The economic meaning of the gradient method

We will now apply the gradient methods of Section II, E to the resource allocation model of Section I, C. The formulation is parallel to the application of Theorem 2 as given in Section III, A. The differential equations (43) and (44) then become

$$(58) \quad dy_i/dt = \begin{cases} 0 \text{ if } y_i = 0 \text{ and } (\partial U/\partial y_i) - p_i < 0, \\ (\partial U/\partial y_i) - p_i \text{ otherwise}; \end{cases}$$

$$(59) \quad dx_j/dt = \begin{cases} 0 \text{ if } x_j = 0 \text{ and } d\pi_j/dx_j < 0, \\ d\pi_j/dx_j \text{ otherwise}; \end{cases}$$

$$(60) \quad dp_i/dt = \begin{cases} 0 \text{ if } p_i = 0 \text{ and } g_i > 0, \\ -g_i \text{ otherwise}. \end{cases}$$

In (59), π_j is the profit evaluated at current prices, as defined in (55).

These equations can be obtained by directly substituting the particular maximand and constraints of the resource allocation problem into the general gradient method. It is perhaps more illuminating to notice that (58) and (59) are direct dynamic counterparts of the conditions (a) and (b) of Theorem 9. Once the problem of the helmsman has been stated as an *unconstrained* maximization, it is natural to transform the static condition of finding the maximum into the gradient method for approaching it; this is precisely (58) (compare Section II, A, 3). Equation (59) has precisely the same relation to condition (b) as (58) has to (a).

But of course we now assume that the maximization processes of (58) and (59) are being applied at any set of prices taken as given to the helmsman and the managers, not merely at the equilibrium set of prices. As the final demands y_i and process scales x_j are varied in accordance with (58) and (59), respectively, the prices which the helmsman and the process managers take as given are themselves being varied in accordance with (60). The meaning of (60) has already been explored in Section II, E.

Thus we see that the gradient method may be given the following institutional interpretation. The helmsman, taking the prices of desired commodities as given, changes each final demand at a rate equal to the difference between marginal utility and price, except that if the final demand for any commodity is zero and the marginal utility is less than the price, the final demand remains at zero (since negative final demands have no meaning). Hence the final demand for a commodity is increased if marginal utility exceeds price and, if not already zero, decreased if marginal utility is less than price. For each process, the manager, taking all prices as given, changes the scale of his process at a rate proportional to its marginal profitability, except that if the scale is zero and the marginal profitability negative, the scale remains at zero. Thus a process increases in scale if the marginal profitability of expansion is positive and decreases in the opposite case if not already zero.

The choice by a manager of his process scale determines the output or input of each commodity in the process. For any one commodity, total the outputs (taking inputs as negative outputs) for all processes, add the initial supply ξ_i, and, in the case of a desired commodity, subtract the final demand determined by the helmsman. The result is the *excess supply*, denoted by g_i, of the desired and primary commodities, respectively. We may imagine for each commodity a *custodian* (again in Koopmans' terminology) who varies the price of the commodity at a rate proportional but opposite in sign to the excess supply, with the qualification that if the price is zero and the excess supply positive the price remains at zero. This instruction is the well-known "law of supply and demand": the price of a commodity rises if demand exceeds supply, falls in the opposite case.

The instructions to the helmsman, the managers, and the custodians represent a high degree of decentralization of the information-gathering and decision-making functions. The helmsman need only know the utility function and the prices of desired commodities to carry out his rule (58). The manager of a process need know only its technology, as represented by the functions $g_{ij}(x_j)$, and the prices of the commodities entering it. A custodian need only know the aggregate difference between demand and supply on his market (not the offers and demands of individual processes or of the helmsman) and the price of his commodity.

D. The conditions for validity of the gradient method

The solution of the system of differential equations (58–60) will not converge for any arbitrary set of functions $U(y_1, \ldots, y_n)$ and $g_{ij}(x_j)$. Not even the concavity of all these functions suffices. As was seen in Section II, D, if all the functions involved are linear, the gradient method will lead to indefinite oscillations in some or all of the variables with no convergence to the optimum solution.

Theorem 5 supplies a sufficient condition for convergence in the general constrained maximization problem but one that, unfortunately, is not applicable to the resource allocation problem. The reason for inapplicability is that the maximand $U(y_1, \ldots, y_n)$ does not contain all the variables with respect to which it is maximized and hence cannot be strictly concave in all the variables.

To obtain the desired results we will now strengthen assumption $(U - C)$ to

$(U - SC)$ $U(y_1, \ldots, y_n)$ is strictly concave in $y_1, \ldots, y_n$.

The justification for $(U - SC)$ is similar to that for $(U - C)$. In consumers' demand theory it is usual to assume not merely that the indifference surfaces are convex to the axes but also that they are not linear or planar and have no linear segments in them. This requirement insures that the demand functions are well-defined (i.e., single-valued) since, for any budget plane, the indifference surface tangent to it has only one point in common with it. We may state this as a requirement on the utility indicator in the terminology of Definition 3:

$(U - SQC)$ $U(y_1, \ldots, y_n)$ is a strictly quasi-concave function.

Under suitable regularity conditions,[51] if $(U - SQC)$ holds, there is a monotonic transform which is strictly concave. Therefore assumption $(U - SC)$ means essentially that a suitable one of the utility indicators has been chosen in the definition of condition (58) of the gradient method.

While assumption $(U - SC)$ is not sufficiently strong to insure that all the variables will converge to their optimal values when the gradient method is applied, it is sufficient to insure that the most important ones do.

Theorem 10.   If $(U - SC)$ and $(P - C)$ hold, and the variables y_i, x_j, p_i are varied in accordance with the gradient method defined by equations (58–60), then, for each desired commodity i, the final demand y_i and the price p_i converge to their optimal values $\bar{y}_i$ and $\bar{p}_i$ $(i = 1, \ldots, n)$. The process scales x_j and the prices of the primary commodities p_i $(i = n + 1, \ldots, s)$ may oscillate indefinitely but cannot diverge.

Further, for any desired commodity for which the optimal final demand is positive, the difference between supply and demand approaches zero. In symbols, for any i for which $\bar{y}_i > 0$,

$$\lim_{t \to \infty} [y_i - \Sigma_{j=1}^m g_{ij}(x_j) - \xi_i] = 0.$$

Although Theorem 10 assures convergence in the most important variables, it is not completely satisfactory. The scales of the processes must, in the limit, supply the equilibrium final demands, but it is not guaranteed that they will satisfy the feasibility constraints with respect to primary commodities. The process scales may instead oscillate indefinitely in such a way that the demand by processes for a primary commodity oscillates indefinitely about the initial supply. Examples can be given to show that this possibility is not ruled out by any assumption thus far made.

As might be expected, the possibility of oscillations is connected with linearity of the production processes. We can say the following:

Remark.   Even if some of the processes are linear, oscillations in the process scales can occur only "by accident," in the sense that special relations must hold among the input-output coefficients which define the different linear processes.

It follows that the gradient method in general provides a satisfactory solution of the resource allocation problem under the assumptions of Theorem 10.

In any case, the absence of linearity is a sufficient condition for convergence in all the variables. We need to assume a sharpened version of $(P - C)$; instead of merely postulating nonincreasing returns, we will wish to assume strictly diminishing returns. In mathematical terms, this means that the functions $g_{ij}(x_j)$ defining a process j are all strictly concave.[52] However, we do not want to assume that the functions $g_{ij}(x_j)$ are strictly concave for all i and j because that would imply that every commodity enters into every process, either as input or as output. We therefore assume the following less stringent sharpening of $(P - C)$:

$(P - SC)$ For each commodity i and process j, the function $g_{ij}(x_j)$ is either strictly concave or identically zero.

We can then state:

Theorem 11.   If $(U - SC)$ and $(P - SC)$ hold, and the variables y_i, x_j, and p_i are varied in accordance with the gradient method defined by equations (58–60), all variables converge to their equilibrium values.[53]

E. The price-adjustment method

We will now apply the price-adjustment method presented for constrained maximum problems in Section II, F, to the resource allocation problem. The formulation is obvious; the price-adjustment is the limiting form of the gradient method of (58–60), where the differential equations (58) and (59) are replaced by the conditions that for any given set of prices the helmsman chooses that set of final demands which maximizes the difference between utility and costs and the manager of each process chooses that scale which maximizes profits (55). The totality of these decisions determines supply and demand on each market; the custodian varies price in accordance with (60).

It must be recalled, as already seen in Section II, F, that the instructions to the managers to choose maximizing values for their scales implies that there exists a maximum and that it is unique. The first condition is satisfied when prices are sufficiently close to their equilibrium values but not necessarily everywhere; the second condition requires that the profit function is strictly concave, which is guaranteed if $(P - SC)$ holds. Similarly, the helmsman has a unique maximum in the final demands when prices are close to equilibrium and the utility function is strictly concave. We shall therefore assume that $(P - SC)$ and $(U - SC)$ are both valid.

For any given set of prices, $p_1, \ldots, p_s$, let the helmsman choose $y_1, \ldots, y_n$ so as to maximize $U(y_1, \ldots, y_n) - \sum_{i=1}^{m} p_i y_i$ and the manager of the jth process choose x_j so as to maximize $\pi_j(x_j)$. Denote the choice of helmsman as a function of the p_i's by

$$\eta_1(p_1, \ldots, p_n), \ldots, \eta_n(p_1, \ldots, p_n).$$

The $\eta_i(p_1, \ldots, p_n)$ is the final demand function for the ith desired commodity. The value of x_j chosen by a manager determines the net output, $g_{ij}(x_j)$, of the ith commodity by the jth process; as a function of the prices, it may be denoted by $\gamma_{ij}(p_1, \ldots, p_s)$, the supply (demand if negative) of the ith commodity by the jth process. The aggregate excess supply for the ith commodity, as a function of prices, is then

$$(61.1) \quad \gamma_i(p_1, \ldots, p_s) = \sum_{j=1}^{m} \gamma_{ij}(p_1, \ldots, p_s) + \xi_i - \eta_i(p_1, \ldots, p_n)$$

$$(i = 1, \ldots, n);$$

$$(61.2) \quad \gamma_i(p_1, \ldots, p_s) = \sum_{j=1}^{m} \gamma_{ij}(p_1, \ldots, p_s) + \xi_i \quad (i = n + 1, \ldots, s).$$

In this notation, the equilibrium conditions for an optimal allocation, as given in Theorem 9, are

$$(62) \quad \gamma_i(\bar{p}_1, \ldots, \bar{p}_s) \geq 0 \quad (i = 1, \ldots, s); \text{ for any } i \text{ such that}$$
$$\gamma_i(\bar{p}_1, \ldots, \bar{p}_s) > 0, \bar{p}_i = 0,$$

that is, the equalization of supply and demand with the necessary qualification for free commodities. The equilibrium values of final demands and process scales are determined from the equilibrium prices by the maximization that determined the supply and demand functions. $\bar{y}_i = \gamma_i(\bar{p}_1, \ldots, \bar{p}_n)$, and $\bar{x}_i$ is the profit-maximizing choice which determined the functions γ_{ij}, evaluated for equilibrium prices.

The dynamics of the price-adjustment method are then simply stated:

$$(63) \quad dp_i/dt = \begin{cases} 0 \text{ if } p_i = 0 \text{ and } \gamma_i(p_1, \ldots, p_s) > 0, \\ -\gamma_i(p_1, \ldots, p_s) \text{ otherwise.} \end{cases}$$

Since the price-adjustment method is simply a limiting form of the gradient method, the conditions for its validity are the same.

Theorem 12.   The price-adjustment method defined by (63) converges under assumptions $(U - SC)$ and $(P - SC)$.

F. Remarks on an alternative form of the price-adjustment method

The static characterization of an optimum given in Section III, B suggests the following alternative form of the price-adjustment method. The supply and demand functions of the processes, $\gamma_{ij}(p_1, \ldots, p_s)$, are generated in the same way as in Section III, E, but the final demand function, $\bar{\eta}_i(p_1, \ldots, p_n)$, are defined by the maximization of $U(y_1, \ldots, y_n)$ subject to the budget restraint, $\sum_{i=1}^{n} p_i y_i = M$. (The dependence of the final demand $\bar{\eta}_i$ on M is not indicated in the notation, since M is taken as a parameter and remains fixed throughout the adjustment process.) Then the definition (61) of excess supply is altered only by replacing $\eta_i(p_1, \ldots, p_n)$ in (61.1) by $\bar{\eta}_i(p_1, \ldots, p_n)$; let $\bar{\gamma}_i(p_1, \ldots, p_s)$ be the excess supply in the new system. Finally the dynamics are supplied by (62), with $\gamma_i(p_1, \ldots, p_s)$ replaced by $\bar{\gamma}_i(p_1, \ldots, p_s)$.

In this form, the system is a special case of a competitive economy, in which the productive units maximize profits at any given level of prices, the consumers (in this case there is only one) maximize utility at any given level of prices, and prices vary according to the law of supply and demand. This is the model sketched by Walras and formulated more precisely by Samuelson. The conditions under which the equilibrium of such an economy is stable are by no means well known, but a number of sufficient conditions have been established.[54]

IV. Modified market mechanisms in absence of decreasing returns

In this section, we will treat the modifications of the market mechanism which might cope with the problems of resource allocation arising under increasing or constant returns. The treatment must, of course, be much more tentative. The possibility of allocative mechanisms which achieve optimal allocation under increasing returns and still have some measure of decentralization is only beginning to be explored.

A. General remarks

As we have seen in several places in Section II, the absence of concavity conditions on the functions involved has two consequences for the characterization of maxima (constrained or unconstrained): the first-order conditions do not completely distinguish maxima from other stationary points, and in any case do not in any way distinguish global from merely local maxima.[55] The latter problem cannot be dealt with by any static characterization which is based on derivatives.

Correspondingly, no variation of the gradient method, which is based on moving uphill as measured solely by local variations, can be expected to insure arrival at the highest of several peaks; at best, only convergence to a local maximum can be expected.

A simple illustration is provided by an economy with one output, one input, and two processes both operating under increasing returns. Let x_i be the input into the ith process, $f_i(x_i)$ the output of the ith process, and ξ the total amount of input available, so that $x_1 + x_2 = \xi$. We assume $f_i'(x_i) > 0, f_i''(x_i) > 0$. We wish to maximize $\psi(x_1) = f_1(x_1) + f_2(\xi - x_1)$. We then have

$$\psi'(x_1) = f_1'(x_1) - f_2'(\xi - x_1),$$

$$\psi''(x_1) = f_1''(x_1) + f_2''(\xi - x_1).$$

We locally maximize $\psi(x_1)$ subject to $0 \leq x_1 \leq \xi$. If the maximizer $\hat{x}_1$ satisfies $0 < \hat{x}_1 < 1$, then we must have $\psi'(\hat{x}_1) = 0, \psi''(\overline{x}_1) \leq 0$. But under the assumptions made $\psi''(x_1) > 0$ for all x_1. Hence either $\hat{x}_1 = 0$ (and $\hat{x}_2 = \xi$) or $\hat{x}_1 = \xi$ (and $\hat{x}_2 = 0$): in any case one of the two processes is at zero level.

Now suppose that $f_1'(\xi) > f_2'(0)$ and also $f_2'(\xi) > f_1'(0)$. Then $\psi'(\xi) > 0$ and $\psi'(0) < 0$, so that $x_1 = \xi$ and $x_1 = 0$ are both *local* maxima. [That this can happen is seen from the example $f_i(x_i) = \alpha_i x_i^2, \alpha_i > 0$.] If $f_1(\xi) \neq f_2(\xi)$, only one of the two local maxima is a global maximum. (Take $\alpha_1 \neq \alpha_2$ in the preceding example.) Hence we may expect to encounter cases of local maxima which are not global.

We will suppose from now on that we know in a general way where the global maximum is; the dynamic problem will be that of locating it precisely. Within the framework of gradient methods, nothing better can be expected.

In any case, we will want to seek processes that do not converge to stationary points that are not even local maxima, while if we do start in the neighborhood of a local maximum we wish our approximation methods to converge to it. These, then, are the criteria by which we will judge modifications of the market mechanisms which seek to yield optimal resource allocations under increasing returns. Our mathematical tools are the static characterizations of Section II, C, and their dynamic counterparts, Theorems 6 and 7 of Section II, E.

B. The unmodified Lagrangian conditions

For static conditions for an optimal allocation, we start with the Kuhn-Tucker Theorem 1, which has in fact been the basis of discussions of optimal allocation to date. The application of Theorem 1 to the resource allocation problem is entirely parallel to that of Theorem 2 in the case where the concavity conditions necessary for the latter, as given in Theorem 9, hold. Each of the four conditions there has a parallel in the more general case.

The analogue of condition (a) is that

(64) $\overline{U}_{y_i} \leq \overline{p}_i$ $(i = 1, \ldots, n)$; if $\overline{U}_{y_i} < \overline{p}_i$, then $\overline{y}_i = 0$.

If we retain the concavity conditions $(U - C)$ for the utility function, then the relations (64) are necessary and sufficient for a maximum of the difference, $U(y_1, \ldots, y_n) - \sum_{i=1}^{n} \bar{p}_i y_i$, so that condition (a) of Theorem 9 remains valid.

The analogue of condition (b) is that

(65) $d\bar{\pi}_i/dx_i \leq 0$ for $x_j = \bar{x}_j$; if $d\bar{\pi}_j/dx_j < 0$, then $\bar{x}_j = 0$.

In (65), the function $\bar{\pi}_j(x_j)$ is the profit, calculated at equilibrium prices, attached to the jth process, as defined just preceding equations (54).

Finally, conditions (c) and (d) remain valid.

Theorem 13.   If $(U - C)$ holds, then the following conditions are necessary for an optimal resource allocation:

(a)   the helmsman chooses the final demands $\bar{y}_1, \ldots, \bar{y}_n$ so as to maximize the difference, $U(y_1, \ldots, y_n) - \sum_{i=1}^{n} \bar{p}_i y_i$, between utility and costs calculated at equilibrium prices;

(b)   each process manager chooses a process scale $\bar{x}_j$ such that $d\bar{\pi}_j/dx_j \leq 0$, but the strict inequality can only hold if $\bar{x}_j = 0$;

(c)   for each commodity i $(i = 1, \ldots, s)$, the excess supply g_i evaluated at equilibrium final demands and process scales must be non-negative; if positive, the price $\bar{p}_i = 0$.[56]

The difference in conditions for optimal resource allocation between the general case discussed here and that in which concavity assumptions are made about production as well as consumption is solely that between condition (b) of Theorem 13 and condition (b) of Theorem 9. The former requires that at equilibrium prices the marginal profitability of each process be non-positive; it can be negative only if the process is operated at zero scale. The last clause is perhaps more intuitively meaningful in its contrapositive form:

(66)   if the marginal profitability is positive at zero output, then the optimal value of the process scale must be positive.

In a general way, the non-negativity clause has been recognized in the literature; it is well known that one of the chief problems in optimal resource allocation under increasing returns is determining which processes are operated at some positive level. Statement (66) supplies a sufficient, though not necessary, condition.

The parallelism between Theorems 9 and 13 suggests a supply-and-demand interpretation. The demand functions of the helmsman are defined precisely as before. For a process manager, however, the supply or demand for each product is defined as a function of all prices by first choosing the process scale x_j so that marginal profitability is zero at the given set of prices (or negative at zero scale) and then finding the corresponding values of $g_{ij}(x_j)$. The equilibrium prices are then defined in the usual way as those which equate supply and demand (or lead to an excess supply with zero price).[57] This interpretation is not as useful as the corresponding one in the case where the concavity conditions on production hold. First, for any given set of prices there is generally more than one value of the process scale which satisfies the stated conditions. Under increasing returns, the marginal profitability can easily increase from a negative value at zero output through zero to positive values. Then both zero and the value of the process scale which makes the marginal profitability zero satisfy the condition. If there is ultimately a phase of diminishing returns, the marginal profitability may again become zero, so there can be three possible values of the process scale. Even more complicated possibilities cannot be excluded. The corresponding supply-and-demand functions are thus multi-valued and not well-defined.

A second difficulty closely related to the first is that the system as a whole will in general have multiple equilibria.[58] We have already seen that this phenomenon is usual in applications of Theorem 1; see the Remark following. Some of these equilibria will not even be local optima.[59]

If we specify in advance a neighborhood of the optimal allocation and consider only alternatives within it, these two difficulties will in general disappear, and Theorem 13 provides a satisfactory static characterization. The next problem is the determination of a dynamic approximation method which converges to the optimum and is consistent with decentralization. Since the proper aim of a process manager may be to minimize rather than maximize profits, the dynamic system of Theorem 10 cannot apply. The above supply-and-demand·interpretation suggests a model in which the dynamic element is simply the adjustment of prices according to supply and demand. The simplest form is the system studied in Theorem 12, with the new interpretation given to the supply-and-demand functions of processes; in this system, price changes at a rate proportional to the negative of excess supply. We will show by example that such a dynamic system can be unstable. However, in Section IV, E below, we will show that the price-adjustment model will be stable with more complicated rules for price changes.

Let there be two commodities and one process. Commodity 1 is a desired commodity with no initial supplies. Commodity 2 is a primary commodity with an initial supply of 1. The one process has commodity 2 as input and commodity 1 as output. If we use the input as the process scale, x_1, the output is assumed to be $x_1{}^2/2$, so that the process displays increasing returns. We assume that the single desired commodity 1 is desired at all levels. Then from an ordinalist point of view the utility function can be any strictly increasing function of the final demand y_1. We choose in particular a strictly concave utility function,

$$(67) \quad U(y_1) = (\log y_1)/2.$$

In our notation, the above model can be written

$$(68) \quad g_{11}(x_1) = x_1{}^2/2, \quad g_{21}(x_1) = -x_1,$$

$$(69) \quad \xi_1 = 0, \quad \xi_2 = 1.$$

Let us derive the supply and demand functions in the notation of Section III, E. First, the demand function of the helmsman is obtained by maximizing the difference, $U(y_1) - p_1 y_1$, so that

(70) $\eta_1(p_1) = 1/2 p_1$.

The process manager chooses x_1 to make the marginal profitability zero. Since $\pi_1(x_1) = p_1 g_{11}(x_1) + p_2 g_{21}(x_1) = (p_1 x_1{}^2/2) - p_2 x_1, d\pi_1/dx_1 = p_1 x_1 - p_2 = 0$, so that $x_1 = p_2/p_1$. This choice of process scale generates the following excess supply functions for the two commodities by substitution into (68):

(71) $\gamma_{11}(p_1, p_2) = p_2{}^2/2 p_1{}^2$, $\gamma_{21}(p_1, p_2) = -(p_2/p_1)$.

The optimal allocation is obvious by inspection; since the output is always desired and is an increasing function of the input, we simply set $x_1 = 1$ and therefore $y_1 = 1/2$. If we start in a neighborhood of the optimum, we can disregard non-negativity considerations. The price-adjustment model, analogous to that of Section III, E, becomes

(72) $dp_1/dt = -\gamma_1(p_1, p_2) = \eta_1(p_1) - \gamma_{11}(p_1, p_2) - \xi_1$

$= (1/2 p_1) - (p_2/p_1)^2/2$,

(73) $dp_2/dt = -\gamma_2(p_1, p_2) = -\gamma_{21}(p_1, p_2) - \xi_2$

$= (p_2/p_1) - 1$.

The equilibrium point of this system can be found by setting the right-hand sides equal to zero, that is, $\gamma_1(\bar{p}_1, \bar{p}_2) = 0, \gamma_2(\bar{p}_1, \bar{p}_2) = 0$. From (73), $p_1 = p_2$ at equilibrium; by substitution into (72), we see that $\bar{p}_1 = \bar{p}_2 = 1$. To investigate the local stability of (72-73) we find the matrix of partial derivatives of the right-hand sides of (72-73) with respect to p_1 and p_2, evaluated at the equilibrium point; the condition for stability is that the real parts of the characteristic roots of this matrix be negative.[60] Straightforward calculation shows that the matrix is

$$\begin{pmatrix} 1/2 & -1 \\ -1 & 1 \end{pmatrix}.$$

The characteristic equation is a quadratic with roots $[3 \pm \sqrt{17}]/4$, so that one characteristic root is positive, and the system (72-73) is unstable.[61]

C. A digression on marginal-cost pricing

Suppose that the jth process has a single output, say commodity 1, and that the scale of the process is taken to be that output. Then $g_{1j}(x_j) = x_j$, and $-g_{ij}(x_j)$ is the input of commodity i needed to produce one unit of commodity 1 ($i = 2, \ldots, s$). Clearly,

(74) $d\bar{\pi}_j/dx_j = \bar{p}_1 - \Sigma_{i=2}^{s} \bar{p}_i[-g_{ij}'(x_j)]$.

Since $-g_{ij}{}'(x_j)$ is the increase in input i per unit increase in output, (74) may be interpreted in familiar fashion; the marginal profitability equals price less marginal cost. Condition (b) then says that at the optimum price equals marginal cost, except that for a process not operated at all price may be less than marginal cost.[62]

We have thus the familiar rule of marginal-cost pricing as a condition for optimal allocation under increasing as well as diminishing returns, that is, that for a process operated at some positive level the output should be chosen so that the marginal cost equals the price. Under diminishing returns, the marginal cost curve will be rising, and the rule then chooses the point of maximum profit. Under increasing returns, however, the marginal cost may be falling, and the (socially) optimal output will yield minimum profit.

Apart from the non-negativity condition, then, the usual marginal-cost-pricing condition is correct when applied, as in our model, to individual processes. But the condition is usually applied to firms, where a firm, in our formulation, is a single decision-making unit having control over several processes. In this form, it is *not* correct, contrary to prevailing opinion, that the optimal allocation corresponds in general to an equality of price and marginal cost, as the latter term is usually defined.

To see this, recall that the cost function is defined in economic literature as the *minimum* cost of producing any given output, prices being taken as given.[63] Marginal cost is then simply the derivative of the cost function with respect to output.

The usual rule of equating marginal cost to price, then, implies that the output of the firm is produced at minimum cost. Despite the reasonable sound of this statement, it is not, in general, a correct rule for optimal resource allocation. Consider for example a firm which has two processes with the same output but different inputs, each process showing increasing returns. Let $f_1(y_1)$ be the amount of input 1 required to produce amount y_1 of the output by process 1, $f_2(y_2)$ the amount of input 2 required to produce amount y_2 of the output by process 2. Let ξ_1 and ξ_2 be the amounts of inputs 1 and 2 initially available. We assume increasing returns, so that $f_1{}''(y_1) < 0, f_2{}''(y_2) < 0$. The rule of minimizing cost at any given output requires the form to choose y_1 and y_2 so as to minimize $p_1 f_1(y_1) + p_2 f_2(y_2)$ subject to the constraint, $y_1 + y_2 = y$, where p_1 and p_2 are the prices of inputs 1 and 2, respectively. This is equivalent to minimizing,

$$\psi(y_1) = p_1 f_1(y_1) + p_2 f_2(y - y_1),$$

with respect to y_1 subject to the inequality constraints $0 \leq y_1 \leq y$. By differentiation, $\psi''(y_1) < 0$ throughout the interval, so that the minimum must occur at either $y_1 = 0$ or $y_1 = y$, i.e., $y_2 = 0$. Thus, no matter what values are assigned for p_1, p_2, and y, one of the two inequalities,

$$f_1(y_1) < \xi_1, \qquad f_2(y_2) < \xi_2,$$

must hold.

On the other hand, socially optimal allocation requires maximizing total output $y_1 + y_2$ subject to the constraints, $f_1(y_1) \leq \xi_1, f_2(y_2) \leq \xi_2$: It is obvious that the maximum is attained by choosing y_1 and y_2 so that,

$$f_1(y_1) = \xi_1, \qquad f_2(y_2) = \xi_2.$$

Therefore it is impossible that the rule of cost minimization lead in this case to an optimal allocation of resources. The minimum cost solution is not socially efficient because it leaves unemployed resources which have positive usefulness, no matter how factor prices are chosen.

D. Optimal allocation through imperfect competition

To deal with the drawbacks of Theorem 1 as a tool for determining optimal resource allocation under increasing returns, we will turn to Theorems 3 and 4 which yield local saddle-point characterizations of the optimal allocation. Unlike Theorem 1, these conditions are satisfied only by local maxima, not by other extrema.

First, consider the application of Theorem 3 to the resource application problem. The concavified Lagrangian with transformed constraints becomes

$$(75) \quad L^*(y_1, \ldots, y_n, x_1, \ldots, x_m; p_1, \ldots, p_s/\eta)$$
$$= U(y_1, \ldots, y_n) + \Sigma_{i=1}^{s} p_i[1 - (1 - g_i)^{1+\eta_i}],$$

where the excess supply $g_i = g_i(x_1, \ldots, x_m, y_1, \ldots, y_n)$ is defined by (46) and (47).

The optimal allocation is characterized as a local saddle-point. Since L^* is linear in the p_i's, with respect to which there is a minimum, we have

$$(76) \quad 1 - (1 - \bar{g}_i)^{1+\eta_i} \geq 0; \text{ for any } i \text{ for which the strict inequality holds,}$$
$$\bar{p}_i = 0.$$

Here, $\bar{g}_i$ is the excess supply at equilibrium, that is, $g_i(\bar{x}_1, \ldots, \bar{x}_m, \bar{y}_1, \ldots, \bar{y}_n)$. However, it is easy to see that the expression,

$$1 - (1 - g_i)^{1+\eta_i},$$

is positive, zero, or negative according as g_i is positive, zero, or negative; indeed it was originally chosen to have this property [see remarks preceding (37) in Section II, C]. Hence (76) is equivalent to

$$(77) \quad \bar{g}_i \geq 0; \text{ if } \bar{g}_i > 0, \text{ then } \bar{p}_i = 0,$$

as was to be expected.

Let us combine the maximization part of the saddle-point criterion with (77).

Theorem 14. Under certain regularity conditions, a necessary and sufficient condition for a locally optimal allocation is that

(a) $\bar{y}_1, \ldots, \bar{y}_n, \bar{x}_1, \ldots, \bar{x}_m$ maximize the expression, $U(y_1, \ldots, y_n) + \Sigma_{i=1}^{s} \bar{p}_i(1 - [1 - g_i(x_1, \ldots, x_m, y_1, \ldots, y_n)]^{1+\eta_i});$

(b) $g_i(\bar{x}_1, \ldots, \bar{x}_m, \bar{y}_1, \ldots, \bar{y}_n) \geq 0$; if $g_i(\bar{x}_1, \ldots, \bar{x}_m, \bar{y}_1, \ldots, \bar{y}_n) > 0$,
then $\bar{p}_i = 0$, where the η_i's have been chosen sufficiently large.

Condition (a) can be given an institutional interpretation. Suppose the helmsman takes over the functions of the process managers in addition to his own, so that he chooses the x_j's as well as the y_i's. At the same time, suppose that the custodian for commodity i purchases any amount u_i available for an amount, $\bar{p}_i[1 - (1 - u_i)^{1+\eta_i}]$. This function is a total revenue function in the ith market. The helmsman then maximizes the sum of his utility and the revenue he obtains by selling the excess supply (the "revenue" would, of course, be negative if there were an excess demand). The helmsman on this interpretation is dealing with a series of markets on which he is a monopolist or monopsonist.

In this formulation, the p_i's do not play the role of competitive prices, but they are parameters which affect the location, though not the general shape, of the revenue functions. We will therefore refer to them as *revenue parameters*. Condition (b) insures that at equilibrium the revenue parameters are chosen so that the helmsman will have zero excess supply for free goods (when $\bar{p}_i = 0$, the revenue is identically zero).

So far the institutional interpretation has been highly centralized. All that has been done is to rephrase the constrained maximization problem as two problems, one an unconstrained maximization and one a feasibility condition. However, any unconstrained maximization has a certain element of decentralization implicit in it. If $\bar{z}_1, \ldots, \bar{z}_p$ maximize a function $f(z_1, \ldots, z_p)$, then it is true that $\bar{z}_1$ maximizes the function $f(z_1, \bar{z}_2, \ldots, \bar{z}_p)$ as a function of the single variable z_1, and similarly with the other z_i's. In the case of Theorem 9, there was an extreme simplification in the unconstrained maximization (given the $\bar{p}_i$'s), since the function to be maximized was a sum of functions each involving a different variable. The maximization in Theorem 14 is not so simple, but along the lines just suggested there is a degree of decentralization which, as we shall see, becomes more pronounced in the dynamic form.

Let,

(78) $h_{ij} = g_i - g_{ij}$ $(i = 1, \ldots, s; j = 1, \ldots, m)$;

(79) $h_i = g_i + y_i$ $(i = 1, \ldots, n)$.

Reference to (46–47) shows that h_{ij} is independent of x_j, though it depends on the scales of all processes other than the jth and, in the case of desired commodities, on y_i. Similarly, h_i depends on the process scales but is independent of the y_i's. If, following the argument above, we maximize with respect to x_j, taking the y_i's and all process scales other than the jth as given at their equilibrium values, we have that

(80) $\bar{x}_j$ maximizes $\Sigma_{i=1}^{s} \bar{p}_i \{1 - [1 - \bar{h}_{ij} - g_{ij}(x_j)]^{1+\eta_i}\}$,

the term $U(\bar{y}_1, \ldots, \bar{y}_n)$ being omitted since it is a constant with respect to x_j. Here as before a bar over a symbol denotes evaluation at equilibrium. Similarly,

(81) $\bar{y}_1, \ldots, \bar{y}_n$ maximizes $U(y_1, \ldots, y_n) + \Sigma_{i=1}^s \bar{p}_i[1 - (1 - \bar{h}_i + y_i)^{1 + \eta_i}]$.

Equations (80) and (81) suggest a degree of decentralization. Each process manager chooses an x_j so as to maximize (80), the helmsman chooses final demands so as to maximize (81). Each is now operating on imperfectly competitive markets. Each now needs somewhat more information from the outside than in the concave case. The manager of the jth process needs to know not only the $\bar{p}_i$'s but also the $\bar{h}_{ij}$'s ($i = 1, \ldots, s$); the helmsman needs to know both $\bar{p}_i$ and $\bar{h}_i (i = 1, \ldots, n)$.

The dynamic counterpart of Theorem 14 is derived from Theorem 6. If we apply the theorem to the resource allocation, we find by straightforward differentiation that

(82) $L_{y_i}{}^* = U_{y_i} - (1 + \eta_i)p_i(1 - g_i)^{\eta_i}$,

(83) $L_{x_j}{}^* = \Sigma_{i=1}^s (1 + \eta_i)p_i(1 - g_i)^{\eta_i}g_{ij}{}'$.

The gradient method based on these derivatives requires the helmsman and the process managers to find the unconstrained maxima of (81) and (80), respectively, with equilibrium replaced by current values. The information required is greater than in the concave case of Theorems 10 and 11, but not too much greater. The helmsman and each process manager must now know the current values of both the revenue parameter and the excess supply for every market, in addition to his utility function or technology, respectively.

The behavior of the revenue parameters is a straightforward dynamic analogue of (76).

Theorem 15.   Under certain regularity conditions and for η_i's sufficiently large, the system of differential equations,

(a) $dy_i/dt = \begin{cases} 0 \text{ if } L_{y_i}{}^* < 0 \text{ and } y_i = 0, \\ L_{y_i}{}^* \text{ otherwise,} \end{cases}$

(b) $dx_i/dt = \begin{cases} 0 \text{ if } L_{x_j}{}^* < 0 \text{ and } x_i = 0, \\ L_{x_j}{}^* \text{ otherwise;} \end{cases}$

(c) $dp_i/dt = \begin{cases} 0 \text{ if } [1 - g_i(x_1, \ldots, x_m, y_1, \ldots, y_n)]^{1 + \eta_i} < 1 \\ \text{and } p_i = 0, \\ [1 - g_i(x_1, \ldots, x_m, y_1, \ldots, y_n)]^{1 + \eta_i} - 1 \text{ otherwise;} \end{cases}$

converges to a local optimum of allocation. Here $L_{y_i}{}^*$ and $L_{x_j}{}^*$ are defined by (82) and (83), respectively.

Theorem 15 thus supplies a dynamic system which converges locally to an optimum and which makes very limited informational demands upon its participants.

Theorem 4 leads to a static characterization of an optimal allocation similar to that of Theorem 14. The new feature is the existence of a set of variables, the w_i's, which, in equilibrium, represent the permissible excess supply. If we refer back to the reasoning leading to Theorem 4, we see that the w_i's were introduced to convert inequality constraints into equality constraints. At equilibrium, then equality must hold in the constraints $g_i(x_1, \ldots, x_m, y_1, \ldots, y_n) - w_i = 0$.

(84)　$\bar{g}_i = \bar{w}_i$; if $\bar{g}_i > 0$, then $\bar{p}_i = 0$.

The second part of (84) is intuitively obvious and can be proved rigorously.

In the saddle-point characterization supplied by Theorem 4, the concavified Lagrangian with quadratic modification has as maximizing variables the w_i's as well as the x_j's and the y_i's. However, if we follow the argument given above about the decentralization implicit in any maximization we may say that the helmsman and the process managers maximize the Lagrangian with respect to the variables under their control, taking as given both the $\bar{p}_i$'s and the $\bar{w}_i$'s. We may refer to the w_i's as the *disposal parameters*. Then, given both the revenue and the disposal parameters, the helmsman and the process managers have, just as in Theorem 14, to maximize a nonlinear function of the inputs and outputs. Again they can be thought of as seeking to maximize profits and utilities by activities which include trading on imperfect markets.

Theorem 16. Under certain regularity conditions and for λ sufficiently large, a necessary and sufficient condition for a locally optimal allocation is that

(a)　$\bar{y}_1, \ldots, \bar{y}_n, \bar{x}_1, \ldots, \bar{x}_m$ maximize the expression,

$$U(y_1, \ldots, y_n) + \Sigma_{i=1}^s [\bar{p}_i(g_i - \bar{w}_i) - \lambda(g_i - \bar{w}_i)^2]:$$

(b)　$\bar{g}_i = \bar{w}_i \geq 0$; if $\bar{w}_i > 0$, then $\bar{p}_i = 0$.

The dynamic counterpart of Theorem 16 derives from application of Theorem 6 to the resource allocation problem. The differentiations involved are straightforward.

Theorem 17. Under certain regularity conditions and for λ sufficiently large, the system of differential equations,

(a)　$dy_i/dt = \begin{cases} 0 \text{ if } L_{y_i}^\dagger < 0 \text{ and } y_i = 0, \\ L_{y_i}^\dagger \text{ otherwise,} \end{cases}$

(b)　$dx_j/dt = \begin{cases} 0 \text{ if } L_{x_j}^\dagger < 0 \text{ and } x_j = 0, \\ L_{x_j}^\dagger \text{ otherwise,} \end{cases}$

(c)　$dw_i/dt = \begin{cases} 0 \text{ if } p_i - 2\lambda(g_i - w_i) > 0 \text{ and } w_i = 0, \\ -p_i + 2\lambda(g_i - w_i) \text{ otherwise,} \end{cases}$

(d)　$dp_i/dt = \begin{cases} 0 \text{ if } g_i > w_i \text{ and } p_i = 0, \\ w_i - g_i \text{ otherwise,} \end{cases}$

converges to a local optimum of allocation. In (a) and (b), respectively,

(e)　$L_{y_i}^{\dagger} = U_{y_i} - p_i + 2\lambda(g_i - w_i)$,

(f)　$L_{x_j} = \sum_{i=1}^{s} [p_i - 2\lambda(g_i - w_i)] g_{ij}'$.

The adjustment formulas for the individual participants are comparatively simple. The helmsman and each process manager have to know, in addition to their own utility function or technology, the revenue parameter, p_i, the disposal parameter, w_i, and the excess supply, g_i, for each commodity. The custodian for commodity i has to know g_i and he can then determine both the revenue and the disposal parameters from the pair of differential equations (c) and (d).

E. Optimal allocation through nonlinear price adjustment

If we examine (82) and (83), we see that there is a common expression in all of them, for which we may introduce a symbol,

(85)　$q_i = (1 + \eta_i) p_i (1 - g_i)^{\eta_i}$.

If we now refer to (a) and (b) of Theorem 15, we see that the helmsman or the process managers can, respectively, be thought of as seeking to maximize the difference between utility and costs or profits, if the q_i's are now regarded as prices. These prices are now determined by a fairly complicated adjustment pattern; first an auxiliary variable p_i is determined by equation (c) of Theorem 15 and then q_i is calculated from (85). However, the informational requirements are low, since the custodian, who is charged with these operations, need still know at any one time only the excess supply g_i.

　　Theorem 18.　　Under certain regularity conditions and for η_i's sufficiently large, the dynamic system,

(a)　$dy_i/dt = \begin{cases} 0 \text{ if } U_{y_i} < q_i \text{ and } y_i = 0, \\ U_{y_i} - q_i \text{ otherwise,} \end{cases}$

(b)　$dx_j/dt = \begin{cases} 0 \text{ if } d\tilde{\pi}_j/dx_j < 0 \text{ and } x_j = 0, \\ d\tilde{\pi}_j/dx_j \text{ otherwise,} \end{cases}$

(c)　$q_i = (1 + \eta_i) p_i (1 - g_i)^{\eta_i}$,

(d)　$dp_i/dt = \begin{cases} 0 \text{ if } g_i > 0 \text{ and } p_i = 0, \\ (1 - g_i)^{1+\eta_i} - 1 \text{ otherwise,} \end{cases}$

converges to a local optimum of allocation. In (b),

(e)　$\tilde{\pi}_j(x_j) = \sum_{i=1}^{s} q_i g_{ij}(x_j)$.

In Theorem 18, the informational requirements on each participant are no different than in the concave case of Theorem 10. The only elements of centralization are that a prior decision must be made on the constants η_i and that a global optimum can only be assured if the initial approximation is sufficiently close.

A limiting case of some interest arises if the adjustment speed of the helmsman and the process managers are increased indefinitely. In that case, for the helmsman we must have $U_{y_i} = q_i$ unless $y_i = 0$ and similarly $d\tilde{\pi}_j/dx_j = 0$ unless $x_j = 0.$[64] Then we return to the supply-and-demand model briefly discussed in Section IV, B. But the price-adjustment rules of (c) and (d) of Theorem 18 now insure stability.

Theorem 19.   Theorem 18 remains valid if (a) and (b), are replaced by

(a′) $U_{y_i} \leqq q_i$; if $U_{y_i} < q_i$, then $y_i = 0$;

(b′) $d\tilde{\pi}_j/dx_j \leqq 0$; if $d\tilde{\pi}_j/dx_j < 0$, then $x_j = 0$.

F. Optimal allocation through price speculation

An alternative institutional interpretation can be given of Theorem 17, in a manner somewhat similar to that which led from Theorem 15 to Theorem 18. If we look at (e) and (f) of Theorem 17, we find it natural to introduce the definition,

(86) $p_i^f = p_i + 2\lambda(w_i - g_i).$

If we now take account of (d) of Theorem 17, we see that, unless both $g_i > w_i$ and $p_i = 0$,

(87) $p_i^f = p_i + 2\lambda(dp_i/dt),$

that is, p_i^f can be considered as an expectation of the price of commodity i in the near future formed by extrapolation of current rates of change.[65] We will now argue that (87) can be made to hold without the exception noted above. As noted in the Remark following Theorem 4, the saddle-point properties of the concavified Lagrangian with quadratic modification hold whether the p_i's are considered to be non-negative or unrestricted as to sign. Relation (d) of Theorem 17 is the appropriate form if the p_i's are restricted to be non-negative. If they are taken to be unrestricted as to sign, then only the second line is relevant; Theorem 17 remains true with this alteration. Then (87) is true in general.

Theorem 20.   Under certain regularity conditions and for λ sufficiently large, the system of differential equations,

(a) $dy_i/dt = \begin{cases} 0 \text{ if } U_{y_i} < p_i^f \text{ and } y_i = 0, \\ U_{y_i} - p_i^f \text{ otherwise,} \end{cases}$

(b) $dx_j/dt = \begin{cases} 0 \text{ if } d\pi_j^f/dx_j < 0 \text{ and } x_j = 0, \\ d\pi_j^f/dx_j \text{ otherwise,} \end{cases}$

(c) $dw_i/dt = \begin{cases} 0 \text{ if } p_i{}^f > 0 \text{ and } w_i = 0, \\ -p_i{}^f \text{ otherwise,} \end{cases}$

(d) $dp_i/dt = w_i - g_i$,

(e) $p_i{}^f = p_i + 2\lambda(dp_i/dt)$,

converges to a local optimum of allocation. In (b),

(f) $\pi_j{}^f(x_j) = \Sigma_{i=1}^{s} p_i{}^f g_{ij}(x_j)$.

Relations (a) and (b) show that the helmsman and the process managers are moving in the direction of maximum benefits computed at expected prices, rather than current ones. Equations (c-e) can be given various institutional interpretations; one is that, taken together, they instruct the custodian how to determine the expected price to be announced to the other participants. It is required that the expected price be sufficiently sensitive to the current rate of change.[66]

G. The linear case

We return finally to the case which started the entire investigation, that where the utility function and all the processes are linear, that is, the case of linear programming. In this case, as we have seen in Section II, D, the gradient method will normally lead to endless oscillations. Since stability has been shown to be related to the strict concavity of the Lagrangian, it is natural to try one of the concavification methods introduced in Section II, C. Since the problem is linear, the Lagrangian is, so to speak, on the borderline of strict concavity, and it might be expected that any modification of the Lagrangian which increases its concavity would suffice. This expectation is correct, at least as far as the method of concavification by transformed constraints.

   Theorem 21.   If $U(y_1, \ldots, y_n)$ and the process functions $g_{ij}(x_j)$ are all linear, then the system of differential equations of Theorem 15, with any $\eta_i > 0$ converges to a global optimum of allocation. Equivalently, the dynamic systems of Theorems 18 and 19 converge to a global optimum under the same condition.[67]

The method of Theorem 21 is by no means the only gradient method for the solution of linear programming problems. Because of their equivalence to zero-sum two-person games,[68] the modified gradient methods developed by Brown and von Neumann for solving the latter can be applied to the former.[69] Of course, there are other methods, of which the best known is the simplex method, which are essentially different from the gradient methods. Although there has been as yet insufficient computational experience, it is very likely that the simplex method is a superior method for computation to any variety of the gradient method. But from the viewpoint of the present study, it lacks the very important virtue of decentralization.

Notes

1 The research reported on in this paper was to a large extent carried on under the auspices of the RAND Corporation. We also wish to thank the Office of Naval Research and the Center for Advanced Study in the Behavioral Sciences for their assistance and M. J. Beckmann and W. M. Gorman for their comments.

2 See L. Walras, *Elements of Pure Economics*, ed. and tr. by W. Jaffé (London: George Allen and Unwin, 1954), pp. 84–86, 90–91, 105–6, 169–172, 243–54, and 184–95. For a vigorous and stimulating analysis of Walras' theory of *tâtonnements* and its central function in seeking to show that economic equilibrium is solved in the market by successive approximations, see D. Patinkin, *Money, Interest, and Prices* (Evanston, Illinois, and White Plains, New York: Row, Peterson and Company, 1956), pp. 377–85.

3 V. Pareto, *Manuel d'économie politique* (Deuxième édition, Paris: Marcel Giard 1927), pp. 233–34. In the terminology of cybernetics, Pareto, crystallizing the usual views of economists, has held that the market mechanism is homeostatic, a position strongly denied by the founder of cybernetics; see N. Wiener, *Cybernetics* (New York and Paris: John Wiley and Sons, and Hermann et Cie., 1948), pp. 185–86. The comparison between the market and a computing machine has also been made by R. M. Goodwin, "Iteration, Automatic Computers, and Economic Dynamics," *Metroeconomica*, III (1951), 1–7.

4 For a possible definition of the term "decentralization" in this context, see L. Hurwicz, "Decentralized Resource Allocation," Cowles Commission Discussion Paper No. 2112, 1955. See also pp. 398–401.

5 See for example A. P. Lerner, *The Economics of Control* (New York: Macmillan, 1946) or J. E. Meade, *Planning and the Price Mechanism* (London: George Allen and Unwin, 1948).

6 F. M. Taylor, "The Guidance of Production in a Socialist State," *American Economic Review*, Vol. 19 (1929), No. 1, reprinted in B. Lippincott (ed.), *On the Economic Theory of Socialism* (Minneapolis: University of Minnesota Press, 1938), pp. 41–54, particularly pp. 50–54.

7 O. Lange, "On the Economic Theory of Socialism," *Review of Economic Studies*, IV, Nos. 1 and 2 (1936–7), reprinted in B. Lippincott, *ibid.*, pp. 57–142, particularly pp. 70–98.

8 P. A. Samuelson, *Foundations of Economic Analysis* (Cambridge, Mass.: Harvard University Press, 1947) pp. 269–75.

9 We follow the discussion in Walras, *op. cit.*, Lesson 22, which treats the adjustment process when there are both consumers and producers. In this lesson, it is also assumed that there is only one output for each process and only one process for producing each commodity (i.e., the assumption of fixed production coefficients), but this assumption is irrelevant to our purposes. Later, Walras considers the production coefficients not as given but as derived by minimization of costs with a given production function (pp. 383–86); but he never successfully integrates this discussion with the earlier discussion of adjustment, as Jaffé points out (pp. 552–53).

10 Walras, *op. cit.*, pp. 253–54; the terminology has been changed to conform to that used below. The reader should be warned that Walras' presentation

is by no means unequivocal, and the interpretation is not the only possible. We have followed the statement which summarizes Lesson 22 on *tatôn-nements* in an economy with consumption and production. But the preceding ten pages, if taken literally, present an adjustment process only distantly related to the summary. Some prices are held constant while others vary independently to clear different markets; similarly quantities are adjusted to make profits zero in each industry, but the adjustment process described takes all prices other than the selling price as given. It is hard to believe that Walras meant to describe reality as if markets and firms came into equilibrium in a preassigned order. It is perhaps this difficulty which led Goodwin (*op. cit.*, p. 5) to deny that Walras meant his adjustment process to be practical, as describing either reality or a device for the operation of a socialist society. However we feel that Walras suffered in his exposition from the crudity of his mathematical tools; he was seeking to explain a simultaneous adjustment in many markets and within many firms without using the concept of a system of differential (or difference) equations and hence was forced to resort to a crude formulation in which some variables changed while others are held constant.

11   *Manuel, op. cit.*, pp. 362–64. There is an amusing misprint, where he speaks of a collectivist society "qui ait pour but de procurer à ses membres le *minimum* d'ophélimité" (p. 362, italics added).

12   *Cours d'économie politique* (Tome Premier, Lausanne, Paris, and Leipzig: F. Rouge, Pichon, Duncker and Humblot, 1896), pp. 45–47.

13   *Ibid.*, p. 25.

14   *Manuel*, pp. 223–24, 232–33.

15   *Ibid.*, pp. 177–79, 185–87.

16   Taylor, *op. cit.*, p. 45.

17   Taylor, *op. cit.*, p. 53.

18   If there is no joint production, then the efficient choice of processes will be the same for all demand functions. See T. C. Koopmans, ed., *Activity Analysis of Production and Allocation*, Cowles Commission Monograph No. 13 (New York and London: John Wiley & Sons and Chapman & Hall, 1951), Chs. VII–X, pp. 142–73. If there is joint production, then the determination of the optimal set of process and therefore of prices according to Taylor's rule cannot be made independently of the demand function.

19   See Section IV, C.

20   Lange, *op. cit.*, fn 43, pp. 89–90.

21   See Section IV, D–F.

22   Lange, *op. cit.*, pp. 90–93.

23   In an unpublished memorandum of 1950; see R. Dorfman, P. A. Samuelson, and R. Solow, *Linear Programming and Economic Analysis* (New York, Toronto, and London: McGraw-Hill, 1958), fn. 1, p. 63. An example is given in Section II, D.

24   T. C. Koopmans, "Analysis of Production as an Efficient Combination of Activities," ch. III in *Activity Analysis*, pp. 33–97, especially pp. 33–34.

25     $f_{z_i}(z_1, \ldots, z_p)$ and $\partial f / \partial z_i$ have the same meaning.

26   See H. B. Curry, "The Method of Steepest Descent for Non-Linear Maximization Problems," *Quarterly of Applied Mathematics*, Vol. 2 (1944),

258–61, who discusses finite difference methods; C. B. Tompkins, "Methods of Steep Descent," ch. 18 in E. F. Beckenbach, ed., *Modern Mathematics for the Engineer* (New York: McGraw-Hill, 1956), pp. 448–79. A brief discussion is also found in Samuelson, *Foundations*, pp. 301–2. Strictly speaking, (7) is only a special case of the gradient method (sometimes called the method of steepest ascent), but since it is the only form with which we shall be concerned, no confusion will result.

27　The gradient process for unconstrained maxima will converge in general to some point at which all derivatives are zero.

28　That is, there is a set of functional relations $z_1 = z_1(z_{r+1}, \ldots, z_p), \ldots,$ $z_r = z_r(z_{r+1}, \ldots, z_p)$ such that $(z_1, \ldots, z_r)$ determined from these relations will satisfy (10).

29　We recall that f is maximized at the point $z = (\bar{z}_1, \bar{z}_2, \ldots, \bar{z}_r, \bar{z}_{r+1}, \ldots, \bar{z}_p)$.

30　A *convex* function is one whose negative is concave; that is, f is convex if $-f$ is concave.

31　See R. G. D. Allen, *Mathematical Analysis for Economists* (London: Macmillan, 1938) pp. 364–83; Samuelson, *Foundations*, pp. 262–64.

32　See O. Lange, "The Foundations of Welfare Economics," *Econometrica*, X (1942), 215–28.

33　See H. W. Kuhn and A. W. Tucker, "Nonlinear Programming," in J. Neyman, ed., *Proceedings of the Second Berkeley Symposium on Mathematical Statistics and Probability* (Berkeley and Los Angeles: University of California Press, 1952), pp. 481–92.

34　Strictly speaking, Theorem 1 is true only if the constraint functions $g_j(z_1, \ldots, z_p)$ satisfy an additional condition, such as that referred to by Kuhn and Tucker as the Constraint Qualification (*op. cit.*, pp. 483–4). A simple condition of this type (used by M. Slater in an unpublished paper) is that there exist some $z_1, \ldots, z_p$ such that $g_j(z_1, \ldots, z_p) > 0$ for all j; in economic terms, that it be possible to choose the economic variables so that there is an excess supply of all resources.

35　For an emphatic statement of this viewpoint, see Samuelson, *Foundations*, pp. 230–31, 234–35.

36　J. von Neumann and O. Morgenstern, *Theory of Games and Economic Behavior* (1st ed.; Princeton, New Jersey: Princeton University Press, 1944). p. 95.

37　Again, Theorem 2 is true only if the constraint qualification holds; see note 34.

38　The equivalence relation between saddle-points and constrained maxima was previously studied in the case where the functions $f(z_1, \ldots, z_p)$, $g_j(z_1, \ldots, z_p)$ are linear, that is, in the case of linear programming, by D. Gale, H. W. Kuhn, and A. W. Tucker, "Linear Programming and the Theory of Games," ch. XIX in *Activity Analysis*, pp. 317–29, and G. B. Dantzig, "A Proof of the Equivalence of the Programming Problem and the Game Problem," ch. XX, *ibid.*, pp. 330–35. The Kuhn-Tucker theorem given in the text presents a somewhat different form of the relation between the two types of extrema as well as an extension to nonlinear maximand and constraints.

39 For a demonstration and more complete spelling out of the regularity conditions, see K. Arrow and L. Hurwicz, "Reduction of Constrained Maxima to Saddle-point Problems," this volume, II.5, pp. 154–177.

40 G. Debreu, "Definite and Semidefinite Quadratic Forms," *Econometrica*, Vol. 20 (1952), 296.

41 See K. Arrow and R. M. Solow, "The Gradient Method for Constrained Maxima Under Weakened Conditions," ch. 10 in K. Arrow, L. Hurwicz, and H. Uzawa, *Studies in Linear and Nonlinear Programming* (Stanford, California: Stanford University Press, 1958), especially section 4. The result is essentially an extension of Debreu's lemma to cover the case of nonnegative variables.

42 The assumptions of (42) insure that there is a saddle-point and that the z-values must be uniquely defined; it is possible however to have more than one set of p-values.

43 The fact that the z-values converge to the z-values of a saddle-point has been proved with local assumptions and conclusions by the authors; see K. J. Arrow and L. Hurwicz, "The Gradient Method for Concave Programming I: Local Results," ch. 6 in Arrow, Hurwicz, and Uzawa, *op. cit.* The corresponding theorem in the large was established by H. Uzawa, "The Gradient Method for Concave Programming II: Global Results," ch. 7, *ibid.* That the p-values also converge is shown in K. J. Arrow and L. Hurwicz, "The Gradient Method for Concave Programming III: Further Global Results with Applications to Resource Allocation," ch. 8, *ibid*, referred to below as, "Gradient Method for Resource Allocation," see section 1. For an earlier exposition of the gradient method as applied to constrained maxima and to saddle-points, see K. J. Arrow and L. Hurwicz, "Gradient Methods for Constrained Maxima," this volume, II.4, pp. 146–153.

44 The nonconvergence of the gradient method in the linear case was observed by Samuelson; see note 23.

45 This fact was one of the reasons for interest in modified Lagrangians where convergence, rather than endless cycling, could be obtained.

46 Despite the importance of this assumption in consumer's demand theory, little attention has been given to its justification. For an argument due to T. C. Koopmans, see K. J. Arrow, "An Extension of the Basic Theorems of Classical Welfare Economics," in *Proceedings of the Second Berkeley Symposium*, pp. 529–30; T. C. Koopmans, *Three Essays on the State of Economic Science* (New York, Toronto, and London: McGraw-Hill, 1957), pp. 26–28. See also W. M. Gorman, "Convex Indifference Curves and Diminishing Marginal Utility," *Journal of Political Economy*, LXV (1957), 40–50.

47 See W. Fenchel, *Convex Cones, Sets, and Functions* (Department of Mathematics, Princeton University, 1953) (mimeographed), pp. 115–37; B. de Finetti, "Sulle stratificazioni convesse," *Annali di Matematica Pura e Applicata*, vol. 30 (1949), 173–83.

48 Equation $y = \bar{y}$ is an abbreviation for the set of equalities $y_1 = \bar{y}_1, y_2 = \bar{y}_2, \ldots, y_n = \bar{y}_n$. Similar notation is used for other sets of variables.

49 We follow the terminology of Koopmans, "Production as an Efficient

Combination. . . ," pp. 93–95, as developed for the linear case; however, the function of the helmsman is somewhat different here.

50 See H. Hotelling, "The General Welfare in Relation to Problems of Taxation and of Railway and Utility Rates," *Econometrica*, Vol. 6 (1938), 212–67; Lange, "Foundations, . . . " *op. cit.*; Koopmans, ch. 1 in *Three Essays, op. cit.*, M. Allais, *Traité d'économie pure* (Paris: Imprimerie Nationale, 1943) III, 604–82; Lerner, *op. cit.*; A. Bergson (Burk), "A Reformulation of Certain Aspects of Welfare Economics," *Quarterly Journal of Economics*, VIII (1938), 310–334.

51 See note 47.

52 The functions $g_{ij}(x_j)$ are here considered to be strictly concave as functions of the process scale x_j. In nonlinear processes, there may be more than one natural definition of a scale. From one point of view, any strictly monotonic transformation of a scale is itself a scale, since it serves equally well as a parameter in defining the different levels of the process. However, the previous theorems have shown that there is an advantage in choosing the scale so that the functions $g_{ij}(x_j)$ are concave. If this condition does not uniquely specify the choice of a scale, then the scale can be so chosen that all the functions g_{ij} which enter the process can be chosen strictly concave.

It may be worth remarking that the condition that it be possible to choose strictly concave input and output functions is stronger than the condition that the process not be linear. The first condition requires that the process have no linear relations between any input and any output.

53 Mathematical proofs of the results in this section will be found in K. Arrow and L. Hurwicz, "Gradient Method for Resource Allocation," *op. cit.*

54 See K. Arrow and L. Hurwicz, "On the Stability of Competitive Equilibrium I," this volume, III.1, pp. 199–228; K. Arrow, H. D. Block, and L. Hurwicz, "On the Stability of Competitive Equilibrium II," this volume, III.1, pp. 228–255.

55 See Sections II, A, 1 and 5, and the Remark to Theorem 1 in Section II, B.

56 It may be remarked that, analogously to Theorem 9, Theorem 13 remains valid when condition (a) is replaced by condition (a′) of Theorem 9′; see Section III, B. Theorem 13 is identical with the propositions of Hotelling, Lange, and Allais, *op. cit.*, note 50, except for the emphasis on the non-negativity conditions.

57 This formulation is employed by Lange, *Socialism*, pp. 81–82.

58 This possibility is admitted by Lange but regarded as exceptional; see *Socialism*, pp. 82, 69–70.

59 There is a third problem, of a type which we have not stressed in this article. If the optimal process scale is such that the marginal profitability is changing from negative values to positive ones, then the position is one of *minimum*, not maximum profits. While this is not a difficulty from the point of view of formal rules of operation, the incentives to the process manager are clearly a good deal less satisfactory than in the concave case where social optima correspond to profit maxima.

60   See Samuelson, *op. cit.*, pp. 270–74.

61   There is another gradient method which corresponds to Theorem 13 (or, more generally, to Theorem 1) and which does converge in general to a local maximum. It is defined by moving in a direction which is as close to the gradient of the unconstrained maximization as possible compatible with satisfying the constraints at all times. In the resource allocation model, this would require that the excess supply for each commodity would have to be zero (apart from free goods) at all points in the approximation process, not merely at equilibrium. There seems no way of satisfying this requirement in a decentralized fashion. For this gradient process, see G. E. Forsythe, "Computing Constrained Minima with Lagrange Multipliers," *Journal of the Society for Industrial and Applied Mathematics*, Vol. 3 (1955), 173–78; Arrow and Solow, *op. cit.*, sec. 3.

62   Actually, this interpretation is not dependent upon identifying the scale of process with the output. We can always write

$$d\tilde{\pi}_j/dx_j = g_{1j}'(x_j) \left\{ \bar{p}_1 - \Sigma_{i=2}^{s} \bar{p}_i \left[-g_{ij}'(x_j)/g_{1j}'(x_j) \right] \right\}.$$

The ratio, $-g_{ij}'(x_j)/g_{1j}'(x_j)$, is clearly the marginal increase in input i for a unit increase in output; hence the term in braces is the difference between price and marginal cost. Since the factor, $g_{1j}'(x_j)$, is necessarily positive, the statement in the text is always equivalent to condition (b).

63   For representative texts, see G. J. Stigler, *The Theory of Price* (rev. ed.; New York: Macmillan, 1952), pp. 127–29; K. E. Boulding, *Economic Analysis* (3rd ed.; New York: Harpers, 1955), ch. 34. This definition of cost is clearly the correct one in the theory of the firm, whether under competition or under monopoly; maximization of profit requires maximizing the difference between revenue and cost as defined in the text, or, equivalently, the equating of marginal revenue and marginal cost.

Writers who have dealt with optimal allocation under increasing returns have usually not been careful to define marginal costs; however, Lange explicitly presents the definition given in the text (pp. 116–17).

64   It should be made clear that in this process x_j is *not* necessarily chosen to maximize process profits, taking the q_i's as given prices. The chosen x_j does maximize the expression (80), with $\bar{p}_i$ and $\bar{h}_{ij}$ being replaced by their current values, p_i and h_{ij}; with the notation of (85), the statement in the text follows. Thus, as Lange correctly noted, the rule that marginal profitability be zero replaces the rule of profit maximization for increasing returns; however, the analysis shows that the price-adjustment rule which leads to a stable allocative system is not a simple one.

65   *Extrapolative expectations* of the type of equation (87) have been studied in connection with inventories by L. Metzler, "The Nature and Stability of Inventory Cycles," *Review of Economic Statistics*, XXIII (1941), 113–29, and in connection with inflationary price movements by A. C. Enthoven, "Monetary Disequilibria and the Dynamics of Inflation," *Economic Journal*, Vol. 66 (1956), 256–70; see also, A. C. Enthoven and K. Arrow, "A Theorem on Expectations and the Stability of Equilibrium," this volume, III.4, pp. 311–317. More detailed study of the system studied in this section will be found in Arrow and Solow, *op. cit.*, sec. 4.

66   The system of Theorem 20 and its interpretation in terms of price expectations is similar but not identical to the proposal of T. Kose, "Solutions of Saddle Value Problems by Differential Equations," *Econometrica*, Vol. 24 (1956), 59–70.

67   For a proof of Theorem 21, see Arrow and Hurwicz, "Gradient Method for Resource Allocation," *op. cit.*, Theorem 3. An illustration of this method with remarks on the problems of machine calculation is found in T. Marschak, "An Example of a Modified Gradient Method for Linear Programming," ch. 9 in Arrow, Hurwicz, and Uzawa, *op. cit.*

68   See note 38.

69   See G. W. Brown and J. von Neumann, "Solutions of Games by Differential Equations," in H. W. Kuhn and A. W. Tucker, eds., *Contributions to the Theory of Games I*, Annals of Mathematics Study No. 29 (Princeton, New Jersey: Princeton University Press, 1950), pp. 73–80. For the application to linear programming, see M. Fukuoka, "A Note on Convergence in Linear Programming Problems," Cowles Commission Discussion Paper: Economics No. 2108, July 14, 1954.

2
STATIC CHARACTERIZATION

Constraint qualifications in maximization problems[1]

KENNETH J. ARROW
LEONID HURWICZ
HIROFUMI UZAWA

Introduction

This article covers an examination of the interrelationships of the additional assumptions under which the following two propositions, both extensions of the classical Lagrange multiplier method ([1], p. 153), are valid:

Quasi-saddle-point condition

If $\bar{x}$ maximizes $f(x)$, subject to the constraints $g(x) \geqq 0$, and $f(x)$ and $g(x)$ are differentiable, then there exists $\bar{y} \geqq 0$, such that $\bar{f}_x + \bar{y}\bar{g}_x = 0, \bar{y}g(\bar{x}) = 0$.[2]

Saddle-point criterion

If $f(x)$ and $g(x)$ are concave, then a necessary and sufficient condition that $\bar{x}$ maximize $f(x)$, subject to the constraints $g(x) \geqq 0$ is that there exist a $\bar{y} \geqq 0$, such that $(\bar{x}, \bar{y})$ is a saddle-point subject to $y \geqq 0$, of the Lagrangian function $f(x) + yg(x)$.

It is known that neither proposition is valid without additional assumptions.[3] Kuhn and Tucker [11] showed that both propositions are valid if f and g are differentiable and the following condition is satisfied:

Constraint qualification KT[4]

For all $\bar{x}$ in the constraint set C [defined by the conditions $g(x) \geqq 0$] and all $\bar{\bar{x}}$ such that $\bar{g}_x^{\ k} \cdot (\bar{\bar{x}} - \bar{x}) \geqq 0$ for each component k of $g(x)$ for which $g^k(\bar{x}) = 0$, there exists a differentiable vector-valued function $\psi(\theta)$ such that $\psi(0) = \bar{x}$, $\psi(\theta)$ belongs to C for all positive θ sufficiently small, and $\psi'(0) = \bar{\bar{x}} - \bar{x}$.

In this article, further results on the subject are discussed and simplified proofs are given. First, Constraint Qualification KT is slightly weakened so that the meaning of the qualification becomes more transparent. Theorem 1 shows that the Lagrangian method can be applied to those constrained maxima for which the weaker version of the Constraint Qualification is satisfied. Next this article shows that the Constraint Qualification in the present formulation is the weakest requirement for the Lagrange method to be applicable; namely, in Theorem 2 below, it is proved that if the Lagrange method is justified for all differentiable maximands (or even all linear maximands), then the constraint function satisfies the Constraint Qualification provided the constraint set is convex.

The direct verification of the Constraint Qualification in specific cases is difficult, and it is useful to find simpler hypotheses which imply it. Several apparently new conditions implying the Constraint Qualification and, therefore, the validity of the Saddle-Point Criterion and the Quasi-Saddle-Point Condition are proved in a later section (A Sufficient Condition for the Constraint Qualification). Note that for differentiable functions $f(x)$ and $g(x)$, the Quasi-Saddle-Point Condition implies the Saddle-Point Criterion. For if $f(x)$ and $g(x)$ are concave, the Lagrangian function, $f(x) + yg(x)$, is concave in x for any given $y \geq 0$; if $\bar{x}$ maximizes $f(x)$ subject to $g(x) \geq 0$, the Quasi-Saddle-Point Condition implies that the Lagrangian function has a zero derivative at $\bar{x}$ and, therefore, as a concave function, must have a maximum there. Since the Lagrangian is linear in y and $g(\bar{x}) \geq 0$, it is obvious that $\bar{y}g(\bar{x}) = 0$ implies that $\bar{y}$ minimizes $f(\bar{x}) + yg(\bar{x})$ subject to $y \geq 0$. The converse part of the Saddle-Point Criterion, that if $(\bar{x}, \bar{y})$ is a saddle-point of the Lagrangian for some $\bar{y}$, subject to $y \geq 0$, then $\bar{x}$ is a constrained maximum of $f(x)$ subject to $g(x) \geq 0$, holds without any assumptions on $g(x)$. (See Kuhn and Tucker [11], Theorem 2.)

Still another constraint qualification has been given by Hurwicz ([5], Chapter 4, Section V.3.3.2). In another section (Equivalence of Constraint Qualifications KT and H), it is shown to be equivalent to Constraint Qualification KT, at least for finite-dimensional spaces.

To state these results more precisely and to relate them to other work, we will introduce some notation and definitions. In the first place, we define the constraint set,

(1) $C = \{x : g(x) \geq 0\}$.

In the second place, we will denote $\bar{x} - x$ by ξ. Finally, to simplify the statement of the conclusion of Constraint Qualification KT, which will appear frequently in the following discussion, we will find it convenient to introduce the following definitions:

Definition 1.   A *contained path* (*with origin $\bar{x}$ and direction ξ*) is an n-vector-valued function $\psi(\theta)$ of a real variable which satisfies:

(2) $\psi(\theta)$ is defined for all $0 \leq \theta \leq \bar{\theta}$ for some $\bar{\theta} > 0$;

(3) $\psi(0) = \bar{x}, \quad \psi(\theta) \in C$ for all $0 \leq \theta \leq \bar{\theta}$;

(4) $\psi(\theta)$ has a right-hand derivative at $\theta = 0$ such that $\psi'(0) = \xi$.

Definition 2.   An n-vector ξ such that there is a contained path with origin $\bar{x}$ and direction ξ will be referred to as an *attainable direction* at $\bar{x}$. The set of attainable directions (at any given $\bar{x}$) will be denoted by A.

The set of indices $\{1, \ldots, m\}$ is divided into two parts, E and F. E is the set of all indices *effective* at $\bar{x}$, namely,

(5) $E = \{j: g^j(\bar{x}) = 0\}$,

and F is the set of all indices *ineffective* at $\bar{x}$, namely,

(6) $F = \{j: g^j(\bar{x}) > 0\}$.

   Definition 3.   An n-vector ξ is termed a *locally constrained direction* if $\bar{g}_x^E \xi \geq 0$ (i.e., $\bar{g}_x^j \xi \geq 0$ *for all* $j \in E$). The set of locally constrained directions will be denoted by L.

   With these definitions the Kuhn-Tucker Constraint Qualification can be written:

Constraint qualification KT

Every locally constrained direction is attainable, i.e., $L \subset A$.

   (Since the definition of a contained path does not require it to be differentiable throughout, this formulation is apparently weaker than Kuhn and Tucker's [11]. We do not know if the weakening is more than apparent when $g(x)$ is differentiable.)

   We now observe that the set L of locally constrained directions is a closed convex cone. (By a cone is meant a set which, if it contains any point x, also contains λx for every scalar $\lambda \geq 0$.) The set A of attainable directions is a cone but is not necessarily convex.

   Definition 4.   Let W be the closure of the convex cone spanned by A, the set of attainable directions (i.e., the smallest closed convex cone containing A). The elements of W will be termed *weakly attainable* directions.

   A weakly attainable direction is, then, the limit of a sequence of nonnegative linear combinations of attainable directions. We now introduce a weaker constraint qualification:

Constraint qualification W

Every locally constrained direction is weakly attainable, i.e., $L \subset W$.[5]

   It will be shown (Theorem 1) that Constraint Qualification W is sufficient for the validity of the Quasi-Saddle-Point Condition and therefore for that of the Saddle-Point Criterion.

   We now turn to some other conditions in the literature which have been found to be sufficient for the Quasi-Saddle-Point Condition. In the usual treatment of the Lagrange multiplier method in the case of equality constraints (Courant [7], p. 198), it is required that the matrix $\bar{g}_x$ of the (partial) derivatives of the constraint functions with respect to the variables have a rank equal to the number of constraints. This condition has been extended to the case of inequalities in [3], p. 8. We write, in the present notation, the

Nondegeneracy condition

The rank of $\overline{g}_x{}^E$ equals the number of effective constraints.

(The condition given in [3] is actually slightly weaker.) It was shown in [3], Appendix I, that the Nondegeneracy Condition implies Constraint Qualification KT. In a later section (A Sufficient Condition for the Constraint Qualification), we will deduce the Nondegeneracy Condition from a more general sufficient condition for Constraint Qualification W.

In concave programming – that is, where the functions $f(x)$ and $g(x)$ are assumed to be concave – there are theorems which state conditions under which the Saddle-Point Criterion is valid but which do not involve Constraint Qualification KT. The simplest case is that of linear programming where the functions $f(x)$ and $g(x)$ are assumed to be linear. In this case, the Saddle-Point Criterion always holds, as is well known ([10], Chapters XIX and XX). Since the constraint qualifications are always assumptions about the constraint functions only and do not involve $f(x)$, the question arises whether or not it is the linearity of $g(x)$ that is vital. The answer is in the affirmative, in the sense that the linearity of $g(x)$ is sufficient for the Quasi-Saddle-Point Condition; see Corollary 2 of Theorem 3.

Another constraint qualification for concave programming has been proposed by Slater [12]:

Constraint qualification S

The function $g(x)$ is concave and, for some x^*, $g(x^*) > 0$.

Slater showed that if the function $f(x)$ is concave, his constraint qualification implied the Saddle-Point Criterion. A simplified proof was given by Uzawa ([5], Chapter 3). Slater's theorem was extended to more general spaces by Hurwicz ([5], Chapter 4, Theorem V.3.1). (Slater's assumption of continuity is dispensable.)

Karlin ([9], Chapter 7, Theorem 7.1.1) suggested still another constraint qualification:

Constraint qualification K

The function $g(x)$ is concave and, for every $y \geqslant 0$, there is an x such that $yg(x) > 0$.

This condition is clearly implied by Constraint Qualification S; Hurwicz and Uzawa ([5], Chapter 5) have shown that in spaces of considerable generality the two conditions are in fact equivalent.

It is natural to investigate the relation between Constraint Qualification S (or K) and the more general Constraint Qualifications, such as KT or W. Obviously, conditions S or K do not require differentiability of $g(x)$, so that they cannot be completely subsumed under conditions KT or W, which do. We may, however, ask whether or not the former do imply the latter conditions under the additional assumption that $g(x)$ is differentiable. In the section devoted to A Sufficient Condition for the Constraint Qualification, it is shown that such is indeed the case; in fact, a single condition (Theorem 3) is given under which all previous conditions can be subsumed as special cases, as well as some conditions not previously given in the literature.

A still weaker version of this condition is presented in Theorem 4. In one of its corollaries, the hypothesis refers to functions which are simultaneously concave and quasi-convex. A characterization of such functions and also of functions which are simultaneously quasi-concave and quasi-convex is presented in the section, A Characterization of Functions Simultaneously Concave and Quasi-Convex; this result may be of interest in other contexts.

In [5], Chapter 4, Section V.3.3.2, Hurwicz introduces the following constraint qualification:

Constraint qualification H

For all $\bar{x} \in C$ and all ξ such that $\bar{g}_x \xi + g(\bar{x}) \geq 0$, ξ is attainable.

Since Constraint Qualification H does not identify separate coordinates, it is meaningful in all linear topological spaces in which a differentiation operation can be defined.[6] It has been shown ([5], Chapter 4, Theorems V.3.3.2 and V.3.3.3) to be a sufficient condition for both the Saddle-Point Criterion and the Quasi-Saddle-Point Condition in spaces of considerable generality. We will show in the section, Equivalence of Constraint Qualifications KT and H, that in finite-dimensional spaces, Constraint Qualifications KT and H are equivalent.

Preliminary lemmas and remarks

Lemma 1.   Every weakly attainable direction is locally constrained.

Proof.   Let ξ be an attainable direction, $\psi(\theta)$ a contained path with origin $\bar{x}$ and direction ξ. Then for some $\bar{\theta} > 0$ and every $j \in E$,

$$g^j[\psi(0)] = 0 \quad \text{and} \quad g^j[\psi(\theta)] \geq 0 \quad (0 \leq \theta \leq \bar{\theta});$$

hence, for $\theta = 0$, $dg^j[\psi/\theta)]/d\theta = \bar{g}_x{}^j \psi'(0) = \bar{g}_x{}^j \xi \geq 0$ for every $j \in E$, so that ξ is locally constrained.[7] That is, A is included in L. Since L is a convex cone, the convex cone spanned by A must also be included in L; and since L is closed, W, the closure of the convex cone spanned by A, must also be included in L.

(Q.E.D.)

Let us define, for $\bar{x} \in C$,

(7) K = closure of the set $\{\lambda(x - \bar{x}): \lambda \geq 0, x \in C\}$.

K is the union of all half-lines from $\bar{x}$ through elements of C, together with the boundary of the union. K is clearly a closed cone. That the set in braces is not necessarily closed is illustrated by the case $g(x, y) = y - x^2$, $\bar{x} = (0, 0)$, where the x-axis belongs to K but not to the set in braces.

Lemma 2.   If the constraint set C is convex, then K is a closed convex cone, and $K \subset W$.

Proof.   The convexity of K follows immediately from that of C.

If $x \in C$, then by the convexity of the set C,

$$\bar{x} + \theta(x - \bar{x}) \in C \qquad \text{for all } 0 \leq \theta \leq 1.$$

Hence, $x - \bar{x}$ is attainable and therefore weakly attainable. Since W is a cone, $\lambda(x - \bar{x}) \in W$ for all $\lambda \geq 0$. (Q.E.D.)

Let B be any set of vectors. The negative polar cone, to be denoted by B', is defined by

$$B' = \{u: ux \leq 0 \qquad \text{for all } x \in B\}.$$

We have (Fenchel [8], pp. 8-10),

(8) B' is a closed convex cone;

(9) $B_1 \subset B_2$ implies that $B_1' \supset B_2'$;

(10)   if B is a closed convex cone, $B'' = B$.

Lagrange regularity and the constraint qualification

Definition 5.   An m-vector-valued function $g(x)$ will be termed *Lagrange regular* if, for any differentiable function $f(x)$, the Quasi-Saddle-Point Condition holds.

Lemma 3.   If $\bar{x}$ maximizes $f(x)$ subject to $x \in C$, then

$$\bar{f}_x \in W'$$

where W' is the negative polar cone of W.

Proof.   Let $\psi(\theta)$ be a contained path with origin $\bar{x}$ and direction ξ; then

$$f[\psi(\theta)] \leq f[\psi(0)] = f(\bar{x}) \qquad \text{for all } 0 \leq \theta \leq \bar{\theta}.$$

Then

$$\bar{f}_x \xi = \bar{f}_x \psi'(0) \leq 0,$$

for any ξ in A and, by continuity and convexity, for any $\xi \in W$ (Definitions 2 and 4). (Q.E.D.)

Theorem 1.   If $g(x)$ satisfies Constraint Qualification W, then $g(x)$ is Lagrange regular.

Proof.   Let $f(x)$ be a differentiable function and $\bar{x}$ maximize $f(x)$ subject to $x \in C$. Then, by Lemma 3, $\bar{f}_x \in W'$. On the other hand, Constraint Qualification W states that $L \subset W$ and therefore implies, from (9), that

$$W' \subset L'.$$

Hence, we have

(11) $\bar{f}_x \in L'.$

If B is the closed convex cone consisting of all vectors $y^E(-\bar{g}_x{}^E)$ with $y^E \geq 0$, then Definition 3 and (11) show that $\bar{f}_x \in B''$, and by (10),

$$-\bar{f}_x = \bar{y}^E \bar{g}_x{}^E \qquad \text{for some } \bar{y}^E \geq 0.$$

Define

$$\bar{y} = (\bar{y}^E, \bar{y}^F) \qquad \text{with } \bar{y}^F = 0.$$

Then $\bar{f}_x + \bar{y}\bar{g}_x = 0, \bar{y}g(\bar{x}) = \bar{y}^E g^E(\bar{x}) = 0$, from (5), so that the Quasi-Saddle-Point Condition is satisfied. (Q.E.D.)

Theorem 1 is the basic necessity theorem for nonlinear programming ([11], Theorem 1) extended to the weaker Constraint Qualification W of this paper.

Theorem 2.   If $g(x)$ is Lagrange regular and if the constraint set C defined by it is a convex set, then $g(x)$ satisfies the Constraint Qualification W.

Proof.   It will be shown first that

(12) $K' \subset L'.$

Let $a \in K'$; then from (7), for $\lambda = 1$,

(13) $a(x - \bar{x}) \leq 0 \qquad \text{for all } x \in C.$

Then $\bar{x}$ maximizes the function $f(x) = ax$ subject to $x \in C$. By the Lagrange regularity of $g(x)$, there is an m-vector $\bar{y}$ such that

(14) $a + \bar{y}\bar{g}_x = 0; \qquad \bar{y} \geq 0,$

and

(15) $\bar{y}g(\bar{x}) = 0.$

Conditions (14) and (15) imply that $\bar{y}^F = 0$ and, thus, that

(16) $a + \bar{y}^E \bar{g}_x{}^E = 0, \qquad \bar{y}^E \geq 0.$

Condition (16) implies that

$$a\xi \leq 0 \qquad \text{for all } \xi \qquad \text{such that } \bar{g}_x{}^E \xi \geq 0;$$

that is,

$$a \in L'.$$

Hence, we have the relation (12). Then, by Eqs. (9) and (10), $K \supset L$. Applying Lemma 2,

$$W \supset K \supset L. \quad \text{(Q.E.D.)}$$

A sufficient condition for the constraint qualification

Theorem 3. If E' is the set of effective constraints which are convex functions, E'' is the set of all other effective constraints, and if there exists ξ^* such that $\bar{g}_x^{E'} \xi^* \geq 0$, $\bar{g}_x^{E''} \xi^* > 0$, then Constraint Qualification W holds.

Proof. Let ξ be any element of L, α any positive real number, and

$$\psi(\theta) = \bar{x} + (\xi + \alpha\xi^*)\theta, \quad \text{for } \theta \geq 0.$$

We will show that $\psi(\theta)$ is a contained path for θ sufficiently small and, hence, $\xi + \alpha\xi^*$ is attainable. If we let α approach zero, it will follow from Definition 4 that ξ belongs to W, in fact to the closure of A, so that we will have shown that $L \subset W$, which is Constraint Qualification W.

For any $j \in E$, at $\theta = 0$,

$$dg^j[\psi(\theta)]/d\theta = \bar{g}_x^j(\xi + \alpha\xi^*) = \bar{g}_x^j\xi + \alpha\bar{g}_x^j\xi^* \geq \alpha\bar{g}_x^j\xi^*,$$

since $\bar{g}_x^j\xi \geq 0$ by definition of L. If $j \in E'$, it follows from the hypothesis of the theorem that

$$dg^j[\psi(\theta)]/d\theta \geq 0 \quad \text{at } \theta = 0,$$

which, for a convex function, implies that $g^j[\psi(\theta)]$ has its minimum for $\theta \geq 0$ at $\theta = 0$. If $j \in E''$, then

$$dg^j[\psi(\theta)]/d\theta > 0 \quad \text{at } \theta = 0,$$

so that $g^j[\psi(\theta)]$ has a local right-hand minimum at $\theta = 0$. It follows that

$$g^E[\psi(\theta)] \geq g^E[\psi(0)] = g^E(\bar{x}) = 0 \quad \text{for } \theta \text{ sufficiently small.}$$

Since, by definition, $g^F[\psi(0)] > 0$, $g^F[\psi(\theta)] \geq 0$ for θ sufficiently small, so that $\psi(\theta) \in C$ for θ sufficiently small, from which the theorem follows, as has previously been shown.

Corollary 1. If $g(x)$ is convex, then $g(x)$ is Lagrange regular.

Proof. In this case, E'' is the null set, and it suffices to set $\xi^* = 0$. The conclusion follows from Theorem 1.

As a special case, we state

Corollary 2. If $g(x)$ is linear, it is Lagrange regular.

Corollary 3. If $g(x)$ is concave, E' the set of the effective constraints which are linear, E'' the set of all other effective constraints, and there exists x^* such that $g^{E'}(x^*) \geq 0$, $g^{E''}(x^*) > 0$, then $g(x)$ is Lagrange regular.

Proof. For any concave function,

$$\bar{g}_x^j(x^* - \bar{x}) \geq g^j(x^*) - g^j(\bar{x}) = g^j(x^*) \quad \text{for } j \in E.$$

Since the only functions which are both concave and convex are linear, the results follow from Theorem 3.

The following special case is precisely Constraint Qualification S.

Corollary 4.   If $g(x)$ is concave and $g(x^*) > 0$ for some x^*, then $g(x)$ is Lagrange regular.

Corollary 4 was originally stated as Theorem 3 in Ref. [4]. The following corollary generalizes Theorem 2 in Ref. [2] which, in turn, generalized Corollary 4.

Corollary 5.   If the constraint set C is convex and possesses an interior, and $\bar{g}_x^j \neq 0$ for each $j \in E$, then $g(x)$ is Lagrange regular.

Proof.   By Lemma 2, $x - \bar{x}$ is weakly attainable for all $x \in C$ and therefore belongs to L by Lemma 1. Since C possesses an interior, L must possess one also and therefore has the full dimensionality of the entire space. If, for some $j \in E$, $\bar{g}_x^j \xi = 0$ for all ξ in L, it follows that $\bar{g}_x^j \xi = 0$ for all ξ, which means that $\bar{g}_x^j = 0$, contrary to hypothesis. Hence, for each $j \in E$, there exists $\xi^j \in L$ such that $\bar{g}_x^j \xi^j \neq 0$; since $\bar{g}_x^j \xi \geq 0$ for all ξ in L by definition, we must have

$$\bar{g}_x^j \xi^j > 0, \qquad \bar{g}_x^j \xi^k \geq 0 \qquad \text{for } j, k \in E.$$

If we let

$$\xi^* = \Sigma_{j \in E} \, \xi^j,$$

we see that

$$\bar{g}_x^E \xi^* > 0,$$

and the conclusion follows trivially from Theorem 3.

Remark.   To establish that C has an interior, it is sufficient that $g(x^*) > 0$ for some x^*; to establish that C is convex, it is sufficient that $g(x)$ be quasi-concave.[8]

We can also relate the Nondegeneracy Condition to this analysis.

Corollary 6.   If the rank of $\bar{g}_x^E$ equals the number of effective constraints, then $g(x)$ is Lagrange regular.

Proof.   Let u be an arbitrary positive column vector; then from the hypothesis, we can find ξ^* such that $\bar{g}_x^E \xi^* = u > 0$.

If we reconsider the proof of Theorem 3, we see that the convexity assumption for the elements of E' is only needed to insure that $g^j[\psi(\theta)]$ has a minimum at $\theta = 0$ for $j \in E'$. For the purposes of the proof, a local minimum is sufficient. It would therefore suffice to define E' as the set of effective constraints which are *locally* convex (i.e., which are convex over some neighborhood of $\bar{x}$), which, for example, would be implied by well-known conditions on the matrix of second partial derivatives of the $g^j(x)$ evaluated at $x = \bar{x}$. It is clear that the larger E' is, the weaker the hypothesis of the theorem.

A somewhat different weakening of Theorem 3 is suggested by observing that if δ^j is the jth unit row vector, then

(17) $-\bar{g}_x{}^j + \delta^j \bar{g}_x{}^E = 0$ for any $j \in E$.

Since $\delta^j \bar{g}_x{}^E(0) = 0$, we see that the Lagrangian conditions for a constrained maximum of $-g^j(\bar{x} + \xi)$ subject to $\bar{g}_x{}^E \xi \geq 0$ are satisfied at $\xi = 0$. Suppose for the moment that the Lagrangian conditions (i.e., those in the Quasi-Saddle-Point Condition) were sufficient to insure a constrained maximum. Then $g^j(\bar{x} + \xi)$ would have a minimum at $\xi = 0$ for $\xi \in L$. Since $(\xi + \alpha \xi^*) \theta \in L$ for all $\theta \geq 0$, this implies that $g^j[\psi(\theta)] \geq g^j[\psi(0)] = 0$, and so the argument of Theorem 3 is still valid if E' is defined to contain all effective constraints for which the Lagrangian conditions are sufficient to insure a constrained maximum for $-g^j(x)$.

A set of hypotheses, under which the Lagrangian conditions are sufficient for a constrained maximum, is presented in [2], Theorem 1. We state the relevant results as a lemma (the statement below is slightly more general in that the domain of definition is not restricted to the nonnegative orthant; the previous proof extends easily).

Lemma 4.   Let $f(x)$ be a differentiable quasi-concave function and $g(x)$ an m-vector valued differentiable quasi-concave function defined over some convex domain D. Let $\bar{x}$ and $\bar{y} \geq 0$ satisfy the Lagrangian conditions, $\bar{f}_x + \bar{y} \bar{g}_x = 0$, $\bar{y} g(\bar{x}) = 0$, and let one of the following conditions be satisfied:

(a) $\bar{f}_x x^1 > \bar{f}_x x^2$ for some $x^1 \in C, x^2 \in D$;
(b) $\bar{f}_x \neq 0$ and $f(x)$ is twice differentiable in a neighborhood of $\bar{x}$;
(c) $f(x)$ is concave.

Then $\bar{x}$ maximizes $f(x)$ subject to the constraints $g(x) \geq 0$.

Lemma 4 can be applied to the preceding argument, with x replaced by ξ, $f(x)$ by $-g^j(\bar{x} + \xi)$, and $g(x)$ by $\bar{g}_x{}^E \xi$. Since the latter is linear and therefore necessarily quasi-concave, the hypotheses of the lemma are equivalent to requiring that one of (a), (b), or (c) hold for the function $-g^j(\bar{x} + \xi)$. The application of (b) and (c) is straightforward. Condition (a) becomes

(18) $\bar{g}_x{}^j \xi^1 < \bar{g}_x{}^j \xi^2$,

for some ξ^1 in the constraint set $\bar{g}_x{}^E \xi \geq 0$ and some ξ^2 for which $\bar{x} + \xi^2$ is in the domain of definition of $g^j(x)$. Since $\bar{g}_x{}^j \xi \geq 0$ for all $\xi \in L$, while $0 \in L$, (18) is equivalent to

$\bar{g}_x{}^j(x - \bar{x}) > 0$,

for some x in the domain of definition of $g^j(x)$. We can thus state the following generalization of Theorem 3:

Theorem 4.   Let E' be the set of effective constraints $g^j(x)$ which are quasi-convex functions and which satisfy one of the following three conditions:

(a) $\bar{g}_x{}^j x > \bar{g}_x{}^j \bar{x}$ for some x for which $g^j(x)$ is defined;

(b) $\bar{g}_x{}^j \neq 0$ and $g^j(x)$ is twice differentiable in a neighborhood of $x = \bar{x}$;
(c) $g^j(x)$ is convex.

If E'' is the set of all other effective constraints and if there exists ξ^* such that $\bar{g}_x{}^{E'}\xi^* \geq 0, \bar{g}_x{}^{E''}\xi^* > 0$, then Constraint Qualification W holds.

From this theorem can be deduced generalizations of some of the corollaries to Theorem 3. Corresponding to Corollary 1 of the latter, we have

Corollary 1.   If $g(x)$ is quasi-convex and each effective component satisfies one of the conditions (a), (b), or (c) of Theorem 4, then $g(x)$ is Lagrange regular.

Corollary 3 of Theorem 3 can be generalized to

Corollary 2.   Suppose $g(x)$ is concave. Let E' be the set of effective constraints which are also quasi-convex and which satisfy one of the following conditions:

(a) $g^j(x) > 0$ for some x;
(b) $\bar{g}_x{}^j \neq 0$ and $g^j(x)$ is twice differentiable in a neighborhood of $x = \bar{x}$;
(c) $g^j(x)$ is linear.

If E'' is the set of all other effective constraints and if there exists ξ^* such that $g^{E'}(x^*) \geq 0, g^{E''}(x^*) > 0$, then $g(x)$ is Lagrange regular.

Proof.   If (a) holds, then, since $g^j(x)$ is concave,

$$\bar{g}_x{}^j(x - \bar{x}) \geq g^j(x) - g^j(\bar{x}) = g^j(x) > 0,$$

so that (a) in Theorem 4 holds. Since (b) is the same in the two statements and (c) here implies (c) in the statement of Theorem 4, E' as defined here satisfies the conditions of Theorem 4. The proof is then the same as that of Corollary 3, Theorem 3.[9]

A characterization of functions simultaneously concave and quasi-convex

To better understand the domain of applicability of Corollary 2 of Theorem 4, it is useful to give a characterization in Lemma 6 of functions which are simultaneously concave and quasi-convex. First, we characterize functions which are simultaneously quasi-concave and quasi-convex. In what follows, an indifference set is a set $\{x: f(x) = c\}$; a maximal (minimal) indifference set is the set on which $f(x)$ attains its maximum (minimum). A set S will be said to be bounded by two noncrossing hyperplanes in D if there exist linear functions, $L_1(x), L_2(x)$, not identically constant in D, such that

(19) $S = \{x \in D: L_1(x) \geq 0, L_2(x) \leq 0\}$,

and

(20) $L_1(x) < 0, \qquad L_2(x) > 0 \qquad$ for no $x \in D$.

A diagram will show that (19) and (20) are algebraic transcriptions of the geometric concept they define.

Lemma 5. A function is both quasi-concave and quasi-convex over a convex domain D if and only if every indifference set not minimal or maximal is bounded by two noncrossing hyperplanes in D.

Proof. Without loss of generality, assume that D is the domain of definition of $f(x)$. We first note that quasi-convexity implies that $\{x: f(x) < c\}$ is convex for all c. Suppose $f(x^0) < c, f(x^1) < c, x^2$ a convex combination of x^0 and x^1. If $c' = \max [f(x^0), f(x^1)]$, we have x^0, x^1 belonging to the set $\{x: f(x) \leq c'\}$, which is convex by definition of quasi-convexity, and hence $f(x^2) \leq c' < c$.

We suppose, without loss of generality, that the linear space is the smallest containing D. Consider any value, c, of $f(x)$, which is neither the maximum nor the minimum. If the set $\{x: f(x) \geq c\}$ did not have the full dimensionality of the space, there would exist a linear function $L(x)$ not identically zero, such that $L(x) = 0$ whenever $f(x) \geq c$. Choose y so that $L(y) \neq 0$, and let $z = y - x$. Then, for any x, $L(x + tz)$ is a linear function of t which is nonzero for $t = 1$ and therefore takes on the value 0 for at most one value of t; hence we can find ϵ arbitrarily small for which $L(x + \epsilon z) \neq 0, L(x - \epsilon z) \neq 0$. Suppose x is an interior point of D. Choose ϵ sufficiently small so that $x \pm \epsilon z \in D$. Since $L(x \pm \epsilon z) \neq 0$, $f(x \pm \epsilon z) < c$; by the convexity of $\{x: f(x) < c\}, f(x) < c$. Since D is convex, it follows by continuity that $f(x) \leq c$ for all $x \in D$, so that c would be the maximum value of $f(x)$, contrary to assumption.

The set $\{x: f(x) \geq c\}$ is convex and has the full dimensionality of the space; the set $\{x: f(x) < c\}$ has been shown to be convex. Hence, there is a separating hyperplane, i.e., a linear function, not constant over the entire space and hence not over D, $L_1(x)$ such that $L_1(x) \leq 0$ for $f(x) < c, L_1(x) \geq 0$ if $f(x) \geq c$ ([8], Theorem 28, p. 48). If $L_1(x) = 0$ whenever $f(x) \geq c$, the set $\{x: f(x) \geq c\}$ would lie in a hyperplane and therefore not have the full dimensionality of the space, a contradiction. Hence, $L_1(x^0) > 0$ for some x^0 for which $f(x^0) \geq c$. Suppose $L_1(x) = 0$ for some x for which $f(x) < c$. Then for y a convex combination of x^0 and x sufficiently close to x, we have $L_1(y) > 0, f(y) < c$, contrary to the separation result. Thus,

$$L_1(x) < 0 \text{ if } f(x) < c, \qquad L_1(x) \geq 0 \text{ if } f(x) \geq c.$$

Since the sets $\{x: f(x) < c\}$ and $\{x: f(x) \geq c\}$ together exhaust D, we have

(21) $\quad \{x: f(x) < c\} = \{x \in D: L_1(x) < 0\}$,

(22) $\quad \{x: f(x) \geq c\} = \{x \in D: L_1(x) \geq 0\}$.

Similarly, from the quasi-concavity of $f(x)$, we find there exists a linear function, $L_2(x)$, such that

(23) $\quad \{x: f(x) \leq c\} = \{x \in D: L_2(x) \leq 0\}$,

(24) $\quad \{x: f(x) > c\} = \{x \in D: L_2(x) > 0\}$.

From (22) and (23), (19) holds for the set $S = \{x\colon f(x) = c\}$. Since the set (24) is included in the set (22), (20) holds.

We now prove the converse theorem. First, consider any c which lies strictly between the maximum and minimum values of $f(x)$. By assumption, the set $S = \{x\colon f(x) = c\}$ satisfies (19) and (20) for some linear functions, $L_1(x)$, $L_2(x)$. Let $\underline{S} = \{x \in D\colon L_1(x) < 0\}$, $\overline{S} = \{x \in D\colon L_2(x) > 0\}$. We will first show that the set $\{x\colon f(x) \leq c\}$ is convex. Since $c < \max_x f(x)$, $f(x^0) - c > 0$ for some x^0.

By (19) we must have $f(x) - c \neq 0$ for all $x \in \underline{S}$, and all $x \in \overline{S}$. Further, $f(x) - c$ cannot assume both signs in $\underline{S}$, for, by the convexity of the set and the continuity of $f(x)$, we would have $f(x) - c = 0$ in that set for some x, which has just been shown impossible. Similarly, $f(x) - c$ must have a single sign in $\overline{S}$.

Suppose $f(x^0) - c > 0$ for some x^0 in $\underline{S}$. We will show that it is impossible that $f(x^1) - c > 0$ for some x^1 in $\overline{S}$. For then, $f(x) - c > 0$ for all $x \in \underline{S}$ and all $x \in \overline{S}$, while $f(x) = c$ for all $x \in S$, and therefore $f(x) \geq c$ for all $x \in D$, contrary to assumption.

Hence, if $f(x^0) > c$ for some x^0 in $\underline{S}$, $f(x) > c$ for all $x \in \underline{S}$, and only for such x. The set $\{x\colon f(x) \leq c\}$ is then precisely the set $\{x \in D\colon L_1(x) \geq 0\}$, which is certainly convex.

Alternatively, we might have $f(x^0) - c > 0$ for some $x^0 \in \overline{S}$. The argument is completely parallel.

We have shown that $\{x\colon f(x) \leq c\}$ is convex for any c neither maximal nor minimal. The proof that $\{x\colon f(x) \geq c\}$ is convex for such c is completely parallel. There remain the cases where $c = \max_x f(x)$ or $\min_x f(x)$. In the first case, the set $\{x\colon f(x) \leq c\}$ is the entire set D and is certainly convex. The set $\{x\colon f(x) \geq c\}$ is the intersection of all the sets $\{x\colon f(x) \geq c'\}$ for $c' < c$; it is an intersection of convex sets and therefore convex. The case where $c = \min_x f(x)$ is handled by the same argument.

Lemma 6.   A concave function is also quasi-convex over a convex domain D if and only if every indifference set not maximal or minimal is the intersection of D with a hyperplane.

Proof.   Let S, as before, be an indifference set, $\{x\colon f(x) = c\}$. We consider five cases:

(a) For some x^0, $x^1 \in S$, $L_1(x^0) > 0$, $L_2(x^1) < 0$. From (19), $L_2(x^0) \leq 0$, $L_1(x^1) \geq 0$. In this case, let $x^2 = (x^0 + x^1)/2$, which belongs to S by convexity,

$$L_1(x^2) > 0, \qquad L_2(x^2) < 0.$$

For any $x \in D$, let $x(\theta) = (1 - \theta)x + \theta x^2$, $g(\theta) = f[x(\theta)]$. Clearly, $x(\theta) \in S$ for θ in the neighborhood of 1, so that $g(\theta) = c$ for all θ in the neighborhood of 1, and $g'(1) = 0$. Since $g(\theta)$ is concave, it has its maximum at $\theta = 1$, and, in particular, $f(x) = g(0) \leq g(1) = c$, so that $c = \max_x f(x)$.

(b) $L_1(x) = 0$ for all $x \in S$, $L_2(x) \leq 0$ for all $x \in D$ for which $L_1(x) = 0$. In this case, $x \in S$, if and only if $x \in D$, $L_1(x) = 0$.   (Q.E.D.)

(c) $L_2(x) = 0$ for all $x \in S$, $L_1(x) \geq 0$ for all $x \in D$ for which $L_2(x) = 0$. In this case, $S = \{x \in D\colon L_2(x) = 0\}$.

(d) $L_1(x) = 0$ for all $x \in S$, $L_2(x^0) > 0$, $L_1(x^0) = 0$, for some $x^0 \in D$. First suppose $L_1(x) < 0$ for some $x \in D$. Then we could find a convex combination of x^0 and x for which L_1 is negative, L_2 positive, contrary to (20).

(25) $L_1(x) \geq 0$ for all $x \in D$.

Since $L_1(x)$ is not identically 0 in D, we can find x^1 so that $L_1(x^1) > 0$. If $L_2(x) < 0$ for some $x \in S$, we can find a convex combination of x, x^1 for which L_1 is positive, L_2 negative, contrary to the assumption that L_1 is zero for all $x \in S$.

(26) $L_2(x) = 0$ for all $x \in S$.

From (25) and (26), the hypotheses of (c) are satisfied.

(e) $L_2(x) = 0$ for all $x \in S$, $L_1(x^0) < 0$, $L_2(x^0) = 0$ for some $x^0 \in D$. This case is completely parallel to (d).

Thus, except in case (a), the indifference sets are the intersections of hyperplanes with D.

The converse follows trivially from Lemma 5; by assumption, for every c not maximal or minimal, there exists a linear function $L(x)$ such that

$$\{x: f(x) = c\} = \{x \in D: L(x) = 0\},$$

so that (19) and (20) are satisfied with $L_1(x) = L_2(x) = L(x)$.

Equivalence of constraint qualifications KT and H

Theorem 5.   In finite-dimensional spaces, Constraint Qualifications KT and H are equivalent.

Proof.   Clearly, the hypothesis of Constraint Qualification KT can be inferred from that of condition H by considering only those components j for which $g^j(\overline{x}) = 0$. Since the conclusions of the two Constraint Qualifications are the same, the KT condition implies condition H.

To establish the converse, suppose Constraint Qualification H and the hypothesis of Constraint Qualification KT hold. Then for any $\epsilon > 0$, if

(28) $g^j(\overline{x}) = 0$, $\overline{g}_x^j \cdot (\epsilon \xi) \geq 0$.

On the other hand, clearly if

(29) $g^j(\overline{x}) > 0$, $g^j(\overline{x}) + \overline{g}_x^j \cdot (\epsilon \xi) \geq 0$ for ϵ sufficiently small.

Since $\overline{x} \in C$, $g^j(\overline{x}) \geq 0$ for all j. From (28) and (29), $g(\overline{x}) + \overline{g}_x(\epsilon \xi) \geq 0$. By Constraint Qualification H, there exists a path $\psi_\epsilon(\theta)$ such that $\psi_\epsilon(0) = \overline{x}$, $\psi_\epsilon(\theta) \in C$ for θ sufficiently small, $\psi_\epsilon{}'(0) = \epsilon \xi$. If we now define $\psi(\theta) = \psi_\epsilon(\theta/\epsilon)$, we have a contained path at $\overline{x}$ in direction ξ.

Notes

1 This work was supported in part by the Office of Naval Research (Task NR-047-004) at Stanford University. Hurwicz's participation was made possible by a Rockefeller Foundation grant to Stanford for mathematical research in the social sciences.

2 Here x is a column vector with components $x_1, \ldots, x_n$, y a row vector with m components, $f(x)$ is a real-valued function of x, $g(x)$ a column vector with real-valued components $g^j(x)$ ($j = 1, \ldots, m$), f_x a row vector with components $f_{x_i} = \partial f/\partial x_i$, g_x a matrix with components $g^j_{x_i} = \partial g^j/\partial x_i$, where i varies over columns and j over rows. Bars over f and g or their derivatives denote evaluation at $\bar{x}$. If v is a vector, $v \geq 0$ means that each component of v is nonnegative; $v > 0$ means that each component is positive.

   A function $f(x)$ of a vector variable is said to be differentiable at $\bar{x}$, if there is a row vector a such that

$$\lim_{h \to 0} [f(\bar{x} + h) - f(\bar{x}) - ah]/|h| = 0.$$

If this condition holds, then the partial derivatives of $f(x)$ all exist at $\bar{x}$ and $\bar{f}_x = a$, but the condition of differentiability at a point is stronger than the existence of partial derivatives.

   The function f is said to be concave, if $f[tx + (1 - t)\bar{x}] \geq tf(x) + (1 - t)f(\bar{x})$ for any pair of vectors, $x, \bar{x}$, and any real number t, $0 \leq t \leq 1$.

   A vector function f is said to be differentiable (or concave), if each component is.

   A saddle-point, subject to $y \geq 0$ of a function $L(x, y)$ of two vectors, is a point $(\bar{x}, \bar{y})$ such that $\bar{x}$ maximizes $L(x, \bar{y})$ and $\bar{y}$ minimizes $L(\bar{x}, y)$ for nonnegative y. The concept is due to Kuhn and Tucker [11]; see their definition of the Saddle Value Problem on p. 482 of Ref. [11]. A quasi-saddle-point is a point where the first-order (necessary) conditions for a saddle-point are satisfied.

   In this article, the variables are not necessarily restricted to be nonnegative. Any such restrictions are therefore assumed to be included among the conditions $g(x) \geq 0$. The formulation of the following conditions therefore differs in detail but not in essence from that of Kuhn and Tucker [11].

3 See, for example, Courant [7], pp. 189–190 and 192–93. For the case of inequalities, the following example is due to Slater [12]: $f(x) = x$, $g(x) = -(1 - x)^2$; here both f and g are concave and differentiable, yet there is no saddle-point and hence no quasi-saddle-point. See also the example of Kuhn and Tucker [11], pp. 483–84.

4 See [11], p. 483. For a corresponding condition in the context of equality constraints, see Bliss [6], p. 210, conclusion of Lemma 76.1.

5 To see that A is not necessarily convex and Constraint Qualification W is truly weaker than Constraint Qualification KT, consider the constraints $x_1 \geq 0, x_2 \geq 0, -x_1 x_2 \geq 0$. The constraint set C consists of the origin and the two positive half-axes. If $\bar{x}$ is taken to be the origin, the set of attainable

directions A is the same as C. The set of weakly attainable directions, W, is the convex cone spanned by this set; that is, the nonnegative quadrant. All constraints are effective, and

$$\bar{g}_x{}^E = \begin{pmatrix} 1 & 0 \\ 0 & 1 \\ 0 & 0 \end{pmatrix},$$

so that the set of locally constrained directions L is defined by $\xi_1 \geq 0$, $\xi_2 \geq 0$, and thus is again the nonnegative orthant. L is therefore contained in W but not in A.

In general, if A were a closed set, then the convex cone spanned by it would also be closed, and the words, "the closure of," in Definition 4 could be deleted without loss of generality. It can be shown fairly easily that it is closed for convex constraint sets. The referee has supplied the following example, which shows that A is not necessarily closed for differentiable $g(x)$ in general:

$$g(x, 0) = -x^2,$$

$$g(x, y) = -r^2 \{\theta^4 \sin^2 (1/\theta) + [\max (r - \sec \theta \tan \theta, 0)]^4\} \quad \text{for } y > 0,$$

where

$$r = (x^2 + y^2)^{1/2}, \quad 0 \leq \theta = \text{arc tan } (y/x) \leq \pi/2,$$

and the domain of definition is the nonnegative quadrant.

Since $g(x, y) \leq 0$ everywhere in the domain of definition, the constraint set

$$C = \{(x, y): g(x, y) \geq 0\} \text{ is the union of the segments}$$

$$\{(x, y): y = x \text{ arc tan } (1/n\pi), x \geq 0, x^2 \leq y\},$$

for all positive integers n. Thus, the attainable directions from $(0, 0)$ include $[1, \text{arc tan } (1/n\pi)]$ for all n, but not $(1, 0)$, so that A is not closed.

6   It is possible, although we have not investigated this point, that Constraint Qualification KT can be extended in a natural form to infinite-dimensional (function) spaces.

7   Note that from the differentiability of $g^j(x)$ and from that of $\psi(\theta)$ at $\theta = 0$, the chain rule for differentiation is valid. Theorem 6.14, p. 113 in [1] may be easily extended to the present case of one-sided differentiation.

8   A function $f(x)$ is quasi-concave if, for all c, the set $\{x: f(x) \geq c\}$ is convex. A function is quasi-convex if it is the negative of a quasi-concave function, so that the sets $\{x: f(x) \leq c\}$ are all convex.

9   It should be stated that the case of nonlinear equality constraints is not well handled by these theorems and corollaries; these all depend on the construction of a linear contained path, but for nonlinear equality constraints none may exist. A form of Corollary 6 to Theorem 3 does remain valid in this case ([3], Appendix 1).

References

[1]   T. M. Apostol, *Mathematical Analysis: A Modern Approach to Advanced Calculus*, Reading, Mass.: Addison-Wesley, 1957.

[2]   K. J. Arrow and A. C. Enthoven, "Quasi-Concave Programming," The RAND Corporation, P-1847, December 16, 1959. (To be published in *Econometrica.*)

[3]   K. J. Arrow and L. Hurwicz, "Reduction of Constrained Maxima to Saddle-Point Problems," *Proceedings of the Third Berkeley Symposium on Mathematical Statistics and Probability*, Berkeley and Los Angeles: University of California Press, 1956, Vol. V, pp. 1–20.

[4]   K. J. Arrow, L. Hurwicz, and H. Uzawa, "Constraint Qualification in Maximization Problems," Office of Naval Research Technical Report No. 64, Department of Economics, Stanford University, 1958.

[5]   K. J. Arrow, L. Hurwicz, and H. Uzawa, *Studies in Linear and Nonlinear Programming*, Stanford: Stanford University Press, 1958.

[6]   G. A. Bliss, *Lectures on the Calculus of Variations*, Chicago: University of Chicago Press, 1946.

[7]   R. Courant, *Differential and Integral Calculus* (E. J. McShane, tr.), Vol. II, New York: Interscience Publishers, 1936.

[8]   W. Fenchel, *Convex Cones, Sets and Functions.* Princeton University, 1953 (hectographed).

[9]   S. Karlin, *Mathematical Methods and Theory in Games, Linear Programming, and Economics*, Vol. I, Reading, Mass.: Addison-Wesley, 1960.

[10]   T. C. Koopmans, Editor, *Activity Analysis of Production and Allocation*, Cowles Commission Monograph No. 13, New York: John Wiley and Sons, 1951.

[11]   H. W. Kuhn and A. W. Tucker, "Nonlinear Programming," in J. Neyman, Editor, *Proceedings of the Second Berkeley Symposium on Mathematical Statistics and Probability*, Berkeley and Los Angeles: University of California Press, 1951, pp. 481–492.

[12]   M. Slater, "Lagrange Multipliers Revisited: A Contribution to Nonlinear Programming," Cowles Commission Discussion Paper, Math. 403, November 1950.

Quasi-concave programming

KENNETH J. ARROW
ALAIN C. ENTHOVEN

1. Introduction

Our problem is to maximize a differentiable function, $f(x)$, of an n-dimensional vector $x = (x_1, \ldots, x_n)$, subject to the constraints $g(x) \geqslant 0$, where $g(x)$ is a differentiable m-dimensional vector function, $g^1(x), \ldots, g^m(x)$, and $x \geq 0$. H. W. Kuhn and A. W. Tucker, in their frequently quoted paper on Nonlinear Programming [4], proved that if $g(x)$ satisfies their *Constraint Qualification*,[1] the necessary conditions for x^0 to maximize $f(x)$ subject to $g(x) \geq 0$ and $x \geq 0$ (the Kuhn-Tucker-Lagrange conditions, or KTL) are

(KTL)
$$f_x^0 + \lambda^0 g_x^0 \leq 0,$$
$$x^0(f_x^0 + \lambda^0 g_x^0) = 0,$$
$$\lambda^0 g(x^0) = 0,$$
$$\lambda^0 \geq 0,$$

where, for example, f_x^0 is the vector of partial derivatives of $f(x)$ evaluated at the point x^0.[2] Kuhn and Tucker also proved that if $f(x)$ and $g(x)$ are *concave* functions, (KTL) are sufficient conditions for a constrained maximum.

A function is *concave* if the chord joining any two points on any plane profile of its graph lies everywhere on or below the function. That is, $f(x)$ is concave if

(1.1) $f[\theta x + (1 - \theta)x^0] \geq \theta f(x) + (1 - \theta)f(x^0)$ $(0 \leq \theta \leq 1)$

for all points x and x^0 in the region of definition of $f(x)$. Write (1.1) in the form

(1.2) $\dfrac{f[x^0 + \theta(x - x^0)] - f(x^0)}{\theta} \geq f(x) - f(x^0)$ $(0 < \theta \leq 1)$

and take the limit of the left-hand side as $\theta \to 0$,[3] to obtain

(1.3) $f_x^0(x - x^0) + f(x^0) \geq f(x)$

which is an alternative definition of concavity for differentiable functions. The inequality (1.3) states that if $f(x)$ is concave, it lies everywhere on or below its tangent planes.

A function is *quasi-concave* if, for each real number c, the set x defined by the inequality

(1.4) $f(x) \geq c$

is convex. That is, $f(x)$ is quasi-concave if

(1.5) $f(x) \geq f(x^0)$ implies $f[\theta x + (1 - \theta)x^0] \geq f(x^0)$

for $0 \leq \theta \leq 1$. Now, for any x satisfying (1.5), let

(1.6) $F(\theta) = f[\theta x + (1 - \theta)x^0] \geq f(x^0) = F(0)$.

Therefore, $F'(0) \geq 0$. Thus, differentiating $F(\theta)$ and setting θ equal to zero, we have

(1.7) $f(x) \geq f(x^0)$ implies $f_x^0(x - x^0) \geq 0$

for differentiable quasi-concave functions.[4]

In speaking of a quasi-concave function, some specific domain of definition, taken to be a convex set, is assumed. Thus, the function $x_1 x_2$ is quasi-concave for nonnegative x_1, x_2, but not for all x. A function which is quasi-concave for a convex domain of definition cannot necessarily be extended to a quasi-concave function over the entire space. (In the same circumstances, a concave function can always be so extended.) In this paper, we shall usually deal with functions quasi-concave over nonnegative values of the variables.

It is clear from (1.1) that all concave functions are quasi-concave. It also can be shown that any monotonic nondecreasing function of a quasi-concave function – and therefore of a concave function – is quasi-concave.[5] However, not every quasi-concave function can be expressed as a monotonic nondecreasing function of a concave function.[6] Thus quasi-concavity is a generalization of the notion of concavity.

In terms of traditional economic theory, a concave function is one that satisfies the second-order conditions for a maximum, that is,

(1.8) $d^2 f = \sum_{i=1}^{n} \sum_{j=1}^{n} f_{x_i x_j} dx_i dx_j \leq 0.$

Quasi-concavity is a weaker condition; (1.8) does not have to hold for quasi-concave functions.[7] A quasi-concave function is one that has a diminishing marginal rate of substitution if $f_x > 0$, or an increasing marginal rate of transformation if $f_x < 0$, between any pair of variables, or between any distinct composite variables. Let x^0 and x^1 be any two nonnegative vectors not zero and not proportional to each other. Then, if we let

(1.9) $g(u, v) = f(ux^0 + vx^1),   u \geq 0, v \geq 0,$

(1.10) $g_u{}^2 g_{vv} - 2g_u g_v g_{uv} + g_v{}^2 g_{uu} \leq 0,$

if $f(x)$ is quasi-concave and twice differentiable. It can also be shown that if (1.10) holds everywhere, $f(x)$ is quasi-concave.

Alternatively, if $f(x)$ is quasi-concave, $(-1)^r D_r \geq 0$, for $r = 1, \ldots, n$ and for all x, where D_r is the bordered determinant

(1.11) $D_r = \begin{vmatrix} 0 & f_{x_1} & & f_{x_r} \\ f_{x_1} & f_{x_1 x_1} & \cdots & f_{x_1 x_r} \\ \cdot & & & \cdot \\ \cdot & & & \cdot \\ \cdot & & & \cdot \\ f_{x_r} & f_{x_r x_1} & \cdots & f_{x_r x_r} \end{vmatrix}.$

Moreover, a sufficient condition for $f(x)$ to be quasi-concave for $x \geq 0$ is that D_r have the sign $(-1)^r$ for all x and all $r = 1, \ldots, n$.[8]

We seek sufficient conditions for $x^0 \geq 0$ to maximize $f(x)$ subject to the constraints $g(x) \geq 0$ when $f(x)$ and $g(x)$ are differentiable quasi-concave functions. It is not true that (KTL) alone are sufficient conditions for a constrained maximum, as the following examples illustrate.

Any monotonic function of one variable is clearly quasi-concave. Let

(1.12) $f(x) = (x - 1)^3,   x \geq 0,$

and maximize it subject to the constraint

(1.13) $g(x) = 2 - x \geqslant 0$.

If $x^0 = 1, \lambda^0 = 0$, (KTL) is satisfied, yet clearly the constrained maximum occurs at $x = 2$, not $x = 1$.

More generally, let $\mathcal{F}(x)$ be any quasi-concave function and x^0 any point, and let

(1.14) $f(x) = [\mathcal{F}(x) - \mathcal{F}(x^0)]^3$.

Then $f(x)$ is quasi-concave and has the same maxima as $\mathcal{F}(x)$. But $f_x{}^0 = 0$, although x^0 was chosen arbitrarily. Moreover, if $g(x)$ is any vector function for which $g(x^0) \geqslant 0$, (KTL) is satisfied if $x = x^0$ and $\lambda^0 = 0$, although x^0 certainly need not be the constrained maximum for $f(x)$ subject to $g(x) \geqslant 0$.

We also state conditions under which (KTL) will be necessary for a constrained maximum, when the constraints are quasi-concave. The following example makes clear the fact that (KTL) are not always necessary conditions, and that some additional condition must be satisfied. Maximize $x_1 x_2$ subject to the constraints $x_1 \geqslant 0, x_2 \geqslant 0$ and

(1.15) $g(x) = (1 - x_1 - x_2)^3 \geqslant 0$.

The constrained maximum occurs at $x_1{}^0 = x_2{}^0 = 1/2$, but there is no value of λ for which (KTL) can be satisfied at that point. This example also illustrates the fact that it is the constraint *functions* and not the constraint *set* which must satisfy the additional condition, for (1.15) and

(1.16) $1 - x_1 - x_2 \geqslant 0$

define the same convex set. Yet (KTL) are satisfied at x^0 with $\lambda^0 = 1/2$ when the constraint is (1.16), and, in fact, in this case (KTL) is a necessary condition for a maximum. The Kuhn-Tucker Constraint Qualification is designed to meet the problem. Since it is rather complicated to apply, in Section 3 below, we present a simpler condition on quasi-concave constraints which, when satisfied, implies that the Constraint Qualification must be satisfied, and therefore that (KTL) are necessary for a constrained maximum.

2. Sufficient conditions for a constrained maximum

Let a *relevant* variable be one which can take on a positive value without necessarily violating the constraints. Or, more formally, x_{i_0} is a *relevant* variable if there is some point in the constraint set, say x^*, at which $x_{i_0}{}^* > 0$. Then we shall prove the following theorem:

Theorem 1.   Let $f(x)$ be a differentiable quasi-concave function of the n-dimensional vector x, and let $g(x)$ be an m-dimensional differentiable quasi-concave vector function, both defined for $x \geqslant 0$. Let x^0 and λ^0 satisfy (KTL), and let one of the following conditions be satisfied:

(a) $f_{x_{i_0}}{}^0 < 0$ for at least one variable x_{i_0};

(b) $f_{x_{i_1}}{}^0 > 0$ for some relevant variable x_{i_1};

(c) $f_x{}^0 \neq 0$ and $f(x)$ is twice differentiable[9] in the neighborhood of x^0;

(d) $f(x)$ is concave.

Then x^0 maximizes $f(x)$ subject to the constraints $g(x) \geqslant 0, x \geqslant 0$.

Only one of these four conditions – and there may be others – need be satisfied for x^0 to maximize $f(x)$ subject to the constraints, if (KTL) is satisfied at x^0.[10] Condition (b) will be satisfied if $x_{i_1}{}^0 f_{x_{i_1}}{}^0 > 0$, if any $f_{x_{i_0}}{}^0 > 0$ and all x_{i_0} are relevant (the usual case in economic theory), or if $f_x{}^0 > 0$ and any x_{i_0} is relevant. If no x_{i_0} is relevant, the problem is trivial. From (a) and (b) it follows that $f_x{}^0 \neq 0$ is sufficient if all x_i are relevant.

Perhaps these conditions can be better understood if we consider what conditions $f(x)$ must satisfy if the theorem does not apply. First, from (d), $f(x)$ must be a quasi-concave function that is not concave; from (a), $f_x{}^0 \geqslant 0$; from (b), $f_{x_i}{}^0 = 0$ for all relevant variables. Then from (c), either $f_x{}^0 = 0$, or $f_{x_i}{}^0 = 0$ for all relevant variables and $f(x)$ is not twice differentiable. Thus, (KTL) fails to be sufficient in the case of the cubic transforms shown in Section 1 because $f_x{}^0 = 0$. An example in which (KTL) fails but $f_x{}^0 \neq 0$ follows this proof.

Proof.   We use the following identity

(2.1) $f_x{}^0 (x^1 - x^0) = (x^1 - x^0)(f_x{}^0 + \lambda^0 g_x{}^0) - \lambda^0 g_x{}^0 (x^1 - x^0).$

If x^0 satisfies (KTL) and x^1 is in the constraint set, the first term on the right-hand side is nonpositive. The second term on the right-hand side is also nonpositive under these conditions. If $\lambda_j{}^0 = 0$, the jth component of the term vanishes. If $\lambda_j{}^0 > 0, g^j(x^0) = 0$, and the fact that x^1 is in the constraint set, that is $g^j(x^1) \geqslant 0$, implies $g^j(x^1) \geqslant g^j(x^0)$ or, by (1.7), $g_x{}^{j0}(x^1 - x^0) \geqslant 0$. Therefore, for $f(x)$ and $g(x)$ quasi-concave,

(2.2) $g(x^1) \geqslant 0, \quad x^1 \geqslant 0$ implies $f_x{}^0 (x^1 - x^0) \leqslant 0$

if x^0 satisfies (KTL).

(a) $f_{x_{i_0}}{}^0 < 0$ for at least one variable x_{i_0}.

Let h be the unit vector in the i_0 th direction.[11] Let $x^2 = x^0 + h$. Then

(2.3) $f_x{}^0 (x^2 - x^0) = f_x{}^0 h = f_{x_{i_0}}{}^0 < 0, \quad x^2 \geqslant 0.$

For any x^1 in the constraint set, let

$x^1(\theta) = (1 - \theta) x^1 + \theta x^2, \quad x^0(\theta) = (1 - \theta) x^0 + \theta x^2.$

Then

(2.4) $f_x{}^0 [x^0(\theta) - x^0] = \theta f_x{}^0 (x^2 - x^0) < 0 \quad$ for $\theta > 0,$

(2.5) $f_x^0 [x^1(\theta) - x^0(\theta)] = (1 - \theta) f_x^0 (x^1 - x^0) \leq 0$ for $\theta \leq 1$,

from (2.2). Adding, we find

(2.6) $f_x^0 [x^1(\theta) - x^0] < 0$ for $0 < \theta \leq 1$,

and from (1.7) this is possible only if

(2.7) $f[x^1(\theta)] < f(x^0)$.

As θ approaches zero, $x^1(\theta)$ approaches x^1, and so $f(x^1) \leq f(x^0)$.

(b) $f_{x_{i_1}}^0 > 0$ for some relevant variable x_{i_1}.

If we exclude case (a), $x^0 f_x^0 > 0$ and (b) are equivalent. Clearly, $x^0 f_x^0 > 0$ implies that (b) is satisfied. For the converse, note that, by (2.2),

(2.8) $f_x^0 x^1 \leq f_x^0 x^0$,

for all x^1 in the constraint set. Excluding (a),

(2.9) $f_x^0 \geq 0$.

But (b) implies that for some x^* in the constraint set and for some i_0, $f_{x_{i_0}}^0 > 0$ and $x_{i_0}^* > 0$, which, together with (2.9) and the nonnegativity of x^*, implies that $f_x^0 x^* > 0$. If we let $x^1 = x^*$ in (2.8), we find that $f_x^0 x^0 > 0$.

If now we let $x^2 = 0$, we see that (2.3) again holds, and the rest of the argument under (a) is valid.

(c) $f_x^0 \neq 0$ and $f(x)$ is twice differentiable in the neighborhood of x^0.

Partition the vector x^0 into two sub-vectors, y^0 and z^0 corresponding to the relevant and irrelevant variables, respectively. Then if we exclude the two cases already covered, but assume $f_x^0 \neq 0$, we have

(2.10) $f_y^0 = 0$, $f_z^0 \geq 0$, $f_{z_{i_0}}^0 > 0$ for some z_{i_0}.

By the definition of an irrelevant variable, $z^0 = 0$ and $z^1 = 0$ for all $x^1 = (y^1, z^1)$ in the constraint set. Therefore, to prove the theorem it is sufficient to prove that $f(y^0, 0) \geq f(y^1, 0)$ for all $y^1 \geq 0$.

Define the function

(2.11) $\phi(u, v) = f[(1 - u) y^0 + u y^1, v\bar{z}] - f(y^0, 0)$

for $0 \leq u \leq 1$, and $v \geq 0$, for any $y^1 \geq 0$ and for any $\bar{z} \geq 0$ such that $\bar{z}_{i_0} > 0$. Because it is essentially $f(x)$ with the range of variation of x restricted to a convex subset of the nonnegative orthant, $\phi(u, v)$ is quasi-concave. Then we have

(2.12) $\phi(0, 0) = 0$,

(2.13) $\phi_u(0, 0) = f_y^0 (y^1 - y^0) = 0$,

and

(2.14) $\phi_v(0, 0) = f_z^0 \bar{z} > 0$.

We want to prove $\phi(1, 0) \leqslant 0$, or to disprove $\phi(1, 0) > 0$. To do so, first we shall establish the fact that within a sufficiently small neighborhood of zero, $\phi(u, 0)$ is either positive, zero, or negative (but not more than one of the three). Then we shall show that $\phi(u, 0) = 0$ and $\phi(u, 0) < 0$ in a neighborhood of zero are incompatible with $\phi(1, 0) > 0$ while $\phi(u, 0) > 0$ contradicts the hypotheses of the theorem.

First, if for some $\bar{u} > 0$, $\phi(\bar{u}, 0) \geqslant 0$, then by quasi-concavity, (1.5), and (2.12), $\phi(u, 0) \geqslant 0$ for all u such that $0 \leqslant u \leqslant \bar{u}$. Thus, either $\phi(u, 0) \geqslant 0$ or $\phi(u, 0) < 0$ for all u in the interval. If $\phi(u, 0) \geqslant 0$, either there exists some sequence of points u_n approaching zero on which $\phi(u, 0) > 0$, or there does not. If there does not, $\phi(u, 0) = 0$ for $u > 0$ sufficiently small. If there does, then, by quasi-concavity and (1.5), $\phi(u, 0) > 0$ in the intervals between the points in the sequence, and therefore $\phi(u, 0) > 0$ for $u > 0$ sufficiently small. Therefore, either $\phi(u, 0) > 0$, or $\phi(u, 0) = 0$, or $\phi(u, 0) < 0$ in a neighborhood of $u = 0$.

Clearly, if $\phi(1, 0) > 0$, by (1.5), $\phi(u, 0) \geqslant 0$ for all u in the interval $0 \leqslant u \leqslant 1$, and $\phi(u, 0)$ cannot be negative.

Now, suppose $\phi(u, 0) = 0$ in the neighborhood of 0. If $\phi(1, 0) > 0$, we must have

(2.15)
$$\phi(u, 0) = 0, \quad 0 \leqslant u \leqslant u^*;$$
$$\phi(u, 0) > 0, \quad u^* < u \leqslant 1;$$

where $u^* > 0$. Since, by (2.14), $\phi_v(0, 0) > 0$, there is a solution, $u(v)$, to the equation

(2.16) $\quad \phi[u(v), 0] = \phi(0, v)$,

with $u(v) \geqslant u^*$, for v sufficiently small. The solution may not be unique, but this does not matter. In any case,

(2.17) $\quad \lim_{v \to 0} u(v) = u^*$.

Let $\theta = 1 - u^*/u(v)$, and form a combination of the points $[u(v), 0]$ and $(0, v)$ with the weights $1 - \theta$ and θ, respectively. Then, (2.16) and (1.5) imply

(2.18) $\quad \phi[(1 - \theta) u(v), \theta v] = \phi(u^*, \theta v) \geqslant \phi(0, v)$.

By Rolle's Theorem (the law of the mean),

(2.19) $\quad \phi_v(u^*, v^*) = \dfrac{\phi(u^*, \theta v) - \phi(u^*, 0)}{\theta v}$

for some v^* in the interval $0 \leqslant v^* \leqslant \theta v$. But $\phi(u^*, 0) = 0$, by (2.15), so that (2.18) and (2.19) imply

(2.20) $\quad \phi_v(u^*, v^*) \geqslant \dfrac{1}{\theta} \dfrac{\phi(0, v)}{v}$.

Now take the limits of both sides as v approaches zero. By (2.17), θ approaches zero as v does. $\phi(0, v)/v$ approaches $\phi_v(0, 0)$ which is positive. Therefore, the right-hand side approaches infinity. Since ϕ_v is differentiable by hypothesis, it is continuous, so that the left-hand side approaches $\phi_v(u^*, 0)$ which is finite. Therefore, the hypotheses lead to a contradiction, and $\phi(u, 0) = 0$ for $u > 0$ and $\phi(1, 0) > 0$ are incompatible.

Finally, suppose $\phi(u, 0) > 0$ for $u > 0$ sufficiently small. Define $u(v)$ as in (2.16). Now

(2.21) $\lim_{v \to 0} u(v) = 0.$

Consider $\phi(u, v)$ on the line connecting the points $(0, v)$ and $[u(v), 0]$. Since $\phi(u, v)$ is quasi-concave, its value along this line must be greater than or equal to its value at the end points. Therefore, the directional derivative of $\phi(u, v)$ at $(0, v)$ in the direction of $[u(v), 0]$ must be nonnegative. That is,[12]

(2.22) $u(v)\, \phi_u(0, v) - v\phi_v(0, v) \geqslant 0.$

This can be written as

(2.23) $u(v)\, \dfrac{\phi_u(0, v)}{v} \geqslant \phi_v(0, v).$

Taking limits as v, and therefore $u(v)$, approach zero, we obtain $\phi_v(0, 0) > 0$ on the right-hand side. On the left-hand side, the limit of $\phi_u(0, v)/v$ as v approaches zero is $\phi_{uv}(0, 0)$. The existence of this derivative is, of course, one of the hypotheses of the theorem. The limit of the left-hand side is zero, which is a contradiction. Therefore, $\phi(u, 0) > 0$ for $u > 0$ sufficiently small contradicts the hypotheses of the theorem, and part (c) of the theorem is proved.

(d) $f(x)$ is concave.[13]

Equations (1.3) and (2.2) imply $f(x^0) \geqslant f(x^1)$ for all $x^1 \geqslant 0, g(x^1) \geqslant 0$. This completes the proof of Theorem 1.

Now we shall construct implicitly a differentiable (in fact, continuously differentiable) quasi-concave function that satisfies (KTL) at a point x^0 with $f_x{}^0 \neq 0$, but which does not have a constrained maximum at that point. The example is designed to show that although the condition of twice differentiability, condition (c) of the theorem, can be weakened, it cannot be dispensed with altogether.

From the proof, it is clear that such an example must be found in a function $f(x, y)$ with $f_x(0, 0) = 0, f(x, 0)$ positive in a right-hand neighborhood, and $f_y(0, 0) > 0$.

The example will be chosen so that $f(0, y) = y, f_x(x, 0) = -1/\log x$ for $x \leqslant 1/2$, and $1/\log 2$ for $x > 1/2$. Given the definition of $f(x, y)$ on the two axes, we complete the definition by requiring that all the level curves be straight lines, which insures the quasi-concavity of the example. Formally, for any fixed value of $f(x, y)$, say z, we define $X(z)$ as the solution of the equation, $f(x, 0) = z$. Then the level curve $f(x, y) = z$ intersects the x-axis at $x = X(z)$ and the y-axis at $y = z$. If the level curve is to be a straight line, and (x, y) is any point on it, we have

(2.24) $\dfrac{x}{X(z)} + \dfrac{y}{z} = 1.$

For fixed x and y, then, $f(x, y)$ is the unique positive value of z for which (2.24) is satisfied [except that $f(x, y) = 0$ for $x = y = 0$].

Since $f_x(0, 0) = 0, f_y(0, 0) = 1$, (KTL) is satisfied at the origin for the constraint, $-y \geqslant 0$, with $\lambda^0 = 1$. But the origin is not a constrained maximum. It remains only to show that f_x and f_y are continuously differentiable. The construction makes clear, and it can be shown analytically, that no difficulty could arise except possibly at the origin. The functions f_x and f_y can be evaluated from (2.24) by implicit differentiation, and careful passage to the limit as x and y both approach zero shows that both are continuous, with f_x approaching zero and f_y approaching 1.

  Remark.[14]   The hypothesis that the constraint function $g(x)$ be quasi-concave was used only to establish that, for all x^1 in the constraint set,

(2.25) $g_x^{j0}(x^1 - x^0) \geqslant 0,$

for all constraints for which $g^j(x^0) = 0$. But for this purpose it suffices that the constraint set be a convex set. For then

  $(1 - \theta) x^0 + \theta x^1$

belongs to the constraint set for $0 \leqslant \theta \leqslant 1$. By definition of the constraint set,

  $g^j[(1 - \theta) x^0 + \theta x^1] \geqslant 0$ for $0 \leqslant \theta \leqslant 1$.

Further, for $\theta = 0$, the left-hand side becomes $g^j(x^0) = 0$, so that the derivative with respect to θ at $\theta = 0$ must be nonnegative. By the chain rule, this statement is equivalent to (2.25).

3. Necessary conditions for a constrained maximum

Kuhn and Tucker [4] showed that (KTL) are necessary conditions for a constrained maximum provided the constraint functions $g(x)$ satisfy a condition termed by them the *Constraint Qualification.* To state the condition, we define a *contained path in the direction* $\xi = (\xi_1, \ldots, \xi_n)$ to be a vector function $\psi(\theta)$, defined for the real variable $\theta \geqslant 0$ in an interval beginning at $\theta = 0$, whose values are points in the constraint set, and differentiable at $\theta = 0$ with $\psi'(0) = \xi$.[15] The Constraint Qualification then requires that for any x^0 in the constraint set, there is a contained path with $\psi(0) = x^0$ in any direction ξ satisfying the conditions

(3.1)   if $g^j(x^0) = 0$,   then $g_x^{j0} \mathcal{E} \geq 0$,

(3.2)   if $x_i^0 = 0$,   then $\mathcal{E}_i \geq 0$.

To grasp the meaning of these conditions, consider any constraint, $g^j(x) \geq 0$, effective at x^0. The tangent hyperplane, $g_x^{j0}(x - x^0) = 0$, then divides the space into two half-spaces (provided $g_x^{j0} \neq 0$), one of which contains the constraint set. Then the directions satisfying (3.1) must point into or along the boundary of that half-space. A similar remark applies to the effective nonnegativity constraints. Then the Constraint Qualification requires that for every direction from x^0 which points into or along the boundaries of the appropriate half-spaces for each effective constraint, there is some path that begins at x^0 in the direction $\mathcal{E}$ all of whose points in some neighborhood of x^0 are in the constraint set. As Kuhn and Tucker point out, the Constraint Qualification is designed to rule out such singularities as outward pointing cusps at the boundary of the constraint set at which λ's satisfying (KTL) may not exist.

In [1], some simpler conditions which, when satisfied, imply that the Constraint Qualification is satisfied were studied. One such condition is that $g(x)$ be linear. Another is that $g(x)$ be concave and that for some $x^* \geq 0, g(x^*) > 0$ (that is, each coordinate is positive).[16] If the constraints $g(x)$ arise from a problem in activity analysis, then this condition means that it is possible to reduce all initial availabilities of primary commodities to some extent and still produce a positive amount of each intermediate and final good.

Since we are interested here in quasi-concave constraints, we shall state a generalization of the latter condition.[17]

Theorem 2.   Let $g(x)$ be an m-dimensional differentiable quasi-concave vector function. Let $g(x^*) > 0$ for some $x^* \geq 0$, and for each j let either

(a) $g^j(x)$ be concave, or
(b)   for each x^0 in the constraint set, $g_x^{j0} \neq 0$.

Then $g(x)$ satisfies the Constraint Qualification.

Therefore, if x^0 maximizes any differentiable function $f(x)$ subject to $g(x) \geq 0$, (KTL) must be satisfied.

If the hypotheses of Theorems 1 and 2 both hold, (KTL) are necessary and sufficient for a constrained maximum.

4. Extensions of the theorems

(1) Dropping the nonnegativity constraints

If $f(x)$ and $g(x)$ are defined for all x, and not just for those values in the non-negative orthant, the conditions (a), (b), and (c) of Section 2 become merely

$f_x{}^0 \neq 0$, for, in effect, all variables become relevant. That is, in the proof of condition (b), we choose x^* so that $f_x{}^0 x^* > 0$. If $f_x{}^0 \neq 0$, this can always be done when x is not restricted to be nonnegative. Thus we can say that (KTL) is sufficient for x^0 to maximize $f(x)$ subject to $g(x) \geq 0$, where $f(x)$ and $g(x)$ are differentiable quasi-concave functions provided that either (a) $f_x{}^0 \neq 0$, or (b) $f(x)$ is concave.

In this case, the first two lines of (KTL) become simply $f_x{}^0 + \lambda^0 g_x{}^0 = 0$.

Actually, the most important consideration is the domain of definition of the functions $f(x)$, $g(x)$ and not the presence or absence of nonnegativity constraints. In the most general case, we may suppose $f(x)$, $g(x)$ defined over a closed convex set D. Then, if we can find any point x^2 satisfying (2.3), with the condition $x^2 \geq 0$ replaced by the condition that x^2 belong to D, the conclusion that x^0 maximizes $f(x)$ follows as in part (a) of the proof of Theorem 1. The statement of (KTL) must be altered to read,

$$(f_x{}^0 + \lambda^0 g_x{}^0)(x^1 - x^0) \leq 0 \quad \text{for all } x^1 \text{ in } D,$$

(KTLD) $$\lambda^0 g(x^0) = 0,$$

$$\lambda^0 \geq 0.$$

An analogue of (c) remains valid. In the context of a general domain of definition, D, the condition $f_x{}^0 \neq 0$ should be altered to read

(4.1) $f_x{}^0(x^2 - x^0) \neq 0$ for some x^2 in D.

(If D has the full dimensionality of the space, as in the case of the nonnegative orthant, this reduces to the condition, $f_x{}^0 \neq 0$.) If the generalized form (2.3) does not hold, then for all x^2 in D,

(4.2) $f_x{}^0(x^2 - x^0) \geq 0$.

In view of (4.1), we can write

(4.3) $f_x{}^0(x^2 - x^0) > 0$ for some x^2 in D.

On the other hand, from (2.2) (with $x^1 \geq 0$ replaced by the condition, x^1 in D) and (4.2),

(4.4) $f_x{}^0(x^1 - x^0) = 0$ for all x^1 in the constraint set.

Then, for any x^1 in the constraint set, define

$$\phi(u, v) = f[(1 - u - v)x^0 + ux^1 + vx^2] - f(x^0).$$

Then it may easily be verified that (2.12–14) still hold, and we seek to prove that $\phi(1, 0) \leq 0$. The rest of the argument under (c) proceeds without change.

Finally, it is obvious that the argument for (d) of Theorem 1 requires no change. We can therefore state the following general theorem, which also incorporates the Remark to Theorem 1.

Theorem 3.   Let $f(x)$ be a differentiable quasi-concave function of the n-dimensional vector x, and let $g(x)$ be an m-dimensional differentiable vector function, both defined for x in a closed convex domain D. Let the set of vectors x in D for which $g(x) \geqslant 0$ be convex, let x^0 and λ^0 satisfy (KTLD), and let one of the following conditions be satisfied:

(a) $f_x^0(x^2 - x^0) < 0$ for some x^2 in D;
(b) $f_x^0(x^2 - x^0) \neq 0$ for some x^2 in D and $f(x)$ is twice differentiable in some neighborhood of x^0;
(c) $f(x)$ is concave.

Then x^0 maximizes $f(x)$ subject to the constraints, $g(x) \geqslant 0, x$ in D.

The analogue of Theorem 2 also holds. If $g(x^*) > 0$ for some x^* in D and for each j, $g^j(x)$ is concave or quasi-concave, and $g_x^{j0} \neq 0$ for all x^0 in the constraint set, (KTLD) are necessary for a constrained maximum.

(2) Equality constraints

The constraint $g(x) = 0$ can be expressed by the two inequality constraints $g(x) \geqslant 0$ and $-g(x) \geqslant 0$. Thus, if $g(x)$ and $-g(x)$ are both quasi-concave, as they will be, for example, if $g(x)$ is linear, Theorem 1 can be applied.

In this case, the last two lines of (KTL) become simply $g(x^0) = 0$.

There is no analogue of Theorem 2 here. However, we have already pointed out that if $g(x)$ is linear, (KTL) is necessary for a maximum.

(3) Unconstrained maxima

First, suppose that all variables must be nonnegative, but that there are no other constraints. Since all variables are relevant, conditions (a), (b), and (c) of Section 2 become $f_x^0 \neq 0$ as in (1) above. (KTL) becomes $f_x^0 \leqslant 0, x^0 f_x^0 = 0$. These statements together imply that x^0 maximizes the quasi-concave function $f(x)$ for $x \geqslant 0$ if either (a) $f_x^0 \leqslant 0, f_x^0 \neq 0$, and $x^0 f_x^0 = 0$ or (b) $f_x^0 = 0$ and $f(x)$ is concave. The first condition requires that the usual first-order conditions for a maximum be satisfied with at least one corner variable. In effect, the existence of the corner variable rules out such possibilities as that the apparent maximum was produced by a cubic transformation.

The Constraint Qualification is automatically satisfied in this case. Hence, for nonnegative variables, $f_x^0 \leqslant 0, x^0 f_x^0 = 0$ is necessary for an unconstrained maximum for any differentiable $f(x)$.

If the variables are unrestricted, (KTL) becomes $f_x^0 = 0$. As the examples at the end of Section 1 show, no conclusion can be drawn in general from (KTL) unless $f(x)$ is concave in which case the condition is clearly sufficient for a maximum.

If the variables are restricted to a general convex domain D, then (KTLD) becomes

$$f_x^0(x^1 - x^0) \leqslant 0 \qquad \text{for all } x^1 \text{ in } D.$$

This condition will be sufficient for a maximum if one of (a), (b), or (c) of
Theorem 3 holds.

5. Economic applications

(1) Consumer demand

The fundamental property of the utility function in the theory of consumer demand is that the indifference curves define convex sets or a diminishing marginal
rate of substitution. Thus, the minimal property of all utility functions is quasi-
concavity. The propositions of consumer demand theory such as the basic Weak
Axiom of Revealed Preference follow directly from quasi-concavity without
appeal to bordered determinants of partial derivatives, monotonic transformations and the like.

Let the utility function $u(x)$ be quasi-concave and assume non-satiation, that
is $u_{x_i}{}^0 > 0$ for some x_i. Then the usual first-order conditions are necessary and
sufficient for a constrained maximum. Let x^0 satisfy the conditions

$$u_{x_i}{}^0 - \lambda^0 p_{x_i} \leq 0 \qquad (i = 1, \ldots, n),$$
$$(5.1) \quad x_i{}^0(u_{x_i}{}^0 - \lambda^0 p_{x_i}) = 0 \qquad (i = 1, \ldots, n),$$
$$\lambda^0(B - \Sigma\, x_i{}^0 p_{x_i}) = 0 \qquad (i = 1, \ldots, n),$$

where $p_{x_i} > 0$ is the price of a unit of x_i and B is the consumer's budget. Then
x^0 maximizes $u(x)$ subject to the constraints $B - \Sigma\, x_i p_{x_i} \geq 0$ and $x \geq 0$. Moreover, if $\lambda^0 > 0$, and the assumption of non-satiation assures that it will be, x^0
minimizes the cost of attaining $u(x^0)$, for it maximizes $-\Sigma\, x_i p_{x_i}$ subject to the
constraints $u(x) - u(x^0) \geq 0$ and $x \geq 0$.[18]

(2) Production

The theory of efficient production can now be extended to include production
functions that are quasi-concave but not concave, that is to those cases in which
there are increasing returns to scale but a diminishing marginal rate of substitution.

Suppose, for example, that an enterprise carries on production in a set of independent processes which transform purchased inputs into intermediate goods
which are not traded on the market, and both into outputs. Let the scale or intensity of the ith process be measured by the variable x_i. Let the jth output or
input into the ith process be a monotonic function $g_{ij}(x_i)$ that is positive if the
commodity in question is an output of the process, negative if it is an input.
Number the final outputs $j = 1, \ldots, m_1$, the purchased inputs, $j = m_1 + 1, \ldots,$
m_2, the intermediate goods, $j = m_2 + 1, \ldots, m$, and let there be n processes.
Then the net output or input of the jth commodity will be

$$(5.2) \quad g_j(x) = \Sigma_{i=1}^{n}\, g_{ij}(x_i).$$

Now, consider the problem of deriving the minimum cost method of producing a fixed set of outputs at given input prices. Let the price of the jth commodity be p_j. Then the problem is to maximize $\sum_{j=m_1+1}^{m_2} p_j g_j(x)$, subject to the output-level constraints $g_j(x) - g_j(x^0) \geqslant 0, j = 1, \ldots, m_1$, and the constraints that the net outputs of the intermediate goods not be negative, or if we let $\mathcal{E}_j$ represent initial stocks, that the net consumption of intermediate goods not exceed the initial stocks, that is $g_j(x) + \mathcal{E}_j \geqslant 0, j = m_2 + 1, \ldots, m$.

Under what conditions will this problem satisfy the hypotheses of Theorem 1? Since any monotonic function of one variable is quasi-concave, the functions $g_{ij}(x_i)$ are quasi-concave. But here we encounter a difference between concave and quasi-concave functions which is important from the point of view of applications to economic theory. While nonnegative linear combinations of concave functions are also concave, nonnegative linear combinations of quasi-concave functions are not necessarily quasi-concave. As a consequence, the hypothesis of quasi-concavity cannot replace the stronger hypothesis of concavity in many parts of economic theory.

Consider one of the output constraints, $g_j(x) - g_j(x^0) \geqslant 0$, or

(5.3) $\sum_{i=1}^{n} g_{ij}(x_i) - g_j(x^0) \geqslant 0.$

For outputs, we have $g_{ij}'(x_i) \geqslant 0$. If $g_{ij}''(x_i) \leqslant 0, g_{ij}(x_i)$ is concave, and therefore, so is $g_j(x_i)$. If $g_{ij}''(x_i) > 0$ for one process, with $g_{ij}''(x_i) \leqslant 0$ for all the others, $g_j(x)$ can be, though is not necessarily, quasi-concave. If $g_{ij}''(x_i) > 0$ for two or more activities, $g_j(x)$ cannot be quasi-concave. For, if $g_j(x)$ is quasi-concave, the marginal rate of substitution between any pair of inputs must be diminishing, all other inputs held constant. That is, from (1.10), holding, for example, $x_3, \ldots, x_n$ constant,[19]

(5.4) $(g_{2j}')^2 g_{1j}'' + (g_{1j}')^2 g_{2j}'' \leqslant 0.$

Thus, it is possible for either g_{1j}'' or g_{2j}'' to be positive without violating (1.10), but clearly both cannot be positive, and similarly for every other pair of processes. Therefore, $g_{ij}''(x_i) > 0$ for at most one process if $g_j(x)$ is to be quasi-concave. The same is true for the constraints on the use of intermediate goods.

What about the maximand, $\sum_{j=m_1+1}^{m_2} p_j g_j(x)$? If the functions $g_j(x)$ are concave, their linear combination will be also. But if any are quasi-concave and not concave, the quasi-concavity of $\sum_{j=m_1+1}^{m_2} p_j g_j(x)$ cannot be guaranteed independently of the prices. Thus, the only way for Theorem 1 to be applicable for all sets of prices is for there to be diminishing or constant returns to scale in the use of the inputs. For any given set of prices we may, however, have a limited amount of increasing returns in the use of inputs measured in money terms.

On the other hand, to apply Theorem 1 to profit maximization, we maximize $\sum_{j=1}^{m_2} p_j g_j(x)$ subject to the constraints $g_j(x) + \mathcal{E}_j \geqslant 0, j = m_2 + 1, \ldots, m$. Now there can be a limited amount of increasing returns with regard to intermediate goods, but not, in general, with regard to outputs or to inputs purchased on the market (unless there is just one output and no purchased inputs). Again, for any given set of prices, a certain amount of increasing returns in outputs or purchased inputs measured in money can be tolerated.

Alternatively, let a firm's production function be

(5.5) $Y = K^\alpha L^\beta$ $(\alpha > 0, \beta > 0)$.

This function will be quasi-concave but not concave when $\alpha + \beta > 1$. Then, Theorem 1 will apply to the problem of determining the efficient combination of inputs, given any specified output, but it will not be applicable to the profit-maximization problem. That is, the problem of minimizing $rK + wL$, or of maximizing $-(rK + wL)$, where r and w are the cost of a unit of K and L respectively, subject to the constraints $Y - Y^0 \geqslant 0, L \geqslant 0, K \geqslant 0$, satisfies the hypotheses of Theorem 1. But the problem of maximizing $\Pi(K, L) = pK^\alpha L^\beta - rK - wL$, subject to $K \geqslant 0, L \geqslant 0$ does not satisfy the hypotheses of Theorem 1 because $\Pi(K, L)$ is not quasi-concave.

(3) Welfare economics

Suppose that society's over-all production possibility function is quasi-concave. The problem of determining an efficient allocation of resources (a Pareto optimum) can then be formulated as the problem of maximizing the utility of one household (a quasi-concave function) subject to the constraints (also quasi-concave) that total output is within society's production possibilities and that the utilities of all other households are at least equal to specified levels.

6. Properties of quasi-concave functions

In Section 1, we gave several alternative definitions of quasi-concavity. Although the equivalence of these definitions, or their relationships when they are not strictly equivalent, seems to be rather generally understood, we have been unable to find in the literature either a proof of the equivalence of quasi-concavity and diminishing marginal rates of substitution (or increasing marginal rates of transformation), or a statement of the relationship between quasi-concavity and the signs of the bordered determinants of partial derivatives of quasi-concave functions.[20] Therefore, we provide both here.

Let $f(x)$ be a twice differentiable quasi-concave function, and let x^0 and x^1 be any two nonnegative vectors, not zero and not proportional to each other. Let

(6.1) $g(u, v) = f(ux^0 + vx^1)$, $u, v \geqslant 0$.

Then $f(x)$ is quasi-concave if and only if $g(u, v)$ is quasi-concave for all x^0 and x^1. Clearly the quasi-concavity of $f(x)$ implies that of $g(u, v)$. On the other hand, if $g(u, v)$ is quasi-concave, then, in particular, for $0 \leqslant \theta \leqslant 1$, we have

(6.2) $\quad f[\theta x^0 + (1 - \theta) x^1] = g(\theta, 1 - \theta) \geqslant \min [g(0, 1), g(1, 0)]$

$$= \min [f(x^0), f(x^1)].$$

If (6.2) holds for all x^0 and x^1, we have the quasi-concavity of $f(x)$ by definition.

Consider any locus of points on which $g(u, v)$ is constant. Along this locus, $du/dv = -g_v/g_u$. If $f_x > 0$ everywhere, as is normally the case in utility theory, $g_u > 0$ and $g_v > 0$, and g_v/g_u is known as *the marginal rate of substitution* between the composite commodities x^0 and x^1. If $f(x)$ is quasi-concave, the marginal rate of substitution is diminishing. That is, $d(g_v/g_u)/dv \leqslant 0$. If $f_x^0 < 0$ everywhere, as is normally assumed in production theory ($-f_x$ being interpreted as marginal costs), $g_u < 0$ and $g_v < 0$, and g_v/g_u is known as *the marginal rate of transformation* between the composite commodities x^0 and x^1, and if $f(x)$ is quasi-concave, the marginal rate of transformation is increasing. That is, $d(g_v/g_u)/dv \geqslant 0$.

In order to prove these statements, observe that

(6.3) $\quad \dfrac{d}{dv} \left(\dfrac{g_v}{g_u} \right) = \dfrac{1}{g_u{}^3} [g_u{}^2 g_{vv} - 2g_u g_v g_{uv} + g_v{}^2 g_{uu}].$

Thus, if $g_u > 0$, we have a diminishing marginal rate of substitution, or if $g_u < 0$, we have an increasing marginal rate of transformation, if the expression in brackets in (6.3) is less than or equal to zero. Therefore, to prove our propositions, we shall prove the following theorem.

Theorem 4. The twice differentiable function $g(u, v)$ with $g_u > 0$ and $g_v > 0$ everywhere, or $g_u < 0$ and $g_v < 0$ everywhere, is quasi-concave if and only if $g_u{}^2 g_{vv} - 2g_u g_v g_{uv} + g_v{}^2 g_{uu} \leqslant 0$.

Proof. Since g_u and g_v are both positive or both negative, the implicit relation $g(u, v) = c$ defines u as a function of v. Let the function be

(6.4) $\quad u = h(v)$.

Consider the case in which $g_u > 0$ and $g_v > 0$. By hypothesis, $d^2 u/dv^2 \geqslant 0$ so that $h(v)$ is a convex function.

Let (u^0, v^0) and (u^1, v^1) be any two points on the level curve $g(u, v) = c$. Then

(6.5) $\quad u^0 = h(v^0), \quad u^1 = h(v^1).$

Let $(u^2, v^2) = (1 - \theta)(u^0, v^0) + \theta(u^1, v^1)$, for $0 \leqslant \theta \leqslant 1$. Then, from (6.5), and the convexity of $h(v)$,

(6.6) $\quad h(v^2) \leqslant (1 - \theta) h(v^0) + \theta h(v^1) = (1 - \theta) u^0 + \theta u^1 = u^2.$

If $g_u > 0$, it follows from the definition of $h(v)$ that

(6.7) $\quad c = g[h(v^2), v^2] \leqslant g(u^2, v^2),$

so that $g(u^0, v^0) = g(u^1, v^1)$ implies

(6.8) $g[(1 - \theta)(u^0, v^0) + \theta(u^1, v^1)] \geqslant g(u^0, v^0)$ $(0 \leqslant \theta \leqslant 1)$.

Quasi-concavity follows immediately. Suppose $g(u^1, v^1) > g(u^0, v^0)$. Let θ' be the largest value of θ for which

$$g[(1 - \theta)(u^0, v^0) + \theta(u^1, v^1)] = g(u^0, v^0).$$

Now, let $(u^2, v^2) = (1 - \theta')(u^0, v^0) + \theta'(u^1, v^1)$. If $0 \leqslant \theta \leqslant \theta'$, we can write $(1 - \theta)(u^0, v^0) + \theta(u^1, v^1) = (1 - t)(u^0, v^0) + t(u^2, v^2)$ where $t = \theta/\theta'$. Since $g(u^2, v^2) = g(u^0, v^0)$, we have shown that

(6.9) $g[(1 - \theta)(u^0, v^0) + \theta(u^1, v^1)]$

$$= g[(1 - t)(u^0, v^0) + t(u^2, v^2)] \geqslant g(u^0, v^0)$$

for $0 \leqslant \theta \leqslant \theta'$. On the other hand, by continuity and the definition of θ',

(6.10) $g[(1 - \theta)(u^0, v^0) + \theta(u^1, v^1)] > g(u^0, v^0)$

for $\theta' < \theta \leqslant 1$. Thus g satisfies (1.5) and is therefore quasi-concave. The theorem can be proved in a similar manner in the case in which $g_u < 0$ and $g_v < 0$ and there is an increasing marginal rate of transformation.

Finally, we shall prove that the quasi-concavity of $g(u, v)$ implies

(6.11) $g_u{}^2 g_{vv} - 2 g_u g_v g_{uv} + g_v{}^2 g_{uu} \leqslant 0$.

Consider any pair of points (u^0, v^0) and (u^1, v^1) such that $g(u^0, v^0) = g(u^1, v^1)$. From (1.7) we have

(6.12)
$$(u^1 - u^0) g_u{}^0 + (v^1 - v^0) g_v{}^0 \geqslant 0,$$
$$(u^0 - u^1) g_u{}^1 + (v^0 - v^1) g_v{}^1 \geqslant 0,$$

which, when added, imply

(6.13) $(g_u{}^0 - g_u{}^1)(u^1 - u^0) + (g_v{}^0 - g_v{}^1)(v^1 - v^0) \geqslant 0$.

Let $k = u^1 - u^0$. In the limit, for k small enough, $v^1 - v^0 = -k g_u{}^0 / g_v{}^0$. Substituting these relationships into (6.13) and dividing through by $-k^2$, we obtain

(6.14) $\dfrac{g_u(u^0 + k, v^0 - k(g_u{}^0/g_v{}^0)) - g_u(u^0, v^0)}{k}$

$$- \frac{g_u{}^0}{g_v{}^0} \frac{g_v(u^0 + k, v^0 - k(g_u{}^0/g_v{}^0)) - g_v(u^0, v^0)}{k} \leqslant 0.$$

Taking limits as k approaches zero, and multiplying both sides by $g_v{}^2$, we obtain (6.11).

Now consider the bordered determinant D_r defined by (1.11). The relationship between the property of quasi-concavity and the signs of D_r is given by the following theorem.

Theorem 5.   A sufficient condition for $f(x)$ to be quasi-concave for $x \geqslant 0$ is that the sign of D_r be the same sign of $(-1)^r$ for all x and all $r = 1, \ldots, n$. A necessary condition for $f(x)$ to be quasi-concave is that $(-1)^r D_r \geqslant 0$, for $r = 1, \ldots, n$, for all x.

Proof.   We shall begin by proving the sufficient condition. If $(-1)^r D_r > 0$ for all r for any point x^0, then, by the usual second-order conditions for a constrained maximum, x^0 is a strict local maximum of $f(x)$ subject to the constraint $f_x{}^0 x = f_x{}^0 x^0$.[21] Let $x^1 \geqslant 0$ be any point x^1 for which

(6.15) $f_x{}^0 x^1 \leqslant f_x{}^0 x^0$.

We shall prove that $f(x^1) \leqslant f(x^0)$, that is, that x^0 is a global constrained maximum subject to (6.15). Let

(6.16) $x(\theta) = (1 - \theta) x^0 + \theta x^1$,

and

(6.17) $F(\theta) = f[x(\theta)]$.

Then let θ_0 be the largest value of θ for which $F(\theta)$ takes its minimum in the interval $[0, 1]$. We shall show that $\theta_0 < 1$ leads to a contradiction.

If $0 < \theta_0 < 1$, then $F'(\theta_0) = 0$ because $F(\theta_0)$ is a minimum. If $\theta_0 = 0$, then $F'(0) \geqslant 0$, so that $f_x{}^0 (x^1 - x^0) \geqslant 0$. But from (6.15), $F'(0) \leqslant 0$, so that $F'(0) = 0$. Hence, in either case, $F'(\theta_0) = 0$, or

(6.18) $f_x{}^{\theta_0} (x^1 - x^0) = 0$ if $0 \leqslant \theta_0 < 1$.

Since $x(\theta_0 + h) - x(\theta_0) = h(x^1 - x^0)$, it follows from (6.18) that

(6.19) $f_x{}^{\theta_0} [x(\theta_0 + h) - x(\theta_0)] = 0$.

But, by assumption, (6.19) implies that $x(\theta_0)$ is a strict local maximum of $f(x)$ subject to $f_x{}^{\theta_0} x = f_x{}^{\theta_0} x(\theta_0)$, so that $f[x(\theta_0 + h)] < f[x(\theta_0)]$, for h positive and sufficiently small. This contradicts the definition of θ_0 as the minimum of $F(\theta)$. It follows that we cannot have $\theta_0 < 1$, so that $\theta_0 = 1$ and in particular, $F(1) \leqslant F(0)$, or $f(x^1) \leqslant f(x^0)$.

We have thus shown that any point x^0 is a global constrained maximum of $f(x)$ subject to the constraints $x \geqslant 0$ and

(6.20) $f_x{}^0 x \leqslant f_x{}^0 x^0$.

Now, let x^0 and x^1 be any two points, and let x^2 be a convex combination (that is, an internal weighted average) of them. Since $f_x{}^2 x^2$ is an internal average of $f_x{}^2 x^0$ and $f_x{}^2 x^1$, it must be at least as great as the lesser. That is, we must have either $f_x{}^2 x^0 \leqslant f_x{}^2 x^1$ or $f_x{}^2 x^1 \leqslant f_x{}^2 x^2$. Since x^2 maximizes $f(x)$ subject to $f_x{}^2 x \leqslant f_x{}^2 x^2$, we must then have either $f(x^2) \geqslant f(x^0)$ or $f(x^2) \geqslant f(x^1)$, and, in either case

(6.21) $f(x^2) \geqslant \min [f(x^0), f(x^1)]$,

so that $f(x)$ is quasi-concave.

To prove the necessity condition, first consider any $x^0 > 0$. If $f_x^0 = 0, D_r = 0$ and the necessity condition is automatically satisfied. If $f_x^0 \neq 0$, consider the maximization of $f(x)$ subject to the constraint (6.20). Since all variables are relevant and (KTL) is satisfied at x^0 with $\lambda^0 = 1$, it follows from Theorem 1 that x^0 is the constrained maximum. Therefore, x^0 certainly is a local constrained maximum of $f(x)$ subject to $f_x^0 x = f_x^0 x^0$, for which the conditions $(-1)^r D_r \geq 0$ are necessary.[22] By continuity, this condition also holds when x^0 has one or more components that are equal to zero.[23]

In Section 5(2), we discussed a necessary condition for the quasi-concavity of a function of the form

(6.22) $g(x) = \Sigma_{i=1}^n g_i(x_i)$.

We now apply Theorem 5 to obtain a necessary and sufficient condition. In this case, $g_{x_i x_j} = 0$ for $i \neq j$. Let $g_{x_i} = g_i'$, and $g_{x_i x_i} = g_i''$, and let

(6.23) $P_r = \Pi_{i=1}^r g_i''$.

Then, by expansion of D_r, it is easy to see that

(6.24) $D_r = -(g_r')^2 P_{r-1} + g_r'' D_{r-1}$.

If we assume, for simplicity, that $g_i'' \neq 0$ for all i, then $D_r/P_r = -(g_r')^2/g_r'' + (D_{r-1}/P_{r-1})$.

Since $D_1/P_1 = -(g_1')^2/g_1''$, it easily follows by induction that

(6.25) $(-1)^r D_r/(-1)^r P_r = -\Sigma_{i=1}^r (g_i')^2/g_i''$.

If $g_i'' < 0$ for all i, then $(-1)^r P_r > 0$ for all r and the right-hand side of (6.25) is positive, from which it follows that $(-1)^r D_r > 0$ for all r, and $g(x)$ is quasi-concave, indeed, concave.

Suppose $g_i'' > 0$ for two or more values of i. By renumbering, we may suppose that $g_1'' > 0, g_2'' > 0$. Then $P_2 > 0$. From (6.25), with $r = 2$, we will have $D_2 < 0$, so that $g(x)$ is not quasi-concave.

In the remaining case, $g_i'' > 0$ for exactly one value of i; we may suppose,

(6.26) $g_i'' < 0 \ (i < n), \qquad g_n'' > 0$.

Then,

(6.27) $(-1)^r P_r > 0 \ (r < n), \qquad (-1)^n P_n < 0$.

The right-hand side of (6.25) is positive for $r < n$; with the aid of (6.27) we have that $(-1)^r D_r > 0$ for $r < n$. To insure quasi-concavity, it is sufficient that $(-1)^n D_n > 0$. In view of (6.27) and (6.25), this is equivalent to

(6.28) $\Sigma_{i=1}^n (g_i')^2/g_i'' > 0$.

Since the first $n - 1$ terms are negative, this means that the last term must outweigh them all, or that g_n'' must be sufficiently small relative to $(g_n')^2$. This places an upper limit on the permissible rate of increasing returns in the nth process. The stronger the rate of diminishing returns in the other processes, the greater is the permissible rate of increasing returns in the nth process.

Notes

1   See [4, pp. 483–484]; also [1].
2   In general, we denote by subscripts partial differentiation with respect to the indicated arguments, and a superscript 0 means evaluation at the point x^0. Then g_x^0 is the $m \times n$ matrix of partial derivatives of the functions $g^j(x)$ with respect to the variables, $x_1, \ldots, x_n$, evaluated at $x = x^0$; λ^0 is an m-vector of Lagrange multipliers, and $\lambda^0 g_x^0$ is an n-vector.
3   See [4, pp. 485–486]. A function, $f(x)$, of several variables is differentiable if $f(x + h) = f(x) + ch + eh$, where c is a vector depending on x but not on h and e is a vector which goes to zero with h. If a function is differentiable, then its partial derivatives exist, and $f_x = c$, but the existence of the partial derivatives does not necessarily imply differentiability; see [2, pp. 59–61]. In particular, $f[x^0 + \theta(x - x^0)] = f(x^0) + f_x^0 \theta(x - x^0) + \epsilon\theta$, where $\epsilon = e(x - x^0)$ goes to zero with θ. Then,

$$\frac{f[x^0 + \theta(x - x^0)] - f(x^0)}{\theta} = f_x^0(x - x^0) + \epsilon \to f_x^0(x - x^0) \text{ as } \theta \to 0.$$

Here $f_x^0(x - x^0)$ is an inner product of the two vectors.
4   The differentiation with respect to θ is, in effect, taking the directional derivative of $f(x)$ at x^0 in the direction of the point x. It is clear from the definition of quasi-concavity that this derivative, $f_x^0[(x - x^0)/d]$, where the terms $(x - x^0)/d$ are the direction cosines $(d = [\Sigma(x - x^0)^2]^{1/2}$, must be nonnegative. For a definition of directional derivatives, see [2, pp. 262–263]. Wold [7] defines a function to be *convex towards the origin* if (1.7) holds (his terminology is geometrically valid in the case he considers, where $f_x > 0$); since (1.7) can be shown to imply quasi-concavity, the two definitions are equivalent.
5   Equation (1.5) can be written $f[\theta x + (1 - \theta)x^0] \geqslant \min[f(x), f(x^0)]$. Let ϕ be a monotonic nondecreasing transformation. Then ϕ does not reverse rankings. That is, $f(x) \geqslant f(x^0)$ implies $\phi[f(x)] \geqslant \phi[f(x^0)]$. Therefore, $\phi\{f[\theta x + (1 - \theta)x^0]\} \geqslant \phi\{\min[f(x), f(x^0)]\}$. Since ϕ does not reverse rankings, $\phi\{\min[f(x), [f(x^0)]\} = \min\{\phi[f(x)], \phi[f(x^0)]\}$ whence $\phi[f(x)]$ is quasi-concave.
6   For example, $f(x, y) = (x - 1) + [(1 - x)^2 + 4(x + y)]^{1/2}$ is quasi-concave. Its contour lines are straight lines that are not parallel. See also the example at the end of Section 2, below. Fenchel [3, p. 134] has proved that such a function cannot be transformed into a concave function by a monotonic nondecreasing transformation
7   For example, $x_1 x_2$ does not satisfy (1.8).
8   These propositions are frequently used in the literature on utility functions,

but rigorous proofs starting from the concept of quasi-concavity seem to be lacking. We give such proofs in Section 4, below.

9   That is, all of the second-order partial derivatives of $f(x)$ exist at x^0. However, they may be equal to zero.

10   In fact, we developed a series of conditions on $g(x)$ analogous to conditions (a) through (d), only to discover that the cases in which they added anything to conditions (a) through (d) were vacuous.

11   For example, h is the unit vector in the direction of x_2 if $h = (0, 1, 0, \ldots, 0)$.

12   This is an application of (1.7) to $\phi(u, v)$.

13   This is more general than the Kuhn-Tucker Theorem because the components of $g(x)$ are assumed to be quasi-concave rather than concave. See [4].

14   We are indebted for this remark to Hirofumi Uzawa.

15   Kuhn and Tucker [4, p. 483], require the path to be differentiable but a careful reading of their proof (p. 484) shows that only differentiability at $\theta = 0$ is used.

16   This condition was used by M. Slater [6] in the case in which $f(x)$ is also assumed concave.

17   This is a special case of Theorem 3, Corollary 5 in [1]. A proof of Theorem 2 appeared in the present manuscript as accepted for publication, but a simpler treatment was subsequently developed in [1].

18   $u_{x_{i_0}}^{\ 0} > 0$, $p_{x_{i_0}} > 0$, and $u_{x_{i_0}}^{\ 0} - \lambda^0 p_{x_{i_0}} \leqslant 0$ imply $\lambda^0 > 0$. The first two lines of (KTL) for the second maximum problem are $-p_{x_i} + \mu^0 u_{x_i}^{\ 0} \leqslant 0$, and $x_i^0(-p_{x_i} + \mu^0 u_{x_i}^{\ 0}) = 0$, or (5.1) with $\mu^0 = 1/\lambda^0$.

 The sufficiency of (5.1) for consumers' demand theory is widely assumed; however, the only rigorous proof, under rather severe regularity conditions, is that of Wold [7, Theorem 6, p. 87].

19   The inequality (5.4) is a necessary condition for (5.3) to be quasi-concave but it is not sufficient. For the corresponding sufficient condition, see Section 6, below.

20   Wold [7, Theorem 5, pp. 85–86] states the relation between the signs of the bordered determinants and convexity of indifference surfaces to the origin, which is equivalent to quasi-concavity (see Theorem 4), under conditions more restrictive than those studied here.

21   See, for example, [5, pp. 376–379].

22   See [5], *ibid.*

23   Let $x^1 > 0$ and $x(t) = (1 - t) x^0 + tx^1$. Then $x(t) > 0$ for $t > 0$, whence $(-1)^r D_r(t) \geqslant 0$ for $t > 0$, where $D_r(t)$ is D_r evaluated at the point $x(t)$. From this it follows that $(-1)^r D_r(0) \geqslant 0$.

References

[1]   Arrow, Kenneth J., Leonid Hurwicz, and Hirofumi Uzawa: "Constraint Qualifications in Maximization Problems," this volume II.2, pp. 96–112.

[2]   Courant, Richard: *Differential and Integral Calculus*, New York: Intersci-
      ence Publishers, 1936.
[3]   Fenchel, Werner: *Convex Cones, Sets and Functions*, Logistics Research
      Project, Princeton University, September, 1953 (mimeographed).
[4]   Kuhn, H. W., and A. W. Tucker: "Nonlinear Programming," in J. Neyman
      (ed.), *Proceedings of the Second Berkeley Symposium on Mathematical
      Statistics and Probability*, Berkeley: University of California Press, 1951,
      pp. 481–492.
[5]   Samuelson, Paul A.: *Foundations of Economic Analysis*, Cambridge: Har-
      vard University Press, 1948.
[6]   Slater, Morton: "Lagrange Multipliers Revisited: A Contribution to Non-
      Linear Programming," Cowles Commission Discussion Paper, Math. 403,
      November, 1950.
[7]   Wold, Herman: *Demand Analysis*, New York: Wiley, 1953.

3
DECENTRALIZATION WITHIN FIRMS

Optimization, decentralization, and internal pricing in business firms

KENNETH J. ARROW

The increasing span of government control over economic life in the last fifty years has directed the attention of economic theorists to the relative merits of centralization and decentralization in economic decision-making.

If the aim of the economic system is something like the maximization of national income, it may be asked whether it is better to make the economic decisions in a central agency where information relating to the entire system can be used or in the many independent units which characterize a capitalist economy such as ours.

In the course of this great debate, the role of the price system in coordinating many individual decisions has been given stronger and stronger recognition, although the idea itself already appears in Adam Smith's famous "invisible hand."

There is also growing concern in the field of industrial management with the administration of large business corporations. Again there arises the issue of centralization vs. decentralization. To what extent is it necessary for the efficiency of a corporation that its decisions be made at a high level where a wide degree of information is, or can be made, available? How much, on the other hand, is gained by leaving a great deal of latitude to individual departments which are closer to the situations with which they deal, even though there may be some loss due to imperfect coordination?

A representative collection of management viewpoints on this issue is found in the proceedings of a conference held in The Netherlands some years ago [1]. It is stressed that the problem of decentralization is basically one of control, information processing, and decision-making, precisely the basic issues in the controversy over the possibility of socialism.

The abstract similarity of the two problems has engaged the attention of some economists [2], but the concept of a price system so central to the economists' understanding of the decentralization problem has not yet penetrated the thinking of the great majority of management theorists [3].

Even such relatively sympathetic organization theorists as March and Simon make only brief reference to the use of the price system for decentralization within business firms and dismiss it, much too hastily in my view [4]; I am not aware of other similar references in the literature on business organization.

In summarizing the results in economic theory relevant to decentralization by means of the price mechanism, I will seek to illustrate as far as possible in terms of the business organization; but it must be understood, of course, that suggestions for application here are the barest beginning. I will feel satisfied if I can make clear the importance and the possibility of price mechanisms as a subject for research by students of business organization.

Doubtless if such devices are used, they will take institutional forms different from the markets that we are accustomed to in relations between firms. A foolish mechanical similarity is not called for. It is rather an understanding of the price mechanism, of its relation to the mathematics and logic of constrained maximization that is called for, so that supple and understanding applications to the operations of business can be devised.

I

Let us represent the operations of a business firm in very general symbolic form. Let $x_1, \ldots, x_n$ be the *decision variables* of the firm. Decision variables are quantitative expressions of the firm's different activities. Some will be purchases of goods from outside the firm; some, production for sale or inventory. Others will be activities for which there need not exist a market counterpart; for example, alternative methods of processing the goods, of routing them from place to place, or storing them in one place rather than another. The aim of the firm is to maximize its profits.[1] It is assumed that profits of the firm are determined by the choices of the decision variables.

More specifically, we can think of a firm as being a conglomeration of processes. These include production processes in the ordinary sense, all items of distribution, warehousing, inventory or transportation, and even general sales efforts, purchasing arrangements, and overhead activities.

The analysis of a firm into such processes may not be a simple matter, but in principle one could always accomplish it. Each process is assumed to be defined as to scale by a single variable x_i. The value of x_i in turn defines the inputs needed for the conduct of the activity or process at that scale and the output or outputs. The inputs may be commodities or services purchased on the open market, but they may also be products of earlier activities within the firm.

Thus an assembly line would be an activity whose inputs include not only labor and the use of certain machines but also parts which are themselves the outputs of other processes in the firm. Similarly, the outputs of a process may not be commodities recognized commercially but items which are only useful as inputs in still other processes of the firm. We will use the term *good* to mean anything which is either input or output as some process in the firm. "Goods" here include services as well as material goods. We will use the term *commodity* for any good which can be purchased from other firms or other individuals, and here again we include services such as labor among commodities.

For each process we assume a set of functions $g_{ij}(x_i)$ which defines the amount of the j-th good produced by the i-th activity when operated at level x_i.

We adopt the convention that an input is regarded as a negative output. Hence the inputs to the i-th process are represented by functions $g_{ij}(x_i)$ which assume a negative value. Let the total number of commodities be p, the total number of goods m ($m \geq p$). We assume that the goods are so numbered that the first p goods are commodities. Then the total output of the j-th commodity is

(1) $y_j = \sum_{i=1}^{n} g_{ij}(x_i)$ $(j = 1, \ldots, p)$

The "output" y_j is understood to be an input if $y_j < 0$.

The net return of a firm derives ultimately from its buying commodities from and selling commodities to the general public. We therefore may designate its profits as $\pi(y_1, \ldots, y_p)$. If the firm is operating under competitive conditions, that is, it is not sufficiently large to affect prices at which it buys or sells, we have a special case:

(2) $\pi(y_1, \ldots, y_p) = \sum_{j=1}^{p} p_j y_j$

However, we may have more general situations in which the firm is of sufficient size that the price at which it can sell its goods is influenced by the amount of goods it offers for sale, or the prices of some or all of the goods and services it buys are influenced by the scale of its operations [5].

II

Let us start with the simplest case, that of perfect competition with all goods being commodities. If we substitute (1) into (2) under these conditions, we see that the aim of the firm is simply to maximize,

(3) $\pi = \sum_{j=1}^{p} p_j \sum_{i=1}^{n} g_{ij}(x_i) = \sum_{i=1}^{n} [\sum_{j=1}^{p} p_j g_{ij}(x_i)]$

Each of these terms,

(4) $\sum_{j=1}^{n} p_j g_{ij}(x_i)$,

depends on a different variable x_i; hence to maximize total profits it is sufficient to maximize each expression (4) separately. But expression (4) is nothing but the profits attributable to operating activity i at level x_i. The optimum policy for the firm is simply to instruct each process manager independently to maximize profits, computed at market prices.

The possibility of complete decentralization appears in this case. The fact that some departments (activities) may be buying from or selling to others in the same firm should not influence their behavior; the same price should be charged or paid as if it were a transaction with another firm [6].

Not only is decentralization possible, but it is advantageous in economizing on the transmission of information. In particular, the detailed technological knowledge of the process need not be transmitted to a central office but can be retained in the department. We are, of course, presupposing that there is a cost to transmission of information. This need not be naively understood to be something like a postage stamp. It is rather the difficulty in terms of time and trouble of transmitting detailed knowledge from one individual to another. Indeed, we may regard it as close to an impossibility for individuals in close contact with the productive processes to transmit their information in all its details to another office. This proposition, long recognized in practice, is the basis of the management literature on the questions of centralization and decentralization.

We will not embark here on a detailed examination of the costs involved in the communication processes. They are complex and in their detailed treatment approximate considerably the internal workings of a great computing machine, such as the IBM 709 at the Western Data Processing Center. A very detailed analysis from a point of view similar to that presented here has been given in the doctoral dissertation of Thomas Marschak [7]. I will simply take for granted the desirability of leaving decisions as far as possible in the hands of those with the most intimate technological knowledge, the only limit being the failure to co-ordinate the activities of the different parts of the firm.

The only remaining problem in decentralization would be to insure that each individual process manager with a knowledge of his own technology should maximize his profits. There may indeed be problems of control to insure that maximization does take place and it is clear that such problems present a challenge to accounting procedures as well as incentive schemes.

It may also be that the process of maximization by a single process manager will still be rather difficult, even though much easier than that of the firm as a whole. In that case, we may substitute for an instantaneous maximization a process of gradual incremental improvement; that is, we may simply direct the manager to alter the activity level by small steps in such a direction as to increase his profits. Such a procedure involves sacrifice of the maximum possible profits but in return it makes less demands upon the computing abilities and powers of the manager. It would have to be examined in individual cases to what extent it pays to improve the optimizing ability of the manager by increasing his computational burden. Such a choice will hinge upon the costs of computing and will change as computing costs continue to decrease sharply.

III

Let us now continue to assume perfect competition but admit the existence of goods which are not commodities, that is, not traded in on the market. It is this case that most brings out the characteristic problems of organization. For simplicity, let us suppose that $p = 2$ and $m = 3$, that is, there are three goods with which the firm deals, one of which, however, does not have a natural market price. In a short-run problem, good 3 might be plant, which is not intended to be bought or sold during the period under consideration, while good 1 might be labor and good 2 the product of the firm. In other contexts, good 3 might be money capital, if we assume that the firm has limitations on the supply of capital available to it. It might also represent some intermediate product, such as heat, which is produced in the course of the production operations but which cannot be bought from outside or sold because of its transitory existence [8]. A transportation service between one part of the firm and another would be still another example of a good which is not a commodity.

The firm itself must produce all of good 3 that it needs, since it cannot buy any. The extent to which it uses good 3 as an input in one or more processes must be at least matched by the output of that good in other processes, so that the activity levels $x_1, \ldots, x_n$ must satisfy the condition

(5) $\sum_{i=1}^{n} g_{i3}(x_i) \geq 0$.

From a mathematical point of view, the problem of the business man is to choose the variables x_i so as to maximize profits (3) subject to the constraint (5). In this case, with $p = 2$, the profits are given by

(6) $\pi = \sum_{i=1}^{n} [p_1 g_{i1}(x_i) + p_2 g_{i2}(x_i)]$.

The crucial difference between this case and the one treated previously is that the process managers cannot choose the x_i's independently of each other because of the condition (5) which involves all or at least some of them. It would appear that decentralization is impossible. But if we follow out the mathematics carefully, we will find that this conclusion is premature.

The problem is one in constrained maximization, and it is known from classical Lagrangian methods in analysis, further developed in modern times, that the maximizing values of the x_i's satisfy the equations

(7) $p_1 g_{i1}'(x_i) + p_2 g_{i2}'(x_i) + \lambda g_{i3}'(x_i) = 0$ $(i = 1, \ldots, n)$

for a suitable λ. (Primes here denote differentiation.) Equation (7), together with equation (5), constitute $n + 1$ equations in the $n + 1$ unknowns $x_1, \ldots, x_n, \lambda$; the x_i's are the maximizing values which are sought [9].

Formula (7) directly suggests an analogy between the Lagrange multiplier λ and the market prices, p_1 and p_2. Note further that in any one equation (7), only one of the variables x_i appears. Hence, if somehow the "*shadow price*" λ were known, we can again have decentralization by instructing the manager of the i-th process to maximize the quantity,

(8) $p_1 g_{i1}(x_i) + p_2 g_{i2}(x_i) + \lambda g_{i3}(x_i)$,

which we may refer to as the *shadow profit*, that is, the profit computed by valuing the two commodities at their market prices and good 3 at its shadow price.

But, it may be thought, we have only evaded the problem, for how is the shadow price to be determined? An answer can be given in terms of a process of successive approximations. To do so we must abandon the impossible ideal of actually achieving a maximum profit at any time. Instead, we must be contented with a procedure which will always lead to an improvement, at least if conditions remain unchanged.[2]

One such process, constructed by analogy with the workings of competitive markets in the economy as a whole, would be the following: Let some central agency within the firm announce a tentative shadow price for the good which is used only internally. Then let the manager of each process maximize his shadow profit, as given by formula (8). As a result, it will be found in general that the total amount demanded of good 3 within the firm is greater or less than the amount available. These demands and supplies are forwarded by the process managers to the central office. If the demand in total exceeds the supply, the shadow price is raised for the next period; otherwise it is lowered. This provides a new shadow price, on the basis of which the process managers again optimize. It can be shown, under certain conditions, that if the process is continued long enough, the operations of the firm will gradually converge to a position of maximum total profitability [10].

The process of successive approximation just described could be thought of as a process to be carried on entirely by computing machines. In other words, it would be equally true that even if all information were centralized, the procedure could be carried on in a way entirely parallel to that just described, except that the decentralized decision-making would be mimicked by the successive approximations on a computer. Such a solution, of course, does not have the advantages of economy on the transmission of information.

IV

To be more specific, suppose we consider in our example that good 3 is money available for investment in a particular process. Since money invested is an input, it will be negative, but we may otherwise take it to be a measure of a scale of activity in the process. Thus we may assume without loss of generality that

$$g_{i3}(x_i) = -x_i.$$

Then the aim of the process manager is to maximize $p_1 g_{i1}(x_i) + p_2 g_{i2}(x_i) - \lambda x_i$. The shadow price λ is the price, then, of investment funds and can be thought of as an internal interest rate. In other words, the firm is fixing a common rate of return in all its processes, and requiring the process manager to act as if he is borrowing money from the firm to carry on his particular process. He thus invests up to the point where the marginal profitability of the process from commodities 1 and 2 alone equals the standard rate of return used for all processes in the firm. If the firm could borrow money freely at a fixed rate of interest, then good 3 would itself be a commodity and the shadow price λ would simply be the market rate of interest. If, however, especially in short periods of time, the firm is forced to rely on internal financing, then the standard rate of return used in examining the profitability of individual processes may be quite different from the market rate of return. Once the standard rate of return λ is announced, individual process managers determine the scale of their activities so as to maximize their profits. If it develops that the funds demanded as a result of these plans exceed those available, the firm must temporarily resort to some rationing device. But then it should change the standard rate of return for a higher level so as to induce managers to retrench in the next period. If, on the other hand, the funds are available and are not used up by the individual process managers, then the standard rate of return should be lowered.

V

We will briefly illustrate the mode of decentralization under imperfect competition. To simplify the discussion, we will assume that all goods are commodities; in particular, we will assume three commodities (two of which are outputs and one an input), two processes (one of which produces output 1 from input 3 and the other of which produces output 2 from input 3). Suppose further that the firm is sufficiently large so that the prices of the two outputs are significantly affected by quantities produced by the firm. Further, suppose that the two commodities are substitutes, so that the price obtainable for either is a function of the amounts of both produced. Let $R(y_1, y_2)$ be the total revenue derived from sale of both outputs in quantities y_1, y_2, respectively, so that profits are given by

$$(9) \quad R(y_1, y_2) - p_3 y_3,$$

where y_i ($i = 1, 2, 3$) is given by (1), which in this case reduces to

$$(10) \quad y_1 = g_{11}(x_1), \qquad y_2 = g_{22}(x_2), \qquad y_3 = g_{13}(x_1) + g_{23}(x_2).$$

If we substitute for y_i from (10) into (9) and differentiate to find a maximum, we have

$$(11) \quad \begin{aligned} (\delta R/\delta y_1) g_{11}'(x_1) - p_3 g_{13}'(x_1) = 0, \\ (\delta R/\delta y_2) g_{22}'(x_2) - p_3 g_{23}'(x_2) = 0. \end{aligned}$$

As before, we can interpret (11) as an instruction to each process manager to maximize his profits, where, in this case, he is to take the *marginal revenue*, $\delta R/\delta y_i$, as a datum. However, the optimizing choices will, in general, affect the marginal revenues. Hence, again, decentralization is possible with the aid of a system of successive approximations. The marginal revenues at each stage must be supplied by a central agency. The process will, under certain conditions, eventually converge to the activity levels which maximize the total profits.

In this case, complete decentralization is not possible, since there has to be some single agency to supply the marginal revenues which are affected by the actions of both process managers. It would not be correct to allow each process manager to maximize his profits taking account of the effect of his output on his own prices but not taking into consideration the effect of his output on the prices received by the other process manager.

VI

The theorem that the price system leads to an optimal allocation of resources is well known to have exceptions. They may be summarized in two categories: (1) there may be relations among the different processes in the firm so that the level of one affects the output of another; (2) more technically, the functions $g_{ij}(x_i)$ may not be concave functions – that is, there may be increasing returns to scale.[3]

Under (1), the existence of *external relations*, we may have for example the case where an outcome of one activity interferes with another. Thus, in the manufacture of phonograph records, if any part of the production process is unusually noisy, it may prevent the recording sessions from taking place in too close proximity. The solution, in principle, is quite simple. It is that every result of one process which has anything to do with the productivity of others is really a good, possibly a good with a negative value as in the case just cited. All that is required is that the accounting of these goods be so complete that every one has a shadow price. In the case of the recording session, we would have to recognize that a negative value must be ascribed to the noise component of the production process. This negative value will be adjusted as a result of successive approximations until there is just exactly the right amount of discouragement to permit the recording to take place or else to require the recording sessions to be elsewhere.

The case under (2), that of *increasing returns*, is more complicated to deal with. What will happen is that the process of successive approximations as described will not converge but will instead oscillate wildly and tend to go off in a direction away from that of maximum profitability. To correct for this, one must introduce modifications into the computations of the profits of individual processes. We will not go into details here, but refer to other works of Leonid Hurwicz and this author [11]. The problem is capable of some kind of solution but it remains to be seen how the rules suggested will work out in any institutional application.

VII

It is interesting to observe that an extension of the mechanism proposed will go some distance toward handling the problems of the reactions of the firm to uncertainty. The essential point is to classify possible alternative states which affect the revenues and costs of the firm. The production or use of a good under one state must be regarded as a different process from producing the same good under another state. The firm, of course, must assign probabilities to occurrences of the different states.

To illustrate, suppose there are two processes in a firm. One uses labor and produces a product which is then, in turn, made use of as an input by the second process which converts it into the final product of the firm. Suppose that what is unknown is the price at which the final product is sold. For simplicity, suppose it could take on only two values p_1 and p_2 with probabilities P and $1 - P$, respectively. Suppose further, however, that the labor used in process 1 must be hired before knowing which price for the final product will prevail, but that the activity level for the second process can be determined after knowing what price will prevail. Let x_1 be the activity level for the first process and also its output; similarly, let x_2 be the output of the second process. Let $c_1(x_1)$ be cost of labor used in running process 1 at level x_1, and $f(x_2)$ the amount of the intermediate product used in producing the final product.

We now distinguish between the output of the intermediate product according as the price of the final product to prevail is p_1 or p_2; let the intermediate products under these two states be termed $(1, 1)$ and $(1, 2)$ respectively, and let their outputs be x_{11} and x_{12}, respectively. Since, however, the decision as to the activity level of process 1 must be made without knowing which price will prevail, we must have

(12) $x_{11} = x_{12} = x_1$.

The (fictitious) goods $(1, 1)$ and $(1, 2)$ will have shadow prices λ_1 and λ_2, respectively. Then the shadow profits for the first activity will be $\lambda_1 x_{11} - c_1(x_1)$ if price p_1 prevails and $\lambda_2 x_{12} - c_1(x_1)$ if price p_2 prevails. From (12), we find that the *expected* profit is

(13) $[\lambda_1 P + \lambda_2(1 - P)] x_1 - c_1(x_1)$.

Level x_1 is chosen to maximize (13).

The activity level for process 2 can be chosen after knowing which price will prevail. Let x_{21} be the activity level of process 2 if price p_1 prevails, and x_{22} the activity level if price p_2 prevails. Then x_{21} is chosen to maximize $p_1 x_{21} - \lambda_1 f(x_{21})$, and x_{22} is chosen to maximize $p_2 x_{22} - \lambda_2 f(x_{22})$. The excess of demand over supply for good $(1, 1)$ is

$f(x_{21}) - x_1$,

and the excess demand for good $(1, 2)$ is

$f(x_{22}) - x_1$.

For any given λ_1 and λ_2, we choose x_1, x_{21}, x_{22} as indicated and then vary λ_1 and λ_2 until the two excess demands both become zero [12].

Again decentralization is possible but there is a complication here; the manager of process 1 would have to know not only his own technology but also the probabilities of the different states with which the firm may be confronted. This information may have to be supplied to him from a different source since it does not normally fall within his range of activities.[4]

VIII

We have just barely touched on many of the implications of price systems for the internal decentralization of large firms. There is no practical experience and very little theorizing in this direction. These suggestions are offered with the hope that they may be useful to students of business organization and accounting. Undoubtedly many specific adaptations of the price mechanism to the internal environment of the firm would be needed before such plans could be made practical, but a deep theoretical analysis of the price system in the economy as a whole has shown convincingly its value and there appears no reason to doubt that, at least in some contexts, it will prove similarly useful inside large business firms, many of which may be greater than the economies of small countries.

Notes

1 Since a firm's activities are extended in time, it is of course understood that we really mean to maximize the sum of the discounted profits of the firm – that is, more nearly its net wealth in ordinary accounting terminology.

2 Indeed, we have already seen that we may wish to limit ourselves to incremental improvement even if all goods are commodities, because of limited computational facilities. The point is very close to H. Simon's emphasis on "satisficing" rather than "optimizing" as typical behavior for organisms; see March and Simon [4], Chapter 6; H. A. Simon, *Models of Man*, New York: John Wiley & Sons, 1957, chapters 15 and 16.

3 These are, in essence, the two objections raised by March and Simon [4] against the price system as a technique of organizational decentralization.

4 The value of *P* may be altered by the transmission of information to and within the organization. The significance of information flows for decentralization has been studied by Jacob Marschak, Chapter XIV in R. M. Thrall, C. H. Coombs, and R. L. Davis (eds.), *Decision Processes*, New York: John Wiley & Sons, 1954.

References

[1]   H. J. Kruisinga (ed.), *The Balance Between Centralization and Decentralization in Managerial Control*, Leiden: H. E. Stenfort Kreese, 1955; for general views, see especially Chapters II (by E. F. L. Brech), III (E. Dale), and IV, Section 1 (H. J. van der Schroeff).

[2]   T. C. Koopmans, "Uses of Prices," in *Proceedings of the Conference on Operations Research in Production and Inventory Control*, Cleveland: Case Institute of Technology, 1954, pp. 1–7; P. W. Cook, Jr., "Decentralization and the Transfer-Price Problem," *Journal of Business*, 28 (1955): 87–94; J. Dean, "Decentralization and Intra-Company Pricing," *Harvard Business Review*, 33 (1955): 65–74; J. Hirshleifer, "On the Economics of Transfer Pricing," *Journal of Business*, 29 (1956): 172–184; and "Economics of the Divisionalized Firm," *Journal of Business*, 30 (1957): 96–108.

[3]   The nearest reference in Kruisinga, *op. cit.*, is emphasis on the separate profitability of departments as one of the criteria by which the central organization exercises control.

[4]   J. G. March and H. Simon, *Organizations*, New York: John Wiley & Sons, 1958, pp. 200–210.

[5]   The activity analysis model used here was developed, in the case where all the functions $g_{ij}(x_i)$ are linear, by T. C. Koopmans, "Analysis of Production as an Efficient Combination of Activities," Chapter III in T. C. Koopmans (ed.), *Activity Analysis of Production and Allocation*, Cowles Commission Monograph No. 13, New York: John Wiley & Sons, 1951. For the nonlinear model, see K. J. Arrow and L. Hurwicz, "Decentralization and Computation in Resource Allocation," this volume, II.1, pp. 41–95.

[6]   This conclusion is, of course, well known and has been stated by the authors cited in [2]; see, for example, Hirshleifer, "On the Economics of Transfer Pricing," pp. 175–176.

[7]   T. Marschak, "Centralization and Decentralization in Economic Organizations," Technical Report No. 42, Contract N6onr-25133, Stanford University, April 22, 1957; *Econometrica* 27 (1959): 399–430.

[8]   The importance of examples of this type for the organization of production has been stressed by S. Reiter, "Trade Barriers in Activity Analysis," *Review of Economic Studies*, 20 (1952–3): 174–180.

[9]   For an exposition of the classical Lagrangian method, see, for example, T. M. Apostol, *Mathematical Analysis*, Reading, Mass.: Addison-Wesley, pp. 152–161. For further modern developments which permit the handling of inequality constraints, see H. W. Kuhn and A. W. Tucker, "Nonlinear Programming," in J. Nevman (ed.), *Proceedings of the Second Berkeley Symposium on Mathematical Statistics and Probability*, Berkeley and Los Angeles: University of California Press, 1951, pp. 481–492.

[10]   See Arrow and Hurwicz, *op. cit.* [5], Part III, pp. 49–68; *ibid.*, "The Gradient Method for Concave Programming III: Further Global Results with Applications to Resource Allocation," Chapter 7 in K. Arrow, L. Hurwicz, and H. Uzawa, *Studies in Linear and Nonlinear Programming*, Stanford: Stanford University Press, 1958. The use of successive approximations in at least one context in decentralization was suggested by Hirshleifer, "Economics of the Divisionalized Firm," *op. cit.* [2], pp. 103–105. Other methods for finding the shadow price than successive approximations are possible; Hirshleifer, in his first article, suggests in effect that each process manager announce the whole function relating

his supply or demand for good 3 to λ. With this information, a central office could choose λ so as to equate supply and demand. This method requires transmitting much more information than the method of the text, but of course the optimum is achieved more rapidly.

[11]   Arrow and Hurwicz, *op. cit.* [5], Part IV, pp. 68–91.

[12]   The essential logic of this approach is found in K. J. Arrow, "Le rôle des valeurs boursières pour la répartition la meilleure des risques," in *Econometrie*, Paris: Centre Nationale de la Recherche Scientifique, 1953, pp. 1–8 (reprinted in Cowles Commission Papers, New Series, No. 77), though in a different context. For a similar formulation within the context of linear programming, see G. B. Dantzig, "Linear Programming under Uncertainty," *Management Science*, 1 (1955): 197–206.

4
DYNAMIC CHARACTERIZATION

Gradient methods for constrained maxima[1]

KENNETH J. ARROW
LEONID HURWICZ

This paper deals with the application of certain computational methods to evaluate constrained extrema, maxima, or minima. To introduce the subject, we will first discuss nonlinear games. Under certain conditions, the finding of the minimax of a certain expression is closely related to, in fact identical with, the finding of a constrained minimum or maximum.[2] Let us consider then a game (in a generalized sense) where player 1 has the choice of a certain set of numbers $x_1, \ldots, x_m$ that are constrained to be nonnegative for present purposes and player 2 selects numbers $y_1, \ldots, y_n$ also constrained to be nonnegative but otherwise unrestricted. The payoff of the game, the payment made by player 2 to player 1, will be a function of the decisions made by the two players, the x's and the y's. This payoff will be designated by $\varphi(x_1, \ldots, x_m; y_1, \ldots, y_n)$. To play the game in an ideal way is to find the minimax solution; we know this solution exists under certain conditions. That is, we arrive at a choice of strategies by the two players where player 1 is maximizing his payoff given the strategy of player 2, and player 2 is minimizing the payoff, given the strategy of player 1.

Suppose we wish to approximate the solution, as we frequently do in an ordinary maximization problem. For ordinary unconstrained maximization problems, we have a method that is satisfactory even for rather complicated problems, the so-called gradient method, which essentially says to move uphill. To maximize a function of several variables, each variable is altered in a direction that is profitable. There are many forms of the gradient method, but one that illustrates the general case is to increase the variable x_i when an increase in x_i will increase the function being maximized. That is, dx_i/dt will be positive if $\partial\varphi/\partial x_i$ is, where $\varphi(x_i, \ldots, x_n)$ is the function being maximized. Similarly, dx_i/dt should be negative if $\partial\varphi/\partial x_i$ is. One system of this type is

(1) $dx_i/dt = \partial\varphi/\partial x_i.$

Since an equation (1) holds for each i, we have a complete system of differential equations, which can be solved numerically. Under suitable conditions, the solution converges to the desired maximum; i.e., by climbing uphill in the steepest way, we finally reach the top.

What is the natural analogous method when applied to a minimax? Here we imagine player 1 and player 2 both experimentally varying their strategy in the light of what the other one has done and what they themselves have done. We assume they are varying their strategies continuously, not in big jumps, so their behavior can be described by a differential equation. Since player 1 is maximizing he behaves at any given moment as if he were just maximizing in an ordinary unconstrained problem with respect to his own variables x_i, taking the values of y_j as fixed at the levels currently set by his opponent. Player 2, however, is trying to minimize, so he goes downhill rather than uphill; he wants to minimize. Player 1's behavior can thus be described by the equations,

(2) $\quad dx_i/dt = \partial\varphi/\partial x_i$,

while player 2's behavior is described by

(3) $\quad dy_j/dt = -(\partial\varphi/\partial y_j)$,

where it will be recalled that φ is a function of $x_1, \ldots, x_m, y_1, \ldots, y_n$.

However, the preceding process [described by (2) and (3)] requires a modification if we are to take into account the fact that the x's and y's are assumed to be nonnegative. The process described by (2) and (3) may hit an impasse. It is possible that at a point where, e.g., $x_1 = 0$, the instructions tell you to continue through the negative area, i.e., $\partial\varphi/\partial x_i < 0$ at that point. Since the variable must be nonnegative, it is frozen at zero. In symbols we modify (2) and (3), respectively, to read:

(4) $\quad \dfrac{dx_i}{dt} = \begin{cases} \partial\varphi/\partial x_i & \text{unless } x_i = 0 \text{ and } \partial\varphi/\partial x_i < 0, \\ 0 & \text{otherwise}; \end{cases}$

(5) $\quad \dfrac{dy_j}{dt} = \begin{cases} -\partial\varphi/\partial y_j & \text{unless } y_j = 0 \text{ and } \partial\varphi/\partial y_j > 0, \\ 0 & \text{otherwise}. \end{cases}$

But does this process converge? Even in ordinary maximization the gradient method may not converge. Whether it does or not depends on the properties of the function being maximized, basically on the *concavity* of the function. We will first define a "strictly concave" function. Take any two different points, say $(x_1', \ldots, x_n')$ and $(x_1'', \ldots, x_n'')$ and the mid-point between these. If the value of the function at the mid-point is greater than the average of values at the two given points, we say the function is strictly concave. Symbolically, we call a function $f(x)$ *strictly concave in* $x = (x_1, \ldots, x_m)$ if, given any pair of points $x' = (x_1', \ldots, x_m')$ and $x'' = (x_1'', \ldots, x_m'')$, we have

(6) $\quad f(\tfrac{1}{2}\{x_1' + x_1''\}, \ldots, \tfrac{1}{2}\{x_m' + x_m''\})$
$$> \tfrac{1}{2}[f(x_1', \ldots, x_m') + f(x_1'', \ldots, x_m'')].$$

If we replaced "greater than" by "greater than or equal to" in (6), we would simply speak of the function's being *concave in* x. (In particular, a linear function is concave but not strictly concave.)

Now, as we shall see shortly, constrained maximization problems can be handled by the gradient method provided the process described in (4) and (5) converges in $x_1, \ldots, x_m$ whenever φ (which is a function of both x and y) is strictly concave in x and linear in y. That this is so was proved by us under considerable restrictions[3]; recently Hirofumi Uzawa[4] showed that these restrictions may be removed. (Uzawa's theorem only guarantees that the x's converge; in fact, however, the y's also converge, as we have shown recently.)

Constrained maxima and games

The preceding discussion has dealt with solving nonlinear games, but we are primarily interested in applying the gradient method to constrained maxima. We have the problem of maximizing a function subject to certain restrictions on the variables. In symbols, we state

Problem I.   To maximize $f(x_1, \ldots, x_m)$ subject to the constraints

$$(7) \quad \begin{aligned} g_j(x_1, \ldots, x_m) &\geq 0, \quad (j = 1, \ldots, n) \\ x_i &\geq 0. \quad (i = 1, \ldots, m) \end{aligned}$$

We have here considered only the case where the restrictions all are of the "greater than or equal to" type. This is just an expository simplification; the case where some restrictions are actually equalities can be handled by a slight extension of the results presented. Similarly, we are going to assume that all the variables are constrained to be nonnegative. Again, the case where some of them are unrestricted as to sign does not have any particularly new points.

We will also consider a second problem, which is to find the saddle point of a certain function, namely, the function being maximized, plus a nonnegative linear combination of the constraints.[5]

Problem II.   To minimax $\varphi(x_1, \ldots, x_m; y_1, \ldots, y_n)$ subject to

$$(8) \quad \begin{aligned} x_1 &\geq 0, \quad (i = 1, \ldots, m) \\ y_j &\geq 0, \quad (j = 1, \ldots, n) \end{aligned}$$

where

$$\varphi(x_1, \ldots, x_m, y_1, \ldots, y_n) = f(x_1, \ldots, x_m) + \Sigma_{j=1}^{j=n} y_j g_j(x_1, \ldots, x_m).$$

This is a function of the x's, of course, and of the y's, the Lagrange multipliers. In this particular case we are going to minimize with respect to the y's and maximize with respect to the x's.

We will first assume that the functions $f(x_1, \ldots, x_m)$, $g(x_1, \ldots, x_m)$ are concave. (Let us remember that a linear function is a particular case of a concave function.) In this case the order in which the operations of maximization and minimization in Problem II is well known to be irrelevant. The significance of this last theorem is the following. Take any solution to Problem I, say $x_1^0, \ldots,$ x_m^0. Then we can find an appropriate set of Lagrange multipliers $y_1^0, \ldots, y_n^0$ (in the context of economics also called "shadow prices") such that the x's and y's together jointly solve Problem II. Conversely, if we can find x_i^0, y_j^0 to solve Problem II, then the numbers $x_1^0, \ldots, x_m^0$ constitute a solution to Problem I.

We will given an illustrative economic interpretation of this. Suppose we regard the x's as the scales at which different productive activities are to be carried on. The function f is the profit derived from these activities. The function g_1, let us say, is determined by the demand for some resource like plant or labor if the various activities 1 to m are carried on at levels x_1 to x_m. To be more precise, g_1 is the available supply of the resource less the total demand generated by carrying on the activities at level x_1 to x_m, and we want the restriction that $g_1 \geqslant 0$ to be interpreted as saying that the demand for utilization of a resource shall not exceed supply, or in other words, that carrying on the activities at scale x_1 to x_m, respectively, is feasible as far as resource 1 is concerned, and similarly with other resources. So g_i can be interpreted as being excess supply (the excess of supply over demand) for the jth resource. In that case, y_j has the interpretation of being the price that the particular resource j would command in a competitive market.

The gradient method for constrained maxima:
the concave case

In Problem II, we are seeking the saddle point of a nonlinear game, and the gradient method can be applied to it provided the concavity properties stated below hold. Applying the method as stated in (4) and (5) to the particular form of the pay-off function given in (8) yields the following set of differential equations:

(9) $\quad \dfrac{dx_i}{dt} = \begin{cases} \partial f/\partial x_i + \sum_{j=1}^{j=n} y_j \, \partial g_j/\partial x_i, \\ 0, \end{cases}$

(10) $\quad \dfrac{dy_j}{dt} = \begin{cases} -g_j, \\ 0. \end{cases}$

In each case the second line applies only when the corresponding variable is 0, and the first line is negative. This says roughly the following: Suppose we are considering an increase in x_1, the scale of the first activity. The first term in the first line of (9) indicates the effect on profits of the increased x_1, and each of the terms $y_j \, \partial g_j/\partial x_i$ indicates the cost of increasing your uses of the resource j as a result of increasing x_i. Increasing the use of resource j is interpreted here as a negative term and is multiplied by the positive price so that this would be a cost. The quantity x_1 should be increased if the increase in profits exceeds the increase in costs, and decreased in the contrary case. The second line of (9) means that if this instruction requires setting one activity at a negative level, which of course is meaningless, just freeze the activity at a zero level. Equation (10) shows that Lagrange multipliers y_j behave analogously to prices in the market. If there is an excess of supply over demand, which would be a positive value of g_j, the policy is to reduce the price y_j, and if there is a negative excess supply (that is, an excess of demand over supply), then you want to raise price y_j. The gradient method just outlined will converge if φ is strictly concave in x, and this will be the case if f is strictly concave and the functions g_j are concave. These assumptions are applicable to a wide range of economic problems, the case loosely referred to as diminishing returns to scale. The gradient method gives a method of handling this problem in general, especially beyond the case where f is quadratic and the functions g_j linear; the gradient method then seems to be almost the only method available.

The nonconcave case

However, there are problems that frequently arise in many practices where we do not have diminishing returns to scale. It is then not the case that the function f is strictly concave and the g_j's are concave. For this case we have a suggested method which has not been given very wide application. We do not know too much about its properties but we know a few things, and we think there will be a wide class of problems where this will be useful. Suppose again we have Problem I. Now the first thing is to note that Problem I can be restated in a new form. Let η stand for any positive, even integer. Then the restriction that $g_j \geqslant 0$ can be written equivalently in the following rather complicated form:

(11) $1 - [1 - g_j(x_1, \ldots, x_m)]^{1+\eta} \geqslant 0.$

Suppose, for example, g_j is greater than or equal to 0. The expression in brackets is less than or equal to 1, and when raised to any odd power is still less than or equal to 1. So that if $x_1, \ldots, x_n$ are a feasible set of activities in the sense of satisfying the constraints of Problem I they will automatically satisfy the more complicated-seeming set of constraints (11) and conversely. We can state

   Problem I(η).   To maximize $f(x_1, \ldots, x_m)$ subject to the constraints (11) and $x_i \geqslant 0$ $(i = 1, \ldots, m)$.

   Problem I(η) is then the same as Problem I but written in a different form. As we have just noted, if the functions f and g_j do not have the right concavity properties, the convergence of the gradient method for Problem II is no longer guaranteed. What we want to do is restate the problem in such a form that the gradient method will have the desirable convergence properties of the concave case.

   Let us take Problem I(η), treat it as if it were Problem I, and discuss the question of converting it to a Problem II(η) which bears the same relation to Problem I(η) as Problem II does to Problem I. That is, in Problem II replace the g_j's wherever they occur by the new sets of constraints (11).

Problem II(η). To minimax $_\pi\varphi(x_1, \ldots, x_m; y_1, \ldots, y_n)$ subject to $x_i \geqslant 0$, $y_j \geqslant 0$, where we define

$$_\eta\varphi(x_1, \ldots, x_m; y_1, \ldots, y_n)$$
$$= f(x_1, \ldots, x_m) + \Sigma_{j=1}^{j=m} y_j \{1 - [1 - g_j(x_1, \ldots, x_m)]^{1+\eta}\}.$$

What is the use of this transformation? When η is zero, we have the original form, and the functions f and g_j are not all concave. The saddle point may not exist or it may exist but bear no resemblance to the solution of Problem I. However, the following theorem can be established: If we pick our η sufficiently large, then Problems II(η) and I(η) are equivalent at least in the small; that is to say, that if we restrict the x's to a sufficiently small range around the optimal values, the expression $_\eta\varphi$ will have a saddle point and the x's which occur in that saddle point will be the x's which solved Problem I(η) and hence Problem I. Furthermore, the expression $_\eta\varphi$ will have the proper concavity properties required here, and therefore the gradient method for solving this will converge to the x-solutions.[6]

Applying the gradient method to the nonlinear game represented by Problem II(η) yields

$$(12) \quad \frac{dx_i}{dt} = \begin{cases} \partial f/\partial x_i + (1+\eta) \Sigma_{j=1}^{j=m} y_j [1 - g_j(x_1, \ldots, x_m)]^\eta \, \partial g_j/\partial x_i, \\ 0. \end{cases}$$

$$(13) \quad \frac{dy_j}{dt} = \begin{cases} [1 - g_j(x_1, \ldots, x_m)]^{1+\eta} - 1, \\ 0. \end{cases}$$

In this non-strictly concave case we have something very similar to what we had in the strictly concave case except that we now have an expression $[1 - g_j]^\eta$ involved. The y_j's qualitatively speaking at least, would be similar in behavior, but the precise relevant prices become somewhat different than they were before. The differential equations will now have the desired property of convergence, though only, as far as we know, locally, and for sufficiently large η. We think this method should be applicable to a class of cases of increasing returns where, for example, the amount of a certain resource that is used does not increase in the same proportion as the output. In this case, the "natural" method of (9) and (10) will not converge, because the activity gets more and more profitable the higher the scale of operations. The tendency is to explode whereas in the modified method of (12) and (13), the exponent works in such a way as to cut down this tendency toward going to extremes.[7]

An illustration of an increasing return problem in which the modified method (12)–(13) is used may be helpful. Suppose a manufacturer can produce two products that are complementary in use (like pen and ink) so that raising the price of either one will reduce the amount he can sell of both. If q_1, q_2 are the amounts produced and sold of the two commodities and if p_1, p_2 are their prices, suppose that the demand functions are

(14) $q_1 = \frac{136}{7} - \frac{16}{7} p_1 - \frac{12}{7} p_2$, $q_2 = \frac{172}{7} - \frac{12}{7} p_1 - \frac{16}{7} p_2$.

Production requires the use of skilled labor and materials. Skilled labor is limited in supply; say only three units are available to the firm, at a total cost of 20. The materials that go into the production of the first commodity cost 3 per unit, while those in the second cost 2.5 per unit, so that the costs of labor and materials are $3q + 2.5q$, and the total profits are

(15) $\pi = p_1 q_1 + p_2 q_2 - 3q_1 - 2.5q_2 - 20$.

In the use of skilled labor, there are increasing returns; suppose that for each commodity the amount of skilled labor required is equal to the square root of the output of that commodity. Then because only three units of labor are available, the outputs must satisfy the constraint

(16) $\sqrt{q_1} + \sqrt{q_2} \leqslant 3$.

The manufacturer seeks to maximize (15) subject to (16).

We can eliminate the prices in (15) by solving for p_1, p_2 in (14) and substituting in (15). Then

$$p_1 = 1 - q_1 + \tfrac{3}{4} q_2, p_2 = 10 + \tfrac{3}{4} q_1 - q_2,$$

and

(17) $\pi = -2q_1 + 7.5q_2 - q_1^2 + 1.5q_1 q_2 - q_2^2 - 20$,

which is to be maximized subject to (16), or, equivalently, subject to

(18) $\tfrac{1}{3} \sqrt{q_1} + \tfrac{1}{3} \sqrt{q_2} \leqslant 1$.

In terms of our previous notation, π corresponds to the function $f(x_1, \ldots, x_m)$, q_1, q_2 to the variables $x_1, \ldots, x_m$, and the left-hand side of (18) to the function $1 - g_1(x_1, \ldots, x_m)$. In terms of Problem II(η), then, we will seek the minimax of

(19) $_\eta \varphi(q_1, q_2, y) = \pi + y \{1 - [\tfrac{1}{3} \sqrt{q_1} + \tfrac{1}{3} \sqrt{q_2}]^{1+\eta}\}$,

where q_1, q_2 are chosen by the first player and y by the second, and all variables are nonnegative. Then, from (12) and (13), the gradient method calls for the solution of the following differential equations:

(20) $dq_1/dt = -2 - 2q_1 + 1.5q_2 - (1 + \eta) y [(\tfrac{1}{3}) \sqrt{q_1} + (\tfrac{1}{3}) \sqrt{q_2}]^{\eta} (1/6\sqrt{q_1})$,

(21) $dq_2/dt = 7.5 + 1.5q_1 - 2q_2 - (1 + \eta) y [(\tfrac{1}{3}) \sqrt{q_1} + (\tfrac{1}{3}) \sqrt{q_2}]^{\eta} (1/6\sqrt{q_2})$,

(22) $dy/dt = [(\tfrac{1}{3}) \sqrt{q_1} + (\tfrac{1}{3}) \sqrt{q_2}]^{1+\eta} - 1$,

with the understanding that the right-hand side of each equation is replaced by zero if the value is negative and the corresponding variable is zero.

It can be shown that if $\eta = 0$, the solution of above differential equations will not converge, but if $\eta = 1$, the solution converges to the desired optimum point, provided the starting point is not too far from the optimum.

Notes

1 The authors wish to thank the Rand Corporation, under whose auspices most of this work was done, and the Office of Naval Research and the Cowles Commission for Research in Economics for additional support and assistance.
2 See A. W. Tucker, "Linear and Nonlinear Programming," *Operations Research*, Vol. 5, No. 2 (1957), pp. 244–257.
3 K. J. Arrow and L. Hurwicz, "A Gradient Method for Approximating Saddle Points and Constrained Maxima," Rand Paper, P-223, June 13, 1951.
4 H. Uzawa, "Notes on a Gradient Method," Tech. Rept. No. 36, O.N.R. Contract N6onr-25133, Department of Economics, Stanford University.
5 See Tucker, *op. cit.*
6 K. J. Arrow and L. Hurwicz, "Reduction of Constrained Maxima to Saddle Point Problems," this volume, II.5, pp. 154–177.
7 The η-method may also be used in the case where φ is concave but not strictly concave, in particular, in the important case of constant returns ("linear programming"). It turns out that if one uses $1 - e^{-\eta g}$, instead of $1 - (1 - g)^{1+\eta}$, convergence in the large can be guaranteed in the linear case.

5
THE HANDLING OF NONCONVEXITIES

Reduction of constrained maxima to saddle-point problems[1]

KENNETH J. ARROW
LEONID HURWICZ

1. Introduction

1.1. The usual applications of the method of Lagrangian multipliers, used in locating constrained extrema (say maxima), involve the setting up of the *Lagrangian expression*,

(1) $\phi(x, y) = f(x) + y'g(x)$,

where $f(x)$ is being (say) maximized with respect to the (vector) variable $x = \{x_1, \ldots, x_N\}$, subject to the constraint $g(x) = 0$, where $g(x)$ maps the points of the N-dimensional x-space into an M-dimensional space, and $y = \{y_1, \ldots, y_M\}$ is the Lagrange multiplier (vector). Here $\{\ \}$ indicates a column vector; the prime indicates transposition, so that y' is a row vector.

The essential step of the customary procedure is the solution for x, as well as y, of the pair of (vector) equations,

(2) $\phi_x(x, y) = 0, \qquad g(x) = 0$,

where $\phi_x(x, y) = \{\partial\phi(x, y)/\partial x_1, \ldots, \partial\phi(x, y)/\partial x_N\}$. Let $(\bar{x}, \bar{y})$ be the solutions of equations (2), while $\hat{x}$ maximizes $f(x)$ subject to $g(x) = 0$. Then, under suitable restrictions,

(3) $\bar{x} = \hat{x}$.

1.2. In [1], Kuhn and Tucker treat the related problem of maximizing $f(x)$ subject to the constraints[2] $g(x) \geq 0$, $x \geq 0$, where, for an arbitrary K-dimensional vector $a = \{a_1, \ldots, a_K\}$, the relation $a \geq 0$ is here defined to mean $a_k \geq 0$ for $k = 1, \ldots, K$. Another definition of vectorial inequalities, permitting greater generality of treatment, will be used in later sections of this paper. There we shall treat directly the class of situations where $f(x)$ is to be maximized subject to $g^{(1)}(x) \geq 0, g^{(2)}(x) = 0, x^{[1]} \geq 0, x^{[2]}$ not restricted as to sign, $x = \{x^{[1]}, x^{[2]}\}$.

Denote by C_g the set of all x satisfying the constraints $g(x) \geq 0, x \geq 0$. The two results stated below are of fundamental importance for the problem considered.

(A) (See theorem 1 [1].) Let g satisfy the following condition (called Constraint Qualification, here abbreviated as C.Q.).[3] If $\tilde{x}$ is a boundary point of C_g

and x satisfies the relations,

(4) $\tilde{g}_x{}^\alpha(x - \tilde{x}) \geqq 0$,

(5) $x^b - \tilde{x}^b \geqq 0$,

where "~" over a symbol denotes its evaluation at $x = \tilde{x}$, $g = \{g^\alpha, g^\beta\}$, $\tilde{g}^\alpha = 0$, $\tilde{g}^\beta > 0$, $x = \{x^a, x^b\}$, $\tilde{x}^a > 0$, and $\tilde{x}^b = 0$, then there exists a differentiable vector-valued function ψ of the real variable θ whose domain is the closed interval $(0, 1)$ and the range is in C_g; that is, $x = \psi(\theta)$, such that $\psi(0) = \tilde{x}$ and $\psi'(0) = \lambda(x - x)$ for some positive scalar λ.

   Under this condition, if all derivatives used below exist and if $\bar{x}$ maximizes $f(x)$ for $x \in C_g$, there exists $\bar{y}$ satisfying the conditions

(6) $\bar{x} \geqq 0$, $\bar{\phi}_x \leqq 0$, $\bar{x}'\bar{\phi}_x = 0$,

(7) $\bar{y} \geqq 0$, $\bar{\phi}_y \geqq 0$, $\bar{y}'\bar{\phi}_y = 0$,

where $\bar{\phi}_x$ and $\bar{\phi}_y$ are partial (vector) derivatives of the Lagrangian expression (1) evaluated at $(\bar{x}, \bar{y})$.

   (B). (See theorem 3 [1].) If the hypotheses specified in (A) hold and, in addition, the functions $f(x), g_m(x), m = 1, \ldots, M$ are *concave*,[4] there exists a pair $(\bar{x}, \bar{y})$, satisfying conditions (6) and (7), such that $(\bar{x}, \bar{y})$ is a *nonnegative saddle-point* (NNSP) of $\phi(x, y)$, that is,

(8) $\phi(x, \bar{y}) \leqq \phi(\bar{x}, \bar{y}) \leqq \phi(\bar{x}, y)$ for all $x \geqq 0, y \geqq 0$;

furthermore, any NNSP $(\tilde{x}, \tilde{y})$ of $\phi(x, y)$ has the property that $\tilde{x}$ maximizes $f(x)$ in C_g. According to lemma 1 [1], conditions (6), (7) are implied by (8) regardless of the nature of $\phi(x, y)$, that is, even if $\phi(x, y)$ is not given by (1).

2. A modified Lagrangian approach

   2.1. Because of the interesting game theoretical and economic implications of the theorem in (B), section 1.2 (which the authors will study elsewhere), the question arises as to the possibility of similar results when some of the conditions of the theorem are relaxed.

   It turns out that results of such nature can be obtained, though not without some sacrifices. The relaxation is primarily with regard to the convexity assumptions which fail to hold in some important economic applications (the case of "increasing returns"). The main sacrifices are (1) the Lagrangian expression is modified, and (2) the results are proved only locally.

   The results are presented below in the form of three theorems. Theorem 1 is auxiliary in nature; theorems 2 and 3 together imply the existence of a local nonnegative saddle-point for the modified Lagrangian expression. Theorem 3 shows this saddle-point to be of the type leading to convergence in gradient procedures described by the authors in [3].

The notation differs in some detail from that introduced in section 1. To facilitate reading, some notational principles are stated in 2.2.1; the main symbols used are listed in sections 2.2.2 and 2.3.4.

2.2.1. Some principles of notation

A K-dimensional column vector $\{a_1, a_2, \ldots, a_K\}$ is denoted by a; dim a denotes the number of components in a. If A is a matrix, A' is its transpose. Hence, in particular, a' is a row vector and $a'b \equiv \Sigma_{k=1}^{K} a_k b_k$ is the inner product of the vectors a and b; $a \cdot b$ is an alternative, and sometimes more convenient, notation for $a'b$.

The $[a_1, a_2, \ldots, a_K]$ is the finite (unordered) set whose elements are $a_1, a_2, \ldots, a_K$. $A \sim B$ is the set of all elements in A but not in B (the set-theoretic difference). The $\{x|p_x\}$ denotes the set of all x possessing the property p_x.

If

(9) $c(a) = \{c_1(a), c_2(a), \ldots, c_P(a)\}$,

(10) $a = \{a_1, a_2, \ldots, a_K\}$,

then

(11) $c_a \equiv c_a(a) = \left\| \dfrac{\partial c_p}{\partial a_k} \right\|$, $p = 1, 2, \ldots, P$; $k = 1, 2, \ldots, K$.

Further, $\bar{c}, \bar{c}_a$ denote, respectively, $c(a)$ and $c_a(a) \equiv c_a$ evaluated at $a = \bar{a}$.

If $\psi(a, b)$ is a real-valued (scalar) function of the vectors $a = \{a_1, a_2, \ldots, a_K\}$, $b = \{b_1, b_2, \ldots, b_R\}$, then

(12) $\psi_{ab} = \left\| \dfrac{\partial^2 \psi}{\partial a_k \, \partial b_r} \right\|$, $k = 1, 2, \ldots, K$; $r = 1, 2, \ldots, R$,

where $\bar{\psi}_{ab}$ denotes ψ_{ab} evaluated at $(\bar{a}, \bar{b})$.

$S_\rho(x^0) = \{x|d(x, x^0) \leq \rho\}$ where $d(x', x'')$ denotes the Euclidean distance between x' and x''.

2.2.2. Some symbols used

(N.1.1) $x = \{x_1, x_2, \ldots, x_N\}$.

X is the Euclidean N-space of the x's.

$\mathfrak{N} = [1, 2, \ldots, N]$.

$\mathfrak{N}'$ is a fixed (possibly empty, not necessarily proper) subset of $\mathfrak{N}$. As will be seen in (N.1.4), the elements of $\mathfrak{N}'$ are the indices of the components of $x^{[1]}$ as defined in the first paragraph of section 1.2.

(N.1.2) $\quad z = \{z_1, z_2, \ldots, z_M\}$.

Z is the Euclidean M-space of the z's.

$\mathfrak{M} = [1, 2, \ldots, M]$.

$\mathfrak{M}'$ is a fixed (possibly empty, not necessarily proper) subset of $\mathfrak{M}$. As will be seen from (N.1.4), (N.2), (N.3), the elements of $\mathfrak{M}'$ are the indices of the components of $g^{(1)}$ as defined in the first paragraph of section 1.2; the elements of $\mathfrak{M} \sim \mathfrak{M}'$ are the indices of $g^{(2)}$ (see same paragraph); g will be defined as $\{g^{(1)}, g^{(2)}\}$.

(N.1.3) $\quad y = \{y_1, y_2, \ldots, y_M\}$.

Y is the Euclidean M-space of the y's. Here Y is the space of the real-valued linear functions on Z. Even in the Euclidean case it is convenient to distinguish between the two, since our definitions of nonnegativity in the two spaces differ.

(N.1.4) $\quad x \geqq 0$ means $\begin{cases} x_n \geqq 0 \text{ for } n \in \mathfrak{N}'. \\ x_n \text{ unrestricted as to sign for } n \notin \mathfrak{N}'. \end{cases}$

X^+ is the set of all $x \geqq 0$.

$z \geqq 0$ means $\begin{cases} z_m \geqq 0 \text{ for } m \in \mathfrak{M}'. \\ z_m = 0 \text{ for } m \notin \mathfrak{M}'. \end{cases}$

$y \geqq 0$ means $\begin{cases} y_m \geqq 0 \text{ for } m \in \mathfrak{M}'. \\ y_m \text{ unrestricted as to sign for } m \notin \mathfrak{M}'. \end{cases}$

For any vector $a = \{a_1, a_2, \ldots, a_k\}$,

$a = 0$ means $a_1 = 0, \quad a_2 = 0, \ldots, a_K = 0$;

$a > 0$ means $a_1 > 0, \quad a_2 > 0, \ldots, a_K > 0$;

$a < 0$ means $-a > 0$.

(N.2.1) $'g$ is a function on X^+ to Z. Hence $'g(x) = \{'g_1(x), 'g_2(x), \ldots, 'g_M(x)\}$ where the $'g_m$, $m \in \mathfrak{M}$ are real-valued functions.

(N.2.2) We shall find it convenient to work with some of the $'g_m$, $m \in \mathfrak{M}'$ replaced by their negatives. More precisely, we write

$$g_m = \begin{cases} 'g_m \text{ if } m \in \mathfrak{M} \sim \mathfrak{M}^- \\ -'g_m \text{ if } m \in \mathfrak{M}^-, \end{cases}$$

where $\mathfrak{M}^- \subseteq \mathfrak{M} \sim \mathfrak{M}'$ will be defined in section 2.3.4.

$g = \{g_1, g_2, \ldots, g_M\}$.

Note. Since $\mathfrak{M}^- \subseteq \mathfrak{M} \sim \mathfrak{M}'$, it is seen that the conditions

$'g(x) \geqq 0, \quad g(x) \geqq 0$

are equivalent. For practical purposes, one could consider the problem as given directly in terms of g, rather than $'g$. We start with $'g$, however, in order to avoid the impression of a loss of generality in connection with the assumptions of section 2.3.4.

(N.3) $C_g = \{x \mid {'g}(x) \geq 0, x \geq 0\} \equiv \{x \mid g(x) \geq 0, x \geq 0\}$

(the "constraint set").

(N.4) f is a real-valued function on X^+ (the "maximand").

(N.5) $O_{fg} = \{x' \mid x' \in C_g \text{ and } f(x) \leq f(x') \text{ for all } x \in C_g\}$

(the "optimal set").

(N.6) $x = \{x^{(1)}, x^{(2)}\}$

where

> $\mathfrak{N}^{(i)}$ = the set of indices of the components of $x^{(i)}$, $i = 1, 2$
>
> $n \in \mathfrak{N}^{(1)}$ if $n \notin \mathfrak{N}'$ or $n \in \mathfrak{N}'$ and $\bar{x}_n > 0$
>
> $n \in \mathfrak{N}^{(2)}$ if $n \in \mathfrak{N}'$ and $\bar{x}_n = 0$

for a given $\bar{x} \in O_{fg}$ and either component may be empty.

Note 1.   When a vector a is partitioned into two subvectors, say

$a = \{a^*, a^{**}\}$

and we say that a^* (or a^{**}) is empty, this means that $a = a^{**}$ (or $a = a^*$).

Note 2.   The above partitioning of the vector x obviously depends on the point $\bar{x}$ in O_{fg} chosen. The same is true of the partitioning in (N.7) below and of various subsequent partitionings of x and g. It is understood that all these partitionings refer to the same choice of $\bar{x}$, and that $\bar{x}$, once chosen, remains fixed.

(N.7) $g = \{g^{[1]}, g^{[2]}\}$

where

$g^{[1]}(\bar{x}) = 0, \qquad g^{[2]}(\bar{x}) > 0$

and either component may be empty.

(N.8) $h(x) = 1 - g(x)$

where 1 denotes the M-dimensional vector with 1's as components; $h^{[i]} = 1 - g^{[i]}$, $i = 1, 2$.

(N.9) $\eta_m p_m(x) = 1 - [h_m(x)]^{1 + \eta_m}, \qquad m \in \mathfrak{M}.$

(N.10) $\eta = \{\eta_1, \eta_2, \ldots, \eta_M\}.$

(N.11) $\eta p(x) = \{\eta_1 p_1(x), \eta_2 p_2(x), \ldots, \eta_M p_M(x)\}.$

(N.12) $\eta \phi(x, y) = f(x) + y'[\eta p(x)]$ (the "modified Lagrangian expression").

2.3.1. A reformulation of Kuhn-Tucker theorem 1

This slight generalization of theorem 1 (see [1], p. 484) is needed here because of the meaning of inequalities given in (N.1.4). [The possibility of this type of generalization is indicated in [1] (see pp. 491–492).][5]

We shall say that g satisfies the Constraint Qualification (C.Q.) at x, if the requirements of the definition in (A) of section 1.2 are satisfied with the inequalities (4), (5) in the same section interpreted in the sense of (N.1.4). Term $\phi(x, y)$ is given by (1) in 1.1. (It is immaterial whether g or $'g$ is used.)

Theorem.   If f and g are differentiable, $\bar{x} \in O_{fg}$ and g satisfy C.Q. at $\bar{x}$, then there exists a $\bar{y} \in Y$ such that

$$\bar{y} \geq 0; \quad \bar{\phi}_y \cdot \bar{y} = 0; \quad \bar{\phi}_y \cdot y \geq 0 \quad \text{for all } y \geq 0;$$

$$\bar{x} \geq 0; \quad \bar{\phi}_x \cdot \bar{x} = 0; \quad \bar{\phi}_x \cdot x \leq 0 \quad \text{for all } x \geq 0.$$

[Note that, by virtue of the definitions in 2.2.2, this means that $\bar{\phi}_{y_m} \geq 0$ if $m \in \mathfrak{M}', \bar{\phi}_{y_m} = 0$ if $m \notin \mathfrak{M}', \bar{\phi}_{x_n} \leq 0$ if $n \in \mathfrak{N}', \bar{\phi}_{x_n} = 0$ if $n \notin \mathfrak{N}'$. The other inequalities of the theorem are also to be interpreted in the sense of (N.1.4).]

2.3.2. Theorem 1

Definition.[6]   An M-dimensional vector $\eta = \{\eta_1, \eta_2, \ldots, \eta_M\}$ is said to be *acceptable* if, for each $m \in \mathfrak{M}$, (1) $\eta_m \geq 0$, and (2) η_m is an even integer if $h_m(\bar{x}) < -1$.

Theorem 1.   If, for some $\rho > 0$, $x \in S_\rho(\bar{x})$, $\bar{x} \in O_{fg}$, f and g are differentiable, and g satisfies C.Q. at $\bar{x}$, then, for any acceptable η, there exists a vector $\bar{y} = \bar{y}(\eta)$ such that

(13) $_\eta\bar{\phi}_x \cdot x \leq 0$ for all $x \geq 0$;

(14) $_\eta\bar{\phi}_x \cdot \bar{x} = 0$;

(15) $\bar{x} \geq 0$;

(16) $_\eta\bar{\phi}_y \cdot y \geq 0$ for all $y \geq 0$;

(17) $_\eta\bar{\phi}_y \cdot \bar{y} = 0$;

(18) $\bar{y} \geq 0$.

The bar over ϕ denotes evaluation at $x = \bar{x}$, $y = \bar{y}(\eta)$.

Note that the relations (13)–(18) are necessary conditions for a nonnegative, in the sense of (N.14), saddle-point of $_\eta\phi(x, y)$ at $(\bar{x}, \bar{y})$. In particular, the relations (13)–(18) are satisfied if one selects $\bar{y} = \bar{y}(\eta)$ such that[7]

(19) $(1 + \eta_m)\bar{y}_m(\eta) = \bar{y}_m(0)$ for all $m \in \mathfrak{M}$.

If the selection is made in accordance with (19), the equality

(20) $_0\bar{\phi}_x = {}_\eta\bar{\phi}_x$

will hold. Here $_0\phi(x,y)$ is $_\eta\phi(x,y)$ with $\eta=0$; this is obviously the same as $\phi(x,y)$ in (1) of 1.1.

Proof. For $\eta=0$, the preceding theorem follows directly from the reformulated version of the Kuhn-Tucker theorem 1 given in 2.3.1. Thus there exists a vector

$$(21) \quad \bar{y}(0) = \{\bar{y}_1(0), \bar{y}_2(0), \ldots, \bar{y}_M(0)\}$$

with the required properties.

Consider now the case $\eta \neq 0$. We shall show that $\bar{y}(\eta)$ defined by (19), that is, explicitly, by

$$(22) \quad y_m(\eta) = \frac{1}{1+\eta_m}\,\bar{y}_m(0), \qquad m \in \mathfrak{M}$$

[where $\bar{y}_m(0)$ is that of (21)], satisfies the relations (13)-(20).

We first observe that (22) yields

$$(23) \quad (1+\eta_m)\,\bar{y}_m(\eta)[h_m(\bar{x})]^{\eta_m} = \bar{y}_m(0), \qquad m \in \mathfrak{M}.$$

[When $h_m(\bar{x})=1$, (23) follows directly from (22). When $h_m(\bar{x}) \neq 1$, we have $_0\phi_{y_m} = g_m(\bar{x}) > 0$, and hence, by (16)-(18), $\bar{y}_m(0)=0$; (22) then yields $\bar{y}_m(\eta)=0$ and (23) follows.]

Since

$$(24) \quad {}_\eta\phi_{x_n} = f_{x_n} + \Sigma_{m=1}^{M}(1+\eta_m)\,y_m(\eta)[h_m(x)]^{\eta_m}\,\frac{\partial g_m(x)}{\partial x_n}, \qquad n \in \mathfrak{N},$$

formula (23) implies

$$(25) \quad {}_\eta\bar{\phi}_{x_n} = \bar{f}_{x_n} + \Sigma_{m=1}^{M}\,\bar{y}_m(0)\,\frac{\partial g_m(\bar{x})}{\partial x_n}, \qquad n \in \mathfrak{N}.$$

Noting that the right member of (25) is identical with $_0\bar{\phi}_{x_n}$, we conclude that the relations (13)-(15) hold for all η with nonnegative components, since they are known to hold for $\eta=0$.

Relation (16) is established by the fact that the right member of

$$(26) \quad {}_\eta\bar{\phi}_{y_m} = {}_\eta p_m(\bar{x}) = 1 - [h_m(\bar{x})]^{1+\eta_m}, \qquad m \in \mathfrak{M},$$

is nonnegative for $m \in \mathfrak{M}'$, zero for $m \notin \mathfrak{M}'$ when η is acceptable (see the definition above) since, for any $m \in \mathfrak{M}$, $h_m(\bar{x}) \leq 1$, and, furthermore, $_\eta\bar{\phi}_{y_m}=0$ if $m \notin \mathfrak{M}'$, in which case $h_m(\bar{x})=1$.

Now suppose that, for some $m_0 \in \mathfrak{M}$, $_\eta\bar{\phi}_{y_{m_0}} > 0$, that is, $h_{m_0}(\bar{x}) < 1$; then, by (16)-(18) for $\eta=0$, $\bar{y}_{m_0}(0)=0$; hence $\bar{y}_{m_0}(\eta)=0$, and, therefore,

$$(27) \quad \bar{\phi}_{y_{m_0}} \cdot \bar{y}_{m_0}(\eta) = 0.$$

Since (27) clearly holds in the alternative case $_\eta\phi_{m_0}=0$, (17) follows.

Finally, (18) holds because $\bar{y}_m(\eta)$ has the same sign as $\bar{y}_m(0)$ and the latter, by (18) for $\eta=0$, is nonnegative if $m \in \mathfrak{M}'$.

2.3.3. Theorem 2

Let, for some $\rho > 0$, $x \in S_\rho(\bar{x})$, $\bar{x} \in O_{fg}$ such that (13)-(20) are satisfied. Then

(28) $_n\phi(\bar{x}, \bar{y}) \leqq {}_n\phi(\bar{x}, y)$ for all $y \geqq 0$.

For we have

(29) $_n\phi(\bar{x}, y) - {}_n\phi(\bar{x}, \bar{y}) = (y - \bar{y}) \cdot {}_n\bar{p} = y \cdot {}_n\bar{p} \geqq 0$ for $y \geqq 0$

where, since

(30) $_n\bar{\phi}_y = {}_n\bar{p}$,

the second equality follows from (17) and the inequality from (16).

2.3.4. Notation

(N.13) $x^{(2)} = \{x^{(21)}, x^{(22)}\}$

where

$$_0\bar{\phi}_{x^{(21)}} = 0, \qquad {}_0\bar{\phi}_{x^{(22)}} < 0$$

and either component may be empty.

(N.14) $x = \{x^I, x^{II}\}$

where

(N.14.1) $\begin{aligned} x^I &= \{x^{(1)}, x^{(21)}\} \\ x^{II} &= x^{(22)}. \end{aligned}$

(Either x^I or x^{II} may be empty.)

It should be noted that, by (13)-(15) and (N.13),

(N.14.2) $\begin{aligned} _0\bar{\phi}_{x^I} &= 0, \\ _0\bar{\phi}_{x^{II}} &< 0. \end{aligned}$

2.3.5. Definition of a regular constrained maximum

In theorem 3 below we use the concept of a *regular* constrained maximum. The definition of such a maximum is given in the last part of this section. To state it, we must first formulate three regularity conditions denoted by R_1, R_2, R_3.

The first regularity condition R_1.   Let $\bar{x}$ be a value maximizing the function $f(x)$ subject to $'g(x) \geqq 0$, $x \geqq 0$, and hence also subject to

(31) $\begin{aligned} g(x) &\geqq 0 \\ x &\geqq 0 \end{aligned}$

where the inequalities are to be interpreted in the sense of (N.1.4).

From (N.6) and (N.7) it is clear that, for sufficiently small variations of x, the constraints

$$(32) \quad \begin{aligned} g^{[2]}(x) &\geq 0 \\ x^{(1)} &\geq 0, \end{aligned}$$

which are a part of (31), can be disregarded. Hence, at $\bar{x}$, $f(x)$ possesses a *local* maximum subject to

$$(33) \quad \begin{aligned} g^{[1]}(x) &\geq 0, \\ x^{(2)} &\geq 0. \end{aligned}$$

Let $g^{\dagger}$ be a subvector of $g^{[1]}$ such that $C_g = C_{\{g^{\dagger}, g^{[2]}\}}$ and write

$$(34) \quad g^{[1]} = \{g^{\dagger}, g^{\dagger\dagger}\}.$$

The components of $g^{\dagger\dagger}$ can be disregarded in the process of maximization, that is, $O_{f,g} = O_{f,\{g^{\dagger}, g^{[2]}\}}$. If the Lagrangian multiplier vector $\bar{y}^{[1]}$ [corresponding to the constraints $g^{[1]}(x) \geq 0$] is partitioned according to

$$(35) \quad \bar{y}^{[1]} = \{\bar{y}^{\dagger}, \bar{y}^{\dagger\dagger}\}$$

it is always possible to put

$$(36) \quad \bar{y}^{\dagger\dagger} = 0,$$

and this will be done in what follows.

Assuming that the constraints (33) are consistent, we may replace them by

$$(37) \quad \begin{aligned} g^{\dagger}(x) &= 0 \\ x^{(2)} &\geq 0. \end{aligned}$$

The *first regularity condition* is

$$(R_1) \quad \text{rank}\,(\bar{g}_{x^{(1)}}{}^{\dagger}) = \dim g^{\dagger} = M^{\dagger},$$

say.

Note 1. R_1 corresponds to the requirement of nondegeneracy in linear programming (see [4], p. 340).

Note 2. R_1 implies C.Q. (see appendix I).

The second regularity condition R_2. Since, by (N.7), (N.6), (N.14.1), and (34),

$$(38) \quad \begin{aligned} g^{\dagger}(\bar{x}) &= 0 \\ \bar{x}^{II} &= 0, \end{aligned}$$

it follows that, as a function of x^I, $f(x^I, \bar{x}^{II}) \equiv f(x^I, 0)$ has at $\bar{x}^I$ a local maximum subject to the constraints

$$(39) \quad \begin{aligned} g^{\dagger}(x^I, \bar{x}^{II}) &\equiv g^{\dagger}(x^I, 0) = 0 \\ x^{(21)} &\geq 0. \end{aligned}$$

The corresponding Lagrangian expression becomes

(40) $\quad _0\phi^I(x^I, y^\dagger) = f(x^I, 0) + y^\dagger \cdot g^\dagger(x^I, 0).$

Using the reformulation of Kuhn-Tucker theorem 1, given in 2.3.1, we may assert the existence of a $\bar{y}^\dagger$ such that

(41) $\quad \bar{x}^I \geq 0; \quad _0\bar{\phi}_{x^I}{}^I = 0;$

(42) $\quad \bar{y}^\dagger \geq 0; \quad _0\bar{\phi}_{y^\dagger}{}^I = 0.$

It might happen that some components of $\bar{y}^\dagger$ vanish. Write $y^\dagger = \{y^*, y^0\}$ where every component of $\bar{y}^*$ is different from zero and

(43) $\quad \bar{y}^0 = 0.$

Let $g^\dagger$ be correspondingly partitioned as

(44) $\quad g^\dagger = \{g^*, g^0\}.$

Now suppose that $_0\phi^I(x^I, y^\dagger)$ has a nonnegative saddle-point at $(\bar{x}^I, \bar{y}^\dagger)$. By theorem 3 in Kuhn-Tucker, a sufficient condition for this is that f and g be both concave. One can then easily verify that

(45) $\quad _0\phi^I(x^I, y^*) \equiv f(x^I, 0) + y^* \cdot g^*(x^I, 0)$

has a nonnegative saddle-point at $(\bar{x}^I, \bar{y}^*)$.

But then $\bar{x}^I$ maximizes $f(x^I, 0)$ subject to $g^*(x^I, 0) \geq 0$ and $x^{(21)} \geq 0$. Hence in this case the components of g^0 could have been disregarded in the original maximization problem $(O_{f,g} = O_{f, \{g^*, g^{[2]}\}})$.

However, complications might arise if $_0\phi^I(x^I, y^\dagger)$ did not have a nonnegative saddle-point at $(\bar{x}^I, \bar{y}^\dagger)$. To take care of this case, one might require that

(46) $\quad g^0$ is empty unless $_0\phi^I(x^I, y^\dagger)$ has a local nonnegative saddle-point at $(\bar{x}^I, \bar{y}^\dagger).$

However, to simplify matters we shall impose the seemingly (see section 2.3.7) stronger condition

(47) $\quad g^0$ is empty.

It follows that

(48) $\quad M^* \equiv \dim g^* = \dim g^\dagger \equiv M^\dagger.$

Let $\mathfrak{M}^*[= \mathfrak{M}^\dagger$ by (47)] denote the set of indices of g^*. Clearly, for $m \in \mathfrak{M}^* \cap (\mathfrak{M} \sim \mathfrak{M}')$, we may have $\bar{y}_m < 0$.

Now suppose the preceding reasoning had been carried out in terms of $'g$ instead of g. Nothing would be changed, except, possibly, the signs of some components of the Lagrangian multiplier, to be denoted by $'\bar{y}$.

That is, we would have $'\bar{y}_m > 0$ for $m \in \mathfrak{M}^* \cap \mathfrak{M}'$ and $'\bar{y}_m > 0$ or $'\bar{y}_m < 0$ for $m \in \mathfrak{M}^* \cap (\mathfrak{M} \sim \mathfrak{M}')$. Let $\mathfrak{M}^-$ be defined by the relation $m \in \mathfrak{M}^-$ if and only if

$m \in \mathfrak{M}^* \cap (\mathfrak{M} \sim \mathfrak{M}')$ and $'\bar{y}_m < 0$. Then, it is clear from (N.2.2) that we may put

(49)
$$\bar{y}_m = '\bar{y}_m \text{ for } m \in \mathfrak{M} \sim \mathfrak{M}^-$$
$$\bar{y}_m = -'\bar{y}_m \text{ for } m \in \mathfrak{M}^-,$$

so that $\bar{y}_m > 0$ for all $m \in \mathfrak{M}^*$.

Hence, *without loss of generality* [as compared with (47)], condition (47) may be restated as the *second regularity condition.*

(R₂)
$$g^0 \text{ is empty and}$$
$$\bar{y}_m > 0 \qquad \text{for all } M \in \mathfrak{M}^*.$$

The first regularity condition then implies

(50) $\text{rank} \, (\bar{g}_{x^{(1)}}^*) = M^*$

where

(51) $M^* = \dim g^*.$

The third regularity condition R_3.   When the first two regularity conditions are satisfied, second derivatives are continuous, and x^I is nonempty, it is possible to show (see appendix II) that a certain quadratic form is nonpositive when some of the variables are restricted in sign. The third regularity condition is a strengthening of (71) requiring that the quadratic form in question be negative under the same restrictions. This condition, analogous to that used by Samuelson (see [5], p. 358) makes it possible to avoid going beyond second-order terms in the expansions used.

The third regularity condition is formulated in terms of a function $q(t)$ of a new variable vector

(52) $t = \{t^*, t^{**}\}$

which is obtained by a transformation of coordinates from x^I after the latter has been partitioned so that

(53) $x^I = \{x^*, x^{**}\},$

where x^* is a subvector of $x^{(1)}$.

We shall (a) define x^* and x^{**}; (b) write down the transformation defining $\{t^*, t^{**}\}$ in terms of $\{x^*, x^{**}\}$; (c) define $q(t)$; and (d) formulate the third regularity condition.

In the remainder of this section it is assumed that R_1 holds; it is also assumed that x^I is not empty.

First case. $M^* = 0$.   Write

(54) $t = t^{**} = x^{**} = x^I,$

so that, by (52) and (53), x^* and t^* are empty, and define

(55) $q(t) = f(x^I, \bar{x}^{II}) = f(t^{**}, 0).$

The third regularity condition for this case is formulated in R_3 below.

Second case. $M^* > 0$.   (a) The definition of x^*. From R_1 it follows that there exists a (nonempty) M^*-dimensional subvector x^* of $x^{(1)}$ such that

(56) $\bar{g}_{x*}^*$ is an M^* by M^* ($M^* \geq 1$) nonsingular matrix.

We then define x^{**} by (53) and $x^{(12)}$ by

(57) $x^{(1)} = \{x^*, x^{(12)}\}$.

Clearly

(58) $x^{**} = \{x^{(12)}, x^{(21)}\}$.

(b) The transformation from x^I to t. Let

(59) $h^* = 1 - g^*$

where 1 is the M^*-dimensional vector with (scalar) 1's as components. $t = \{t^*, t^{**}\}$ is then defined by the transformation

(60) $t^* = h^*(x^*, x^{**}, \bar{x}^{II})$

(61) $t^{**} = x^{**}$.

We also partition t^{**} by

(62) $t^{**} = \{t^{(12)}, t^{(21)}\}$

where

(63) $\begin{aligned} t^{(12)} &= x^{(12)}, \\ t^{(21)} &= x^{(21)}. \end{aligned}$

This is obviously consistent with (57) and (61).

(c) The definition of $q(t)$. By (59), the Jacobian H of the transformation (58)–(59) is

(64) $H = \begin{pmatrix} h_{\dot{x}*}^* & h_{x**}^* \\ 0 & I \end{pmatrix} = - \begin{pmatrix} g_{x*}^* & g_{x**}^* \\ 0 & -I \end{pmatrix}$,

so that, by (56),

(65) $|\bar{H}| = \pm |\bar{g}_{x*}^*| \neq 0$,

that is,

(66) $\bar{H}$ is nonsingular.

Hence, locally, (60)–(61) can be solved for x^I in terms of t; we may write this solution as

(67) $x^I = r(t)$

where

(68) $r = \{r^*, r^{**}\}$

and

(69) $x^* = r^*(t), \qquad x^{**} = r^{**}(t) = t^{**}.$

The function $q(t)$ is now defined as $f(x)$ evaluated at $x^{II} = \bar{x}^{II}$ and with x^I expressed in terms of t, that is,

(70) $q(t) = f[r(t), \bar{x}^{II}] \equiv f[r^*(t^*, t^{**}), t^{**}, 0]$.

The statement of the third regularity condition. We have now defined $q(t)$ for all M^* provided the first regularity condition R_1 is satisfied and x^I is non-empty. It is shown in appendix II that, assuming R_1, R_2, and the continuity of the second derivatives, unless x^{**} is empty, there exists $\rho > 0$ such that, for all $t^{**} \in S_\rho(\bar{x}^{**})$,

(71) $(t^{**} - \bar{x}^{**})' \bar{q}_{t^{**}t^{**}}(t^{**} - \bar{x}^{**}) \leqq 0, \qquad \text{if } t^{(21)} \geqq 0.$

The *third regularity condition* is a strengthening of the preceding inequality. It states that

(a) x^{**} is empty or

(R$_3$) (b) there exists $\rho > 0$ such that, for all $t^{**} \in S_\rho(\bar{x}^{**})$,

$(t^{**} - \bar{x}^{**})' \bar{q}_{t^{**}t^{**}}(t^{**} - (\bar{x}^{**}) < 0 \text{ if } t^{(21)} \geqq 0 \text{ and } t^{**} \neq \bar{x}^{**}.$

Note. The situation covered by (a) of R_3 is of importance since it permits the treatment of a large class of cases where f and g are linear.

Definition. $f(x)$ is said to have a *regular maximum* at $\bar{x}$ subject to $g(x) \geqq 0$, $x \geqq 0$, if the three regularity conditions R_1, R_2, R_3 are satisfied at $\bar{x}$ and $\bar{x} \in O_{fg}$.

2.3.6. Theorem 3

If, for some $p > 0, x \in S_\rho(\bar{x}), \bar{x}$ a regular maximum[8] of $f(x)$ subject to $g(x) \geqq 0$ and $x \geqq 0, f$ and g are differentiable (with regard to x), and furthermore, when x^I is nonempty, have continuous second-order derivatives with regard to x^I, then, for all acceptable[9] η sufficiently large in each component.

(72) x^I is empty,

or

(73) $(x^I - \bar{x}^I)'_\eta \bar{\phi}_{x^I x^I}(x^I - \bar{x}^I) < 0 \qquad \text{if } x^{(21)} \geqq 0, x^I \neq \bar{x}^I,$

and for some $\rho' > 0$, and all $x \in S_{\rho'}(\bar{x})$ such that $x \geqq 0, x \neq \bar{x}$,

(74) $_\eta \phi[x, \bar{y}(\eta)] < _\eta \phi[\bar{x}, \bar{y}(\eta)]$

where $_\eta \phi$ and $\bar{y}(\eta)$ are defined as in theorem 1.

Note.[10] Theorem 3 is valid for f, g linear if x^{**} is empty (regardless of whether x^* is empty), provided the first two regularity conditions hold. However, if both x^* and x^{**} are empty, x^I is empty, and the theorem follows from the first case considered below. If x^{**} is empty while x^* is nonempty, use the

first two cases below together with (90) (since g^* is nonempty and t^{**} is empty).
Note that x^{**} is empty at the basic solutions of a linear programming problem.

2.3.7. Proof of theorem 3

First it is shown that (72) or (73) implies (74). Then it is shown that (72) or
(73) is true.

It can be seen that if theorem 3 is established for the case of $\{g^{\dagger\dagger}, g^0\}$
empty, then theorem 3 is also true if (i) $g^{\dagger\dagger}$ is not empty, and/or (ii) g^0 is not
empty but $_0\phi^I(x^I, y^\dagger)$ has a nonnegative saddle-point at $(\bar{x}^I, \bar{y}^\dagger)$, since in
either case $\bar{x}$ remains unchanged and the additional terms in the modified Lagrangian expression vanish at $\bar{y}$ [compare equations (36) and (43)].

Hence, with no loss of generality, we may henceforth assume $\{g^{\dagger\dagger}, g^0\}$ to be
empty, that is,

(75) $g^{[1]} = g^*$.

We now show that (72) or (73) implies (74), that is, that in a sufficiently
small neighborhood, if (72) or (73) is assumed to be valid and the inequalities
$x \geq 0$, $x \neq \bar{x}$ hold, the conclusion of (74) follows. We write ϕ instead of $_n\phi$
throughout. Also (72) or (73), $x \geq 0$, $x \neq \bar{x}$, is assumed.

Let

(76) $\xi = x - \bar{x}$

(77) $\xi^i = x^i - \bar{x}^i$, $i = I, II$.

First case: $\xi^{II} \neq 0$. By (20) and (N.14.2),

(78) $\bar{\phi}_x \cdot \xi = \bar{\phi}_{x^I} \cdot \xi^I + \bar{\phi}_{x^{II}} \cdot \xi^{II} < 0$.

But then the conclusion of (74) follows from the well-known "Fréchet"
property of differentials[11] which, as applied to the present case, states that,
given any $\sigma > 0$, there exists an $\epsilon > 0$ such that

(79) $\left| \dfrac{1}{|\xi|} [\phi(x, \bar{y}) - \phi(\bar{x}, \bar{y}) - \bar{\phi}_x \cdot \xi] \right| < \sigma$

if $|\xi| < \epsilon$.

Choose

(80) $\sigma = - \dfrac{1}{|\xi|} \bar{\phi}_x \cdot \xi$

which is positive by (78). Then, for a sufficiently small $|\xi|$, we have by (79)

(81) $\left| \dfrac{1}{|\xi|} [\phi(x, \bar{y}) - \phi(\bar{x}, \bar{y}) + \sigma] \right| < \sigma$

which implies

(82) $\dfrac{1}{|\xi|}\,[\phi(x,\bar{y}) - \phi(\bar{x},\bar{y})] < 0$

and hence the conclusion of (74).

If x^I is empty, this completes the proof of the theorem 3, since $x \neq \bar{x}$ then implies $\xi^{II} \neq 0$. If x^I is not empty, we must consider the

Second case: $\xi^{II} = 0.$ Since it is assumed that $x \neq \bar{x}$, $\xi^{II} = 0$ implies

(83) $\xi^I \neq 0.$

By virtue of the existence of the second derivatives of ϕ with regard to x^I (by definition of ϕ, and the assumptions concerning the second derivatives of f and g with regard to x^I) we have, by Taylor's theorem,

(84) $\phi(x,\bar{y}) - \phi(\bar{x},\bar{y}) = \bar{\phi}_{x^I} \cdot \xi^I + \tfrac{1}{2}\,(\xi^I)'\tilde{\phi}_{x^I x^I}\xi^I,$

where $\phi_{x^I x^I}$ denotes $\phi_{x^I x^I}$ evaluated at $x = \tilde{x}$, $\tilde{x} = \bar{x} + \theta\xi, 0 < \theta < 1$. It now suffices to note that $(\xi^I)'\phi_{x^I x^I}\xi^I$ is negative at $\bar{x}$ [since (72) or (73) is assumed to hold and its hypotheses are satisfied] and continuous in the neighborhood of $\bar{x}$ (by the hypotheses of the theorem concerning the second derivatives of f and g), so that, for a sufficiently small $|\xi^I|$, $(\xi^I)'\tilde{\phi}_{x^I x^I}\xi^I < 0$. Since $\bar{\phi}_{x^I} \cdot \xi^I = 0$ by (N.14.2), (74) follows.

We now show that (72) holds if x^I is nonempty.

First case: g^* *empty.*   By equation (75), $g^{[1]}$ is also empty. Hence, by (13)–(15) in theorem 1,

(85) $\bar{y}(\eta) = \bar{y}^{[2]}(0) = 0$

and, using (N.12),

(86) $_\eta\phi[x,\bar{y}(\eta)] = f(x).$

Since g^* is empty, we have $M^{*'} = 0$, and, therefore, the definition (55) of q applies, so that (since x^* is empty but x^I is not) t^{**} is not empty and

(87) $\bar{q}_{t^{**}t^{**}} = \bar{f}_{x^{**}x^{**}} = _\eta\bar{\phi}_{x^I x^I}.$

Equations (86) and (87), together with the third regularity condition R_3, yield (73) for a sufficiently small neighborhood of $\bar{x}$.

Second case: g^* *nonempty.*   Write

(88) $\psi(t,y) = \phi[r(t), \bar{x}^{II}, y]$

where $r(t)$ is defined in (67). (Where it is desired to indicate the dependence of ψ on η, we may write $_\eta\psi$ instead of ψ.)

Then, by (66), that is, R_1, we have

(89) $\bar{\psi}_{tt} = \psi_{tt}|_{t=\bar{t}} = (\bar{H}^{-1})'_\eta\bar{\phi}_{x^I x^I}\bar{H}^{-1}, \qquad \bar{t} = \{h^*(\bar{x}), \bar{x}^{**}\},$

since $_\eta\bar{\phi}_{x^I} = _0\bar{\phi}_{x^I} = 0$ by (20) and (N.14.2).

We shall now show that (73) is implied by

(90) $\tau'\overline{\psi}_{tt}\tau < 0$,   if $\tau^{(21)} \geq 0$,   and $\tau \neq 0$

where the partitioning of τ corresponds to that of t. We show later that (90) holds.

To see that (90) implies (73), let x^I satisfy the inequalities $x^{(21)} \geq 0$, $x^I \neq \overline{x}^I$. Choose

(91) $\begin{pmatrix} \tau^* \\ \tau^{**} \end{pmatrix} = \tau = \overline{H}(x^I - \overline{x}^I) = \begin{pmatrix} \overline{h}_{x^*}{}^* & \overline{h}_{x^{**}}{}^* \\ 0 & I \end{pmatrix} \begin{pmatrix} x^* - \overline{x}^* \\ x^{**} - \overline{x}^{**} \end{pmatrix}$.

Since, by (66), $\overline{H}$ is nonsingular, $x^I \neq \overline{x}^I$ implies $\tau \neq 0$. Also, (91) yields

(92) $\tau^{**} = x^{**} - \overline{x}^{**}$,

hence, in particular,

(93) $\tau^{(21)} = x^{(21)} - \overline{x}^{(21)}$.

But

(94) $\overline{x}^{(21)} = 0$,

since $x^{(21)}$ is a component of $x^{(2)}$ by (N.13), and $\overline{x}^{(2)} = 0$ by (N.6). Hence

(95) $\tau^{(21)} = x^{(21)}$

and thus $x^{(21)} \geq 0$ implies $\tau^{(21)} \geq 0$.

Having shown that the hypotheses of (73) imply those of (90), we see that the hypotheses of (73), together with the validity of the assertion in (90), yield

(96) $\tau'\overline{\psi}_{tt}\tau < 0$.

But, using in succession (91), (89), and simplifying, we have

(97) $\tau'\psi_{tt}\tau = (x^I - \overline{x}^I)'\overline{H}'\overline{\psi}_{tt}\overline{H}(x^I - \overline{x}^I)$

$= (x^I - \overline{x}^I)'\overline{H}'(\overline{H}^{-1})'_{\eta}\phi_{x^I x^I}\overline{H}^{-1}\overline{H}(x^I - \overline{x}^I)$

$= (x^I - \overline{x}^I)'_{\eta}\phi_{x^I x^I}(x^I - \overline{x}^I)$.

Formulas (96) and (97) yield the conclusion of (73). Thus it has been established that (90) implies (73). It remains to be shown that (90) is valid. It is convenient to write $\overline{\psi}_{tt}$ in the partitioned form

(98) $\overline{\psi}_{tt} = \begin{pmatrix} \overline{\psi}_{t^*t^*} & \overline{\psi}_{t^*t^{**}} \\ \overline{\psi}_{t^{**}t^*} & \overline{\psi}_{t^{**}t^{**}} \end{pmatrix} \equiv \begin{pmatrix} A & B \\ B' & C \end{pmatrix}$

where t^{**} may be empty; t^* is assumed nonempty, since the case of t^* empty was treated earlier.

It will now be shown that A, that is, $\overline{\psi}_{t^*t^*}$ [compare (98)], which depends on η, can be made negative definite by a suitable choice of η.

Recalling that $\mathfrak{m}^*$ denotes the set of indices of the components of g^*, and using (N.9) and (60), we see that, for $m \in \mathfrak{m}^*$,

(99) $\eta_m p_m(x) = 1 - t_m^{1+\eta_m}$

where t_m is a component of t^*.

Since, by theorem 1 and equation (75),

(100) $\bar{y}_m(\eta) = 0$ for $m \in \mathfrak{m} \sim \mathfrak{m}^*$,

we have, from the definitions of $\psi, q,$ and $_\eta\phi$ [equations (88), (70), and (N.12), respectively], and the preceding relations (99) and (100), the equality

(101) $\psi[t, \bar{y}(\eta)] = q(t) + \sum_{m \in \mathfrak{m}^*} [\bar{y}_m(\eta)] (1 - t_m^{1+\eta_m}).$

Writing

(102) $F = \bar{q}_{t^*t^*},$

we have, from (101) and the definition of A that

(103) $A = F - D,$

where $D = \|d_{m,m'}\|, m \in \mathfrak{m}^*, m' \in \mathfrak{m}^*,$ is a diagonal matrix [that is, $d_{m,m'} = 0$ for $m \neq m'$] with

(104) $d_{m,m} = [\bar{y}_m(\eta)] (1 + \eta_m) \eta_m = \bar{y}_m(0) \eta_m,$ $m \in \mathfrak{m}^*,$

where the second equality follows from (19).

Let λ denote the largest characteristic root of F. Since, by the second regularity condition R_2, $\bar{y}_m(0) > 0$ if $m \in \mathfrak{m}^*$, we may choose η_m^0, for each $m \in \mathfrak{m}^*$, to be a positive even integer satisfying

(105) $\eta_m^0 > \lambda/\bar{y}_m(0),$

so that

(106) $\min_{m \in \mathfrak{m}^*} d_{m,m} > \lambda$

for all acceptable $\eta_m \geq \eta_m^0$.

Then, for any $t^* \neq 0$, and each acceptable $\eta_m \geq \eta_m^0$, we have

(107) $t^{*\prime}Ft^* \leq \lambda t^{*\prime}t^* \equiv \lambda \sum_{m \in \mathfrak{m}^*} t_m^2 < \sum_{m \in \mathfrak{m}^*} d_{m,m} t_m^2$

$\equiv t^{*\prime}Dt^*,$

that is, $t^* \neq 0$ implies $t^{*\prime}(F - D) t^* < 0$ for all sufficiently large acceptable η, or A is negative definite for all sufficiently large acceptable η.

This suffices to establish (90) and, therefore, (73) if t^{**} is empty.

Now assume t^{**} not empty. Write

(108) $P = \begin{pmatrix} I & -A^{-1}B \\ 0 & I \end{pmatrix}$

and

(109) $\quad {}_\eta\Omega = P'{}_\eta\bar{\psi}_{tt}P.$

Then methods used to show that (90) implies (73) can be used to show that

(110) $\quad w'{}_\eta\Omega w < 0 \quad$ for $w \neq 0,\ w^{(21)} \geq 0$

implies (90). This is because

(111) $\quad P^{-1} = \begin{pmatrix} I & A^{-1}B \\ 0 & I \end{pmatrix}$

and, like its analogue $\bar{H}$, performs an identity transformation on t^{**}, so that the condition $t^{(21)} \geq 0$ is transformed into the condition $w^{(21)} \geq 0$. It remains to establish (110). Now from (109), (108), and (98), we have

(112) $\quad {}_\eta\Omega = \begin{pmatrix} A & 0 \\ 0 & C - B'A^{-1}B \end{pmatrix},$

so that $w'{}_\eta\Omega w = w^{*\prime}Aw^* + w^{**\prime}(C - B'A^{-1}B)w^{**}.$

Now, we may take A as negative definite, and hence, to establish (110), it will suffice to show that

(113) $\quad Q \equiv w^{**\prime}(C - B'A^{-1}B)w^{**} < 0, \quad$ if $w^{**} \neq 0,\ w^{(21)} \geq 0.$

Before doing so, we shall obtain an auxiliary result.

It will now be shown that the norm of A^{-1} can be made arbitrarily small by choosing η sufficiently large. It does not matter which of the many norms is used (see Bowker [6]). Note that, denoting by $N(X)$ the norm of the matrix X, we have $N(A + B) \leq N(A) + N(B),\ N(AB) \leq N(A)N(B)$; if all the elements of a matrix approach 0, so does its norm. If I denotes the identity matrix, $N(I) = 1$.

D^{-1} is a diagonal matrix whose nonzero elements approach zero for η large; hence, the same is true of $D^{-1}F$. Therefore, η can be chosen sufficiently large so that

(114) $\quad I - D^{-1}F$ is nonsingular,

and

(115) $\quad N(D^{-1}F) < 1.$

Following Waugh (see p. 148, [7]), we use the identity, valid because of (114),

(116) $\quad (I - D^{-1}F)^{-1} = I + (I - D^{-1}F)^{-1}D^{-1}F,$

and the properties of the norm to derive the relation,

(117) $\quad N[(I - D^{-1}F)^{-1}] \leq 1 + N[(I - D^{-1}F)^{-1}]\,N(D^{-1}F).$

From (117) and (115), it follows that

(118) $N[(D^{-1}F - I)^{-1}] \leqq \dfrac{1}{1 - N(D^{-1}F)}$.

Since $A = F - D = D(D^{-1}F - I)$, it follows that $A^{-1} = (D^{-1}F - I)^{-1}D^{-1}$, and hence

(119) $N(A^{-1}) \leqq N(D^{-1}) N[(D^{-1}F - I)^{-1}] \leqq \dfrac{N(D^{-1})}{1 - N(D^{-1}F)}$

which can be made arbitrarily small for η large.

Consider now the quadratic form Q in (113). We have shown, using (101), that

(120) $C = \bar{\psi}_{t^{**}t^{**}} = \bar{q}_{t^{**}t^{**}}$.

Hence the third regularity condition, R_3, implies

(121) $w^{**\prime}Cw^{**} < 0$ if $w^{**} \neq 0$, $w^{(21)} \geqq 0$.

As shown earlier $N(B'A^{-1}B) \leqq N(B') N(A^{-1}) N(B) = N(A^{-1})[N(B)]^2$ can be made arbitrarily small by choosing a large enough η. Now

(122) $|w^{**\prime}B'A^{-1}Bw^{**}| \leqq N(B'A^{-1}B) w^{**\prime}w^{**}$,

since the characteristic roots of a matrix are bounded in absolute value by its norm.

Also, denoting by μ the maximum of $w^{**\prime}Cw^{**}$ subject to $w^{**\prime}w^{**} = 1$, $w^{(21)} \geqq 0$, we have

(123) $w^{**\prime}Cw^{**} \leqq \mu w^{**\prime}w^{**}$

and, by (121), $\mu < 0$. With the aid of (122),

(124) $Q < [\mu + N(B'A^{-1}B)] w^{**\prime}w^{**}$ if $w^{**} \neq 0$, $w^{(21)} \geqq 0$.

By choosing η sufficiently large, so that

(125) $\mu + N(B'A^{-1}B) < 0$,

we establish (113), which, in turn, yields (110), (90), (73), and hence theorem 3.

Appendix I[12]

Let the first regularity condition R_1 hold. Consider $\bar{x}$ such that

(126) $g^{[1]}(\bar{x}) = 0$, $g^{[2]}(\bar{x}) > 0$, $\bar{x} \geqq 0$,

and x such that

(127) $\bar{g}_x^{[1]}(x - \bar{x}) \geqq 0$, $x^{(2)} - \bar{x}^{(2)} \geqq 0$,

where all inequalities are to be interpreted in the sense of (N.14). Define now the function $g^{\#}$ of $\bar{x}$ by

(128) $g^{\#}(x) = \{g^{\dagger}(x), x^{**}, x^{II}\}$

where x^{**} is defined by (58). Notice that assuming g^0 to be empty as in (47), $g^{\#}$, like x, has N dimensions. It follows that

$$(129) \quad g_x{}^{\#} = \begin{pmatrix} g_{x*}{}^{\dagger} & g_{x**}{}^{\dagger} & g_{xII}{}^{\dagger} \\ 0 & I & 0 \\ 0 & 0 & I \end{pmatrix}$$

and hence

(130) $|\bar{g}_x{}^{\#}| = |\bar{g}_{x*}{}^{\dagger}| \neq 0.$

Consider now the relation which associates with a real number a the values $\bar{\bar{x}}$ of x for which the equation

(131) $g^{\#}(\bar{\bar{x}}) = g^{\#}(\bar{x}) + a\bar{g}_x{}^{\#}(x - \bar{x})$

is satisfied. By virtue of the implicit function theorem, for sufficiently small values of a (131) defines $\bar{\bar{x}}$ as a (single-valued) differentiable function of a, say

(132) $\bar{\bar{x}} = \psi_1(a),$

such that

(133) $\psi_1(0) = \bar{x}.$

Differentiating (131) with respect to a and setting $a = 0$, we have

(134) $\bar{g}_x{}^{\#}\psi_1'(0) = \bar{g}_x{}^{\#}(x - \bar{x})$

and hence, because of (130),

(135) $\psi_1'(0) = x - \bar{x}.$

We shall now show that

(136) $\psi_1(a) \in C_g$ for $a \geq 0$, a sufficiently small.

By (131), (126), and (127)

(137) $g^{\dagger}(\bar{\bar{x}}) = a\bar{g}_x{}^{\dagger}(x - \bar{x}) \geq 0$ for $a \geq 0$.

It follows that

(138) $g^{[1]}(\bar{\bar{x}}) \geq 0$ for $a \geq 0$,

which together with

(139) $g^{[2]}[\psi_1(a)] \geq 0$ for a sufficiently small,

yields

(140) $g[\psi_1(a)] \geq 0$ for $a \geq 0$ sufficiently small.

Now, since x^* is a subvector of $x^{(1)}$, $x^{(2)}$ is a subvector of $\{x^{**}, x^{II}\}$, hence (127) and (131) imply

(141) $\bar{\bar{x}}^{(2)} = \psi_1{}^{(2)}(a) = \bar{x}^{(2)} + a(x^{(2)} - \bar{x}^{(2)}) \geq 0$ for $a \geq 0$

which, together with

(142) $\bar{\bar{x}}^{(1)} = \psi_1{}^{(1)}(a) \geq 0$ for a sufficiently small,

yields

(143) $\psi_1(a) \geq 0$ for $a \geq 0$, a sufficiently small.

In turn, (140) and (143) yield (136).

Now let us interpret "a sufficiently small" as $0 \leq a \leq \lambda$ where $\lambda > 0$ and define the function ψ by

(144) $\psi(\theta) = \psi_1(\lambda\theta)$ for all $0 \leq \theta \leq 1$.

Then

$$\psi(0) = \bar{x},$$
(145) $$\psi'(0) = \lambda\psi_1{}'(0) = \lambda(x - \bar{x}), \qquad \lambda > 0,$$
$$\psi(\theta) \in C_g, \qquad 0 \leq \theta \leq 1.$$

Since (145) are precisely the requirements of C.Q., it has been shown that R_1 implies C.Q.

Appendix II

We shall now show that, if the first two regularity conditions hold and if in a neighborhood of $\bar{x}$, f and g are assumed to possess continuous derivatives of second order with regard to x^I, then (71) is valid.

Let x^{**} be nonempty. Then, writing

(146) $\bar{t}^* = h^*(\bar{x}) = 1$ (a vector of 1's),

(147) $\bar{t}^{**} = \bar{x}^{**}$,

we have, using Taylor's theorem,

(148) $q(\bar{t}^*, t^{**}) - q(\bar{t}^*, \bar{t}^{**})$

$$= \bar{q}_{t**} \cdot (t^{**} - \bar{t}^{**}) + \tfrac{1}{2}(t^{**} - \bar{t}^{**})'\tilde{q}_{t***t**}(t^{**} - \bar{t}^{**}),$$

where "—" over a symbol denotes the evaluation at $t = \bar{t}$, while "~" over a symbol denotes evaluation at $t = \tilde{t}$, where $\tilde{t} = \bar{t} + \theta(t^{**} - \bar{t}^{**})$, $0 < \theta < 1$. Now suppose it has been shown that (a) $q(\bar{t}^*, t^{**})$ has, as a function of t^{**}, subject to the constraint $t^{(21)} \geq 0$, a local maximum at $t^{**} = \bar{t}^{**}$, and (b) $\bar{q}_{t**} = 0$. From (a) it follows that, in a sufficiently small neighborhood, the left member of (148) is nonpositive if $t^{(21)} \geq 0$. But then, using (b), we see that the quadratic form in the right member of (148) is nonpositive. Since, by hypothesis, $q_{t^{**}t^{**}}$ is a continuous function of t^{**}, we have, for $t^{(21)} \geq 0$, and in a sufficiently small neighborhood of $\bar{t}$,

(149) $(t^{**} - \bar{t}^{**}) \bar{q}_{t^{**}t^{**}} (t^{**} - \bar{t}^{**}) \geq 0$

which is the desired result (71). Hence it remains to prove (a) and (b).

(a) $q(\bar{t}^*, t^{**})$ has, as a function of t^{**}, subject to $t^{(21)} \geq 0$, a local maximum at $t^{**} = \bar{t}^{**}$.

It follows from the remarks at the beginning of the discussion of the second regularity condition that $f(x^I, 0)$, as a function of x^I, has a local maximum at $x^I = \bar{x}^I$, subject to the constraints

(150) $g^\dagger(x^I, 0) = 0, \quad x^{(21)} \geq 0$.

Hence, subject to the same constraints, $q(t)$ has a local maximum at $\bar{t}$. Now we must distinguish the two ways in which the "milder" (46) second regularity condition R_2 may be satisfied.

First way. $_0\phi^I(x^I, y^\dagger)$ has a nonnegative saddle-point at $(\bar{x}^I, \bar{y}^\dagger)$, that is, locally, since $\bar{y}^0 = 0$ by (43),

(151) $f(x^I, 0) + \bar{y}^* \cdot g^*(x^I, 0) \leq f(\bar{x}^I, 0) + \bar{y}^* \cdot g^*(\bar{x}^I, 0)$

for all x^I such that $x^{(21)} \geq 0$.

But $g^*(\bar{x}^I, 0) = 0$ because of (150), and $g^*(x^I, 0)$ in the left member of (151) vanishes for $t^* = \bar{t}^*$. Hence (151) yields, locally and for $t^{(21)} \geq 0$,

(152) $f[r^*(\bar{t}^*, t^{**}), t^{**}, 0] \leq f[r^*(\bar{t}^*, \bar{t}^{**}), \bar{t}^{**}, 0]$

which means precisely that $q(\bar{t}^*, t^{**})$ has a local maximum at $\bar{t}^{**}$ subject only to $t^{(21)} \geq 0$.

Second way. g^0 is empty. In this case (150) is equivalent to

(153) $g^*(x^I, 0) = 0$,

(154) $x^{(21)} \geq 0$.

But (153) is necessarily satisfied if $t^* = \bar{t}^*$ and hence can be disregarded. Since $q(t)$ was seen to have a local maximum at $\bar{t}$ subject to (150), it follows that $q(\bar{t}^*, t^{**})$ will have a local maximum at $\bar{t}^{**}$ subject only to $t^{(21)} \geq 0$.

(b) $\bar{q}_{t^{**}} = 0$.

We have

(155) $\bar{q}_{t^{**}} = \bar{f}_{x^*} \bar{r}_{t^{**}}^* + \bar{f}_{x^{**}}$.

We now evaluate the three expressions on the right-hand side of (155). We start with $\bar{r}_{t^{**}}^*$. Noting that

(156) $g^* \{ [r^*(\bar{t}^*, t^{**}), t^{**}], 0 \} = 0 \qquad \text{for all } t^{**},$

we obtain by differentiation with respect to t^{**}, using (60) and (69), and evaluating at $t = \bar{t}$,

(157) $\bar{g}_{x*}{}^*\bar{r}_{t**}{}^* + \bar{g}_{t**}{}^* = 0;$

in virtue of R_1 this can be solved yielding

(158) $\bar{r}_{t**}{}^* = -(\bar{g}_{x*}{}^*)^{-1}\bar{g}_{t**}{}^*.$

To find $\bar{f}_{x*}, \bar{f}_{x**}$, we write the condition that $_0\bar{\phi}^I x^I = 0$, using equation (41) in the form

(159) $\begin{aligned}\bar{f}_{x*} + \bar{g}_{x*}{}^*\bar{y}^* &= 0, \\ \bar{f}_{x**} + \bar{g}_{x**}{}^*\bar{y}^* &= 0.\end{aligned}$

The terms involving g^0 vanish, of course.

Substituting (159) and (158) into (155), we have

(160) $\begin{aligned}\bar{q}_{t**} &= (-\bar{y}^* \cdot g_{x**}{}^*) + (-\bar{y}^* \cdot g_{x*}{}^*)[-(\bar{g}_{x*}{}^*)^{-1}\bar{g}_{x**}{}^*] \\ &= (-\bar{y}^* \cdot \bar{g}_{x**}{}^*) + (\bar{y}^* \cdot \bar{g}_{x**}{}^*) = 0.\end{aligned}$

This completes the proof of (71).

Notes

1   Most of the work of this paper was done under the auspices of The RAND Corporation, with additional support and assistance from the Cowles Commission for Research in Economics and the Office of Naval Research.
2   In [1] our f and g are respectively written as g and F. The symbol in [1] for the Lagrange multiplier (our y) is u.
3   This restriction "is designed to rule out singularities on the boundary of the constraint set, such as an outward-pointing 'cusp'" (see p. 483 in [1]). It should be noted, however, that because of (4), C.Q. is a property of g, not merely of C_g. Thus $g(x) \equiv -(x - 1)^3$, x one-dimensional, lacks C.Q., while $g(x) \equiv -(x - 1)$, with the same C_g, does have it.
4   A function $f(x)$ is said to be concave if

$$(1 - \theta) f(x^0) + \theta f(x) \leq f[(1 - \theta) x^0 + \theta x]$$

for all $0 \leq \theta \leq 1$ and all x^0 and x in the region where $f(x)$ is defined (see [1], pp. 10–11).
5   See also Hurwicz [9], pp. VIII–2–6.
6   In many applied problems, $h_m(x) \geq 0$ for all m and all $x \geq 0$. It was pointed out by Dr. Masao Fukuoka that, in the absence of such an assumption, the requirement of nonnegativity of the components of η is insufficient for the proof of the theorem.
7   $\bar{y}_m(0) = \bar{y}$ in Kuhn-Tucker theorem 1 (see section 2.3.1).
8   The term "regular maximum" is defined at the end of section 2.3.5.
9   The term "acceptable" is defined at the beginning of section 2.3.2.

10 The desirability of explicit treatment of the linear case was emphasized by Dr. Masao Fukuoka.
11 See Hille [10], p. 72, definition 4.3.4, equation (iii).
12 This appendix parallels lemma 76.1 in Bliss [11].

References

[1] H. W. Kuhn and A. W. Tucker, "Nonlinear programming," *Proceedings of the Second Berkeley Symposium on Mathematical Statistics and Probability*, Berkeley and Los Angeles, University of California Press, 1951, pp. 481–492.

[2] T. C. Koopmans, "Analysis of production as an efficient combination of activities," edited by T. C. Koopmans, *Activity Analysis of Production and Allocation*, Cowles Commission Monograph No. 13, New York, John Wiley and Sons, 1951, pp. 33–97.

[3] K. J. Arrow and L. Hurwicz, "A gradient method for approximating saddle-points and constrained maxima," P-223, The RAND Corporation, 1951 (hectographed).

[4] G. B. Dantzig, "Maximization of a linear function of variables subject to linear inequalities," *Activity Analysis of Production and Allocation*, edited by T. C. Koopmans, Cowles Commission Monograph No. 13, New York, John Wiley and Sons, 1951, pp. 339–347.

[5] P. A. Samuelson, *Foundations of Economic Analysis*, Cambridge, Harvard University Press, 1948.

[6] A. H. Bowker, "On the norm of a matrix," *Annals of Math. Stat.*, Vol. 18 (1947), pp. 285–288.

[7] F. V. Waugh, "Inversion of the Leontief matrix by power series," *Econometrica*, Vol. 18 (1950), pp. 142–154.

[8] P. A. Samuelson, "Market mechanisms and maximization," P-69, The RAND Corporation, 1949 (hectographed).

[9] L. Hurwicz, "Programming in general spaces," Cowles Commission Discussion Paper, Economics No. 2109, 1954 (hectographed).

[10] E. Hille, *Functional Analysis and Semi-Groups*, New York, American Mathematical Society Colloquium Publications, Vol. 31, 1948.

[11] G. A. Bliss, *Lectures on the Calculus of Variations*, Chicago, The University of Chicago Press, 1946.

A general saddle point result for constrained optimization

K. J. ARROW,[1]
F. J. GOULD,[2]
S. M. HOWE[2]

1. Introduction

In the context of nonlinear programming theory, the characterization of a constrained optimum as a saddle point of the Lagrangian function is known to be heavily dependent upon convexity properties of the underlying problem. In particular, for a concave program satisfying the Slater condition with a solution x^*, there is a u^* such that x^*, u^* is a saddle point of the Lagrangian function. Conversely, each saddle point x^*, u^* of the Lagrangian function yields a solution x^* to the concave program. In 1956, motivated by game-theoretical and economic implications, Arrow and Hurwicz [1] demonstrated that the concavity assumptions could be relaxed via a modified Lagrangian approach. The results in [1] were presented in terms of a specific modified Lagrangian formulation. In 1958, in a discussion of gradient methods, Arrow and Solow [2, Ch. 11] presented additional saddle point results in terms of a different modified Lagrangian function. Another specific result along the same lines was presented by Gould and Howe [5] in 1971.

In this work we both generalize and simplify the above presentations. Conditions will be given under which, for a nonconcave (as well as a concave) program, a quite general function P (i.e., a parameterized class of functions) will possess the property that local saddle points and program solutions correspond. Moreover, the function P will be concave (locally) in the primal and convex in the dual variables just as in the concave case. Specific realizations of this P-function will be the modified Lagrangian expressions discussed by the above-mentioned authors. The results presented herein serve not only to unify the above works. Certain general properties of multiplier functions are postulated which help to explain why these palpably different avenues in fact lead to special cases of the same general result.

While this contribution has theoretic interest in programming and games, there is also the suggestion of numerical application to the computation of solutions for nonconvex problems. Previous literature indicates a general interest in this approach. For example as early as 1958, Arrow, Hurwicz, and Uzawa [2, Chs. 6–8] described small step gradient methods for saddle point computation. In 1970, Rockafellar [8] noted that the saddle point approach lends insight into the underlying dual structure of the problem. He also discussed the theoretic versatility of this approach, proposed a new modified Lagrangian function (which is also included in the P-class), and noted the lack of computational development. In 1971, Martinet [6] proposed new computational techniques for saddle point approximation in a convex environment. In a 1972 dissertation, Merrill [7] applied complementary pivot theory on pseudomanifolds to the solution of min-max problems via Kakutani fixed points. Also in a 1972 dissertation, Buys [3] discussed computational procedures for a dual algorithm approach to constrained optimization problems. The approach, in common with all dual approaches, essentially involves the computation of a saddle point of our P-function.

In summary it can be stated that the concave-convex properties of the P-function will serve to legitimize the (local) use of the computing methods referred to above. However, it must also be stated that at present the computational evidence on the practical feasibility of the saddle point approach is exceedingly scarce. Even tentative conclusions will have to await further applied results.

2. Reduction to an unconstrained problem

We formulate the nonlinear program with both equality and inequality constraints:

(P) $\max_{x \in \mathbf{R}^n} f(x)$.

subject to $g_i(x) \leqslant 0$, $i = 1, \ldots, m$,
$h_j(x) = 0$, $j = 1, \ldots, p$.

Throughout the paper it is assumed that all functions in (P) are twice differentiable.

Corresponding to the inequality constraints (the correspondence will be clear from the P-function formulation), let $\lambda(\xi, \eta, \alpha): \mathbf{R} \times \mathbf{R}_+ \times \mathbf{R}_{++} \to \mathbf{R}$ be a multiplier function,[3] continuous in ξ, where we employ the notation $\partial \lambda / \partial \xi = \lambda_1$, $\partial^2 \lambda / \partial \xi^2 = \lambda_{11}$. Impose the following properties on λ:

(i)   for any $\alpha > 0$, $\lambda_1(0, \eta, \alpha) = \eta$ for every $\eta \geqslant 0$;
(ii) for any $\alpha > 0$, $\lambda_1(\xi, 0, \alpha) = 0$ for every $\xi < 0$;
(iii) for each fixed $\eta > 0$, $\lambda_{11}(0, \eta, \alpha) \to \infty$ as $\alpha \to \infty$.

Corresponding to the equality constraints, let $\varphi(\xi, \eta, \alpha): \mathbf{R} \times \mathbf{R} \times \mathbf{R}_{++} \to \mathbf{R}$ be a multiplier function such that

(iv) for any $\alpha > 0$, $\varphi_1(0, \eta, \alpha) = \eta$ for every $\eta \in \mathbf{R}$;
(v)   for each fixed $\eta \in \mathbf{R}$, $\varphi_{11}(0, \eta, \alpha) \to \infty$ as $\alpha \to \infty$.

Note. It is assumed that all above-mentioned derivatives exist; also, (ii) implies that, for any $\alpha > 0$, $\xi < 0$, $\lambda_{11}(\xi, 0, \alpha) = 0$.

Examples of the λ functions are

M1 $\eta[(\xi + 1)^{1+\alpha} - 1]/(1 + \alpha)$, α an even integer;

M2 $(\eta/\alpha)[\exp(\alpha \xi) - 1]$;

$$M3 \quad \begin{cases} -\eta/4\alpha, & \xi \leq -1/2\alpha, \\ \eta\alpha\xi^2 + \eta\xi, & \xi > -1/2\alpha, \end{cases}$$

$$M4 \quad \begin{cases} \eta^2/4\alpha, & \xi \leq -\eta/2\alpha, \\ \alpha\xi^2 + \eta\xi, & \xi > -\eta/2\alpha. \end{cases}$$

An example of the φ function is

M5 $\alpha\xi^2 + \eta\xi$.

Now define the modified Lagrangian function $P: \mathbf{R}'' \times \mathbf{R}_+{}^m \times \mathbf{R}^p \times \mathbf{R}_{++} \to \mathbf{R}$ as follows:

$$P(x, \mu, \psi, \alpha) = f(x) - \Sigma_{i=1}^m \lambda(g_i(x), \mu_i, \alpha) - \Sigma_{j=1}^p \varphi(h_j(x), \psi_j, \alpha).$$

If the multiplier functions are chosen as in M1 or M5, one obtains, respectively, the P-functions studied by Arrow and Hurwicz [1] and by Arrow and Solow [2, Ch. 11]. By the choice M2, one obtains the P-function studied by Gould and Howe [5]. The choice M4 appears to have been first discussed by Rockafellar [8].

The following result, sometimes referred to as Finsler's Lemma, will be used (see [4], or the appendix to this paper).

Lemma 2.1 (Finsler's Lemma).   Let Q be a real $n \times n$ matrix and let L be a real $m \times n$ matrix. Suppose $z^\mathrm{T} Q z < 0$ for every $z \neq 0$ such that $Lz = 0$. Then, for all α sufficiently large, $z^\mathrm{T}[Q - \alpha L^\mathrm{T} L] z < 0$ for all $z \neq 0$. That is, if Q is negative definite on the null space of L, then for α sufficiently large $Q - \alpha L^\mathrm{T} L$ is negative definite on the whole space.

Let $L(x, \mu, \psi) = f(x) - \langle \mu, g(x) \rangle - \langle \psi, h(x) \rangle$, which is the usual Lagrangian function.

The first result of this paper is the following:

Theorem 2.2.   Suppose (x^*, μ^*, ψ^*) satisfy the second-order sufficiency conditions for x^* to be an isolated local solution to (P) and suppose strict complementarity holds. That is, we assume

(a) $\nabla L(x^*, \mu^*, \psi^*) = 0$:
(b) $g_i(x^*) \leq 0, i = 1, \ldots, m, h_j(x^*) = 0, j = 1, \ldots, p$;
(c) $\mu_i^* \geq 0, \mu_i^* > 0$ if and only if $g_i(x^*) = 0, i = 1, \ldots, m$;
(d) $y^\mathrm{T} \nabla^2 L(x^*, \mu^*, \psi^*) y < 0$ for every nonzero y such that $y^\mathrm{T} \nabla g_i(x^*) = 0$, $i \in I$, and $y^\mathrm{T} \nabla h_j(x^*) = 0, j = 1, \ldots, p$, where I denotes the active inequality constraints, that is, $I = \{i: g_i(x^*) = 0\}$.

Then:

(1) If α is sufficiently large, the function $P(x, \mu^*, \psi^*, \alpha): \mathbf{R}'' \to \mathbf{R}$ has an unconstrained isolated local maximum at x^*;

(2) if α is sufficiently large, and if for all i the expressions $\lambda_{11}(\xi, \eta, \alpha)$ are continuous at the points $(g_i(x^*), \mu_i^*, \alpha)$ and the expressions $\varphi_{11}(\xi, \eta, \alpha)$ continuous at the points $(0, \psi_i^*, \alpha)$, then, for all (μ, ψ) sufficiently close to (μ^*, ψ^*), $P(x, \mu, \psi, \alpha)$ is strictly concave in x close to x^*.[4]

Proof. For any $\alpha > 0$,

$$\nabla P(x^*, \mu^*, \psi^*, \alpha) = \nabla f(x^*) - \Sigma_{i=1}^m \lambda_1(g_i(x^*), \mu_i^*, \alpha) \nabla g_i(x^*)$$
$$- \Sigma_{j=1}^p \varphi_1(h_j(x^*), \psi_j^*, \alpha) \nabla h_j(x^*)$$
$$= \nabla f(x^*) - \Sigma_I \mu_i^* \nabla g_i(x^*) - \Sigma_{j=1}^p \psi_j^* \nabla h_j(x^*)$$
$$= \nabla L(x^*, \mu^*, \psi^*) = 0 \qquad \text{by (a)}.$$

$$\nabla^2 P(x^*, \mu^*, \psi^*, \alpha) = \nabla^2 f(x^*) - \Sigma_{i=1}^m [\lambda_1(g_i(x^*), \mu_i^*, \alpha) \nabla^2 g_i(x^*)$$
$$+ \lambda_{11}(g_i(x^*), \mu_i^*, \alpha) \nabla g_i(x^*) \nabla^T g_i(x^*)]$$
$$- \Sigma_{j=1}^p [\varphi_1(h_j(x^*), \psi_j^*, \alpha) \nabla^2 h_j(x^*)$$
$$+ \varphi_{11}(h_j(x^*), \psi_j^*, \alpha) \nabla h_j(x^*) \nabla^T h_j(x^*)]$$
$$= \nabla^2 L(x^*, \mu^*, \psi^*) - \Sigma_I \lambda_{11}(g_i(x^*), \mu_i^*, \alpha) \nabla g_i(x^*)$$
$$\cdot \nabla^T g_i(x^*) - \Sigma_{j=1}^p \varphi_{11}(h_j(x^*), \psi_j^*, \alpha) \nabla h_j(x^*)$$
$$\cdot \nabla h_j^T(x^*).$$

Defining

$$J^T = [\nabla g_i(x^*), \dots, i \in I, \nabla h_1(x^*), \dots, \nabla h_p(x^*)],$$

note that $y^T \nabla^2 L(x^*, \mu^*, \psi^*) y < 0$ for every nonzero y such that $Jy = 0$, by (d). By Lemma 2.1, $\nabla^2 L(x^*, \mu^*, \psi^*) - kJ^T J$ is negative definite for some scalar k sufficiently large. Now if α is sufficiently large, we can obtain

$$\lambda_{11}(g_i(x^*), \mu_i^*, \alpha) > k \qquad \text{for each } i \in I,$$

$$\varphi_{11}(h_j(x^*), \psi_j^*, \alpha) > k \qquad \text{for each } j = 1, \dots, p,$$

whence

$$\nabla^2 P(x^*, \mu^*, \psi^*, \alpha) = \nabla^2 L(x^*, \mu^*, \psi^*) - kJ^T J$$
$$+ \Sigma_I [k - \lambda_{11}(g_i(x^*), \mu_i^*, \alpha)] \nabla g_i(x^*) \nabla g_i^T(x^*)$$
$$+ \Sigma_{j=1}^p [k - \varphi_{11}(h_j(x^*), \psi_j^*, \alpha)] \nabla h_j(x^*) \nabla h_j^T(x^*),$$

which, for all α sufficiently large, is negative definite, since large α implies that each of the dyadic terms has a negative coefficient and is hence negative semi-definite. By continuity, $\nabla^2 P(x, \mu, \psi, \alpha)$ is negative definite for any (x, μ, ψ) sufficiently close to (x^*, μ^*, ψ^*).

3. A local saddle point result

To obtain the main result, it is necessary to impose the further assumptions on λ:

(vi) if $\alpha > 0, \eta \geqslant 0$, then $\lambda(0, \eta, \alpha) = 0$ and $\lambda(\xi, \eta, \alpha)$ is monotonically nondecreasing over $\xi \in (-\infty, 0]$; if $\alpha > 0$ and $\xi \in \mathbf{R}$, then $\lambda(\xi, \eta, \alpha)$ is concave in $\eta \geqslant 0$;

(vii)   if $\alpha > 0$, $\eta \in \mathbf{R}$, then $\varphi(0, \eta, \alpha) = 0$; if $\alpha > 0$ and $\xi \in \mathbf{R}$, then $\varphi(\xi, \eta, \alpha)$ is concave in $\eta \in \mathbf{R}$.

It should be noted that conditions (vi) and (vii) are satisfied by the examples M1-M5.

Theorem 3.1.   If the multiplier functions satisfy properties (i)-(vii), then under the conditions of Theorem 2.2, if α is sufficiently large,

$$P(x, \mu^*, \psi^*, \alpha) \leqslant P(x^*, \mu^*, \psi^*, \alpha) \leqslant P(x^*, \mu, \psi, \alpha)$$

for every x in some neighborhood N of x^* and every point $(\mu, \psi) \in \mathbf{R}_+^m \times \mathbf{R}^p$. Furthermore, for all (μ, ψ) sufficiently close to (μ^*, ψ^*), $P(x, \mu, \psi, \alpha)$ is strictly concave in x close to x^*, and, for each $x \in \mathbf{R}^n$, $P(x, \mu, \psi, \alpha)$ is convex in $(\mu, \psi) \in \mathbf{R}_+^m \times \mathbf{R}^p$.

Proof.   In view of Theorem 2.2, we need only prove the second inequality and the convexity of P in (μ, ψ). Since $g_i(x^*) = 0, i \in I, h_j(x^*) = 0, j = 1, \ldots,$ p, it follows from (vi), (vii) that, for $(\mu, \psi) \in \mathbf{R}_+^m \times \mathbf{R}^p$,

$$P(x^*, \mu, \psi, \alpha) = f(x^*) - \Sigma_{i \notin I} \lambda(g_i(x^*), \mu_i, \alpha).$$

For $i \notin I$, $\mu_i^* = 0$. Integration of (ii) from $g_i(x^*)$, to 0, together with (vi), shows that $\lambda(g_i(x^*), \mu_i^*, \alpha) = 0$ for $i \notin I$. Thus the complementary slackness conditions $\lambda(g_i(x^*), \mu_i^*, \alpha) = 0, i = 1, \ldots, m$, hold. From the monotonicity property in (vi), for each i, $\lambda(g_i(x^*), \mu_i, \alpha) \leqslant \lambda(0, \mu_i, \alpha) = 0$ for any $\mu_i \geqslant 0$. It follows immediately that $P(x^*, \mu^*, \psi^*, \alpha) \leqslant P(x^*, \mu, \psi, \alpha)$ for all $(\mu, \psi) \in \mathbf{R}_+^m \times \mathbf{R}^p$. The convexity of P in (μ, ψ) is directly implied by (vi), (vii).

Finally, under assumptions (i)-(vii), plus two additional multiplier assumptions, it can be shown that, given a fixed α, if the triple $(x^*, \mu^*, \psi^*) \in \mathbf{R}^n \times \mathbf{R}_+^m \times \mathbf{R}^p$ is a local (global) saddle point of $P(x, \mu, \psi, \alpha)$, then x^* is a local (global) solution to the nonlinear program (P).[5] In particular, assume:

(viii)   for any $\alpha > 0, \xi > 0, \lambda(\xi, \eta, \alpha)$ is strictly increasing in $\eta \geqslant 0$;

 (ix)   for any $\alpha > 0, \xi \neq 0, \varphi(\xi, \eta, \alpha)$ is either strictly increasing or strictly decreasing in $\eta \in \mathbf{R}$.

Again it can be noted that the functions M1-M5 satisfy the above two conditions.

Theorem 3.2.   Let the multiplier functions satisfy properties (i)-(ix), and suppose that, for some α, the function $P(x, \mu, \psi, \alpha)$ has a saddle point at (x^*, μ^*, ψ^*) for x in some convex set N, $(\mu, \psi) \in \mathbf{R}_+^m \times \mathbf{R}^p$. Then x^* is a solution to the nonlinear program (P) further constrained by the requirement $x \in N$,

Remark 3.3.   If N is a neighborhood of x, then x^* is a local solution to (P); if $N = \mathbf{R}^n$, then x^* is a global solution.

Proof of Theorem 3.2.   The hypothesis states that

$$P(x, \mu^*, \psi^*, \alpha) \leqslant P(x^*, \mu^*, \psi^*, \alpha) \leqslant P(x^*, \mu, \psi, \alpha)$$

for all $x \in N$ and every point $(\mu, \psi) \in \mathbf{R}_+^m \times \mathbf{R}^p$. Transposing the left-hand inequality immediately gives, for all $x \in N, f(x^*) \geqslant f(x) + A$, where

$$A = \Sigma_{j=1}^m \left[\lambda(g_i(x^*), \mu_i^*, \alpha) - \lambda(g_i(x), \mu_i^*, \alpha) \right]$$
$$+ \Sigma_{j=1}^p \left[\varphi(h_j(x^*), \psi_j^*, \alpha) - \varphi(h_j(x), \psi_j^*, \alpha) \right].$$

If it can be shown that x^* is feasible and that A is nonnegative for every x in the intersection of N with the constraint set, the result will be proved. Note that the right-hand saddle point inequality yields

R $\quad \Sigma_{i=1}^m \lambda(g_i(x^*), \mu_i, \alpha) + \Sigma_{j=1}^p \varphi(h_j(x^*), \psi_j, \alpha)$

$$\leqslant \Sigma_{i=1}^m \lambda(g_i(x^*), \mu_i^*, \alpha) + \Sigma_{j=1}^p \varphi(h_j(x^*), \psi_j^*, \alpha).$$

Since the left-hand side is a sum of functions of different independent variables, R holds for all $(\mu, \psi) \in \mathbf{R}_+^m \times \mathbf{R}^p$ if and only if

$$\lambda(g_i(x^*), \mu_i, \alpha) \leqslant \lambda(g_i(x^*), \mu_i^*, \alpha) \qquad \text{for all } \mu_i \geqslant 0, \ i = 1, \dots, m;$$
$$\varphi(h_j(x^*), \psi_j, \alpha) \leqslant \varphi(h_j(x^*), \psi_j^*, \alpha) \qquad \text{for all } \psi_j \in \mathbf{R}, j = 1, \dots, p.$$

But from (viii) and (ix), these inequalities can hold only if $g_i(x^*) \leqslant 0, i = 1, \dots, m, h_j(x^*) = 0, j = 1, \dots, p$, so that x^* is feasible. From the first of these inequalities, with $\mu_i = 0$, and (vi),

$$\lambda(g_i(x^*), 0, \alpha) \leqslant \lambda(g_i(x^*), \mu_i^*, \alpha) \leqslant \lambda(0, \mu_i^*, \alpha) = 0;$$

but, as already shown in the proof of Theorem 3.1, $\lambda(g_i(x^*), 0, \alpha) = 0$ if $g_i(x^*) \leqslant 0$. Hence the complementary slackness conditions

$$\lambda(g_i(x^*), \mu_i^*, \alpha) = 0, \qquad i = 1, \dots, m$$

hold. [Since $\mu_i^* g_i(x^*) = 0$ is not here assumed, the demonstration of complementary slackness is slightly more involved than in Theorem 3.1.] For any x in the intersection of N and the constraint set, $h_j(x) = 0 = h_j(x^*)$. Therefore,

$$A = - \Sigma_{i=1}^m \lambda(g_i(x), \mu_i^*, \alpha)$$

for all such x. But from (vi) and the condition that $g_i(x) \leqslant 0, \lambda(g_i(x), \mu_i^*, \alpha) \leqslant \lambda(0, \mu_i^*, \alpha) = 0$, so that $A \geqslant 0$, as was to be proved.

We thus have a saddle point theory for nonconvex programs which completely parallels that for convex programs conjoined with the usual Lagrangian formulation.

Appendix

We here give a proof of Lemma 2.1 (Finsler's Lemma). This result will be corollary to the following more general statement.

Theorem A.1.   If $f(x)$ and $g(x)$ are continuous functions on a compact set K and $g(x) \geqslant 0$ for all $x \in K$, then the following two statements are equivalent in K:

(a) $f(x) > 0$ whenever $g(x) = 0$;
(b)   for all α sufficiently large, $f(x) + \alpha g(x) > 0$ for all x.

   Proof.   Trivially (b) implies (a). We establish the converse.
   Let K' be the subset of K on which $f(x) \leqslant 0$. Clearly K' is compact. Since $g(x) \geqslant 0$ on K, we have

(A.1) $f(x) + \alpha g(x) \geqslant f(x) > 0$ for all $x \in K \backslash K'$ and all $\alpha \geqslant 0$.

If K' is empty, there is nothing left to prove. If K' is nonempty, let μ_f and μ_g denote the minima of f and g, respectively, on K'. Then $\mu_g = g(x^*)$ for some $x^* \in K'$. By hypothesis $g(x^*) \geqslant 0$. But if $g(x^*) = 0$, then, by (a), $f(x^*) > 0$, contrary to the definition of K'. Hence, $g(x^*) > 0$, or

(A.2) $\mu_g > 0$.

Now clearly for all α sufficiently large, we have

(A.3) $\mu_f + \alpha \mu_g > 0$.

Then, for any $x \in K'$, by definition of a minimum,

(A.4) $f(x) + \alpha g(x) \geqslant \mu_f + \alpha \mu_g > 0$ for all α sufficiently large.

This, together with (A.1) implies (b).
   To obtain Finsler's Lemma from this result, assume that $x^T Q x < 0$ for every $x \neq 0$ such that $Lx = 0$. In the above theorem, take $f(x) = -x^T Q x$, $g(x) = x^T L^T L x$, and take K to be the unit sphere $x^T x = 1$. Then, by assumption, condition (a) in the theorem is satisfied. Hence, from (b), for all α sufficiently large, $x^T (Q - \alpha L^T L) x < 0$ for $x^T x = 1$ and, hence, whenever $x \neq 0$.

Notes

1   Sponsored in part by the Office of Naval Research under Grant No. N00014-67A-0298-0019 (NR047-004).
2   Sponsored in part by the Office of Naval Research under Grant No. N00014-67A-0321-0003 (NR047-096).
3   The $\mathbf{R}_+^k$ will denote the nonnegative orthant of $\mathbf{R}^k$; the $\mathbf{R}_{++}^k$ denotes the positive orthant of $\mathbf{R}^k$.
4   Note that under the strict complementarity conditions the additional continuity postulates hold for functions M1–M5.
5   The local/global distinction is with respect to the x-variables. In both cases (local and global) the values of μ are always constrained to $\mathbf{R}_+^m$, while the values of ψ are unconstrained in $\mathbf{R}^p$.

References

[1]   K. J. Arrow and L. Hurwicz, "Reduction of constrained maxima to saddle-point problems," this volume, II.5, pp. 154–177.

[2]   K. J. Arrow, L. Hurwicz, H. Uzawa, *Studies in linear and nonlinear programming* (Stanford University Press, Stanford, Calif., 1958).

[3]   J. D. Buys, "Dual algorithms for constrained optimization problems," Dissertation, University of Leiden, Leiden (1972).

[4]   G. Debreu, "Definite and semidefinite quadratic forms," *Econometrica* 20 (1952) 295–300.

[5]   F. J. Gould and S. M. Howe, "A new result on interpreting Lagrange multipliers as dual variables," Institute of Statistics Mimeo Series No. 738, Dept. of Statistics, University of North Carolina, Chapel Hill, N.C. (January 1971).

[6]   B. Martinet, "Dual methods for the approximate solution of convex constrained optimization problems – applications," Working Paper, Département d'Informatique, Centre d'Etudes Nucléaires de Grenoble, Grenoble (1971).

[7]   O. H. Merrill, "Applications and extensions of an algorithm that computes fixed points of certain upper semi-continuous point to set mappings," Dissertation, University of Michigan, Ann Arbor, Mich. (1972).

[8]   R. T. Rockafellar, "New applications of duality in nonlinear programming," presented at 7th International Symposium on Mathematical Programming, The Hague (September 1970).

Convexity of asymptotic average production possibility sets

LEONID HURWICZ
HIROFUMI UZAWA

Let there exist a denumerable set $S = \{s\}$ of firms, labeled $s = 1, 2, \ldots, ad\ inf.$ For each firm s, the production processes are described by the production possibility set Y^s; it will be assumed that each Y^s is a nonempty subset of the (m-dimensional) commodity space $E = E^m$.

We define the (*asymptotic*) *average production possibility set* Y as the set of all commodity bundles y for which there exist a sequence of firms $\langle s_1, s_2, \ldots \rangle$ and a sequence of vectors $\langle y^{s_1}, y^{s_2}, \ldots \rangle$ such that $\{s_1, s_2, \ldots\} \subseteq S$ and $s_1 <$

$s_2 < \cdots$ (order is preserved):

$$y = \lim_{n \to \infty} \frac{1}{n} \Sigma_{j=1}^{n} y^{s_j},$$

$$y^{s_j} \in Y^{s_j} \quad (j = 1, 2, \ldots),$$

and, for some K,

$$\| y^{s_j} \| \leq K \quad (j = 1, 2, \ldots),$$

where $\| y^{s_j} \|$ stands for the length of vector $y^{s_j} = (y_1{}^{s_j}, \ldots, y_m{}^{s_j})$,

$$\| y^{s_j} \| = [\Sigma_{k=1}^{m} (y_k{}^{s_j})^2]^{1/2}.$$

In symbols,

$$(1) \quad Y = \left\{ y \in E: \ y = \lim_{n \to \infty} \frac{1}{n} \Sigma_{j=1}^{n} y^{s_j}, \ y^{s_j} \in Y^{s_j}, \ j = 1, 2, \ldots \right.$$

$$\left. \text{and} \ \langle y^{s_1}, y^{s_2}, \ldots \rangle \ \text{is a bounded sequence} \right\}.$$

The average production possibility set Y is uniquely determined by a sequence of production possibility sets $\langle Y^1, Y^2, \ldots \rangle$ and may be denoted by

$$Y = Y[Y^1, Y^2, \ldots].$$

A class of production sets $\{Y^1, Y^2, \ldots\}$ is called *uniformly bounded* if there exists a finite number K such that

$$\| y^s \| \leq K, \quad \text{for all } y^s \in Y^s, \text{ and } s = 1, 2, \ldots, ad \ inf.$$

Theorem 1. If the class of production possibility sets $\{Y^1, Y^2, \ldots\}$ is uniformly bounded, then the average production possibility set $Y = Y[Y^1, Y^2, \ldots]$ is a compact (= bounded and closed) convex subset of the commodity space E.

Theorem 2. For any sequence of production possibility sets $\langle Y^1, Y^2, \ldots \rangle$, the average production possibility set $Y = Y[Y^1, Y^2, \ldots]$ is a convex subset of the commodity space E.

Theorem 2 is easily derived from Theorem 1. In fact, for any positive number K, let us define

$$Y_K^s = \{y^s \in Y^s: \ \| y^s \| \leq K\} \quad (s = 1, 2, \ldots, ad \ inf.)$$

and

$$Y_K = Y[Y_K{}^1, Y_K{}^2, \ldots].$$

The class of production possibility sets $\{Y_K{}^1, Y_K{}^2, \ldots\}$ *is* uniformly bounded; hence, by applying Theorem 1 to $\{Y_K{}^1, Y_K{}^2, \ldots\}$, the average production possibility sets Y_K is a *convex* subset of the commodity space E. On the other hand, by the definition (1) of the average production possibility set Y, we have

$$Y = \bigcup_{K=1}^{\infty} Y_K.$$

Since $Y_{K_1} \subseteq Y_{K_2}$ for $K_1 < K_2$, and each Y_K is convex, the set Y is also *convex*. The proof of Theorem 1 will be preceded by some definitions and lemmas.

For any denumerable class of production possibility sets $\{Y^1, Y^2, \ldots\}$, we define:

(2) $A = A[Y^1, Y^2, \ldots] = \{a \in E: a = \lim_{j \to \infty} y^{s_j}$, for some

subsequence $\langle s_1, s_2, \ldots \rangle$ of firms $\{s_1, s_2, \ldots\} \subseteq \{1, 2, \ldots\}$,

$s_j < s_{j+1}$ $(j = 1, 2, \ldots)$ and some convergent sequence $\langle y^{s_1}, y^{s_2}, \ldots \rangle$

from $\langle Y^{s_1}, Y^{s_2}, \ldots \rangle\}$

(3) $B = B[Y^1, Y^2, \ldots] = \{b \in E: b = \sum_{i=1}^{r} \lambda_i a_i$, for some finite number of

positive real numbers $\lambda_1, \ldots, \lambda_r$ such that $\sum_{i=1}^{r} \lambda_i = 1$ and of

vectors $a_1, \ldots, a_r \in A\}$.

Lemma 1. $Y \supseteq B$.

Proof. By definition (3) of B, we have to prove that, for any finite number of vectors $a_1, \ldots, a_r \in A$ and of real numbers $\lambda_1, \ldots, \lambda_r$, such that

$$\sum_{i=1}^{r} \lambda_i = 1, \quad \lambda_i > 0 \quad (i = 1, \ldots, r),$$

the linear combination

$$\sum_{i=1}^{r} \lambda_i a_i$$

belongs to the average production possibility set Y.

Let $a_1, \ldots, a_r$ be any finite number of vectors from A and $\lambda_1, \ldots, \lambda_r$ be real numbers, such that

(4) $\sum_{i=1}^{r} \lambda_i = 1, \quad \lambda_i > 0 \quad (i = 1, \ldots, r)$.

By definition (2) of A, for each $i = 1, \ldots, r$, there exists a subsequence of firms $\langle s_i(1), s_i(2), \ldots \rangle$ and a sequence of vectors $\langle y^{s_i(1)}, y^{s_i(2)}, \ldots \rangle$ such that

(5) $a_i = \lim_{n \to \infty} y^{s_i(n)}, \quad y^{s_i(n)} \in Y^{s_i(n)}$

$$(n = 1, 2, \ldots, ad\ inf.; i = 1, \ldots, r).$$

For each $i = 1, \ldots, r$, the sequence $\langle y^{s_i(1)}, y^{s_i(2)}, \ldots \rangle$ is convergent, hence is bounded; that is, for some $K_i > 0$,

$$\|y^{s_i(n)}\| \leq K_i \quad (n = 1, 2, \ldots, ad\ inf.).$$

Let K be the maximum of $K_1, \ldots, K_r$; then we have

(6) $\|y^{s_i(n)}\| \leq K, \quad (n = 1, 2, \ldots, ad\ inf.; \ i = 1, \ldots, r)$.

Now let $\langle p_i{}^1, p_i{}^2, \ldots \rangle$, $i = 1, \ldots, r$, be r sequences of nonnegative integers for which

(7) $\lambda_i = \lim_{n \to \infty} p_i{}^n / p^n$ $(i = 1, \ldots, r)$

and

(8) $\lim_{n \to \infty} \dfrac{p^{n+1}}{q^n} = 0,$

where

(9) $p^n = p_1{}^n + \cdots + p_r{}^n$

(10) $q^n = p^1 + \cdots + p^n$ $(n = 1, 2, \ldots, ad\ inf.)$.

It is possible to construct r sequences of nonnegative integers $\langle p_i{}^1, p_i{}^2, \ldots \rangle$ satisfying conditions (7) and (8). For example, let us define, for $n = 1, 2, \ldots$, *ad inf.*,

(11) $\begin{cases} p_i{}^n = [\lambda_i n] & (i = 1, \ldots, r-1) \\ p_r{}^n = n - \sum_{i=1}^{r-1} [\lambda_i n], \end{cases}$

where $[\lambda_i n]$ is the maximum integer that does not exceed the number $\lambda_i n$; hence

(12) $[\lambda_i n] \leqq \lambda_i n < [\lambda_i n] + 1.$

Thus, for any n and i, $p_i{}^n$ is a nonnegative integer and

(13) $p^n = p_1{}^n + \cdots + p_r{}^n = n.$

By dividing (12) by n and substituting (11) and (13), we get

(14) $\dfrac{p_i{}^n}{p^n} \leqq \lambda_i < \dfrac{p_i{}^n}{p^n} + \dfrac{1}{n}$ $(i = 1, \ldots, r-1)$

and, hence,

(15) $\lambda_i = \lim_{n \to \infty} \dfrac{p_i{}^n}{p^n}$ $(i = 1, \ldots, r-1)$.

But,

$\dfrac{p_r{}^n}{p^n} = 1 - \sum_{i=1}^{r-1} \dfrac{p_i{}^n}{p^n},$

which, together with (4) and (15), implies that

(16) $\lambda_r = \lim_{n \to \infty} \dfrac{p_r{}^n}{p^n}$

On the other hand,

$$q^n = p^1 + \cdots + p^n = 1 + \cdots + n = \frac{n(n+1)}{2}$$

and, hence,

(17) $\lim_{n \to \infty} \dfrac{p^{n+1}}{q^n} = \lim_{n \to \infty} \dfrac{n+1}{n(n+1)/2} = 0.$

Therefore, the sequences $\langle p_i{}^1, p_i{}^2, \ldots \rangle$ $(i = 1, \ldots, r)$, constructed by (11), satisfy conditions (7) and (8).

We now define a sequence of firms $\langle t_1, t_2, \ldots \rangle$ and a sequence of vectors $\langle y^{t_1}, y^{t_2}, \ldots \rangle$ by the following procedures.

First, let us define a function $i = \psi(n)$ as follows:

Function $i = \psi(n)$ if and only if there exists an integer k for which

(18) $q^{k-1} + (p_1{}^k + \cdots + p_{i-1}^k) < n \le q^{k-1} + (p_1{}^k + \cdots + p_i{}^k),$

where q^{k-1} is defined by (10).

Second, we define $n' = \phi(n)$ by the following recursive formula:

(19) $n' = \phi(n)$ is the minimum integer for which

$$s_{\psi(n)}(n') > s_{\psi(0)}(\phi(0)), s_{\psi(1)}(\phi(1)), \ldots, s_{\psi(n-1)}(\phi(n-1)),$$

where $s_{\psi(0)}(\phi(0)) = 0.$

Finally, we define

(20) $t_n = s_{\psi(n)}(\phi(n))$ $\quad (n = 1, 2, \ldots, ad\ inf.)$

and

(21) $y^{t_n} = y^{s_{\psi(n)}(\phi(n))}$ $\quad (n = 1, 2, \ldots, ad\ inf.).$

We shall prove that

(22) $\lim_{N \to \infty} \dfrac{1}{N} \sum_{j=1}^{N} y^{t_j} = \sum_{i=1}^{r} \lambda_i a_i.$

In order to see (22), we shall first show that

(23) $\lim_{n \to \infty} \dfrac{1}{q^n} \sum_{j=1}^{q^n} y^{t_j} = \sum_{i=1}^{r} \lambda_i a_i.$

In fact, we have the identity,

(24) $\sum_{j=1}^{q^n} y^{t_j} = \sum_{i=1}^{r} \sum_{j \in Q_i(n)} y^{t_j}$

where

(25) $Q_i(n) = \{ j : 1 \le j \le q^n, \ \psi(j) = i \}$

$$(i = 1, \ldots, r; \quad n = 1, 2, \ldots, ad\ inf.).$$

From (18), the number of integers in the set $Q_i(n)$ is equal to

(26) $q_i(n) = p_i^1 + \cdots + p_i^n$ $(i = 1, \ldots, r)$.

Let

(27) $Q_i(n) = \{j_i^1, \ldots, j_i^{q_i(n)}\}$

and

(28) $n_i(k) = \phi(j_i^k)$ $[k = 1, \ldots, q_i(n)]$.

From (21), (25), and (28), we have

(29) $\sum_{j \in Q_i(n)} y^{tj} = \sum_{j \in Q_i(n)} y^{s_i(\phi(j))} = \sum_{k=1}^{q_i(n)} y_i^{s_i(n_i(k))}$.

From (24) and (29), we have

(30) $\dfrac{1}{q^n} \sum_{j=1}^{q^n} y^{tj} = \sum_{i=1}^{r} \dfrac{q_i(n)}{q^n} \cdot \dfrac{1}{q_i(n)} \sum_{k=1}^{q_i(n)} y_i^{s_i(n_i(k))}$.

But, from (5) we have

(31) $\lim_{n \to \infty} y^{s_i(n_i(k))} = a_i$

because $n_i(k)$ tends to infinity as $k \to \infty$.

Hence, by a fundamental theorem on Césaro sum (see, for example, T. M. Apostol, *Mathematical Analysis*, Reading, Mass.: Addison-Wesley, 1957, Theorem 12-48, p. 378), (31) implies

(32) $\lim_{n \to \infty} \dfrac{1}{q_i(n)} \sum_{k=1}^{q_i(n)} y^{s_i(n_i(k))} = a_i$ $(i = 1, \ldots, r)$.

On the other hand, from (16) we have

(33) $\lim_{n \to \infty} \dfrac{q_i(n)}{q^n} = \lambda_i$,

where $q_i(n)$ and q^n are, respectively, defined by (26) and (10).

Relation (33) may be proved as follows: Let

(34) $\epsilon_i^n = \dfrac{p_i^n}{p^n} - \lambda_i$ $(n = 1, 2, \ldots; i = 1, \ldots, r)$,

then from (15) and (16),

(35) $\lim_{n \to \infty} \epsilon_i^n = 0$.

From (26), (10), and (34), we have

$$\dfrac{q_i(n)}{q^n} = \lambda_i + \dfrac{\epsilon_i^1 p^1 + \cdots + \epsilon_i^n p^n}{p^1 + \cdots + p^n}$$

and, hence,

$$\left[\frac{q_i(n)}{q^n} - \lambda_i\right] = \frac{\epsilon_i^{\,1} p^1 + \cdots + \epsilon_i^{\,n} p^n}{p^1 + \cdots + p^n},$$

which by (35) tends to zero as $n \to \infty$.

From (30), (32), and (33), we have

$$\lim_{n \to \infty} \frac{1}{q^n} \Sigma_{j=1}^{q^n} y^{tj} = \Sigma_{i=1}^{r} \lambda_i a_i,$$

thus proving relation (23).

We next show that

(36) $\lim_{n \to \infty} \dfrac{1}{q^n} \Sigma_{j=1}^{q^n} y^{tj} - \lim_{N \to \infty} \dfrac{1}{N} \Sigma_{j=1}^{N} y^{tj} = 0$

For any given N, let n be the integer for which

(37) $q^n \le N < q^{n+1}$;

namely, in view of (10),

(38) $0 \le N - q^n < p^{n+1}$.

Such an n always exists because $\{q^n\}$ is a monotonically increasing unbounded sequence of positive integers.

Now we have

(39) $\dfrac{1}{N} \Sigma_{j=1}^{N} y^{tj} - \dfrac{1}{q^n} \Sigma_{j=1}^{q^n} y^{tj}$

$$= \left(\frac{1}{N} \Sigma_{j=1}^{q^n} y^{tj} + \frac{1}{N} \Sigma_{j=q^n+1}^{N} y^{tj}\right) - \frac{1}{q^n} \Sigma_{j=1}^{q^n} y^{tj}$$

$$= \left(\frac{1}{N} - \frac{1}{q^n}\right) \Sigma_{j=1}^{q^n} y^{tj} + \frac{1}{N} \Sigma_{j=q^n+1}^{N} y^{tj}$$

$$= Q_1 + Q_2, \quad \text{say}.$$

Then

(40) $|Q_1| \le \left(\dfrac{1}{q^n} - \dfrac{1}{N}\right) q^n K = \dfrac{N - q^n}{N} K,$

where K is a number such that

$\|y^{s_i(n)}\| \le K, \quad (i = 1, \ldots, r \text{ and } n = 1, 2, \ldots, ad \text{ } inf.)$.

Inequality (40), together with (37) and (38), imply that

(41) $|Q_1| \le \dfrac{p^{n+1}}{q^n} K.$

On the other hand,

$$(42) \quad |Q_2| \leq \frac{1}{N}(N - q^n) K \leq \frac{p^{n+1}}{q^n} K$$

From (39), (41), and (42),

$$\left| \frac{1}{N} \sum_{j=1}^{N} y^{tj} - \frac{1}{q^n} \sum_{j=1}^{q^n} y^{tj} \right| \leq 2K \frac{p^{n+1}}{q^n},$$

which, together with (8), imply

$$\overline{\lim}_{N \to \infty} \left| \frac{1}{N} \sum_{j=1}^{N} y^{tj} - \frac{1}{q^n} \sum_{j=1}^{q^n} y^{tj} \right| = 0$$

because $n \to \infty$ as $N \to \infty$; thus (36) is proved.

Relations (23) and (36) imply relation (22); this completes the proof of Lemma 1. Q.E.D.

Lemma 2. $Y \subseteq \overline{B}$, where $\overline{B}$ is the closure of the set B.

Proof.   Suppose

$$(43) \quad Y \nsubseteq \overline{B}.$$

Then there exists a vector y_0 such that

$$(44) \quad y_0 \in Y, \quad \text{but } y_0 \notin \overline{B}.$$

Since B is a convex set, the closure $\overline{B}$ is a closed convex set. Hence, relation (44) implies, by the separation theorem that there exists a vector c such that

$$(45) \quad cy_0 > cb \quad \text{for all } b \in B.$$

By definition (1) of Y, there exists a sequence of firms $\langle s_1, s_2, \ldots \rangle$ and a bounded sequence $\langle y^{s_1}, y^{s_2}, \ldots \rangle$ such that

$$(46) \quad y_0 = \lim_{n \to \infty} \frac{1}{n} \sum_{j=1}^{n} y^{s_j}, \quad y^{s_j} \in Y^{s_j} \quad (j = 1, 2, \ldots, ad \ inf.).$$

From (46), we have

$$(47) \quad cy_0 = \lim_{n \to \infty} \frac{1}{n} \sum_{j=1}^{n} cy^{s_j},$$

where the sequence $\langle cy^{s_1}, cy^{s_2}, \ldots \rangle$ is necessarily bounded.

Let

$$(48) \quad \beta = \overline{\lim}_{j \to \infty} cy^{s_j};$$

namely, for any $\epsilon > 0$ there exists a j_ϵ such that

$$(49) \quad cy^{s_j} < \beta + \epsilon \quad (j \geq j_\epsilon).$$

Let ϵ be an arbitrarily given positive number; then, from (49),

(50) $\dfrac{1}{n} \Sigma_{j=1}^{n} cy^{s_j} = \dfrac{1}{n} \Sigma_{j=1}^{j_\epsilon} cy^{s_j} + \dfrac{1}{n} \Sigma_{j=j_\epsilon+1}^{n} cy^{s_j}$

$< \dfrac{1}{n} \Sigma_{j=1}^{j_\epsilon} cy^{s_j} + \dfrac{n - j_\epsilon}{n} (\beta + \epsilon).$

If we let $n \to \infty$, then (50) implies that (fixing ϵ, hence j_ϵ)

(51) $\lim_{n \to \infty} \dfrac{1}{n} \Sigma_{j=1}^{n} cy^{s_j} \leqq \beta + \epsilon.$

Since (51) holds for any positive ϵ, we get

(52) $\lim_{j \to \infty} \dfrac{1}{n} \Sigma_{j=1}^{n} cy^{s_j} \leqq \beta,$

where β is defined by (48).

From (48) and (52), then, there exists a subsequence $\langle s_{v(1)}, s_{v(2)}, \ldots \rangle$ of $\langle s_1, s_2, \ldots \rangle$ such that

(53) $\lim_{n \to \infty} \dfrac{1}{n} \Sigma_{j=1}^{n} cy^{s_j} \leqq \lim_{j \to \infty} cy^{s_{v(j)}},$

(54) $\lim_{j \to \infty} y^{s_{v(j)}}$ exists and, say, $= a_0.$

Hence

(55) $\lim_{n \to \infty} \dfrac{1}{n} \Sigma_{j=1}^{n} cy^{s_j} \leqq ca_0.$

where $a_0 \in A$.

From (47) and (55), we have

(56) $cy_0 \leqq ca_0, \qquad a_0 \in A \subseteq B$

contradicting (45).

Thus assumption (43) does not hold.

Lemma 3. Let $\langle Y^1, Y^2, \ldots \rangle$ be a uniformly bounded sequence of production possibility sets. Then set $B = B[Y^1, Y^2, \ldots]$ is a compact convex set.

Proof. The convexity of set B is evident from definition (3). In order to show the compactness of set B, it suffices to show that set $A = A[Y^1, Y^2, \ldots]$, defined by (2), is compact.

Since $\langle Y^1, Y^2, \ldots \rangle$ is uniformly bounded, there exists a positive number k such that

(57) $\| y^s \| \leqq k, \qquad$ for all $y^s \in Y^s \qquad (s = 1, 2, \ldots).$

From (1) and (57), we have

(58) $\|a\| \leq k, \quad (a \in A)$.

On the other hand, let

(59) $a = \lim_{n \to \infty} a_n, \quad a_n = \lim_{j \to \infty} y_0 {}^{s_j(n)}, \quad y_0 {}^{s_j(n)} \in Y^{s_j(n)}$

$$(n = 1, 2, \ldots ; j = 1, 2, \ldots).$$

Let $\langle t_1, t_2, \ldots \rangle$ and $\langle y^{t_1}, y^{t_2}, \ldots \rangle$ be defined by

(60) $t_n = \min \{s_j(n): s_j(n) > t_1, \ldots, t_{n-1}\}$.

Then we have

$$a = \lim_{n \to \infty} a^{t_n}$$

thus proving that set A is closed.   Q.E.D.

Proof of Theorem 1.   From Lemma 1 and Lemma 2, we have

$$B \subseteq Y \subseteq \overline{B}$$

But, for a uniformly bounded sequence $\langle Y^1, Y^2, \ldots \rangle$, we have by Lemma 3 that B is compact and convex.

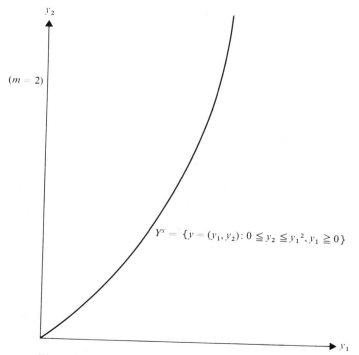

$Y^s = \{y = (y_1, y_2): 0 \leq y_2 \leq y_1{}^2, y_1 \geq 0\}$

$(m = 2)$

Figure 1

Hence

$$Y = B$$

and Y is compact and convex.   Q.E.D.

Corollary.   The (asymptotic) average production possibility set $Y = Y[Y^1,$ $Y^2, \ldots]$ is determined independently of the order in which all the firms are labeled.

Proof.   By definition (2), set A, hence set B, does not depend on the order in which firms are labeled. But from the proof of Theorem 1, $Y = B$.   Q.E.D.

Example 1.   See Figure 1. $Y = B$ is not closed.

$$A = A[Y^1, Y^2, \ldots] = Y^1 = Y^2 = \cdots$$

$$B = B[Y^1, Y^2, \ldots] = \{y = (y_1, y_2): y = (0, 0) \text{ or } y_1 > 0 \text{ and } y_2 \geq 0\};$$

B is not closed.

Example 2. $Y^* \neq Y, \overline{Y}$, where

$(m = 1)$,

$$Y^* = \left\{ y \in E: y = \lim_{n \to \infty} \frac{1}{n} \Sigma_{j=1}^{n} \, y^{s_j}, \quad \begin{matrix} (s_1, s_2, \ldots, \text{arb.}) \\ (y^{s_1}, y^{s_2}, \ldots, \text{arb.}) \end{matrix} \right\}$$

$$Y^s = \{0, s\}, \quad (s = 1, 2, \ldots);$$

$$A = \{0\}$$

$$Y = B = \{0\}; \quad \overline{Y} = Y = \{0\}$$

$$Y^* = \{y: 0 \leq y < \infty\}$$

PART III

Economies with multiple objectives

1

STABILITY OF COMPETITIVE EQUILIBRIUM

On the stability of the competitive equilibrium, I[1]

KENNETH J. ARROW
LEONID HURWICZ

Introduction

1.

A great deal of work has been done recently on what one may call the *static* aspects of competitive equilibrium, its existence, uniqueness, and optimality.[2] This work is characterized, in the main, by being based on models whose assumptions are formulated in terms of certain properties of the individual economic units, although in the last analysis it is the nature of the aggregate excess demand functions that determines the properties of equilibria.

With regard to *dynamics*, especially the *stability* of equilibrium, much remains to be done. The concept of stability, used already by the nineteenth century economists[3] in its modern sense, did not receive systematic treatment in the context of economic dynamics until Samuelson's paper of 1941 [32]. Samuelson, however, did not fully explore the implications of the assumptions underlying the perfectly competitive model. He (as well as Lange [20], Metzler [24], and Morishima [25]) focused attention on the relationship between "true dynamic stability" and the concept of "stability" as defined by Hicks in *Value and Capital* [16], rather than on whether under a given set of assumptions stability (in either sense) would prevail or not.[4] Even though the Hicksian concept does not, in general, coincide with that of "true dynamic stability," it is of considerable interest to us for two reasons: first, as shown by the writers just cited, there are situations where the two concepts are equivalent; second, because the equilibrium whose "stability" Hicks studied is indeed *competitive* equilibrium.[5] But again, little is known about conditions under which Hicksian stability prevails. There is thus a gap in this field and our aim is to help fill it. The task consists in constructing a formal dynamic model whose characteristics reflect the nature of the competitive process and in examining its stability properties, given assumptions as to the properties of the individual units or of the aggregate excess demand functions. The results here presented cover certain special classes of cases and many important questions remain open.

2. Dynamic concepts

We shall be dealing with only one type of dynamic system, that of a set of simultaneous ordinary differential equations (with time not appearing explicitly). Let these equations be written as

(1') $dp_j/dt = f_j(p_1, \ldots, p_m)$ $(j = 1, \ldots, m; \; m \geqslant 1)$,

or, in vector form,

(1") $dp/dt = f(p)$

where $p = (p_1, \ldots, p_m)$.

Function $\Psi(t; p^0)$ is said to be a *solution* ("path") of (1) with p^0 as the *initial value* if and only if

(2.1) $\partial\Psi(t; p^0)/\partial t = f[\Psi(t; p^0)]$ for all $t \geqslant 0$,

and[6]

(2.2) $\Psi(0; p^0) = p^0$.

A point $\bar{p}$ in the m-dimensional space of the vectors $p = (p_1, \ldots, p_m)$ is called an *equilibrium point* of (1) if and only if (cf. note 17)

(3) $f(\bar{p}) = 0$.

An equilibrium point $\bar{p}$ is said to be *locally stable* if there exists a neighborhood $N(\bar{p})$ of $\bar{p}$ such that for any point p^0 of the neighborhood $N(\bar{p})$ every[7] solution Ψ converges to $\bar{p}$, i.e.,

(4) $\lim_{t \to \infty} \Psi(t; p^0) = \bar{p}$.

(This is Samuelson's "stability of the first kind in the small.")

An equilibrium point is said to be *locally unstable* if it is not locally stable. If an equilibrium point $\bar{p}$ has the property

(5) $\lim_{t \to \infty} \Psi(t; p^0) = \bar{p}$

for all p^0 (and for every solution Ψ), it is said to be *globally stable* ("stability of the first kind in the large").

We shall encounter situations where (3) has more than one solution, i.e., where there are multiple equilibria (or where at least the possibility of multiple equilibria cannot be excluded). When there are two or more equilibria, it cannot be the case that all equilibrium points are globally stable,[8] but the *system* as a whole may still be endowed with an important stability property. Denote by E the set of all equilibrium points. We shall call the *system* (1) *stable* if and only if

(6)   for each p^0 there is some equilibrium point $\bar{p}$ in E such that
       $\lim_{t \to \infty} \Psi(t; p^0) = \bar{p}$,

i.e., no matter where one starts, there is a tendency to approach *some* equilibrium point. Clearly, when equilibrium is unique [i.e., when (3) has only one solution $\bar{p}$], if the *system* is stable in the sense of the preceding definition, the unique equilibrium point $\bar{p}$ is globally stable.[9]

3. The adjustment process

From among the many possible dynamic versions of the market process,[10] we have chosen two particular ones, here labelled, respectively, (A) *the instantaneous adjustment process*, and (B) *the lagged adjustment process*. The instantaneous adjustment process is well-known and is of particular interest because it is close to the formulations of Walras, Hicks, and many other writers, and because (comparatively) a great deal is known about it. The lagged adjustment process is of interest in the context of various gradient processes,[11] but our main emphasis is on the instantaneous process defined below. The lagged process is defined, and some of its properties examined, in the Appendix to Part I.

The instantaneous adjustment process.   In this process the variables (as anticipated by the notation of the preceding section) are the ("normalized") prices $p_1, p_2, \ldots, p_m$ of the m commodities (other than the numéraire) in terms of another commodity called the numéraire whose price is set at 1. (For labelling purposes the numéraire is characterized by the subscript 0. Counting the numéraire, there are $m + 1$ commodities. We use the terms "commodity" and "good" interchangeably.)

The instantaneous adjustment process is defined by the differential equations,

$$(1) \quad dp_j/dt = f_j(p_1, p_2, \ldots, p_m) \quad (j = 1, 2, \ldots, m)$$

where p_r denotes the price of the rth commodity in terms of the numéraire and f_j is the *aggregate excess (net) demand function* for the jth commodity. To make (1) meaningful, the f_j are assumed to be single-valued. Lange [20], Metzler [24], and others have studied a class of processes [of which (1) is a special case] where the speeds of adjustment may vary from one market to another; a process of this class is given by the differential equation system

$$(2) \quad dp_j/dt = k_j f_j(p_1, \ldots, p_m), \quad k_j > 0, \quad (j = 1, 2, \ldots, m).$$

Clearly, (2) can be reduced to (1) by a suitable choice of units of measurement for each of the m commodities. Now the assumptions on the excess demand functions made in the course of our analysis of stability of competitive equilibria are invariant under a change of units of measurement. Hence in each case where (dynamic) stability of equilibria of (1) has been established, (dynamic) stability of (2) follows.

This phenomenon is of interest because of Metzler's result [24, p. 282] that Hicks's "perfect stability" is a necessary condition for the stability of (2) with all possible choices of the k_j's. Hence, in each case where the results of this paper yield (dynamic) stability, Hicks's "perfect stability" conditions must be satisfied at equilibrium. These conclusions may be summarized in the following:

Remark.   Let M be a class of models (systems of excess demand functions) such that if m belongs to M, then so does any m' obtained from m by a change of units of measurement of the commodities. Then the (dynamic) stability of

(1) for all m's in M implies (a) the (dynamic) stability of (2) for all choices of the k_j and all m's in M, and (b) the Hicksian "perfect stability" for all m's in M.

4. Excess demand under perfect competition

Each of the n economic units is assumed to be maximizing an entity (utility, profit) which is a function of the prices. By definition, under perfect competition, prices are treated by each unit as fixed parameters. In particular, under pure exchange the ith unit's (individual) excess demand function is obtained by maximizing the utility function

(1) $u^i(X_0^i, X_1^i, \ldots, X_m^i)$

subject to the budget constraint (taken as an equation[12])

(2) $\Sigma_{k=0}^m p_k X_k^i = \Sigma_{k=0}^m p_k \overset{0}{X}_k^i$

and to the conditions

(3) $X_k^i \geq 0$ $(k = 0, 1, \ldots, m)$.

[Here X_k^i denotes the amount of the kth good *finally obtained* (consumed) by the ith unit; $\overset{0}{X}_k^i$ is the amount of the kth good *initially held* by the ith unit. p_k denotes the ("normalized") price of the kth good in terms of the 0th commodity (numéraire); hence $p_0 = 1$.]

Let u^i (the ith unit's utility function), as given in (1), be maximized subject to (2) and (3). The solution for the X's obviously depends on the prices (as well as the amounts initially held and the shape of the utility function) and may be written as[13]

(4) $\hat{X}_k^i = \overset{0}{X}_k^i + f_k^i(p_1, \ldots, p_m)$ $(k = 0, 1, \ldots, m)$

where j_k^i is the ith unit's (individual) excess demand function for the kth good. The *aggregate excess demand function for the kth good*, $f_k(p_1, \ldots, p_m)$ is then defined by

(5) $f_k(p_1, \ldots, p_m) = \Sigma_{i=1}^n f_k^i(p_1, \ldots p_m)$ $(k = 0, 1, \ldots, m)$.

It is this latter function that forms the right-hand side of the differential equations defining the instantaneous adjustment process [Section 3, (1)].

5. Aggregate excess demand functions

Had the procedure of the preceding section been carried out in a manner symmetric with regard to all $m + 1$ goods (without singling out one of them as numéraire), we would have written the ith budget constraint as

(1) $\Sigma_{k=0}^m P_k X_k^i = \Sigma_{k=0}^m P_k \overset{0}{X}_k^i$

where the P_k are non-normalized prices. (The normalized prices p_k used earlier are then obtained from $p_k = P_k/P_0$.) The aggregate excess demand function for the kth good could then be written as[14]

(2) $\quad F_k(P_0, P_1, \ldots, P_m)$.

The existence of *competitive equilibrium* means that there exists a vector

(3.1) $\quad \bar{P} = (\bar{P}_0, \bar{P}_1, \ldots, \bar{P}_m)$

such that

(3.2) $\quad F_k(\bar{P}) = 0 \quad (k = 0, 1, \ldots, m)$

and[15]

(3.3) $\quad \bar{P} \geqslant 0$.

Now, recent work[16] shows that a sufficient condition for the existence of such an equilibrium is the continuity (together with single-valuedness) of the functions F_k.[17] We shall be using this result in what follows and we shall assume that P_0 is among the positive components of $\bar{P}$. (This merely means that we shall not use as numéraire a good which would be free at equilibrium!) Thus we may go back to the formulation in terms of the relative prices $p_j (j = 1, 2, \ldots, m)$; here the existence of competitive equilibrium means that there exists a vector

(4.1) $\quad \bar{p} = (\bar{p}_1, \ldots, \bar{p}_m)$

such that

(4.2) $\quad f_j(\bar{p}) = 0 \quad (j = 1, \ldots, m)$

and

(4.3) $\quad \bar{p} \geq 0$.

[Note that the inequality (4.3) is weaker than (3.3) and $\bar{p}$ might have all zero components.]

From the recent literature various sets of conditions on the individual units are known to be sufficient for the continuity and single-valuedness of the aggregate excess demand functions. For the case of pure exchange one may, for instance, postulate strict quasi-concavity and continuity of the individual preferences together with one of the several possible restrictions on the initial holding vectors $\overset{0}{X}{}^i = (\overset{0}{X}{}^i_0, \overset{0}{X}{}^i_1, \ldots, \overset{0}{X}{}^i_m), i = 1, 2, \ldots, n$. The strongest of these is

(5) $\quad \overset{0}{X}{}^i_k > 0 \quad$ for all $i = 1, 2, \ldots, n$ and all $k = 0, 1, \ldots, m$.

But while (5) cannot be dispensed with entirely, a considerable weakening is possible.[18]

The existence of such results makes it possible, to some extent at least, to have a "two-level" structure of analysis. At one level, one makes assumptions, viz., those of continuity and single-valuedness, on the (individual or aggregate) excess demand functions. These assumptions are essential statically in that they guarantee the existence of equilibrium, but also dynamically in that they make the adjustment equations meaningful, and they furthermore guarantee the existence of solutions (paths) to the differential equation systems.[19] At another level, static analysis of the maximum conditions for the firm or a household has been used (as just indicated) to derive the properties of the excess demand functions, such as continuity and single-valuedness, from assumptions about the individual units. The two levels can be combined, so that dynamic properties are implied by assumptions about individual units, the implication running by way of the properties of excess demand functions. In some cases it is obvious how this can be done, and we confine ourselves to the statement of the "first level" dynamic results. But in some cases (e.g., Appendix to Part II) we derive some additional results in the theory of individual units which we need for dynamic implications.

6. Summary of results

In the present paper we have examined several classes of cases from the viewpoint of their stability properties. In Part I we mainly study situations where there is no trade at equilibrium; in particular, this covers the case of identical individuals and the case of a Pareto-optimal initial resource distribution; for technical reasons, the case of a market satisfying the weak revealed preference axiom is also treated there. Part II is devoted to the case of two commodities, one of which is used as numéraire; this case is of interest because it can be treated more completely and also because it has implications (via composite commodity construction) for cases of more than two commodities. Part III deals with the case where all goods are gross substitutes at all prices; it is also shown that certain other situations one might wish to study by analogous methods (such as universal prevalence of gross complementarity or the Morishima (see [25]) case extended to all $m + 1$ commodities) contradict the postulates underlying the usual competitive equilibrium analysis. (The latter findings may be of some interest even apart from their dynamic implications.)

In each of these cases we took advantage of the findings and conjectures to be found in the work of Walras, Hicks, Samuelson, Lange, Metzler, and others; on the other hand, we have also tried to show how our results are related to some of the problems they have posed.

Whenever possible, we took the global viewpoint, but in some cases (e.g., the case of universal gross substitutability where there are more than three goods) we had to be satisfied with local results. (Further global results will be found in [3].)

The nature of our findings can be summarized very simply by saying that *in none of the cases studied have we found the system to be unstable under the* (*perfectly competitive*) *adjustment process*, whether instantaneous or lagged. To put it in the more positive form: (a) where equilibrium is unique (as, for instance, in the gross substitution case) we have found global stability in some of the cases studied, while in others local stability has been proved (with the question of global stability remaining unresolved); (b) where there is a possibility of multiple equilibria (as in Part II), we have found in the class of cases studied that the *system* is stable (in the sense of our definition in Section 2), even though some equilibria may be locally unstable.

It should be emphasized that because of the fragmentary nature of the present study, no general assertions about the stability of the system under competition can as yet be made. It is conceivable, for instance, that (outside the class of situations here treated) an example of unstable unique competitive equilibrium may be found. On the other hand, none of the results so far obtained contradicts the proposition that under perfect competition, with the customary assumptions as to convexity, etc., the *system* is always stable. If the latter proposition turns out to be true, Samuelson's "correspondence principle" [30, p. 258] would then provide no information that could not be deduced from micro-economic considerations under competition, at least for the particular class of adjustment processes considered.[20] At the moment, however, the question remains open.

Part I: The case of absence of trade at equilibrium and related results

7. Global stability when there is no trade at equilibrium

Let D denote the distance from an arbitrary point p (in the price space) to some (fixed) equilibrium point $\bar{p}$, so that

(1) $\quad D^2 = \Sigma_{k=0}^{m} (p_k - \bar{p}_k)^2 = \Sigma_{j=1}^{m} (p_j - \bar{p}_j)^2$

(where the second equality follows from $p_0 = \bar{p}_0 = 1$), and consider the time derivative dD/dt. We shall show that under certain conditions $dD/dt < 0$. It then follows[21] that $p \to \bar{p}$ as $t \to \infty$. We shall find it more convenient to work with the expression

(2) $\quad V = (1/2) D^2.$

We have

(3) $\quad dV/dt = \Sigma_{j=1}^{m} (p_j - \bar{p}_j)(dp_j/dt) = \Sigma_{j=1}^{m} (p_j - \bar{p}_j) x_j$

where $x_k = f_k(p_1, \ldots, p_m)$, $k = 0, 1, \ldots, m$, is the aggregate net amount of the kth good demanded. Write x_k^i to denote the net amount of the kth good demanded by the ith individual, so that [with $\hat{X}_k^i$ the maximizing amount finally held (consumed)].

(4) $\quad x_k^i = \hat{X}_k^i - \overset{0}{X}_k^i, \qquad x_k = \Sigma_{i=1}^{n} x_k^i.$

We have from (3)

(5) $dV/dt = \sum_{j=1}^{m} p_j x_j - \sum_{j=1}^{m} \bar{p}_j x_j = \sum_{j=1}^{m} p_j \sum_{i=1}^{n} x_j^i - \sum_{j=1}^{m} \bar{p}_j x_j$

$= \sum_{i=1}^{n} (\sum_{j=1}^{m} p_j x_j^i) - \sum_{j=1}^{m} \bar{p}_j x_j.$

Now, because of the budget constraint (under non-saturation) with $p_0 = 1$,

(6) $\sum_{k=0}^{m} p_k x_k^i = 0.$

Substituting (6) into (5), we get (utilizing the fact that $\bar{p}_0 = p_0 = 1$)

(7) $dV/dt = \sum_{i=1}^{n} (-p_0 x_0^i) - \sum_{j=1}^{m} \bar{p}_j (\sum_{i=1}^{n} x_j^i) = -\sum_{i=1}^{n} (\sum_{k=0}^{m} \bar{p}_k x_k^i).$

Lemma 1.   Let each unit satisfy the "weak axiom of revealed preference."[22] Then, under non-saturation, the equalities

$\bar{x}_k^i = f_k^i (\bar{p}_1, \ldots, \bar{p}_m) = 0$ for all $i = 1, \ldots, n$ and $k = 0, 1, \ldots, m,$

imply

(8) $-\sum_{j=1}^{m} (p_j - \bar{p}_j) x_j^i = \sum_{k=0}^{m} \bar{p}_k x_k^i > 0$ unless $x_k^i = 0$ for all $i, k.$

Proof.   The equality in (8) follows from operations in (3)–(7) performed in the case of a single individual. The inequality in (8) is obtained as follows. By definition, $\bar{x}^i \equiv (\bar{x}_0^i, \bar{x}_1^i, \ldots, \bar{x}_m^i)$ maximizes the ith unit's utility subject to $\bar{P} \cdot x^i = 0$. However, since $\bar{x}^i = 0, P \cdot \bar{x}^i = 0$ also. Thus the antecedent of the revealed preference axiom holds in the form $P \cdot \bar{x}^i \leqslant P \cdot x^i$, since, in fact, $P \cdot \bar{x}^i = 0$ as just shown, and $P \cdot x^i = 0$ by the budget constraint. It follows that $P \cdot x^i > P \cdot \bar{x}^i$ unless $\bar{x}^i = x^i$; this yields $\bar{P} \cdot x^i > 0$ unless $x^i = 0$, since $\bar{P} \cdot \bar{x}^i = 0$. Dividing both sides of $\bar{P} \cdot x^i > 0$ by $\bar{P}_0$, we obtain the inequality of the lemma.

Thus it follows that $dV/dt < 0$ unless $x^i = 0$, i.e., unless $x^i = \bar{x}^i$ for all i. But if $x^i = \bar{x}^i$ for all units i, it follows that

(9) $u_k^i(x^i) = u_k^i(\bar{x}^i)$ for all $i, k,$

where $u_k^i \equiv \partial u/\partial x_k^i$.

In turn, at an individual maximum (with the whole budget spent)

(10) $p_j = u_j^i/u_0^i.$

Hence we have that $dV/dt < 0$ unless

(11) $p_j = \dfrac{u_j^i (\bar{x}^i)}{u_0^i (\bar{x}^i)} = \bar{p}_j,$

i.e., when

(12) $p_j = \bar{p}_j$ for $j = 1, 2, \ldots, m$

so that the system is in equilibrium. Hence

$\lim_{t \to \infty} \Psi(t; p^0) = \bar{p}$ for all $p.$

Bearing in mind that global stability implies the uniqueness of equilibrium (see note 8), we then have

Theorem 1. Suppose that every individual excess demand function is continuous and single-valued and no individual is saturated. Let $\bar{x}^i = 0$ for all $i = 1, 2, \ldots, m$. Then the instantaneous adjustment process is stable under pure trade. Furthermore, it has a unique (and, of course, globally stable) equilibrium price vector.[23,24]

This theorem has a number of interesting consequences.

I. Identical individuals.[25] By symmetry of the problem, we have (for each k)

$$\bar{x}_k^{\,1} = \bar{x}_k^{\,2} = \cdots = \bar{x}_k^{\,n}.$$

On the other hand, competitive equilibrium requires that

$$\Sigma_{i=1}^n \, \bar{x}_k^{\,i} = 0.$$

Hence

$$\bar{x}_k^{\,i} = 0 \qquad \text{for all } i, k.$$

This makes Theorem 1 applicable and we have

Corollary 1.1. If all individuals are identical (see definition, note 25) the instantaneous adjustment process is convergent and the (unique) equilibrium point is globally stable.[26]

Note. In particular, this is so for $n = 1$.

II. Pareto-optimal initial resource distribution. Let the initial holdings n-tuple $\overset{0}{X} \equiv (\overset{0}{X}^1, \overset{0}{X}^2, \ldots, \overset{0}{X}^n)$, where $\overset{0}{X}^i = (\overset{0}{X}_0^{\,i}, \overset{0}{X}_1^{\,i}, \ldots, \overset{0}{X}_m^{\,i})$ be Pareto-optimal. Then it follows from the results of Arrow, Debreu, and others (see note 2) that $\overset{0}{X}$ is an equilibrium position, i.e., that in this case $\bar{x}^1 = \bar{x}^2 = \cdots = \bar{x}^n = 0$. Again, Theorem 1 is applicable and we have

Corollary 1.2. If the initial resource allocation is Pareto-optimal, the instantaneous adjustment process is convergent and the (unique) equilibrium point is globally stable.

8. Weak axiom of revealed preference for the market

It is known that the aggregate demand functions need not satisfy the ("weak") revealed preference axiom. Nevertheless (see, e.g., Wald [36, pp. 375–76]), it is of interest to investigate the special class of cases where the aggregate demand functions do satisfy this axiom,[27] i.e., suppose that $P' \cdot (x'' - x') \leqslant 0, x'' \neq x'$, implies $P'' \cdot (x'' - x') < 0$, and $x = (x_0, x_1, \ldots, x_n)$ where $x_k = \Sigma_{i=1}^n x_k^i$.

Now, since $\bar{x}_k = 0$ for all $k = 0, 1, \ldots, m$ by definition of equilibrium, and $\Sigma_{k=0}^m p_k x_k^i = 0$ by virtue of the individual budget constraints, we have

(1) $\quad \Sigma_{k=0}^m p_k \bar{x}_k = \Sigma_{k=0}^m p_k x_k \; (= 0).$

The application of the revealed preference axiom for the market then yields

$$\sum_{k=0}^{m} \bar{p}_k \bar{x}_k < \sum_{k=0}^{m} \bar{p}_k x_k \qquad \text{provided } \bar{x}_k \neq x_k \text{ for some } k.$$

Since $\bar{x}_k = 0, k = 0, 1, \ldots, m$, this yields

(2) $\quad \sum_{k=0}^{m} \bar{p}_k x_k > 0 \qquad$ unless $x_k = 0$ for $k = 0, 1, \ldots, m$.

Hence Equation (7) of Section 7 yields

$$dV/dt = - \sum_{i=1}^{n} \sum_{k=0}^{m} \bar{p}_k x_k{}^i = - \sum_{k=0}^{m} \bar{p}_k \sum_{i=1}^{n} x_k{}^i = - \sum_{k=0}^{m} \bar{p}_k x_k < 0$$

where the last inequality follows from (15). This establishes, as before,

   Theorem 2.   If the aggregate excess demand functions satisfy the weak axiom of revealed preference, then the instantaneous adjustment process is stable in the x_j's and in the p_j's, and the equilibrium is unique.

9. Relationship to Hicksian stability; cases involving symmetry

Theorem 1 and its corollaries are global in nature. Similar local results can be derived immediately (and this may have been noted somewhere in the literature) in the context of the work of Hicks, Mosak, and Samuelson. Samuelson[28] pointed out that when the matrix $\| \bar{a}_{rs} \|$, $\bar{a}_{rs} = \partial f_r / \partial P_s$ (evaluated at $P = \bar{P}$) is symmetric, local dynamic stability (real parts of characteristic roots negative) is equivalent to Hicksian "perfect stability." Now

$$a_{rs} = \sum_{i=1}^{n} \bar{a}_{rs}{}^i, \qquad \bar{a}_{rs}{}^i = \partial f_r{}^i / \partial P_s \qquad \text{(evaluated at } P = \bar{P})$$

and[29]

(1) $\quad a_{rs}{}^i = (\overset{0}{X}_s{}^i - X_s{}^i) a_r{}^i + \beta_{rs}{}^i = -x_s{}^i a_r{}^i + \beta_{rs}{}^i$

where $a_r{}^i$ and $\beta_{rs}{}^i$ depend on the individual's utility function and initial holdings (they are the income and substitution terms, respectively). Evaluating at equilibrium (as indicated by bars over symbols),

(2) $\quad \bar{a}_{rs}{}^i = -\bar{x}_s{}^i a_r{}^i + \beta_{rs}{}^i.$

Suppose now

(3) $\quad \bar{x}_s{}^i = 0 \qquad$ for all i and all s.

We then have

(4) $\quad \bar{a}_{rs}{}^i = \beta_{rs}{}^i = \beta_{sr}{}^i,$

where the last equality, implying the symmetry of $\| \bar{a}_{rs} \|$, follows from the well-known properties of the substitution term. The remarks made (apparently independently) by Hicks, Mosak, and Samuelson subsequent to the publication of the first edition of *Value and Capital* [16] note that the matrix $\| \beta_{rs}{}^i \|$ satisfies the conditions of Hicks's "perfect stability." Application of the Samuelson proposition on equivalence of the two stability concepts when $\| \bar{a}_{rs} \|$ is symmetric then yields local dynamic stability of equilibrium. More direct proof is, of course, possible.

The preceding is but a special case of

Theorem 3. If all the aggregate income effects vanish at a given equilibrium point $\bar{p}$, i. e., if

$$\Sigma_{i=1}^n \bar{x}_s^i \bar{a}_r^i = 0 \quad \text{for all } s, r, = 0, 1, \ldots, m,$$

then $\bar{p}$ is locally (dynamically) stable.[30]

It will be noted that the local stability in the case of Theorem 3 is due to the fact that the matrix

$$\bar{A} = \| \bar{a}_{rs} \| \quad (r, s = 1, 2, \ldots, m)$$

of the partial derivatives of aggregate excess demand with respect to prices (which we may here take in the normalized form) is negative definite. Obviously, if $\bar{A}$ is negative definite for any reason (not necessarily the vanishing of income effects), the same conclusion follows.[31] But a stronger, global result can be obtained (A' is the transpose of the matrix A):

Theorem 4. If the matrix $A + A'$ is negative definite, then there is global stability.

Proof. It is sufficient to show that, for $V = (1/2) \Sigma_{j=1}^m f_j^2$, the inequality $dV/dt < 0$ holds unless $f_j = 0$ for all j. We have

$$dV/dt = \Sigma_{j,r} f_j (\partial f_j/\partial p_r) (dp_r/dt) = \Sigma_{j,r} f_j a_{jr} f_r,$$

i.e., in vector form, with $f = \{ f_1, f_2, \ldots, f_m \}$,

$$dV/dt = f'Af = f' [(1/2)(A + A')] f < 0.$$

where the last inequality follows from the hypothesis of the theorem.

Appendix to Part I

We consider an alternative type of adjustment process, to be called a lagged adjustment process, where individuals are not in general on the budget plane but tend toward it.

The process is of the gradient variety, based on a game interpretation of competition. As before, we denote by x_k^i the amount of commodity k in the hands of the individual i expressed as a deviation from his initial holdings. The utility function is written as $u^i(x^i)$ and the budget constraint[32]

$$P \cdot x^i \equiv \Sigma_{k=0}^n P_k x_k^i = 0, \quad P = (P_0, P_1, \ldots, P_m).$$

The bar over a symbol indicates evaluation at equilibrium.

The Lagrangian expression for the ith individual's maximization problem is

$$\Phi(x^i, \lambda^i) = u^i(x^i) - \lambda^i \Sigma_{k=0}^m P_k x_k^i.$$

We imagine three kinds of participants in this "game," controlling respectively the x^i, λ^i and P_k ($2n + m + 1$ participants altogether). Their "payoffs" are respectively Φ, $-\Phi$, and $P_k \sum_{i=1}^{n} x_k{}^i$. Each participant follows the gradient (marginal profitability) principle. Hence the dynamic adjustment equations are given by

$$(1) \quad \begin{cases} dx_k{}^i/dt = \dfrac{\partial \Phi}{\partial x_k{}^i} & (i = 1, 2, \ldots, n; k = 0, 1, \ldots, m), \\[2ex] d\lambda^i/dt = -\dfrac{\partial \Phi}{\partial \lambda^i} & (i = 1, 2, \ldots, n), \\[2ex] dP_k/dt = \dfrac{\partial\,(P_k \sum_{i=1}^{n} x_k{}^i)}{\partial P_k} & (k = 0, 1, \ldots, m). \end{cases}$$

When the right-hand rows are evaluated, this yields (writing $\partial u^i/\partial x_k{}^i = u_k{}^i$)

$$(2) \quad \begin{cases} dx_k{}^i/dt = u_k{}^i - P_k\lambda^i, \\[1ex] d\lambda^i/dt = \sum_{k=0}^{m} P_k x_k{}^i, \\[1ex] dP_k/dt = \sum_{i=1}^{n} x_k{}^i & (i = 1, 2, \ldots, n; k = 0, 1, \ldots, m). \end{cases}$$

To explore the stability properties of this system along the lines of Liapounoff's "second method" we define a "weighted distance" function V by the relation

$$(3) \quad 2V = \sum_{i,k} (x_k{}^i - \bar{x}_k{}^i)^2/\bar{\lambda}^i + \sum_{i=1}^{n} (\lambda^i - \bar{\lambda}^i)^2/\bar{\lambda}^i + \sum_{k=0}^{m} (P_k - \bar{P}_k)^2.$$

Clearly, $V \geqslant 0$ always and $V = 0$ if and only if the system is at equilibrium. We now investigate conditions under which $dV/dt < 0$.

Differentiating (3) and substituting from (2), we have

$$(4) \quad dV/dt = \sum_{i,k} \frac{1}{\bar{\lambda}^i} (x_k{}^i - x_k{}^i) \frac{dx_k{}^i}{dt} + \sum_{i=1}^{n} \frac{1}{\bar{\lambda}^i} (\lambda^i - \bar{\lambda}^i) \frac{d\lambda^i}{dt}$$

$$+ \sum_{k=0}^{m} (P_k - \bar{P}_k) \frac{dP_k}{dt}$$

$$= \sum_{i,k} \frac{1}{\bar{\lambda}^i} (x_k{}^i - \bar{x}_k{}^i)(u_k{}^i - P_k\lambda^i) + \sum_{i=1}^{n} \frac{1}{\bar{\lambda}^i}(\lambda^i - \bar{\lambda}^i)$$

$$\cdot \sum_{k=0}^{m} P_k x_k{}^i + \sum_{k=0}^{m} (P_k - \bar{P}_k) \sum_{i=1}^{n} x_k{}^i.$$

Write $w^i = \lambda^i/\bar{\lambda}^i$. Then

$$(5) \quad (u_k{}^i - \lambda^i P_k)/\bar{\lambda}^i = [(u_k{}^i - \bar{u}_k{}^i)/\bar{\lambda}^i] + [\bar{u}_k{}^i/\bar{\lambda}^i] - w^i P_k$$

$$= [(u_k{}^i - \bar{u}_k{}^i)/\bar{\lambda}^i] + \bar{P}_k - w^i P_k,$$

since utility maximization at equilibrium implies $\bar{u}_k{}^i = \bar{\lambda}^i \bar{P}_k$.

Substituting (5) in (4) and expanding, we obtain

(6) $\quad dV/dt = \Sigma_i \left[\Sigma_k (x_k^i - \bar{x}_k^i)(u_k^i - \bar{u}_k^i)/\lambda^i \right] + \Sigma_{i,k} x_k^i \bar{P}_k - \Sigma_{i,k} \bar{x}_k^i \bar{P}_k$

$\qquad - \Sigma_{i,k} x_k^i w^i P_k + \Sigma_{i,k} \bar{x}_k^i w^i P_k + \Sigma_{i,k} w^i P_k x_k^i - \Sigma_{i,k} P_k x_k^i$

$\qquad + \Sigma_{i,k} P_k x_k^i - \Sigma_{i,k} \bar{P}_k x_k^i.$

Of the nine terms in the right member of (6), the following pairs cancel: second and ninth, fourth and sixth, seventh and eighth. Also,

(7) $\quad \Sigma_{i,k} \bar{x}_k^i \bar{P}_k = \Sigma_k \bar{P}_k \Sigma_{i=1}^n \bar{x}_k^i = 0,$

since at equilibrium

$\Sigma_{k=0}^m \bar{x}_k^i = 0$

by definition. Hence,

(8) $\quad dV/dt = \Sigma_i \left[\Sigma_k (x_k^i - \bar{x}_k^i)(u_k^i - \bar{u}_k^i) \right] /\bar{\lambda}^i + \Sigma_{i,k} \bar{x}_k^i w^i P_k.$

Now (see Lemma 2 below), if u^i is strictly concave, it follows that

(9) $\quad \Sigma_k (x_k^i - \bar{x}_k^i)(u_k^i - \bar{u}_k^i) < 0 \qquad$ unless $x_k^i = \bar{x}_k^i$ for all k.

Since the second term in the right member of (8) vanishes when

(10) $\quad \bar{x}_k^i = 0 \qquad$ for all i, k

(i.e., in the absence of trade at equilibrium), it follows that (8), (9), and (10) yield

(11) $\quad dV/dt < 0 \qquad$ unless $x_k^i = 0$ for all i, k.

Since the condition $\bar{x}_k^i = 0$ means that there is no trade at equilibrium, one obtains a result analogous to that underlying Theorem 1 and its corollaries; however, since the budget constraint need not be satisfied, the convergence in the x's does not imply that in the P's. We have

Theorem 5. Let the utility function be strictly concave. If there is no trade at equilibrium (the initial holdings equal equilibrium holdings), the lagged budget adjustment process converges (in the large) in the quantities held. In particular, there is such convergence if the initial resource holdings distribution is Pareto-optimal or if all the individuals are identical.

It remains to establish the following

Lemma 2. Let $f(x)$ be a real-valued strictly concave function of the vector x. Then for any two points $x \neq \tilde{x}$,

$$(x - \tilde{x})'(f_x - \tilde{f}_x) < 0,$$

where $f_x, \tilde{f}_x$ are evaluated at $x, \tilde{x}$, respectively.

Proof.   For a real number t, let

$$g(t) = f[xt + (1 - t)\tilde{x}].$$

Then

$$g'(t) = (x - \tilde{x})' f_x[tx + (1 - t)\tilde{x}].$$

Since, $g(t)$ is a strictly concave function of the real variable t, $g'(1) < g'(0)$; the conclusion of the lemma follows.

Part II: A two-commodity economy $(m = 1)$[33]

10. A one-individual market $(n = 1)$

Consider a market where there are only two goods (X_0, X_1) and only a single ith individual. Under the assumptions of Part I [the existence of single-valued continuous excess demand functions $f_k{}^i(p_1)$, $k = 0, 1$], there exists (by virtue of the results referred to in the Introduction) an equilibrium price $\bar{p}^i$ such that

(1.1) $\infty > \bar{p}^i \geqslant 0$

and (cf. 17)

(1.2) $f^i(\bar{p}^i) = 0.$

Under the hypotheses of Theorem 1, Part I, it follows that $\bar{p}^i$ is unique and the weak axiom of revealed preference holds. It follows from Lemma 1 of Part I that (under non-saturation)

(2) $\sum_{j=1}^{m} (p_j - \bar{p}_j{}^i) x_j{}^i < 0$ for $p \neq \bar{p}^i.$

Applying this to the case $m = 1$ and dropping the subscript 1, we have

(3) $(p - \bar{p}^i) x^i < 0$

so that

(4.1) $x^i < 0$ for $p > \bar{p}^i$

and

(4.2) $x^i > 0$ for $p < \bar{p}^i.$

[If $\bar{p}^i = 0$, (4.2) holds, vacuously.]

11. A market with n-individuals.

We may now distinguish two cases according to the values of $\bar{p}^i$, as defined in Equation (1.2), Section 10.

(I) $\bar{p}^i = 0$ for all $i = 1, 2, \ldots, n.$

Here[34]

$$f(p) = \Sigma_{i=1}^n f^i(p) \begin{cases} = 0 & \text{for } p = 0, \\ < 0 & \text{for } p > 0. \end{cases}$$

It then follows that $dp/dt = f(p) < 0$, so that $\Psi(t; p^0)$ is decreasing so long as it is positive, and

$$\lim_{t \to \infty} \Psi(t; p^0) = 0 \qquad \text{for all } p^0 \geq 0;$$

that is, we have stability in the large for the (unique) equilibrium point $\bar{p} = 0$ and, of course, the system is stable.

(II) $\quad \bar{p}_0{}^i > 0 \qquad$ for some i_0.

Since there are only finitely many $\bar{p}^i$'s and $f^i(p) < 0$ for $p > \bar{p}^i$, it is clear that $f(p) < 0$ for p sufficiently large.

If $f_0{}^i(p)$ is continuous[35] we have either

(II*) $\quad \infty > f_0{}^i(0) > 0$

or

(II**) $\quad \lim_{p \to +0} f_0{}^i(p) = +\infty.$

Hence, assuming $f^i(p)$ to be single-valued, since

$$f^i(0) \geq 0 \qquad \text{for all } i = 1, 2, \dots, n.$$

it follows that

$$\infty \geq f(0) > 0.$$

If $f(p)$ is assumed continuous at $p = 0$, it follows that, for some $\epsilon > 0$.

$$f(p) > 0 \qquad \text{if } 0 \leq p < \epsilon.$$

Now let p^0 be any point in the interval $(0, \infty)$. If $f(p^0) > 0$, by the continuity of f there exists an equilibrium point $\bar{p} > p^0$ since $f(p) < 0$ for p sufficiently high. Let

$$\tilde{p} = \inf_p \{\bar{p}: f(\bar{p}) = 0, \bar{p} > p^0\}.$$

Now, by the continuity of f, $\tilde{p}$ is itself an equilibrium point [i.e., $f(\tilde{p}) = 0$] and it is clear that the solution of the dynamic system $\Psi(t; p^0)$ will increase steadily with t from p^0, since $dp/dt = f(p) > 0$, but cannot go beyond the equilibrium point $\tilde{p}$. Hence

$$\lim_{t \to \infty} \Psi(t; p^0) = \tilde{p}.$$

Similar reasoning applies to the case $f(p^0) < 0$, while if $f(p^0) = 0$, then

$$\lim_{t \to \infty} \Psi(t; p^0) = p^0.$$

Theorem 6.   For two commodities (of which one is the numéraire), if the individual excess demand functions are single-valued and continuous and no individual unit is saturated, the system is stable.

12.

Suppose the ith individual has a differentiable utility function φ^i and there is no saturation with respect *to either good*. Then with $\varphi^i = \varphi^i(x_0{}^i, x_1{}^i)$

(1)
$$\varphi_0{}^i = \partial\varphi^i/\partial x_0{}^i = \lambda^i \qquad (p_0 = 1),$$
$$\varphi_1{}^i = \partial\varphi^i/\partial x_1{}^i = \lambda^i p \qquad (p = p_1).$$

Hence

(2) $\varphi_1{}^i = p\varphi_0{}^i.$

Utilizing the budget constraint $x_0{}^i + px_1{}^i = 0$, we have

(3) $\varphi_1{}^i(-px_1{}^i, x_1{}^i) = p\varphi_0{}^i(-px_1{}^i, x_1{}^i).$

Differentiating with regard to p in (3) and omitting superscripts, we get (with $f' = dx_1/dp$),

(4) $\varphi_{10}(-x_1 - pf') + \varphi_{11}f' = \varphi_0 + p[\varphi_{00}(-x_1 - pf') + \varphi_{01}f']$

or

(5) $(\varphi_{11} - 2p\varphi_{10} + p^2\varphi_{00})f' = \varphi_0 + x_1[\varphi_{10} - p\varphi_{00}].$

Now the coefficient of f' in the left member of (5) is necessarily negative (see Hicks [17, Appendix]), while, by assuming non-saturation with respect to both commodities, we obtain $\varphi_0 > 0$.

Hence, for an individual, since $\bar{x} = 0$, it follows that, at equilibrium (if it exists),

(6) $f' < 0,$

i.e., at equilibrium the excess demand curve has a negative slope. Given (from assumptions guaranteeing the continuity and single-valuedness of the f^i) the existence of a (necessarily unique) $\bar{p}^i$ such that $f^i(\bar{p}^i) = 0$ with $0 \leqslant \bar{p}^i < \infty$, it follows again (by continuity of f^i and the uniqueness of $\bar{p}^i$) that

$$f^i(p) < 0 \qquad \text{for } p > \bar{p}^i$$

and

$$f^i(p) > 0 \qquad \text{for } 0 \leqslant p < \bar{p} \text{ if } \bar{p} > 0.$$

This yields a theorem close to Theorem 6, at least for pure exchange. (A generalization to the case involving production is straightforward.) This approach has the disadvantage of using the differentiability properties of the utility function but is closer to the "classical" methods of mathematical economics.

Note. If the utility function is additive and strictly concave, ($\varphi_{00}{}^i < 0$, $\varphi_{11}{}^i < 0$, $\varphi_{10}{}^i = 0$), it follows from (5) that $f' < 0$ for all $x_1{}^i \geq 0$, not only for $x_1{}^i = 0$. Walras [37, Appendix I], seems to have utilized this case to prove the counterpart of Theorem 6. However, he seems to ignore the possibility $\bar{p} = 0$ and, while in some respects exploiting the assumption of non-saturation, assumes saturation in other contexts. Hence, it is difficult to form a judgment as to the quality of his proof.

13. Giffen's paradox; complementarity

The results of the preceding two sections imply that in the case of two goods ($m = 1$), unique equilibrium is necessarily stable. Now at a stable equilibrium the excess demand function cannot be sloping upward. Hence, "Giffen's paradox" must be absent (a good cannot be "inferior") at a unique equilibrium in the case of two goods.

Now let us see whether there can be complementarity between the two goods at equilibrium. As Hicks has pointed out [17, Appendix] (net) complementarity, as he has defined the term, cannot be present unless there are at least three goods but we may ask whether there can be gross complementarity defined by the inequalities[36]

(1) $a_{rs} < 0$ $(r \neq s)$.

Now, for $m = 1$, the matrix

$$A = \begin{Vmatrix} a_{00} & a_{01} \\ a_{10} & a_{11} \end{Vmatrix}$$

is subject to the set of restrictions:

(2.1) $\Sigma_{r=0}^{1} P_r a_{kr} = 0$ $(k = 0, 1)$

[which[37] is due to the fact that demand is homogeneous of degree zero in the non-normalized price vector (P_0, P_1)] and (because of "Walras' Law"[38])

(2.2) $\Sigma_{k=0}^{1} \bar{P}_k \bar{a}_{kr} = 0$ $(r = 0, 1)$.

At a point (P_0, P_1) of *stable equilibrium,* we have

(3) $\bar{a}_{11} \leq 0$.

Hence, restrictions (2.1) and (2.2) for $k = 1$ and $r = 1$, respectively, imply

(4) $\bar{a}_{kr} \geq 0$, $k \neq r$ at a point of stable equilibrium.

We may summarize in the following

Remark. At any point of stable equilibrium, hence, in particular, if there is only one equilibrium (which we know to be stable), $\bar{a}_{01} \geq 0$ and $\bar{a}_{10} \geq 0$. Hence, there can be *no gross complementarity at such equilibrium points.*

Appendix to Part II

A. II.1 The result stated in Theorem 6 depends on the continuity of the individual excess demand function in the sense of note 35. The following theorem defines one class of situations where such continuity is obtained.

To simplify notation, since there are only two commodities, we shall use X to denote the numéraire and Y to denote the other good. Also, we omit until further notice the superscript i referring to the individual.

It is assumed that the individual has a continuous strictly quasi-concave utility function[39] strictly increasing in both variables and to be written as $u(X, Y)$, i.e.,

$$(1) \quad \begin{cases} & u(X, Y') > u(X, Y'') \quad \text{if } Y' > Y'' \\ \text{and} \\ & u(X', Y) > u(X'', Y) \quad \text{if } X' > X''. \end{cases}$$

Let $\overset{0}{X}, \overset{0}{Y}$ denote the quantities initially held by the individual, p denote the price of Y in terms of X (the price of X being equal to 1), and $f(p), g(p)$ denote the respective excess demand functions of the individual for X and Y.

We then have

Theorem 7.   If there is no saturation with regard to either commodity [i.e., if (1) holds], $\overset{0}{X} > 0$ implies $\lim_{p \to +0} g(p) = \infty$. Similarly, if $\overset{0}{Y} > 0$, $\lim_{p \to +\infty} f(p) = \infty$.

Proof.   Suppose the theorem is false. Then there exists a sequence $\{p_1, p_2, \ldots, p_n, \ldots\}$ and a number M such that

$$(2) \quad \lim_{n \to \infty} p_n = 0, \quad g(p_n) \leq M \quad \text{for all } n.$$

Since necessarily $g(p_n) \geq -\overset{0}{Y}$, it follows (using the budget constraint) that

$$(3) \quad \lim_{n \to \infty} f(p_n) = -\lim_{n \to \infty} [p_n g(p_n)] = 0.$$

Define the following two sequences:

$$(4) \quad \begin{cases} x_n = -p_n \dfrac{M+1}{1+p_n}, \\ \\ y_n = \dfrac{M+1}{1+p_n}, \end{cases}$$

so that the budget constraint is satisfied, i.e.,

$$(5) \quad x_n + p_n y_n = 0.$$

Now $\overset{0}{X} > 0$ by hypothesis and $\lim_{n \to \infty} x_n = 0$. Hence

$$(6) \quad \overset{0}{X} + x_n \geq 0 \quad \text{for } n \text{ sufficiently large.}$$

Also, if M is chosen to be positive (as one always may),

$$(7) \quad \overset{0}{Y} + y_n > \overset{0}{Y} \geq 0.$$

Hence, since f and g are defined to maximize utility under the budget constraint, for n sufficiently large, we have[40]

(8) $\quad u[\overset{0}{X} + f(p_n), \overset{0}{Y} + g(p_n)] \geq u[\overset{0}{X} + x_n, \overset{0}{Y} + y_n]$.

From (2) and the monotonicity (non-saturation) of u, it follows that

(9) $\quad u[\overset{0}{X} + f(p_n), \overset{0}{Y} + g(p_n)] \leq u[\overset{0}{X} + f(p_n), \overset{0}{Y} + M]$.

Inequalities (8) and (9) yield

(10) $\quad u[\overset{0}{X} + f(p_n), \overset{0}{Y} + M] \geq u[\overset{0}{X} + x_n, \overset{0}{Y} + y_n]$.

But then, let n approach infinity. By continuity of the utility function we can substitute in (10) the limits of $f(p_n), x_n$, and y_n from (3) and (4), thus obtaining

(11) $\quad u[\overset{0}{X}, \overset{0}{Y} + M] \geq u[\overset{0}{X}, \overset{0}{Y} + M + 1]$.

which contradicts the monotonicity (non-saturation) assumption with regard to the utility function. This completes the proof of the first assertion of the theorem.

By interchanging X and Y and replacing p by $1/p$, we obtain the analogous proof of the second assertion.

A. II.2. Consider the market with n individuals. Then the preceding theorem yields global stability of the system if all individuals have non-saturated utilities and the following conditions hold:

$$\Sigma_{i=1}^{n} \overset{0}{X}^i > 0, \quad \Sigma_{i=1}^{n} \overset{0}{Y}^i > 0,$$

i.e., we have

Theorem 8. Let $\Sigma_{i=1}^{n} \overset{0}{X}^i > 0$ and $\Sigma \overset{0}{Y}^i > 0$, and suppose the utility functions of all individuals are monotone in each commodity and continuous. Then $g(p)$ is continuous, at least one equilibrium point $\bar{p}$ exists, $g(p) > 0$ for all $0 < p < p'$, and $g(p) < 0$ for all $p > p''$, where p', p'' are two (finite) positive numbers. Hence, the system is stable.

The proof follows easily from Theorem 7 and the reasoning in the rest of Part II, where we note that $g(p) = -(1/p) f(p)$.

A. II.3. It is worth noting that multiplicity of equilibria and hence the presence of unstable equilibria does in fact occur under the assumptions of the present section. The following pair of utility functions yields such an outcome. We write

$$x = X - \overset{0}{X}, \quad y = Y - \overset{0}{Y}.$$

1st individual: $u(x, y) = -10^{-x} - 10^{-y}$,
2nd individual: $u(x, y) = 10^{-.04x} - 10^{-40y}$.

It is seen that these functions are monotone in both variables and strictly concave. The proof of the multiplicity of equilibria will be published elsewhere.[41]

Part III: The case of gross substitutability

14.

Gross substitutability is said to prevail in the system if

(1) $a_{rs} \equiv \partial f_r / \partial p_s \geqq 0$ $(r \neq s; r = 0, 1, \ldots, m; s = 1, 2, \ldots, m)$.

[In terms of individual units, an obvious sufficient condition for (1) is given by

(1') $(a_{rs}^{\,1}, a_{rs}^{\,2}, \ldots, a_{rs}^{\,n}) \geqslant 0$ $(r \neq s; r = 0, 1, \ldots, m; s = 1, 2, \ldots, m)$

where $a_{rs}^{\,i} \equiv \partial f_r^{\,i} / \partial p_s$. (For the vectors $a, b, a \geqslant b$ means $b \neq a \geqq b$.)]

It was shown by Metzler [24] that when gross substitutability prevails in the system, local dynamic stability (real parts of characteristic roots negative) prevails if and only if the system is perfectly stable in Hicks's sense.[42] This, of course, means that under gross substitutability we either have both types of stability or neither. The question may then be raised if there would be stability (necessarily in both senses) when not only gross substitutability but also competition is assumed.

In the original version of this paper, as submitted for publication, there were established several results on local and global stability under gross substitutability. Subsequently, H. D. Block and the authors found more general theorems, which under mild restrictions show that gross substitutability implies global stability (see [3, Theorems 1 and 2]).

In the present version of this section we therefore merely state without proof two of the original theorems, establishing local stability in general and global stability for the case where the initial price values are such as to produce positive aggregate excess demands for all commodities (or negative excess demands for all commodities) other than the numéraire. In the next section, we state and prove a theorem on global stability in the case of three commodities; the simple semi-graphic analysis possible in this case will provide a useful introduction to the more difficult proofs for the general case.

Theorem 9.   Suppose $\bar{p} > 0$ and the matrix $A = \| \bar{a}_{rs} \|$, $\bar{a}_{rs} = \partial f_r / \partial p_s |_{p = \bar{p}}$, to be nonsingular. Assume also that $\partial f_k / \partial p_j \geqq 0$ for all $k \neq j$ $(k = 0, 1, \ldots, m; j = 1, \ldots, m)$ (gross substitutability). Then the equilibrium point $\bar{p}$ is locally stable.[43]

Theorem 10.   Assume the uniqueness[44] of the solution $\Psi(t; p^0)$. Assume all $a_{kj} > 0$, $k = 0, \ldots, m; j = 1, \ldots, m$, $k \neq j$ [strong (gross) substitutability] and suppose $f(p^0) > 0$ or $f(p^0) < 0$. Then

$$\lim_{t \to \infty} \Psi(t; p^0) = \bar{p}$$

where $\bar{p}$ is the (unique) equilibrium point.

15. The case of three goods (m = 2)

Theorem 11.   Let there be only two goods other than the numéraire $(m = 2)$ and suppose strong (gross) substitutability prevails, i.e., $a_{kj} > 0$ $(k \neq j; k = 0, 1,$

$2; j = 1, 2)$. Assume also that for every value of p_1 there is a finite p_2 such that $f_2(p, p_2) = 0$ and that for every value of p_2 there is a finite value of p_1 such that $f_1(p_1, p_2) = 0$.[45]

Then the (unique) equilibrium point $\bar{p}$ is globally stable.

15.1. The proof is based on Figure 1. In this section, we shall assume that the basic features of Figure 1 are correct, i.e., that (a) on the curves $f_1 = 0$ and $f_2 = 0$, p_2 is a monotone increasing function of p_1, (b) f_1 is positive to the left and negative to the right of the curve $f_1 = 0$ and similarly f_2 is negative above and positive below the curve $f_2 = 0$, and (c) the curve $f_1 = 0$ cuts the curve $f_2 = 0$ from below. Subsequently (a) and (b) will be established in 15.2 and (c) in 15.3.

First consider a point on that boundary of quadrant I for which $f_1 = 0$. Then $f_1 = 0, f_2 < 0$; since $dp_1/dt = f_1, dp_2/dt = f_2$, the path from that point must descend vertically and therefore enter quadrant I. Similarly the path from any point on the other boundary of quadrant I (for which $f_2 = 0$) must enter quadrant I. If the path from any interior point eventually enters another quadrant, it must pass through the boundary into some quadrant other than I, which is impossible.

It follows that the path from any point in quadrant I (including the boundary) must remain in quadrant I. Since $f_1 \leq 0, f_2 \leq 0$ in quadrant I, p_1 and p_2 are both steadily decreasing. From the diagram, $p_1(t)$ and $p_2(t)$ must converge to $\bar{p}_1$ and $\bar{p}_2$, respectively.

We thus see that if the path starts in quadrant I or ever enters it, it must converge to $\bar{p}$. The same conclusion clearly holds for quadrant II. This result is in fact Theorem 10 for two commodities.

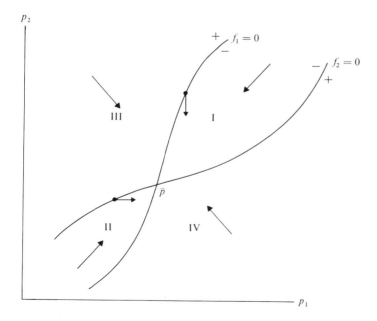

Figure 1

Now suppose p^0 is, say, in region IH. (The case of region IV is analogous.) The arrow in the diagram indicating the direction of adjustment shows that either p will converge to $\bar{p}$ or it will hit the upper boundary of region I or of region II.

Suppose p hits a point of the boundary between III and I. As we shall show below, p_2 is a monotone increasing function of p_1, on the curve $f_1(p_1, p_2) = 0$. But this means that from the boundary point p will move into the region where $f_1(p) < 0$ and $f_2(p) < 0$. The previous argument then guarantees the convergence to $\bar{p}$.

On the other hand, suppose p hits a point on the boundary of regions III and II. Here we use the fact (to be shown below) that p_2 is a monotone increasing function of p_1 on the curve $f_2(p_1, p_2) = 0$ to conclude that p will enter the interior of region II and hence converge to $\bar{p}$.

15.2. We now establish properties (a) and (b) stated in 15.1.

Consider the effect of a proportionate increase in the three non-normalized prices P_0, P_1, P_2 on the demand for the kth good ($k \geq 1$). We have (with λ as the proportionality factor)

$$\frac{dx_k}{d\lambda} = \Sigma_{r=0}^m \frac{\partial F_k}{\partial P_r} \frac{dP_r}{d\lambda}.$$

But $dx_k/d\lambda = 0$ (homogeneity of zero degree), $dP_r/d\lambda = P_r$, and $P_0 \, \partial(F_k/\partial P_r) = a_{kr}$. Hence

$$\Sigma_{r=0}^m a_{kr} P_r = 0$$

and, for $P > 0$, it cannot be that all $a_{kr}, r = 0, 1, \ldots, m$, are positive. Hence, if $a_{kr} > 0$ for $k \neq r$ (strong gross substitutability), it follows that $a_{kk} < 0$. This argument applies to $k = 1, 2$.

We have, along $f_1 = 0$,

$$0 = a_{11} dp_1 + a_{12} dp_2$$

$$dp_2/dp_1 = -a_{11}/a_{12}$$

while along $f_2 = 0$,

$$dp_2/dp_1 = -a_{21}/a_{22}.$$

Now, a_{12} and a_{21} are positive while a_{11} and a_{22} are negative; both derivatives therefore are positive and this establishes property (a) for the two curves.

Property (b) follows from the negative values of a_{11} and a_{22}.

15.3. To demonstrate property (c), we suppose that it is false and derive a contradiction. If property (c) did not hold, then Figure 1 would be replaced by Figure 2. For any point p in quadrant I we have then $f_1(p) > 0, f_2(p) > 0$; also, from the monotonicity of the curves $f_1 = 0$ and $f_2 = 0$, we must have $p_1 > \bar{p}_1$, $p_2 > \bar{p}_2$. But then, by gross substitutability, $f_0(p) > f_0(\bar{p}) = 0$ (by definition of equilibrium), so that the excess demands for all commodities are positive, which is impossible by Walras' Law.

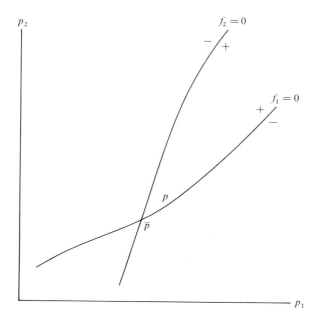

Figure 2

16. Remarks on complementarity and stability

The power of the assumption of gross substitutability of all commodities in yielding positive implications of stability raises the question of possible generalizations which admit some (gross) complementarity, a point which has already been touched on for the case of two commodities ($m = 1$) in Section 13 of Part II. Two possible special cases which come to mind are the one in which all commodities are gross complements ($a_{rs} < 0, r \neq s$) and the case suggested by Morishima [25] in which (a) a_{rs} and a_{sr} have the same sign, and (b) the sign of a_{rt} is the same as that of $a_{rs} a_{st}$, for r, s, t distinct.[46] The Morishima case is interesting not only for its intuitive appeal but also because here, as in the case of universal gross substitution, the Hicksian conditions are necessary and sufficient for dynamic stability.

As Morishima has shown, an alternative formulation of his case is the following: The set of all commodities k ($k = 0, \ldots, m$) can be divided into two non-overlapping subsets R and S, such that $a_{rs} > 0$ (gross substitutability) if both r and s are in the same subset and such that $a_{rs} < 0$ if r and s are in different subsets.[47]

We shall now prove a theorem which shows that neither the case of universal complementarity nor the Morishima case can hold for all values of the price vector if the excess demand functions are assumed to be homogeneous of degree zero in the non-normalized prices and are assumed to satisfy Walras' Law. More precisely, we show this impossibility for a class of cases which includes these two.

Theorem 12.   It is not possible to divide all the commodities (including the numéraire) into two non-empty sets R and S such that $\partial f_r/\partial p_s < 0$ for all $r \in R$, $s \in S$, and all price vectors p.

Proof.   Suppose the theorem is false. We may then define two composite commodities, a, which consists of the elements of R, each with weight 1, and b, which consists of the elements of S, each with weight 1. Let f_a denote the excess demand for a, i.e.,

(1) $f_a = \Sigma_{r \in R} \, f_r.$

Let p_0 be the price of commodity b in terms of a. Then

(2) $df_a/dp_0 = \Sigma_{r \in R}(1) \, \Sigma_{s \in S}(1) \, (\partial f_r/\partial p_s) < 0.$

This means that commodity b is a gross complement to commodity a for all p_0. However, as noted in the Remark of Section 13, Part II, gross complementarity cannot hold for all prices when $m = 1$, and, in particular, not for stable equilibrium. The contradiction establishes the theorem.

Corollary 12.1.   For any number of commodities, it is impossible that every pair be gross complements for all values of the price vector.

Proof.   Otherwise any partition of the commodities into two non-overlapping non-null sets would satisfy the hypotheses of Theorem 12.

Corollary 12.2.   The Morishima conditions cannot hold for all values of the price vector.

Theorem 12 suggests the possibility that complementarity situations which might upset stability may be incompatible with the basic assumptions of the competitive process.

In view of these results, it is worthwhile to observe that, unlike these cases, the case of universal gross substitutability is indeed possible. For instance, we may assume that all utility functions are of the form:

$$\Sigma_{k=0}^m \, \alpha_k \log X_k \quad (\alpha_k > 0)$$

or

$$\Sigma_{k=0}^m \, \gamma_k \, X_k^{\alpha_k} \quad (\gamma_k > 0, 0 < \alpha_k < 1).$$

The latter case satisfies Wald's Condition 5 [36, pp. 383–85], which as he has shown implies gross substitutability.

Notes

1   Research done partly under contract with the Office of Naval Research and partly under the auspices of the Center for Advanced Study in the Behavioral Sciences. An earlier version of this paper was circulated as Technical

Report No. 46, Project on Efficiency of Decision-Making in Economic Systems, July, 1957.

2   Without any claim to completeness, some of the more important references may be listed here: Wald [34, 35, 36]; Hotelling [18]; Lange [19]; Debreu [11, 12, 13]; Arrow [2]; Arrow and Debreu [4]; McKenzie [22, 23]; Nikaidô [29]; Gale [14]; and Uzawa [33].

3   Cournot [10, p. 89]; Walras [37, p. 109]; Marshall [21, p. 806].

4   Samuelson's analysis of the symmetric case [30, p. 270 ff.] is one of the exceptions. It may be pointed out that even for the problem of the relationship of the two concepts of stability (dynamic *versus* Hicksian), the implications of the competitive model are not known. Thus, for instance, we do not know whether Samuelson's example in which Hicksian perfect stability is present but dynamic stability is lacking [31; 30, p. 273] is compatible with competitive equilibrium, convex preferences, etc.

5   When there are only two goods in the economy, the "true dynamic" and Hicksian concepts coincide. The stability of competitive equilibrium in this case was studied by Walras [37, Lesson 7], although without a formal dynamic framework.

6   For the fundamental theorems concerning the existence and uniqueness of solutions the reader may wish to consult Coddington and Levinson [9].

7   It is conceivable that there might be more one solution ("path") Ψ with a given initial value. This should be distinguished from the possibility of multiple equilibria, i.e., multiple solutions (points) $\bar{p}$ of (3).

8   Let p^{-1} and p^{-2} be two distinct equilibrium points. Consider the solution $\psi(t; p^{-1})$. If it converges to one of the two equilibrium points, the other one, by definition, lacks global stability; if it converges to a third equilibrium point, neither p^{-1} nor p^{-2} is globally stable. (We may note for later reference that global stability of an equilibrium point, therefore, implies uniqueness of equilibrium.)

9   When needed, we refer to the *stability* concepts defined in this section as *dynamic*, to distinguish them, for instance, from Hicksian "stability."

10   See Samuelson, *Foundations* [30, p. 263 ff.].

11   See Arrow and Hurwicz [5].

12   Throughout this paper it is assumed that the budget constraint is satisfied as an *equality* for each individual maximizing his utility. This is called *non-saturation* of the individual (with regard to some commodity at least). Non-saturation with regard to each commodity is a much stronger condition: it means that an individual's utility can always be increased by giving him more of any one commodity while the amounts of all other commodities remain constant.

13   In general, the amount $\hat{X}_k{}^i$ maximizing u^i subject to (2) and (3) need not be a single-valued function of the prices, but we shall confine ourselves to situations where they are because otherwise the precise meaning of the adjustment equations becomes problematical.

14   We may note for later reference that F_k is homogeneous of degree zero in $(P_0, P_1, \ldots, P_m)$.

15   We follow the current usage for vectorial inequalities. Thus, for any two vectors a, b, $a \geqslant b$ means that every component of a is at least as large as

the corresponding component of b, and furthermore, at least one component of a is larger than the corresponding component of b.

16   See references in note 2.

17   More precisely, in the definition of equilibrium, (3.2) should read:

$$F_k(P) \leqq 0 \qquad P_k = 0 \qquad \text{if } F_k(P) < 0.$$

For simplicity, we assume in this paper that $F_k(\overline{P}) = 0$, i.e., that no commodities have positive excess supplies at equilibrium.

18   See Arrow and Debreu [4, Theorem II].

19   More stringent assumptions on the aggregate excess demand functions are needed to guarantee either the uniqueness of equilibrium or the uniqueness of solutions (paths) through any given initial value. Several cases treated in the present paper have special properties implying uniqueness of equilibrium, while some results are valid under conditions compatible with the existence of multiple equilibria. Uniqueness of solutions of the differential equation system is postulated in some of the theorems of Part III.

20   The "correspondence principle" could still be highly useful in other contexts, e.g., in macroeconomics.

21   See Arrow and Hurwicz [5]. This is a special case of Liapounoff's "second method" for proving stability.

22   Let $>$ denote the preference relation on the space of the vectors x. Suppose x' and x'', $x' \neq x''$, are the *unique* maximal elements in the sets defined respectively by the constraints $P' \cdot x \leqq 0$ and $P'' \cdot x \leqq 0$. Since under these conditions

the inequality (*) $P' \cdot x'' \leqq P' \cdot x'$ implies $x' > x''$

and

the inequality (**) $P'' \cdot x' \leqq P'' \cdot x''$ implies $x'' > x'$,

it follows that the inequalities (*) and (**) cannot both be true.

   The proposition that $x' \neq x''$ and the inequality (*) together imply the falsity of the inequality (**) is called the "weak axiom of revealed preference." (See Wald [36, pp. 375–76], and Samuelson [30, pp. 110–111].) As here stated, the axiom may be applied not only to pure trade but also to a production economy. The use of budget constraints in the equality form $P \cdot x = 0$ (rather than weak inequality) is justified when the individual is not saturated (i.e., no interior point of the set $P \cdot x \leqq 0$ is preferable to some point on $P \cdot x = 0$). (In this note, $P \cdot x$ denotes the inner product of the vectors P and x.)

23   With regard to a production economy, it is still true that $x_k{}^i \to \overline{x}_k{}^i$ as $t \to \infty$, but we have no basis for making the corresponding assertion with regard to prices.

24   A local version of this theorem was established under special conditions by M. Morishima [26, pp. 203–205].

25   We say that all individuals are identical if all the individual excess demand functions are identical. This would occur under pure trade if the functions $\omega^i(x^i)$ defined by $u^i(X^i) = ui(\overset{0}{X}{}^i + x^i) = \omega^i(x^i)$ were identical for all individuals. (u^i is the ith utility function.) The simplest case, of course, is

that in which all the utility functions u^i are identical and so are all the initial holdings vectors $\overset{0}{X}{}^i$.

26 A local version of this corollary was established by M. Allais [1, Tome II, pp. 486–493].

27 That this is not impossible for $n > 1$ is shown by the case of identical individuals (Cor. 1.1).

28 *Foundations* [30, pp. 270–72].

29 See Hicks, *Value and Capital* [17, Appendix, p. 313].

30 See Samuelson [30, p. 270], concerning the economic interpretation of the vanishing of income effects. Cf. also Hicks [17, p. 72]: "The only possible ultimate source of instability is strong asymmetry in the income effects."

In Sec. 15 of the first edition of *Value and Capital* [16] this was shown explicitly for the case of two goods, by examining a diagonal term a_{rr}; in the second edition, the case of more goods is also covered. Hicks's remarks were meant to apply to "perfect stability."

31 Cf. Samuelson [31, p. 271].

32 We do not normalize prices here.

33 In this part we drop the subscript 1 in f_1, p_1, etc. wherever convenient.

34 $\bar{p} = 0$ is the unique equilibrium point.

35 Here we find it convenient to write $f(0) = +\infty$ if $\lim_{p \to +0} j(p) = +\infty$ and $f(p)$ is said to be *continuous* at $p = 0$ if either $\lim_{p \to +0} f(p) = \infty$ or $\lim_{p \to +0} f(p) = f(0)$.

36 See Section 9 above for the definition of a_{rs}.

37 For derivation, see Section 15.2 below.

38 Equation (2.2) holds only at equilibrium; (2.1) everywhere, including equilibrium.

The "Walras Law," resulting directly from aggregating the individual budget equations, states that

$$\Sigma_{k=0}^{m} P_k x_k = 0 \qquad \text{for all } (P_0, P_1, \ldots, P_m).$$

Upon differentiating with respect to, say, P_r (cf. Hicks [17, Appendix, p. 308, Eq. (7.1)]), this yields

$$\Sigma_{k=0}^{m} P_k \frac{\partial x_k}{\partial P_r} = -x_r$$

and hence, at equilibrium, in view of $x_r = 0$,

$$\Sigma_{k=0}^{m} \bar{P}_k \bar{a}_{kr} = 0.$$

39 The argument could be carried out in terms of an ordering relation.

40 Bundle $(\overset{0}{X} + x_n, \overset{0}{Y} + y_n)$ satisfies the budget constraint for p_n.

41 Cf. Wald [36, pp. 387–88]. However, Wald's case involves nonisolated equilibrium points. The issue of the possibility of multiple equilibria (with consequent instability of some) was argued between Auspitz and Lieben, on the one side and Walras, on the other. While one of the former later conceded the possibility, an actual example of this type does not seem to have been constructed.

42 It is worth mentioning at this point that Wald [36] proved the uniqueness of equilibrium when gross substitutability prevails in the system. (See also Gale [14].)

43 For the case $m = 2$, this result has already been established by Bushaw and Clower [8, p. 81]. The general case has been demonstrated independently by Hahn [15] and Negishi [28].

44 E.g., $f(p)$ satisfies the Lipschitz condition. See Coddington and Levinson [9].

45 These properties can be derived from utility maximization considerations via a composite commodity argument.

46 In words, if commodity r is a gross substitute (complement) for commodity s, then commodity s is a gross substitute or complement, respectively, for commodity r; substitutes of substitutes and complements are substitutes; and substitutes of complements and complements of substitutes are complements.

47 Morishima in his own analysis of dynamic stability applied the above-stated conditions only to the non-numéraire commodities $1, 2, \ldots, m$. In the following analysis, however, we have used the term, "Morishima case," in the sense of the above paragraph, that is, applying to all commodities.

References

[1] Allais, Maurice: *Traité d'Economie Pure,* Paris: Imprimerie Nationale, 1943.

[2] Arrow, Kenneth J.: "An Extension of the Basic Theorems of Classical Welfare Economics," in J. Neyman (ed.), *Proceedings of the Second Berkeley Symposium on Mathematical Statistics and Probability,* Berkeley and Los Angeles: University of California Press, 1951, pp. 507–532.

[3] Arrow, Kenneth J., Henry D. Block, and Leonid Hurwicz: "On the Stability of the Competitive Equilibrium, II," this volume, III.1, pp. 228–255.

[4] Arrow, Kenneth J., and Gerard Debreu: "Existence of an Equilibrium for a Competitive Economy," *Econometrica,* 22: 265–290 (July, 1954).

[5] Arrow, Kenneth J., and Leonid Hurwicz: "A Gradient Method for Approximating Saddle Point and Constrained Maxima," P-223, the RAND Corporation, Santa Monica, California, June, 1951 (to appear in a somewhat modified form in K. Arrow, L. Hurwicz, and H. Uzawa, *Studies in Linear and Non-Linear Programming,* Stanford University Press).

[6] Arrow, Kenneth J., and Marc Nerlove: "A Note on Expectations and Stability," this volume, III.4, pp. 317–325.

[7] Bellman, Richard: *Stability Theory of Differential Equations,* New York: McGraw-Hill, 1953.

[8] Bushaw, D. W., and R. W. Clower, *Introduction to Mathematical Economics,* Homewood, Illinois: Richard D. Irwin, 1957.

[9] Coddington, E. A., and N. Levinson: *Theory of Ordinary Differential Equations,* New York: McGraw-Hill, 1955.

[10]   Cournot, Antoine Augustin: *Researches into the Mathematical Princi-
        ples of the Theory of Wealth* (N. T. Bacon, tr.), New York: The
        MacMillan Company, 1897.
[11]   Debreu, Gerard: "The Coefficient of Resource Utilization," *Econo-
        metrica*, 19: 273–292 (July, 1951).
[12]   Debreu, Gerard: "Market Equilibrium," *Proceedings of the National
        Academy of Sciences*, 42: 876–878, (November, 1956).
[13]   Debreu, Gerard: "Valuation Equilibrium and Pareto Optimum," *Pro-
        ceedings of the National Academy of Sciences*, 40: 588–592 (July,
        1954).
[14]   Gale, David: "The Law of Supply and Demand," *Math. Scand.* 3: 155–
        169 (1955).
[15]   Hahn, Frank: "Gross Substitutes and the Dynamic Stability of General
        Equilibrium," *Econometrica* 26: 169–170 (January, 1958).
[16]   Hicks, John R.: *Value and Capital*, 1st ed., Oxford: Oxford University
        Press, 1939.
[17]   Hicks, John: *Value and Capital*, 2nd ed., Oxford: Oxford University
        Press, 1946.
[18]   Hotelling, Harold: "The General Welfare in Relation to Problems of
        Taxation and Railway and Utility Rates," *Econometrica*, 6: 242–269
        (July, 1938).
[19]   Lange, Oskar: "The Foundations of Welfare Economics," *Econometrica*,
        10: 215–228 (July–October, 1942).
[20]   Lange, Oskar: *Price Flexibility and Employment*, Bloomington, Indiana:
        The Principia Press, 1944, Appendix.
[21]   Marshall, Alfred: *Principles of Economics*, 8th ed., New York: The
        MacMillan Company, 1948.
[22]   McKenzie, Lionel W.: "Competitive Equilibrium with Dependent Con-
        sumer Preferences," in United States Air Force, the *Second Symposium
        on Linear Programming*, Washington, D.C., January, 1955, pp. 277–294.
[23]   McKenzie, Lionel: "On Equilibrium in Graham's Model of World Trade
        and Other Competitive Systems," *Econometrica*, 22: 147–161 (April,
        1954).
[24]   Metzler, Lloyd: "Stability of Multiple Markets: the Hicks Conditions,"
        Econometrica, 13: 277–292 (October, 1945).
[25]   Morishima, Michio: "On the Laws of Change of the Price-system in an
        Economy which Contains Complementary Commodities," *Osaka Eco-
        nomic Papers*, I: 101–113 (May, 1952).
[26]   Morishima, Michio: "Notes on the Theory of Stability of Multiple Ex-
        change," *Review of Economic Studies*. XXIV: 203–208 (May, 1957).
[27]   Mosak, Jacob L: *General Equilibrium Theory in International Trade*,
        Bloomington, Indiana: The Principia Press, 1944.
[28]   Negishi, Takashi: "A Note on the Stability of an Economy where All
        Goods are Gross Substitutes," *Econometrica*, 26: July, 1958.
[29]   Nikaidô, Hukukane: "On the Classical Multilateral Exchange Problem,"
        Metroeconomica, VIII: 135–145 (August, 1956).
[30]   Samuelson, Paul A.: *Foundations of Economic Analysis*, Cambridge,
        Massachusetts: Harvard University Press, 1948.

[31]   Samuelson, Paul: "The Relation between Hicksian Stability and True Dynamic Stability," *Econometrica*, 12: 256–257 (July–October, 1944).

[32]   Samuelson, Paul: "The Stability of Equilibrium: Comparative Statics and Dynamics," *Econometrica*, 9: 97–120 (January, 1941).

[33]   Uzawa, Hirofumi: "Note on Existence of an Equilibrium for a Competitive Economy," Technical Report No. 40, Project on Efficiency of Decision-Making in Economic Systems, Stanford University, November, 1956.

[34]   Wald, Abraham: "Über die eindeutige positive Lösbarkeit der neuen Produktionsgleichungen," *Ergebnisse eines mathematischen Kolloquiums*, Heft 6: 12–20 (1933–34), Vienna: F. Deuticke, 1935.

[35]   Wald, Abraham: "Über die Produktionsgleichungen der Ökonomischen Wertlehre (II. Mitteilung)," *Ergebnisse eines mathematischen Kolloquiums*, 7: 1–6 (1934–35), Vienna: F. Deuticke, 1935.

[36]   Wald, Abraham: "On Some Systems of Equations of Mathematical Economics," *Econometrica*, 19: 368–403 (October, 1951).

[37]   Walras, Léon: *Elements of Pure Economics* (William Jaffé, tr.), London: George Allen & Unwin, and Homewood, Illinois: Irwin, 1954.

On the stability of the competitive equilibrium, II[1]

KENNETH J. ARROW
H. D. BLOCK
LEONID HURWICZ

Introduction

In this paper we present several extensions of the results on the stability of the competitive equilibrium contained in [2].

One such extension establishes the stability in the large, when substitution prevails in the system, for commodity spaces of arbitrary finite dimensionality; in [2], the results obtained for the case of substitutability were local, or limited to spaces of low dimensionality, or valid for special initial positions only.

Horizons are also broadened with regard to the adjustment processes considered. In [2], only processes with a numéraire commodity singled out (its price fixed throughout the process) were treated (the "normalized process"). Here we obtain in virtually every case parallel results for the "non-normalized process" where all commodities are treated symmetrically and there is no numéraire.

Furthermore, in some cases (including that of substitutability) we find it possible to relax the assumptions concerning the dependence of the rate of change in prices on the excess demand for the relevant commodity: instead of postulating simple proportionality, we only require that the rate of price change be a single-valued sign-preserving function of the excess demand. This is an interesting example of a situation where only the "qualitative" features of the dynamic process are of importance.

Finally, we prove that competitive equilibrium is stable in a class of cases ("dominant diagonal") where the demand for each particular commodity is more sensitive (in a sense to be specified) to a change in the price of that commodity itself than it is to a price change in any other commodity.

1. The model (statics)

We assume that there are $m + 1$ commodities, labeled $0, 1, \ldots, m$. The (non-normalized) price of the kth commodity is denoted by P_k and is always assumed to be nonnegative, i.e.,

(1) $\quad P_k \geqq 0 \quad (k = 0, 1, \ldots, m)$.

The excess demand (= demand − supply) of the ith individual ($i = 1, 2, \ldots, n$) for the kth commodity is denoted by x_k^i. The budget constraint for the ith individual is written in the form

(2') $\quad \Sigma_{k=0}^{m} P_k x_k^i = 0$,

or, in the inner product notation,

(2'') $\quad P \cdot x^i = 0$,

where

(2''') $\quad P = (P_0, P_1, \ldots, P_m) \quad$ and $\quad x^i = (x_0^i, x_1^i, \ldots, x_m^i)$.

The budget constraint (2'') does not exclude the possibility that the excess demands for some products with zero prices may be finite.

The aggregate excess demand for the kth commodity is defined as

(3) $\quad x_k = \Sigma_{i=1}^{n} x_k^i$.

The summation of the budget constraints (2) for all individuals yields the so-called *Walras Law* (W):

$$\Sigma_{k=0}^{m} P_k x_k \equiv P \cdot x = 0,$$

where

(4'') $\quad x = (x_0, x_1, \ldots, x_m)$.

Each individual's excess demand is a function of the prices, written

(5) $\quad x_k^i = F_k^i(P)$.

It is frequently assumed that the $F_k{}^i$ are positively homogeneous of degree zero in P, so that

(6) $F_k{}^i(\lambda P) = F_k{}^i(P)$ for any $\lambda > 0$.

[The homogeneity property can be derived from the assumption that the individual is maximizing his satisfaction (utility) subject to the budget constraint (2).]

The aggregate excess demand function is defined by

(7) $F_k(P) = \sum_{i=1}^n F_k{}^i(P)$.

If the individual excess demand functions are positively homogeneous of degree zero, then so is the aggregate function, and we have

(8) $F_k(\lambda P) = F_k(P)$ for any $\lambda > 0$.

The aggregate excess demand function vector

(9) $F = (F_0, F_1, \ldots, F_m)$

is said to possess an equilibrium price (vector) $\overline{P}$ if the relations

(10) $F(\overline{P}) \le 0$, $\overline{P} \ge 0$, $\overline{P}_k = 0$ if $F_k(\overline{P}) < 0$,

are satisfied.[2]

It is known from recent contributions (see [1, 4, 7, 8, 11, 13]) that, with certain additional assumptions concerning the nature of the economy, F will possess an equilibrium price vector if every component of F is a continuous function single-valued except at the origin; in what follows we shall assume that F has the latter two properties (so that the differential equation systems being studied are meaningful and possess solutions) and that at least one equilibrium price vector exists. If positive homogeneity is assumed, any positive (scalar) multiple of an equilibrium price vector is also an equilibrium price vector.

In the present paper we shall confine attention to the case where the equilibrium is not characterized by any "corner" components [k is a "corner" component if $F_k(\overline{P}) < 0$, $\overline{P}_k = 0$]. Then (10) is replaced by

(10′) $F(\overline{P}) = 0$, $\overline{P} \ge 0$.

It is sometimes convenient to single out one commodity, say that bearing the subscript 0, as the "numéraire" in terms of which other prices are expressed. Assuming $P_0 > 0$, we write

(11′) $p_k = P_k/P_0$ $(k = 0, 1, \ldots, m)$

and

(11″) $p = (p_1, p_2, \ldots, p_m)$.

p and its components are referred to as *normalized*, while P and its components are called *non-normalized*.

When the F_k are assumed positively homogeneous in P and $P_0 > 0$, we have

(12) $F_k(P) = F_k(P_0, P_1, \ldots, P_m) = F_k(1, p_1, \ldots, p_m)$.

We shall write

(13') $f_k(p) = f_k(p_1, \ldots, p_m) = F_k(1, p_1, \ldots, p_m)$

and

(13") $\bar{p}_k = \bar{P}_k / \bar{P}_0$

for $k = 0, 1, \ldots, m$.

2. The model (dynamics)

We shall consider two classes of price adjustment processes: (I) non-normalized and (II) normalized.

The *non-normalized* process (I) is governed by the differential equation system (with the symbols P, F as defined in the preceding section)

(1) $dP_k/dt = H_k[F_k(P)]$ $(k = 0, 1, \ldots, m)$

where t denotes time. A *solution of* (1) *through* P^0 is an $m + 1$ dimensional function $\Psi^I(t; P^0)$ of time such that

(2.1) $\Psi^I(0; P^0) = P^0$

and the kth component $\Psi_k{}^I$ of Ψ^I satisfies the identity

(2.2) $d\Psi_k{}^I/dt = H_k\{F_k[\Psi^I(t; P^0)]\}$ for all $t \geqq 0$.

The normalized process (II) is governed by the differential equation system (with the symbols p, f as defined in the preceding section)

(3) $dp_j/dt = h_j[f_j(p)]$ $(j = 1, 2, \ldots, m)$.

A *solution of* (3) *through* p^0 is an m-dimensional function $\psi^{II}(t; p^0)$ of time such that

(4.1) $\psi^{II}(0; p^0) = p^0$

and the jth component $\psi_j{}^{II}$ of ψ^{II} satisfies the identity

(4.2) $d\psi_j{}^{II}/dt = h_j\{f_j[\psi^{II}(t; p^0)]\}$ for all $t \geqq 0$.

The functions H_k and h_j are always assumed to be continuous and *sign-preserving*. [A function g is said to be sign-preserving if sgn $(g(s)) = $ sgn s.]

A differential *system* is said to be *stable (in the large)* if, given any initial value, every solution of the system through that value converges to some equilibrium point of the system.

It may be helpful to point out that one can study the behavior of the normalized prices under the non-normalized process and vice versa. Thus, under the non-normalized process (I), we have from the definition of the normalized price

$$p_j = \frac{\Psi_j^I(t; P^0)}{\Psi_0^I(t; P^0)} \equiv \psi_j^I(t; p^0)$$

where

$$p^0 = (P_1^0/P_0^0, \ldots, P_m^0/P_0^0).$$

On the other hand, we may "embed" (3) in an expanded differential system

$$(3') \quad \begin{cases} d(P_j/P_0)/dt = h_j[f_j(P_1/P_0, \ldots, P_m/P_0)], \\ dP_0/dt = 0, \end{cases}$$

which yields the same behavior of $p(t)$ as (3), but also defines the behavior of $P(t)$, to be written, say, as $\Psi^{II}(t; P^0)$.

We note that, in general, Ψ^{II} is different from Ψ^I, even though they both describe the behavior of the non-normalized price vector P. Similarly, ψ^{II} is, in general, different from ψ^I; that is the behavior of the normalized price vector differs depending on whether process (I) or process (II) is assumed, and the same is true of the behavior of the non-normalized price vector.

In what follows, we shall confine ourselves to the study of the behavior of the non-normalized price vector P under the non-normalized process (Ψ^I) and of the normalized price vector p under the normalized process (ψ^{II}).

3. The concept of substitutability and some of its static properties

The concept of substitutability used here (as also in [2]) is "gross" (as in Metzler [9] and Mosak [10]) rather than "net" (as in Hicks [5]). The basic idea of the gross substitutability concept is this: if one commodity price goes up while all other prices remain unchanged, there will be an increase in excess demand for every commodity whose price has remained constant. In symbols, for two (non-normalized) price vectors

$$P' = (P_0', \ldots, P_m'), \quad P'' = (P_0'', \ldots, P_m'')$$

and any integer k_0 in $\{0, 1, 2, \ldots, m\}$, we have the following condition[3] (*gross substitutability, finite increment form*):

$$(S_F) \quad \begin{cases} \text{the relations} & \begin{array}{ll} P_r' = P_r'' & \text{for all } r \neq k_0, \\ P_{k_0}' < P_{k_0}'' & \end{array} \\ \text{imply} & F_r(P') < F_r(P'') \quad \text{for all } r \neq k_0. \end{cases}$$

Now (S_F) as just defined is implied by, but not equivalent to, the condition (*gross substitutability, differential form*)[4]:

(S_D) $\left\{\begin{array}{l}\text{the functions } F_k \text{ and all the partial derivatives } F_{rk} = \partial F_r/\partial P_k \ (r, k = 0, \\ 1, \ldots, m) \text{ exist and are continuous (though possibly infinite-valued,} \\ \text{and, for all } P, F_{rs} = \partial F_r/\partial P_s > 0, \text{ for all } r \neq s \ (r, s = 0, 1, \ldots, m).\end{array}\right.$

The advantage of (S_D) is that, in addition to implying (S_F), it also yields (with the help of the Walras Law) another needed property, viz. the positiveness of the equilibrium price vector. Because of its importance for subsequent developments, we state this as a corollary to

Lemma 1. If the excess demand functions are positive homogeneous (H) and satisfy the differential form (S_D) of gross substitutability, then the excess demand for any free good is positive infinite, provided not all goods are free; i.e.,

if $P \geqslant 0$ and, for some $r \geq 0$, $P_r = 0$, then $F_r(P) = +\infty$.

Proof. For any price vector P, whether or not it has zero components, and any component r, define

(1) $g(p_1, \ldots, p_m) = F_r(1, p_1, \ldots, p_m)$.

By homogeneity (H), for $P_0 > 0$,

(2) $F_r(P) = F_r(P_0, \ldots, P_m) = g(P_1/P_0), \ldots, P_m/P_0)$,

so that, for $r > 0$,

(3) $\left\{\begin{array}{l} F_{rj} = g_j/P_0 \qquad \text{for } j > 0, \\ F_{r0} = \sum_{s=1}^{m}(-g_s)\,(P_s/P_0^2), \end{array}\right.$

and, therefore,

(4) $F_{r0} = -(\sum_{s=1}^{m} P_s F_{rs})/P_0$.

Let P^0 be any point for which some but not all components are zero; without loss of generality we suppose $P_0^0 > 0$. Let

$A = \{s \colon P_s^0 = 0\}, \qquad B = \{s \colon P_s^0 > 0, s > 0\}.$

Define a variable point P^t, $t \geq 0$, by the conditions

(5) $P_s^t = t \qquad \text{for } s \in A, P_s^t = P_s^0 \text{ otherwise.}$

Choose any fixed r in A; then by the assumption (S_D), $F_{r0} > 0$, $F_{rs} > 0$ for $s \in B$. With the aid of (3) and (4), we have, for $P = P^t$, $t \geq 0$,

$\sum_{s \in A} P_s^t F_{rs} < -\sum_{s \in B} P_s^t F_{rs} < 0;$

hence, because of (5),

(6) $t \sum_{s \in A} F_{rs} < 0$.

The left-hand side is clearly $t\,[dF_r(P^t)/dt]$. Since the inequality holds for all $t \geq 0$ and since the partial derivatives are all continuous, we can find c and t_0

such that

(7) $t[dF_r(P^t)/dt] < c < 0$ for $0 \leqq t \leqq t_0$.

Divide through in (7) by t and integrate from ϵ to t_0. After rearrangement, we have

(8) $F_r(P^\epsilon) > F_r(P^{t_0}) + c \log \epsilon - c \log t_0$.

If we now let ϵ approach zero and recall that $c < 0$, we see that $F_r(P^0) = +\infty$.

Q.E.D.

Corollary to Lemma 1.[5]   Under the conditions of Lemma 1, if $\overline{P}$ is an equilibrium price vector, then $\overline{P} > 0$, and $F(\overline{P}) = 0$.

Proof.   If $\overline{P}$ is an equilibrium price vector, then by definition (10), section 1, at least one component is positive. If some component $\overline{P}_r$ is zero, then $F_r(\overline{P}) = +\infty > 0$ by Lemma 1, contrary to (10), section 1.

In deriving Theorem 2 below, we find it convenient to use a condition of substitutability, to be denoted by (S_F') which is shown to be equivalent to (S_F) in

Lemma 2.   The condition

(S_F') $\left\{ \begin{array}{l} \text{the relations } P' \leqslant P'', P_r' = P_r'' \text{ for all } r \in R \subset \{0, 1, \ldots, m\} \\ \text{imply } F_r(P') < F_r(P'') \text{ for all } r \in R, \end{array} \right.$

is equivalent to the condition (S_F) as defined above.

Proof.   That (S_F') implies (S_F) is seen by taking $R = \{0, 1, \ldots, m\} - k_0$. To see that (S_F) implies (S_F'), let

$P_k'' = P_k' + h_k$

with

$h_k > 0$ for $k \in \{k_1, k_2, \ldots, k_v\} = \{0, 1, \ldots, m\} - R$.

Consider the sequence of price vectors defined by

$\left\{ \begin{array}{l} P^0 = P', \\ \ldots \\ P^1 = P^0 + (0, \ldots, 0, h_{k_1}, 0, \ldots, 0), \\ P^s = P^{s-1} + (0, \ldots, 0, h_{k_s}, 0, \ldots, 0), \quad s = 1, 2, \ldots, v, \\ \ldots \\ P^v = P''. \end{array} \right.$

By (S_F),

$F_w(P^s) > F_w(P^{s-1})$ for $w \neq k_s$,

and, since R and $\{k_1, \ldots, k_v\}$ are disjoint, we have, for any $r \in R$,

$F_r(P'') = F_r(P^v) > F_r(P^{v-1}) > \cdots > F_r(P') > F_r(P^0) = F_r(P')$,

and the conclusion of (S_F') follows.

In deriving Theorem 1 we use yet another condition related to substitutability (meaningful only when $\overline{P} > 0$):

$$(S^*) \begin{cases} \text{if } F(P) \neq 0, F(\overline{P}) = 0, P_{K'}/\overline{P}_{K'} = \max_{k \in \{0,1,\dots,m\}}(P_k/\overline{P}_k), \\ \text{and } P_{K''}/\overline{P}_{K''} = \min_{k \in \{0,1,\dots,m\}}(P_k/\overline{P}_k), \\ \text{then } F_{K'}(P) < 0 \text{ and } F_{K''}(P) > 0. \end{cases}$$

Since the proof of stability of equilibrium in Theorem 1 uses (S^*) as its hypothesis, it becomes crucial to know under what conditions (S^*) holds. This question is answered by

Lemma 3. Substitutability (S_F'), together with positiveness of the equilibrium price vector (E^+) and positive homogeneity (H) of the excess demand functions, implies condition (S^*), provided $P > 0$.[6,7]

Proof. Let $F(P) \neq 0$, $F(\overline{P}) = 0$, and $P_{K'}/\overline{P}_{K'} \geq P_k/\overline{P}_k$ for all k in $\{0, 1, \dots, m\}$. We must have

$$P_{K'}/\overline{P}_{K'} > P_{k_0}/\overline{P}_{k_0} \qquad \text{for some } k_0,$$

since otherwise

$$P = \lambda \overline{P} \qquad \text{for some } \lambda > 0,$$

and hence [by (H)], $F(P) = 0$, which contradicts the hypothesis. Since $P_{K'} > 0$, we can define

$$P^* = (\overline{P}_{K'}/P_{K'})P.$$

Then, by hypothesis, $P^* \leq \overline{P}$ and $P_{K'}^* = \overline{P}_{K'}$. Hence by (H) and (S_F'),

$$F_{K'}(P) = F_{K'}(P^*) < F_{K'}(\overline{P}) = 0.$$

Similarly, with K'' as in (S^*), we define

$$P^{**} = (\overline{P}_{K''}/P_{K''})P$$

and obtain $\overline{P} \leq P^{**}$, $\overline{P}_{K''} = P_{K''}^{**}$, so that, by (H) and (S_F'),

$$0 = F_{K''}(\overline{P}) < F_{K''}(P^{**}) = F_{K''}(P).$$

Since the uniqueness of the "equilibrium price ray" is used in the proofs of Theorems 1 and 2, it is of interest to see that

Lemma 4. (S^*) and (H) imply uniqueness of the equilibrium price ray, i.e.,

(U)   if $F(\overline{P}'') = F(\overline{P}') = 0$,   then $\overline{P}'' = \lambda \overline{P}'$ for some $\lambda > 0$.

Proof. We follow Wald [14, pp. 385–7]. Suppose $F(\overline{P}') = F(\overline{P}'') = 0$, and let $\overline{P}_{K'}'/\overline{P}_{K''}'' = \min_{k \in \{0,1,\dots,m\}}(\overline{P}_k'/\overline{P}_k'')$. By (H), we may replace $\overline{P}''$ by $\overline{P}'''$ such that $\overline{P}''' = \mu \overline{P}''$, $\mu > 0$, and $\overline{P}_{K'}' = \overline{P}_{K}'''$. If $\overline{P} \neq \lambda \overline{P}''$ for all $\lambda > 0$, $\overline{P}''' \leq \overline{P}'$, and hence by (S^*), $F_K(\overline{P}''') > 0$, which contradicts the assumption that $\overline{P}''$ (and, therefore, $\overline{P}'''$) is an equilibrium price vector.

3.1. In this section we shall establish another (static) result, to be used in the proof of Theorem 2 in section 4.2. It is included here because of its static nature, but it is not used in the proof of Theorem 1 of section 4.1 and its reading may be postponed until after section 4.1 is completed.

Lemma 5.   If the equilibrium vector $\overline{P} > 0$ and gross substitutability (S_F') prevails and the Walras Law (W) together with positive homogeneity (H) hold, then, for any non-equilibrium vector $P > 0$, we have[8]

(1) $\overline{P} \cdot F(P) \equiv \Sigma_{k=0}^{m} \overline{P}_k F_k(P) > 0.$

3.1.1. Proof of Lemma 5.

3.1.1.0. Suppose the Lemma has been shown to hold for the special case where,[9]

$$\overline{P} = \lambda 1 \equiv (\lambda, \lambda, \ldots, \lambda), \qquad \lambda > 0,$$

so that

(2) $F(P) \neq 0$ implies $\Sigma_{k=0}^{m} F_k(P) > 0.$

We shall show that this implies the validity of the Lemma in the general case. This is accomplished by showing that the general case can be reduced to the special. Let asterisks denote the entities in the general case and transform the variables by changing to new units of measurement in such a way that in the new units of measurement (entities without asterisks) $P_k = P_k^*/\overline{P}_k^*$, so that $\overline{P} = \lambda 1$, $\overline{P}_k F_k(P) = \overline{P}_k^* F_k^*(P^*)$, and $\overline{P} \cdot F(P) = \overline{P}^* \cdot F^*(P^*)$. But then $\overline{P}^* \cdot F^*(P^*) = \lambda \Sigma_{k=0}^{m} F_k(P)$ and the latter expression is positive by (2) if $F^*(P^*) \neq 0$. Hence it will suffice to prove (2) and the Lemma will follow.

3.1.1.1. We now assume that the equilibrium vector is of the form $(\lambda, \lambda, \ldots, \lambda)$ and it is our purpose to show that, for a positive non-equilibrium P,

(3) $1 \cdot F(P) = \Sigma_k F_k(P) > 0.$

Without loss of generality we may so number the commodities that

(4) $P_0 \leqq P_1 \leqq \cdots \leqq P_m.$

Furthermore, since P is non-equilibrium, it cannot have all components equal [by (H)], and hence one of the inequalities in (4) must be strict, say

(5) $P_v < P_{v+1}$ for some $0 \leqq v < m.$

We now define a sequence of $m + 1$ dimensional vectors $P^0, P^1, \ldots, P^m$ by the relations

(6)
$$
\begin{cases}
P^0 = (P_0, P_0, P_0, \ldots, P_0), \\
P^1 = (P_0, P_1, P_1, \ldots, P_1), \\
P^2 = (P_0, P_1, P_2, \ldots, P_2), \\
\cdots \\
P^s = (P_0, P_1, \ldots, P_{s-1}, P_s, P_s, \ldots, P_s), \\
\cdots \\
P^m = (P_0, P_1, \ldots, P_m),
\end{cases}
$$

where the P_j are the components of P, so that

(7) $P^m = P$.

The excess demand vector corresponding to P^s will be denoted by x^s, i.e.,

(8) $x^s = F(P^s)$.

In particular, since P^0 has equal components,

(9) $x^0 = F(P^0) = 0$.

The inequality (3) we are about to prove may be rewritten as

(10) $1 \cdot x^m > 0$.

Now

(11) $x^m = (x^m - x^{m-1}) + (x^{m-1} - x^{m-2}) + \cdots + (x^2 - x^1) + (x^1 - x^0) + x^0$.

and, because of (9), the last term on the right drops out. Hence (10) will have been proved if we show that the sum of components of every difference in parentheses on the right of (11) is nonnegative and at least one is positive. Specifically, we shall show that

(12) $1 \cdot (x^{s+1} - x^s) \geq 0$ for $s = 0, 1, \ldots, m - 1$

and

$1 \cdot (x^{v+1} - x^v) > 0$.

Before proceeding with the proof, we introduce some additional notation. We define

(13) $\begin{cases} b_0 = 1, \\ b_j = (1/P_0)(P_j - P_{j-1}), \end{cases}$

so that

(14) $\begin{cases} b_k \geq 0 \quad \text{for } k = 0, 1, \ldots, m, \text{ and} \\ b_{v+1} > 0. \end{cases}$

For $s < m$, let k' range over $\{0, 1, \ldots, s\}$ and k'' over $\{s + 1, s + 2, \ldots, m\}$.[10] We then have

(15.1) $P_{k'}{}^{s+1} = P_{k'}{}^s$,

(15.2) $P_{k''}{}^{s+1} = P_{k''}{}^s + P_0 b_{s+1} = P_m{}^{s+1}$,

(15.3) $P_{k'}{}^s \leq P_{k''}{}^s = P_m{}^s$.

Now because of zero degree homogeneity (H) of the excess demand functions,

(16) $x^{s+1} = F(P^{s+1}) = F(Q^{s+1})$

where

(17) $Q^{s+1} = [(1 + b_1 + \cdots + b_s)/(1 + b_1 + \cdots + b_s + b_{s+1})]P^{s+1}$.

We then have

(18.1) $Q_{k''}{}^{s+1} = P_{k''}{}^{s}$

while

(18.2) $Q_{k'}{}^{s+1} \leqq P_{k'}{}^{s}$;

moreover,

(18.3) $Q_{w'}{}^{v+1} < P_{w'}{}^{v}$ for $w' \in \{0, 1, \ldots, v\}$.

It then follows from the assumption of substitutability (S_F') that

(19.1) $x_{k''}{}^{s+1} \leqq x_{k''}{}^{s}$ (so that $x_{k''}{}^{s+1} \leqq x_{k''}{}^{s} \leqq \cdots \leqq x_{k''}{}^{0} = 0$)

and

(19.2) $x_{w''}{}^{v+1} < x_{w''}{}^{v}$ (so that $x_{w''}{}^{v+1} < x_{w''}{}^{v} \leqq \cdots \leqq x_{w''}{}^{0} = 0$ for $w'' \in \{v + 1, v + 2, \ldots, m\}$).

Also, since $P_{k''}{}^{s+1} \geqq P_{k''}{}^{s}$, while $P_{k'}{}^{s+1} = P_{k'}{}^{s}$ substitutability implies

(19.3) $x_{k'}{}^{s+1} \geqq x_{k'}{}^{s}$.

Write now, for $s < m$,

(20) $P_* = (P_0, \ldots, P_s)$, $P_{**} = (P_{s+1}, \ldots, P_m)$

with the corresponding symbols for the x's. (This partitioning depends on s, even though the dependence is not shown by the symbols.) From (6), (13) and (15) it then follows that

(21.1) $P_*{}^{s+1} = P_*{}^{s}$,

(21.2) $P_{**}{}^{s+1} = P_{**}{}^{s} + P_0 b_{s+1} \mathbf{1} = P_m{}^{s+1} \mathbf{1}$, $\mathbf{1} = (1, 1, \ldots, 1)$.

Now consider the expression

(22) $D = P^{s+1} \cdot x^{s+1} - P^s \cdot x^s$.

By the Walras Law both inner products in (22) vanish, hence

(23) $D = 0$.

Therefore, partitioning according to (20) and using (22) and (23), we have

(24) $O = D = P_*{}^{s+1} \cdot x_*{}^{s+1} + P_{**}{}^{s+1} \cdot x_{**}{}^{s+1} - P_*{}^{s} \cdot x_*{}^{s} - P_{**}{}^{s} \cdot x_{**}{}^{s}$

$\qquad = P_*{}^{s} \cdot (x_*{}^{s+1} - x_*{}^{s}) + P_{**}{}^{s+1} \cdot x_{**}{}^{s+1} - P_{**}{}^{s} \cdot x_{**}{}^{s}$

$\qquad\qquad\qquad\qquad\qquad\qquad\qquad\qquad\qquad$ [by (21.1)]

$\qquad = P_*{}^{s} \cdot (x_*{}^{s+1} - x_*{}^{s}) + P_{**}{}^{s+1} \cdot x_{**}{}^{s+1}$

$\qquad\quad - (P_{**}{}^{s+1} - P_0 b_{s+1} \mathbf{1}) \cdot x_{**}{}^{s}$ [by (21.2)]

$\qquad = P_*{}^{s} \cdot (x_*{}^{s+1} - x_*{}^{s}) + P_{**}{}^{s+1} \cdot (x_{**}{}^{s+1} - x_{**}{}^{s}) + P_0 b_{s+1} (\mathbf{1} \cdot x_{**}{}^{s})$

$$= P_*^{\ s} \cdot (x_*^{\ s+1} - x_*^{\ s}) + P_m^{\ s+1} [1 \cdot (x_{**}^{\ s+1} - x_{**}^{\ s})]$$
$$+ P_0 b_{s+1} (1 \cdot x_{**}^{\ s}) \qquad [\text{by } (21.2)]$$
$$\leqq P_m^{\ s+1} [1 \cdot (x_*^{\ s+1} - x_*^{\ s})] + P_m^{\ s+1} [1 \cdot (x_{**}^{\ s+1} - x_{**}^{\ s})]$$
$$+ P_0 b_{s+1} (1 \cdot x_{**}^{\ s}) \qquad [\text{by } (15.1)\,(15.3)\,(19.3)]$$
$$= P_m^{\ s+1} [1 \cdot (x^{s+1} - x^s)] + P_0 b_{s+1} (1 \cdot x_{**}^{\ s}).$$

This may be written as

$$(25) \quad 1 \cdot (x^{s+1} - x^s) \geqq -(P_0/P_m^{\ s+1})\, b_{s+1} (1 \cdot x_{**}^{\ s}).$$

It follows that the left member of (25) is nonnegative, since the prices are positive, $b_{s+1} \geqq 0$ by (14) and $(1 \cdot x_{**}^{\ s}) \leqq 0$ by (19.1). Furthermore, $b_{v+1} > 0$, and $(1 \cdot x_{**}^{\ v}) < 0$ by (19.2). Hence (12) follows and the proof is complete.

4. Stability of equilibrium under substitutability

4.0. As seen from Lemma 4, if a positive equilibrium price vector $\overline{P}$ exists and gross substitutability [even in its weakest form (S*)] is assumed, it follows that all other equilibrium price vectors are positive scalar multiples of $\overline{P}$. We express this geometrically by saying that there is a unique "equilibrium ray" $E = \{\lambda \overline{P} : \lambda > 0\}$. It follows that the normalized equilibrium price vector $\overline{p} = (\overline{P}_1/\overline{P}_0, \ldots, \overline{P}_m/\overline{P}_0)$ is also unique.

To establish the stability of the normalized process (II),[11] we shall show that the distance $D(t)$ from the variable point $p(t) = \psi^{II}(t; p^0)$ to the (unique) normalized equilibrium price vector $\overline{p}$ tends to zero as time tends to infinity. Where this distance has a continuous time derivative $\dot{D}(t)$, the convergence $p(t) \to \overline{p}$ is established by showing that $\dot{D}(t) < 0$ unless $f[p(t)] = 0$, i.e., when $p(t)$ is the equilibrium vector.

In the non-normalized process (I) we proceed in a similar fashion, except that here, because of the non-uniqueness of the equilibrium vector, we consider the distance from the variable point $P(t) = \Psi^{I}(t; P^0)$ to any (arbitrarily selected) equilibrium price vector $\overline{P}$. Where this distance has a continuous time derivative $\dot{D}(t)$, we show that $\dot{D}(t) < 0$ unless $F[P(t)]p = 0$, i.e., unless $P(t)$ is an equilibrium price vector (possibly different from $\overline{P}$), and it follows that $P(t) \to \overline{P}'$ where $\overline{P}'$ is some equilibrium price vector.

Interestingly enough, there is some latitude in the selection of the norm (metric) in terms of which distance is measured. If we use the Euclidean[12] norm $\| \ \|_2$ and postulate (H), (W), (E$^+$) and (S$_F'$), we find that the (Euclidean) distance function $D_2(t)$ does have a continuous derivative for all $t \geqq 0$ in the class of non-normalized differential processes given by

$$(\mathrm{I}') \quad \dot{P}_k = A_k F_k(P), \quad A_k > 0,$$

as well as in the class of normalized differential processes given by

(II') $\quad \dot{p}_j = a_j f_j(p), \quad a_j > 0.$

Because of the continuity of $\dot{D}_2$ it is then relatively simple to prove convergence (hence stability of equilibrium) from the fact that $\dot{D}_2 = -\overline{P} \cdot F(P) < 0$ (by Lemma 5) always. Furthermore $\dot{D}_2 < 0$ means that the convergence is *monotone*, i.e., the Euclidean distance from $p(t)$ to $\overline{p}$ decreases throughout the process.

On the other hand, we may use the "maximum norm" $\| \ \|_M$, where the length of a vector equals the largest of the absolute values of its components.[13] The corresponding distance is denoted by D_M.

We assume[14] (H), (E$^+$), and (S*) and consider the processes[15] given by

(I) $\quad \dot{P}_k = H_k[F_k(P), \quad$ where H_k is continuous and sign-preserving,

(II) $\quad \dot{p}_j = h_j[f_j(p)] , \quad$ where h_j is continuous and sign-preserving.

Here it is not true that $\dot{D}_M$ always exists, but when it does we have, for the non-normalized process $\dot{D}_M = -|H_K [F_K(P)] / \overline{P}_K|$ where K is such that

$$\left| \frac{P_K}{\overline{P}_K} - 1 \right| = \max_k \left| \frac{P_k}{\overline{P}_k} - 1 \right|,$$

with an analogous formula for the normalized process. By Lemma 3, $\dot{D}_M < 0$. With some complications due to the fact that $\dot{D}_M$ does not exist everywhere, we again are able to conclude convergence and also find this convergence to be monotone in the $\| \ \|_M$ norm, i.e., the distance to equilibrium decreases throughout the process.

Since the $\| \ \|_M$ approach uses weaker assumptions and applies to a broader class of processes than the $\| \ \|_2$ approach, it is important to realize that this does not make the Euclidean approach superfluous, since monotonicity of convergence in the $\| \ \|_M$ norm does not imply monotonicity of convergence in $\| \ \|.$[16]

4.1. Theorem 1. (Stability of equilibrium under substitutability; monotone convergence in the maximum norm). Assume that the excess demand functions $F_k(P)$ are single-valued, continuous, and positively homogeneous (H) of degree zero; assume further that there exist positive equilibrium price vectors $(\overline{P} > 0)$ and that substitutability (S*) prevails.[17]

Then, for $P^0 > 0$,

(a_1) every[18] solution through P^0 of the non-normalized process (I) with the functions H_k continuous and sign-preserving, i.e., every $\Psi^I(t; P^0)$, converges to some equilibrium price vector $\overline{P}$, and

(a_2) the convergence of $\Psi^I(t; P^0)$ is strictly monotone in the norm $\| \ \|_M$ defined below;

and for $p_r^{\ 0} > 0,$

(b_1) every[18] solution through p^0 of the normalized process (II) with the functions h_j continuous and sign-preserving, i.e., every $\psi^{II}(t; p^0)$, converges to the (unique) normalized equilibrium price vector $\bar{p}$, and

(b_2) the convergence of $\psi^{II}(t; p^0)$ is strictly monotone in the norm $\| \ \|_M$ defined below.

[$\Psi^I(t; P^0)$ and $\psi^{II}(t; p^0)$ are respectively solutions of (1) and (3) in section 2.]

Outline of proof. Assertions (a_1), (a_2) are proved in 4.1.2; their proof is based on Lemma 6 in 4.1.1. Assertions (b_1) and (b_2) are proved in 4.1.4 on the basis of Lemma 7 given in 4.1.3.

4.1.1. Lemma 6.[19,20] Let $Q = (Q_0, Q_1, \ldots, Q_m)$ denote an $m + 1$-tuple of real numbers. For $k = 0, 1, \ldots, m$, let G_k be a continuous real-valued function defined on the space of positive Q's (i.e., Q's whose every component is positive). It is assumed that the functions G_k satisfy Condition (S)[21]:

Condition (S): $\begin{cases} \text{if } Q \text{ is such that } G(Q) \neq 0 \text{ and } Q \neq \lambda 1 \text{ for all } \lambda > 0 \\ \text{(where } 1 \text{ denotes a vector all of whose components are 1's),} \\ \text{then } Q_{K'} = \max Q_k \text{ implies } G_{K'}(Q) < 0 \text{ and} \\ Q_{K''} = \min_k Q_k \text{ implies } G_{K''}(Q) > 0. \end{cases}$

Then the differential system

(1) $dQ/dt = G(Q)$ for $t \geq 0$, with $Q(0) = Q^0 > 0$

(A) has a solution $Q(t)$ for all $t \geq 0$ which

(B) is contained in the "cube" $B = \{Q: 0 < \alpha \leq Q_k \leq \beta$ for all $k\}$, where $\alpha = \min_k Q_k^0$ and $\beta = \max_k Q_k^0$. Furthermore,

(C) let $Q(t)$ be a solution of (1), satisfying the condition $Q(t) \notin E$ for all t in the interval $0 \leq t' \leq t \leq t'' \leq \infty$, with E denoting the "equilibrium ray," $E = \{\lambda 1; \lambda > 0\}$, and, for some fixed positive $\bar{\lambda}$, write $D_M(t) = \max_k |Q_k(t) - \bar{\lambda}|$; then $D_M(t)$ is a continuous strictly decreasing function of t on the closed interval $[t', t'']$, and

(D) as $t \to \infty$, $Q(t) \to \lambda_0 1$ for some $\lambda_0 > 0$.

Proof. In the "cube" $B' = \{Q: 0 < \alpha/2 \leq Q_k \leq \beta + \alpha/2$ for all $k\} \supset B$ the functions G_k are bounded, say

$$\max_k \max_{Q \in B'} |G_k(Q)| \leq M.$$

By the Cauchy-Peano existence Theorem,[22] the differential system has, therefore, a solution remaining within B' for $0 \leq t \leq \beta/M \equiv \nu$. However, in virtue of condition (S), the solution will actually stay within the smaller cube B. For, by condition (S), $Q_{K'} < 0$, so that $Q_{K'}(t) \leq \beta$ implies $Q_{K'}(t + h) \leq \beta$ for $h > 0$. The reasoning for $Q_{K''}$ is analogous.

Because the solution stays within B, the initial conditions for the time interval $(\nu, 2\nu)$ are the same as those for the interval $(0, \nu)$ and the solution can be continued, still within B. In this manner a solution staying in B can be found for all $t \geq 0$. This establishes assertions (A) and (B) of the Lemma.

Now let $\bar{\lambda}$ be a fixed positive number and define $D_M(t)$ as in assertion (C) of the Lemma. That $D_M(t)$ is a *continuous* function of t, follows from its definition. To show that it is *strictly decreasing* when $Q(t) \notin E$, we proceed as follows. First, we consider a special relatively simple case where $\max_k |Q_k(t) - \bar{\lambda}|$ is achieved for a unique value K of k. Then we revert to the general case where K need not be unique. (The consideration of the special case may be omitted without invalidating the proof; it is included for expository purposes only.)

When K is unique, then in a sufficiently small neighborhood of t, say $(t - \Delta t, t + \Delta t)$ it remains, by continuity, the unique maximizer, so that $D_M(t)$ has a derivative

(2) $dD_M/dt = [\mathrm{sgn}\,(Q_K(t) - \bar{\lambda})]\,dQ_K/dt = [\mathrm{sgn}\,(Q_K(t) - \bar{\lambda})]\,G_K.$

If $Q_K(t) - \bar{\lambda} > 0$, it follows that $Q_K(t)$ is maximal among the $Q_k(t)$ and, by condition (S), $G_K < 0$; therefore, the rightmost member of (2) is negative. When $Q_K(t) - \bar{\lambda} < 0$, we see that $Q_K(t)$ is minimal among the $Q_k(t)$ and, by condition (S), $G_K > 0$; here again the rightmost member of (2) is negative. Since $Q_K(t) - \bar{\lambda} = 0$ is prohibited by the requirement that $Q \notin E$, we have established that when K is unique,

(3) $dD_M/dt = -|G_K| < 0$ for Q not in E.

Now we drop the assumption of a unique K and thus return to the general case, where the existence of a derivative for D_M cannot be assured. Consider the value $Q(t)$ of a solution of (1) and let К denote the non-empty subset of $\{0, 1, \ldots, m\}$ such that the maximum over k in $\{0, 1, \ldots, m\}$ of $|Q_k(t) - \bar{\lambda}|$ is achieved for all the members of К and no others. Then, for $h > 0$,

(4) $\lim \sup_{h \to 0} \dfrac{D_M(t + h) - D_M(t)}{h} \leqq \max_{k \in К} (-|G_k[Q(t)]|) < 0,$

since

$$\lim \sup_{h \to 0} \left\{ \max_{k \in К} \left| \frac{Q_k(t + h) - \bar{\lambda}}{h} \right| - \max_{k \in К} \left| \frac{Q_k(t) - \bar{\lambda}}{h} \right| \right\}$$

$$\leqq \lim \sup_{h \to 0} \left\{ \max_{k \in К} \left[\frac{|Q_k(t + h) - \bar{\lambda}| - |Q_k(t) - \bar{\lambda}|}{h} \right] \right\}$$

$$= \max_{k \in К} \left\{ (\mathrm{sgn}\,[Q_k(t) - \bar{\lambda}])\,\frac{dQ_k}{dt} \right\} = \max_{k \in К} (-|G_k|).$$

By (4), for sufficiently small $h > 0$, $D_M(t + h) < D_M(t)$, and thus assertion (C) of the Lemma is established.

To prove convergence to some point on the "equilibrium ray" E, we consider the path $Q(t)$ as $t \to \infty$. There are two possibilities: either this path stays a finite distance away from E, or it comes arbitrarily close to E. We shall see below that the former supposition leads to a contradiction; hence we must examine the case where $Q(t)$ comes arbitrarily close to E as $t \to \infty$. Here for any positive ϵ_ν we can find a time-point t_ν such that $\max_k |Q_k(t_\nu) - \bar{\lambda}^\nu| < \epsilon_\nu$ for some $\bar{\lambda}^\nu$. We note that, by the already established assertion (C) of the Lemma,

$$\max_k |Q_k(t) - \bar{\lambda}^\nu| < \epsilon_\nu$$

for all $t > t_\nu$. Therefore, by selecting a sequence of numbers $\epsilon_\nu > 0$, we obtain a corresponding sequence of nested "parallelepipeds" with centers on the segment of $E = \lambda \mathbf{1}$ given by $0 < \alpha \leq \lambda \leq \beta$ and diameters tending to zero such that $Q(t)$ must lie in each for all t sufficiently large. The unique common point must obviously lie on E and may be written as, say, $\lambda_0 \mathbf{1}$. It is the limit of $Q(t)$ as $t \to \infty$ and thus assertion (D) of the Lemma follows.

It remains to be shown that the path cannot stay a finite distance away from E as $t \to \infty$. If it did, it would remain within a set

$$\tilde{S}_\epsilon = \{Q: \inf_{\bar{Q} \in E} \max_k |Q_k - \bar{Q}_k| \geq \epsilon\}.$$

Now let us select (arbitrarily) a fixed positive number λ_1, and, for each k in $\{0, 1, \ldots, m\}$ define the sets

$$T_k = \{Q: |Q_k - \lambda_1| = \max_{k'} |Q_{k'} - \lambda_1|\},$$

$$H_k = B \cap \tilde{S}_\epsilon \cap T_k.$$

Note that, for Q not in E,

$$|Q_k - \lambda_1| = \max_{k'} |Q_{k'} - \lambda_1| \quad \text{implies } G_k \neq 0,$$

as shown earlier [following equation (2)[23] with the help of condition (S)]. It follows that $|G_k| > 0$ on points of T_k that are not in E, and hence $|G_k| > 0$ on H_k. Since $|G_k|$ is continuous on H_k, we may conclude (because of the compactness of H_k) that

$$|G_k| \geq \delta_k > 0 \quad \text{on } H_k.$$

Now consider the distance from $Q(t)$ to $\lambda_1 \mathbf{1}$ on E. This distance is given by $D_M(t) = \max_{k'} |Q_{k'}(t) - \lambda_1|$. Because it is monotone and continuous [by assertion (C)] it has a time derivative dD_M/dt almost everywhere[24] and, as seen above, for a point of H_k, it is given by $-|G_k|$. Since every point in the intersection $B \cap \tilde{S}_\epsilon$ belongs to H_k for some k in $\{0, 1, \ldots, m\}$, it follows that, where the derivative exists,

$$|dD_M(t)/dt| \geq \min_k \delta_k \equiv \delta > 0.$$

Using again the fact that D_M is a monotone decreasing continuous function of time, we have[24]

$$D_M(0) \geq D_M(0) - D_M(t) \geq \int_0^t \left[-\frac{d}{dt} D_M(t) \right] dt = \int_0^t \left| \frac{d}{dt} D_M(t) \right| dt \geq \delta \cdot t$$

which yields a contradiction for t sufficiently large.

4.1.2. Proof of assertions (a_1) and (a_2) of Theorem 1.   (Stability and mono-tone convergence of the non-normalized process under substitutability; maxi-mum norm.) Consider the non-normalized differential equation system

$dP_k/dt = H_k[F_k(P)]$ $(k = 0, 1, \ldots, m)$,

with $P^0 > 0$, $F(P^0) \neq 0$.

Let $\overline{P}$ be some fixed equilibrium price vector. Since $\overline{P}$ is positive by the hypothesis of the theorem, we may perform the transformation of variables

$Q_k = P_k/\overline{P}_k$ $(k = 0, 1, \ldots, m)$.

We then obtain a differential equation system

$\overline{P}_k \dot{Q}_k = H_k[F_k(Q_0 \overline{P}_0, Q_1 \overline{P}_1, \ldots, Q_m \overline{P}_m)]$

or

(1) $\dot{Q}_k = G_k(Q)$, $Q_k^0 = P_k^0/\overline{P}_k$,

where we define

$G_k(Q) = (1/\overline{P}_k) H_k[F_k(Q_0 \overline{P}_0, \ldots, Q_m \overline{P}_m)]$.

We shall now verify that the system (1) satisfies the hypotheses of Lemma 6. Clearly $Q^0 > 0$ since $P^0 > 0$ and $\overline{P} > 0$; also, G_k is continuous since both F_k and H_k are continuous. It remains for us to verify condition (S) of Lemma 6. Now if $Q_{K'} = \max_k Q_k$, we have (by definition of the Q_k)

$P_{K'}/\overline{P}_{K'} \geqq P_k/\overline{P}_k$ for all k.

Now let $G(Q) \neq 0$. Since the H_k are sign-preserving, it follows that $F(P) \neq 0$ also. The substitutability condition (S*) then implies $F_{K'}(P) < 0$, and hence $G_{K'}(Q) = (1/\overline{P}_{K'}) H_{K'}[F_{K'}(P)] < 0$ in view of the sign-preserving property of $H_{K'}$. The proof that $Q_{K''} = \min_k Q_k$ implies $G_{K''}(Q) > 0$ is analogous. Hence Lemma 6 applies to the system (1).

Therefore, there exists a positive number λ_0 such that $Q(t)$ converges to $\lambda_0 1$ as $t \to \infty$; i.e., for each k,

$P_k(t)/\overline{P}_k \to \lambda_0$ as $t \to \infty$,

or, equivalently,

$P(t) \to \lambda_0 \overline{P}$ as $t \to \infty$.

By homogeneity (H), $\lambda_0 \overline{P}$ is an equilibrium price vector, since $\overline{P}$ is 1.

Furthermore, this convergence is, by assertion (C) of Lemma 6, strictly mono-tone in the norm $\| P \|_M = \max_k (| P_k |/\overline{P}_k$ where $\overline{P}$ is any equilibrium price vec-tor; i.e., the distance $D_M(t)$ from $P(t)$ to any equilibrium price vector $\overline{P}$, given by $D_M(t) = \max_k (| [P_k(t) - \overline{P}_k]/\overline{P}_k |)$, decreases, since this decrease is equivalent to a decrease in $\max_k | Q_k(t) - 1 |$ implied by Lemma 6.

4.1.3. Lemma 7.   This Lemma is used in the proof of convergence of the normalized process in the same way as Lemma 6 is used in the proof of convergence of the non-normalized process. As in the context of Lemma 6, the reader may find it helpful to have an economic interpretation: q is the normalized (m-dimensional price vector), $g(q)$ the corresponding excess demand function, and the equilibrium price vector is $(1, 1, \ldots, 1)$.

Lemma 7.   Let $q = (q_1, q_2, \ldots, q_m)$ denote an m-tuple of real numbers. For $j = 1, 2, \ldots, m$, let g_j be a continuous real-valued function defined on the space of positive q's (i.e., q's whose every component is positive). It is assumed that the functions $\bar{g}_j$ satisfy Condition(s)[25]:

$$
\text{Condition (s)} \begin{cases}
\text{If } q \neq 1 \text{ [where } 1 = (1, 1, \ldots, 1)] \\
\text{then } q_{J'} = \max_j q_j \geq 1 \quad \text{implies } g_{J'}(q) < 0; \\
\text{and } q_{J''} = \min_j q_j \leq 1 \quad \text{implies } g_{J''}(q) > 0.
\end{cases}
$$

Then the differential system

(1) $dq/dt = g(q)$ for $t \geq 0$, $q(0) = q^0 > 0$,

(A) has a solution $q(t)$ for all $t \geq 0$ which

(B) is contained in the "cube" $A = \{q : 0 < \alpha \leq q_j \leq \beta \text{ for all } j\}$ where $\alpha = \min(\min_j q_j^0, 1)$ and $\beta = \max(\max_j q_j^0, 1)$. Furthermore,

(C) $D_M(t) = \max_j |q_j(t) - 1|$ is a continuous strictly decreasing function in the interval $[t', t'']$, $0 \leq t' \leq t \leq t'' \leq \infty$, in which $q(t) \neq 1$, and

(D) as $t \to \infty$, $q(t) \to 1$.

Proof.   The proof is very similar to that of Lemma 6. By constructing a cube $A' = \{q : 0 < \alpha/2 \leq q_j \leq \beta + \alpha/2 \text{ for all } j\} \supset A$ and proceeding with A' and A, respectively, as we did with B' and B, respectively, in the proof of Lemma 6, we establish assertions (A) and (B) of the present Lemma. The continuity of D_M is again established by appeal to its definition. Its decreasing nature is again easy to show when the value J of j maximizing the expression $|q_j(t) - 1|$ over all j is unique. For in this case

$dD_M/dt = \text{sgn}(q_{J'} - 1) g_{J'}$

and the right member of this derivative is negative by condition (s) (substitutability) when $q \neq 1$. In the general case (when J need not be unique) the argument is parallel to that in Lemma 6 and involves showing that

$$\limsup_{h \to 0} (1/h) [D_M(t + h) - D_M(t)] \leq \max_{j \in \mathfrak{z}} (- |g_j(q(t))|) < 0$$

where $\mathfrak{z}$ is the set of maximizing subscripts for $|q_j(t) - 1|$.

It remains to establish (D). Here again we distinguish two cases, depending on whether $q(t)$ has 1 as a limiting point for $t \to \infty$. If 1 is a limiting point for $q(t)$, then it must be that $q(t)$ converges to 1 since D_M has just been shown to decrease in a monotone fashion. Hence the proof will be complete if we can show that 1 must be a limiting point of $q(t)$.

Suppose not. Then $q(t)$ will stay away a distance of at least ϵ, i.e., it will stay within the set $\tilde{S}_\epsilon = \{q : \max_j |q_j - 1| \geq \epsilon\}$. Now define, for each j the set $T_j = \{q : |q_j - 1| = \max_{j'} |q_{j'} - 1|\}$. Also, write $H_j = A \cap \tilde{S}_\epsilon \cap T_j$.

Using condition (s) we show that $|g_j| > 0$ on H_j. By compactness of H_j and continuity of $|g_j|$ we conclude that $|g_j| \geq \delta_j > 0$ on H_j. By steps identical with those for Lemma 7, it follows that $D_M(t)$ as defined in assertion (C) of the present Lemma has a time derivative almost everywhere and that

$$|dD_M/dt| \geq \min_j \delta_j > \delta > 0,$$

and, following the last phases of the proof of Lemma 7, we again have a contradiction.

4.1.4. Proof of assertions (b_1) and (b_2) of Theorem 1. (Stability and monotone convergence of the normalized process under substitutability; maximum norm.) This proof is parallel to that of section 4.1.2; it involves going over from the differential system

(1) $\dot{p}_j = h_j[f_j(p)] \qquad (j = 1, 2, \ldots, m)$

to the system

(2) $\dot{q}_j = g_j(q) \qquad (j = 1, 2, \ldots, m)$

where $q_j = p_j/\bar{p}_j$. The assertions of the theorem are easily established for the p's if the hypotheses of Lemma 7 can be verified for the system (2). This verification raises no new problems except for justifying condition (s) of Lemma 7. This is accomplished by taking condition (S*), involving non-normalized prices P_k as the starting point and observing that, for instance,

$$P_{K'}/\bar{P}_{K'} \geq P_k/\bar{P}_k \qquad \text{for all } k \text{ in } \{0, 1, \ldots, m\}$$

is equivalent to

$$p_{K'}/\bar{p}_{K'} \geq p_k/\bar{p}_k \qquad \text{for all } k \text{ in } \{0, 1, \ldots, m\},$$

where $p_0 = 1$, and this in turn is implied by

$$q_{J'} = \max_j q_j \geq 1 \qquad \text{(with } j \text{ ranging over } \{1, 2, \ldots, m\})$$

if K' is put equal to J'.

The minimal subscript J'' is treated in an analogous manner.

4.2 Theorem 2.   *(Stability of equilibrium under substitutability; and monotone convergence in the Euclidean norm.)*

In this section we obtain a theorem similar to Theorem 1, but there are two important differences. The class of differential processes is narrower, in that the right members of the differential equations must be proportional to the excess demands instead of merely sign-preserving functions; also, the Walras Law is here included among the assumptions, while it was not used in the proof of Theorem 1. The proof of convergence uses one of the results of Lemma 6, hence is not completely independent of the results of section 4.1.

4.2.1. The non-normalized process (I′). In this section we consider processes defined by the differential equation system

(1′) $dP_k/dt = A_k F_k(P)$, $P^0 > 0$ $(k = 0, 1, \ldots, m)$,

where the A_k are positive constants. [This is a special case of $\dot{P}_k = H_k[F_k(P)]$ with sign-preserving H_k, i.e., of process (I).]

The (weighted) Euclidean norm of a vector P will be defined as

(1) $\|P\|_2 = (\Sigma_k P_k{}^2/A_k)^{1/2}$.

Hence the square of the distance from the moving point $P(t) = P$ to an equilibrium point $\bar{P}$ is given by

(2) $D_2 = \Sigma_k V_k$

where

(3) $V_k = (1/A_k)(P_k - \bar{P}_k)^2$.

Differentiating the latter expression we obtain

(4) $\frac{1}{2} dV_k/dt = (1/A_k)(P_k - \bar{P}_k)(dP_k/dt) = (1/A_k)(P_k - \bar{P}_k)A_k F_k(P)$

$$= (P_k - \bar{P}_k) F_k(P).$$

Hence

(5) $\frac{1}{2} dD_2/dt = \Sigma_k (P_k - \bar{P}_k) F_k(P) = -\Sigma_k \bar{P}_k F_k(P)$

where the second equality follows from the Walras Law.

Now, by assertions (A) and (B) of Lemma 6, (I′) has a solution and $P^0 > 0$ implies $P(t) > 0$ for all $t \geq 0$. Therefore, the derivative dD_2/dt exists for all $t \geq 0$, is continuous [by the continuity of $F_k(P)$ and $P(t)$], and, furthermore, by Lemma 5 applied to equation (5),

(6) $dD_2/dt < 0$ if $\bar{P} > 0$ and $F(P) \neq 0$.

Hence the convergence of $P(t)$ to some equilibrium point (already guaranteed by Theorem 1) is monotone in the Euclidean norm. (One could also establish this convergence directly from the continuity of dD_2/dt as a function of time.) Thus we have

Theorem 2.1. Assume the excess demand functions to be continuous, single-valued, and positively homogeneous of degree zero (H). Suppose furthermore that the Walras Law (W) and gross substitutability (S_F) prevail and $\bar{P} > 0$ exists. Then, for $P^0 > 0$, the system (I′) is stable (i.e., there is convergence to some equilibrium point) and the convergence to an equilibrium price vector is monotone in the weighted Euclidean norm given by equation (1).

4.2.2. The normalized process (II′). In this section we consider processes defined by the differential equation system

(II′) $dp_j/dt = a_j f_j(p)$, $p^0 > 0$ $(j = 1, 2, \ldots m)$,

where the a_j are positive constants. [This is a special case of process (II).]
We proceed in a manner parallel to that of section 4.2.1, using, respectively, p, j, a for P, F, A and with summations on j ranging over $\{1, 2, \ldots, m\}$ instead of those on k ranging over $\{0, 1, \ldots, m\}$. For the squared distance here given by

(1) $D_2 = \frac{1}{2} \Sigma_j (1/a_j)(p_j - \bar{p}_j)^2$

we find

(2) $dD_2/dt = \Sigma_{j=1}^{m} (p_j - \bar{p}_j) f_j(p)$.

Now, as indicated in section 2, we may embed (II′) in a process such as that given by equation (3′) of section 2. This amounts to replacing p_j by P_j/P_0 and specifying a (constant) value for P_0. Because $P_0(t)$ is constant, we may, if we put $P_0 = \bar{P}_0 = 1$, rewrite equation (2) as

(3) $dD_2/dt = \Sigma_{k=0}^{m} (P_k - \bar{P}_k) F_k(P)$.

From here on, we again proceed again as in 4.2.2, thus obtaining the counterpart of Theorem 2.1 above for the normalized process. This may be labeled

Theorem 2.2. (The wording is exactly as that of Theorem 2.1, except that P is replaced by p and I′ by II′.) The two theorems 2.1 and 2.2 together are referred to as *Theorem 2*.

4.3. Combining information provided by the two norms

It was mentioned in 4.0 that information concerning the path of convergence can be obtained from the use of the two norms in the proof of convergence. To see this, consider the special case where, for the normalized process (19), all the $a_j = 1$ and all the $\bar{p}_j = 1$. Suppose we are at the point p. Where shall we be a short time interval later?

To answer the question consider the following two sets: $S_2(P)$, the m-dimensional sphere with center at the equilibrium point and going through the point p; $S_M(P)$ the m-dimensional "cube" with center at the equilibrium point and walls parallel to the coordinate planes. The proof using $\| \ \|_2$ tells us that p will travel into the interior of $S_2(p)$; the proof using $\| \ \|_M$ tells us that p will travel into the interior of $S_M(p)$. Hence p will have to travel into the interior of the intersection of the two sets. Since, in general, neither set contains the other, there is a clear gain of information in using both norms rather than either one alone. At special points, however, the cube is a subset of the sphere or vice versa and there is no gain of information.

Figure 1 shows a few situations for the case $m = 2$, where the "sphere" is a circle and the "cube" a square. The shaded area is the intersection of the two sets.

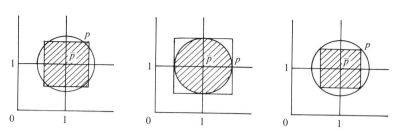

Figure 1

5. Dominant negative diagonal

5.1. In this section we establish stability in the large for a class of cases closely related to that of substitutability.[26] We shall deal only with the normalized process. The method of proof used is in some respects analogous to that of 4.1 above.

Theorem 3.   The normalized process (II′) is stable in the large if there exists a set of positive constants $(c_1, c_2, \ldots, c_m)$ such that, for each $j = 1, 2, \ldots, m$ the inequalities

(1) $f_{jj} < 0,$

(2) $c_j |f_{jj}| > \Sigma_{s \neq j} c_s |f_{js}|$

(where $f_{js} = \partial f_j / \partial p_s$) are satisfied.

Proof.   We show that, for

(3) $V = \max_j |a_j f_j| / c_j$

we have, wherever dV/dt exists,

(4) $dV/dt < 0$ except at equilibrium.

Let

(5) $|a_J f_J| / c_J \geq |a_j f_j| / c_j$ for all j,

so that

(6) $V = |a_J f_J| / c_J.$

Therefore

(7) $\dfrac{dV}{dt} = \left(\dfrac{a_J}{c_J}\right) (\text{sgn } f_J) \, \Sigma_j \, f_{Jj} \left(\dfrac{dp_j}{dt}\right)$

$\qquad = \left(\dfrac{a_J}{c_J}\right) (\text{sgn } f_J) \, \Sigma_j \, f_{Jj} f_j a_j.$

Clearly, $dV/dt = 0$ at equilibrium where all the f_j vanish. But suppose we are not at equilibrium. Then at least one of the f_j must be different from zero.

Hence by (5), $|f_J| > 0$. In this case, using (2) for $j = J$, and multiplying by $|f_J|$ on both sides of the inequality, we obtain

(8) $c_J |f_{JJ}| \cdot |f_J| > \Sigma_{s \neq J} c_s |f_{Js}| \cdot |f_J|$

$\geq \Sigma_{s \neq J} c_s |f_{Js}| (c_J a_s / a_J c_s) \cdot |f_s|$

$= (c_J / a_J) \Sigma_{s \neq J} |f_{J\epsilon}| \cdot |f_s| a_s$ [by (5)].

Hence

(9) $|f_{JJ}| \cdot |f_J| a_J > \Sigma_{s \neq J} |f_{Js}| \cdot |f_s| a_s$,

i.e., because of (1),

(10) $-f_{JJ} (\operatorname{sgn} f_J) f_J a_J > \Sigma_{s \neq J} |f_{Js}| \cdot |f_s| a_s \geq (\operatorname{sgn} f_J) \Sigma_{s \neq J} f_{Js} f_s a_s$.

Writing this as

(11) $(\operatorname{sgn} f_J) \Sigma_j f_{Jj} f_j a_j < 0$

we see that the right member of (7) is negative. The case in which dV/dt does not exist may be dealt with as in the proofs of Lemmas 6 and 7.

5.2. The domain of applicability of the preceding result remains to be explored. In particular, the results in section 4 concerning the stability *in the large* under gross substitutability do not seem to follow from Theorem 3. Locally, on the other hand, the stability under substitution can be derived from Theorem 3 through the utilization of the Euler equation $\Sigma_{k=0}^{m} P_k F_{kr} = 0$ (implied by the homogeneity of the F's): the $\bar{P}_j$ can be used as the c_j of the theorem. (In the large, one is tempted to try the use of the P_j, even though variable, in the same way as the c_j's. This introduces additional terms in dV/dt which make trouble when $f_J < 0$.)

One could obtain the analogue of Theorem 3 for the non-normalized process (II') by a procedure similar to that of 4.1, but here even the local version of the substitution case does not seem to follow.

5.3. For purposes of economic interpretation, it is easiest to deal with the special case of (2) where all the $c_j = 1$, so that

$$|f_{jj}| > \Sigma_{s \neq j} |f_{js}|$$

and, also, $f_{jj} < 0$. (The c_j's can be made $= 1$ by a suitable change of measurement of the commodities.) Suppose now that the price of the jth commodity (non-numéraire) is changed, either up or down, by an amount K, while the other $m - 1$ (non-numéraire) commodities undergo changes (either up or down) whose magnitude does not exceed K. (They need not all move in the same direction, and some may remain unchanged.) Then the excess demand for the jth commodity will have gone up or down according to whether the change in p_j had been downward or upward.

Walras' argument [15, lesson 12, pp. 170–172] is perhaps based on such an assumption.

6. Other results on stability for the non-normalized process (I')

In this section it is shown that three of the results obtained in [2] for the normalized process (II') can also be obtained for the non-normalized process (I'). Without loss of generality, we put, in (I'), $A_k = 1$ for $k = 0, 1, \ldots, m$, so that the process may now be written as

(1) $dP_k/dt = F_k(P)$ $(k = 0, 1, \ldots, m)$.

Using inner product notation, the Walras Law is written as

(2) $P \cdot F(P) = 0$.

6.1 The aggregate excess demand functions satisfy the Weak Axiom of Revealed Preference. (See [2, Theorem 2].)

We say that the aggregate excess demand functions satisfy the Weak Revealed Preference Axiom if

(3) $P' \cdot [F(P'') - F(P')] \leqq 0$, $F(P'') \neq F(P')$

$$\text{imply } P'' \cdot [F(P'') - F(P')] < 0.$$

Now let $P'' = \bar{P}$ and $P' = P$. Then the first inequality of (3) is fulfilled because of the Walras Law (2) and by definition of equilibrium $F(\bar{P}) = 0$. Also, if P is not an equilibrium price vector, we have $F(P) \neq 0$, hence the second inequality of (3) is also satisfied. It follows that

(4) $-\bar{P} \cdot F(P) < 0$ if P is not an equilibrium price vector.

Now define, as before,

(5) $D_2 = (1/2)(P - \bar{P}) \cdot (P - \bar{P})$.

Then

(6) $dD_2/dt = (P - \bar{P}) \cdot F(P) = P \cdot F(P) - \bar{P} \cdot F(P)$

$$= -\bar{P} \cdot F(P) \quad \text{[by (2)]}$$

$$< 0 \quad \text{[by (4)]}$$

which implies stability.

When there is only one individual ($n = 1$), or when all individuals are identical, the preceding results also imply stability.

6.2. The case of "no trade" at equilibrium

This case (see [2, Theorem 1]) arises when

(7) $F^i(\bar{P}) = 0$ $(i = 1, 2, \ldots n)$

where the superscript refers to the individual. By methods very close to those of the preceding section, the proof of Theorem 1 in [2] can be adapted to non-normalized process (I'). For every individual i, we find that (7) implies the fulfillment of the antecedent of the (individual) weak revealed preference axiom, viz.,

(8) $P \cdot [F^i(\bar{P}) - F^i(P)] \leqq 0,$

and $F^i(P) \neq F^i(\bar{P})$ since we assume that P is non-equilibrium. It follows that

(9) $\bar{P} \cdot [F^i(\bar{P}) - F^i(P)] < 0,$

i.e., because of (7),

(10) $-\bar{P} \cdot F^i(P) < 0$

and, by aggregation,

(11) $-\bar{P} \cdot F(P) < 0.$

Using D_2 as defined in (5), we see that the left member of (11) equals dD_2/dt which completes the proof.

6.3. The case of two commodities ($m = I$). (See [2, Theorem 6].)

First, let us make the following observation, valid for *any* m:

(12) $\sum_{k=0}^{m} P_k^2 = \text{constant}$ along a solution of (1) subject to (2).

[This is because $d(\sum_k P_k^2)/dt = 2 \sum_k P_k(dP_k/dt) = 2 \sum_k P_k F_k(P)$ and the last expression vanishes by (2).]

Secondly, also for any m, by zero degree homogeneity,

(13) $F_k(P) = f_k(p)$ $(k = 0, 1, \ldots, m)$

where $p = (P_1/P_0, \ldots, P_m/P_0)$.

Now put $m = 1$, so that $p = P_1/P_0$. Then, by the Walras Law, the two functions $f_0(p)$ and $f_1(p)$ have the same zeros and opposite signs when they are not zero.

Suppose that, at the initial point $(P_0^0, P_1^0) = P^0, f_1(p^0) > 0$ where $p^0 = P_1^0/P_0^0$. Then $F_1(P^0) > 0$ and $F_0(P^0) < 0$ by (13) and the Walras Law; hence P_1 will be increasing and P_0 decreasing by (1), and thus p will increase towards the zero of $f_1(p)$ next above p^0, say $\bar{p}$. Hence the ratio P_1/P_0 converges to $\bar{p}$, while the sum $P_0^2 + P_1^2$ remains constant by (12). It follows that $P(t)$ converges to some $\bar{P}$ as t tends to infinity. The rest of the proof is carried out in terms of the argument used in establishing Theorem 6 in [2].

Remark.   The results for $m = 1$ can easily be extended to the generalized adjustment processes of section 4 above, since the signs of $f_k(p)$ are again decisive.

Notes

1   Research sponsored by the Office of Naval Research. An earlier version of this paper was circulated as an ONR project report, February, 1958.

2   We follow the usual conventions for vector inequalities. For a vector v, $v \geqq 0$ means that all components of v are nonnegative; $v \geq 0$ means $v \geqq 0$ and $v \neq 0$ (i.e., at least one component of v is positive and none is negative); $v > 0$ means that every component of v is positive.

3   See Wald [14, pp. 385–87], where it is shown that, under (S_F) and homogeneity, $F(\bar{P}') = F(\bar{P}'') = 0$ implies $P' = \lambda P''$ for some $\lambda > 0$, which means that the normalized equilibrium price vector is unique. See also Gale [4, p. 163], and Lemma 4, below.

4   Labeled, in a slightly different form, "strong gross substitutability" in [2, p. 546, Theorem 10].

5   The authors were led to a reformulation of an earlier version of this Lemma as a result of correspondence with F. H. Hahn of the University of Birmingham.

6   Surprisingly enough, the Walras Law is not used. However, one may regard (W) as the rationale underlying the formulation of (S_F).

7   Lemma 3 shows that [given (E^+) and (H)] (S^*) is no stronger than (S_F'). In fact, (S^*) is weaker. This can be seen when the functions $F_K(P)$ are replaced by $H_k[F_k(P)]$ where the H_k are sign-preserving but not monotone; in this case (S^*) still holds, but (S_F') can easily be violated.

8   The relation (1) may be interpreted as stating that, under gross substitutability, the weak revealed preference axiom holds for any pair of price vectors, one of which is an equilibrium price vector.

9    $\mathbf{1} = (1, 1, \ldots, 1)$.

10   The ranges of k' and k'' depend on s, but this dependence is not shown in the symbols.

11   Because it has a unique equilibrium point, its stability properties are somewhat simpler to discuss. Therefore we start with this case.

12   Actually a "weighted" Euclidean distance is used:

$$\|P\|_2 = [\Sigma_k P_k{}^2 / A_k]^{1/2}$$

where the A_k's are the constants in (I') below.

13   $\|P\|_M = \max_k |P_k|$.

14   These assumptions are weaker than those for $\| \ \|_2$, since (W) is not used at all, and (S^*) in conjunction with (H) and (E^+) is weaker than (S_F'). See note 7 above.

15   These are, of course, respectively more general than (I') and (II').

16   Most stability proofs in [2] were carried out in terms of $\| \ \|_2$. On the other hand, the method used in [2] for proving stability in the large for $m = 2$ under substitutability has a close relationship to the approach using $\| \ \|_M$.

17   We recall that, for instance, under homogeneity, the differential form of substitutability (S_D) implies both (S^*) and $P > 0$.

18   We do not assume or assert the uniqueness of these solutions, thus relaxing the conditions under which some of the results in [2] had been obtained

19 In developing the proof of Lemmas 6 and 7, we benefited from a suggestion due to Professor J. Blackman of Syracuse University.

20 While Lemma 6 is stated abstractly, the reader may find it helpful to think of Q as a non-normalized price vector, $G_k(Q)$ as the excess demand function for the kth commodity, with the units of measurement selected in such a manner that every equilibrium price vector has equal components, i.e., is of the form $(a, a, \ldots, a)$.

21 It is understood throughout 4.1.1 that k ranges over $\{0, 1, \ldots, m\}$.

22 See, e.g., Coddington and Levinson [3, Theorem 1.2, p. 6 and remarks on p. 19].

23 The argument given there does not depend on the uniqueness of K.

24 See, for instance, Kestelman [6, Theorem 258, p. 178].

25 In 4.1.3, it is understood that j ranges over $\{1, 2, \ldots, m\}$.

26 This line of inquiry was suggested by the corresponding local results (unpublished), due to F. H. Hahn, and R. M. Solow, Massachusetts Institute of Technology.

References

[1] Arrow, Kenneth J., and Gerard Debreu: "Existence of an Equilibrium for a Competitive Economy," *Econometrica*, 22: 256–290 (July, 1954).

[2] Arrow, Kenneth J., and Leonid Hurwicz: "On the Stability of the Competitive Equilibrium, I," this volume, III.1, pp. 199–228.

[3] Coddington, Earl A., and Norman Levinson: *Theory of Ordinary Differential Equations*. New York: McGraw Hill, 1955.

[4] Gale, David: "The Law of Supply and Demand," *Math. Scand.* 3: 155–169 (1955).

[5] Hicks, J. R.: *Value and Capital*. Oxford, 1939.

[6] Kestelman, H.: *Modern Theories of Integration*. Oxford, 1937.

[7] McKenzie, Lionel W.: "Competitive Equilibrium with Dependent Consumer Preferences," in United States Air Force, the *Second Symposium on Linear Programming*. Washington, D.C., January, 1955.

[8] McKenzie, Lionel W.: "On Equilibrium in Graham's Model of World Trade and Other Competitive Systems," *Econometrica*, 22: 147–161 (April, 1954).

[9] Metzler, Lloyd: "Stability of Multiple Markets: the Hicks Conditions," *Econometrica*, 13: 277–292 (October, 1954).

[10] Mosak, Jacob L.: *General Equilibrium Theory in International Trade*. Bloomington, Indiana: The Principia Press, 1944.

[11] Nikaidô, Hukukane: "On the Classical Multilateral Exchange Problem," *Metroeconomica*, VIII: 135–145 (August, 1956).

[12] Samuelson, P. A.: *Foundations of Economic Analysis*. Cambridge, 1955.

[13] Uzawa, Hirofumi: "Note on Existence of an Equilibrium for a Competitive Economy," Technical Report No. 40, Project on Efficiency of

Decision-Making in Economic Systems, Stanford University, November, 1956.

[14]   Wald, Abraham: "On Some Systems of Equations of Mathematical Economics," *Econometrica*, 19: 368–403 (October, 1951).

[15]   Walras, Léon: *Elements of Pure Economics* (William Jaffé, tr.). London: George Allen & Unwin, and Homewood, Illinois: Irwin.

On the stability of the competitive equilibrium, II: postscript

KENNETH J. ARROW
LEONID HURWICZ

Hotaka [1] has shown that several of the proofs in section 3 of the preceding article are fallacious or misleading, although the conclusions used in later sections are undisturbed. For the most part, these criticisms can be met by minor changes, but one of them suggests a better approach to Lemma 1 and its Corollary.

1. Hotaka argues that the statement and proof of Lemma 1 are false because the excess demand function vector $F(P)$ is not defined on the boundary (where some prices are zero). Actually, this is rather a matter of careless or misleading notation than a genuine error; since Lemma 1 asserts that $F_r(P) = +\infty$ if $P_r = 0$, therefore $F(P)$ is certainly not finite-valued at the boundary and might be said to be undefined. In the definition of the assumption (S_D), the values of the partial derivatives $F_{rk} = \partial F_r / \partial P_k$ at a boundary point should be understood to be the limit as the price vector P approaches the boundary point from the interior; the limits are assumed to exist, though possibly infinite-valued. Thus, if P^0 is a boundary point, (S_D) asserts that

$$\lim_{P \to P^0} F_{rs}(P)$$

exists and is positive (possibly $+\infty$) if $r \neq s$. Hotaka's "counter-example" ([1], top of p. 306) does not satisfy this condition. Then in the proof of Lemma 1, the statements, "$F_{r0} > 0, F_{rs} > 0$ for $s \in B$" [the two lines following (5)], are understood to be statements about the limits as $t \to \infty$. Hence, (6) is correct for $t \geq 0$ if it is understood to read,

$$\lim_{t \to 0+} t \sum_{s \in A} F_{rs} < 0$$

and the rest of the proof is valid.

However, the conclusion of Lemma 1 is not stated correctly; all that has been proved is that, if the prices of several commodities approach zero along a particular path (where they are equal, in the argument used), then the excess demand for each of these commodities approaches plus infinity. It is easy to modify the proof to show that the result holds if the prices of these commodities approach zero along any path for which the ratio of any two is bounded away from zero. But the conclusion does not hold in general if some prices are approaching zero faster than others.

If Lemma 1 were restated to meet this difficulty, the Corollary would still be valid; since the existence of an equilibrium is assumed in the hypothesis, it would follow even from a corrected version of Lemma 1 that the equilibrium cannot be located on the boundary and therefore must be interior.

2. Nevertheless, Hotaka's comments do suggest the desirability of an alternative approach in which (S_D) is dispensed with and reference made only to (S_F). This is especially desirable, since (S_D) is stronger than (S_F); its implications have not been fully explored but appear to be undesirably strong. It is, indeed, possible to construct an example of excess demand functions derived from utility maximization and satisfying (S_F), namely, for a consumer with a Cobb-Douglas utility function and strictly positive endowments of all commodities.

A more satisfactory treatment can, in our view, be found in Arrow and Hahn [2, pp. 221-22], which we summarize here. The approach is based on the following continuity theorem on excess demand functions derived from utility maximization, whether or not the commodities are gross substitutes [2, Theorem 4.8, p. 102]. First, we state an extended definition of continuity appropriate for excess demand functions [2, Assumption 2.6, p. 31].

(C') $F(P)$ is continuous in its domain of definition, which includes all strictly positive price vectors, and, for any price vector $P^0 \geqslant 0$ for which $F(P)$ is not defined,

(1) $\lim_{P \to P^0} \sum_{r=0}^{m} F_r(P) = +\infty$

Theorem A.   If $F(P)$ is the excess demand function vector derived by maximizing a strictly quasi-concave utility function, where income is positive for all semipositive price vectors, then $F(P)$ satisfies (C').

A sum of excess demand function vectors, each satisfying (C'), also satisfies (C'). Hence, we can postulate that (C') holds for the market excess demand function.

Now, following Hotaka's remarks [1, p. 305] (see also [2, Theorem 6, p. 221]), we note that, on the boundary, (S_F) is incompatible with the homogeneity of the excess demand functions.

Lemma A.   If the excess demand functions are positive homogeneous of degree zero (H) and satisfy (S_F), then the excess demand functions are not defined if any good is free, i.e.,

if $P \geqslant 0$ and, for some r, $P_r = 0$, then $F(P)$ is not defined

Proof.   Let P^0 be a boundary point, $A = \{r | P_r^0 = 0\}$, $B = \{r | P_r^0 > 0\}$; by hypothesis, A and B are both nonempty. Choose any $\lambda > 1$. Then $\lambda P_r^0 = P_r^0$

for $r \in A$, $\lambda P_r^0 > P_r^0$ for $r \in B$. By Lemma 2 (whose proof does not depend on Lemma 1 or its Corollary), if $F(P)$ were defined at P^0.

$$F_r(P_0^0, \ldots, P_m^0) < F_r(\lambda P_0^0, \ldots, \lambda P_m^0) \qquad \text{for } r \in A$$

On the other hand, by (H), for any r,

$$F_r(P_0^0, \ldots, P_m^0) = F_r(\lambda P_0^0, \ldots, \lambda P_m^0)$$

a contradiction.

This version of Lemma 1 is adequate for the proof of the Corollary as it stands, since the excess demand functions must be defined at an equilibrium price vector. But more insight can be obtained by noting that, from Theorem A, and Lemma A, equation (1) must hold at every boundary point. On the one hand, this assures us that the equilibrium cannot occur on the boundary; on the other hand, (C'), together with the Walras Law (W), is sufficient to insure the existence of an equilibrium [2, Theorem 2.2, p. 33] (the theorem as stated also includes in its hypothesis the boundedness of the excess demand functions from below, but this hypothesis is nowhere used in the proof). Hence, we can conclude that an equilibrium does exist, and a strengthened version of the Corollary to Lemma 1 holds.

Lemma B. If $F(P)$ satisfies the Walras Law (W), extended continuity (C'), and (S_F), then there must exist at least one interior equilibrium, $\overline{P} > 0$, for which $F(\overline{P}) = 0$, and there are no boundary equilibria.

Remark. Hotaka's Lemma 1(W) [1, p. 306] *assumes* the existence of an interior equilibrium and deduces that $F_r(P) \to +\infty$ if $P_r \to 0$. He considers only the case where one price approaches zero, all others being bounded away from zero, but his argument could be extended to show that equation (1) holds as the price vector approaches any boundary point. Hence, a converse of Lemma B holds; if (W) and (S_F) hold, then the existence of an interior equilibrium implies (C').

3. Hotaka [1, pp. 306-7] objects to the statement of Lemma 4 because (S*) and (H) do not imply the result. Indeed, if $F(\overline{P}'')$ and $F(\overline{P}')$ are both zero, then (S*) as stated does not apply. This is best rectified by restating (S*):

(S**) if $F(\overline{P}) = 0, P \neq \lambda \overline{P}$ for all $\lambda > 0$, $P_{K'}/\overline{P}_{K'}$

$= \max_{k \in \{0,1,\ldots,m\}}(P_k/\overline{P}_k), P_{K''}/\overline{P}_{K''}$

$= \max_{k \in \{0,1,\ldots,m\}}(P_k/\overline{P}_k),$

then $F_{K'}(P) < 0, F_{K''}(P) > 0$.

Then Lemmas 3 and 4 remain valid if (S*) is replaced by (S**) in the conclusion of Lemma 3 and in the hypothesis of Lemma 4. The proof of Lemma 4 is valid as it stands; in the proof of Lemma 3, is it only necessary to delete the condition, "$F(P) \neq 0$," in the first line.

Condition (S*) is used in the proof of Theorem 1 (see the preceding article, section 4.1.2) in the original form. However, from (H), it is obvious that $F(P) \neq 0$, $F(\bar{P}) = 0$, imply that $P \neq \lambda \bar{P}$ for all $\lambda > 0$. Hence, (S**) and (H) imply (S*).

4. In the proof of Lemma 5, Hotaka [1, p. 307] notes that the step, "$(1 \cdot x_{**}^{v}) < 0$ by (19.2)," in the last line of the proof is not valid if v happens to be 0. He points out, however, that (S_F') implies that

$$x_k^{v+1} > x_k^{v} \qquad k \leq v.$$

It follows that the inequality in the next-to-last line of equation (24) is strict for $s = v$, and the same, therefore, holds in equation (25), so that equation (12) again follows, and Lemma 5 is proved.

References

[1]   Hotaka, Ryosuke: "Some Basic Problems on Excess Demand Functions," *Econometrica*, 39: 305-7.
[2]   Arrow, Kenneth J., and Frank H. Hahn: *General Competitive Analysis.* San Francisco: Holden-Day, 1971.

Some remarks on the equilibria of economic systems

KENNETH J. ARROW
LEONID HURWICZ[1]

1. Uniqueness

1.1. In an earlier paper dealing with problems of stability, we asserted that the competitive equilibrium is unique if the excess demand functions satisfy the weak axiom of revealed preference [4, p. 208]. This assertion is correct if the equilibrium set is assumed to consist of isolated points, but examples can be constructed (see 1.5 below) where there is a multiplicity of (non-isolated) equilibrium points. In general, one is only entitled to say that the equilibrium set is *convex*. Hence, in Theorem 2 of [4], the term "unique" should be replaced by "convex," with the assertion concerning stability remaining unchanged. Thus we obtain[2]

Theorem 1.   If the aggregate excess demand functions satisfy the weak axiom of revealed preference, then (a) the instantaneous adjustment process is stable (whether or not there is a numéraire), and (b) the set of equilibrium points is convex.

Proof.   (a) As essentially shown in [4], the weak axiom of revealed preference implies that

(1) $\Sigma_{k=0}^{m} \overline{P}_k x_k > 0$ unless $x_k \leqslant 0$ for all $k = 0, \ldots, m$,

where $x_k = F_k(P)$, the excess demand for the kth good at price vector P, and $\overline{P}$ is any equilibrium price vector. Let,

(2) $V_{\overline{P}} = \Sigma_{k=0}^{m} (P_k - \overline{P}_k)^2 = D_{\overline{P}}^2$,

where D_P is the (Euclidean) distance from the given price vector $P(t)$ on the solution [of the differential system (3) below] to any equilibrium price vector $\overline{P}$. If there is no numéraire, a dynamic system defining the motion of the price is

(3) $dP_k/dt = \begin{cases} 0 & \text{if } P_k = 0, x_k < 0, \\ x_k & \text{otherwise.} \end{cases}$

(The condition in the first line prevents prices from becoming negative.) Let

(4) $T = \{k \colon P_k = 0, x_k < 0\}$,

and $\tilde{T}$ be its complement. Then, along the path,

(5) $dV_{\overline{P}}/dt = \Sigma_{k=0}^{m} (P_k - \overline{P}_k) \cdot dP_k/dt = \Sigma_{k \in \tilde{T}} (P_k - \overline{P}_k) x_k$

$\qquad = \Sigma_{k=0}^{m} (P_k - \overline{P}_k) x_k - \Sigma_{k \in T} (P_k - \overline{P}_k) x_k$

$\qquad = \Sigma_{k=0}^{m} P_k x_k - \Sigma_{k=0}^{m} \overline{P}_k x_k - \Sigma_{k \in T} P_k x_k + \Sigma_{k \in T} \overline{P}_k x_k.$

The first term vanishes by Walras's Law. By definition of T, $P_k = 0, x_k < 0$ for all $k \in T$; therefore, the third term vanishes and the fourth is nonpositive. From (1), it follows that

(6) $dV_{\overline{P}}/dt < 0$ unless $P(t)$ is an equilibrium point.

If the equilibrium price vector $\overline{P}$ were known to be unique, then it would follow by Lyapunov's so-called second method[3] that the solution $\psi(t; P^0)$ must converge to $\overline{P}$.

But even if there is a possibility of non-uniqueness of equilibrium, we may conclude that (i) the solution path is bounded (since its distance from any given equilibrium point is non-increasing), and (ii) any limit point of the path must itself be an equilibrium point.[4] Given (i) and (ii), by reasoning analogous to that of [1],[5] we then conclude that convergence to some equilibrium point will take place, which (by definition) means that the system is globally stable.

We have so far assumed that there is no numéraire, so that the dynamics are described by (3). If commodity 0 is the numéraire, then (3) continues to hold for $k \geqslant 1$, while,

$P_0 \equiv \overline{P}_0$,

where $\bar{P}_0$ is a positive number (1 if the units are chosen properly). Then (5) becomes

$$dV_{\bar{P}}/dt = \Sigma_{k \in \widetilde{T} \atop k \neq 0} (P_k - \bar{P}_k) x_k$$

$$= \Sigma_{k=0}^{m} P_k x_k - \Sigma_{k=0}^{m} \bar{P}_k x_k - \Sigma_{k \in T} P_k x_k$$

$$+ \Sigma_{k \in T} \bar{P}_k x_k - (P_0 - \bar{P}_0) x_0.$$

Since $P_0 = \bar{P}_0$, the last term vanishes; the first four terms are the same as before, so that (6) again holds, and we have global stability of the system.

(b) Let $\bar{P}^{\alpha}(\alpha = 1, 2)$ be two equilibrium price vectors and P^* a convex combination of them, say $P^* = \lambda \bar{P}^1 + (1 - \lambda) P^2, 0 < \lambda < 1$. Consider the solution $\psi(t; P^*)$ starting from P^*, and suppose that P^* is not an equilibrium point. Then, for both $\alpha = 1$ and $\alpha = 2$, by (6), the distance $D[\psi(t; P^*), \bar{P}^{\alpha}]$ from the moving point to the equilibrium point $\bar{P}^{\alpha}$ is less than the distance $D[P^*, \bar{P}^{\alpha}]$ from P^* to $\bar{P}^{\alpha}$ if $t > 0$. Hence the sum $D[\psi(t; P^*), \bar{P}^1] + D[\psi(t; P^*)\bar{P}^2]$ of the distances from the moving point to the two equilibria must be less than the sum of the distances $D[P^*, \bar{P}^1] + D[P^*, \bar{P}^2]$ from P^* to the two equlibria. But P^* lies on a straight line segment between $\bar{P}^1$ and $\bar{P}^2$, and hence must minimize the sum of distances from any point to the two equilibria. This contradiction shows that P^* must be an equilibrium point and hence that any convex combination of equilibria must itself be equilibrium.

1.2. Remark.   The "dynamic" approach used in the preceding proof of the convexity of the set of equilibrium points is natural to use in connection with investigations of stability and has the merit of applicability in more general situations. For the case of weak revealed preference, however, a direct "static" proof can also be given. Let again $P^* = \lambda \bar{P}^1 + (1 - \lambda) \bar{P}^2, 0 < \lambda < 1$, and denote by $x_k^*, k = 0, 1, \ldots, m$, the excess demand at P^* for the kth good. Suppose P^* is not an equilibrium point. Then, by (1),

(3) $\Sigma_{h=0}^{m} \bar{P}_h^{\alpha} x_h^* > 0$ for $\alpha = 1, 2$.

Hence

(4) $\Sigma_{k=0}^{m} P_k^* x_k^* = \Sigma_{k=0}^{m} [\lambda \bar{P}_k^1 + (1 - \lambda) \bar{P}_k^2] x_k^*$

$$= \lambda \Sigma_{k=0}^{m} \bar{P}_k^1 x_k^* + (1 - \lambda) \Sigma_{k=0}^{m} \bar{P}_k^2 x_k^* > 0$$

which contradicts the Walras Law requirement that $\Sigma_{k=0}^{m} P_k^* x_k^* = 0$.

1.3. It can be noted that the proof of Theorem 1 made use of the weak axiom of revealed preference only to establish (1). That is, it was only used to compare the excess demands at an equilibrium price vector with that at a disequilibrium price vector. We may therefore strengthen Theorem 1 to

Theorem 2.   If the aggregate excess demand functions $F_k(p)$ satisfy the condition that

$$\Sigma_{k=0}^{m} \bar{P}_k F_k(p) > 0$$

whenever $\bar{P}$ is an equilibrium and P is not, then the instantaneous adjustment process is stable (whether or not there is a numéraire), and the set of equilibrium point is convex.

1.4. In [1], Lemma 5, it was shown that the hypothesis of Theorem 2 was valid if all commodities were strong gross substitutes ($\partial F_r / \partial p_s > 0$ for $r \neq s$). In this case, the last part of the theorem is uninteresting because the equilibrium is in fact unique. A modification of the proof, however, shows that the lemma is still valid for weak gross substitutes ($\partial F_r / \partial p_s \geqslant 0$ for $r \neq s$) (see [2, Theorem 1]). Hence,

Corollary.   If all commodities are weak gross substitutes, the instantaneous adjustment process is stable and the set of equilibria is convex.

Related results are to be found in unpublished papers by Uzawa [7], McKenzie [5], and Morishima [6]. In particular, McKenzie has demonstrated the convexity of the set of equilibria for the case of weak gross substitutes.

1.5. Finally, it may be useful to give two examples of non-unique equilibrium in which the weak axiom of revealed preference holds for the aggregate excess demand functions. This will certainly be true if there is only one individual in the market or, more generally, if the aggregate excess demand function could be that of a single utility-maximizing individual. In the following examples, E is the initial endowment, I the indifference curve through E, and P^1 and P^2 two possible budget lines through E such that the individual will in fact demand E; hence the negative of the slope of either line is an equilibrium price ratio.

In the first example (Figure 1), the possibility of multiple equilibria rests on a (commodity space) corner maximization of utility. (Note this is not the same as a

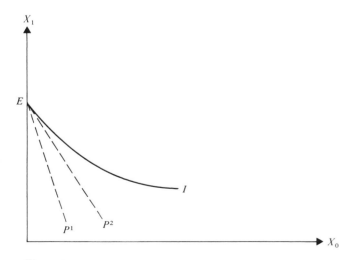

Figure 1

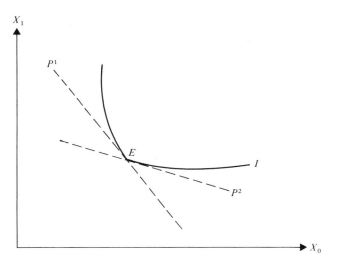

Figure 2

(price space) *corner equilibrium of the market* since supply equals demand, and both prices can be positive.) It requires that there exist no initial endowment of commodity 1, a condition which is somewhat peculiar for a pure exchange economy but which is natural enough in a production economy. The second example (Figure 2) requires a kink in the indifference curve, again a condition very possible in an economy with production but which is inconsistent with the smooth indifference curves usually postulated for a pure exchange economy.

2. Existence

A clarification is also in order concerning a statement [4, p. 203] that the continuity and single-valuedness of the excess demand functions (with positive homogeneity of degree zero and Walras's Law also assumed) imply the existence of a competitive equilibrium. This statement is correct if continuity is understood in the usual sense, so that the function is finite-valued everywhere. It is frequently convenient, however, to permit the excess demand for a good to tend to infinity as its price tends to zero. This will be true of any commodity which always has a positive marginal utility (cf. [4, Theorem 7]); in [1, Lemma 1], infinite excess demands are shown to be a consequence of strong gross substitutability.

In such cases, the concept of continuity may be broadened to permit an infinite value for $F_k(P)$ and continuity defined by the condition $\lim_{n \to \infty} F_k(P^n) = +\infty$ for any sequence $\{P^n\}$ such that $P^n \to P$ (cf. [4, footnote 35, p. 225]). With this definition, it is true that continuity, single-valuedness, and the boundedness from below of the excess demand function (together with homogeneity and

Walras's Law) imply the existence of competitive equilibrium. Boundedness from below prevails, for example, under pure trade (absence of production) where the excess supply cannot be higher than the initial endowment.

The following example shows that the condition of boundedness from below cannot be dispensed with.[6] Let $m = 1$ (i.e., only one commodity other than numéraire), $p = P_1/P_0$ (the price of the non-numéraire good in terms of numéraire), the excess demand for numéraire $x_0 = -p$, the excess demand for the non-numéraire good $x_1 = +1$ for all p. Then all the conditions other than boundedness from below are satisfied, yet equilibrium obviously does not exist since the excess demand for the non-numéraire good is always positive.

3. Inferior goods and Giffen's paradox

The need for the following correction in [4] has been pointed out to us by Robert Mundell. On p. 215 we note that, " 'Giffen's paradox' must be absent (a good cannot be 'inferior') at a unique equilibrium point in the case of two goods." The statement is correct except for the assertion in parentheses which, of course, is not equivalent to the absence of Giffen's paradox. In an earlier version of the present note,[7] an example was given to illustrate this point.

Notes

1 Participation made possible by a Rockefeller Foundation grant. We are also indebted to the Office of Naval Research (Task NR-047-004) for additional assistance.
2 We use the notations and definitions of [4]. Unlike [4], we do not ignore "corner" equilibria (where $\bar{x}_r < 0$ with $\bar{P}_r = 0$).
3 See, for example, [3, p. 124]. A generalization of Lyapunov's result is to be found in [8].
4 This can be proved by the method of [3].
5 The proof of convergence in Lemma 6 of [1, pp. 242–3, (following eq. (4))] goes over, except that the Euclidean norm replaces that based on the maximal component of the vector.
6 It may, of course, be replaced by other conditions.
7 Circulated as Technical Report No. 76, Office of Naval Research, Contract Nonr-225(50) (NR-047-004), Stanford University, July 23, 1959.

References

[1] Arrow, Kenneth J., Henry D. Block, and Leonid Hurwicz: "On the Stability of the Competitive Equilibrium, II," this volume, III.1, pp. 228–255.
[2] Arrow, Kenneth J., and Leonid Hurwicz: "Competitive Stability under

Weak Gross Substitutability: The 'Euclidean Distance' Approach," this volume, III.2, pp. 265–275.

[3]   Arrow, Kenneth J., and Leonid Hurwicz: "The Gradient Method in Concave Programming: Local Results," Chapter 6 in K. J. Arrow, L. Hurwicz, and H. Uzawa, *Studies in Linear and Nonlinear Programming*, Stanford, California, Stanford University Press, 1959.

[4]   Arrow, Kenneth J., and Leonid Hurwicz: "On the Stability of the Competitive Equilibrium, I," this volume, III.1, pp. 199–228.

[5]   McKenzie, Lionel: "A Contribution to the Theory of Stability of Competitive Equilibrium," unpublished manuscript, 1959.

[6]   Morishima, Michio: "Gross Substitutability, Homogeneity, and the Walras Law," unpublished manuscript, 1959.

[7]   Uzawa, Hirofumi: "An Alternative Proof of the Stability in the Gross Substitute Case," Technical Report No. 60, Office of Naval Research Contract N60nr-25133, Stanford University, October 8, 1958.

[8]   Uzawa, Hirofumi: "On the Stability of Dynamic Processes," Technical Report No. 61, Office of Naval Research, Contract N60nr-25133, Stanford University, November 28, 1958.

2

COMPETITIVE STABILITY UNDER WEAK GROSS SUBSTITUTABILITY

---

*Competitive stability under weak gross substitutability:
the "Euclidean distance" approach*

KENNETH J. ARROW
LEONID HURWICZ[1]

1. Introduction

1.1. In earlier papers [3, 1], the global stability of the competitive equilibrium was investigated under different assumptions on the excess demand functions. For the most part, the dynamic assumption was that the price of each commodity moved proportionately to its excess demand; there may or may not be a commodity distinguished as *numéraire* whose price is held fixed at 1.

Let there be $m + 1$ commodities, numbered $0, \ldots, m$; the *numéraire*, if any, is commodity 0. Let P_k be the price of commodity k, P the vector with components P_k $(k = 0, \ldots, m)$, and p the vector with components P_j $(j = 1, \ldots, m)$; the components of p are sometimes also denoted by p_j. All prices are non-negative, and at least one is positive. Let $F_k(P)$ be the excess demand for commodity k at price vector P; we assume,

(W) $P \cdot F(P) = 0$,

and, for each $k = 0, 1, \ldots, m$,

(H) $F_k(P)$ is (positively) homogeneous of degree 0;

(C) $F_k(P)$ is continuous and differentiable;

(B) $F_k(P)$ is bounded from below.

Assumption (H) is usual and follows from utility maximization subject to the budget constraint.

The assumption (C) of continuity is to be understood here in an extended sense which permits positive infinite values of demand [negative infinite values are excluded by (B)]. If $F_j(P)$ is finite at some P, then continuity has the usual meaning; if infinite, then continuity means that

$$\lim_{n \to \infty} F_j(P^n) = +\infty,$$

for any sequence $\{P^n\}$ converging to P.[2] It may be remarked that, because of assumptions (W) and (B), $F_j(P)$ can only be infinite when $P_j = 0$. Admitting infinite excess demands for free goods does not seem unreasonable; if, however, the reader prefers to insist on continuity in the stricter sense which requires finite-valuedness, all the results of this paper will, of course, be *a fortiori* true.[3]

Assumption (W) is Walras' Law.

Assumption (B) is reasonable for the case of pure trade, in which case the maximum excess supply which an individual can offer is his initial holdings (see also [2], Section 2).

1.2. If (a) there is *no numéraire*, the dynamic system is

$$(1) \quad \dot{P}_k = \begin{cases} 0 & \text{if } P_k = 0, F_k(P) < 0, \\ F_k(P) & \text{otherwise } (k = 0, \ldots, m). \end{cases}$$

If (b) there is *a numéraire*, let $f_j(p) = F_j(1, p)$ be the excess demand for commodity j as a function of $p_1, \ldots, p_m$, when $P_0 = 1$. The dynamic system in this case is

$$(2) \quad dp_j/dt = \begin{cases} 0 & \text{if } p_j = 0, f_j(p) < 0, \\ f_j(p) & (j = 1, \ldots, m). \end{cases}$$

In both cases, the price of each commodity (other than the *numéraire*) varies proportionately to excess demand with an exception to prevent prices from becoming negative. By choice of suitable units of measurement, we may assume that the rate of change of prices equals excess demand; i.e., there is no loss of generality in choosing all proportionality coefficients equal to unity.

The dynamic system (1) will be referred to as the *non-numéraire* system, (2) as the *numéraire* system (the less descriptive terms, "non-normalized," and "normalized," respectively, were used in [1], Section 2).

1.3. In [3] and [1] considerable attention was given to the case where the commodities are all gross substitutes, that is $\partial F_j/\partial P_k > 0$, for all $j \neq k$. It was shown that both the *numéraire* and *non-numéraire* systems were stable in the (rather strong) sense that, beginning with any starting point, the solution of the differential equations (1) or (2) converged to the (unique) equilibrium point (see [1], Section 4). Two methods of proof were given; in one, the "maximum norm" method, it was shown that the expression,

$$\max_k |(P_k/\overline{P}_k) - 1|,$$

where $\overline{P}$ is any equilibrium point, was necessarily decreasing along any solution of (1) or (2) which did not start from an equilibrium point. In the second, the "Euclidean distance" approach, it was shown similarly that the square of the distance to any equilibrium,

$$\Sigma_{k=0}^{m} (P_k - \overline{P}_k)^2,$$

was decreasing along solutions of (1) and (2). The last fact follows from the statement that

$$(3) \quad \overline{P} \cdot F(P) > 0, \quad \text{provided } \overline{P} \text{ is equilibrium and } P \text{ is not.}$$

Statement (3) can, as shown in [3], p. 534, be interpreted as saying that Samuelson's Weak Axiom of Revealed Preference holds between any pair of price vectors of which exactly one is an equilibrium price vector.[4]

In subsequent unpublished work, Uzawa [6], McKenzie [4], and Morishima [5], extended these results to the case where the commodities are *weak* gross substitutes, that is, where it is only assumed that

(S) $\begin{cases} \text{the derivatives } \partial F_j/\partial P_k \text{ exist for all } j, k, \\ \text{and } \partial F_j/\partial P_k \geqslant 0 \quad \text{for all } j \neq k. \end{cases}$

All three made assumptions which implied the existence of an equilibrium price vector with all components positive. In this note we remove these restrictions by an extension of the "Euclidean distance" argument. That is, we show that (S) in conjunction with the other assumptions is sufficient to imply stability even if the equilibrium points have some zero components.

1.4. In the case of weak gross substitutes the equilibrium is not necessarily unique. As a result, there is more than one conceivable meaning of stability. Both Uzawa and McKenzie demonstrate the following property, called by Uzawa "quasi-stability" ([7], pp. 3–4): every solution (path) of the differential equations (1) or (2) is bounded, and the distance from the moving point to the *set* of equilibria approaches zero. [Both Uzawa and McKenzie have dynamic systems more general than (1) and (2).] It does not follow from quasi-stability that the solution approaches any limit; for instance, it might oscillate in some way about the set of equilibrium points. The "Euclidean distance" method, however, establishes that in fact each solution does converge to a limit, which must, of course, be an equilibrium. Thus we establish the stability of the system in the sense used in [3], p. 524.[5]

1.5. In this paper we confine ourselves to the dynamic systems (1) and (2). In [1], Theorem 1, it was shown that the "maximum norm" argument demonstrated the stability of more general dynamic systems, in which the rate of change of prices may be, for example, a non-linear function of excess demand. The results of Uzawa and McKenzie apply to these more general systems. It is not known whether or not their theorems generalize to the case where there does not exist at least one strictly positive equilibrium vector; it can be shown that if equilibria with some zero components are admitted, the solutions to the dynamic system which generalizes (1) can be unbounded.

1.6. Our procedure is based on previous results which showed that (3) implies both global stability and convexity of the set of equilibrium points (see [2], Theorem 2), provided solutions of (1) or (2) exist and are unique and continuous with respect to the starting point. Hence, we need only demonstrate that (3) holds. We first show that weak gross substitutability implies that the excess demand for a free good must be independent of the prices of all other goods. Second, we show that if there exists a positive equilibrium price vector, then (3) holds in the case of weak gross substitutes; the method is a modification of the argument used in [1] for the case of strong gross substitutes. From these two results we can derive the validity of (3) (see Theorem 1 below).

In the argument use is made several times of a reduction of the commodity space to a smaller number of dimensions in the following sense: if the prices of a set S of commodities are put equal to zero ($P_k = 0$ for $k \in S$), and if the excess demands for the free goods are non-positive, then the system of excess demand functions for the remaining commodities, $F_k(P)$ ($k \notin S$), satisfies all the assumptions, (H), (C), (W), (B), and (S), considered as functions of the remaining prices, P_k ($k \notin S$). Any results proved for such systems of functions can be applied to the reduced system (see Lemma 3).

2. Excess demand for free goods

For any vector X and any set of indices S, we will denote by X_S the vector with components $X_j(j \in S)$; thus $P_S = \{P_{j_1}, \ldots, P_{j_s}\}$, where $j_1, \ldots, j_s$ are the elements of S. The notation $F_S(P)$ is understood similarly. Also, $\tilde{S}$ is the complement of S with respect to the set of indices $\{0, \ldots, m\}$.

We first demonstrate:

Lemma 1.   If (H), (C), (W), (B), and (S) hold, then there are constants F_j^0 such that $F_j(P) = F_j^0$ for all P such that $P_j = 0$. Equivalently, under the assumptions listed, if P' and P'' are the price vectors such that $P_j' = P_j'' = 0$, then $F_j(P') = F_j(P'')$.

Proof: Let P be any fixed vector such that $P_j = 0$, k any fixed index, $k \neq j$. Write

(4) $S = \{r: P_r = 0\}$, so that $P_S = 0$ always,

and

(5) $T = \{r: P_r > 0, r \neq k\}$.

First, suppose $P_k > 0$, and consider two subcases, according as T is or is not null. In the first case,

$$F_j(P) = F_j(P_S, P_k) = F_j(0, P_k) = F_j(0, 1),$$

by (H), so that F_j is independent of P_k. In the second case, $F_j(P) = F_j(0, P_T, P_k)$. By homogeneity and Euler's equation,

$$\Sigma_{r \in T} (\partial F_j / \partial P_r) P_r + (\partial F_j / \partial P_k) P_k = 0.$$

From (S), each term is non-negative, hence they must all be zero. In particular,

$$\partial F_j / \partial P_k = 0.$$

Thus F_j is independent of P_k for all P_k positive and, by continuity (C) of $F_j(P)$, for $P_k = 0$; since this holds for all $k \neq j$, the lemma is proved.

In the case of strict gross substitutability ($\partial F_j / \partial P_k > 0$ for $j \neq k$), it was shown in [1], Lemma 1, that the excess demand for a free good is necessarily infinite, a special case of Lemma 1 of the present paper.

Lemma 2. If $F_j(P^1) \leqslant 0$ for some P^1 for which $P_j^1 = 0$, then $F_j(P) \leqslant 0$ for all P.

Proof. For any P, define Q so that

(6) $\quad Q_j = 0, \qquad Q_k = P_k \qquad$ for all $k \neq j$.

From (H) and (S) it easily follows that $F_j(P)$ is a non-increasing function of P_j; from (6),

(7) $\quad F_j(P) \leqslant F_j(Q)$.

From Lemma 1, $F_j(Q) = F_j(P^1) \leqslant 0$, by hypothesis; the lemma follows from (7).

Lemma 3. If assumptions (H), (C), (W), (B), and (S) hold for a vector $F(P)$ of excesss demand functions, and if, for some set S of indices, the inequality $F_{\widetilde{S}}(P) \leqslant 0$ holds for all P, then the vector of excess demand functions $F_s(P_s, 0)$ also satisfies (H), (C), (W), (B), and (S) as functions of P_s; further, if $\overline{P}_s$ is any equilibrium point for $F_s(P_s, 0)$, then $(\overline{P}_s, 0)$ is an equilibrium point for $F(P)$.

Proof. That assumptions (H), (C), (B), and (S) hold for $F_s(P_s, 0)$ is obvious. If the excess demand functions $F(P)$ are bounded from above as well as from below, (W) obviously holds also. However, we need to show that no difficulty will arise when $F(P)$ may be unbounded from above. Since (W) holds for $F(P)$, we can write

$$P \cdot F(P) = P_s \cdot F_s(P_s, P_{\widetilde{s}}) + P_{\widetilde{s}} \cdot F_{\widetilde{s}}(P_s, P_{\widetilde{s}}) = 0 \qquad \text{for all } P.$$

If we let $P_{\widetilde{s}}$ approach zero monotonically, it follows from (S) that F_s is monotone decreasing and therefore bounded by (B). At the same time $F_{\widetilde{s}}$ is bounded from below by (B), and from above by the hypothesis $F_{\widetilde{s}}(P) \leqslant 0$; hence, in the limit we have

$$P_s \cdot F_s(P_s, 0) = 0,$$

which is the assertion (W) for the set of functions $F_s(P_s, 0)$.

If $\overline{P}_s$ is an equilibrium for $F_s(P_s, 0)$, then by definition

$$F_s(\overline{P}_s, 0) \leqslant 0.$$

Since $F_{\widetilde{s}}(\overline{P}_s, 0) \leqslant 0$ by hypothesis, $F(\overline{P}_s, 0) \leqslant 0$, so that $(\overline{P}_s, 0)$ is an equilibrium by definition.

3. The "revealed preferences" relation between equilibrium and disequilibrium points

Theorem 1. If $F(P)$ is a vector of excess demand functions satisfying (H), (C), (W), (B), and (S), then

$$\overline{P} \cdot F(P) > 0$$

provided $\overline{P}$ is an equilibrium price vector and P is not $(P \neq 0)$.

In Section 3.1 we prove the theorem for the case $\overline{P} > 0$; in 3.2 the general case is established.

3.1. The proof follows in general the lines of [1], Lemma 5. However, some modifications are needed: (1) In [1] the proof made essential use of the assumption of gross substitutability in the strict sense; as we shall see, this assumption is not needed.[6] In [1] it was assumed that the disequilibrium price vector was positive; again we shall find this assumption unnecessary.

3.1.1. The magnitude $\overline{P} \cdot F(P)$ is measured in money and is independent of the units in which commodities are measured. Since (in 3.1) $\overline{P} > 0$, we may, without loss of generality, assume that

(8') $\overline{P}_k = 1$ $(k = 0, \ldots, m)$,

so that

(8") $F(\overline{P}) = 0$.

For a given non-zero vector $P \equiv (P_0, P_1, \ldots, P_m)$ assume the commodities so numbered that

(9') $P_k \geqslant P_{k+1}$ $(k = 0, \ldots, m - 1)$,

and hence, by $P \neq 0$,

(9") $P_0 > 0$.

Then define a sequence of vectors $P^s(s = 0, \ldots, m)$ by the conditions that

(10) $P_k{}^s = \max (P_s, P_k)$.

It may easily be seen from (9') and (10) that for $P^s = (P_0{}^s, P_1{}^s, \ldots, P_m{}^s)$

(11) $P_k{}^s = \begin{cases} P_k & (k \leqslant s), \\ P_s & (k > s), \end{cases}$

and

(12) $P_k{}^{s+1} = \begin{cases} P_k & (k \leqslant s), \\ P_{s+1} & (k > s). \end{cases}$

Thus the change from P^s to P^{s+1} consists in changing the last $m - s$ components from P_s to P_{s+1}. In more detail, we see that

$$P^0 = (P_0, \ldots, P_0),$$

$$P^1 = (P_0, P_1, P_1, \ldots, P_1),$$

$$\cdots$$

$$P^s = (P_0, \ldots, P_{s-1}, P_s, P_s, \ldots, P_s),$$

$$P^{s+1} = (P_0, \ldots, P_{s-1}, P_s, P_{s+1}, \ldots, P_{s+1}),$$

$$\cdots$$

$$P^m = (P_0, \ldots, P_{m-1}, P_m).$$

From (8′) we see that $P^0 = P_0 \bar{P}$; it follows from (H), (9″), and (8″) that

(13) $F(P^0) = 0$.

Also, we note that

(14) $P^m = P$.

The last $m - s$ components of P^{s+1} are, from (11), (12), and (9′), not greater than the corresponding components of P^s, while the first $s + 1$ components are the same. Hence, by substitutability (S)

(15) $F_k(P^{s+1}) \leqslant F_k(P^s)$ $(k \leqslant s)$.

Suppose for the moment that $P_{s+1} > 0$; then from (9′) $P_s > 0$. Write $Q^{s+1} = (P_s/P_{s+1})P^{s+1}$. Since by (9′) $P_s/P_{s+1} \geqslant 1$, we have $Q_k^{s+1} \geqslant P_k^s$ $(k \leqslant s)$, $Q_k^{s+1} = P_k^s$ $(k > s)$ from (11) and (12). By (S) $F_k(Q^{s+1}) \geqslant F_k(P^s)$ $(k > s)$; since by (H) $F_k(Q^{s+1}) = F_k(P^{s+1})$, we have

(16) $F_k(P^{s+1}) \geqslant F_k(P^s)$ $(k > s)$.

The assumption that $P_{s+1} > 0$ may now be dropped, since, by continuity (C), (16) also holds if $P_{s+1} = 0$.

The inequality (16) can also be written in the form

$F_k(P^{t+1}) \geqslant F_k(P^t)$ $(k > s \geqslant t \geqslant 0)$.

By induction $F_k(P^{t+1}) \geqslant F_k(P^0)$, $(k > s \geqslant t \geqslant 0)$. But the right member of the last inequality vanishes by (13), and if we set t equal to $s - 1$, we get

(17) $F_k(P^s) \geqslant 0$ $(k > s)$.

3.1.2. In 3.1.3 below we shall use the results of 3.1.1 to establish the following inequalities:

(18) $\Sigma_{k=0}^m F_k(P^{s+1}) \geqslant \Sigma_{k=0}^m F_k(P^s)$ $(s = 0, 1, \ldots, m - 1)$,

(19) $\Sigma_{k=0}^m F_k(P^{s+1}) > \Sigma_{k=0}^m F_k(P^s)$ $\begin{cases} \text{if } P^s \text{ is an equilibrium vector,} \\ P^{s+1} \text{ a disequilibrium vector,} \\ s = 0, 1, \ldots, m - 1. \end{cases}$

From (18) it follows by induction that $\Sigma_{k=0}^m F_k(P^s) \geqslant \Sigma_{k=0}^m F_k(P^0)$ for all s. Set $s = m$ and recall (13), then

$\Sigma_{k=0}^m F_k(P^m) \geqslant 0$.

From (8′) and (14) we can write

(20) $\bar{P} \cdot F(P) \geqslant 0$ for all P.

If, in addition, we assume that $P = P^m$ is a disequilibrium vector, then, since P^0 is an equilibrium vector, there must be some s for which P^s is an equilibrium vector, P^{s+1} a disequilibrium vector. Then with the aid of (19) we have by the same argument

(21) $\bar{P} \cdot F(P) > 0$ for any disequilibrium P,

which is the assertion of the theorem.

3.1.3. To prove (18) and (19), we consider *three cases: (a)* $P_s = P_{s+1}$; *(b)* $P_s > P_{s+1}$ and $F_{k'}(P^{s+1}) < F_{k'}(P^s)$ for some $k' \leqslant s$; *(c)* $P_s > P_{s+1}$ and $F_k(P^{s+1}) = F_k(P^s)$ for all $k \leqslant s$. [In view of (9) and (15), these cases are exhaustive.]

(*a*) In this case, from (10) $P^s = P^{s+1}$; hence

(22) $\sum_{k=0}^{m} F_k(P^{s+1}) = \sum_{k=0}^{m} F_k(P^s)$ if $P_s = P_{s+1}$.

(*b*) In this case we have

(23) $P_{k'}[F_{k'}(P^{s+1}) - F_{k'}(P^s)] < P_{s+1}[F_{k'}(P^{s+1}) - F_{k'}(P^s)]$,

since $P_{k'} \geqslant P_s > P_{s+1}$ by the assumption that $k' \leqslant s$ and (9). From (15)

$P_k[F_k(P^{s+1}) - F_k(P^s)] \leqslant P_{s+1}[F_k(P^{s+1}) - F_k(P^s)]$ $(k \leqslant s)$.

This, in conjunction with (23), yields

(24) $\sum_{k=0}^{s} P_k[F_k(P^{s+1}) - F_k(P^s)] < P_{s+1} \sum_{k=0}^{s} [F_k(P^{s+1}) - F_k(P^s)]$.

Now by (W) we have

$\sum_{k=0}^{m} P_k{}^s F_k(P^s) = 0 = \sum_{k=0}^{m} P_k{}^{s+1} F_k(P^{s+1})$,

and therefore, with the aid of (11) and (12) and then (24),

(25)
$$
\begin{aligned}
0 &= \sum_{k=0}^{m} P_k{}^{s+1} F_k(P^{s+1}) - \sum_{k=0}^{m} P_k{}^s F_k(P^s) \\
&= \sum_{k=0}^{s} P_k[F_k(P^{s+1}) - F_k(P^s)] + P_{s+1} \sum_{k=s+1}^{m} [F_k(P^{s+1}) - F_k(P^s)] \\
&\quad + (P_{s+1} - P_s) \sum_{k=s+1}^{m} F_k(P^s) < P_{s+1} \sum_{k=0}^{m} [F_k(P^{s+1}) - F_k(P^s)] \\
&\quad + (P_{s+1} - P_s) \sum_{k=s+1}^{m} F_k(P^s) \leqslant P_{s+1} \sum_{k=0}^{m} [F_k(P^{s+1}) - F_k(P^s)],
\end{aligned}
$$

the last inequality following from (17) and the fact that $P_{s+1} - P_s < 0$. From (25) we must have $P_{s+1} > 0$, and therefore (25) yields

(26) $\sum_{k=0}^{m} F_k(P^{s+1}) > \sum_{k=0}^{m} F_k(P^s)$ $\left\{ \begin{array}{l} \text{if } P_{s+1} < P_s \text{ and} \\ F_{k'}(P^{s+1}) < F_{k'}(P^s) \text{ for some } k' \leqslant s. \end{array} \right.$

(*c*) In this case by assumption

$\sum_{k=0}^{s} F_k(P^s) = \sum_{k=0}^{s} F_k(P^{s+1})$,

so that from (16)

(27) $\sum_{k=0}^{m} F_k(P^{s+1}) \geqslant \sum_{k=0}^{m} F_k(P^s)$ $\left\{ \begin{array}{l} \text{if } P_s > P_{s+1} \text{ and} \\ F_k(P^{s+1}) = F_k(P^s) \text{ for all } k \leqslant s, \end{array} \right.$

which are the assumptions of this case.

Suppose now that P^s is an equilibrium, P^{s+1} a disequilibrium vector. Then $F(P^s) \leqslant 0$, so that from (15) $F_k(P^{s+1}) \leqslant 0$ $(k \leqslant s)$. Since P^{s+1} is not an equilibrium vector, $F_k(P^{s+1}) > 0$ for some k so that

$$F_{k''}(P^{s+1}) > 0 \quad \text{for some } k'' > s.$$

Since $F_{k''}(P^s) \leqslant 0$, $F_{k''}(P^{s+1}) > F_{k''}(P^s)$, therefore, because of (16),

(28) $\quad \Sigma_{k=0}^{m} F_k(P^{s+1}) > \Sigma_{k=0}^{m} F_k(P^s)$ $\left\{ \begin{array}{l} \text{if } P_s > P_{s+1} \text{ while} \\ F_k(P^{s+1}) = F_k(P^s) \text{ for all } k \leqslant s, \text{ with} \\ P^s \text{ equilibrium, } P^{s+1} \text{ disequilibrium.} \end{array} \right.$

Then (18) follows from (22), (26), and (27). If P^s is equilibrium and P^{s+1} is disequilibrium, then $P^s \neq P^{s+1}$ and therefore $P_s > P_{s+1}$; then (19) follows from (26) or (28). Hence, by the argument of Section 3.1.2, (20) and (21) are demonstrated.

3.1.4. *Remark.* Let P be any equilibrium point; then $F(P) \leqslant 0$. From (20) it follows that

(29) $\left\{ \begin{array}{l} \text{if there exists a positive equilibrium, then } F(P) = 0 \\ \text{for every equilibrium price vector } P. \end{array} \right.$

3.2. We now consider the general case where the equilibrium $\overline{P}$ may have zero components. Write

(30) $\quad S = \{k: \overline{P}_k > 0\}.$

Then $\overline{P}_{\tilde{s}} = 0$. By definition of equilibrium $F(\overline{P}) \leqslant 0$ and, in particular, $F_{\tilde{s}}(\overline{P}) \leqslant 0$; by Lemma 2,

(31) $\quad F_{\tilde{s}}(P) \leqslant 0 \quad \text{for all } P.$

Then from (B), $F_{\tilde{s}}(P)$ is finite-valued, so that the product $\overline{P}_{\tilde{s}} \cdot F_{\tilde{s}}(P)$ is well defined and equal to zero. Hence,

(32) $\quad \overline{P} \cdot F(P) = \overline{P}_s \cdot F_s(P) + \overline{P}_{\tilde{s}} \cdot F_{\tilde{s}}(P) = \overline{P}_s \cdot F_s(P).$

Since $P_{\tilde{s}} \geqslant 0$, it follows from (S) that

(33) $\quad F_s(P) = F_s(P_s, P_{\tilde{s}}) \geqslant F_s(P_s, 0),$

so that

(34) $\quad \overline{P}_s \cdot F_s(P) \geqslant \overline{P}_s \cdot F_s(P_s, 0).$

From (31) and Lemma 3 the function $F_s(P_s, 0)$ satisfies all the assumptions (H), (C), (W), (B), and (S). Further, it has a positive equilibrium $\overline{P}_s$. Hence, we can apply the results (21) and (29) of Section 3.1 and conclude that

(35) $\quad \overline{P}_s \cdot F_s(P_s, 0) > 0 \quad \text{if } P_s \text{ is not an equilibrium of } F_s(P_s, 0),$

(36) $\quad F_s(P_s, 0) = 0 \quad \text{if } P_s \text{ is an equilibrium of } F_s(P_s, 0).$

If P_s is not an equilibrium of $F_s(P_s, 0)$, then $\overline{P} \cdot F(P) > 0$ from (32), (34–35). If it is, then $F_s(P) \geqslant 0$ from (33) and (36). If $F_s(P) = 0$, then, from (31), P is an equilibrium. Hence, if P is a disequilibrium vector, $F_s(P) \geqslant 0$, $F_s(P) \neq 0$, so that

$$\overline{P}_s \cdot F_s(P) > 0,$$

and, by (32), $\overline{P} \cdot F(P) > 0$ even if P_s is an equilibrium of $F_s(P_s, 0)$.

4. Statement of theorem on stability and convexity of equilibria

In [1], as part of the proof of Theorem 2, it was shown that the condition $\overline{P} \cdot F(P) > 0$ was sufficient for the convergence of solutions of both the *non-numéraire* and *numéraire* systems; for further discussion see [2], Theorem 2, where "corners" are explicitly treated, and it is also shown that the same condition insures the set of equilibria is convex. Hence, Theorem 1 implies

   Theorem 2.   If $F(P)$ is a vector of excess demand functions which are homogeneous of degree zero, continuous, bounded from below, if Walras' Law holds, and if all commodities are weak gross substitutes, then both the *non-numéraire* and *numéraire* adjustment systems [Equations (1) and (2) above] are stable[7] and the set of equilibria is convex.[8]

Notes

1   The authors acknowledge the assistance of a grant from the Rockefeller Foundation to Stanford University for mathematical research in the social sciences, and additional help from the Office of Naval Research, Task NR-047-004.

2   Cf. [3], Theorem 7 and footnote 36; also [2], Section 2.

3   It should be noted that the excess demand function resulting from maximizing any utility function with the frequently assumed property of positive marginal utilities (e.g., $\sum_{k=0}^{m} \alpha_k \log X_k, \alpha_k > 0$) will tend to infinity as the corresponding price tends to zero; the function is continuous in the extended sense used here, but is not bounded as price varies over the unit simplex.

4   This is, of course, considerably weaker than assuming that the Weak Axiom of Revealed Preference holds for *all* pairs of price vectors.

5   Morishima's assumptions implied the uniqueness of equilibrium, so this question does not arise in his proof.

6   Morishima [5] replaced the assumption of strict gross substitutability by one of indecomposability, but this is also unnecessary.

7   In the sense that every solution (path) converges to some equilibrium point.

8   The convexity of the set of equilibria when all commodities are weak gross substitutes was observed by McKenzie [4].

References

[1]   Arrow, Kenneth J., Henry D. Block, and Leonid Hurwicz, "On the Stability of the Competitive Equilibrium, II," this volume, III.1, pp. 228–255.

[2]   Arrow, Kenneth J., and Leonid Hurwicz, "Some Remarks on the Equilibria of Economic Systems," this volume, III.1, pp. 258–264.

[3]   Arrow, Kenneth J., and Leonid Hurwicz, "On the Stability of the Competitive Equilibrium, I," this volume, III.1, pp. 199–228.

[4]   McKenzie, Lionel, "A Contribution to the Theory of Stability of Competitive Equilibrium," unpublished manuscript, 1959.

[5]   Morishima, Michio, "Gross Substitutability, Homogeneity, and the Walras Law," unpublished manuscript, 1959.

[6]   Uzawa, Hirofumi, "An Alternative Proof of the Stability in the Gross Substitute Case," Technical Report No. 60, Office of Naval Research, Contract N6onr-25133, Stanford University, October 8, 1958.

[7]   Uzawa, Hirofumi, "On the Stability of Dynamic Processes," Technical Report No. 61, Office of Naval Research, Contract N6onr-25133, Stanford University, November 28, 1958.

Competitive stability under weak gross substitutability: nonlinear price adjustment and adaptive expectations

KENNETH J. ARROW
LEONID HURWICZ[1]

1. Introduction

In earlier papers by the authors [4 (218–21)], and in collaboration with H. D. Block [1 (240–49)], the global stability of the competitive equilibrium was studied in the case where all commodities are gross substitutes, that is, $\partial F_j/\partial P_k > 0$ for all $j \neq k$, where F_j is the excess demand for commodity j and P_k is the price of commodity k. Two dynamic systems were considered: one a *linear* system in which the price of each commodity moved proportionately to its excess demand, and the other a more general *nonlinear* system in which the rate of change of each price was a sign-preserving function of the excess demand (in both cases, with the possible exception of a numéraire). For both systems it was demonstrated that global stability held in the strong sense that for any arbitrary starting point the prices converged to a limit which was necessarily the competitive equilibrium point (unique up to a proportionality factor under the assumptions made). For the latter system, the proof of convergence depended upon showing that the "maximum norm,"

$$\max_k \left| (P_k/\overline{P}_k) - 1 \right|,$$

where $\overline{P}$ is an equilibrium vector, was necessarily decreasing so long as prices were not at equilibrium.

Subsequently, the stability of nonlinear adjustment processes was studied by Uzawa [15] and McKenzie [12] for the case of weak gross substitutes, i.e., where $\partial F_j/\partial P_k \geqq 0$ for $j \neq k$. In this case, the equilibrium may not be unique up to a proportionality factor, but it has been shown by McKenzie [12 (Theorem 1)] that the set of equilibria must form a convex set. See also [2 (Theorem 2)]. Both Uzawa and McKenzie explicitly or implicitly assumed that there exists at least one equilibrium vector positive in all components. Uzawa assumed that the rate of change of each price was a monotone increasing function of excess demand which vanishes for zero excess demand, a more restrictive dynamic system than that considered in [1]; McKenzie assumed that the rate of change of each price (other than a possible numéraire) was a function of all prices which, however, had the same sign as the excess demand. Both proved that their respective processes had the property that Uzawa called "quasi-stability" [15 (618)]; the price movement starting from any initial point is always bounded, and the distance from the moving point to the *set* of equilibria approaches zero. Equivalently, the second part of the definition can be replaced by the conditions that every path is bounded and every limit point of a path is an equilibrium.[2] This is a weaker property than convergence to a limit along any path, which we have called (global) stability. Uzawa showed that for weak gross substitutes quasi-stability implies stability.

In this paper, we shall consider McKenzie's dynamic system, which is the most general yet proposed, and demonstrate that if there exists at least one strictly positive equilibrium, then the path defined by the dynamic system from any starting point will converge to a limit which, of course, must be an equilibrium. This theorem is stronger than McKenzie's in the sense that the type of stability proved is somewhat stronger. The method of proof is perhaps novel, though related to the methods of [1] and of Uzawa [15].

The results are extended to the case where current excess demand depends upon expected future prices as well as current prices. It is assumed that all commodities, present and future, are weak gross substitutes, and that expectations about future prices are formed from present and past prices according to the principle of adaptive expectations used by Cagan [7], Friedman [9 (143–52)], and Nerlove [13] in empirical studies. This hypothesis requires that expected price be changed at a rate proportional to the difference between current actual and current expected price. It has been shown by Nerlove and one of the present authors [5] that local stability can be established for adjustment systems where all commodities are gross substitutes and expectations are adaptive. In this paper, we show that such adjustment systems are globally stable, provided that all equilibria are strictly positive.

We start by proving in Section 2 a general theorem on stability of dynamic systems. This theorem is used in Sections 3 and 5 to prove the stability of the systems without and with expected prices, respectively. In Section 4, it is shown, by example, that if we do not assume the existence of at least one positive equilibrium, the nonlinear process may lead to unbounded solutions. This possibility does not arise in linear systems, where there is always global stability under conditions of weak gross substitutability, as shown in [2 (Theorem 2)].

It may be of some interest to note that weak gross substitutability constitutes a genuine generalization of gross substitutability compatible with the assumption that excess demand functions are determined by utility maximization under competitive conditions. Let the demand of the i-th individual be determined as the vector, X^i, which maximizes a utility function $U_i(X^i)$ subject to the constraints, $X^i \geq 0$, and $P \cdot X^i \leq P \cdot \overline{X}^i$, where P is the vector of prices and $\overline{X}^i$ the initial endowment vector of the i-th individual. It will be shown possible to select utility functions, $U_i(X^i)$, not all the same, and initial endowment vectors, $\overline{X}^i$, so that $\partial X_j^i/\partial P_k \geq 0$ for all $j \neq k$, with the equality holding for all individuals i for a subset of the commodities (specifically, for commodities $2, \ldots, m$) in a range of prices. Since the market excess demand function is the sum of the individual demand functions less a constant (the sum of the individual initial endowment vectors), it follows that all commodities are weak gross substitutes, with $\partial F_j/\partial P_k = 0$ for $j, k = 2, \ldots, m, j \neq k$, over some range of prices.

To construct such an example, first define a function $\phi(u)$, which is equal to $\log u$ for $u \geq 1$, quadratic for $u \leq 1$, and twice continuously differentiable at $u = 1$. It is easily verified that $\phi'(u) = 2 - u$ for $u \leq 1$. Thus, $\phi(u)$ is concave.

For any individual, choose a utility function,

$$U(X) = \sum_{j=1}^{m} a_j \phi(X_j - \overline{X}_j),$$

where $a_1 = 1, a_j > 0, j = 2, \ldots, m$. The initial endowments $\overline{X}_j$ can be chosen arbitrarily, except that it will be required that

$$\overline{X}_1 \geq (1 + a)^{1/2} - 1,$$

where we define, $a = \sum_{j=2}^{m} a_j$. Finally, define,

$$\lambda = (1 + a)^{1/2} + 1.$$

Suppose $P_1 = 1, P_j < a_j/\lambda, j = 2, \ldots, m$. Then, under the above conditions, it may be verified that the vector X which maximizes utility is given by

$$X_1 = \overline{X}_1 - \frac{a}{\lambda},$$

$$X_j = \overline{X}_j + \frac{a_j}{\lambda P_j}, \quad j \geq 2.$$

The conditions stated show that $X_1 \geq 0$, $X_1 - \overline{X}_1 < 0 < 1$, $X_j - \overline{X}_j > 1$ for $j > 1$. Then the first-order conditions for a constrained maximum are satisfied, with λ as the Lagrange multiplier. We see immediately that for any $j \geq 2$, X_j is independent of P_k for $k \geq 2$, $k \neq j$.

For each individual, we can choose a utility function of the above form and an initial endowment vector. Then, for each individual $\partial X_j{}^i/\partial P_k = 0$ for j, $k \geq 2$, $j \neq k$, for $P_1 = 1, P_2, \ldots, P_m$ sufficiently small. Homogeneity of the demand functions implies that the independence of demands holds whenever P_j, $j \geq 2$, are sufficiently small relative to P_1, which is the desired example.

2. A theorem on stability

In this section, we consider a general dynamic system,

(1) $dP/dt = H(P)$,

and state a set of sufficient conditions for the stability of its solutions.

First we state a lemma which is closely related to Lyapunov's "second method" for proving stability and which has been used implicitly in several earlier papers. See especially [3].

Lemma 1.   Constancy of functions on limit paths. Suppose that for any P^0 there is a solution $P(t)$ of equation (1) with $P(0) = P^0$ and that, for fixed t, $P(t)$ is a continuous function of P^0. Suppose further that $\Phi(P)$ is a continuous function of P, $P(t)$ any solution of (1), and $P^*(t)$ a limit path of $P(t)$, i.e., a solution of (1) with $P^*(0) \equiv P^* = $ a limit point of $P(t)$. Then if $\Phi[P(t)]$ converges to a limit, say Φ^*, $\Phi[P^*(t)] \equiv \Phi^*$, the identity holding in t.

Proof.   Use the notation $P(t|P^0)$ to denote the solution with $P(0|P^0) = P^0$. By definition of a limit point, there is a sequence $\{t_n\}$ such that $\lim_{n \to \infty} P(t_n) = P^*$. From continuity in the starting point and uniqueness of the solution,

$$P^*(t) = P(t|P^*) = \lim_{n \to \infty} P[t|P(t_n)]$$

$$= \lim_{n \to \infty} P[t + t_n|P(0)] = \lim_{n \to \infty} P(t + t_n).$$

From continuity of Φ,

$$\Phi[P^*(t)] = \Phi[\lim_{n \to \infty} P(t + t_n)] = \lim_{n \to \infty} \Phi[P(t + t_n)] = \Phi^*,$$

for any t.

Theorem 1.   Suppose the system (1) satisfies the following conditions.

(a) There exists at least one positive equilibrium, that is, a point $\overline{P} > 0$ for which $H(\overline{P}) = 0$;

(b) for every positive equilibrium $\overline{P}$ and every solution $P(t)$, $\max_j P_j(t)/\overline{P}_j$ is monotone decreasing and $\min_j P_j(t)/\overline{P}_j$ is monotone increasing;

(c) for any P^0 there is a unique solution $P(t)$ with $P(0) = P^0$; further, for fixed t, $P(t)$ is a continuous function of P^0;

(d) if $P(t)$ is a solution which has at least one component not eventually constant,[3] and $P^*(t)$ is a limit path of $P(t)$, then at least one eventually constant component of $P^*(t)$ is not eventually constant in $P(t)$.

Then every solution $P(t)$ of (1) for which $P(0) > 0$ converges to a limit.

Proof. Let the vector P have m components. For any solution $P(t)$, let c be the number of its eventually constant components. The conclusion holds trivially for any solution for which $c = m$. We shall prove it for all solutions by backward induction on c.

Suppose that the theorem is valid for all solutions with $c > c_0$ eventually constant components, and let $P(t)$ be any solution with c_0 eventually constant components. Let $\overline{P}$ be any positive equilibrium. From (b) and the assumption that $P(0) > 0$, we have, for all $t \geq 0$,

$$(2) \quad \max_j P_j(0)/\overline{P}_j \geq \max_j P_j(t)/\overline{P}_j \geq P_j(t)/\overline{P}_j \geq \min_j P_j(t)/\overline{P}_j$$
$$\geq \min_j P_j(0)/\overline{P}_j > 0.$$

Since $\max_j P_j(t)/\overline{P}_j$ is monotone decreasing and bounded from below, it must approach a limit. We may, therefore, define

$$(3) \quad \lim_{t \to \infty} \max_j P_j(t)/\overline{P}_j = \overline{\mu}(\overline{P}).$$

A similar remark holds for $\min_j P_j(t)/\overline{P}_j$; since it is monotone increasing from a positive beginning, we can write

$$(4) \quad \lim_{t \to \infty} \min_j P_j(t)/\overline{P}_j = \underline{\mu}(\overline{P}) > 0.$$

It follows from (2) that $P(t)$ is bounded and hence has a limit point P^*. Let $P^*(t)$ be the solution with $P^*(0) = P^*$. It follows from (3), (4), and Lemma 1 that

$$(5) \quad \max_j P_j^*(t)/\overline{P}_j \equiv \overline{\mu}(\overline{P}), \quad \min_j P_j^*(t)/\overline{P}_j \equiv \underline{\mu}(\overline{P}),$$

the identity holding with respect to t.

For all j such that $P_j(t)$ is eventually constant, it is certainly convergent. By Lemma 1, $P_j^*(t)$ is constant (hence eventually constant). From (d), $P^*(t)$ has at least one eventually constant component that had not been eventually constant in $P(t)$. Therefore, the number of eventually constant components in $P^*(t)$ is greater than c_0, and by the induction hypothesis,

$$(6) \quad \lim_{t \to \infty} P^*(t) = P^{**},$$

for some P^{**}, which must be an equilibrium. See, e.g., [6 (Lemma 1, p. 77)]. If we replace $P(t)$ by $P^*(t)$ in (2) and use (4) and (5),

$$P_j^*(t) \geq \overline{P}_j \, \underline{\mu}(\overline{P}) > 0 \quad \text{for all } t,$$

so that

$$(7) \quad P^{**} \text{ is a positive equilibrium.}$$

By definition of a limit, $\lim_{t\to\infty} P_j^*(t)/P_j^{**} = 1$ for all j, so that

(8) $\lim_{t\to\infty} \max_j P_j^*(t)/P_j^{**} = 1 = \lim_{t\to\infty} \min_j P_j^*(t)/P_j^{**}$.

From (7), (5) holds with $\bar{P} = P^{**}$. By (8), then, $\bar{\mu}(P^{**}) = 1 = \underline{\mu}(P^{**})$. If in (2) we replace $P(t)$ by $P^*(t)$ and $\bar{P}$ by P^{**}, we see, in view of (5), that $P^*(t) = P^{**}$ for all t. In particular, this holds for $t = 0$, so that $P^* = P^*(0) = P^{**}$, and hence by (7),

(9) P^* is a positive equilibrium.

Since P^* was any limit point, the quasi-stability of the system has been shown. However, from the quasi-stability and (b), it will be shown that stability in the stronger sense follows.[4] For by definition of a limit point and positivity of P^*, there must exist a sequence $\{t_n\}$ such that $P_j(t_n)/P_j^*$ approaches 1 for each j. Hence,

(10) $\lim_{t\to\infty} \max_j P_j(t_n)/P_j^* = \lim_{t\to\infty} \min_j P_j(t_n)/P_j^* = 1$.

But since $\max_j P_j(t)/P_j^*$ and $\min_j P_j(t)/P_j^*$ both converge, (10) implies that they must both converge to 1. From (2), with $\bar{P} = P^*$, $P_j(t)/P_j^*$ converges to 1 for each j, which demonstrates the conclusion.

3. Stability under weak gross substitutability without expectations

3.1. We assume that there are m commodities, numbered $1, \ldots, m$. Let P be the vector of their prices and $F(P)$ the vector of excess demands as a function of P. We make the following assumptions.

(W) $P \cdot F(P) = 0$;

for each $j = 1, \ldots, m$,

(H) $F_j(P)$ is homogeneous of degree 0,

(C) $F_j(P)$ is continuous,

(B) $F_j(P)$ is bounded from below,

and

(S) $\partial F_j/\partial P_k \geqq 0$ for all $j \neq k$.

The dynamic system we assume is that introduced by McKenzie. We assume

(D.1) $\dot{P}_j = \begin{cases} H_j(P) & \text{if } P_j > 0 \text{ or } H_j(P) > 0, \\ 0, & \text{otherwise,} \end{cases}$

where, for each j,

(D.2) $\operatorname{sgn} H_j(P) = \operatorname{sgn} F_j(P)$ for all P or $H_j(P) \equiv 0$,

the latter holding for at most one commodity j.

The functions H are assumed to be continuous.

The dynamic system (D.1–2) is formulated to include both numéraire and nonnuméraire systems; when $H_j(P) \equiv 0$ for some j, then j is a numéraire. The second part of (D.1) insures that any solution is nonnegative. Any nonnegative ($\neq 0$) initial position is possible, except, of course, that the numéraire price must be positive.

3.2. In this subsection we show that in studying the stability of solutions of (D.1–2) we can confine ourselves to solutions $P(t)$ which are positive everywhere so that, in particular, $P(0) > 0$. It follows that we can disregard the second part of (D.1). We make use of some lemmas proved in [2].

Lemma 2.   Let $P(t)$ be any solution of the system (D.1–2), where $F(P)$ satisfies conditions (W), (H), (C), (B), and (S). Then there exists a possibly empty set of indices Z and a time t_0 such that:

(a) $P_Z(t) \equiv 0$ for $t \geq t_0$;

(b) $P_{\tilde{Z}}(t) > 0$ for all t;

(c) $\dot{P}_{\tilde{Z}} = H_{\tilde{Z}}[0, P_{\tilde{Z}}(t)]$ for $t \geq t_0$;

(d) $\operatorname{sgn} H_j(0, P_{\tilde{Z}}) = \operatorname{sgn} F_j(0, P_{\tilde{Z}})$ for $j \in \tilde{Z}$, except for the numéraire, if any;

(e)   the function $F_{\tilde{Z}}(0, P_{\tilde{Z}})$ satisfies (H), (C), (B), (W), and (S);

(f)   if $\overline{P}$ is any equilibrium of the excess demand functions $F(P)$, then $\overline{P}_{\tilde{Z}}$ is an equilibrium for the excess demand functions $F_{\tilde{Z}}(0, \overline{P}_{\tilde{Z}})$ in the space consisting only of the commodities in $\tilde{Z}$.

Proof.   Suppose that on the solution, $P(t)$, commodity j has a zero price at some time $t_1 > 0$. It cannot be that $H_j[P(t_1)] > 0$; for then, by continuity, $H_j[P(t)] > 0$ for $0 \leq t_1 - \epsilon < t \leq t_1$. By (D.1), $\dot{P}_j(t) > 0$ in this interval. Since $P_j(t_1 - \epsilon) \geq 0, P_j(t_1) > 0$, contrary to assumption. Hence

(11) $H_j[P(t_1)] \leq 0$.

Since j cannot be the numéraire (which can never have a zero price because it starts at a positive value and remains constant), it follows from (D.2) that $F_j[P(t_1)] \leq 0$, while $P_j(t_1) = 0$. By Lemma 2 of [2], however, if $F_j(P^1) \leq 0$ for any P^1 for which $P_j^{\,1} = 0$, then $F_j(P) \leq 0$ for all P. Now define

(12) $Z = \{j: P_j(t) = 0 \text{ for some } t > 0\}$.

Then we have shown that

(13) $F_Z(P) \leq 0$ for all P.

It follows from (D.1-2) that $\dot{P}_z \leq 0$. In particular, if $P_j(t_1) = 0$ for some $j \in Z$, then $P_j(t) = 0$ for all $t \geq t_1$. Since this holds for each $j \in Z$, (a) holds for some t_0, and (b) follows by definition of Z. By (D.1), (c) follows from (a) and (b), while (d) is a special case of (D.2).

Finally, that (e) and (f) follow from (13) is precisely the assertion of Lemma 3 of [2].

3.3. To prove stability with the aid of Theorem 1, we have to establish or assume conditions (a)–(d) of that theorem. We will assume (a) and (c) hold. We have then to establish (b) and (d). These assertions, which are dynamic in character, will be shown to follow from the following static lemma. An analogue of this lemma was proved for the case of gross substitutes in the strict sense in [1] (see Lemma 3); a weaker form was established by Uzawa [15 (Lemma 2)]. We make use of some steps similar to those in the proof of Theorem 1 of [2].

Lemma 3. If $\overline{P}$ is a positive equilibrium vector, P a positive disequilibrium vector, $\pi(i)$ any permutation of the indices $1, \ldots, m$ such that

$$P_{\pi(j)}/\overline{P}_{\pi(j)} \leq (\text{resp. } \geq) P_{\pi(j+1)}/\overline{P}_{\pi(j+1)},$$

and J is defined as max $\{j : F_{\pi(j)}(P) \neq 0\}$, then $F_{\pi(J)}(P) < (\text{resp. } >) 0$.

Proof. As in the proof of Theorem 1 of [2], we may assume without loss of generality that $\overline{P}_j = 1$ for all j. Also without loss of generality we may suppose the numbering of the commodities such that $P_j \leq P_{j+1}, j = 1, \ldots, m$. Define a sequence of price vectors, P^*, by the relation

(14) $\quad P_j^s = \min(P_s, P_j)$,

so that, in particular, P^1 is an equilibrium vector, with all components equal to P_1, and $P^m = P$. From (14) and the conventions just made, we see easily that

$$(15) \qquad P_j^s = \begin{cases} P_j, & j \leq s, \\ P_s, & j > s, \end{cases}$$

$$(16) \qquad P_j^{s+1} = \begin{cases} P_j, & j \leq s, \\ P_{s+1}, & j > s. \end{cases}$$

Thus a change from P^s to P^{s+1} involves no change in the first s prices and an increase (or at least no decrease) in the last $m - s$. From (S),

(17) $\quad F_j(P^{s+1}) \geq F_j(P^s), \quad j \leq s.$

If we write, P_{s+1} being positive by hypothesis,

$$Q^{s+1} = (P_s/P_{s+1}) P^{s+1},$$

we see that the last $m - s$ components of Q^{s+1} are the same as those of P^s while the first s components are smaller or the same. Hence, by (S),

$$F_j(Q^{s+1}) \leq F_j(P^s), \quad j > s.$$

But by (H), $F_j(Q^{s+1}) = F_j(P^{s+1})$, so that

(18) $F_j(P^{s+1}) \leq F_j(P^s)$, $j > s$.

From (18),

$F_j(P^{s+1}) \leq F_j(P^s)$ if $j \geq J > s$.

By induction on s, it follows that

$F_j(P^{s+1}) \leq F_j(P^1)$ if $j \geq J > s$.

Since P^1 is a positive equilibrium vector, $F_j(P^1) = 0$. If we set $s = J - 1$, and distinguish the two cases, $j = J, j > J$, we have

(19) $F_J(P^J) \leq 0$,

(20) $F_j(P^J) \leq 0$ for $j > J$.

From (20),

$\Sigma_{j=J+1}^m P_j^J F_j(P^J) \leq 0$.

By (W), $\Sigma_{j=1}^m P_j^J F_j(P^J) = 0$, so that

$\Sigma_{j=1}^J P_j^J F_j(P^J) \geq 0$.

From (15), $P_j^J = P_j$ for $j \leq J$, so that

(21) $\Sigma_{j=1}^J P_j F_j(P^J) \geq 0$.

From (17), $F_j(P^{s+1}) \geq F_j(P^s)$ for $j \leq J \leq s$. By induction on s,

$F_j(P^J) \leq F_j(P^s)$ for $j \leq J \leq s$.

In particular, let $s = m$, and recall that $P^m = P$.

(22) $F_j(P^J) \leq F_j(P)$ for $j \leq J$.

Finally, by (W),

$0 = \Sigma_{j=1}^m P_j F_j(P) = \Sigma_{j=1}^J P_j F_j(P^J) + \Sigma_{j=1}^J P_j[F_j(P) - F_j(P^J)]$

$+ \Sigma_{j=J+1}^m P_j F_j(P)$.

The first summation is nonnegative, by (21). Each term of the second summation is nonnegative, by (22). Finally, $F_j(P) = 0$ for $j > J$ by hypothesis. Hence, each term in the second summation must be zero, i.e.,

$F_j(P) = F_j(P^J)$ for $j \leq J$.

In particular, let $j = J$ and recall (19). Since $F_J(P) \neq 0$ by definition, we must have $F_J(P) < 0$.

The other half of the lemma is proved in exactly the same way.

3.4. In this subsection we derive the dynamic implications of Lemma 3; we shall show that the system (D.1–2) has certain properties, which in the next subsection will be shown to imply hypotheses (b) and (d) of Theorem 1 and therefore stability.

Lemma 4.   Let S be any set of commodities containing the numéraire, if any, and $\bar{P}$ any positive equilibrium. Then: (A) For any given time interval, if $P_j(t)$ is identically constant for all $j \notin S$, then $\max_{j \in S}$ (resp., $\min_{j \in S}$) $P_j(t)/\bar{P}_j$ is monotonic decreasing (resp., increasing); (B) if $P_j(t)$ is constant for all $t \geq 0$ for all $j \notin S$, and if $\max_{j \in S}$ (resp., $\min_{j \in S}$)$P_j(t)/\bar{P}_j$ is constant for all $t \geq 0$, then there exists a commodity $k \in S$ such that

$$\max_{j \in S} \text{ (resp., } \min_{j \in S}\text{) } P_j(t)/\bar{P}_j = P_k(t)/\bar{P}_k$$

for all t sufficiently large.

Proof.   (A) For convenience, define

(23) $\bar{V}(P, \bar{P}: S) = \max_{j \in S} P_j/\bar{P}_j,$

(24) $M(t) = \{j: \ j \in S, P_j(t)/\bar{P}_j = \bar{V}[P(t), \bar{P}: S]\}.$

For any fixed t' in the interval, let j' be any element of $M(t')$. Renumber the commodities in increasing order of $P_j(t')/\bar{P}_j$. Since this ratio is the same for all elements of $M(t')$, choose the numbering so that j' is the last element of $M(t')$. Then $P_j(t')/\bar{P}_j > \max_{k \in S} P_k(t')/\bar{P}_k$ for $j > j'$, so that $j \notin S$ for $j > j'$ and, therefore, $P_j(t)$ is identically constant over the given time interval, by hypothesis about elements $\notin S$. By (D.1) and Lemma 2, for $j > j'$, $H_j[P(t)] = 0$ over the interval. Since, for $j > j'$, j cannot be the numéraire (which belongs to S), (D.2) implies that $F_j[P(t)] = 0$ for all points of the time interval and therefore in particular for t', so that

(25) $F_j[P(t')] = 0$ for $j > j'$.

But now by Lemma 3, $F_{j'}[P(t')] \leq 0$. Since j' was any element of $M(t')$,

(26) $F_j[P(t')] \leq 0$ for all $j \in M(t')$.

If j is the numéraire, then $H_j \equiv 0$; if not, then from (D.2) and (26), $H_j[P(t')] \leq 0$. Hence, from (D.1),

(27) $\dot{P}_j \leq 0$ for all $j \in M(t')$, for all t' in the interval.

By definition of $M(t)$, $\bar{V}[P(t'), \bar{P}: S] = \bar{V}[P(t'), \bar{P}: M(t')] > P_j(t')/\bar{P}_j$ for all $j \in S - M(t')$. Hence, for t sufficiently close to t',

(28) $\bar{V}[P(t), \bar{P}: S] = \bar{V}[P(t), \bar{P}: M(t')].$

By definition of $M(t)$,

(29) $P_j(t')/\bar{P}_j = \bar{V}[P(t'), \bar{P}: M(t')]$ for all $j \in M(t')$.

We will examine the right- and left-hand derivatives of $\bar{V}[P(t), \bar{P}: S]$ at $t = t'$. From (28),

(30) $\quad \overline{V}[P(t'+h), \overline{P}: S] - \overline{V}[P(t'), \overline{P}: S]$

$$= \overline{V}[P(t'+h), \overline{P}: M(t')] - \overline{V}[\overline{P}(t'), \overline{P}: M(t')]$$

$$= \max_{j \in M(t')} P_j(t'+h)/\overline{P}_j - \max_{j \in M(t')} P_j(t')/\overline{P}_j$$

$$= \max_{j \in M(t')} [P_j(t'+h) - P_j(t')]/\overline{P}_j,$$

from (29). For $h > 0$, then

(31) $\quad \{\overline{V}[P(t'+h), \overline{P}: S] - \overline{V}[P(t'), \overline{P}: S]\}/h$

$$= \max_{j \in M(t')} [P_j(t'+h) - P_j(t')]/(h\overline{P}_j).$$

If we let h approach zero from the right, the right-hand derivative is, then,

$$\max_{j \in M(t')} \dot{P}_j/\overline{P}_j \leq 0,$$

by (27). Similarly, the left-hand derivative is

$$\min_{j \in M(t')} \dot{P}_j/\overline{P}_j \leq 0.$$

Hence, both the right- and left-hand derivatives of $\overline{V}[P(t), \overline{P}: S]$ exist and are nonpositive, so that $\overline{V}[P(t), \overline{P}: S]$ is monotone decreasing, while a similar argument shows that

$$\min_{j \in S} P_j(t)/\overline{P}_j$$

is monotone increasing; this is assertion (A).

(B) By hypothesis,

(32) $\quad \overline{V}[P(t), \overline{P}: S] \equiv \overline{\mu},$

say. If the numéraire j_0 belongs to $M(t)$ for some value of t, then $P_{j_0}/\overline{P}_{j_0} = \overline{\mu}$. Thus the numéraire belongs to $M(t)$ for all t, so that (B) holds. Let us now assume that the numéraire belongs to $M(t)$ for no value of t. For each $t, M(t)$ is nonnull and so contains a positive integral number of elements. Choose t_0 so that $M(t_0)$ has fewest elements. For simplicity, let

(33) $\quad M = M(t_0), \quad N = S - M(t_0).$

By construction, N contains the numéraire. By definition,

(34) $\quad \overline{V}[P(t), \overline{P}: S] = \max \{\overline{V}[P(t), \overline{P}: M], \overline{V}[P(t), \overline{P}: N]\},$

(35) $\quad \overline{V}[P(t_0), \overline{P}: M] > \overline{V}[P(t_0), \overline{P}: N].$

Consider any t for which $\overline{V}[P(t), \overline{P}: M] > \overline{V}[P(t), \overline{P}: N]$. From (34), $M(t)$ must be disjoint from N and therefore a subset of M. But $M(t)$ cannot contain fewer elements than $M(t_0)$, so that if

(36) $\quad \overline{V}[P(t), \overline{P}: M] > \overline{V}[P(t), \overline{P}: N], \quad$ then $M(t) = M.$

Suppose $\overline{V}[P(t), \overline{P}: N] = \overline{V}[P(t), \overline{P}: S]$ for some $t > t_0$. Let t_1 be the earliest such t. In view of (34) and (35),

(37) $\overline{V}[P(t), \overline{P}: M] > \overline{V}[P(t), \overline{P}: N]$ for $t_0 < t < t_1$.

Hence, by (36), $M(t) = M$ in this interval. From (32), $P_j(t)$ must be identically constant for all $j \in M$ in this interval. If $j \notin N$, then $j \in M$ or $j \notin S$; in either case, $P_j(t)$ is constant in the interval. Since N contains the numéraire, we can apply part (A) of this lemma to the set N; $\overline{V}[P(t), \overline{P}: N]$ is monotone decreasing in (t_0, t_1), so that

$$\overline{V}[P(t_1), \overline{P}: N] \leq \overline{V}[P(t_0), \overline{P}: N] < \overline{V}[P(t_0), \overline{P}: M]$$

$$= \overline{\mu} = \overline{V}[P(t_1), \overline{P}: S],$$

by (35), (34), and (32), contradicting the definition of t_1. Hence,

$$\overline{V}[P(t), \overline{P}: S] > \overline{V}[P(t), \overline{P}: N]   \text{for all } t > t_0;$$

from (34) and (36), $M(t) = M(t_0)$ for all $t > t_0$. Therefore (B) holds for any $k \in M(t_0)$.

Again the argument for the minimum is entirely parallel.

3.5. The proof of stability is now an easy consequence of Theorem 1 and Lemma 4.

Theorem 2.   If $F(P)$ satisfies (W), (H), (C), (B), and (S), and if it possesses a positive equilibrium, then the dynamic system defined by

(D.1) $\dot{P}_j = \begin{cases} H_j(P) & \text{if } P_j > 0 \text{ or } H_j(P) > 0, \\ 0 & \text{otherwise}, \end{cases}$

where

(D.2) $\operatorname{sgn} H_j(P) = \operatorname{sgn} F_j(P)$ for all P or $H_j(P) \equiv 0$,

the latter holding for at most one j, is globally stable in the sense that every solution converges, provided the solutions are unique and continuous in the starting point.

Proof.   By Lemma 2, we can assume that $\dot{P} = H(P)$ and that $P(0) > 0$. Conditions (a) and (c) of Theorem 1 have been assumed here; it remains to demonstrate (b) and (d).

If we let S be the set of all commodities $1, \ldots, m$, then assertion A of Lemma 4 is hypothesis (b) of Theorem 1.

To verify (d) of Theorem 1, let C be the set of components of $P(t)$ which are eventually constant other than the numéraire, if any. Then for t sufficiently large, $\widetilde{C}$ satisfies the conditions for the set S in Lemma 4 (assertion A), so that

$$\max_{j \in \widetilde{C}} P_j(t)/\overline{P}_j$$

is monotone decreasing, and

$$\min_{j \in \widetilde{C}} P_j(t)/\overline{P}_j$$

is monotone increasing. Since $\max_{j\in\tilde{C}} P_j(t)/\bar{P}_j \geq \min_{j\in\tilde{C}} P_j(t)/\bar{P}_j \geq 0$, both functions are bounded and hence convergent.

Let $P^*(t)$ be a limit path of $P(t)$. Then, by Lemma 1,

(38) $\max_{j\in\tilde{C}} P_j^*(t)/\bar{P}_j \equiv \bar{\mu}, \quad \min_{j\in\tilde{C}} P_j^*(t)/\bar{P}_j \equiv \mu,$

for suitably chosen constants $\bar{\mu}, \mu$.

Also, by definition of the set C, $P_j(t)$ is convergent for $j \in C$. Again by Lemma 1,

(39) $P_j^*(t)$ is identically constant for $j \in C$.

If $\bar{\mu} = \mu$, then $P_j^*(t)$ would be constant for all j in $\tilde{C}$, from (38). In conjunction with (39), all components of $P^*(t)$ would be constant, so that (d) would certainly be satisfied.

Otherwise, $\bar{\mu} > \mu$. From (38), (39), and Lemma 4, assertion (B), there exist commodities $j', j'' \in \tilde{C}$ such that

(40) $P_{j'}^*(t)/\bar{P}_{j'} \equiv \bar{\mu}, \quad P_{j''}^*(t)/\bar{P}_{j''} \equiv \mu, \quad$ for t sufficiently large.

Both j' and j'' are eventually constant. They cannot be the same, since $\bar{\mu} > \mu$ and, therefore, they cannot both be the numéraire. Hence at least one was not eventually constant along $P(t)$. Hence (d) follows, completing the proof of Theorem 2.

4. An example of instability in the absence of a positive equilibrium

When there is gross substitutability in the strict sense, there must be a positive equilibrium [1 (88)]. However, condition (S) in its present form is not sufficient to guarantee this, so the assumption of a positive equilibrium is an additional one. Further, it will now be shown, by means of an example, that Theorem 2, at least in its present form, would not remain valid if this assumption were dropped.

Suppose there are two commodities, with excess demand functions,

(41) $F_1(P) = P_2^2/P_1^2, \quad F_2(P) = -P_2/P_1.$

These excess demand functions satisfy the conditions (W), (H), (C), and (S). They do not satisfy (B) as they stand; however, we can regard (41) as valid only for $P_2/P_1 \leq 1$, and define the excess demand functions for $P_2/P_1 \geq 1$, by

$F_1 = 2(P_2/P_1) - 1, \quad F_2 = (P_1/P_2) - 2.$

The modified functions satisfy all conditions. In the example, we shall need the definition of the functions only in the region, $P_2/P_1 \leq 1$.

Note that the only equilibrium points are those for which $P_2 = 0, P_1 > 0$. Hence, there is no positive equilibrium.

We now define the adjustment process. Let

(42) $\Phi(u) = 2ue^{-1/u}$.

This function is zero when $u = 0$ and positive for all positive values of u, approaching infinity as u approaches infinity. By differentiation, it is easy to see that Φ is strictly increasing. Hence, it has a well-defined inverse $\psi(v)$ for all non-negative v with

(43) $\operatorname{sgn} \psi(v) = \operatorname{sgn} v$.

We now let

(44) $H_1(P) = \psi(P_2/P_1)$, $H_2(P) = -P_2/P_1 = F_2(P)$.

From (41), $\operatorname{sgn} F_1 = \operatorname{sgn}(P_2/P_1)$; hence from (43) and (44), $\operatorname{sgn} F_1 = \operatorname{sgn} H_1$, while the condition, $\operatorname{sgn} F_2 = \operatorname{sgn} H_2$, is trivially satisfied. In fact, since $H_1 = \psi(\sqrt{F_1})$, H_1 and H_2 are actually monotonically increasing as well as sign-preserving functions of F_1 and F_2, respectively.

The dynamic system, $\dot{P} = H(P)$, can be written, in view of the definitions, as

(45) $\Phi(\dot{P}_1) = P_2/P_1$, $\dot{P}_2 = -P_2/P_1$.

It is easily verified that the pair of functions

$$P_1(t) = \sqrt{t + 1}, \qquad P_2(t) = \exp(-2\sqrt{t + 1})$$

constitute a solution of (45). Along this path, $P_2(t)/P_1(t) \leq e^{-2} < 1$, so that confining ourselves to (41) involves no loss of generality. But then $P_1(t)$ approaches infinity, and the solution is not convergent in the usual sense.

Nevertheless, it must be noted that there is a kind of convergence, for $P_2(t)$ approaches zero, so that the solution does approach the set of equilibria (which includes all points with $P_2 = 0$). Put slightly differently, the relative prices converge, though the absolute prices are in part unbounded.

5. Stability under expectations

5.1. We now suppose that the demand for commodities depends on both current prices and expected future prices. Let current prices be denoted by $P_j, j = 1, \ldots, m$, while expected future prices are denoted by $P_j, j = m + 1, \ldots, 2m$, where P_{j+m} is the expected future price of commodity j. The vector P will have $2m$ components; we will also write P^1 for the vector of current prices, $P_1, \ldots, P_m$ and P^2 for the vector of future prices.

Given the vector P, each individual, and therefore the market, determines a $2m$-vector of excess demands, $F(P)$. The first m components, $F^1(P) = F^1(P^1, P^2)$, are excess demands for current goods. The last m components, $F^2(P)$, are planned excess demands for the future. In the absence of futures markets, these planned excess demands can have no influence on prices.[5] We will then suppose that the dynamic relations (D.1–2) of Section 3 apply only to current prices:

(DE.1) $\dot{P}_j = \begin{cases} H_j(P) & \text{if } P_j > 0 \text{ and } H_j(P) > 0, \\ 0 & \text{otherwise}, \quad j = 1, \dots, m, \end{cases}$

where

(DE.2) $\text{sgn } H_j(P) = \text{sgn } F_j(P)$ or $H_j(P) \equiv 0,$

the latter holding for at most one j.

Since P^2 enters F^1, this dynamic theory is not complete. It is necessary to postulate that P^2 is determined by the expectations of the market, which in turn will be determined by past experience in some way. We shall adopt here the hypothesis of *adaptive expectations* (see Section 1), which can be written

(DE.3) $\dot{P}_j = a_j(P_{j-m} - P_j),$ $j = m + 1, \dots, n,$ $a_j > 0.$

If there is a numéraire, j_0, then we can assume that the market has a perfect expectation of its price. This can be achieved without modifying (DE.3) by assuming that for any solution the starting values, $P_{j_0}(0)$ and $P_{j_0+m}(0)$, are the same.

The market interpretation of this dynamic system deserves some consideration. When only current prices affect excess demand, there are two possible interpretations of the adjustment process studied in Section 3. One is the usual recontracting interpretation of the Walrasian *tâtonnement*; no transactions actually take place during the process until equilibrium is achieved. A second interpretation, however, seems more interesting to us. All the magnitudes, demands and initial endowments alike, are flows of instantaneously perishable goods, with no interdependence in utility between commodities at different dates. At each moment of time, transactions can indeed take place, but they do not affect decisions taken at any subsequent period.

Analogues of both interpretations are possible in this two-period case. Imagine that each individual can issue notes or make deposits freely during the first period; he is obliged to redeem his notes or use up his deposits in the second. Then Walras's Law holds for his total of current and planned expenditures but not in each period separately. Under the recontracting interpretation, then, at each moment of time, the individual is faced with a set of current prices on the market and a set of expected prices which he has formed from the past history of prices during the recontracting period. He determines his excess demands for both the current and the future periods by maximizing utility under a budget constraint; the current excess demands, which do not necessarily satisfy a budget constraint, determine the rate of change of current prices, while the individual's expectation of prices changes adaptively. If the monetary aggregate of current excess demands is positive, the individual is supposed to issue notes, to be redeemed in the future, when, from the budget constraint, he is planning an equal monetary aggregate of excess supply. If the monetary aggregate of current excess demands is negative, the individual is supposed to be able to deposit the difference and draw on it in the next period.

The second interpretation, in terms of flows of perishable goods, is also possible here, if we add the hypotheses that the utility for present and future goods is the sum of utilities of present goods and of future goods and that the two utility functions have the same mathematical form. The "future" here is supposed to be only infinitesimally far off. Then, when the future arrives, the individual is in exactly the same situation he was to begin with, and the process continues. In this interpretation, the equations describe the changes of prices in real time.

It should be remarked that this model ignores any discounting of the future; the notes and deposits bear no interest.

Remark 1. We do not have to worry about the expected prices becoming negative. From (DE.1), $P_j(t) \geq 0$ for $j \leq m$. Then if $P_j(t) = 0$ for some $j > m$, $P_{j-m}(t) \geq 0$, so that, from (DE.3), $\dot{P}_j \geq 0$.

A point $\bar{P}$ satisfying the conditions,

$$F^1(\bar{P}) \leq 0, \qquad \bar{P}^1 \cdot F^1(\bar{P}) = 0, \qquad \bar{P}^1 = \bar{P}^2,$$

is necessarily an equilibrium of the dynamic system (DE.1–3). We shall postulate that there exist competitive equilibria with respect to the entire set of excess demand functions (including those for future goods) for which the current and future expected prices are equal; these will be termed *stationary equilibria*. This assumption could be deduced from some stationarity conditions on the excess demand functions or the utility functions underlying them. For such an equilibrium, by definition,

$$F(\bar{P}) \leq 0, \qquad \bar{P}^1 = \bar{P}^2,$$

and, by (W),

$$\bar{P} \cdot F(\bar{P}) = 0 = \bar{P}^1 \cdot F^1(\bar{P}) + \bar{P}^2 \cdot F^2(\bar{P}).$$

Since each term is nonpositive,

$$\bar{P}^1 \cdot F^1(\bar{P}) = 0,$$

and so, by the previous remarks, a stationary equilibrium is an equilibrium of the dynamic system (DE.1–3).

We shall, in fact, postulate the existence of stationary equilibria not only for the original system but also for all systems formed from it by combining a set of commodities into a composite commodity.

(SE)   There exists $\bar{P}^1$ such that $F(\bar{P}^1, \bar{P}^1) \leq 0$;

further, if we define, for a given set of commodities S and a given weight vector $\pi_{\bar{S}}$,

$$G_j(P_S^1, p_0^1, P_S^2, p_0^2) = F_j(P_S^1, p_0^1 \pi_{\bar{S}}, P_S^2, p_0^2 \pi_{\bar{S}}), \qquad j \in S \text{ or } j - m \in S,$$

$$G_0^1(P_S^1, p_0^1, P_S^2, p_0^2) = \Sigma_{j \in \bar{S}} \pi_j F_j(P_S^1, p_0^1 \pi_{\bar{S}}, P_S^2, p_0^2 \pi_{\bar{S}}),$$

$$G_0^2(P_S^1, p_0^1, P_S^2, p_0^2) = \Sigma_{j \in \bar{S}} \pi_j F_{j+m}(P_S^1, p_0^1 \pi_{\bar{S}}, P_S^2, p_0^2 \pi_{\bar{S}}),$$

so that we are forming a composite commodity from a set $\tilde{S}$ of the current commodities and another composite commodity from the corresponding set of future commodities, then there exist $\bar{P}_S{}^1, \bar{p}_0{}^1$ such that

$$G(\bar{P}^1, \bar{p}_0{}^1, \bar{P}^1, \bar{p}_0{}^1) \leqq 0.$$

To simplify matters, we ignore, unlike in the previous parts of the paper, the difficulties of corner equilibria by postulating positive demand for free goods,

(PF)   if $P_j = 0$,   then $F_j(P) > 0$, $j = 1, \ldots, m$.

Remark 2. From (PF), we cannot have $\bar{P}_j = 0$ for any j in (SE). Hence, we certainly have a positive equilibrium, and condition (a) of Theorem 1 is fulfilled. Also, the second line of (DE.1) becomes superfluous, for suppose $P_j(t) = 0$ for some $t > 0$, and $j \leqq m$. Then $F_j > 0$, while commodity j cannot be a numéraire; therefore $H_j > 0$. Further, then $\dot{P}_j(t) > 0$, so that $P_j(t - \epsilon) < P_j(t)$ for ϵ sufficiently small. Since $P_j(t - \epsilon) \geqq 0$, $P_j(t) > 0$. Hence, we can assume that $P(0) > 0$ without loss of generality.

5.2. Theorem 3. Under assumptions (W), (H), (C), (B), (S), (SE), and (PF), the dynamic system defined by (DE.1–3) is globally stable in the sense that every solution converges, provided the solutions are unique and continuous in the starting point.

Proof. As before, we use Theorem 1. Hypothesis (a) is implied by assumption (PF). See Remark 2 of 5.1. Hypothesis (c) is explicitly stated. It remains to verify hypotheses (b) and (d).

By (SE) and (PF), we can choose a positive equilibrium $\bar{P}$ with

(46) $\bar{P}_j = \bar{P}_{j+m}$, $j = 1, \ldots, m$.

Suppose j is such that

(47) $P_j(t)/\bar{P}_j = \max_k P_k(t)/\bar{P}_k$.

If $j \leqq m$, we may apply Lemma 3; we must have $F_j[P(t)] \leqq 0$, and therefore $H_j[P(t)] \leqq 0$. If $j > m$, then, by assumption,

$$P_j(t)/\bar{P}_j \geqq P_{j-m}(t)/\bar{P}_{j-m}.$$

From (46), $P_j(t) \geqq P_{j-m}(t)$, and by (DE.3), $\dot{P}_j(t) \leqq 0$. Since this holds for all j for which (47) holds, it follows from the proof of Lemma 4(A) that

(48) $\max_k P_k(t)/\bar{P}_k$ is monotonic decreasing.

An exactly parallel argument applies to $\min_k P_k(t)/\bar{P}_k$, so that hypothesis (b) of Theorem 1 is verified.

We have finally to verify hypothesis (d) of Theorem 1. As in the proof of Theorem 2, we let C be the eventually constant set of components of $P(t)$ other than the numéraire. Let

$$C_1 = \{j: j \leqq m, j \in C\}, \quad C_2 = \{j: j \leqq m, j + m \in C\}.$$

The set C is completely determined by C_1 and C_2. If $j \in C_2$, then from (DE.3), $P_j(t) \equiv P_{j+m}(t)$ for t sufficiently large; since $P_{j+m}(t)$ is constant for t sufficiently large, by definition, we must have $j \in C_1$.

$$C_2 \subset C_1.$$

Let $P^*(t)$ be a limit path of $P(t)$. We must show that at least one element not eventually constant on $P(t)$ is eventually constant on $P^*(t)$. We consider two cases. First suppose that there is at least one j in C_1 but not in C_2. Since $P_j(t)$ is constant for t sufficiently large, the differential equation (DE.3), with j replaced by $j + m$, becomes a single differential equation with a stable solution, so that $P_{j+m}(t)$ converges. Then by Lemma 1, $P_{j+m}{}^*(t)$ is constant. Since j did not belong to C_2, this means there is at least one more eventually constant component in $P^*(t)$ than in $P(t)$.

Now suppose that $C_1 = C_2$. For t sufficiently large, $P_j(t)$ and $P_{j+m}(t)$ are constant for $j \in C_1$. From (DE.3), we must have $P_j(t) = P_{j+m}(t)$. Let the common constant values form a vector π_{C_1}. By Lemma 1, we must also have

$$P_j{}^*(t) \equiv P_{j+m}{}^*(t) \equiv \pi_j, \quad j \in C_1.$$

Now form all the commodities in C_1, together with the numéraire, if any, into a single composite commodity. Let V be the remaining current commodities. Call the new set of excess demand functions $G(P)$; they are defined as in the statement of assumption (SE). The corresponding dynamic system is

$$
(49) \quad
\begin{aligned}
dP_j/dt &= H_j(P) = H_j(P_{\tilde{C}_1}{}^1, \pi_{C_1}, P_{C_1}{}^2, \pi_{C_1}), \quad && j \in V, \\
dP_{j+m}/dt &= a_{j+m}(P_j - P_{j+m}), && j \in V.
\end{aligned}
$$

The system (49) is satisfied by $P(t)$, for t sufficiently large, and $P^*(t)$. It also satisfies all the conditions of the Theorem, in view of (SE), so that we can conclude that (48) holds for this system. Let W be the variables of (49), including the composite numéraire. Then, by Lemma 1,

$$(50) \quad \max_{j \in W} P_j{}^*(t)/\bar{P}_j \equiv \bar{\mu}, \quad \min_{j \in W} P_j{}^*(t)/\bar{P}_j \equiv \mu.$$

In the next subsection, 5.3, we will demonstrate by Lemma 5 that from (50), we can infer the existence of $j', j'' \in W$ such that

$$(51) \quad P_{j'}{}^*(t)/\bar{P}_{j'} \equiv \bar{\mu}, \quad P_{j''}{}^*(t)/\bar{P}_{j''} \equiv \mu.$$

If $\bar{\mu} = \mu$, then $P_j{}^*(t)$ must be constant for all $j \in W$ and therefore for $j \in C_1$ or j such that $j - m \in \tilde{C}_1$. Since the other variables are certainly constant, then all variables are constant, and (d) is satisfied.

If $\bar{\mu} > \mu$, then j' and j'' are distinct and cannot both be the composite numéraire. Neither j' nor j'' belong to C so that (d) is again verified.

5.3 We have only to prove the following lemma:

Lemma 5. If $\max_j$ (resp., $\min_j$) $P_j(t)/\bar{P}_j$ is identically constant, then there is some j' such that

$$P_{j'}(t)/\bar{P}_{j'} \equiv \max_j P_j(t)/\bar{P}_j$$

for t sufficiently large.

Proof. Suppose not.

(52) $\quad \max_j P_j(t)/\bar{P}_j \equiv \bar{\mu}.$

Then in particular,

(53) $\quad P_j(t) < \bar{\mu}\bar{P}_j$

in some time interval for $j \leq m$. From (DE.3),

(54) $\quad P_{j+m}(t) = e^{-a_j t} [P_{j+m}(0) + a_j \int_0^t e^{a_j s} P_j(s) \, ds].$

Since, by (52),

$$P_{j+m}(0) \leq \bar{\mu}\bar{P}_j, \qquad P_j(s) \leq \bar{\mu}\bar{P}_j \qquad \text{for all } s,$$

it follows from (54) that

$$P_{j+m}(t) \leq e^{-a_j t} [\bar{\mu}\bar{P}_j + a_j \bar{\mu}\bar{P}_j \int_0^t e^{a_j s} \, ds] = \bar{\mu}\bar{P}_j.$$

Indeed, $P_{j+m}(t)$ is, in effect, a weighted average of $P_{j+m}(0)$ and past values of $P_j(s)$. Further, the strict inequality holds if $P_j(s) < \bar{\mu}\bar{P}_j$ over some s-interval. In view of (53), we can conclude

(55) $\quad P_{j+m}(t)/\bar{P}_j < \bar{\mu} \qquad$ for all t sufficiently large.

Let

(56) $\quad M(t) = \{ j: P_j(t)/\bar{P}_j = \bar{\mu} \}, \qquad F = \{ j: j > m \}.$

From (56), (55) can be written

(57) $\quad M(t)$ is disjoint from F for $t \geq t_0$,

for suitable t_0.

Among values of $t \geq t_0$, choose t_1 so that the number of elements of $M(t)$ is minimal. Let

(58) $\quad M = M(t_1), \qquad N = \{ j: j \leq m, j \notin M \}.$

Suppose $\bar{V}[P(t), \bar{P}: M] > \bar{V}[P(t), \bar{P}: N]$. In view of (57), it follows that $M(t) \subset M$. But for $t \geq t_0$, it follows from the choice of t_1 that $M(t)$ cannot be a proper subset of M.

(59) $\quad$ If $\bar{V}[P(t), \bar{P}: M] > \bar{V}[P(t), \bar{P}: N]$, then for $t \geq t_0, M(t) = M$.

Suppose for some $t \geq t_1$,

$$\bar{V}[P(t), \bar{P}: M] = \bar{V}[P(t), \bar{P}: N].$$

Let t_2 be the smallest such t. Then, since $\bar{V}[P(t_1), \bar{P}: M] > \bar{V}[P(t_1), \bar{P}: N]$ by definition of t_1, we must have $t_2 > t_1$, and

(60) $\quad \overline{V}[P(t), \overline{P}\colon M] > \overline{V}[P(t), \overline{P}\colon N] \qquad$ for $t_1 \leqq t < t_2$,

(61) $\quad \overline{V}[P(t_2), \overline{P}\colon M] = \overline{V}[P(t_2), \overline{P}\colon N]$.

Let

(62) $\quad N(t) = \{j\colon \; j \in N, P_j(t)/\overline{P}_j = \overline{V}[P(t), \overline{P}\colon N]\}$.

From (59) and (60), $M(t) = M$ for $t_1 \leqq t < t_2$. In a sufficiently small left-hand neighborhood of t_2, it follows from (61) and (55) that $P_j(t)/\overline{P}_j$ has a greater value for $j \in N(t)$ than for $j > m$. Hence, if the commodities (present and future together) are ranked in increasing order of $P_j(t)/\overline{P}_j$, the elements of M will be the highest, those in $N(t)$ the next highest.

At the same time, if M contained the numéraire, the conclusion of the lemma would hold, contrary to supposition. Since $P_j(t)/\overline{P}_j \equiv \overline{\mu}$ for $j \in M$, for $t_1 \leqq t < t_2$, $P_j(t)$ is identically constant over this interval, so that $H_j[P(t)] \equiv 0$. Since j is not the numéraire,

(63) $\quad F_j[P(t)] \equiv 0 \qquad$ for $t_1 \leqq t < t_2$.

In view of the ranking found in the preceding paragraph, it follows from (63) and Lemma 3 that $F_j[P(t)] \leqq 0$ for all $j \in N(t)$. This implies that $H_j[P(t)] \leqq 0$ and for all $j \in N(t)$, and hence, by the reasoning used in the proof of Lemma 4(A), $\overline{V}[P(t), \overline{P}\colon N]$ is monotone decreasing in a left-hand neighborhood of t_2. But then it is impossible, as implied by (60) and (61), that

$$\overline{V}[P(t), \overline{P}\colon N] < \underline{\mu} \qquad \text{for } t < t_2, \qquad \overline{V}[P(t_2), \overline{P}\colon N] = \underline{\mu}.$$

Notes

1 Arrow's work was done with the help of the Office of Naval Research (Task 047), Hurwicz's with the partial support of a grant from the Rockefeller Foundation to Stanford University for mathematical research in the social sciences.

2 The second of these two formulations is Uzawa's definition. McKenzie [12 (606, n. 3)] asserts that the first formulation is a stronger property than the second, but this is clearly wrong. According to the second, (a) every sequence of points along the path has a convergent subsequence, and (b) the distance from any point of a convergent sequence to a particular equilibrium, and hence to the set of equilibria, approaches zero. From (a) and (b), it follows that the distance to the set of equilibria must approach zero along the path.

3 A component, $P_j(t)$, is said to be eventually constant if it is constant for all $t \geqq t_0$, for some t_0.

4 This argument is used by Uzawa [15 (Stability Theorem 3)]. Thus, in the theorem of the following section, it would have been possible to infer stability in our sense from the results of McKenzie. We adopt the present approach partly as a variant but mainly because it also supplies a technique for handling the case of adaptive expectations.

5   That current and planned excess demands depend on current and expected prices is, of course, a standard doctrine; see, e.g., Hicks [10] or Lange [11]. These works do not, however, have an explicit formulation of stability as related to price adjustment. Patinkin [14 (Chapters IV, X)] and Enthoven [8] have formulated dynamic models in which current excess demands influence current prices but planned excess demands have no relevance to price movements. As here, it becomes necessary to introduce expectational assumptions; Patinkin uses static assumptions, Enthoven an assumption of extrapolation from current values on the basis of the current rate of change.

References

[1]   Arrow, K. J., H. D. Block, and L. Hurwicz, "On the Stability of the Competitive Equilibrium, II," this volume, III.1, pp. 228–255.

[2]   Arrow, K. J., and L. Hurwicz, "Competitive Stability under Weak Gross Substitutability: The 'Euclidean Distance' Approach," this volume, III.2, pp. 265–275.

[3]   Arrow, K. J., and L. Hurwicz, "Gradient Method for Concave Programming, I: Local Results," *Studies in Linear and Non-Linear Programming*, eds. K. J. Arrow, L. Hurwicz, and H. Uzawa (Stanford: Stanford University Press, 1959), 117–26.

[4]   Arrow, K. J., and L. Hurwicz, "On the Stability of the Competitive Equilibrium, I," this volume, III.1, pp. 199–228.

[5]   Arrow, K. J., and M. Nerlove, "A Note on Expectations and Stability," this volume, III.4, pp. 317–325.

[6]   Bellman, R., *Stability Theory of Differential Equations* (New York: McGraw-Hill, 1953).

[7]   Cagan, P., "The Monetary Dynamics of Hyper-Inflation," *Studies in the Quantity Theory of Money*, ed. M. Friedman (Chicago: University of Chicago Press, 1956), 25–117.

[8]   Enthoven, A., "Monetary Disequilibria and the Dynamics of Inflation," *Economic Journal*, LXVI (June, 1956), 256–70.

[9]   Friedman, M., *A Theory of the Consumption Function* (Princeton: Princeton University Press, 1957).

[10]   Hicks, J. R., *Value and Capital*, 2nd ed. (Oxford: Oxford University Press, 1946).

[11]   Lange, O., *Price Flexibility and Employment* (Bloomington, Indiana: The Principia Press, 1944).

[12]   McKenzie, L., "Stability of Equilibrium and the Value of Positive Excess Demand," *Econometrica*, XXVIII (July, 1960), 606–17.

[13]   Nerlove, M., *The Dynamics of Supply: Estimation of Farmers' Responses to Price* (Baltimore: Johns Hopkins University Press, 1958).

[14]   Patinkin, D., *Money, Interest, and Prices* (Evanston, Illinois: Row, Peterson and Company, 1956).

[15]   Uzawa, H., "The Stability of Dynamic Processes," *Econometrica*, XXIX (October, 1961), 617–31.

3
STABILITY IN OLIGOPOLY

Stability of the gradient process in n-person games

KENNETH J. ARROW
LEONID HURWICZ [1]

1. Introduction

1.1. In an n-person game the ith player has at his disposal the (vector) *strategy* variable $x^i = (x_1{}^i, \ldots, x_{m_i}{}^i)$ which he chooses from the domain X^i in such a manner as to maximize his gain, as defined by the (real-valued) *payoff function* $\phi^i(x^1, x^2, \ldots, x^n)$. An n-tuple $\bar{x} = (\bar{x}^1, \bar{x}^2, \ldots, \bar{x}^n)$ of strategies is said to be an *equilibrium point* (cf. Nash [4]) of the *game* $\phi = (\phi^1, \phi^2, \ldots, \phi^n)$ (i.e., of the game defined by these payoff functions), if no player can profit by being the only one departing from the equilibrium strategy while others retain theirs, i.e., if the inequality

$$\phi^i(\bar{x}) \geq \phi^i(\bar{x}^1, \ldots, \bar{x}^{i-1}, x^i, \bar{x}^{i+1}, \ldots, \bar{x}^n) \qquad \text{(for all } x^i \text{ in } X^i\text{)}$$

holds for every i.

Suppose the game $\phi = (\phi^1, \phi^2, \ldots, \phi^n)$ is to be played repeatedly by a group of n players. If the strategies used by players $1, 2, \ldots, n$ in the tth play were respectively $x^1(t), x^2(t), \ldots, x^n(t)$, it might be natural for the ith player to choose his strategy $x^i(t + 1)$ for the $t + 1$ play in such a way as to maximize the value of $\phi^i[x^1(t), \ldots, x^{i-1}(t), x^i, x^{i+1}(t), \ldots, x^n(t)]$ over the domain X^i; this could be rationalized by imputing to the ith player the belief that no other player would depart from the strategy used in the tth play. A somewhat more cautious approach would call for selecting $x^i(t + 1)$ in such a way that, if possible,

$$\phi^i[x^1(t), \ldots, x^{i-1}(t), x^i(t + 1), x^{i+1}(t), \ldots, x^n(t)]$$

is greater than $\phi^i[x(t)]$, but without going all the way to the maximum. If the time parameter, t, is made continuous, one method for doing this is the *gradient process* defined by

$$(1) \qquad \frac{dx^i}{dt} = \lambda_i \frac{\partial \phi^i}{\partial x^i}, \qquad \lambda_i > 0 \qquad (i = 1, 2, \ldots, n),$$

with additional rules to cover the case where the process defined in (1) would lead outside the permissible strategy region $X^1 \times X^2 \times \cdots \times X^n$. It is easily seen that all the coefficients λ_i may be put equal to 1 without loss of generality by a suitable scale transformation for each of the variables x^i. Hence in what follows we shall write the gradient process in the simpler form

$$(2) \quad \frac{dx^i}{dt} = \frac{\partial \phi^i}{\partial x^i} \quad (i = 1, 2, \ldots, n),$$

again with suitable modification insuring that the boundaries of strategy domains are not violated.

It may be noted that, for $n = 1$, this is the classical "steepest ascent" method of handling maximization problems. For $n = 2$, $\phi^1 + \phi^2 = 0$, i.e., a two-person zero-sum game, such a gradient process was considered by the authors in [1], Chs. 6 and 8, and by Uzawa [1], Ch. 7.

The interest in the gradient method in the case previously studied was due to the fact that, under certain conditions, the solutions $x(t)$ of the (ordinary) differential equation system defined by the gradient relations (2) were found to converge to the maximum (for $n = 1$) or the saddle-point (for $n = 2$, $\phi^1 + \phi^2 = 0$). In this paper we show that, under suitable assumptions involving primarily the convexity properties of the payoff functions, the solution of the gradient process (2) converges to an equilibrium point, at least in some of its components. The earlier results for $n = 1, 2$ may be regarded as special cases of those found in the present paper.

The convergence of the gradient process solution is, of course, of interest for computational reasons; under the convexity assumptions made here, the gradient method provides a practical method for computing an equilibrium point. For an example of a two-person zero-sum game solved by gradient methods, see T. Marschak [1], Ch. 9.

In addition, as explained in the preceding paragraphs, the gradient method is at least a plausible mode of behavior for players in games which are played over and over again. Even in the one-person game, if it is too difficult to locate the maximum by a direct calculation, it is a reasonable hypothesis that the "player" approaches his maximum by successive improvements. The same argument applies to the n-person game. Hence it is of considerable behavioral as well as computational importance to determine conditions under which the gradient process converges.

As an illustration, the gradient method is applied to the n-person game *par excellence* of economics, the theory of oligopoly originated by Cournot. The stability of oligopolistic equilibrium is explored in Section 8, and some light is thereby cast on the range of applicability of the Theorem of this paper.[2]

1.2. The proof of convergence of the gradient process (2), suitably modified at the boundaries,[3] is analogous to that used in [1], Chs. 6–8. It is accomplished by showing that, for any equilibrium point $\bar{x} = (\bar{x}^1, \ldots, \bar{x}^n)$, the Euclidean distance $D_{\bar{x}}$ from the moving point $x(t) = [x^1(t), \ldots, x^n(t)]$ to $\bar{x}$ is a nonincreasing (and, away from equilibrium, decreasing) function of time.[4]

This behavior of the distance $D_{\bar{x}}$ is due to certain convexity properties imposed on the payoff functions ϕ^i. That some such properties would be sufficient is suggested by the consideration of the two special cases already known, viz., (a) the case $n = 1$, and (b) the case $n = 2$ with $\phi^1 + \phi^2 = 0$ (the zero-sum two-person game). In the case (a), convergence is assured by postulating that $\phi^1(x^1)$ is strictly concave in x^1. In the case (b), it was assumed in [1], Ch. 6, that (say) $\phi^1(x^1, x^2)$ is convex in x^2 and strictly concave in x^1.

Now in a zero-sum two-person game the requirement that the first player's payoff should be concave in x^1 and convex in x^2 implies that, similarly, the second player's payoff is concave in x^2 and convex in x^1. If the zero-sum restriction is dropped or the number of players exceeds two, the payoffs of the players are no longer related in this manner. Hence it becomes natural to try to obtain convergence by imposing restrictions on each player's payoff function; for instance, in the general (not necessarily zero-sum) two-person case, one might be inclined to postulate that for each i, $\phi^i(x^1, x^2)$ be convex in $x^j (j \neq i)$ and concave for x^i, and that, for at least one i, ϕ^i be strictly concave in x^i. But it turns out that these assumptions would not guarantee convergence and that even in this simple case, the "natural" generalization from the zero-sum case is of a somewhat different nature.

Such a generalization, for a game involving an arbitrary number of players and without the zero-sum restriction, is obtained through a reduction of the problem of convergence in the general n-person case to that of certain associated zero-sum two-person (i.e., saddle-point) problems. If S is a coalition (a subset of players) and $\tilde{S}$ its complement, the *associated S-game* is defined as the zero-sum two-person game where the payoff to the first player is given by

$$g^S = f^S - (x - \bar{x}) \cdot \bar{f}_x^S,$$

the strategy variable of the first player is the vector x^S whose components are the x^i, i in S, and the strategy variable of the second player is x^S whose components are the x^i, $i \in \tilde{S}$. The function f^S in the definition of g^S is the difference between the aggregate payoff to the members of S and that to the members of $\tilde{S}$, i.e.,

$$f^S = \Sigma_{i \in S} \phi^i - \Sigma_{i \in \tilde{S}} \phi^i,$$

and $\bar{f}_x^S$ is the vector whose components are the partial derivatives $\partial f^S / \partial x^i$ evaluated at $x = \bar{x}$. (We may note that g^S differs from f^S by a linear term only, so that their convexity properties are identical.)

It is shown below (Section 7.1) that the distance $D_{\bar{x}}$ will have the desired decreasing behavior if every associated S-game is monotonically convergent in the Euclidean (distance) norm, for which, as we know from [1], a sufficient condition is that $g^S(x^S, x^{\tilde{S}})$ be convex in $x^{\tilde{S}}$ and strictly concave in x^S, i.e., that $f^S(x^S, x^{\tilde{S}})$ be convex in $x^{\tilde{S}}$ and strictly concave in x^S. But the requirement that, for *each* set S of players, the payoff difference f^S be *strictly* concave in x^S is unnecessarily strong; for instance, in the case of the Lagrangian saddle-point (which may be treated as a two-person zero-sum game) the Lagrangian function is linear in the "multipliers" and hence the strict concavity condition would not be satisfied for the second player. On the other hand, it is known (cf. Samuelson [5], pp. 17–22) that under linearity there need not be any convergence even in the saddle-point case. This leads to an intermediate assumption, viz., that (a) each $f^S(x^S, x^{\tilde{S}})$ be concave in x^S and convex in $x^{\tilde{S}}$, and in addition that (b) for *some* set of players S^0, the difference f^{S^0} be convex in $x^{\tilde{S}^0}$ and *strictly* concave in x^{S^0}.[5]

It is hardly surprising that the latter assumption yields a weaker conclusion. In general, we may only assert that the components of x^{S^0} will converge to their equilibrium values, while the question of the convergence of the other x^i remains open. But for $n = 2$, whether the game is or is not of the zero-sum type, it turns out that the convergence of x^{S^0} implies the convergence of the whole vector x (cf. Section 7.2 below).

For the sake of concreteness, we provide an explicit statement for $n = 2$ and $n = 3$. First, consider the case $n = 2$, zero-sum. Suppose the payoff to the first player ϕ^1 is convex in x^2 and strictly concave in x^1. It follows that $f^1 = \phi^1 - \phi^2 = 2\phi^1$ has the same properties. It follows that $f^2 = -2\phi^1$ is concave in x^2 and convex in x^1. Finally, $f^{\{1,2\}} = \phi^1 + \phi^2 = 0$ is concave in (x^1, x^2). This disposes of all nonempty subsets of the set of players; the general theorem then implies that $x^1(t)$ must converge to one of its equilibrium values; in fact (cf. Section 7.2 below), $x^2(t)$ is also convergent here. Of course, the results of [1] cover this case.

Second, let $n = 2$, but without the zero-sum restriction. To apply the theorem, we require that $f^{\{1\}} = \phi^1 - \phi^2$, $f^{\{2\}} = \phi^2 - \phi^1$, and $f^{\{1,2\}} = \phi^1 + \phi^2$ be respectively concave in x^1, x^2, and (x^1, x^2); furthermore, at least one of these three concavity properties must hold in the strict sense. With the help of remarks in Section 7.2 below, we use the theorem of the present paper to conclude the convergence of both $x^1(t)$ and $x^2(t)$.

Now consider the case $n = 3$. Suppose that we wish to guarantee the convergence of $x^2(t)$. (The convergence of the other components would not necessarily follow.) To apply the theorem, we then assume that $f^{\{2\}} = \phi^2 - \phi^1 - \phi^3$, $f^{\{1,2\}} = \phi^1 + \phi^2 - \phi^3$, $f^{\{2,3\}} = \phi^2 + \phi^3 - \phi^1$, $f^{\{1,2,3\}} = \phi^1 + \phi^2 + \phi^3$ be respectively concave in x^2, (x^1, x^2), (x^2, x^3), (x^1, x^2, x^3); that $f^{\{2\}}$, $f^{\{1,2\}}$, $f^{\{2,3\}}$ be respectively convex in (x^1, x^3), x^3, x^1; and that at least one of the four concavity properties hold in the strict sense.

2. Notation

$I = \{1, 2, \ldots, n\}$: the set of all players.

S: a generic symbol for a subset of I.

$A \sim B$: the set of all elements in A but not in B (the set-theoretic difference).

$\tilde{S} = I \sim S$: the complement of S with respect to I.

$)i(\, = I \sim \{i\}$: the set of all players other than i.

$[i] = \{S\colon S \subseteq I, i \in S\}$: the collection of all sets of players containing the ith player.

$2^I = \{S\colon S \subseteq I\}$: the power set of I.

For a collection $A = \{S_1, S_2, \ldots, S_m\}$ of m subsets S_j of I, we write $N(A) = m$: the number of sets in the collection A.

X^i: the domain of strategy of the ith player.

x^i: a point in X^i (a strategy of the ith player).

$x^S = (x^{i_1}, x^{i_2}, \ldots, x^{i_{n(S)}})$ where $S = \{i_1, i_2, \ldots, i_{n(S)}\} \subseteq I$.

$x = x^I = (x^1, x^2, \ldots, x^n)$.

$x^{)i(} = (x^1, \ldots, x^{i-1}, x^{i+1}, \ldots, x^n)$.

$\phi^i\colon X^1 \times X^2 \times \cdots \times X^n \to$ reals (the payoff function of the ith player).

$f^S = \sum_{i \in S} \phi^i - \sum_{i \in \tilde{S}} \phi^i$, i.e., $f^S(x) = \sum_{i \in S} \phi^i(x) - \sum_{i \in \tilde{S}} \phi^i(x)$.

For a vector-valued function $g(z)$ on a vector space z, g_z denotes the matrix $\|\partial g_i / \partial z_j\|$; $g_z{}^0$ and $\bar{g}_z$ denote evaluation at z^0 and $\bar{z}$, respectively. If $z^{(1)}$ and $z^{(2)}$ are two vectors, their inner product is denoted by $z^{(1)} \cdot z^{(2)}$. Expression $z \geq 0$ means that every component of z is nonnegative; the set of all $z \geq 0$ is the nonnegative orthant.

3. Auxiliary results

In this section we present certain known propositions to be used in the proof of the convergence theorem below.

3.1. Lemma A.   Let Z be a convex set, and f a real-valued differentiable concave function defined on Z. Then:

(1) $f(z) \leq f(z^0) + f_z{}^0 \cdot (z - z^0)$ for any (z, z^0) in $Z \times Z$;

(2) for $Z = \{z\colon z \geq 0\}$ = the nonnegative orthant, (a) $z^0 \geq 0$ maximizes $f(x)$ over Z if $f_z{}^0 \leq 0$, $z^0 \cdot f_z{}^0 = 0$ (hence, in particular, if $f_z{}^0 = 0$), and (b) the function $F(z; f, z^0)$ defined on Z by

$$F(z) \equiv F(z; f, z^0) \equiv f(z) - (z - z^0) \cdot f_z{}^0$$

assumes its maximum over Z at the point $z = z^0$.

Lemma A.1, which is Lemma 3 in Kuhn-Tucker [3], implies 2(a); 2(b) follows from 2(a), since $F_z{}^0 = 0$.

3.2. In Lemmas B and C below, let $\mathfrak{U}$ and $\mathfrak{V}$ be vector spaces of m_u and m_v dimensions, respectively, $\mathfrak{W} = \mathfrak{U} \times \mathfrak{V}$, $W = \{(u, v)\colon u \geq 0, v \geq 0\}$ = the nonnegative orthant of $\mathfrak{W}$, and $g(u, v)$ a real-valued differentiable function defined on W, concave in u for each v and convex in v for each u.

Lemma B.   For any $u^0 \geq 0$, $v^0 \geq 0$, the function $G(u, v; g, u^0, v^0)$ defined on W by $G(u, v) \equiv G(u, v; g, u^0, v^0) \equiv g(u, v) - (u - u^0) \cdot g_u{}^0 - (v - v^0) \cdot g_v{}^0$ has a saddle-point over W at (u^0, v^0), i.e.,

$$G(u, v^0) \leq G(u^0, v^0) \leq G(u^0, v) \qquad \text{[for all } (u, v) \text{ in } W] .$$

This follows from Lemma A.2 (b), since $G_u^0 = 0$, $G_v^0 = 0$.

Lemma C (Uzawa). Let $\overline{w} = (\overline{u}, \overline{v})$ be a saddle-point of g over W. Define the gradient equation by

$$\frac{du}{dt} = \alpha g_u, \qquad \frac{dv}{dt} = \beta g_v,$$

where

$$\alpha \equiv \alpha(u, v) = \begin{pmatrix} \alpha_1(u, v) & & 0 \\ & \ddots & \\ 0 & & \alpha_{m_u}(u, v) \end{pmatrix}$$

$$\beta \equiv \beta(u, v) = \begin{pmatrix} \beta_1(u, v) & & 0 \\ & \ddots & \\ 0 & & \beta_{m_v}(u, v) \end{pmatrix}$$

$$\alpha_i(u, v) = \begin{cases} 0 & \text{if } u_i = 0 \text{ and } g_{u_i}(u, v) < 0, \\ 1 & \text{otherwise,} \end{cases}$$

$$\beta_j(u, v) = \begin{cases} 0 & \text{if } v_j = 0 \text{ and } g_{v_j}(u, v) > 0, \\ -1 & \text{otherwise.} \end{cases}$$

Also, write

$$D(t) = \tfrac{1}{2} \left[(u - \overline{u}) \cdot (u - \overline{u}) + (v - \overline{v}) \cdot (v - \overline{v}) \right] .$$

Then, for all (u, v) in W,

$$(u - \overline{u}) \cdot \alpha g_u - (v - \overline{v}) \cdot \beta g_v \leq 0$$

and

$$\frac{dD}{dt} \leq 0.$$

Furthermore, if $g(u, v)$ is strictly concave in u for each v, then all saddle-points over W of $g(u, v)$ have the same u-component, $\overline{u}$, and, for any (u, v) in W, $u \neq \overline{u}$,

$$(u - \overline{u}) \cdot \alpha g_u - (v - \overline{v}) \cdot \beta g_v < 0$$

and

$$\frac{dD}{dt} < 0.$$

See Uzawa's Theorem [1], Ch. 7, and parts (b) and (c) of the proof.

4. A property of equilibrium points

4.1. For the sake of clarity, we provide the following formal

Definition. $\bar{x} \in X^1 \times X^2 \times \cdots X^n$ is said to be an *equilibrium point* of the game [defined by the n-tuple of payoff functions] $\phi \equiv (\phi^1, \phi^2, \ldots, \phi^n)$ if, for each $i \in I$,

$$\phi^i(\bar{x}) \geq \phi^i(x^i, \bar{x}^{)i(}) \qquad \text{(for all } x^i \in X^i\text{)}.$$

4.2. Lemma D.   (1) Let $\bar{x}$ be an equilibrium point of the game $\phi \equiv (\phi^1, \phi^2, \ldots, \phi^n)$ such that (a) for each $S \subseteq I$, the function

$$f^S(x^S, x^{\widetilde{S}}) = f^S(x) = \Sigma_{i \in S} \, \phi^i(x) - \Sigma_{i \in \widetilde{S}} \, \phi^j(x)$$

is concave in x^S for each $x^{\widetilde{S}}$ and convex in $x^{\widetilde{S}}$ for each x^S.
Then the function

$$g^S(x^S, x^{\widetilde{S}}) = f^S(x^S, x^{\widetilde{S}}) - (x - \bar{x}) \cdot \bar{f}_x{}^S$$

has a saddle-point over $X^1 \times X^2 \times \cdots \times X^n$ at $(\bar{x}^S, \bar{x}^{\widetilde{S}})$.

(2) If the above condition (a) holds, and furthermore, (b) for some $S^0 \subseteq I$, the function $f^{S^0}(x^{S^0}, x^{\widetilde{S}^0})$ is strictly concave in x^{S^0} for each $x^{\widetilde{S}^0}$, then all equilibrium points of ϕ have the same $x^{\widetilde{S}^0}$ component, i.e., given two equilibrium points of ϕ, say $\bar{x} = (\bar{x}^{S^0}, \bar{x}^{\widetilde{S}^0})$ and $\bar{\bar{x}} = (\bar{\bar{x}}^{S^0}, \bar{\bar{x}}^{\widetilde{S}^0})$, the equality of $\bar{x}^{S^0} = \bar{\bar{x}}^{S^0}$ holds.

Proof.   (1) follows from Lemma B, since the function g^S is concave in x^S, and convex in $x^{\widetilde{S}}$.

By (1), if $\bar{x}$ and $\bar{\bar{x}}$ are two equilibrium points of ϕ, they are both saddle-points of g^{S^0}. Since g^{S^0} is strictly concave in x^{S^0}, the uniqueness of $\bar{x}^{S^0}$ follows from Lemma C.

5. The gradient method in an n-person game

For each $i \in I$, let X^i be the nonnegative orthant of the m_i-dimensional Euclidean space $\mathcal{X}^i$.[6] The *gradient relations* for the game $\phi = (\phi^1, \ldots, \phi^n)$ are written

$$(1) \qquad \frac{dx^i}{dt} = \gamma^i \phi_x{}^{ii} \qquad (i = 1, 2, \ldots, n)$$

where

$$\gamma^i = \begin{pmatrix} \gamma_1{}^i(x) & & 0 \\ & \ddots & \\ 0 & & \gamma_{m_i}{}^i(x) \end{pmatrix},$$

$$\gamma_r{}^i(x) = \begin{cases} 0 & \text{if } x_r{}^i = 0 \text{ and } \phi_{x_r}^i{}^i < 0, \\ 1 & \text{otherwise,} \end{cases}$$

$r = 1, 2, \ldots, mi; x^i = (x_1{}^i, \ldots, x_{m_i}{}^i), x = (x^1, x^2, \ldots, x^n)$. The n-tuple

$$\xi[t; x(0)] = (\xi^1[t; x(0)], \ldots, \xi^n[t; x(0)]), \qquad \xi^i[t; x(0)] \in X^i,$$

is said to be a solution of (1) through $x(0)$ if, for each $i \in I$,

$$\frac{d\xi^i}{dt} = \gamma^i \phi_x{}^i(\xi[t; x(0)]) \qquad \text{(for all } t \geq 0)$$

and

$$\xi^i[0; x(0)] = x^i(0).$$

6. Theorem

Let $\bar{x} = (\bar{x}^1, \bar{x}^2, \ldots, \bar{x}^n)$ be an equilibrium point of the game $\phi \equiv (\phi^1, \phi^2, \ldots, \phi^n)$ such that (a) for each $S \subseteq I$, the function

$$f^S(x^S, x^{\tilde{S}}) \equiv f^S(x) = \Sigma_{i \in S}\, \phi^i(x) - \Sigma_{i \in \tilde{S}}\, \phi^i(x)$$

is concave in x^S for each $x^{\tilde{S}}$, convex in $x^{\tilde{S}}$ for each x^S; and (b) for some $S^0 \subseteq I$, the function

$$f^{S^0}(x^{S^0}, x^{\tilde{S}^0})$$

is strictly concave in x^{S^0} for each $x^{\tilde{S}^0}$.

Let the gradient system (1) of Section 5 above have a unique solution $\xi[t; x(0)]$, continuous in $[t; x(0)]$ for every initial value $x(0)$.[7] Then, for any player $i_0 \in S^0$, $\xi^{i_0}[t; x(0)]$ converges to the (uniquely determined) $\bar{x}^{i_0}$ as $t \to \infty$.

7. Proof

7.0. Write

$$D = \tfrac{1}{2}(x - \bar{x}) \cdot (x - \bar{x}).$$

In 7.1 we show that $\dot{D} = dD/dt \leq 0$ for all x in $X^1 \times X^2 \times \cdots \times X^n$ and, furthermore, that $\dot{D} < 0$ for all $x = (x^{S^0}, x^{\tilde{S}^0})$ such that $x^{S^0} \neq \bar{x}^{S^0}$. By reasoning fully analogous to that used in the proof of Uzawa's Theorem [1], Ch. 7, convergence follows.

7.1.1. In 7.1.2 we shall show that, for an arbitrary $i_1 \in I$,

$$(1) \quad \dot{D} \leq \frac{1}{2^{n-1}} \Sigma_{S \in [i_1]} \left[(x^S - \bar{x}^S) \cdot \gamma^S g_{x^S}{}^S - (x^{\tilde{S}} - \bar{x}^{\tilde{S}}) \cdot \gamma^{\tilde{S}} g_{x^{\tilde{S}}}{}^{\tilde{S}} \right]$$

where

$$[i_1] = \{S \subseteq I: i_1 \in S\}, \qquad \gamma^S = \begin{pmatrix} \gamma^{i_1} & & 0 \\ & \ddots & \\ 0 & & \gamma^{i_{m(S)}} \end{pmatrix},$$

$S = \{i_1, \ldots, i_{m(S)}\}$, and, for any $S \in [i_1]$, $g^S(x^S, x^{\tilde{S}})$ is the function defined in Lemma D.

Now, by Lemma D, g^S has a saddle-point at $(\bar{x}^S, \bar{x}^{\tilde{S}})$. Hence, by Lemma C, for each $S \in [i_1]$,

(2) $\quad (x^S - \bar{x}^S) \cdot \gamma^S g_{x^S}^S - (x^{\tilde{S}} - \bar{x}^{\tilde{S}}) \cdot \gamma^{\tilde{S}} g_{\tilde{x}^S}^S \leqq 0,$

and hence $\dot{D} \leqq 0$. Furthermore, if g^{S^o} is strictly concave in x^{S^o} for each $x^{\tilde{S}^o}$, then, again by Lemma C, the left member of (2) is less than zero unless $x^{S^o} = \bar{x}^{S^o}$.

7.1.2.1. In 7.1.2.2 we shall show that

(1) $\quad \phi^i = \dfrac{1}{2^{n-1}} \Sigma_{S \in [i]} f^S$

where, as before,

(2) $\quad f^S = \Sigma_{i \in S} \phi^i - \Sigma_{i \in S} \phi^i.$

With g^S again defined by

(3) $\quad g^S = f^S - (x - \bar{x}) \cdot \bar{f}_x^S,$

equation (1) yields, upon differentiation with respect to x^i,

(4) $\quad \begin{aligned} 2^{n-1} \phi_{x^i}^{\ i} &= \Sigma_{S \in [i]} f_{x^i}^{\ S} = \Sigma_{S \in [i]} (g_{x^i}^{\ S} + \bar{f}_{x^i}^{\ S}) \\ &= \Sigma_{S \in [i]} g_{x^i}^{\ S} + 2^{n-1} \bar{\phi}_{x^i}^{\ i}. \end{aligned}$

Turning now to the gradient process, we have

(5) $\quad \dot{D} = \Sigma_{i=1}^n (x^i - \bar{x}^i) \cdot \dot{x}^i = \Sigma_{i=1}^n (x^i - \bar{x}^i) \cdot \gamma^i \phi_{x^i}^{\ i}.$

Hence

(6) $\quad \begin{aligned} 2^{n-1} \dot{D} &= \Sigma_{i=1}^n (x^i - \bar{x}^i) \cdot \gamma^i 2^{n-1} \phi_{x^i}^{\ i}, \\ &= \Sigma_{i=1}^n (x^i - \bar{x}^i) \cdot \gamma^i [\Sigma_{S \in [i]} g_{x^i}^{\ S} + 2^{n-1} \bar{\phi}_{x^i}^{\ i}] \\ &= \Sigma_{i=1}^n \Sigma_{S \in [i]} (x^i - \bar{x}^i) \cdot \gamma^i g_{x^i}^{\ S} + 2^{n-1} \Sigma_{i=1}^n (x^i - \bar{x}^i) \cdot \gamma^i \bar{\phi}_{x^i}^{\ i}. \end{aligned}$

By definition of an equilibrium point and of γ^i, $\gamma^i \bar{\phi}_{x^i}^{\ i} \leqq 0$ and $\bar{x}^i \cdot \gamma^i \bar{\phi}_{x^i}^{\ i} = 0$. Hence, since $x^i \geqq 0$ by hypothesis on X^i,

(7) $\quad 2^{n-1} \Sigma_{i=1}^n (x^i - \bar{x}^i) \cdot \gamma^i \bar{\phi}_x^{\ ii} \leqq 0,$

and (6) implies

(8) $\quad 2^{n-1} \dot{D} \leqq \Sigma_{S \in 2^I} \Sigma_{i \in S} (x^i - \bar{x}^i) \cdot \gamma^i g_{x^i}^{\ S} = \Sigma_{S \in 2^I} (x^S - \bar{x}^S) \cdot \gamma^S g_{x^S}^{\ S}.$

For an arbitrary $i_1 \in I$, (8) may be written as

(9) $\quad 2^{n-1} \dot{D} \leqq \Sigma_{S \in [i_1]} (x^S - \bar{x}^S) \cdot \gamma^S g_{x^S}^{\ S} + \Sigma_{S \in 2^{I} \sim [i_1]} (x^S - \bar{x}^S) \cdot \gamma^S g_{x^S}^{\ S}.$

Now each element of $2^I \sim [i_1]$ is the complement (with respect to 2^I) of an element of $[i_1]$. Hence (9) may be rewritten as

$$
(10) \quad
\begin{aligned}
2^{n-1}\dot{D} &\leq \Sigma_{S \in [i_1]} [(x^S - \bar{x}^S) \cdot \gamma^S g_{x^S}{}^S + (x^{\tilde{S}} - \bar{x}^{\tilde{S}}) \cdot \gamma^{\tilde{S}} g_{x^S}{}^{\tilde{S}}] \\
&= \Sigma_{S \in [i_1]} [(x^S - \bar{x}^S) \cdot \gamma^S g_{x^S}{}^S - (x^{\tilde{S}} - \bar{x}^{\tilde{S}}) \cdot \gamma^{\tilde{S}} g_{x^S}{}^{\tilde{S}}],
\end{aligned}
$$

since $g^{\tilde{S}} = -g^S$ by definition. Thus (1) of 7.1.1 has been obtained.

7.1.2.2. It remains to establish (1) of 7.1.2.1, i.e., the relation

$$\Sigma_{S \in [i]} f^S = 2^{n-1} \phi^i.$$

Now, with $\delta_{iS} = 1$ if $i \in S$ and $\delta_{iS} = -1$ if $i \in \tilde{S}$, we have

$$
(1) \quad
\begin{aligned}
\Sigma_{S \in [i]} f^S &= \Sigma_{S \in [i]} (\Sigma_{j \in I} \delta_{jS} \phi^j) \\
&= \Sigma_{j \in I} (\Sigma_{S \in [i]} \delta_{jS}) \phi^j \\
&= \Sigma_{j \in I} [N([i] \cap [j]) - N([i] \sim [j])] \phi^j
\end{aligned}
$$

where $N(A)$ is defined in Section 2 above.

We shall show below that

$$
(2) \quad
\begin{aligned}
&(2.1) \ N([i] \cap [i]) = 2^{n-1} \\
&(2.2) \ N([i] \sim [i]) = 0 \\
&(2.3) \ N([i] \cap [j]) = N([i] \sim [j]) \text{ for } i \neq j.
\end{aligned}
$$

Hence (1) reduces to

$$(3) \quad \Sigma_{S \in [i]} f^S = N([i] \cap [i]) \phi^i = 2^{n-1} \phi^i$$

which is the desired result. It remains to justify (2).

Clearly, $[i] \cap [i] = [i]$. $S \subseteq [i]$ if, and only if, $S = \{i\} \cup T$, where T is a subset of $I \sim \{i\}$. There are 2^{n-1} such sets T, hence (2.1). Since $[i] \sim [i]$ is null, (2.2) follows. Finally, with each set $S \in [i] \cap [j]$, $i \neq j$, associate $A(S) = \tilde{S} \cup \{i\}$. A defines a one-to-one correspondence between $[i] \cap [j]$ and $[i] \sim [j]$ which implies (2.3).

7.2. Uzawa's Theorem in [1], Ch. 7, is a special case of the preceding result for $n = 2$, $\Sigma_{i \in I} \phi^i = 0$. (The corresponding local results are those of Ch. 6 in [1].) Now it was shown in the authors' Ch. 8 of [1] that, for $n = 2$, $\Sigma_{i \in I} \phi^i = 0$, ϕ^i concave in x^i, and, say, ϕ^1 strictly concave in x^1, the gradient process converges not only in the x^1-component, but also in the x^2-component. It is natural to inquire whether the result of the present paper could be correspondingly strengthened. The answer, in general, is in the negative. Thus for $n = 3$, $\phi^1(x) = \psi_1(x^1)$, $\phi^2(x) = \psi_2(x^2, x^3)$, $\phi^3 = -\psi_2(x^2, x^3)$, there is no convergence in (x^2, x^3) if ψ_2 is linear in (x^2, x^3), even if ψ_1 is strictly concave in x^1. In fact, even the zero-sum condition would not guarantee convergence in all components, as shown by the following modification of the preceding example:

$$\phi^1 = \psi_1(x^1), \qquad \phi^2 = -\tfrac{1}{2}\psi_1(x^1) + \psi_2(x^2, x^3),$$
$$\phi^3 = -\tfrac{1}{2}\psi_1(x^1) - \psi_2(x^2, x^3).$$

However, there is convergence in both x^1 and x^2 components in the two-person game, even if the zero-sum condition is not satisfied. This follows from a consideration of the "limit cycle" (with $x^1 = \bar{x}^1$) of the gradient process along the lines of the argument in Ch. 8 of [1]. One finds that, with $x^1 = \bar{x}^1$, the gradient process reduces to $dx^2/dt = \phi^2(\bar{x}^1, x^2)$ which necessarily converges when $\phi^2(\bar{x}^1, x^2)$ is concave in x^2. It then follows that, for $n = 2$, under the hypothesis of the theorem in Section 6 above, $\xi^1(t) \to \bar{x}^1$ and $\xi^2(t) \to \bar{x}^2$ as $t \to \infty$.

8. The Cournot oligopoly theory

For an application of the theorem, we shall consider the well-known Cournot oligopoly case ([2], pp. 79 ff.); it will serve to illustrate the range of applicability of the convexity conditions on the payoff functions. There are n sellers of the identical product. Each seller determines his own output $x^i, x^i \geq 0$, for which he incurs a cost, $C_i(x^i)$. The price $p > 0$ of the product is a function of the total supply on the market, that is,

$$p = D(\Sigma_{i=1}^n x^i).$$

Hence, the profit (payoff) of the ith oligopolist is

$$\phi^i(x) = x^i D(\Sigma_{i=1}^n x^i) - C_i(x^i) \qquad (i = 1, \ldots, n).$$

The equilibrium point was defined by Cournot to be a vector of outputs, $\bar{x}^1, \ldots, \bar{x}^n$, such that each oligopolist is maximizing his profits by choosing $x^i = \bar{x}^i$ when every other oligopolist, j, chooses $x^j = \bar{x}^j$. A natural postulate about the behavior of the oligopolist in general (nonequilibrium) situations is that he varies his output so as to increase his profits under the assumption that the outputs of all other oligopolists remain constant. The gradient method described in Section 5 represents behavior of this type. We will use our Theorem to derive some sufficient conditions for the stability of equilibrium, that is, for the convergence of the gradient system to the equilibrium.

We now construct the functions f^S of the Theorem. For stability, we need to show that each one is concave in x^S for fixed $x^{\tilde{S}}$, with, for each i^0, the strict concavity holding for some $S^0, i^0 \in S^0$. Since $f^S = -f^{\tilde{S}}$, and the negative of a concave function is a convex function, the convexity of f^S in x^S for fixed $x^{\tilde{S}}$ follows automatically from the concavity of all f^S in x^S for fixed $x^{\tilde{S}}$.

(1)
$$f^S = \Sigma_{i \in S}\,[x^i D(\Sigma_{i=1}^n x^i)] - \Sigma_{i \in \tilde{S}}[x^i D(\Sigma_{i=1}^n x^i)]$$
$$- \Sigma_{i \in S}\, C_i(x^i) + \Sigma_{i \in \tilde{S}}\, C_i(x^i).$$

Write

(2) $X^S = \Sigma_{i \in S} x^i$ (for any S).

Then (1) can be written,

(3) $f^S = (X^S - X^{\tilde{S}}) D(X^S + X^{\tilde{S}}) - \Sigma_{i \in S} C_i(x^i) + \Sigma_{i \in \tilde{S}} C_i(x^i)$.

The terms $C_i(x^i)$ ($i \in \tilde{S}$) are fixed if $x^{\tilde{S}}$ is fixed. Hence it is sufficient (though certainly not necessary) for the concavity of f^S in x^S that each of the remaining terms, $(X^S - X^{\tilde{S}}) D(X^S + X^{\tilde{S}})$, $- C_i(x^i)$ ($i \in S$), be concave in X^S. The first term depends on x^S only through the sum of its components, so that concavity in x^S is equivalent to concavity in X^S; each term $C_i(x^i)$ depends only on a single output x^i. Hence a sufficient condition for the concavity of f^S is that

(4) $(X^S - X^{\tilde{S}}) D(X^S + X^{\tilde{S}})$ is concave in X^S for each $X^{\tilde{S}}$,

and

(5) $C_i(x^i)$ is convex for each $i \in S$.

Since we seek conditions to insure that f^S be concave for *all* S, we will assume, in line with (5), that

(6) $C_i(x^i)$ is convex for each i ($i = 1, \ldots, n$).

Condition (6) is the familiar economic condition of *nondecreasing marginal costs*.[8]

In Condition (4), the set S plays no role; X^S and $X^{\tilde{S}}$ can be thought of as any two nonnegative numbers. Let

(7) $X = X^S + X^{\tilde{S}}$, $Y = X^{\tilde{S}}$,

so that $X - Y \geq 0$, $Y \geq 0$, and (4) becomes

(8) $(X - 2Y) D(X)$ is concave in X for all Y, $X \geq Y \geq 0$.

If $D(X)$ has two derivatives, concavity is equivalent to the nonnegativity of the second derivative with respect to X.

(9) $(X - 2Y) D''(X) + 2D'(X) \leq 0$ (for all $X \geq Y \geq 0$).

Since the left-hand side is linear in Y, it follows that, for any given X, the inequality holds for all Y in the indicated range if and only if it holds for $Y = 0$ and $Y = X$. The two resulting inequalities can be written as

(10) $2D'(X) \leq XD''(X) \leq -2D'(X)$.

If (10) is satisfied, then $D'(X) \leq 0$. To avoid some tedious special cases, we will assume that

(11) $D'(X) < 0$,

which simply asserts that price decreases when total quantity available increases, a customary assumption in the present context.[9]

Relations (10) and (11) suggest one simple sufficient condition, namely, that $D''(X) = 0$, i.e., that demand is linear. In that case, from (11), (10) is satisfied with strict inequality, so that the first term of f^S will be strictly concave in X^S. If S^0 consists of any single element, say i^0, then $X^{S^0} = x^{i^0}$, so that f^{S^0} is strictly concave in x^{i^0}.

Proposition 1.   If the demand function is linear and decreasing and marginal costs are nondecreasing, the Cournot oligopoly equilibrium is stable.

Another form of (10) may be more intuitively meaningful. First, divide through in (10) by the positive number, $-D'(X)$.

(12) $-2 \leqq -XD''/D' \leqq 2.$

Now introduce the familiar economic concept of the *elasticity of demand*,

(13) $\eta = -(p/X)(dX/dp),$

that is, the proportional effect on demand of a given proportional change in price. Now the demand function $p = D(X)$ used here expresses price in terms of quantity, so that $dX/dp = 1/D'$; hence,

(14) $\eta = -(D/XD') > 0,$

where the inequality follows from (11). Now consider the elasticity of η with respect to changes in the quantity X, that is,

(15) $E\eta/EX = (X/\eta)(d\eta/dX) = d(\log \eta)/d(\log X).$

From (14),

$$\log \eta = \log D - \log X - \log (-D'),$$

so that, from (15),

(16)
$$E\eta/EX = d(\log D)/d(\log X) - 1 - XD''/D'$$
$$= -(1/\eta) - 1 - XD''/D'.$$

Substitute (16) into (12) and simplify.

(17) $-3 \leqq (1/\eta) + (E\eta/EX) \leqq 1.$

Thus (17), together with (11), is equivalent to (12) and hence to (4). Therefore (17), (11), and (6) imply the concavity of f^S in x^S for all S. To insure the strict concavity of f^{S^0} in x^{S^0}, where S^0 contains the single element i^0, it is sufficient that strict inequality hold in (17).[10]

Proposition 2.   If the elasticity of demand, η, is positive, and satisfies the condition,

$$-3 < (1/\eta) + (E\eta/EX) < 1,$$

and if marginal costs are nonincreasing, the Cournot oligopoly equilibrium is stable.

As a special case, we have the following

Corollary. If the elasticity of demand is constant and greater than 1 and if marginal costs are nonincreasing, the Cournot oligopoly equilibrium is stable.[11]

Proposition 2 gives a general idea of the range of applicability of the concavity conditions of the Theorem, as applied to the Cournot oligopoly case.

Notes

1   Arrow's participation was made possible by the Office of Naval Research (Task NR-047-004); Hurwicz's work was partly done as Fellow of the Center for Advanced Study in the Behavioral Sciences, 1955–56.
2   For a stability proof in an alternative dynamic model of Cournot duopoly, see Wald [6], pp. 391–403.
3   The precise form of the gradient relations is to be found in equation (1) of Section 5.
4   In the proof (see Section 7), D denotes half the distance squared.
5   The following is equivalent to part (a) of the assumption: For each set S of players, $f^S(x^S, x^{\tilde{S}})$ is a concave function of x^S, for $f^{\tilde{S}} = -f^S$, so that the concavity of $f^{\tilde{S}}$ with respect to $x^{\tilde{S}}$ is equivalent to the convexity of f^S with respect to $x^{\tilde{S}}$.
6   More general cases can also be considered; the case where only some (but not all) components, or even none, are required to be nonnegative can be handled by analogous methods.
7   See Uzawa's Theorem in [1], Ch. 7, for conditions under which these requirements are satisfied.
8   To avoid misunderstanding, note that (4) and (6) are sufficient but not necessary conditions for the concavity of f^S. It can be shown, however, that the concavity of f^S for all S implies that not more than one oligopolist can operate under decreasing marginal costs (strict concavity of C_i).
9   Although the case where $D'(X) > 0$ over certain ranges of X is not without interest in certain economic situations.
10   An alternative sufficient condition for strict concavity of f^{S^0} in x^{i^0} is that $C_i^0(x^{i^0})$ be strictly concave.
11   As a curiosity, it may be noted that the hypothesis of Proposition 2 implies that $\eta > 1$ for all X even when it is not constant. To see this, write $u = \log X$; then

$$E\eta/EX = (1/\eta)\, \eta'(u),$$

where the prime denotes differentiation. The right-hand inequality in the hypothesis of Proposition 2 can then be written,

$$d\eta/du < \eta - 1.$$

If $\eta(u_0) \leqq 1$ for some u_0, then $\eta'(u_0) < 0$. If $\eta'(u) \geqq 0$ for some $u > u_0$, let u_1 be the smallest such u. Since $\eta'(u) < 0$, $u_0 \leqq u < u_1$, $\eta(u_1) < \eta(u_0)$; hence $\eta'(u_1) < \eta(u_1) - 1 < \eta(u_0) - 1 < 0$, a contradiction. Therefore, $\eta(u)$ is strictly decreasing for $u > u_0$, and $\eta'(u) < \eta(u) - 1 < \eta(u_0) - 1 < 0$, which implies that $\eta(u)$ is negative for u (or X) sufficiently large. This contradicts the assumption that $\eta > 0$.

References

[1]   Kenneth J. Arrow, Leonid Hurwicz, and Hirofumi Uzawa, *Studies in Linear and Non-Linear Programming*, Stanford Univ. Press, 1958.

[2]   Augustin Cournot, *Researches into the Mathematical Principle of the Theory of Wealth* (1838), translation by Nathaniel T. Bacon, with a bibliography of mathematical economics by Irving Fisher, Macmillan, New York, 1897.

[3]   Harold W. Kuhn, and Albert W. Tucker, *Nonlinear programming*, Proceedings of the Second Berkeley Symposium in Mathematical Statistics and Probability (J. Neyman, ed.): Univ. of Calif. Press, 1951, pp. 481–492.

[4]   John F. Nash, Jr., *Equilibrium points in n-person games*, Proc. Nat. Acad. Sci. U.S.A., 36 (1950), pp. 48–49.

[5]   Paul A. Samuelson, *Market mechanisms and maximization*, RAND report No. P-69, The RAND Corp., Santa Monica, Calif., March 28, 1949.

[6]   Abraham Wald, *On some systems of equations of mathematical economics*, Econometrica, 19 (1951), pp. 368–403. (Translation from *Über einige Gleichungssysteme der mathematischen Ökonomie*, Z. Nationalökonomie, 7 (1936), pp. 637–670.)

4
STUDIES IN LOCAL STABILITY

A theorem on expectations and the stability of equilibrium

ALAIN C. ENTHOVEN
KENNETH J. ARROW[1]

The conditions under which a Walrasian system of multiple markets will be stable have been investigated by a number of authors under the implicit assumption of static expectations [3, 5, 6, 7]. It often has been assumed that expectations based upon an extrapolation of current rates of change (rather than upon the assumption that the future would be like the present) would prevent the system from converging onto its equilibrium position at all.[2] Since interesting results have been scarce and difficult to achieve even in the case of static expectations, it is not surprising that little has been done with the relationship between extrapolative expectations and dynamic stability. In this paper, we shall introduce, under rather restrictive assumptions, a type of extrapolative expectations and we shall test its effects on the stability of a dynamic system.

Excess demands in a multiple market system are usually taken to be functions of the current prices of all goods. Ideally, it would be desirable also to include expected prices for all future time periods and for all individuals and all assets as arguments of the excess demand functions. A theory of such formal generality, however, would be necessarily devoid of much content. Abstractions and simplifying assumptions are necessary. There are many possible expectations functions by which people might relate current and expected prices, and there is a variety of ways to represent plausibly the type of extrapolative expectations which we wish to describe. Our choice was made largely on the grounds of mathematical simplicity. Though our assumptions are quite special, we believe that the results have more general significance in that they show that a stable dynamic system can have "room" for some extrapolative expectations and that the critical amount of extrapolation, from the point of view of stability, is related to the inertia of the system.

First of all, we assume that for any price, the expectations of all individuals can be represented adequately by those of a "representative individual." This device, traditional in economic theory, can be justified by the argument that whatever amount the market demands, there is some price expectation which, if held by everybody, would result in the same demand. Secondly, we assume away "cross effects" of price expectations on excess demand, i.e., only the expected price for the ith good significantly affects excess demand for that good. Though obviously not realistic, this assumption is a natural first approximation to reality.

It is difficult to justify the frequently made assumption that expectations for all future time periods can be represented by one "expected price." For given current prices and given expected prices one month hence, demand can still vary with expectations for subsequent months. Reactions to price changes which are thought to be one-way movements will differ from reactions to changes which are expected to be reversed. This difficulty can be avoided partially by the introduction of the distinction between induced and autonomous expectations of price change. The difference between any expected price and its corresponding current price can be thought of as divisible into two components. One part is, from the point of view of a short-run dynamic model, autonomous. It is the result of knowledge about price histories and causal factors relating to particular prices. A new invention may set up the expectation that a certain price will fall when the invention is applied to production. This sort of expectation can be taken as exogenous. On the other hand, part of the expected price change is induced by actual changes in current prices. These expectations are definitely endogenous to the dynamic system and dynamic stability can be affected by them. The induced component of expected price changes for all future periods is much more likely to have the same sign as the autonomous part. In the analysis that follows, we assume that induced expectations can be represented by one "expected price" for each good and that autonomous expected price changes are small. We shall also assume that during the time interval under consideration, changes in the asset structure, as such, can be neglected.

Letting P_i represent the current price of the ith good and P_i', the expected price, excess demand functions for the n goods can be written

(1) $X_i = X_i(P_1, \ldots, P_n, P_i')$ $(i = 1, \ldots, n)$.

In equilibrium,

(2) $X_i = 0$ $(i = 1, \ldots, n)$

and

(3) $P_i' = P_i$ $(i = 1, \ldots, n)$.

The latter conditions are necessary for equilibrium, for if expected prices do not equal present prices, the latter cannot be in equilibrium (except possibly for an instant). If the expectations are correct, prices will change, whence they were not in equilibrium. If the expectations are incorrect, then current behavior is based upon false expectations and hence it will be modified as the expectations fail to be verified. Equations (1), (2), and (3) are sufficient to determine the equilibrium values of all the variables.[3]

If all prices are flexible, their dynamic behavior can be approximated by equations of the form

(4) $\dot{P}_i = K_i X_i$ $(i = 1, \ldots, n)$

where the K_i are positive constants. We shall assume that induced changes in expected prices are governed by the relationship

(5) $P_i' = P_i + \eta_i \dot{P}_i$ $(i = 1, \ldots, n)$.

This is a simple variant of Metzler's "coefficient of expectations" [5]. When $\eta_i = 0$, expectations are static and current prices are expected to persist. When $\eta_i > 0$, expected prices are an extrapolation of the trend in current prices and expectations may be described as "extrapolative." When $\eta_i < 0$, expectations in that market might be described as conservative in that expected prices lag behind current prices.

By Taylor's theorem, we can approximate (1) in the neighborhood of equilibrium by the linear expression

(6) $X_i = \Sigma_j a_{ij}(P_j - P_j^0) + b_i(P_i' - P_i^0)$ $(i = 1, \ldots, n)$

where $a_{ij} = \partial X_i/\partial P_j$, and $b_i = \partial X_i/\partial P_i'$, both evaluated in the neighborhood of equilibrium. Substituting (5) and (6) into (4), we obtain the linear system

(7) $\dot{P}_i = K_i \Sigma_j a_{ij}(P_j - P_j^0) + K_i b_i(P_i - P_i^0) + K_i b_i \eta_i \dot{P}_i$ $(i = 1, \ldots, n)$.

If all $\eta_i = 0$, the roots of the system with static expectations are the characteristic roots of the matrix

$$A = \begin{vmatrix} K_1(a_{11} + b_1) & \cdots & K_1 a_{1n} \\ \vdots & & \vdots \\ K_n a_{n1} & \cdots & K_n(a_{nn} + b_n) \end{vmatrix}.$$

Metzler [5] has shown that if all goods are gross substitutes, i.e., all of the off-diagonal elements are positive, then necessary and sufficient conditions for stability are that the principal minors of the matrix alternate in sign, with sign $(-1)^n$, where n is the order of the minor.[4] Metzler's result can be extended to include non-static expectations.

Theorem.   If the parameters of the system with static expectations fulfil the conditions for the Metzler theorem, then a necessary and sufficient condition for the stability of the system (7) with any expectations is that $1/K_i > b_i \eta_i$ for all markets.

The stability conditions on expectations require that the reciprocal of the price reaction coefficients, i.e., the coefficients of insensitivity of prices to excess demand, be greater than the destabilizing force of the extrapolative expectations. Only in the limiting case of infinite K_i will $\eta_i \leq 0$ be necessary for stability. In other cases, the effects of the expectations may be damped by the friction and inertia of the system and the system may asymptotically converge to equilibrium.

For any real square matrix A, let $\phi(A)$ be the largest of the real parts of the characteristic roots. A is said to be *stable* if and only if $\phi(A) < 0$.

The characteristic equation of (7) can be written

(8) $\det |DA - \lambda I| = 0$

where D is a diagonal matrix with elements $d_i = (1 - K_i b_i \eta_i)^{-1}$. Given that A is stable, we shall prove that $R(\lambda) < 0$ if and only if the elements of D are positive.

Sufficiency.   If all of the elements of D are positive, the signs of the elements and the signs of the minors of DA will be the same as those of the corresponding elements and minors of A since each of the latter will have been multiplied by a positive factor. Hence, DA will also fulfil the conditions of the Metzler theorem and it will be stable.

Necessity.   In order to prove that the stability of DA implies that $d_i > 0$, we must first prove three lemmas.

Lemma 1.   If no off-diagonal element of A is negative, then $\phi(A)$ is a characteristic root of A and it does not decrease when any off-diagonal element of A increases.

Proof.   Choose s so that $s + a_{ii} > 0$ for all i. Then $sI + A$ is a positive matrix whose characteristic roots are s greater than those of A. If λ is a characteristic root of A, $\lambda + s$ is a characteristic root of $sI + A$. $sI + A$ has a real characteristic root, λ_0, such that $|\lambda + s| \leq \lambda_0$.[5] Since $R(z) \leq |z|$ for any complex number, $R(\lambda + s) = R(\lambda) + s \leq \lambda_0$ or $R(\lambda) \leq \lambda_0 - s$. Since $\lambda_0 - s$ is a characteristic root of A and a real number, clearly, $\phi(A) = \lambda_0 - s$.

The second part of the Lemma is a well known property of λ_0, and hence of $\lambda_0 - s$ if the diagonal elements are constant so that s need not vary.[6]

Lemma 2.   If A is a nonnegative matrix and if $Ax \geq \lambda x$ for some real λ and for some $x \geqslant 0$ ($\geqslant$ indicating that not all $x = 0$), then $\lambda \leq \phi(A)$.

Proof.   Wielandt[7] has shown that for any nonnegative indecomposable matrix

$$\lambda_0 = \max_{x \geq 0} \min_i \left(\Sigma_{j=1}^n a_{ij} x_j / x_i \right)$$

where λ_0 is defined as it is in the proof of Lemma 1. For positive A, clearly $\lambda_0 = \phi(A)$. Then, for the particular λ and x in the hypothesis

$$\phi(A) = \lambda_0 \geq \min_i \left(\Sigma_{j=1}^n a_{ij} / x_i \right) \geq \lambda.$$

Lemma 3.   Let A be a stable matrix with only nonnegative off-diagonal elements and D a nonsingular diagonal matrix. Then $\phi(DA) \neq 0$.

Proof.   Choose s so that $B = sI + A$ is a nonnegative matrix. Suppose $\phi(DA) = 0$. Then DA has a pure imaginary characteristic root, λ, and a characteristic vector, $x \neq 0$, such that $DAx = \lambda x$. Multiplying by D^{-1} and adding sx to both sides, we obtain the system of equations

(9) $Bx = (sI + \lambda D^{-1})x.$

Consider the absolute values of both sides of each equation. The absolute value of the sum on the left-hand side is less than or equal to the sum of the absolute values. On the right-hand side, $sI + \lambda D^{-1}$ is a diagonal matrix, so that the absolute value of each is the absolute value of a single non-zero term. Therefore, letting the elements of B be b_{ij},

(10) $\quad \Sigma_j b_{ij} |x_j| \geq |s + \lambda/d_i| \cdot |x_i|$.

Let $\mu = \min_i |s + \lambda/d_i|$ and $y_i = |x_i|$. Then (10) implies

(11) $\quad By \geq \mu y, \quad y \geq 0$.

However, by Lemma 2,

(12) $\quad \mu \leq \phi(B) = s + \phi(A)$.

Since λ is a pure imaginary number and d_i is real, it is easy to see that $|s + \lambda/d_i| \geq s$ for each i whence $\mu \geq s$. But this and (12) imply $\phi(A) \geq 0$ which is a contradiction since A was assumed stable.

Theorem. [8] If A has all negative diagonal elements and no negative off-diagonal elements, D is a diagonal matrix, and both A and DA are stable, then the diagonal elements of D are positive.

Proof. If D were singular, then DA would be singular and have 0 as a characteristic root, so that $\phi(DA) \geq 0$, contrary to hypothesis. Therefore

(13) $\quad D$ is nonsingular and $d_i \neq 0$.

Let the variable matrix $A(t)$ be defined for $0 \leq t \leq 1$ as

$$a_{ij}(t) = a_{ij} \qquad \text{for } i \leq j,$$
$$a_{ij}(t) = (1 - t)a_{ij} \qquad \text{for } i > j.$$

Then

(14) $\quad A(t)$ has nonnegative off-diagonal elements for $0 \leq t < 1$,

and $A(0) = A$.

As t increases, some elements decrease while none increase. Thus (14) and Lemma 1 imply that $\phi[A(t)]$ is a non-increasing function of t for $0 \leq t < 1$. Hence, $\phi[A(t)] \leq \phi[A(0)] = \phi(A) < 0$, the latter inequality being true by hypothesis. Therefore,

(15) $\quad A(t)$ is a stable matrix for $0 \leq t < 1$.

From (13), (14), and (15) and Lemma 3, $\phi[DA(t)] \neq 0$ for $0 \leq t < 1$. By hypothesis, $DA = DA(0)$ is stable, so that $\phi[DA(0)] < 0$. Since $\phi[DA(t)]$ is a continuous function of t, it follows that $\phi[DA(t)] < 0$ for $0 \leq t < 1$, and hence, by continuity,

(16) $\quad \phi[DA(1)] \leq 0$.

But $A(1)$, and hence $DA(1)$, has only zeroes below the diagonal so that its characteristic roots are precisely its diagonal elements, $d_i a_{ii}$. Equation (16) implies, then, that $d_i a_{ii} \leq$ for all i. Since $a_{ii} < 0, d_i \geq 0$ and (13) implies that $d_i > 0$.

Therefore, the stability of DA implies that $d_i > 0$ whence the condition $1/K_i > b_i \eta_i$ is necessary as well as sufficient for stability.

Notes

1   The authors wish to express their gratitude to Professor Robert Solow for his valuable suggestions in the preparation of this paper.
2   See Hicks [3], p. 225.
3   It is easy enough to construct examples in which the equations (1), (2), and (3) have either no meaningful solution or several. In the latter case, the "local" results of this note can be taken to apply in the neighborhood of any such equilibrium. We do not consider the problem of stating sufficient conditions that at least one equilibrium point actually exists. But see Arrow and Debreu [1].
4   This condition on the minors is known as the Hicks condition. See the mathematical appendix of [3]. The condition is also necessary and sufficient when the matrix is symmetric regardless of the signs of the elements.
5   See Debreu and Herstein [2], Theorem I.
6   *Ibid.*
7   Wielandt [8], equation (4). Though the Wielandt result is stated only for nonnegative indecomposable matrices, the validity of the lemma for all nonnegative matrices can be shown from the present proof by a trivial limiting argument.
8   The A matrix of this theorem is more general than that of the Metzler theorem which must have positive off-diagonal elements. The extension of the Metzler theorem follows as a special case.

References

[1]   Arrow, K. J., and G. Debreu: "Existence of an Equilibrium for a Competitive Economy," *Econometrica*, Vol. 22, No. 3, July, 1954, pp. 265–290.
[2]   Debreu, G., and I. N. Herstein: "Nonnegative Square Matrices," *Econometrica*, Vol. 21, No. 4, October 1953, pp. 597–607.
[3]   Hicks, J. R.: *Value and Capital*, Second Edition, Oxford University Press, London, 1946.
[4]   Metzler, L. A.: "The Nature and Stability of Inventory Cycles," *Review of Economic Statistics*, Vol. XXIII, August, 1941.
[5]   Metzler, L. A. : "Stability of Multiple Markets: The Hicks Conditions," *Econometrica*, Vol. 13, No. 4, October 1945, pp. 277–292.
[6]   Samuelson, P. A.: "The Stability of Equilibrium: Comparative Statics and Dynamics," *Econometrica*, Vol. 9, No. 2, April 1941, pp. 97–120.
[7]   Samuelson, P. A.: "The Relation Between Hicksian Stability and True Dynamic Stability," *Econometrica*, Vol. 12, Nos. 3 & 4, July–October, 1944, pp. 256–257.

[8]   Wielandt, H.: "Unzerlegbare, nicht negative Matrizen," *Mathematische Zeitschrift*, Vol. 52, March 1950, pp. 642–648.

A note on expectations and stability [1]

KENNETH J. ARROW
MARC NERLOVE

In a recent article, Enthoven and Arrow [5] examine the relationship between extrapolative expectations and the dynamic stability of a multiple market system. They show, for a simple expectations function, that a stable dynamic system can absorb the effects of some extrapolation of price movements and remain stable. This note discusses the relationship between dynamic stability and a somewhat more complicated expectations function suggested by Hicks' definition of the elasticity of expectations.

1. Hicksian expectations

In the notation of Enthoven and Arrow, P_i represents the current price of the ith commodity and P_i', the expected future price of the ith commodity. It is assumed that changes in the expected future price of the ith good, induced by changes in actual prices, are governed by the relationship

(1) $P_i' = P_i + \eta_i \dot{P}_i,$

where $\dot{P}_i$ is the derivative of P_i with respect to time, and η_i is a constant.[2] When $\eta_i = 0$, current prices are expected to persist, and we say that expectations are static. When $\eta_i > 0$, some multiple of the change in prices is added to current price in arriving at expected price; hence, expectations may be described as extrapolative. When $\eta_i < 0$, expected prices do not change as much as actual prices.[3]

In their discussion Enthoven and Arrow assume that expectations ". . . for all future time periods can be represented by one 'expected' price" ([5], p. 312). As they indicate, this frequently made assumption is difficult to justify. Justification becomes easier, however, if we consider, not expectations of particular future prices, but expectations of the average level about which future prices are expected to fluctuate. It then becomes quite natural to think of changes in current price as affecting people's expectation of this level of future prices.[4] In what follows we call the average level about which future prices are expected to fluctuate "expected normal price."

If more specific information is not available, it seems reasonable to suppose that expected normal price depends in some way on what actual prices have been in the past. Such an assumption corresponds to the distinction made by Enthoven and Arrow between the "induced" and "autonomous" components of a change in expected price. Induced changes in expected price, or the dependence of expected normal price on past prices, are the only things we can study outside the context of a specific situation. Factors, other than past prices, which influence expected prices cannot readily be incorporated into a discussion of dynamic stability.

Each past price represents only a short-run market phenomenon, an equilibrium of those forces present in the market at the time. It is for precisely this reason that the assumption of static expectations (i.e., the assumption that people expect current prices to persist) is not plausible. This does not mean, however, that the past or the present has no relevance for the future. Past and present prices reflect forces which determine the level about which future prices may be expected to fluctuate: the more recent the past price the more it expresses the operation of those forces relevant to expectations.[5] Hence, we assume that the influence of more recent prices on expectations should be greater than the influence of less recent prices. A more specific assumption would be that expected normal price is a weighted average of past prices, where the weights decline as one goes back in time.[6]

Hicks may have had this notion in mind when he defined ". . . the elasticity of a particular person's expectations of the price of a commodity x as the ratio of the proportional rise in [all] expected future prices of x to the proportional rise in its current price" ([7], p. 205). Hicks, it will be remembered, distinguished two pivotal cases: (1) an elasticity of zero, implying no effect of a change in current price upon expected future prices; and (2) an elasticity of one, implying that if prices were previously expected to remain constant, i.e., were at their long-run equilibrium level, they will now be expected to remain constant at the level of current price. By allowing for a range of elasticities between the two, Hicks implicitly recognized that a particular past price may have something, but not everything, to do with people's notion of what the normal price will be.

Hicks' definition of the elasticity of expectations implies that prices have actually been normal (i.e., that the system has been in equilibrium) up to the time when some change occurred. But, of course, we know that conditions are seldom normal in the real world; furthermore, "normality" itself is a subjective matter. It is useful, therefore, to express current price, not as a deviation from what prices have been in the past, but from what people had previously thought of as the normal (i.e., people's previous expected normal price). If we think of time as a discontinuous variable, and let $P_i'(t)$ be the normal price of the ith commodity during period t expected at the start of the period and $P_i(t)$ be the actual price, we may express the expectations model suggested by Hicks' definition of the elasticity of expectations as

(2) $\dfrac{P_i'(t) - P_i'(t - 1)}{P_i(t - 1) - P_i'(t - 1)} = \beta_i,$

where the prices are expressed in logarithms and β_i is the elasticity of expectations of the price of the ith commodity, assumed to be constant. When $\beta_i = 0$, changes in actual price have no effect on expected normal price; when $\beta_i = 1$, current price is projected forward as people's expectations of the level of future prices.

If we drop the assumption that prices are expressed in logarithms, the differential equation analogue[7] of (2) is

(3) $\dot{P_i'} = \beta_i(P_i - P_i'), \qquad \beta_i \geqslant 0.$

When $\beta_i = 0$, changes in current price have no effect on expected normal price. Note, however, that the case of static expectations is now $\beta_i = +\infty$, as can be seen more rigorously by letting β_i approach $+\infty$ in (4) below. For a given time path of prices $P_i(t)$, equation (3) has the solution

(4) $P_i'(t) = P_i'(0) e^{-\beta_i t} + e^{-\beta_i t} \int_0^t \beta_i P_i(u) e^{\beta_i u} \, du,$

where $P_i'(0)$ is the initial value of expected normal price. If the origin is in the sufficiently distant past, the term in (4) involving $P_i'(0)$ is negligible; hence, $P_i'(t)$ may be taken as an exponentially weighted average of past prices.[8] Consequently, the model of expectation formation suggested by Hicks' definition of the elasticity of expectations leads to a reasonable representation of expected normal price in terms of past prices. In what follows we call expectations generated by equations such as (3) *adaptive* expectations.

2. Stability under adaptive expectations

Enthoven and Arrow [5] assume that there are no "cross-effects" of price expectations on excess demand, i.e., that only the expected price of the ith good significantly affects the excess demand for that good. Under adaptive expectations, however, we may allow for possible cross-effects; consequently we may write the excess demand functions for the n goods in our system as

(5) $x_i = x_i(P_1, \ldots, P_n, P_1', \ldots, P_n') \qquad (i = 1, \ldots, n),$

where x_i represents the excess demand for the ith commodity. In equilibrium, demand equals supply in each of the n markets and all expectations are fulfilled, i.e.,

(6) $x_i = 0 \qquad (i = 1, \ldots, n)$

and

(7) $P_i' = P_i \qquad (i = 1, \ldots, n).$

As in [5], we approximate the dynamic behavior of prices by equations of the form

(8) $\dot{P}_i = K_i x_i$ $(i = 1, \ldots, n)$,

where the K_i are positive constants. We assume that expectations are generated by equations such as (3) above.

By Taylor's theorem, we can approximate (5) in the neighborhood of equilibrium by the linear expressions

(9) $x_i = \Sigma_j a_{ij}(P_j - P_j^0) + \Sigma_i b_{ij}(P_j' - P_j^0)$ $(i = 1, \ldots, n)$,

where the P_j^0 are prices which simultaneously satisfy equations (5)-(7), and where $a_{ij} = \partial x_i/\partial P_j$ and $b_{ij} = \partial x_i/\partial P_j'$, both evaluated in the neighborhood of equilibrium. Substituting (9) into (8), we have

(10) $\dot{P}_i = \Sigma_j K_i a_{ij}(P_j - P_j^0) + \Sigma_j K_i b_{ij}(P_j' - P_j^0)$ $(i = 1, \ldots, n)$.

Adding and subtracting $\beta_i P_i^0$ on the right-hand side of equation (3), we obtain

(11) $\dot{P}_i' = \beta_i(P_i - P_i^0) - \beta_i(P_i' - P_i^0)$ $(i = 1, \ldots, n)$.

Equations (10) and (11) constitute the dynamic system, the properties of which we wish to investigate.

In order to simplify matters, we assume that all present commodities are gross substitutes for one another and also that each future commodity is a gross substitute for each present commodity (see Metzler [9]). That is, we assume that

(12) $a_{ij} \geqslant 0$ for all $i \neq j$

and

$b_{ij} \geqslant 0$ for all i and j.

As indicated above K_i and β_i are assumed to be positive. The dynamic system (10)-(11) has a matrix of the form

(13) $C = \begin{pmatrix} A & B \\ \beta & -\beta \end{pmatrix}$,

where A is a matrix $(K_i a_{ij})$, B is a matrix $(K_i b_{ij})$, and β is a diagonal matrix with the elements β_i along the diagonal and 0 elsewhere. Under the assumptions all the off-diagonal elements of C are nonnegative.

When the β_i are infinitely large equations (3) reduce to

$P_i' = P_i$ $(i = 1, \ldots, n)$,

which, as we have indicated, defines static expectations. Subtracting P_i^0 from both sides of these equations, we have

(14) $P_i' - P_i^0 = P_i - P_i^0$ $(i = 1, \ldots, n)$.

Substituting (14) into (10), we have

(15) $\quad \dot{P}_i = \Sigma_j K_i (a_{ij} + b_{ij})(P_j - P_j{}^0) \quad (i = 1, \ldots, n).$

Equations (15) define a dynamic system under static expectations; the matrix of this system is $A + B$.

Consider the case in which no expected prices enter the excess demand functions, i.e., in which the excess demand function may be written

(16) $\quad x_i = x_i(P_1, \ldots, P_n) \quad (i = 1, \ldots, n).$

The matrix of the dynamic system defined by (16) and (8) is the matrix A defined above. Metzler [9] has shown that if all present goods are gross substitutes, i.e., if all off-diagonal elements of the matrix A are positive, the system with matrix A is stable if and only if the principal minors of A alternate in sign, with sign $(-1)^n$ where n is the order of the minor. This, of course, implies that all the elements of A along the diagonal are negative, since any commodity can be taken as the first. It is suggested below that $A + B$ is stable when derived from competitive supply and demand functions.

We shall prove the following theorem:

Theorem. The system (10)-(11), with matrix C, is stable if and only if the system (15) with matrix $A + B$ is stable.

That is, we shall prove that a system of multiple markets is stable under Hicksian expectations if and only if it is stable under static expectations. We argue below that stability under static expectations is plausible.

In order to prove the theorem, we must first prove two lemmas:

Lemma 1. If M is a matrix with nonnegative off-diagonal elements, then there exists a vector $x \geqslant 0$ such that $Mx = \phi(M)x$, where $\phi(M)$ is the largest of the real parts of the characteristic roots of M.

Proof. Choose a real number s so that $s + m_{ii} \geq 0$ for all i. Then $sI + M$ is a nonnegative matrix whose characteristic roots are s greater than those of M. If λ is a characteristic root of M, $\lambda + s$ is a characteristic root of $sI + M$. $sI + M$ has a real characteristic root, λ_0, such that $|\lambda + s| \leq \lambda_0$, and with λ_0 there can be associated an eigenvector $x \geqslant 0$.[9] The real part of $\lambda + s$ does not exceed $|\lambda + s|$ and hence does not exceed λ_0. Thus the real part of λ does not exceed $\lambda_0 - s$; since λ was any characteristic root of M, it follows by definition that $\phi(M) \leq \lambda_0 - s$. But $\lambda_0 - s$ is a real characteristic root of M, so that $\phi(M) = \lambda_0 - s$; since $(sI + M)x = \lambda_0 x$, the vector x fulfills the conditions of the lemma.

Lemma 2. If M is a matrix with nonnegative off-diagonal elements, then $\phi(M) \geq 0$ if and only if there exists a vector $x \geq 0$ such that $Mx \geq 0$.

Proof. Consider the matrix $sI + M$. Suppose there exists an x as given by the hypothesis. Since $sI + M$ is nonnegative by definition,

(17) $\quad sI + M \geq 0.$

Since $Mx \geqslant 0$, it follows by adding sx to both sides that

(18) $(sI + M)x \geqq sx$,

where $x \geqslant 0$. Lemma 2 in Enthoven and Arrow [5] states that for any non-negative matrix A, if $Ax \geqq \lambda x$ for some real λ and some $x \geqslant 0$, then $\lambda \leqq \phi(A)$. It follows from (17) and (18) that

(19) $s \leqq \phi(sI + M)$,

so that $\phi(M) \geqq 0$.

Conversely suppose that $\phi(M) \geqq 0$. By Lemma 1, there exists an $x \geqslant 0$ such that $Mx = \phi(M) x$, so that $Mx \geqq 0$.

We are now in a position to prove the theorem stated above.

Recall that a system with matrix M is stable if and only if all characteristic roots have negative real parts, i.e., if and only if $\phi(M) < 0$.

To prove necessity, we shall show that the instability of $A + B$ implies the instability of C. If $A + B$ is unstable, then $\phi(A + B) \geqq 0$. The matrix $A + B$ clearly has nonnegative off-diagonal elements. Hence, by Lemma 2, there exists a vector $p \geqslant 0$ such that

(20) $(A + B) p \geqq 0$,

or,

(21) $Ap + Bp \geq 0$.

Also, $\beta p - \beta p = 0$. Comparison with (13) shows that $Cq \geq 0$, where q is the vector $\binom{p}{p}$, so that $q \geqslant 0$. It follows from Lemma 2 that $\phi(C) \geqq 0$, so that the system (10)–(11), with matrix C, is unstable.

To prove *sufficiency* we shall show that the instability of C implies the instability of $A + B$. Suppose that system (10)–(11) is unstable, then, by Lemma 2, there exists a vector q of length $2n$ such that

(22) $Cq \geqq 0$,

and

(23) $q \geqslant 0$.

Let p be the first n elements of q, and $\bar{p}$ be the remaining n elements. Equation (22) may then be expanded into

(24) $Ap + B\bar{p} \geqq 0$,

and

(25) $\beta p - \beta \bar{p} \geqq 0$.

Equation (23) implies

(26)   either $p \geqslant 0$ or $\bar{p} \geqslant 0$.

Equation (25) can be rewritten

$$\beta_i(p_i - \bar{p}_i) \geq 0 \qquad (i = 1, \ldots, n)$$

which is equivalent to

(27) $p \geq \bar{p}.$

since $\beta_i > 0$ for all i. By (27) we see that if $\bar{p} \geqslant 0$, then $p \geqslant 0$; hence (26) and (27) together imply that

(28) $p \geqslant 0.$

Since, under the assumptions, each future commodity is a gross substitute for each present commodity, the matrix B is nonnegative. Hence, (27) implies that $Bp \geq B\bar{p}$. Consequently, (24) implies that

(29) $(A + B)p \geq 0.$

Since all present commodities are gross substitutes for each other, the matrix A has nonnegative off-diagonal elements and, hence, so has $A + B$. Hence, (28) and (29) together imply that $\phi(A + B) \geq 0$, by Lemma 2. Consequently, the system under static expectations, with matrix $A + B$, is unstable.

We have shown that the instability of $A + B$ is a necessary and sufficient condition for the instability of C; or, what is the same, we have shown that C is stable if and only if $A + B$ is stable.

3. Conclusions

Enthoven and Arrow [5] show that a stable dynamic system can absorb the effects of some extrapolation of price movements and yet remain stable. The critical amount of extrapolation is related to the inertia of the system, i.e., the size of the parameters K_i which enter equations (8). We show that under adaptive expectations, a dynamic system, stable under static expectations, remains stable no matter what the inertia of the system or the elasticities of expectations. Under the assumption that expectations for all future time periods can be represented by one "expected" price, adaptive expectations appear to be a more reasonable formulation than extrapolative expectations.

The relevance of the theorem proved above can be further extended: It can be argued that the stability of the dynamic system under static expectations, (15), is plausible,[10] hence, by the theorem proved, stability, under the more general assumption of adaptive expectations is plausible. Consider any possible way of dividing the n commodities into two groups. Suppose that the relative prices within each group remain constant, so that each group can be regarded as a composite commodity in the sense of Hicks.[11] Let the price ratio between the two composite commodities vary. If individuals maximize profit or utility under competitive conditions, and if the market demand and supply functions are the sums of the individual demand and supply functions, it can be shown that the excess demand for the first composite commodity will be negative for a sufficiently high relative price and positive for a sufficiently low relative price. If all present commodities are gross substitutes, it can then be shown that a system such as (16)-(8), which does not involve expectations of the future, is necessarily stable. Suppose now that expectations of future prices are introduced. In equilibrium the planned excess demands for any future time will be the same as the current excess demands if expectations are static. Under the same assumption, expectations may differ from current prices, but expected future prices for the same commodity relative to one another are constant and indeed identical. Hence, the same commodity at different points in future time is a composite commodity in the sense of Hicks, and the same reasoning used to show that a system such as (16)-(8) is stable may be used to show that a system such as (15) is stable.

Notes

1 The research underlying this paper was done in part under contract with the Office of Naval Research and in part under authority of the Agricultural Marketing Act of 1946 (RMA, Title II). We are indebted to A. Okun, Cowles Foundation for Research in Economics, for helpful comments.

2 Equation (1) is related to the naive models used to test the forecasts of econometric models. (See Christ [3], pp. 55-59.) It is also related to an expectations model presented by Metzler in his analysis of inventory cycles [8].

3 In a model formulated in terms of periods, the case $\eta_i < 0$ corresponds to taking expected price as a weighted average of actual prices lagged one and two periods.

4 See Nerlove [11], pp. 41-54.

5 It should be noted that this statement may not hold in specific situations, although we might expect it to hold "on the average." For example, the sharp increase in the prices of certain commodities after the outbreak of the Korean conflict probably did not have much to do with shaping people's long-run price expectations. If we examine expectations over long periods, however, and abstract from changes in price expectations due to factors which are exogenous, the statement in the text is plausible.

6 As indicated in note 3, the model expressed by equation (1) allows a representation of expected price in terms of only two past prices, when time is treated as a discontinuous variable. If expectations for all future time periods are to be represented by one "expected price," the formulation in (1) does not, therefore, seem plausible.

7 The model in this from has been used by Phillip Cagan in his study of hyper-inflation [2], and by Milton Friedman in his study of the consumption function [6]. The model has also been applied in the form suggested

by equation (2) to the study of supply functions for agricultural commodities by Nerlove [10] and [11].

8 Since $e^{-\beta_i t} \int_0^t \beta_i \, e^{\beta_i u} \, du \approx 1$, if t is sufficiently large.

9 See Debreu and Herstein [4], p. 600, Theorem I*. For a vector x, $x \geq 0$ means $x_i \geq 0$ for all i, $x \geqslant 0$ means $x \geq 0$, $x \neq 0$.

10 See K. Arrow and L. Hurwicz [1].

11 See Hicks [7], pp. 312–313.

References

[1]   Arrow, Kenneth J., and Leonid Hurwicz: "On the Stability of the Competitive Equilibrium I," this volume, III.1, pp. 199–228.

[2]   Cagan, Phillip: "The Monetary Dynamics of Hyper-Inflation," in M. Friedman (ed.), *Studies in the Quantity Theory of Money*, Chicago: University of Chicago Press, 1956, pp. 25–117.

[3]   Christ, Carl: "A Test of an Econometric Model for the United States, 1921–47," *Proceedings of the Conference on Business Cycles*, New York: National Bureau of Economic Research, 1951, pp. 35–129.

[4]   Debreu, G., and I. N. Herstein: "Non-negative Square Matrices," *Econometrica*, Vol. 21, No. 4, October, 1953, pp. 597–607.

[5]   Enthoven, Alain C., and Kenneth J. Arrow: "A Theorem of Expectations and the Stability of Equilibrium," this volume, III.4, pp. 311–317.

[6]   Friedman, Milton: *A Theory of the Consumption Function*, Princeton, N.J.: Princeton University Press, 1957.

[7]   Hicks, J. R.: *Value and Capital*, Second Edition, Oxford: Oxford University Press, 1946.

[8]   Metzler, Lloyd A.: "The Nature and Stability of Inventory Cycles," *Review of Economic Statistics*, Vol. 23, No. 3, August, 1941, pp. 113–129.

[9]   Metzler, Lloyd A.: "Stability of Multiple Markets: The Hicks Condition," *Econometrica*, Vol. 13, No. 4, October, 1945, pp. 277–292.

[10] Nerlove, Marc: "Estimates of the Elasticities of Supply of Selected Agricultural Commodities," *Journal of Farm Economics*, Vol. 38, No. 2, May, 1956, pp. 496–509.

[11] Nerlove, Marc: "Estimates of the Elasticities of Supply of Corn, Cotton, and Wheat," unpublished Ph.D. dissertation, The Johns Hopkins University, November, 1956.

A note on dynamic stability

KENNETH J. ARROW
MAURICE McMANUS[1]

1. Introduction

In a recent issue of *Econometrica*, A. C. Enthoven and K. J. Arrow [1] were interested in the following problem. Let $\phi(A)$ be the largest of the real parts of the characteristic roots of the real, square matrix A. Then A is said to be *stable* if and only if $\phi(A) < 0$. Now if A is stable, in what circumstances is DA stable, where D is diagonal? Their theorem is that if A has nonnegative off-diagonal elements, this being a generalized version of the type examined by L. A. Metzler [3], then DA is stable if and only if the diagonal elements of D are all positive. The purpose of this note is to examine the same problem for certain other classes of matrices.[2] The importance of the results for economic dynamics is discussed at the end of the paper.

2. Three theorems on stability

Definition 1. A real, square matrix M is called negative (resp., positive) quasi-definite if and only if $h'Mh$ is negative (resp., positive)[3] for every real, non-null column vector h.[4]

Remarks. Definiteness is the special case of quasi-definiteness where M is symmetric; if M is negative (resp., positive) quasi-definite, it is nonsingular and its inverse is correspondingly quasi-definite, for

$$k'M^{-1}k = k'M^{-1\prime}M'M^{-1}k = h'M'h = h'Mh,$$

where $h = M^{-1}k$; the inverse of a nonsingular symmetric matrix S is also symmetric, since $S^{-1\prime} = S^{-1\prime}SS^{-1} = S'^{-1}S'S^{-1} = S^{-1}$.

Lemma 1. Any real symmetric matrix S can be transformed by a real orthogonal matrix P into a diagonal matrix $D = P'SP$. The diagonal elements of D are the characteristic roots of S; they are real, and they are all positive (resp., negative) if and only if S is positive (resp., negative) definite.

Lemma 2. Negative quasi-definite matrices are stable.

These lemmas are classical results. A proof of the second is given by Samuelson [7], p. 438. It also follows directly from the remarks and equation (2) below with $S = I$.

Definition 2. A matrix M is said to be S-stable if, for symmetric matrices S, SM is stable if and only if S is positive definite.

Definition 3. A matrix M is said to be D-stable if, for diagonal matrices D, DM is stable if and only if $d_{ii} > 0$ for every i, where the d_{ii} denote the diagonal elements of D.

Remarks. S-stability implies D-stability, for diagonal matrices are symmetric and are positive definite if and only if all their diagonal elements are positive; S-stability or D-stability implies stability.

We are now in a position to state and prove

Theorem 1. Negative quasi-definite matrices are S-stable.

The proof turns upon

Lemma 3. If A is negative quasi-definite and S is nonsingular and symmetric, then no characteristic root of SA has a zero real part.

Proof of Lemma 3. If λ is any characteristic root of SA, there exists a non-null vector x such that $SAx = \lambda x$. Premultiply both sides by $\bar{x}'S^{-1}$, where $\bar{x}$ denotes the complex conjugate of x:

(1) $\bar{x}'S^{-1}SAx = \bar{x}'Ax = \lambda \bar{x}'S^{-1}x.$

Write $x = y + iz$, $\lambda = \alpha + i\beta$, where y, z, α and β are all real. Equating real parts of (1),

(2) $y'Ay + z'Az = \alpha(y'S^{-1}y + z'S^{-1}z),$

for, by the remarks, the real coefficient of β is zero. By hypothesis the left-hand side of (2) is negative and so $\alpha \neq 0$.

Proof of Theorem 1. Let A be negative quasi-definite. If S is singular it is not definite and SA is singular; hence det. $(SA - \lambda I) = 0$ for $\lambda = 0$. Therefore, the theorem is satisfied if det. $S = 0$. Now assume that S is not singular. If it is positive definite it follows from (2) that $\alpha < 0$. This proves the sufficiency part of the theorem, though both parts are simultaneously deduced in what follows. Define

$A(t) = (1 - t)A - tI, \qquad 0 \le t \le 1.$

$A(t)$ is negative quasi-definite for all t since $h'A(t)h = (1 - t)h'Ah - th'h < 0$ because A is negative quasi-definite. Hence, by Lemma 3, $\phi[SA(t)] \neq 0$ for all t. By continuity, therefore, $\phi[SA(t)]$ is either positive for all t or else negative for all t. In particular,

$\phi[SA(0)] < 0$ if and only if $\phi[SA(1)] < 0.$

But $A(0) = A$ and $A(1) = -I$. Hence the characteristic roots of $SA(1)$ are those of $-S$. By Lemma 1 they are all real and are all negative if and only if S is positive definite. Thus $\phi(SA)$, i.e., $\phi[SA(0)]$, is negative if and only if S is positive definite.

The sufficiency part of Theorem 1 was stated by Samuelson [7], p. 275.[5] M. Sono [8] proved that if S is symmetric and if both A and SA are negative quasi-definite, then S is positive definite. This is a special case of the necessity part of Theorem 1 above.[6]

Since S-stability implies D-stability, we immediately get the

Corollary.   Negative quasi-definite matrices are D-stable.

This corollary is the counterpart of the Enthoven-Arrow Theorem, proved for the negative quasi-definite type of stable matrix instead of the "generalized Metzlerian" type, i.e., stable matrices with all off-diagonal elements nonnegative.[7]

A useful extension of the Enthoven-Arrow Theorem and the Corollary to Theorem 1 is provided by

Theorem 2.   Let E be a nonsingular diagonal matrix. C is D-stable if and only if $A = ECE^{-1}$ is D-stable.

The proof makes use of

Lemma 4.   Any matrix B is stable if and only if GBG^{-1} is stable for nonsingular G.

Proof. B and GBG^{-1} are *similar* matrices, having the same characteristic roots.

Proof of Theorem 2.   Since diagonal matrices are commutative in multiplication, $DA = DECE^{-1} = E(DC)E^{-1}$. By Lemma 4, therefore, DC is stable if and only if DA is. Hence if the positivity of the d_{ii} is decisive for the stability of DA it must be for the stability of DC too, and vice versa.

Corollary.   Let C be such that, for some diagonal matrix E, $A = ECE^{-1}$ is either negative (quasi-) definite or has all off-diagonal elements nonnegative and is stable. Then DC is stable if and only if every d_{ii} is positive.

Proof.   By the corollary of Theorem 1 and the Enthoven-Arrow Theorem – as the case may be – the matrix A of the corollary has the property stipulated for A in Theorem 2.

Theorem 2 is important because if A is generalized Metzlerian, or symmetric, or quasi-definite, $E^{-1}AE = C$ need be none of these.[8]

The following theorem describes how certain product matrices using diagonal matrices as premultipliers are related to other matrix products using symmetric matrices as premultipliers.

Theorem 3.   Given C and a certain symmetric matrix $\overline{S}$, let P be such that $P'\overline{S}P = \overline{D}$ where $\overline{D}$ is diagonal, and define $\overline{C} = P'CP$. Assume that $\overline{D}\,\overline{C}$ is stable if and only if all the diagonal elements of $\overline{D}$ are positive. For example, for some diagonal E, $A = EP'CPE^{-1}$ may be either negative quasi-definite or generalized Metzlerian and stable. Then $\overline{S}C$ is stable if and only if $\overline{S}$ is positive definite.

Proof.   By Lemma 1, P is orthogonal and so $\overline{DC} = P'\overline{S}PP'CP = P^{-1}(\overline{S}C)P$. The roots of $\overline{DC}$ and $\overline{S}C$ are the same by dint of Lemma 4, and by hypothesis $\overline{DC}$ is stable if and only if all the $\bar{d}_{ii}$ are positive. By Lemma 1, however, $\overline{D}$ is positive definite if and only if $\overline{S}$ is. Hence $\overline{S}C$ is stable if and only if $\overline{S}$ is positive definite.

In Theorem 3, C does not have to be D-stable, for the question of the stability of $\overline{DC}$ is confined to the case where D is the given matrix $\overline{D}$. In the same way C is not necessarily S-stable, whether or not $\overline{C}$ is D-stable. Theorem 3 adds something new to the results discussed previously, for they do not cover those cases where either $\overline{C}$ is not D-stable or where $\overline{S} \neq \overline{D}$ and either A is generalized Metzlerian and stable or, for some $E \neq I$, A is negative quasi-definite.[9]

3. Economic application

The Enthoven-Arrow dynamic general equilibrium system can be written as

(3) $\dot{p} = Kx; \quad x = Q(p - p^0) + B(p^f - p^0); \quad p^f = p + \eta\dot{p}.$

Here p is the column vector of all the other prices in terms of the numéraire, the dot represents differentiation with respect to time, the superscript "0" denotes "equilibrium" levels and p^f is the vector of expected future relative prices, while x is the vector of the corresponding excess-demands, K is the matrix of speeds of adjustment of prices to excess-demands, $Q = [dx/dp']^0$, $B = [dx/dp^{f'}]^0$, and η is the matrix of "extrapolative price-expectational coefficients." In the original model, K, B, and η are all diagonal matrices. Eliminating x and p^f, (3) yields the set of linear differential equations,

(4) $\dot{p} = (I - KB\eta)^{-1}K(Q + B)(p - p^0).$

Enthoven and Arrow [1] have D and A refer to $(I - KB\eta)^{-1}$ and $K(Q + B)$, respectively. It will now be more convenient, however, to rewrite (4) as

(5) $\dot{p} = (K^{-1} - B\eta)^{-1}(Q + B)(p - p^0),$

and let D (or S) refer to $(K^{-1} - B\eta)^{-1}$ and A (or C) to $(Q + B)$. The Samuelsonian expectationless model is a special case with $\eta = B = 0$. Denote the elements of matrices by the corresponding small letters with appropriate row and column suffixes. Then the corollary to Theorem 2 tells us that if $E(Q + B)E^{-1}$ is either negative (quasi-)definite or generalized Metzlerian and stable for some E (including, of course, $E = I$), the expectationless system is stable if and only if all the k_{ii} are positive – the usual behavior. Moreoever, for the same $(Q + B)$, the introduction of the expectational coefficients does not upset stability if and only if $1/k_{ii} > b_{ii}\eta_{ii}$ for all i.

Since the same conclusions do not hold for arbitrary stable $(Q + B)$,[10] it is fortunate that some of the types that are covered by the theorems are of particular interest to the economist. If income effects are either absent or else symmetrical, $Q + B$ is symmetric. Alternatively, if the system contains no gross complements,[11] then $Q + B$ has nonnegative off-diagonal elements. In any actual economy, however, we must be prepared to find substantial, asymmetrical income effects and a goodly sprinkling of gross complementarity. It is desirable, therefore, to try to find other classes of matrices about which useful statements about stability can be made. An important stride in this direction was made by Samuelson [7] in his consideration of non-symmetric, negative, quasi-definite matrices, and the E transformation provides a way of generating further types out of the two or three basic ones. If, for example, A is generalized Metzlerian and the elements of E are of mixed signs, then $E^{-1} AE$ is of the type which has been examined in detail by M. Morishima [4].

An additional interest in Theorems 1 and 3 lies in the fact that S need not be diagonal, only symmetric. This has an application in terms of the above model. The speed of price adjustment in any one market may depend upon the excess demands in other markets as well as in its own, as has been argued cogently by D. Patinkin [6], p. 157; it is quite feasible that some excess demands partly depend upon expected prices in other markets; it may well be that expected prices are influenced by what is happening to several different current prices. In general, any combination of these makes $(I - KB\eta)^{-1}$ or $(K^{-1} - B\eta)^{-1}$ non-diagonal.

Samuelson [7, pp. 274-5] subjects the original variables p and x to a contragredient transformation $\bar{p} = c'p; x = c\bar{x}$.

The system (5) becomes

(6) $\dot{p} = c'(K^{-1} - B\eta)^{-1} cc^{-1}(Q + B)c'^{-1}(\bar{p} - p^0).$

The transformation of Lemma 1 as used in Theorem 3 is a special case where c is the orthogonal P. Using this interpretation, SC and DC would refer to the *same* economic system, but one in which two different ways of describing and measuring the given number of commodities are considered.

Notes

1   Arrow's participation was supported by the Office of Naval Research. This paper will be reprinted as a Cowles Foundation Paper. The authors are indebted to Gerard Debreu for his comments.

2   For a different approach to closely related questions see M. McManus [2].

3   A prime after a vector or matrix denotes its transpose.

4   See P. A. Samuelson [7, p. 140] for an equivalent definition.

5   Actually he claims that, in terms of our notation, if A is negative quasi-definite then it is sufficient for the stability of, say, HA that H^{-1} (and so, by the Remarks, H) be only positive *quasi*-definite. This, however, goes too far, as the following counterexample shows:

$$\text{Let } H = \begin{bmatrix} 1 & 2 \\ -1 & 1 \end{bmatrix} \text{ and } A = \begin{bmatrix} -1 & -1 \\ 2 & -1 \end{bmatrix}; \text{ then } HA = \begin{bmatrix} 3 & -3 \\ 3 & 0 \end{bmatrix}$$

is unstable, although H is positive quasi-definite and A negative quasi-definite.

6　An example suffices to show that Sono's Theorem does not apply to as wide a class of matrices as does Theorem 1.

$$\text{Let } S = \begin{bmatrix} 1 & 1 \\ 1 & 2 \end{bmatrix} \text{ and } A = \begin{bmatrix} -1 & 1 \\ -1 & -1 \end{bmatrix}, \text{ so that } SA = \begin{bmatrix} -2 & 0 \\ -3 & -1 \end{bmatrix}.$$

Now S is positive definite and A is negative quasi-definite, but SA, though stable, is not quasi-definite.

7　The question may be raised as to whether or not stable generalized Metzlerian matrices are S-stable. The following two examples show that they are not.

$$(1) \quad S_1 = \begin{bmatrix} 1 & 1 \\ 1 & 2 \end{bmatrix}, \quad M_1 = \begin{bmatrix} -1 & 3 \\ .2 & -1 \end{bmatrix};$$

S_1 is positive definite, M_1 is stable Metzlerian, but $S_1 M_1$ is not stable.

$$(2) \quad S_2 = \begin{bmatrix} -1 & -.5 \\ -.5 & -.27 \end{bmatrix}, \quad M_2 = \begin{bmatrix} -1 & 4 \\ 1 & -5 \end{bmatrix};$$

S_2 is symmetric but not positive definite, M_2 is a stable Metzlerian matrix, yet $S_2 M_2$ is stable.

8　We do not know how wide the class of D-stable matrices is. Certainly not all stable matrices are D-stable. For example,

$$\begin{bmatrix} -2 & -3 \\ 1 & 1 \end{bmatrix} \text{ is stable, yet } \begin{bmatrix} 1 & 0 \\ 0 & 3 \end{bmatrix}\begin{bmatrix} -2 & -3 \\ 1 & 1 \end{bmatrix} \text{ is unstable and}$$

$$\begin{bmatrix} -1 & 0 \\ 0 & -3 \end{bmatrix}\begin{bmatrix} -2 & -3 \\ 1 & 1 \end{bmatrix} \text{ is stable.}$$

It may be that all D-stable matrices are of the form $E^{-1}AE$, where E is diagonal and A is either generalized Metzlerian and stable or else negative quasi-definite. If this is so, Theorem 2 and its corollary are equivalent.

9　If $\overline{C}$ itself is negative quasi-definite, then C is too (see Samuelson [7, pp. 140–1]), so Theorem 1 applies.

10　See note 8.

11　The adjective "gross" indicates that income effects are being taken into account. The name is due to J. Mosak [5].

References

[1]　Enthoven, A. C., and K. J. Arrow: "A Theorem on Expectations and the Stability of Equilibrium," this volume, III.4, pp. 311–317.

[2]　McManus, M.: "Transformations in Economic Theories," *Review of Economic Studies*, Vol. XXV, 2 (67), pp. 97–108.

[3]   Metzler, L. A.: "Stability of Multiple Markets: The Hicks Conditions," *Econometrica*, Vol. 13, No. 4, October, 1945, pp. 277–292.
[4]   Morishima, M.: "On the Laws of Change of the Price-System in an Economy Which Contains Complementary Commodities," *Osaka Economic Papers*, Vol. I, No. 1, May, 1952, pp. 101–113.
[5]   Mosak, J.: *General Equilibrium Theory in International Trade*, Bloomington, Ind.: Principia Press, 1944.
[6]   Patinkin, D.: *Money, Interest and Prices*, Evanston, Ill., and White Plains, N.Y.: Row, Peterson and Co., 1956.
[7]   Samuelson, P. A.: *Foundations of Economic Analysis*, Cambridge, Mass.: Harvard University Press, 1947.
[8]   Sono, M.: "Positive and Negative Relations and Stability Conditions," *Osaka Economic Papers*, Vol. VIII, No. 3, March, 1955, pp. 15–28.

Stability independent of adjustment speed [1]

KENNETH J. ARROW

I. Introduction

In his classic work, Hicks [5] introduced for serious consideration by economists the problem of analyzing stability in multiple markets. He defined a concept of *perfect stability*, in which one market was singled out and the remaining markets were divided into two sets; in one, all prices were held fixed at their equilibrium values, while, as the singled-out price varied, all prices in the second set were continuously adjusted to keep supply and demand on all the markets in that set constant. Under these conditions, excess demand was defined as a function of the singled-out price. If the resulting function was downward sloping for all ways of singling out a price and all ways of dividing the remaining markets into two sets as indicated, then the economy was said to be *perfectly stable*. It was demonstrated that a necessary and sufficient condition for perfect stability was that the Jacobian matrix of the excess demand functions (omitting one commodity and one price, chosen as numéraire) have the property that the principal minors of odd order have negative determinants and those of even order have positive determinants.

Matrices with this property have continued to be of great interest. The negative of such a matrix has the property that all its principal minors have positive determinants; such matrices have become known as *P matrices* (for this name, see Gale and Nikaidô [4]).

Samuelson [8] insisted that the definition of stability must be grounded in an explicit dynamic system, specifically.

(1) $dp_i/dt = H[z_i(p)]$ $(i = 1, \ldots, n)$

where i runs over the nonnuméraire commodities, p_i is the price of the ith commodity, z_i the excess demand for the ith commodity, p the vector of (non-numéraire) prices, and H an increasing function, with $H(0) = 0$. (Local) stability requires that every solution of the system of differential equations (1) whose starting point lies in some neighborhood of the equilibrium point p^0, defined by $z(p^0) = 0$ (where z is the vector of excess demands), converge to p^0. By well-known theorems, the stability of equilibrium is equivalent (apart from border-line cases) to the condition that the characteristic roots of the Jacobian of the right-hand side of (1) have negative real parts. A matrix with this property will be termed *stable*.

The function H indicates the adjustment of price to excess demand. The imposed conditions imply that a price rises if the corresponding excess demand is positive and falls otherwise. The derivative $H'(0)$ can be regarded as the speed of adjustment in the neighborhood of equilibrium.

There is no reason for the function H to be the same for all commodities; indeed, simple dimensional considerations show that this cannot be true in general. For suppose the units in which commodity i is measured are changed, for example each unit is twice as large. Then the measured excess demand is half as much, while the price is twice as great. The rate of change of price per unit time is also doubled; hence, the speed of adjustment of that commodity is quadrupled, while leaving the speeds of adjustment of other commodities unchanged. Thus equal speeds of adjustment on all markets can hold only for one particular choice of units.

If one assumes a single speed of adjustment, then the Jacobian of the right-hand sides of (1) can be written simply $H'(0)X$, where X is the Jacobian of the excess demand functions. The characteristic roots of $H'(0)X$ are simply those of X multiplied by the positive scalar $H'(0)$, and hence the stability of the dynamic system (1) depends only on the properties of the excess demand functions. Here, Samuelson noted that the condition that X be the negative of a P matrix was not necessary for the stability of (1); and later [9], he gave an example due to W. Hurewicz which showed that this condition was not sufficient either.

Meanwhile Lange [6, pp. 94–97] first explicitly stated that the adjustment functions might differ from one commodity to another. Then (1) is generalized to

(2) $dp_i/dt = H_i[z_i(p)]$ $(i = 1, \ldots, n)$

where $H_i(0) = 0, H_i' > 0$. The Jacobian of the right-hand sides of (2) can be written as DX, where D is a diagonal matrix with $d_{ii} = H_i'(0) > 0$. In general, then, stability depends not only on the properties of the excess demand functions but also on the speeds of adjustment.

It is against this background that the brilliant and exciting paper of Metzler [7] appeared. Metzler accomplished two rehabilitations of the Hicks conditions. The second of his propositions [7, p. 285] has had the greatest impact; if one confines oneself to what have become known as *Metzler matrices*, that is, matrices with nonnegative off-diagonal elements, then a matrix X is stable if and only if its negative is a P matrix. But the first of his two propositions has been much less remarked. He noted that Hicks' definition of perfect stability could be thought of as dealing with varying speeds of adjustment. On some markets adjustment is infinitely rapid, on others infinitely slow; the criterion of perfect stability is that stability hold no matter how the markets are divided into these two classes. This suggests the following question: Under what conditions is the stability of the system independent of the speeds of adjustment? In mathematical terms, we are asking when a matrix X has the property that DX is stable for all positive diagonal matrices D. We will call this property D stability. Metzler showed [7, pp. 280-283] that a *necessary* condition for D stability is that $-X$ be a P matrix.

As to why this question is economically interesting, one can do no better than to quote Metzler's [7] own statement:

> Two answers may be given. . . . First, the extent to which the stability of a group of markets depends upon speeds of adjustment is a question of considerable interest. It is important to know, for example, whether the inflexibility of certain prices is a stabilizing factor or whether the markets would be stable even if all prices were responsive to discrepancies between supply and demand. If the Hicks conditions of perfect stability are not satisfied, stability of the system clearly depends upon a relative inflexibility of certain prices. Second, and more important, the conditions which govern price responsiveness are much more obscure than are the static supply and demand conditions in individual markets. Economists are usually more confident of their knowledge of supply and demand conditions than of their knowledge of such dynamic factors as speeds of adjustment. If possible, it is therefore desirable to describe market systems in terms which are independent of speeds of adjustment [p. 284].

Metzler's first theorem, in turn, opens up two questions, with which this paper is concerned. (1) The property that X is D stable is a statement about the characteristic roots of the family of matrices DX, with X fixed and D varying over the positive diagonal matrices. As we have seen, stability and a fortiori, D stability, is stronger than being the negative of a P matrix. Is there some other statement about the characteristic roots of the family DX which is exactly equivalent to being the negative of a P matrix? It is shown in Section II that roughly speaking, X is a P matrix if and only if, for every positive diagonal matrix D, every *real* characteristic root of DX is positive. (Hence, if X is the *negative* of a P matrix, every real characteristic root of DX is negative.) A more exact statement is to be found below. It is interesting to note that Metzler's example [7, pp. 284-285] to show that one can have a negative of a P matrix whose stability depends upon speed of adjustment illustrates this property; it is the *complex* roots which can have positive real parts for suitably chosen adjustment speeds, but the real roots are always negative, as Metzler explicitly notes.

(2) Another question is that of sufficient conditions for D stability. Some answers have been given in earlier papers (Enthoven and Arrow [2], Arrow and McManus [1]). There was some resemblance among the proofs of these apparently diverse theorems. In Sections III-VI, I develop a general theoretical structure from which the previous results (somewhat generalized) can easily be deduced. Actually, as already seen implicitly in the article by Enthoven and Arrow [2], these methods can yield more information. It is sometimes economically meaningful to consider the stability of matrices DX where D is diagonal but the diagonal elements are not necessarily positive. We actually find sufficient conditions on X that the number of characteristic roots of DX with positive, zero, and negative real parts, be equal respectively to the number of diagonal elements of D which are positive, zero, and negative. (In particular, then, when these conditions hold, $-X$ is stable when D is positive diagonal, for then every characteristic root of X has a positive real part, or, equivalently, every characteristic root of $-X$ has a negative real part.)

II. Real characteristic roots of products of positive diagonal and P matrices

As can be seen from the sometimes tortured language used above, it is easier to reverse the signs of the usual stability criteria. It is linguistically easier to talk about matrices with positive or nonnegative principal minors than about matrices whose principal minors have alternating signs. Hence, throughout this chapter we shall be concerned with criteria for characteristic roots to have *positive* real parts or to be positive reals. Of course, any result found here has an obvious counterpart by simply reversing the sign of the matrix and therewith of all its characteristic roots.

In this section we will therefore be concerned with conditions on X which ensure that the real characteristic roots of DX be nonnegative for all positive diagonal D. It is necessary to shift from positive to nonnegative to achieve definite results. A careful reading of Metzler's first proposition and its proof will reveal that, strictly speaking, what he showed was that if the characteristic roots of DX have nonnegative real parts for all positive diagonal D, then the principal minors of X have nonnegative determinants. He states the result with the signs reversed, with the word "positive" instead of "nonnegative" in both places, but the proof involves a passage to a limit in which the determinants might approach zero. A counterexample to the stronger assertion is

$$X = \begin{pmatrix} 1 & 1 \\ -1 & 0 \end{pmatrix};$$

it is easy to calculate that the two characteristic roots of DX are real and positive if $4d_{22} \leqq d_{11}$, and complex conjugate with real part $d_{11}/2 > 0$ if $4d_{22} > d_{11}$. Thus X is D stable but has a principal minor which is zero. The same example shows that Theorem 1(c) below is no longer valid if "P_0 matrix" is replaced by "P matrix" and "nonnegative" by "positive."

Definition 1. X is a P matrix if every principal minor has a positive determinant.

Definition 2. X is a P_0 matrix if every principal minor has a nonnegative determinant.

Notation 1.   If x is a vector with n components and S a subset of the integers $1, \dots, n$, then x_S is the vector with components $x_i (i \in S)$.

Notation 2.   If A is a square matrix of order n and S and T are subsets of the integers $1, \dots, n$, then A_{ST} is the matrix with elements $a_{ij} (i \in S, j \in T)$.

Notation 3.   If x and y are vectors, then $x \geqq y$ means $x_i \geqq y_i$, all i; $x > y$ means $x_i \geqq y_i$, all i, $x_i > y_i$, at least one i; $x \gg y$ means $x_i > y_i$, all i.

Notation 4.   If x is a vector, $\hat{x}$ is the diagonal matrix defined by $\hat{x}_{ii} = x_i$, $\hat{x}_{ij} = 0$ for $i \neq j$.

Notation 5.   The vector e is defined by $e_i = 1$, all i.

From Notations 4 and 5, we note immediately that $\hat{x}e = x$.

We now state the basic result of this section.

Theorem 1.   Each of the following conditions is necessary and sufficient that X be a P_0 matrix.

(a) $X + D$ is a P matrix for all positive diagonal D.

(b)   If $x \neq 0$ and $y = Xx$, then there exists i such that $x_i \neq 0, x_i y_i \geqq 0$.

(c)   For all positive diagonal matrices D, every real root of DX is nonnegative.

Note.   The new result established here is Theorem 1(c). Theorem 1(b) is part of Theorem 1.3 of Fiedler and Pták [3, p. 164] and Theorem 1(a) is implicit in their proof. The parallel results for P matrices had also been obtained by Gale and Nikaidô [4]. We reprove these results here to make the exposition self-contained.

Proof. X is a P_0 matrix if and only if (a): Use the notation A^{ii} to mean the minor obtained by deleting the ith row and column. Then,

$$\partial \det (X + D)/\partial d_{ii} = \det (X + D)^{ii}.$$

We proceed by induction on the order of X. Clearly the equivalence holds if $n = 1$; suppose it is true for matrices of order $n - 1$. If X is a P_0 matrix, then so is X^{ii}; hence by induction $(X + D)^{ii} = X^{ii} + D^{ii}$ is a P matrix and, in particular, $\det (X + D)^{ii} > 0$. Thus $\det (X + D)$ is a strictly increasing function of the d_{ii}'s in the region where all are positive. It immediately follows that $\det (X + D) > \det X \geqq 0$ if X is a P_0 matrix. Conversely, if $X + D$ is a P matrix for all positive D, $\det (X + D) > 0$ for all such D; by continuity, $\det X \geqq 0$. But for any S which is a proper subset of the integers $1, \dots, n$, $X_{SS} + D_{SS}$ is a P matrix for all positive diagonal D_{SS}; by the induction hypothesis, X_{SS} is a P_0 matrix and in particular det $X_{SS} \geq 0$.

Before proceeding with the proof of the theorem, we prove the following lemma, based on the result just proved.

Lemma 1. If X is a P_0 matrix and $y = Xe$, then $y_i \geq 0$, for some i.

Proof of Lemma 1. By assumption, $Xe = \hat{y}e$, so that

$$(X - \hat{y})e = 0;$$

$X - \hat{y}$ is singular and cannot be a P matrix. By Theorem 1(a), $-\hat{y}$ cannot be a positive diagonal matrix, which means that $\hat{y}$ has at least one nonnegative diagonal element, or $y_i \geq 0$, some i.

We now return to the proof of Theorem 1. X a P_0 matrix implies (b): Note that since $\hat{x}$ is a diagonal matrix

$$(\hat{x}X\hat{x})_{SS} = \hat{x}_S X_{SS} \hat{x}_S,$$

and therefore det $(\hat{x}X\hat{x})_{SS} = (\det \hat{x}_S)^2 \det X_{SS} \geq 0$ for all S, so that $\hat{x}X\hat{x}$ is also a P_0 matrix. Since any principal minor of a P_0 matrix is trivially a P_0 matrix, $(\hat{x}X\hat{x})_{SS} = \hat{x}_S X_{SS} \hat{x}_S$ is a P_0 matrix. Let

$$z_S = \hat{x}_S X_{SS} x_S = (\hat{x}_S X_{SS} \hat{x}_S) e_S.$$

By Lemma 1, we must have $z_i \geq 0$ for some $i \in S$. Choose now $S = \{i | x_i \neq 0\}$. Let $y = Xx$. Then,

$$y_S = X_{SS} x_S + X_{S\tilde{S}} x_{\tilde{S}} = X_{SS} x_S$$

where $\tilde{S}$ is the set of indices i not in S; by construction, $x_{\tilde{S}} = 0$. Since $z_S = \hat{x}_S y_S$, $z_i = x_i y_i$ for $i \in S$. It has been shown that $x_i y_i \geq 0$ for some i for which $x_i \neq 0$, by the definition of S.

Condition (b) implies (c): For any positive diagonal D, let λ be a real characteristic root of DX and x a corresponding real characteristic vector:

$$DXx = \lambda x, \quad x \neq 0,$$

so that

$$y = Xx = \lambda D^{-1}x.$$

Since $y_i = \lambda x_i/d_{ii}$, it follows from (b) that $\lambda x_i^2/d_{ii} \geq 0$ for some i for which $x_i \neq 0$. As $x_i^2/d_{ii} > 0$, it must be that $\lambda \geq 0$.

Condition (c) implies that X is a P_0 matrix: For any fixed S, we seek to show that det $X_{SS} \geq 0$. If det $X_{SS} = 0$, the result is true, so assume that det $X_{SS} \neq 0$. Then no characteristic root of X_{SS} is zero. Define, for each $t > 0$, the positive diagonal matrix.

$$D(t) = \begin{pmatrix} I_{SS} & 0 \\ 0 & tI_{\tilde{S}\tilde{S}} \end{pmatrix}$$

where I is the identity matrix with appropriate indices. The characteristic roots of $D(t)X$ are continuous functions of t. Since

$$D(0)X = \begin{pmatrix} X_{SS} & X_{S\tilde{S}} \\ 0 & 0 \end{pmatrix},$$

its nonzero characteristic roots are precisely the characteristic roots of X_{SS}, with the same multiplicities. Choose ϵ to be greater than 0 and less than the smallest absolute value of a characteristic root of X_{SS}. Then as t approaches 0, some of the characteristic roots of $D(t)X$ approach those of X_{SS}, while the remainder approach 0; for t sufficiently small those approaching the roots of X_{SS} will be above ϵ in absolute value while the remainder are below. Call the first set the *large* roots. Since the conjugate of a complex number has the same absolute value and since the complex roots of $D(t)X$ come in conjugate pairs, the product of the complex large roots must be positive. By hypothesis, the real roots of $D(t)X$ are nonnegative for $t > 0$. Hence, the product of the large roots is non-negative for $t > 0$. Since the large roots approach the roots of X_{SS}, the product of the characteristic roots of X_{SS} must be nonnegative. But this product is equal to det X_{SS}.

We have now shown that if X is a P_0 matrix, then (b) holds; if (b) holds, then (c) holds; and if (c) holds, X is a P_0 matrix. Hence, the three conditions are equivalent, as was to be proved.

For a linear system or within the linear approximation around equilibrium to a nonlinear system, the motion of the system can be expressed as a sum of monotonic motions, corresponding to the real characteristic roots, and oscillatory motions, corresponding to the complex roots. What is established here is that the Hicksian conditions tell us about the stability of monotonic motions. This result therefore makes clear the extent to which the Hicksian conditions are useful in stability analysis.

III. Some notes on connected sets·

We digress here to introduce a mathematical concept which may seem unrelated. Let K be a subset of a finite-dimensional space.

Definition 3. N is a *neighborhood relative to K* if it is the nonnull intersection of a neighborhood with K, i.e., if N is nonempty and if N can be written as $N = N' \cap K$, where N' is a neighborhood in the usual sense.

Definition 4. C is *open relative to K* if C is a subset of K such that for every element $x \in C$, there is a neighborhood N relative to K such that $x \in N \subset C$.

Definition 5. A sequence $\{x^v\}$ converges to x^0 relative to K if, for every neighborhood N relative to K and containing x^0, $x^v \in N$ for all v sufficiently large.

Definition 6. The subset C of K is *closed relative to K* if it contains all x^0 to which sequences in C converge relative to K.

To illustrate, the half-open interval $[0, 1)$ is open relative to the nonnegative reals; for the neighborhoods of 0 relative to the nonnegative reals are the half-open intervals $[0, \epsilon)$.

For later use, also remark that if a set C is closed (respectively, open) relative to K and if $K' \subset K$, then $C \cap K'$ is closed (respectively, open) relative to K'.

Now consider the set K made of the two closed intervals $[0, 1]$ and $[2, 3]$. It is easy to verify that $[0, 1]$ is both open and closed relative to K. This fact is clearly related to the observation that K is made up of two distinct parts. This example leads to the formal definition.

Definition 7. A set K is said to be *connected* if it does not contain any proper nonempty subset which is both open and closed relative to K. (A *proper* subset is one that does not contain every member of the set.)

In the sequel, we will be concerned with connected sets of matrices; the square matrices of any given order clearly constitute a finite-dimensional space.

(All the preceding definitions can be stated more abstractly and are in standard works on analysis. But only the preceding definitions are needed here.)

An obvious restatement of the definition is contained in the following lemma.

Lemma 2. K is connected if and only if it cannot be partitioned into a family containing two or more open nonnull subsets.

Proof. If K is not connected, it contains a nonnull proper subset C which is both open and closed in K. Hence C is open in K, and $K \sim C$ (the set-theoretic difference between K and C, i.e., the set of all elements of K not in C) is open in K, since the complement of a closed set relative to K is open relative to K. These two sets constitute a partition into two nonnull subsets open relative to K.

Conversely, if such a partition exists, let C be any member of the partition and C', the union of all other members. Both are nonnull; since C' is a union of open sets, it is open. Hence, C is the complement of an open set and therefore closed; it is also proper, since its complement is nonnull.

We state first of all a theorem about connected sets which will be used subsequently.

Theorem 2. Let f be a function from a connected set K to any range. If $f^{-1}(y)$ is open for every y in the range of f, then f is a constant.

Notation 6. If f is a function, $f(K) = \{y \mid y = f(x) \text{ for some } x \in K\}$, $f^{-1}(y) = \{x \mid f(x) = y\}$.

Proof. Since f is a function, $f(x)$ is single-valued; hence the family of sets $f^{-1}(y)$ as y varies over $f(K)$ is a partition of K (that is, every element of K is in one and only one member of the family). If each set is open, it follows from Lemma 2 and the connectedness of K that the partition can have but one member.

We also need some method of establishing whether a set is connected. First, note that the interval $[0, 1]$ is connected. For suppose it contained a proper nonnull subset C both closed and open in $[0, 1]$. Since C has 1 as an upper bound, it possesses a supremum, say $\dot{M}$. If $M < 1$, the open intervals $(M - \epsilon, M + \epsilon)$ are neighborhoods relative to $[0, 1]$ for ϵ sufficiently small; if $M = 1$, then the half-open intervals $(1 - \epsilon, 1]$ are neighborhoods relative to $[0, 1]$. In either case, by definition of a supremum, each such neighborhood must contain a point of C; since C is closed, $M \in C$. But since C is open, if $M < 1$, then some neighborhood of M is included in C, which means that C contains an element greater than M, in contradiction to the definition of a supremum. Therefore, $M = 1$, and $1 \in C$. But the complement of C in $[0, 1]$ is also open and closed in $[0, 1]$ and therefore also contains 1, a contradiction since the two sets are disjoint.

Second we note:

Lemma 3.   If f is a continuous function and K is connected, then $f(K)$ is connected.

Proof.   Suppose $f(K)$ were the union of two disjoint sets Y and Y', each nonnull and open in $f(K)$. Then K would be the union of $f^{-1}(Y)$ and $f^{-1}(Y')$. If $y_0 \in Y$, then there is a neighborhood N of y_0 relative to $f(K)$ contained in Y. Let $y_0 = f(x_0)$; then for x sufficiently close to x_0, $f(x) \in N$, since f is continuous. Then $f(x) \in Y$, or $x \in f^{-1}(Y)$, for those x. Hence, $f^{-1}(Y)$ is open relative to K; so would be $f^{-1}(Y')$, in contradiction to the connectedness of K.

A *line segment* $[x^0, x^1]$ in some finite-dimensional space consists of all points $x = (1 - t)x^0 + tx^1$ for some t, $0 \leq t \leq 1$. If we write $f(t) = (1 - t)x^0 + tx^1$, we can say that $[x^0, x^1]$ is the image of $[0, 1]$ under the continuous function $f(t)$; since $[0, 1]$ is connected, so is every line segment.

We now state a general condition by which we can prove that many sets are connected, given that we know that some, like line segments, are.

Definition 8.   A family F of sets is said to be a *connected family* if, for every proper nonnull subfamily F', there is at least one set $S \in F'$ and one set $T \in F \sim F'$ such that $S \cap T$ is nonnull.

Notation 7.   If F is a family of sets, then $U(F)$ is the union of all the sets in F, i.e., the set consisting of all elements which belong to at least one member of F.

Theorem 3.   The union of a connected family of connected sets is a connected set.

Proof.   Let F be the connected family of connected sets. Suppose $U(F)$ is not connected; then it possesses a proper nonnull subset L which is both open and closed in $U(F)$. If $K \in F$, $K \subset U(F)$); as remarked earlier, $K \cap L$ is both open and closed in K. But K is connected so that $K \cap L$ cannot be a proper nonnull subset of K for each $K \in F$: either $K \cap L$ is null or $K \cap L = K$. Let F' be the subfamily of F for which the latter condition holds; it is equivalent to the statement $K \subset L$. Notice that if $K \cap L$ were null for all $K \in F$, L would have to be null, while if $K \subset L$, all $K \in F$, $U(F) \subset L$, and L would not be a proper subset of $U(F)$, both contrary to assumption. Hence, F' is a proper nonnull subfamily of F.

But now, any set belonging to F' is included in L while any set belonging to $F \sim F'$ is disjoint from L, so that their intersection must be null, contrary to the defintion of a connected family. Hence the supposition $U(F)$ not connected has led to a contradiction.

Corollary 3. A convex set is connected.

Proof. If C is a convex set, let F be the family of all line segments joining any pair of elements of C. As already noted, every member of F is a connected set. Further, any set in F is a subset of C by the definition of a convex set, so that $U(F) \subset C$; but every member of C belongs to at least one member of F, so that $C \subset U(F)$. Hence, $C = U(F)$. By Theorem 3, it suffices to show that F is a connected family.

Let F' be any proper nonnull subfamily of F, L' any line segment belonging to F', and L'' any line segment belonging to $F \sim F'$. Choose any points $x' \in L'$ and $x'' \in L''$; both are members of C. Finally, let L be the line segment $[x', x'']$; it belongs to F. If $L \in F'$, note that $L \cap L''$ contains the point x'' and is therefore nonnull; if $L \in F \sim F'$, then note that $L \cap L'$ contains the point x' and is nonnull. In either case, there is a set belonging to F' which intersects a set belonging to $F \sim F'$, and therefore F is a connected family.

IV. Location of characteristic roots of matrices

From now on, it will be more convenient to deal with complex matrices even though the intended application is to real matrices.

Notation 8. For any complex number λ and any matrix X, $\mu(X, \lambda)$ is the algebraic multiplicity of λ as a characteristic root of X. (If λ is not a characteristic root of X, this value is 0.)

Notation 9. For any set C of complex numbers and any matrix X, $\mu(X, C)$ is the sum of the multiplicities of all the characteristic roots of X which lie in the set C.

(We are going to be interested in such sets as those with positive or negative real parts.)

In what follows we will have occasion to use the continuity of the characteristic roots as a function of the matrix. We may enumerate the n roots of a matrix of order n as, say, $\lambda_1, \ldots, \lambda_n$, where each multiple root appears the number of times given by its multiplicity. But of course the order of the roots has no significance; in particular, a permutation of them would be no difference at all. Hence, the distance between two sets of roots $\lambda_1, \ldots, \lambda_n$ and $\lambda_1', \ldots, \lambda_n'$ has to be defined in a way which is invariant under permutation. We can define the distance in some conventional way provided we first permute the subscripts so as to make the measure of distance as small as possible.

Definition 9.   Let λ and λ' be two n-tuples of complex numbers. The distance between them will be defined as

$$\rho(\lambda, \lambda') = \min_\pi \left[\Sigma_{i=1}^n \mid \lambda_i - \lambda_{\pi(i)}' \mid^2 \right]^{1/2}$$

where π varies over all permutations of the integers $1, \ldots, n$ into themselves.

Then the characteristic roots of X are continuous functions of X in the sense that as X approaches a fixed matrix X_0, the distance between the n-tuple of characteristic roots of X and that of X_0 approaches 0, when distance is understood in the sense of Definition 9.

We now discuss the behavior of $\mu(X, \lambda)$ and $\mu(X, C)$, as X varies locally.

Suppose $\mu(X_0, \lambda_0) = m$. Let N be a neighborhood of λ_0 sufficiently small to exclude any other characteristic roots. Then $\mu(X_0, N) = m$. Now let X vary in a neighborhood of X_0. Clearly m of the roots have to remain near λ_0, i.e., in N. It is not excluded, however, that additional roots may enter the neighborhood N:

$$\mu(X, N) \geqq \mu(X_0, N) = m \qquad \text{for } X \text{ close to } X_0.$$

Now consider an open set C with several distinct roots λ_i $(i = 1, \ldots, p)$ of X_0. We can find a neighborhood N_i for each λ_i which is entirely contained in C and so that the neighborhoods N_i are disjoint.

By definition,

$$\mu(X, C) \geqq \Sigma_{i=1}^p \mu(X, N_i),$$

while from the previous remark, we have, for X sufficiently close to X_0,

$$\mu(X, N_i) \geqq m_i,$$

the multiplicity of λ_i as a root of X_0. Hence, for X sufficiently close to X_0,

$$\mu(X, C) \geqq \Sigma_{i=1}^p m_i = \mu(X_0, C).$$

Now consider a partition of the complex numbers into sets, all but one of which is open (the application we make is into the sets of complex numbers with positive real parts, negative real parts, and zero real parts). Let the sets be $C_j (j = 0, \ldots, m)$, with C_j open for $j \geqq 1$. Further, we will let X vary over a connected set K, and we will assume that $\mu(X, C_0)$ is constant over K. Since the sum of the multiplicities of the characteristic roots is n, we must have

$$\Sigma_{j=0}^m \mu(X, C_j) = n.$$

If $\mu(X, C_0)$ is constant, then

$$\Sigma_{j=1}^m \mu(X, C_j) \text{ is constant for } X \in K.$$

But as we have just seen,

$$\mu(X, C_j) \geqq \mu(X_0, C_j) \qquad (j = 1, \ldots, m)$$

for X sufficiently close to X_0. If we combine these two remarks, we see that, as X varies over a neighborhood of X_0 relative to K,

$$\mu(X, C_j) = \mu(X_0, C_j) \quad (j = 1, \ldots, m).$$

Let $\mu(X)$ be the function of X defined as the vector of nonnegative integers with components $\mu(X, C_j)$ $(j = 1, \ldots, m)$, and let $r = (r_1, \ldots, r_m)$ be any realized value of this vector. We have shown that if $\mu(X_0) = r$, then $\mu(X) = r$ for all X in a neighborhood of X_0 relative to K, that is, we have shown that $\mu^{-1}(r)$ is open relative to K for each r. But now Theorem 2 immediately assures us that $\mu(X)$ must be a constant, that is, $\mu(X, C_j)$ is a constant on K for each j.

Theorem 4. If C_j $(j = 0, \ldots, m)$ is a partition of the complex numbers, with C_j open for $j \geq 1$ and if $\mu(X, C_0)$ is constant as X varies over a connected set of matrices K, then $\mu(X, C_j)$ is constant on K for all j.

The point of this result is that the constancy of the numbers of characteristic roots in each set follows from the constancy on the single set which, so to speak, separates all the others.

V. Constancy of the inertia of a matrix

As already indicated, we now specialize to partitions defined by the real parts of characteristic roots of matrices.

Notation 10. $R(\lambda)$ is the real part of λ.

Notation 11.

$$C^+ = \{\lambda \mid R(\lambda) > 0\}, \quad C^0 = \{\lambda \mid R(\lambda) = 0\}, \quad C^- = \{\lambda \mid R(\lambda) < 0\}.$$

Notation 12. $v^k(X) = \mu(X, C^k)$ $(k = +, 0, -)$.

Definition 10. The *inertia* of a matrix X (denoted by in X) is the triple $v^+(X), v^0(X), v^-(X)$.

(This is a standard definition in matrix theory.) With this definition, Theorem 4 specializes as follows:

Corollary 4. If $v^0(X)$ is constant for X on a connected set K, then in X is constant on that set.

This corollary could itself be the basis of ordinary stability proofs. Suppose that K contains at least one stable member, so that in $X = (0, 0, n)$ for that matrix. Then if we can show that $v^0(X)$ is always 0 on K, that is, no $X \in K$ is singular or has purely imaginary roots, we have shown that all members of K are stable. We will not pursue this matter here but consider instead the application of this corollary to D stability and related matters.

Let D be any fixed matrix (we will in the sequel assume it to be a real diagonal matrix, but for the moment that is unnecessary). If X varies over a connected set K, DX varies over a connected set, so that on such a set the constancy of $\nu^0(DX)$ implies that of in DX. If in particular $I \in K$, where I is the identity matrix, then the constancy of $\nu^0(DX)$ is the same as the statement that $\nu^0(DX) = \nu^0(D)$, and similarly with the constancy of in DX. Finally, if the statement that $\nu^0(DX) = \nu^0(D)$ holds for all D in some class A as well as for all $X \in K$, then the conclusion in DX = in D holds for the same range of D and X.

    Theorem 5.   If K is a connected set of matrices, with $I \in K$, and if $\nu^0(DX) = \nu^0(D)$ for all D in some set A and all $X \in K$, then in DX = in D for all $D \in A$ and $X \in K$.

    If we consider A to be the class of positive diagonal matrices, then in $D = (n, 0, 0)$, and $\nu^0(D) = 0$. Then Theorem 5 tells us that if DX has no zero or purely imaginary roots for all $X \in K$ and all positive diagonal D, then the characteristic roots of DX have positive real parts for all $X \in K$ and all positive diagonal D. That is, the negatives of the members of K are D stable.

    If instead we take A to be the set of *all* diagonal matrices, and if the hypotheses hold, then we have identified a class of matrices such that the number of characteristic roots of DX whose real parts have given signs is the same as the numbers of diagonal elements of D with those signs. In particular, it means that stability fails to hold when the diagonal matrix is not positive (if the sign of X is reversed).

    Just how important economically is the stronger question of the last paragraph is hard to answer. The problem was raised in the Enthoven–Arrow model on the basis of an expectational model which is perhaps none too satisfactory. Assume that excess demand for a commodity is made up of two parts, the ordinary excess demand which depends on current prices as usual, and a speculative demand which depends only on the rate of change of the price of that commodity. Then excess demand for commodity i can be written

$$z_i(p_1, \ldots, p_n) + w_i(dp_i/dt),$$

or, to a linear approximation,

$$\Sigma_{i=1}^{n} X_{ij}(p_j - \bar{p}_j) + w_i'(0)\,(dp_i/dt)$$

where $X_{ij} = \partial z_i/\partial p_j$, and $(\bar{p}_1, \ldots, \bar{p}_n)$ is the equilibrium. As before, let $H_i'(0)$ be the speed of adjustment on the ith market in the neighborhood of equilibrium, so the linear approximation to the dynamic system is

$$dp_i/dt = H_i'(0)\,[\Sigma_{j=1}^{n} X_{ij}(p_j - \bar{p}_j) + w_i'(0)\,(dp_i/dt)],$$

or

$$[1 - H_i'(0)\,w_i'(0)]\,dp_i/dt = H_i'(0)\,\Sigma_{j=1}^{n} X_{ij}(p_i - \bar{p}_j),$$

so that the stability of the system is determined by the matrix DX, where now D is a diagonal matrix with the ith diagonal element being

$$H_i'(0)/[1 - H_i'(0)\,w_i'(0)].$$

As can be seen, if the speculative demand is sufficiently responsive, i.e., $w_i'(0)$ large enough, some of the diagonal elements can be negative. It is interesting to conclude that not only is there stability when the d_{ii}'s are all positive but that it fails when $d_{ii} < 0$ for some i.

VI. Conditions that DX and D have the same number of characteristic roots with zero real part

In view of Theorem 5, it is useful to characterize matrices X for which $v^0(DX) = v^0(D)$ for all D in some set A. If we can find the class of matrices X with that property, we then will seek a connected subset K which also contains I; K will then satisfy the conclusions of the theorem.

We will first take the case where A is the set of all diagonal matrices. Of course, conditions sufficient for this case are sufficient for any other set A, though one might hope to find weaker conditions valid for smaller sets. While such weaker conditions are stated, it has so far not been found possible to make effective use of them.

Consider then first the condition on a matrix X that the property which I will denote by (A) holds:

(A) $v^0(DX) = v^0(D)$ for all real diagonal D.

In what follows, the phrase "real diagonal matrix" will be abbreviated to "rdm," to avoid offensive repetition. For any such matrix, we define:
Notation 13. $\Sigma(D) = \{i \mid d_{ii} \neq 0\}$.

The $\Sigma(D)$ is a function defined on matrices whose values are sets of integers; hence the notation $\Sigma^{-1}(S)$ means the set of diagonal matrices whose diagonal elements are nonzero precisely for $i \in S$.

If $S = \Sigma(D)$, then we can write

$$DX = \begin{pmatrix} D_{SS} & 0 \\ 0 & 0 \end{pmatrix} \begin{pmatrix} X_{SS} & X_{S\bar{S}} \\ X_{\bar{S}S} & X_{\bar{S}\bar{S}} \end{pmatrix} = \begin{pmatrix} D_{SS}X_{SS} & D_{SS}X_{S\bar{S}} \\ 0 & 0 \end{pmatrix},$$

so that

$$\det(DX - \lambda I) = \det \begin{pmatrix} D_{SS}X_{SS} - \lambda I_{SS} & D_{SS}X_{S\bar{S}} \\ 0 & -\lambda I_{\bar{S}\bar{S}} \end{pmatrix}$$

$$= (-\lambda)^{n-\#S} \det(D_{SS}X_{SS} - \lambda I_{SS})$$

where we use:
Notation 14. $\#S$ is the number of elements in the set S.

Clearly, if $\lambda \neq 0$, then $\mu(DX, \lambda) = \mu(D_{SS}X_{SS}, \lambda)$, while $\mu(DX, 0) = \mu(D_{SS}X_{SS}, 0) + n - \#S$. If we sum over all characteristic roots with zero real parts, we have

$$v^0(DX) = v^0(D_{SS}X_{SS}) + n - \#S.$$

By construction D_{SS} is nonsingular, so that it does not have zero as a characteristic root, while, being real diagonal, it has no purely imaginary roots. That is, $v^0(D_{SS}) = 0$. If we set $X = I$ in the above equation, we have

$$v^0(D) = v^0(D_{SS}) + n - \#S = n - \#S,$$

so that

$$v^0(DX) = v^0(D_{SS}X_{SS}) + v^0(D).$$

Thus, for rdm's in $\Sigma^{-1}(S)$, condition (A) is equivalent to the condition that $v^0(D_{SS}X_{SS}) = 0$. Note that by varying D over all members of $\Sigma^{-1}(S)$, we can make D_{SS} any nonsingular rdm of order $\#S$. Write the condition

(B) $v^0(DX) = 0$ for all nonsingular rdm's D.

Then it has been shown that (A) holds for a matrix X if and only if (B) holds for all principal minors of X. Let us then examine the conditions for (B) to hold.

Note that $v^0(DX) = 0$ if and only if both $\mu(DX, 0) = 0$ and $\mu(DX, ia) = 0$ for every real $a \neq 0$. The first condition is the same as the nonsingularity of DX; for D nonsingular, this is equivalent to the nonsingularity of X. The second condition is that of the nonsingularity of $DX - iaI$. Since D is nonsingular, we can write

$$DX - iaI = D(X - iaD^{-1}),$$

and nonsingularity of this matrix is equivalent to that of $X - iaD^{-1}$. But as a varies over nonzero reals and D over nonsingular rdm's, $-aD^{-1}$ varies over all nonsingular rdm's. Thus (B) holds if and only if both X is nonsingular and $X + iE$ is nonsingular for all nonsingular rdm's E. This yields the following condition for (A).

Theorem 6.   A necessary and sufficient condition that $v^0(DX) = v^0(D)$ for all rdm's D is that both X_{SS} be nonsingular for all S and $X_{SS} + iE_{SS}$ be nonsingular for all S and all nonsingular rdm's E_{SS} of order $\#S$.

For completeness, we state the criterion that $v^0(DX) = v^0(D)$ for all rdm's D in some arbitrary set A and sketch the proof which uses the same reasoning as the foregoing.

For any given A, $A \cap \Sigma^{-1}(S)$ is the subset of A for which $d_{ii} \neq 0$ for precisely the members of S. For D in this set, D_{SS} is nonsingular.

Notation 15. A_S is the image of $A \cap \Sigma^{-1}(S)$ under the mapping $D \rightarrow D_{SS}$.

Notation 16.   If B is a set of nonsingular matrices, B^{-1} is the image of B under the operation of taking the inverse of the matrix.

Notation 17.   If B is any set of matrices, define the double cone spanned by B as

$$dk(B) = \{X \mid X = t \, Y \text{ for some real } t \text{ and some } Y \text{ in } B\}.$$

Then the condition $v^0(DX) = v^0(D)$ for all $D \in A$ becomes, following the preceding reasoning,

$$v^0(DX_{SS}) = 0 \quad \text{for all } D \in A \cap \Sigma^{-1}(S).$$

But this means $DX_{SS} - ia I_{SS}$ is nonsingular for all real a, or, since D is nonsingular, that

$X_{SS} - ia D^{-1}$ is nonsingular for all real a and all D in $A \cap \Sigma^{-1}(S)$,

that is, that $X_{SS} + iE$ is nonsingular for all $E \in dk(A_S^{-1})$.

Theorem 7.   A necessary and sufficient condition that $v^0(DX) = v^0(D)$ for all $D \in A$ is that $X_{SS} + iE$ is nonsingular for every S and E for which $E \in dk(A_S^{-1})$.

To illustrate this theorem, we may consider the problem of D stability in its original form, where we simply ask that DX be stable (with reversal of sign, so that we seek that all roots have positive real parts) for all positive rdm's. In this case, A is the set of positive rdm's. Then $\Sigma(D)$ is the entire set of integers $1, \ldots, n$ for all D, and therefore $\Sigma^{-1}(S)$ is null for S a proper subset of them. When S is the entire set of integers, $A \cap \Sigma^{-1}(S) = A$; A^{-1} is again the set of positive rdm's, and $dk(A^{-1})$ is the set of all one-signed rdm's (i.e., those for which either all diagonal elements are positive, all are negative, or all are zero). In this case, of course, $v^0(D) = 0$ for all $D \in A$.

Corollary 7.   A necessary and sufficient condition that $v^0(DX) = 0$ for all positive rdm's is that $X + iE$ be nonsingular for all one-signed rdm's E.

VII. A general class of matrices for which the inertia of DX is equal to that of D

In this section, we draw together Theorems 5 and 6 to find a very broad class K with the property that in $DX = $ in D for all rdm's D and all $X \in K$. Finally, we show that some earlier results actually identified subsets of this class.

Theorem 8.   Let X have the property that, for every real $a \geq 0$, every principal minor of $X + aI$ is nonsingular, and for any nonsingular rdm E every principal minor of $X + iE + aI$ is nonsingular. Then in $DX = $ in D for all rdm's D.

Proof.   The hypothesis can be restated: For every real $a \geq 0$ and every rdm $E = 0$ or nonsingular, every principal minor of $X + iE + aI$ is nonsingular. Let K be the class of all such matrices. The hypothesis, for $a = 0$, implies, according to Theorem 6, that $v^0(DX) = v^0(D)$ for all rdm's and all $X \in K$.

If $X = I$, $X + iE + aI = (1 + a)I + iE$, a diagonal matrix. Since the real part of every diagonal element is $1 + a \geq 1 > 0$, every principal minor is certainly nonsingular; hence, $I \in K$.

By Theorem 5, it suffices to show that K is connected. For each X in K, consider the line segment $[X, I]$. Let F be the family of such line segments. Each member of the family is convex and therefore connected, by Corollary 3. Any two members of the family have the element I in common; hence, no matter how F is partitioned into two nonnull subfamilies, every member of one intersects every member of the other, and, by Definition 8, F is a connected family. By Theorem 3, the union of F is a connected set; we need only show that $K = U(F)$.

Since $X \in [X, I]$, every member of K belongs to at least one member of F, so that $K \subset U(F)$. We need therefore only show that $[X, I] \subset K$ for each $X \in K$, for then the union of all those segments must also be included in K; since $K \subset U(F)$, K would equal $U(F)$.

We already know that $I \in K$. Consider any member of $[X, I]$ other than I, say $Y = (1 - t) X + tI, 0 \leq t < 1$. For any rdm $E = 0$ or nonsingular,

$$Y + iE + aI = (1 - t) X + iE + (a + t) I = (1 - t) (X + iE' + bI)$$

where

$$E' = E/(1 - t), \qquad b = (a + t)/(1 - t).$$

Clearly, E' is again a rdm and $b \geq 0$; further $E' = 0$ if $E = 0$ and is nonsingular if E is nonsingular. Since $X \in K$, every principal minor of $X + iE' + bI$ is nonsingular, and this property remains valid when the matrix is premultiplied by the positive scalar $1 - t$. Hence Y satisfies the defining characteristic of K.

We now give two classes of matrices which will be shown to be subsets of the class defined by Theorem 8.

Notation 18.   If X is a matrix, X' is its transpose and $\overline{X}$ its conjugate (formed by taking the conjugate of each element).

Notation 19. $X^* = X + \overline{X}'$.

Definition 11. X is Hermitian if X^* is real positive definite symmetric.

We will show that Hermitian matrices are included in the set defined by Theorem 8. If we restrict ourselves to real matrices, as one would in economic theory, this class contains those for which $X + X'$ is positive definite, i.e., the class sometimes called *positive quasidefinite*.

It is obvious from the definition that any principal minor of a Hermitian matrix is Hermitian. It is also well known that Hermitian matrices are nonsingular. To see this, consider any vextor x for which

$$Xx = 0.$$

Multiply on the right by $\overline{x}'$; then $\overline{x}'Xx = 0$. This expression is a real scalar and therefore equal to its conjugate transpose, which can be written

$$\overline{x}'\overline{X}'x = 0.$$

Adding these last two equations, we have $\overline{x}'X^*x = 0$. Since X^* is real and positive definite, this is possible only if $x = 0$, so we have shown that $Xx = 0$ implies $x = 0$, i.e., X is nonsingular.

From these remarks, it is obvious that every principal minor of a Hermitian matrix is nonsingular. To show that every Hermitian matrix satisfies the conditions of Theorem 9, it suffices then to show that if X is Hermitian, then $Y = X + iE + aI$ is also. But

$$Y^* = X^* + (iE)^* + aI = X^* + aI,$$

which is certainly real positive definite and symmetric if X^* is.

Corollary 8.1. If X is positive Hermitian, then in DX = in D for all rdm's D.

This generalizes the result of Arrow and McManus [1] in one direction. It is weaker in another, because the result was found there to be true for all symmetric matrices, not merely for diagonal matrices.

This generalization is, however, an implication of Corollary 8.1. Note the following facts: If R is a real orthogonal matrix, then (a) RXR' has the same characteristic roots as X and therefore in X = in RXR', and (b) if X is positive Hermitian, then so is RXR'. Further, if M is real symmetric, then we can find real orthogonal R and real diagonal D such that $RMR' = D$. Then

in MX = in $RMXR'$ = in $RMR'RXR'$ = in $D(RXR')$.

If X is positive Hermitian, then so is RXR', and by Corollary 8.1,

in $D(RXR')$ = in D = in $R'DR$ = in M.

Corollary 8.2. If X is positive Hermitian, then in MX = in M for all real symmetric M.

We now consider a class of matrices which have dominant diagonals.

Definition 12. X has a (weighted) dominant diagonal if there exist positive numbers $w_1, \ldots, w_n$ such that, for each i, $w_i |X_{ii}| > \Sigma_{i \neq j} w_j |X_{ij}|$.

It is, of course, very well known that any principal minor of a dominant diagonal matrix has a dominant diagonal and that dominant diagonal matrices are nonsingular.

Notation 20. For any matrix X, we define X^{**} to be obtained by replacing the diagonal element X_{ii} by its real part $R(X_{ii})$.

We consider the class of matrices for which X^{**} is positive dominant diagonal. For real matrices, of course, this reduces to the usual class of positive dominant diagonal matrices. Since stable Metzler matrices have a negative dominant diagonal, their negatives form a subclass; it is the last set which was studied by Enthoven and Arrow [2].

Since $|X_{ii}| \geq R(X_{ii}) = X_{ii}^{**}$, while $X_{ij}^* = X_{ij}$ for $i \neq j$, it is obvious that if X^{**} has a dominant diagonal, then so has X, and therefore every principal minor of a matrix in this class is nonsingular.

It remains to show that if X belongs to the class under consideration, so does

$Y = X + iE + aI$; then, as in the case of Hermitian matrices, we will have verified that the class is a subset of that specified in Theorem 9. But obviously $Y_{ij}{}^{**} = X_{ij} = X_{ij}{}^{**}$ for $i \neq j$, since $iE + aI$ is a diagonal matrix; while $Y_{ii}{}^{**} = X_{ii}{}^{**} + a \geq X_{ii}{}^{**}$. Hence if X^{**} has a positive dominant diagonal, so has Y^{**}.

Corollary 8.3.   If X^{**} (obtained from X by replacing the diagonal elements by their real parts) has a positive dominant diagonal, then in $DX =$ in D for all rdm's D.

For the record, we state a generalization of Theorem 8, corresponding to the generalization from Theorem 6 to Theorem 7. The proof completely parallels that of Theorem 8 and is omitted.

Theorem 9.   Let A be a class of rdm's, and let X have the property that $X_{SS} + iE + aI$ is nonsingular for every $a \geq 0$ and every S and E for which $E \in dk(A_S{}^{-1})$. Then in $DX =$ in D for all $D \in A$.

Corollary 9.   If $X + iE + aI$ is nonsingular for every $a \geq 0$ and every one-signed rdm E, then X is D stable.

We may conclude with one tiny generalization, which nevertheless gives rise to a new stability result.

Theorem 10.   If in $DX =$ in D for all rdm's D and if P is positive diagonal, then in $DPX =$ in D for all rdm's D.

Proof.   Since DP is a rdm, it follows immediately from the hypothesis that in $DPX =$ in DP. But, for each i, the sign of $d_{ii}p_{ii}$ is the same as that of d_{ii}. Since the characteristic roots of D are the numbers d_{ii} and those of DP are the numbers $d_{ii}p_{ii}$, we clearly have in $DP =$ in D.

In conjunction with Corollary 8.1, we then see:

Corollary 10.   If X is Hermitian and P positive diagonal, then in $DPX =$ in D for all rdm's D.

Thus, PX is D stable for positive diagonal P and Hermitian (e.g., quasidefinite) X, a result which, though obvious once stated, seems not to have been noticed in stability theory.

No similar generalization can be derived from Corollary 8.3; if a matrix of the class defined there is premultiplied by a positive diagonal matrix, another matrix of the same class results.

Note

1   I am very grateful to John S. Chipman for his comments, which have markedly improved the exposition.

References

[1] Arrow, K. J., and McManus, M., "A Note on Dynamic Stability," this volume, III.4, pp. 326–332.

[2] Enthoven, A. C., and Arrow, K. J., "A Theorem on Expectations and the Stability of Equilibrium," this volume, III.4, pp. 311–317.

[3] Fiedler, M., and Pták, V., "Some Generalizations of Positive Definiteness and Stability," *Numerische Mathematik*, Vol. 9 (1966), 163–172.

[4] Gale, D., and Nikaidô, H., "The Jacobian Matrix and Global Univalence of Mappings," *Mathematische Annalen*, Vol. 159 (1965), 159–183.

[5] Hicks, J. R., *Value and Capital*. London and New York: Oxford Univ. (Clarendon) Press. 1939.

[6] Lange, O., *Price Flexibility and Employment*. Bloomington, Indiana: Principia Press, 1944.

[7] Metzler, L. A., "Stability of Multiple Markets: The Hicks Conditions," *Econometrica*, Vol. 13 (1945), 277–292.

[8] Samuelson, P. A., "The Stability of Equilibrium: Comparative Statics and Dynamics," *Econometrica*, Vol. 9 (1941), 97–120.

[9] Samuelson, P. A., "The Relation between Hicksian Stability and True Dynamic Stability," *Econometrica*, Vol. 12 (1944), 256–257.

5
DYNAMIC SHORTAGES

Dynamic shortages and price rises: the engineer-scientist case[1]

KENNETH J. ARROW
WILLIAM M. CAPRON

The frequent and loud complaints of a shortage of engineers and scientists heard over the past eight years or so might be taken as indicating a failure of the price mechanism and indeed have frequently been joined with (rather vaguely stated) proposals for interference with market determination of numbers and allocation. It is our contention that these views stem from a misunderstanding of economic theory as well as from an exaggeration of the empirical evidence. On the contrary, a proper view of the workings of the market mechanism, recognizing, in particular, the dynamics of market adjustment to changed conditions, would show that the phenomenon of observed shortage in some degree is exactly what would be predicted by classical theory in the face of rapidly rising demands.

In this paper we present a model which explains the dynamics of the market adjustment process and apply the conclusions drawn from this analysis to the scientist-engineer "shortage."

Equality of supply and demand is a central tenet of ordinary economic theory, but only as the end result of a process, not as a state holding at every instant of time. On the contrary, inequalities between supply and demand are usually regarded as an integral part of the process by which the price on a market reaches its equilibrium position. Price is assumed to rise when demand exceeds supply and to fall in the contrary case.[2] A shortage, in the sense of an excess of demand over supply is then the normal concomitant of a price rise.

If we assume stability of the market mechanism, the shortage observed during the equilibrating process is transitory and tends to disappear as the price approaches equilibrium. If, however, the demand curve is steadily shifting upward at the same time, the shortage will persist, and the price will continue to rise. We argue that the interaction of rising demand with price movements which do not instantaneously equate supply and demand provides a plausible interpretation of the recent history of the engineer-scientist market in the United States from about 1950 to date. We also suggest a more detailed account of the price-adjustment mechanism than the bare statement that price varies according to the inequality between supply and demand.

I. Shortages and price rises

In what follows, we use the terms supply and demand to mean the aggregation of *the choices made by all firms and individuals in equilibrium at a given price* on a given market. Thus for a firm, the quantity demanded or supplied at a given price is that which maximizes profits. The equilibrium of each firm does not, of course, imply the equilibrium of the market, since the aggregate of the decisions of all firms need not lead to equality of supply and demand. At any given moment, the decision made by a firm or individual need not be optimal from its point of view at the given price, since economic agents require time to make decisions and to learn. It is assumed that each agent gradually corrects its errors, but in the process the firm or individual will not, by definition, be on its demand or supply curve. We hold that the process by which an economic agent moves toward its own internal equilibrium is an integral part of the process by which the market as a whole comes into equilibrium.

In Marshall's formulation, two equilibria were distinguished, short-run and long-run. A movement along a long-run demand or supply curve manifests itself as a shift in the short-run curve. Market price at any moment may diverge from *both* equilibrium prices. In comparative static analysis all that is shown is that under certain assumptions about the nature of supply and demand functions, price will tend to move toward both short-run and long-run equilibrium price, given a shift in one or both of these functions. Over short periods of time, in which we are interested, the shift of the short-run demand or supply functions can be taken as exogenous trends, and will be so treated in this paper. Our analysis is, in Marshallian terms, short-run; but it differs from the neoclassical analysis in that we are presenting a model which explains not only the direction of price adjustment (i.e., toward equilibrium) but the rate of adjustment in the face of continued shifts in the short-run functions.

For purposes of comparison we draw the usual price-quantity diagram (Figure 1). If P_1 is the initial price, we expect the existence of a shortage to raise the price gradually to the equilibrium value P. During the process the shortage decreases to zero. The shortage can persist only if the price is held at some value such as P_1 by an outside force, such as price control. In that case we have a shortage due to a fundamental imperfection of the market.

Now suppose that we have a market which is initially in equilibrium. For concreteness, we may think of it as the market for engineers and scientists. Suppose further that the price of a commodity that uses engineers in its production has increased. Assume further that each firm producing this commodity was in equilibrium before the increase in the commodity price, that is, that it had as many engineers as it wished to hire at a given salary level. Under the new conditions, the number of engineers that it would pay the firm to hire at the previous salary has gone up, and therefore the market demand has risen. The change from

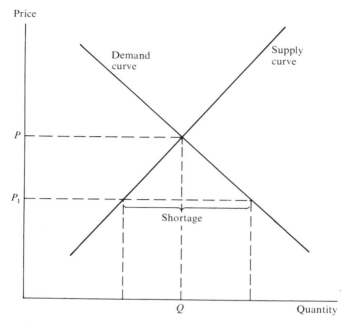

Figure 1

the old situation to the new is illustrated in Figure 2. Here D_1 represents the original demand curve for engineers. Curve D_2 represents the new demand arising from some change in external conditions, in this instance the rise in the price of the commodity in whose production the engineers are engaged. Recall that for present purposes we define demand as the amount which the firm would choose to buy after careful calculation. At any given moment of time the firm may not be fully aware of what its demand (in our sense) is and seek to hire more or fewer engineers. But we do assume that the firm will gradually become aware of any such errors and correct them.

In Figure 2, P_1 represents the equilibrium price when the demand curve is D_1. Let us assume that in fact P_1 was the price prevailing just before the shift in the demand curve. After the demand curve has shifted to D_2, the price that would bring supply and demand into equilibrium is P_2. But movement to this price or salary level typically will take time.

Consider the situation of a firm just after the shift of the demand curve to D_2. A comparison of Figures 1 and 2 shows a strong analogy, not to say identity. At the moment of the shift, the market is experiencing a shortage, which is in many respects comparable to what it would face under price control. Each firm seeks to hire additional engineers at the price it currently pays, but there are no more engineers available at this price. We do not assume that each firm recog-

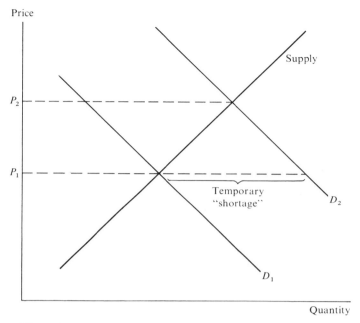

Figure 2

nizes fully its demand, that is, how many engineers it would be best to have under the new conditions. All that is required is that each firm realize it wants more engineers than it now has. Then there will be unfilled vacancies so long as the firms do not raise salaries above what they are currently paying.

II. Empirical evidence of a shortage in the engineer-scientist market

Is there any evidence of a shortage in the sense just described? In view of all the discussion of the "shortage" problem, it is remarkable how little direct evidence is available. The National Science Foundation in 1953 asked officials in large companies whether or not they were experiencing a shortage of engineers and scientists for research and development purposes,[3] but no clear operational definition of the term "shortage" was supplied to these officials. It is plausible to suppose that a respondent would interpret the term to mean the existence of unfilled vacancies with salaries equal to those of engineers and scientists now employed by the firm and performing equivalent services. At least half of the firms reported that they were unable to hire enough research scientists and engineers to meet their needs, although, except for the aircraft industry, there was no industry in which all firms reported such a shortage.

The picture given by the National Science Foundation study is similar to that given by G. W. Beste in a study of the chemical industry.[4] Referring to the Ethyl Corporation, Beste states, "We employ 370 chemical engineers today but need an additional 39. This 39 represent the accumulated deficiency of the last five years."[5] The meaning of the term "deficiency" is not explained, but it is perhaps fair to assume that it means the inability to fill vacancies at salaries then being paid to employees. If Beste and the respondents to the National Science Foundation's survey have understood the term "shortage" in this way, there is then fragmentary evidence of a shortage as manifested by unfilled vacancies, but this shortage is not large. Such a situation is to be expected when the demand curve has shifted and the price does not immediately rise to the level that would equate supply and demand.

III. The process of adjustment in the market

We will trace briefly the sequence of events that will be observed in the market as a result of the shift in the demand curve from D_1 to D_2. At the moment, any individual firm may not have fully calculated how many more engineers it could profitably hire, but we may suppose that it will be aware of wanting more engineers than it now employs. It will begin by seeking to hire more engineers at the going salary but will find that there are none to be had. Its advertised vacancies find no takers; its offers are refused. The firm becomes aware that in order to hire additional engineers it must pay higher salaries, and it will now have to calculate whether or not the additional product derivable from additional engineers will be sufficient to cover the higher level of salaries. In the situation envisaged, the firm will indeed eventually decide to hire some additional engineers at a higher salary, but the decision will take time. First, there must be recognition of the need for higher salaries, then approval must be obtained from various echelons of management, and finally orders must be issued to hire.

Thus the time lag in the firm's reaction is spent partly in learning about the supply conditions in the market and partly in determining the profitability of additional hiring under the new supply conditions. This, however, is only one step in the process of adjustment. First of all, the firm may not yet have fully adjusted to the new demand curve; it has hired some more engineers than before but possibly not as many as would achieve maximum profitability. But, second, even if the firm has hired as many as would be profitable at the new salary level, the market as a whole would still not be in equilibrium, because the firm is now paying a lower salary to its old employees than to the new ones, and there is really more than one price being paid for the identical services rendered by different individuals. The multiplicity of prices is characteristic of disequilibrium situations, but in any well-developed market it cannot persist indefinitely. What happens is that other firms, also experiencing shortages, bid for the services of the engineers belonging to the firm we have been considering. While old employees will probably have some reluctance to move, this reluctance is certainly not absolute and can be overcome by a sufficiently high salary offer. That engineers do change jobs in sufficient numbers to suggest a responsiveness to market forces has been shown by Blank and Stigler.[6] However, we would again expect a lag in information.[7] An employed engineer may not be in touch with current salary offers, and it may take some time before he is aware that the salary he is receiving is below what he might receive elsewhere. We would, however, certainly expect that he will become informed eventually, and that the discrepancy between his actual and his possible salary will tend to be reduced over time. While some individuals will not be tempted to move even in the presence of considerable possible salary increases, many would be willing to do so; either they will in fact move or the hiring firm, to keep them, will raise their salaries to the competitive level. Thus the initial tendency within the firm for new employees to enjoy higher salaries than old ones will gradually be overcome as the salaries of the latter are raised in response to competition.

There is another mechanism which will work to eliminate salary differences within a firm but at the expense of slowing down the firm's willingness to raise salary offers for new personnel. Salary differences within the firm are certain to be a source of morale problems to the extent that they are known, and clearly complete secrecy is out of the question. There will be pressure on the firm to increase the salaries of all its employees (in the same category) to the new higher levels. The lag in adjustment of the salaries of already employed engineer-scientists is thereby reduced, but, on the other hand, the firm is more reluctant to increase its salary offers to new employees because it realizes it must incur the increased cost not only for the new employees but also for the old ones. In effect the additional cost of the salary rise is recognized by the firm to be much greater if it has to extend the increase to all employees.

The total lag in the response of salaries to a shortage (in the sense of an excess of demand over supply) is then compounded out of the time it takes the firm to recognize the existence of a shortage at the current salary level, the time it takes to decide upon the need for higher salaries and the number of vacancies at such salaries, and either the time it takes employees to recognize the salary alternatives available and to act upon this information or the time it takes the firm to equalize salaries without outside offers.

IV. A model of dynamic shortages and price rises

While there is, strictly speaking, no one market price during the process of adjusting supply to increased demand, a multiplicity of prices being characteristic, we may focus attention on the average price being paid for engineering services. The preceding discussion makes clear that the average price will tend to rise so long as there is an excess of demand over supply, but it will not rise instantaneously to the level that will bring supply and demand into equality (P_2 in Figure 2). Further, the forces that induce price rises will clearly operate more strongly the greater the excess of demand over supply. Hence we find it reasonable to accept the usual view that the rate of increase of price per unit of time is greater the greater the excess of demand over supply. As a corollary, price will cease rising when the price is such that demand equals supply. Recall that demand and supply at any given price are defined as the quantities demanded and supplied after complete rational calculation.

Call the ratio of the rate of price rise to the excess of demand over supply the *reaction speed*. Then the amount of shortage will tend to disappear faster the greater the reaction speed and also the greater the elasticity of supply (or demand).[8]

We have thus far been sketching a way of looking at the response of the market to a single shift of the demand curve; we have suggested that the price will tend to move to the new equilibrium but with a lag. This analysis has been preliminary to our main purpose, which is to consider a situation of *continuing* change in demand (or supply). We will suggest that this has been the case for engineer-scientists in the period beginning about 1950. If, for example, the demand curve is rising steadily, then as the market price approaches the equilibrium price the latter steadily moves away from the former. There will be a chronic shortage in the sense that, as long as the rise in demand occurs, buyers at any given moment will desire more of the commodity at the average price being paid than is being offered, and the amount of the shortage will not approach zero. The price will increase steadily and indefinitely but always remain below the price that would clear the market. This condition will continue as long as demand is increasing.[9]

In the market for engineer-scientists or for any other commodity we expect that a steady upward shift in the demand curve over a period of time will produce a shortage, that is, a situation in which there are unfilled vacancies in positions where salaries are the same as those being currently paid in others of the same type and quality. Such a shortage we will term a *dynamic shortage*. The magnitude of the dynamic shortage depends upon the rate of increase in demand, the reaction speed in the market, and the elasticity of supply and demand. The reaction speed in any particular market depends partly on institutional arrangements, such as the prevalence of long-term contracts, and partly on the rapidity with which information about salaries, vacancies, and availability of personnel becomes generally available throughout the market. In the case of an organized exchange, such as those for securities or certain agricultural products, we should expect the information to be passed on so rapidly that the reaction speed is virtually infinite and dynamic shortages virtually nonexistent.[10] In the following section we will advance evidence for the hypothesis that the engineer-scientist market for the last seven or eight years has shown a dynamic shortage in the sense just defined.

V. Dynamic shortage in the engineer-scientist market

The preceding analysis has been very abstract. Though we have referred to the market for engineer-scientists for the sake of concreteness, actually everything said would be equally applicable to any other market. We want to argue here that because of the character of the engineer-scientist market and the demands made on it over the last few years, the magnitude of the dynamic shortage may well have been sufficient to account for a great proportion of the complaints. It should be made clear that we are not arguing that the market is subject to unusual imperfections. Rather the very way in which the market performs its functions leads to the shortage in this particular period.

A dynamic shortage is a possible explanation of the observed tensions in the engineer-scientist market because (1) there has been a rapid and steady rise in demand, (2) the elasticity of supply is low, especially for short periods, and (3) the reaction speed on the engineer-scientist market may, for several reasons, be expected to be slow. The hypothesis stated in the previous section would imply that under such conditions a dynamic shortage could be expected. And we believe that such a shortage would largely explain such reactions as intensified recruiting and attempts at long-range policy changes observable in the industries affected.

(1) The market on which the tensions seem to be focused is not the engineer-scientist market in general but the market for engineers and scientists for research and development purposes. It is a matter of common knowledge that there has been a very rapid increase in demand in this market. During the year 1951 the total number of research engineers and scientists in industry rose from 74,028 to 91,585, an increase of 17,557 or 23.7 per cent.[11] Such an increase is clearly capable of putting a strain on the smooth functioning of almost any market.

The increase in demand is, in turn, to be explained chiefly by the action of the government in contracting for research and development work by private industry. The increase in the number of research engineers and scientists employed on government contracts during the year 1951 was 15,547,[12] so that virtually the whole increase in employment of research engineers and scientists was due to government demand. The importance of the increase in government demand as the chief explanation of shortages has also been stressed by some observers, such as C. B. Jolliffe, of the Radio Corporation of America.[13] Jolliffe also states that the type of research and development done on military contract is more complicated than the usual industrial work. This would imply that there is some differentiation between the markets for engineer-scientists in military and in other research and development, so that the full force of the increased demand would fall on the former.

(2) The elasticity of the supply of engineer-scientists with respect to price changes may be expected to be small but not zero over short periods of time, owing to the length of time it takes to train new personnel. Over longer periods,

higher salaries will certainly elicit a greater supply, though again because of the importance of noneconomic factors in choosing a career and because of the uncertainty of rewards in the distant future, the responsiveness of supply will be less for commodities such as manufactured goods. Hence while it would be totally incorrect to deny the influence of price on supply, the responsiveness is sufficiently low to add to the possibility of a dynamic shortage.

(3) There are three reasons why it might be expected that the speed of reaction in the engineer-scientist market would be slower than that in the markets for other commodities, such as manufactured goods, or even than in other labor markets. They are the prevalence of long-term contracts, the influence of the heterogeneity of the market in slowing the diffusion of information, and the dominance of a relatively small number of firms in research and development.

Typically, for the engineer-scientist already employed by the government, a university, or a private industrial firm, there will be no instantaneous adjustment in the price he receives even in the face of demand changes, since contracts are not subject to daily renegotiation. Even in the absence of specific contractual elements of this sort, reaction is slowed down because of the greater job security which comes with long service with a particular employer. Professorial tenure is an extreme and institutionalized form of this phenomenon.

We have remarked earlier that the market for engineer-scientists is not a single one. The heterogeneity of the market may interfere with the diffusion of information because an individual engineer-scientist may not know to which market he belongs. He may be aware that an associate is getting a higher salary, which may suggest that he ought to look around for another position. But he may very well wonder whether the associate's higher salary is perhaps due to superior ability or to the fact that somewhat different skills are being rewarded more highly at the moment. Because of his doubts he may be delayed in ascertaining his alternative opportunities. Thus the length of time before he actually does achieve a higher salary, either from another firm or from his own, will be longer, and the reaction speed will be correspondingly less.

Finally, one special characteristic of the market for engineers and scientists in research and development is that the typical buyer is large; in particular a single buyer, the government, directly and indirectly accounts for about half of total demand.[14] Up to a certain point a large firm with large competitors has an incentive to keep salaries down rather than bid engineer-scientists away from competitors. Any one firm in an industry dominated by a few large ones will fear that increasing salaries in order to attract more scientists and engineers may set off competitive bidding that will end up with no substantial change in the distribution of scientists and engineers among firms but a considerably higher salary bill. This is especially likely to be the attitude of firms if the total supply of the engineer-scientists for which they are competing is not likely to change much in response to higher prices.

The desire to avoid competitive bidding sometimes takes the form of "no-raiding" agreements, drawn up among otherwise competing firms in the same industry. Such a situation is alleged to exist to some extent in the electrical equipment and electronics industries, dominated by General Electric, Westing-house, and the Radio Corporation of America, and in aircraft, where a handful of firms account for the bulk of the research and development and of output.

But in no case do the large firms dominate the research and development market to such an extent that "no-raiding" agreements or other devices to limit competition in hiring can be effective indefinitely. If nothing else happens, the competition of smaller firms forces the large firms to match their offers. There is no evidence that attempts by large firms to avoid competitive bidding can in the long run prevent the market price from reaching its equilibrium level. But they certainly can slow down the speed with which prices will rise in response to an excess of demand over supply and so, in accordance with the analysis of the preceding section, increase and prolong the dynamic shortage.

VI. Alternate definitions of a shortage

It is not our purpose here to present an exhaustive review of alternate concepts of shortage. However, it is appropriate to call attention to the discussion of the alleged shortage of scientists and engineers presented in the recently published, important study of the engineer-scientist market by Blank and Stigler.[15]

After considering several definitions of the term "shortage," the authors settle on the following: "A shortage exists when the number of workers available (the supply) increases less rapidly than the number demanded *at the salaries paid in the recent past.* Then salaries will rise, and activities which were once performed by (say) engineers must now be performed by a class of workers less well trained and less expensive."[16] Blank and Stigler rely primarily on a comparison of the earnings of engineers with the earnings of other professional groups and wage earners in order to test the hypothesis of a shortage of engineers. By definition a shortage exists if the relative earnings of engineers have risen.

The authors look at such data as are available going back to 1929, in more detail at the period since 1939, and in still greater detail at the post-World War II period. They say[17]:

> We summarize these pieces of information on engineering earnings as follows. Since 1929, engineering salaries have declined substantially relative to earnings of all wage earners and relative to incomes of independent professional practitioners. Especially since 1939 engineering salaries have declined relative to the wage or salary income of the entire group of professional, technical and kindred workers, as well as to the working population as a whole. After the outbreak of the Korean War there was a minor increase in the relative salaries of engineers (and of other college trained workers), but this was hardly more than a minor cross-current in a tide. Relative to both the working population as a whole and the professions as a separate class, then, the record of earnings would suggest that up to at least 1955 there had been no shortage – in fact an increasingly ample supply – of engineers.

The Blank–Stigler conclusion that there has been no significant shortage must be viewed not only in the light of their definition but also in the context of their major concern with long-run trends, not short-run phenomena. It might be pointed out, however, that it is only in the post-Korean era that there have been any complaints of shortages in this market. Therefore even if one is primarily concerned with the broad sweep of events, it seems proper to suggest that the period of real interest as far as possible shortage goes is that of the last few years, and with this interest in mind one may legitimately view "the minor cross-current" as being significant. The reason that Blank and Stigler adduce for dismissing the evidence of a shortage (by their own definition as tested by their own data) in the years since 1950 is that the relative change in salaries of engineers has been so slight that the shortage could not have been serious. But concluding that the market is a free, competitively working market, they do not consider the suggestion put forward here, namely, that even though there may be no obvious imperfections in the market, there may be a considerable lag in the adjustment of salaries in response to changes in demand.

It is worth noting just what the Blank–Stigler data do show. By their definition a shortage exists whenever the price of a given commodity rises. From 1950 to 1956 they show a rise in average starting salaries for college graduates with an engineering degree of 51.5 per cent.[18] Since increases in starting salaries for college graduates in other fields have been roughly comparable (though none are quite so high for this same period), this merely indicates, by their definition, that there has been a shortage of college graduates in general, i.e., a rise in their relative wages. (The same table shows that, for the period 1950–55, starting engineers' salaries increased by 38.0 per cent compared with an increase for manufacturing wage earnings of 31.8 per cent.)

Blank and Stigler acknowledge that there has been considerable talk about a shortage of engineers and scientists, but having concluded that there has not in fact been a "shortage" of the price-rise type of any significance, they make no attempt to explain all the talk except to point to the use of the word "shortage" as embodying some social criterion. It may be their hypothesis that the recent complaints of "shortage" have been based solely on this use of the term.

As we have recognized elsewhere,[19] there are other possible explanations for at least some of the public concern over the "shortage" of scientists and engineers in recent years. It should be emphasized that many of those who have discussed this problem have been using the term "shortage" in a very different sense from that we have employed here. In particular, careful reading of such statements indicates that the speakers have in effect been saying: There are not as many engineers and scientists as this nation should have in order to do all the things that need doing such as maintaining our rapid rate of technological progress, raising our standard of living, keeping us militarily strong, etc. In other words, they are saying that (in the economic sense) demand for technically skilled manpower *ought* to be greater than it is – it is really a shortage of *demand* for scientists and engineers which concerns them. A somewhat different implicit

definition of shortage which has been applied asserts that since we are not producing scientists and engineers at as fast a rate as the Soviet Union we have a
"shortage." Still another explanation of the complaints may be found if one
recalls the servant shortage of World War II days. In that situation, there is no
evidence that the market did not respond to changed supply and demand conditions; alternative opportunities for employment developed for those who had
previously been servants; the higher wages in these alternate lines of employment
lured many to these occupations so that, *at the price they had been paying for
household help*, many families found they could no longer find such people.
Rather than admit that they could not pay the higher wages necessary to keep
help, many individuals found it more felicitous to speak of a "shortage." There is
reason to think that at least some of the complaints of shortage in the scientist-
engineer market have the same cause. Indeed, in any market when there is a
relatively sudden and dramatic change in either demand or supply which results
in large price increases, we may find complaints of a "shortage" while people
get used to the fact that the price has risen significantly.

VII. Conclusion

It is our view that the model of dynamic shortage developed in this paper is useful in helping to understand the behavior of the market for scientists and engineers in the past several years. The very rapid increase in demand in the market
during this period has led to "shortage" conditions resulting basically from a
failure of the price of such services to adjust upward as rapidly and by as large
an amount as warranted by the increasing demand, given the supply schedule of
such services. This lag in adjustment, so far as we can see, can be attributed to a
significant extent, not to any successful overt attempt to control prices artifi-
cially, but to certain inherent characteristics of supply and demand conditions
and of the operation of the market. While the relative rigidity of supply in the
short run is unpleasant (from the buyers' standpoint), and the price rise required
to restore the market to equilibrium may seem to be very great, it is only by permitting the market to react to the rising demand that, in our view, it can allocate
engineer-scientists in the short run and call forth the desired increase in supply
in the longer run.

Notes

1   This paper is part of an economic analysis of the engineer-scientist market
     conducted for The RAND Corporation, A. A. Alchian, K. J. Arrow, and
     W. M. Capron, RM-2190-RC, "An Economic Analysis of the Market for
     Scientists and Engineers," 6 June 1958.
2   See, for example, Marshall's well-known analysis of the equilibrating pro-
     cess on the corn market, *Principles of Economics*, 8th ed., pp. 332–34.

P. A. Samuelson has shown the fundamental importance of the law of supply and demand in stability analysis; see *Foundations of Economic Analysis*, pp. 263, 269–70.

3   See National Science Foundation, *Scientific Manpower Bulletin No. 6*, August 1, 1955.

4   G. W. Beste, "A Case Study of the Shortage of Scientists and Engineers in the Chemical Industry," presented at the second meeting of the National Committee for the Development of Scientists and Engineers, June 21, 1956.

5   Actually, this deficiency turns out to be largely the product of the two years, 1955 and 1956. It is typical of the lack of historical perspective in the engineer-scientist shortage discussion that such short-run phenomena are made the basis for discussion of long-run policies.

6   David M. Blank and George J. Stigler, *The Demand and Supply of Scientific Personnel* (New York: National Bureau of Economic Research, 1957), pp. 29–30.

7   We might note that in some markets, such as the organized exchanges for securities or commodities, information is available very quickly, indeed almost instantaneously, but this is clearly accomplished only because it has been found worthwhile for those who buy and sell on these markets to pay the costs of the operation of such exchanges. No such exchange exists for scientists and engineers, and one can understand why: the product is not homogeneous, and each unit of supply is controlled by a different owner (i.e., the individual scientist or engineer himself).

8   Let p be the (average) price, k the reaction speed, D demand, S supply, and t time. The movement of the market over time is determined, in the above model, by the following relations (using linear approximations for the demand and supply functions):

(1) $dp/dt = k(D - S)$,

(2) $D = -ap + c$,

(3) $S = bp + d$.

Equation (1) expresses the assumption in the text about the relation between price rises and the difference between supply and demand; equations (2) and (3) are simple assumptions about the nature of the demand and supply functions, as represented graphically in Figures 1 and 2.

Let X represent the shortage, i.e., $X = D - S$. From (2) and (3),

(4) $X = -(a + b) p + (c - d)$.

Differentiate (4) with respect to time; then $dX/dt = -(a + b) (dp/dt)$. If we then substitute from (1) and replace $D - S$ by X, we have

(5) $dX/dt = -k(a + b) X$.

Thus for any given shortage X, the speed of convergence is greater the greater $k(a + b)$. In particular, other things being equal, the smaller the value of b (which is closely related to the elasticity of supply), the slower will be the convergence of the shortage X to zero.

9   The steady upward shift in demand may be represented by adding a trend
     term to the demand as given by (2) in note 8,

(6) $D = -ap + c + et$,

where t represents time and e the rate of increase of demand with time for
any given price. Let X be the amount of shortage, i.e., $D - S$. From (3) and
(6),

(7) $X = -(a + b)p + (c - d) + et$.

Differentiate all the terms of (7) with respect to time.

(8) $dX/dt = -(a + b)(dp/dt) + e$.

In view of the definition of X, (1) can be written

(9) $dp/dt = kX$.

Substitute from (9) for dp/dt into (8):

(10) $dX/dt = -(a + b)kX + e$.

Assume that at the beginning, there is no shortage, so that $S = D$, or $X = 0$.
Then from (10) we see that $dX/dt > 0$, so that the shortage X starts increasing and must continue to increase (since if dX/dt ever reached zero, it
would remain at zero thereafter). It is also easy to see that

(11) $\lim_{t \to \infty} X(t) = e/(a + b)k$,

so that the shortages tend to a limit which is greater the greater the rate of
increase of demand and the slower the speed of adjustment would have
been with an unshifting demand schedule.
     Let p' be the rate of increase of prices, i.e., dp/dt. Differentiate (9) with
respect to time, and then substitute from (8):

(12) $dp'/dt = k\,dX/dt = -k(a + b)p' + ke$.

By the same reasoning as with (10), p' must be increasing over time and
approaching a limit. Since it is zero to begin with, it follows that p' must
be positive for all t, so that, by the definition of p', the price p must be
increasing steadily.
     Let p^* be the price at any time which would clear the market, that is,
which would make $X = 0$. In view of (7), p^* satisfies the equation,

(13) $0 = -(a + b)p^* + (c - d) + et$.

Multiply through in (13) by k:

(14) $0 = -k(a + b)p^* + k(c - d) + ket$.

Let q be the excess of the market-clearing price over the actual price, i.e.,
$q = p^* - p$. Substitute from (7) into (9):

(15) $p' = -k(a + b)p + k(c - d) + ket$.

Subtract (14) from (15) and use the definition of q:

(16) $p' = k(a + b)q$.

Since p' is positive and increases from zero to a limit, the same must be true of q. Thus the actual price will always remain below the market-clearing price and indeed the gap will actually widen with time, but the two time paths will approach parallelism.

The discussion to this point has dealt with a single market. In the real world there are a number of related markets. Firms in different industries, in different localities, etc., may in any given case compete for the services of engineer-scientists of certain specified skills. Therefore the firms in any one industry will find that the supply available to them depends not only on their own salary offers but on the salary levels in all industries buying similar skills. In short, the demand for engineer-scientists comes from a whole series of interrelated markets. This situation cannot be represented graphically, but the general conclusions just drawn remain valid. See K. J. Arrow, "Price-Quantity Adjustments in Multiple Markets with Rising Demands," this volume, III.5, pp. 367–379.

10   Thus, in Marshall's example of the corn market (*op. cit.*) the adjustment process took a day. In the market for scientists and engineers the "day" will be much longer – say several weeks or even months.

11   See U.S. Department of Labor, Bureau of Labor Statistics, *Scientific Research and Development in American Industry: A Study of Manpower and Costs*, Bulletin No. 1148, 1953, Tables C-5 (p. 62) and C-11 (p. 68). This source gives the January 1952 employment and the percentage increase; the other figures were calculated from these two.

12   *Ibid.*, Table C-13 (p. 70), shows that the number employed on government contracts in January 1952 was 45,425 and that this figure was an increase of 52 per cent over that of January 1951. The figure in the text is calculated from these two.

13   C. B. Jolliffe, "Electronics: A Case Study of the Shortage of Scientists and Engineers," delivered to the President's Committee for the Development of Scientists and Engineers, 21 June 1956. In discussing his own company, Jolliffe says, "We could use one thousand more right now without any question. Where could we use them? Mainly on military contracts because it is here – rather than in consumer and industrial electronics – that the pinch is tightest." (p. 6)

14   Bureau of Labor Statistics Bulletin No. 1148, *op. cit.*, presents some relevant figures for 1951. In that year, seven companies spent 26 per cent of the total expenditures on research and development in industry (p. 21), and the government financed 46.8 per cent of all such expenditures (Table 4) in addition to research performed directly by the government.

15   Blank and Stigler, *op. cit.*, p. 9; Chap. II, p. 2.

16   *Ibid.*, p. 24. Italics by Blank and Stigler.

17   *Ibid.*, pp. 28–29.

18   *Ibid.*, Table 14, p. 28.

19   Alchian, Arrow, Capron, *op. cit.*

Price-quantity adjustments in multiple markets with rising demands[1]

KENNETH J. ARROW

1. Introduction

In the classical account of the law of supply and demand, it is assumed that the price on any market moves upward if demand exceeds supply and downward in the opposite case. The discrepancy between supply and demand is assumed to have a real, if transitory, significance. Thus a sudden upward shift in the demand curve gives rise to an excess demand or "shortage," which in turn causes a rise in price that eventually wipes it out.[2] From the point of view of market behavior, a shortage manifests itself as unfilled orders. In the case of a labor market, this means unfilled vacancies; that is, firms are willing to hire more workers than they can find at the wage they are currently paying.

In the previous study by W. M. Capron and myself [3] , it has been suggested that an extension of this analysis explains some aspects of the observed shortage of engineers and scientists in the United States over the greater part of the postwar period. If the demand curve for a commodity, in this case the services of engineers and scientists, is rising over time, in this case primarily because of increasing government demand, the equilibrating effects of the rising price can be offset by the rise in the demand curve, which raises the equilibrium price as fast as the market price moves toward it. A shortage, in the sense of an excess of demand over supply, may therefore persist for an extended period of time, during which the market price is steady rising. The observed phenomenon of persistent complaints about unfilled vacancies is therefore not incompatible with the usual assumptions about the working of the market.

In the present paper, account is taken of the fact that there is not one market for engineers and scientists but many interrelated markets; that there are many different types of engineers (chemical, mechanical, civil, etc.) and scientists (mathematicians, physicists, etc.); and that within each type there are many grades of ability and specialty. To a considerable extent, these different types and grades are substitutes for each other on either the demand side or the supply side or both. Thus, many engineers can perform the functions of mathematicians or physicists, or, if theoretical mathematicians are expensive, they can to a certain extent be replaced by increased computing, which in turn leads to demands for electrical engineers as well as for less well-qualified mathematicians.

The model, which will be formulated abstractly, then consists of a set of markets. On each one the demand is a function of all prices; a rise in the price on any market decreases the demand in that market but increases the demand in some or all other markets, since all the commodities (types of services) are substitutes. Similarly, the supply on each market is, in general, a function of all prices; a rise in any one price increases supply on that market but decreases it (or at least does not increase it) on all other markets, since it draws the supply to that market if there is any possibility of transfer. It is assumed that the price on each market obeys the law of supply and demand.[3] In the absence of disturbances, the prices will eventually approach equilibrium, with equality of supply and demand on all markets.

This paper studies the effect of steady upward shifts in some or all demand functions on the adjustment path of all these prices and quantities. It is shown that the shortage on each market increases to a limiting value, while prices rise with a rate of increase that itself increases to a limiting value depending only on supply and demand conditions, independent of the speed of adjustment.

When prices are changing, it is natural to suppose that supply and demand may be influenced by expectations of future prices, as well as by current prices. If the price of certain types of engineers is expected to be high in the future, the entrepreneur will seek in the present to change to production processes that economize on the use of the relatively expensive services. It is shown that, under a plausible and empirically supported assumption about the formulation of expectations, the qualitative behavior described in the previous paragraph continues to hold.

2. Interrelated markets in the absence of trends

We suppose there are n services or commodities that can be supplied from the same or related sources and that are demanded by the same or related industries. Let $p_i (i = 1, \ldots, n)$ be the price of the service or commodity on the ith market, and let S_i be the supply forthcoming at any moment of time. The supply of any one commodity will depend not only on its price but also on the prices of all other commodities, since higher prices on other markets will draw supplies away from the given market. We can thus write

(1) $S_i = S_i(p_1, \ldots, p_n)$,   with $\partial S_i / \partial p_i > 0, \partial S_i / \partial p_j \leq 0$ for $i \neq j$.

In a linear approximation, we can write

(2) $S_i = \sum_{j=1}^{n} a_{ij} p_j + c_i$ $(i = 1, \ldots, n)$,

with

(3) $a_{ii} > 0$, $a_{ij} \leq 0$ for $i \neq j$.

Similarly, the demands for the different commodities may be interrelated: an increase in the price of one commodity will cause demand to shift from it to other commodities that are substitutes for it.

(4) $D_i = D_i(p_i, \ldots, p_n)$,   with $\partial D_i / \partial p_i < 0, \partial D_i / \partial p_j \geq 0$ for $i \neq j$.

Because of the weak inequalities in the last clause, the case where all demands are independent, that is, where D_i depends only on p_i, is included as a special case. As a linear approximation to (4), we have

(5) $\quad D_i = \Sigma_{j=1}^n b_{ij} p_j + d_i,$ $\quad$ with $b_{ii} < 0, b_{ij} \geq 0$ for $i \neq j.$

On each market, there will usually be a "shortage," i.e., the difference between demand and supply, which we will denote by X_i:

(6) $\quad X_i = D_i - S_i.$

(Of course, X_i might be negative, in which case there is a "surplus.")

We assume that on each market the price moves as directed by the shortage X_i, rising if the shortage X_i is positive, decreasing if negative, and remaining stationary if zero. To a linear approximation,

(7) $\quad dp_i/dt = k_i X_i,$ $\quad$ with $k_i > 0$ $\quad (i = 1, \ldots, n).$

Substitute from (2) and (5) into (6):

(8) $\quad X_i = \Sigma_{j=1}^n (b_{ij} - a_{ij}) p_j + (d_i - c_i)$ $\quad (i = 1, \ldots, n).$

For convenience, let

(9) $\quad m_{ij} = b_{ij} - a_{ij},$ $\quad n_i = d_i - c_i.$

Then (8) can be written

(10) $\quad X_i = \Sigma_{j=1}^n m_{ij} p_j + n_i$ $\quad (i = 1, \ldots, n).$

From (9), (3), and (5) we see that

(11) $\quad m_{ii} < 0,$ $\quad m_{ij} \geq 0$ $\quad$ for $i \neq j.$

The equilibrium situation is one of equality of supply and demand on all markets; that is, $X_i = 0$ for all i. Then (10) yields a system of linear equations that can be solved for the equilibrium price. The approach to equilibrium is described by equations (7) and (10). These combine to yield

(12) $\quad dp_i/dt = k_i \Sigma_{j=1}^n m_{ij} p_j + k_i n_i$ $\quad (i = 1, \ldots, n).$

Equation (12) constitutes a system of simultaneous differential equations whose solution yields the time paths for each price. We will assume that the system is *stable*, that is, that each price approaches its equilibrium value.[4]

Let us rewrite the above in vector notation. Let x be the vector with components X_i, p the vector with components p_i, K the matrix with diagonal elements k_i and off-diagonal elements 0, M the matrix with elements m_{ij}, and n the vector with components n_i. Then (7), (10), and (12) can be written

(13) $\quad dp/dt = Kx,$

(14) $\quad x = Mp + n,$

(15) $\quad dp/dt = KMp + Kn.$

We have assumed that the system (15) is stable. The stability depends only on the matrix of coefficients of p, so that we will also say that KM is a *stable matrix*, which we will define as one whose characteristic roots all have negative real parts (this is slightly stronger than the condition that the system of differential equations be stable). Also, a matrix with non-negative off-diagonal elements will be termed a *Metzler* matrix [12]. Since the elements of KM are $k_i m_{ij}$, it follows from (7) and (11) that KM is also a Metzler matrix.

(16) KM is a stable Metzler matrix.

3. Some mathematical properties of Metzler matrices

As a preliminary to the subsequent analysis, we will need some mathematical properties of Metzler matrices.

   Theorem.   If A is a Metzler matrix, $b \geq 0, y(0) \geq 0$, and $dy/dt = Ay + b$, then $y(t) \geq 0$ for all t.

   Proof.   Suppose the set of times t such that $t \geq 0$ and $y_j(t) < 0$ for some j is non-null. Let t_0 be the greatest lower bound of such t-values. If $t_0 > 0$, then by definition $y(t) \geq 0$ for $t < t_0$, so that, by continuity,

(17) $y(t_0) \geq 0$.

If $t_0 = 0$, then (17) holds by hypothesis.

   First suppose that $b > 0$ (strictly positive in all components). Let S be the set of indices j such that $y_j(t_0) = 0$, $\widetilde{S}$ the complementary set on which $y_j(t_0) > 0$. By defintion of t_0, S is non-null. From the definitions we can write

(18) $y_S(t_0) = 0$, $y_{\widetilde{S}}(t_0) > 0$,

where the subscript S means the sub-vector composed of components with indices in S.

   Let B be the principal minor of A with rows and columns in S, C the minor with rows in S and columns in $\widetilde{S}$. Then, by hypothesis,

(19) $\dot{y}_S(t_0) = By_S(t_0) + Cy_{\widetilde{S}}(t_0) + b_S$,

where the dot denotes differentiation with respect to time. From the first part of (18), $By_S(t_0) = 0$. Since A is a Metzler matrix, all the elements of C are non-negative; from the second part of (19), $Cy_{\widetilde{S}}(t_0) \geq 0$. Finally, $b_S > 0$, since $b > 0$.

(20) $\dot{y}_S(t_0) > 0$.

From (18) and (20),

(21) $y(t) > 0$ for $t_0 < t < t_0 + \epsilon$,

for some $\epsilon > 0$, which contradicts the definition of t_0.

   The theorem has therefore been shown to hold if $b > 0$. Since the solution is a continuous function of the parameters, the theorem remains true for $b \geq 0$ by continuity.[5]

Corollary. If A is a stable Metzler matrix, then $-A^{-1}$ is non-negative.[6]

Proof. Let b be any non-negative vector and $y(t)$ a solution of the differential equation $dy/dt = Ay + b$, with $y(0) \geqq 0$. Since A is stable, $y(t)$ converges to a limit, which is the value of y that makes the right-hand side zero.

(22) $\lim_{t \to \infty} y(t) = -A^{-1}b.$

Since $y(t) \geqq 0$ by the theorem, $-A^{-1}b \geqq 0$. Since b was any non-negative vector, the corollary follows.

We also restate two lemmas that have been proved in earlier papers in slightly different forms.

Lemma 1. If M is a Metzler matrix and K a diagonal matrix with positive elements on the diagonal, then M is stable if and only if KM is stable and also if and only if MK is stable.

Proof. That the stability of M implies that of KM was remarked in Enthoven and Arrow [8, p. 291]. Since K^{-1} is also a diagonal matrix with positive elements on the diagonal, KM is a Metzler matrix, and $M = K^{-1}(KM)$, it follows that the stability of KM implies that of M. Since $MK = K^{-1}(KM)K$, the characteristic roots of MK and KM are the same, so that the stability of either implies the stability of the other.

Lemma 2. If M is a Metzler matrix, M' is a non-negative matrix, and $M + M'$ is stable, then the matrix

$$M'' = \begin{pmatrix} M & M' \\ I & -I \end{pmatrix}$$

is a stable Metzler matrix.

This is a special case of the theorem in [5, p. 321].

4. The adjustment process with steadily increasing demands

We shall now examine the process of adjustment described in Sections 1 and 2 when the demand is shifting steadily upward in time on some or all of the inter-related markets. For simplicity, we assume that the supply curve is not changing; however, the following analysis would remain valid if the supply were also shifting upward in time but not more rapidly than the demand. We shall also assume that, to begin with, supply and demand are equal.

We shall then continue to assume that (2) holds but that (5) becomes

(23) $D_i = \sum_{j=1}^{n} b_{ij} p_j + d_i + e_i t$, with $b_{ii} < 0$, $b_{ij} \geqq 0$ for $i \neq j$, and $e_i \geqq 0$.

The definition of the shortage X_i remains as before, and the adjustment of prices continues to be described by (7). Then the discussion following (7) remains valid with slight modification. A term $e_i t$ is added on the right side of (8) and, equivalently, of (10). Let e be the vector whose components are e_i. Then in vector notation (13) remains valid, while (14) becomes

(24) $x = Mp + n + et$,   where $e \geq 0$.

M still satisfies (11). Further, we shall assume that the system defined by (13) and (24) would be stable in the absence of trends, i.e., if $e = 0$, so that (16) remains valid.

From Lemma 1,

(25) MK is a stable Metzler matrix.

Differentiating (24) with respect to time, we obtain

(26) $\dot{x} = M\dot{p} + e$,

where, it will be recalled, dots denote differentiation with respect to time. Substituting for $\dot{p}$ from (13) into (26), we obtain

(27) $\dot{x} = MKx + e$.

From (25) we see that the solution $x(t)$ of the differential equation (27) converges to a limit, which must be such that $\dot{x} = 0$.

(28) $\lim_{t \to \infty} x(t) = -K^{-1}M^{-1}e$.

The assumption that supply and demand are equal at the beginning can be expressed by saying that

(29) $x(0) = 0$,

where $t = 0$ is taken as the beginning of the process. Let $t = 0$ in (27); from (29) and (24).

(30) $\dot{x}(0) = e \geq 0$.

Differentiating (27) with respect to time, we obtain

(31) $d\dot{x}/dt = MK\dot{x}$.

We can apply the theorem with y replaced by $\dot{x}$, b by 0, and A by MK; the hypotheses are satisfied, according to (25), (30), and (31), so that

(32) $\dot{x}(t) \geq 0$ for $t \geq 0$.

Thus,

   Proposition 1.   The shortage on each market increases from the initial value of 0 toward the asymptotic limit given by (28).

   In particular,

(33) $x(t) \geq 0$ for $t \geq 0$.

From (13) and (33),

(34) $\quad \dot{p}(t) \geqq 0 \qquad$ for $t \geqq 0$,

so that the price on each market is increasing over time. Differentiating (13) with respect to time, we obtain

(35) $\quad d\dot{p}/dt = K\dot{x}$.

Substituting for $\dot{x}$ from (26), we obtain

(36) $\quad d\dot{p}/dt = KM\dot{p} + Ke$.

From (16) and (36) it follows that $\dot{p}$ converges to a limit as t approaches infinity:

(37) $\quad \lim_{t \to \infty} \dot{p}(t) = -(KM)^{-1} Ke = -M^{-1} e$.

From (34) and (37) we arrive at the following proposition:

Proposition 2. Prices rise on all markets, and the increase approaches a constant rate that will usually be positive on all markets, even those that do not themselves have an upward shift in demand; the limiting rate of price increase depends only on supply and demand conditions and is independent of the speeds of adjustment.

At any time t, let p^* be the vector of prices that would clear the market, i.e., make the shortage zero. From (24),

(38) $\quad 0 = Mp^* + n + et$.

Multiplying through in (38) by K yields

(39) $\quad 0 = KMp^* + Kn + Ket$.

Substituting from (24) into (13), we obtain

(40) $\quad \dot{p} = KMp + Kn + Ket$.

Finally, let q be the difference between the market-clearing price p^* and the actual price p, i.e., $p^* \stackrel{?}{-} p$. Subtracting (40) from (39), we obtain

(41) $\quad -\dot{p} = KMq$,

or

(42) $\quad q = -(KM)^{-1}\dot{p}$.

From (16) and the Corollary, $-(KM)^{-1}$ is a non-negative matrix. Then from (34), we obtain

(43) $\quad q(t) \geqq 0 \qquad$ for all $t \geqq 0$,

while from (42) and (37),

(44) $\quad \lim_{t \to \infty} q(t) = (KM)^{-1} M^{-1} e = M^{-1} K^{-1} M^{-1} e$.

Thus,

Proposition 3.   The actual price is always below the price that would clear the market, the difference approaching a limit that decreases as the speeds of reaction on the different markets increase.

It can also be shown that the difference between the actual and the market-clearing price widens as time goes on.

5. The effect of expectations on the adjustment process

If prices are changing, it is reasonable to suppose that demand and supply decisions will depend on expectations of future prices as well as on current prices. Future and current usage of the services of engineers and scientists are to a certain extent substitutes. Hence, it is not unreasonable to assume that current excess demand is a function of both current and expected prices, and that an increase in any expected price will increase (or at least not decrease) the current excess demands for all services. Let p' be the vector of expected prices; then we generalize (24) to

(45) $x = Mp + M'p' + n + et.$

From the previous remarks, we assume that

(46) M is a Metzler matrix, M' a non-negative matrix.

We continue to assume that price movements are governed by the law of supply and demand (13). To complete the system, it is necessary to make some assumption about the formation of expectations.

The simplest assumption is that of *static expectations*; at each instant of time, expected future price equals current price:

(47) $p' = p.$

In this case, (45) collapses into

(48) $x = (M + M')p + n + et.$

The system is therefore the same as that analyzed in the previous section, with M replaced by $M + M'$, which is a Metzler matrix, from (46). Because of (47), the market acts as if the price ratio between any given current service and the same service in the future were constant (equal to 1); hence, each such pair can be treated as a composite commodity. We shall assume then that the resulting system is stable in the absence of trend,[7] so that, by analogy with (25),

(49) $(M + M')K$ is a stable Metzler matrix.

The reasoning of the previous section holds, and we can thus read the following conclusion:

Proposition 4.   Propositions 1, 2, and 3 remain valid under the assumption of static expectations.

We shall now study the adjustment process under a more general assumption concerning the formation of expectations. In recent empirical studies by Cagan [6], Friedman [9, pp. 143–52], and Nerlove [14], it has been found that many observed phenomena can be explained by the assumption of *adaptive expectations* (see Arrow and Nerlove [5, sec. 1]). By this is meant that at each instant of time the economic agent compares the actual price (income, in Friedman's work) with his previous expectation of it and then forms a new expectation by revising his previous one in the direction of the actual price. Thus the rate of change of the expected price will have the same sign as the difference between actual and expected price; in a linear approximation, we may assume proportionality between the two. In symbols,

$$dp_i'/dt = k_i'(p_i - p_i'),$$

or, in matrix notation,

$$(50) \quad dp'/dt = K'(p - p'),$$

where

(51) K' is a diagonal matrix with positive elements on the diagonal.

This hypothesis also appears to be compatible with some results in the theory of learning.

In the present context of steadily rising demands, there is one unsatisfactory feature about (50). By integration, it implies that the expected price at any time is a weighted average of all past prices (see, for example, [5, p. 319] or [14, pp. 54–55].). If prices have been rising steadily, this means that expected price at any time is below the present price, which does not seem reasonable if prices have in fact been rising. We shall therefore follow Friedman [9, p. 144] in generalizing the hypothesis to admit that prices may be expected to rise even if current price equals expected price. In symbols, the hypothesis of *adaptive-trend expectations* will be written

$$(52) \quad dp'/dt = K'(p - p') + n^0,$$

where K' still satisfies (51).[8]

The adjustment process is now decribed by equations (13), (45), and (52). In addition to current prices, p, and excess demands, x, the process now involves a new set of variables, expected prices, p'.

By a suitable notation, we shall show that the adjustment process with adaptive-trend expectations is mathematically isomorphic to the adjustment process without expectations, so that the results of Section 4 can be used. First, define $n' = (K')^{-1}n^0$. From (51) and (52),

$$dp'/dt = K'(p - p' + n').$$

Let

(53) $x' = p - p' + n';$

then

(54) $dp'/dt = K'x'.$

Now define the following vectors of length $2n$ and square matrices of order $2n$:

(55) $p'' = \begin{pmatrix} p \\ p' \end{pmatrix}, \quad x'' = \begin{pmatrix} x \\ x' \end{pmatrix}, \quad M'' = \begin{pmatrix} M & M' \\ I & -I \end{pmatrix},$

$$K'' = \begin{pmatrix} K & 0 \\ 0 & K' \end{pmatrix}, \quad n'' = \begin{pmatrix} n \\ n' \end{pmatrix}, \quad e'' = \begin{pmatrix} e \\ 0 \end{pmatrix}.$$

Then, from (45), (53), and (55),

(56) $x'' = M''p'' + n'' + e''t,$

while from (13), (54), and (55),

(57) $dp''/dt = K''x''.$

Equations (56) and (57) have exactly the same form as (13) and (24), the system analyzed in Section 4. From (24) and (55),

(58) $e'' \geq 0.$

From (49) and Lemma 1, $M + M'$ is a stable Metzler matrix. By Lemma 2, M'' is a stable Metzler matrix. Also, K'' is obviously a diagonal matrix with positive diagonal elements, so that, by Lemma 1,

(59) $M''K''$ is a stable Metzler matrix.

Hence, all the assumptions of Section 4 are satisfied, and the propositions proved there remain valid, with x and p replaced by x'' and p'', respectively.

The analog of Proposition 1 holds for each component of x''; in particular, it holds for the first n components, which form the vector x of shortages. Therefore,

Proposition 5.   Under adaptive-trend expectations, the shortage on each market increases from the initial value of 0 toward an asymptotic limit.

Similarly, Proposition 2 holds for all components of p'', including in particular the elements of p. The analog of (37) is

(60) $\lim_{t \to \infty} \dot{p}''(t) = -(M'')^{-1}e'',$

which is independent not only of K'' but also of n'', and, in particular, of n'.

Proposition 6. Under adaptive-trend expectations, prices rise on all markets, and the increase approaches a constant rate that will usually be positive on all markets, even those that do not themselves have an upward shift in demand; the limiting rate of price rise depends only on supply and demand conditions and is independent of the speeds of adjustment and of the parameters in the expectation relation.

Since p'' includes the components of p' as well as of p, Proposition 6 is equally valid for expected prices. Thus dp'/dt approaches a limit; from (52), this implies that $p - p'$ approaches a limit, and therefore the limiting rate of increase of p must be the same as that of p'.

Proposition 7. Under adaptive-trend expectation, each expected price rises, and the increase approaches the same limit as that of the actual price.

An analog of Proposition 3 can be stated, but the generalization of market-clearing prices is rather complicated in meaning.

6. Non-linear trends

When this paper was read at the symposium, David G. Kendall asked to what extent the results were dependent on the linearity of the trend. We may first observe that the proof of the theorem remains valid if the constant b is replaced by any non-negative function $b(t)$.

Theorem*. If A is a Metzler matrix, $b(t) \geqq 0$, $y(0) \geqq 0$, and $dy/dt = Ay + b(t)$, then $y(t) \geqq 0$ for all t.

Let us now suppose that the upward trend in demand is a non-linear function of time. Then (24) becomes

(61) $\quad x = Mp + n + e(t)$, where $e'(t) \geqq 0$.

Then (27) can be written

(62) $\quad \dot{x} = MKx + e'(t)$.

We may apply this last theorem directly to (62) and derive

Proposition 8. For any (not necessarily linear) upward trend, there will be excess demands and therefore rising prices on all markets.

More specific results depend upon more specific assumptions. The interesting case raised by Kendall was that of an increase toward an asymptote: for example, an increase in government spending toward a higher constant level. Asymptotically, of course, excess demands will approach zero and prices will approach the equilibrium levels corresponding to the asymptotic level of the shift function. From Proposition 8, there will be excess demands and rising prices on all markets during the adjustment process.

Notes

1   This paper is part of an economic analysis of the engineer-scientist market conducted for the RAND Corporation in collaboration with A. Alchian and W. Capron [1]. An earlier version was circulated as a RAND paper, P-1364-RC, 7 May 1958. I am indebted to G. Debreu for comments.

2   See, e.g., Marshall's account of the path to equilibrium on a corn market [11, pp. 332–34]. For the interpretation of the law of supply and demand in interrelated markets, see Samuelson [15, pp. 270–73].

3   The individual behavior underlying the law of supply and demand is itself in need of further explanation. A discussion in terms of the engineer-scientist market is presented by Arrow and Capron [3, pp. 356–57]; for a somewhat different, though not incompatible, analysis, see [2].

4   Under the assumptions stated, it can be shown that stability follows from the usual competitive assumptions if we take all commodities other than the services here studied as a composite numéraire and if there is gross substitutability between the services and all other commodities; see Hahn [10], Negishi [13], or Arrow and Hurwicz [4, Theorem 9]. Under this interpretation, the prices in the text are to be taken as relative to the general price level.

5   I am indebted to my colleague S. Karlin for the perturbation argument of this paragraph.

6   This well-known proposition is, for example, equivalent to Theorem III* in [7, p. 601].

7   See note 4 and the discussion in Arrow and Nerlove [5, sec. 3].

8   Equation (52) is equivalent to asserting that there is an expected linear trend in prices and that the hypothesis of adaptive expectations is applied to deviations from that trend. Friedman's hypothesis about income expectations is the same, except that his expected trend is exponential rather than linear.

References

[1]   Alchian, A. A., K. J. Arrow, and W. M. Capron, "An Economic Analysis of the Market for Scientists and Engineers," Santa Monica, Calif.: The RAND Corporation, RM-2190-RC, 6 June 1958.

[2]   Arrow, K. J., "Toward a Theory of Price Adjustment," this volume, III.6, pp. 380–390.

[3]   Arrow, K. J. and W. M. Capron, "Dynamic Shortages and Price Rises: The Engineer-Scientist Case," this volume, III.5, pp. 352–366.

[4]   Arrow, K. J. and L. Hurwicz, "On the Stability of Competitive Equilibrium, I," this volume, III.1, pp. 199–228.

[5]   Arrow, K. J. and M. Nerlove, "A Note on Expectations and Stability," this volume, III.4, pp. 317–325.

[6]   Cagan, P., "The Monetary Dynamics of Hyper-Inflation," in M. Fried-
        man, ed., *Studies in the Quantity Theory of Money*, Chicago: University
        of Chicago Press, 1956, pp. 25–117.

[7]   Debreu, G. and I. N. Herstein, "Nonnegative Square Matrices," *Econo-
        metrica*, Vol. 21 (1953), 597–607.

[8]   Enthoven, A. and K. J. Arrow, "A Theorem on Expectations and the
        Stability of Equilibrium," this volume, III.4, pp. 311–317.

[9]   Friedman, M., *A Theory of the Consumption Function*, Princeton, N.J.:
        Princeton University Press, 1957.

[10]   Hahn, F., "Gross Substitutes and the Dynamic Stability of General Equi-
        librium," *Econometrica*, Vol. 26 (1958), 169–70.

[11]   Marshall, A., *Principles of Economics*, 8th ed., New York: Macmillan,
        1948.

[12]   Metzler, L., "Stability of Multiple Markets: the Hicks Conditions," *Econ-
        ometrica*, Vol. 13 (1945), 277–92.

[13]   Negishi, T., "A Note on the Stability of an Economy Where All Goods
        Are Gross Substitutes," *Econometrica*, Vol. 26 (1958), 445–47.

[14]   Nerlove, M., *The Dynamics of Supply: Estimation of Farmers' Responses
        to Price*, Baltimore, Md.: Johns Hopkins University Press, 1958.

[15]   Samuelson, P. A., *Foundations of Economic Analysis*, Cambridge, Mass.:
        Harvard University Press, 1947.

6
FOUNDATIONS OF PRICE DYNAMICS

Toward a theory of price adjustment

KENNETH J. ARROW

The role of price adjustment equations in economic theory

In this essay, it is argued that there exists a logical gap in the usual formulations of the theory of the perfectly competitive economy, namely, that there is no place for a rational decision with respect to prices as there is with respect to quantities. A suggestion is made for filling this gap. The proposal implies that perfect competition can really prevail only at equilibrium. It is hoped that the line of development proposed will lead to a better understanding of the behavior of the economy in disequilibrium conditions.

In the traditional development of economic theory, the usual starting point is the construction for each individual (firm or household) of a pattern of reactions to events outside it (examples of elements of a reaction pattern: supply and demand curves, propensity to consume, liquidity preference, interindustrial movements of capital and labor in response to differential profit and wage rates). This point of view is explicit in the neoclassicists (Cournot, Jevons, Menger, and successors) and strongly implicit in the classicists (from Smith through Cairnes) in their discussion of the motivations of capitalists, workers, and landlords which lead to establishment of the equilibrium price levels for commodities, labor, and the use of land. The basic logic of Marx's system brings it, I believe, into the same category, although some writers have referred to his theories as being "class" economics rather than "individual" economics.[1] Although the dialectical discussion of value in the opening sections of Volume I of *Capital*[2] lends some credence to this view, it is already clear in Marx's discussion of relative surplus value (Volume I, Part IV)[3] that the introduction of new production processes is based on the profit-maximizing behavior of the individual entrepreneur; and the role of the individual behavior reaction is basic in Marx's discussion of the equalization of profit rates in different industries in Volume III (especially Chapter X). In the opinion of most contemporary Marxist economists, such as Dobb [3] and Sweezy [4] and of sympathetic critics such as Lange [5],[4] the value theory of Volume I is to be regarded only as a first approximation to that of Volume III, so that the latter must be regarded as the basic part of Marx's price theory.[5]

There remains one school which might be interpreted as objecting to the development of economics from the viewpoint of individual reaction patterns.

These are the institutionalists, such as Veblen [8], who attacked the behavior patterns hypothesized by contemporary economists for stressing the passive reacting character of individual behavior; but this argument seems partly a terminological question and partly an attack on the limited, excessively hedonistic expositions of the marginal utility theory current about 1900. Elsewhere both Veblen [9] and Mitchell [10] have emphasized the importance for the course of economic activity of the behavior of individuals, especially profit-making by firms.

In this individualistic framework, every relevant variable, except those classified as exogenous for the whole economic system, is the result of a decision on the part of some one individual unit of the economy. This paper considers the theoretical analysis of the decisions as to prices.

The standard development of the theory of behavior under competitive conditions has made both sides of any market take prices as given by some outside agency. Thus, for a single market,

(1) $\quad D = f(p), \quad S = g(p)$

where D is the demand for the commodity, S its supply, and p its price. The functions $f(p)$ and $g(p)$ represent the behavior of consumers and producers, respectively. But relation (1) constitutes only two equations in the three unknowns D, S, and p.

The theoretical structure is usually completed by adding the condition of equality of supply and demand,

(2) $\quad S = D.$

What is the rationale of relation (2)? In the usual treatise on economics, a great deal of attention is paid to the derivation of the functions entering into relation (1), but equation (2) is usually taken pretty much for granted. If we look further into the reasoning given by such writers as do not regard equation (2) as completely self-evident, it is clear that it is regarded as the limit of a trial-and-error process describable by an equation of the general type

(3) $\quad dp/dt = h(S - D)$

where

(4) $\quad h' < 0, \quad h(0) = 0.$

(Here and below, primes denote differentiation, so that h' is the rate of change of the function h with respect to an increase in the excess supply.)

Relation (3) is, of course, the well-known "Law of Supply and Demand." It asserts that price rises when demand exceeds supply and falls in the contrary case. Equations (1) and (3) together define a dynamic process in which supply, demand, and price vary in a prescribed way over time. If the process is stable, these three magnitudes approach limits. At the limiting values, there can be no pressure for any of the variables to change. In view of equations (3) and (4), price will remain stationary if and only if equation (2) holds; but if price remains stationary, demand and supply will do so also, by relation (1). (See Samuelson [11] and Arrow and Hurwicz [12].)

The Law of Supply and Demand may be a useful basis for interpreting some empirical phenomena, particularly the course of prices in markets subject to rapid changes in supply or demand conditions, although in fact few such applications have been made; however, the Law is not on the same logical level as the hypotheses underlying equation (1). It is not explained whose decision it is to change prices in accordance with equation (3). Each individual participant in the economy is supposed to take prices as given and determine his choices as to purchases and sales accordingly; there is no one left over whose job it is to make a decision on price.[6]

Price adjustment under monopoly

Before discussing the mechanics of price adjustment under competitive conditions, we may consider the determination of price under monopoly. Here, there is no question of the locus of price decisions. In the standard theory (essentially unchanged from Cournot's original presentation), the monopolist fixes his price and output to maximize $R(x) - C(x)$, where x is output, $R(x)$ the total revenue curve, and $C(x)$ the total cost curve. Price and output are related by the demand curve, and the firm's output will, therefore, always equal demand. This theory clearly presupposes that the monopolist knows the true demand curve confronting him.

Lange [14] has sought to develop a theory of price adjustment for monopolies analogous to the Law of Supply and Demand under competition. Let $U(p)$ be the profit of the entrepreneur if he sets price p, assuming that the output has been fixed in accordance with the demand curve. Then Lange suggests

(5) $dp/dt = F(U')$

where

(6) $F' > 0, \quad F(0) = 0.$

Rules (5) and (6) amount to saying that the entrepreneur varies his price in that direction which leads to an increased profit. The rules are of the type referred to in mathematics as gradient methods of maximization.

These rules have concealed in them implicit assumptions about the monopolist's knowledge of the demand curve facing him (I assume he has complete knowledge of his cost curve). Since Lange assumes that output equals sales, the monopolist must know the demand at the price chosen, and, to make equation (5) operationally meaningful, he must know the elasticity of demand at that price. On the other hand, the monopolist presumably does not know the entire demand curve, for otherwise he would jump immediately to the optimal position. Further, his knowledge must be changing over time. To see this, let p_0 be the price set at some time t_0 and p_1 the price at some later time t_1. Since the monopolist is increasing his profit by his successive trial prices, the profit $U(p_1)$ at time t_1 must be greater than $U(p_0)$, the profit at time t_0. If, at time t_0, the monopolist had known the demand at price p_1, he would have known that p_0 was not the point of maximum profit and would have chosen p_1, or, possibly, some price which yielded a still higher profit. Thus the value of demand at p_1 is knowledge which is available to the monopolist at time t_1 but not at time t_0.

Uncertainty, then, is a crucial consideration in the theory of monopolistic price adjustment. We cannot completely follow Lange in assuming that the monopolist never wets his toes in the cold waters of uncertainty as to the demand curve. It may be that, without knowing the exact value of demand at p_1, the monopolist knows that even under the worst possible conditions the profit will be greater than at p_0, where the demand is known. Indeed, it suffices that the expected profit corresponding to p_1 be sufficiently greater than the known profit at p_0 to overcome the entrepreneur's distaste for the greater uncertainty. Hence we must admit the possibility of a discrepancy between output and demand for a monopolist. The discrepancy once observed has a twofold significance for price adjustment. On the one hand, it informs the monopolist of the extent to which he is in error and yields knowledge to estimate better his demand curve; on the other hand, the discrepancy alters his stock of inventories, which may in turn affect his cost situation in the next period.[7] The latter effect would, of course, not apply to cases where either no inventories can be accumulated, as with services, or where the carrying costs (including storage, depreciation, and foregone liquidity) are very high. It seems reasonable to conclude that price adjustment will be slower in the last-mentioned case than where inventories can be accumulated or decumulated more readily.

Thus, if demand is higher than anticipated, the monopolist will, in general, raise his price because both his marginal cost and anticipated marginal revenue curves have shifted upwards, and conversely for demands lower than anticipated. If the true demand and cost curves remain unchanged in the process, the monopolist will gradually converge towards his optimal price-quantity position. If, however, the demand and cost curves are shifting over time in response to influences exogenous to the market under consideration, the monopolist's price adjustment relations become part of a general dynamic system which is not necessarily stable. I will not elaborate here a more complete model, which can become very complicated.[8]

Competitive price adjustment

The above sketch of monopolistic price adjustment theory has been introduced here not only for its own sake, but for the purpose of laying the foundations for a theory of price adjustment under competitive circumstances. As has been understood since the days of Cournot and emphasized in more recent times by Chamberlin and Joan Robinson, the competitive firm is a monopolist with a special environment.

Ordinarily, the firm acting under competitive conditions is pictured as a monopolist confronted with a perfectly elastic demand curve. More explicitly, it is assumed that there exists a price, which we may refer to as the market price, such that the firm can sell any output it desires at a price not exceeding the market price, but can sell nothing at a higher price.

Triffin [16] has criticized this criterion of perfect elasticity of demand as a definition of pure competition, arguing that such a demand situation is itself a consequence of the fundamental technological and test factors involved. He defines perfect competition instead in terms of certain cross-elasticities of supply and demand as between different firms.

Indeed, suppose we have a situation which conforms in all the aspects of homogeneity of output and multiplicity of firms to the usual concept of perfect competition, but in which the aggregate supply forthcoming at the "market" price exceeds the demand at that price. Then the individual firm cannot sell all it wishes to at the market price; i.e., when supply and demand do not balance, even in an objectively competitive market, the individual firms are in the position of monopolists as far as the imperfect elasticity of demand for their products is concerned.

What is the meaning of market price in such a situation? We are always told by the textbooks that there is one price in a competitive market at a given time. But what determines this one price? The answer has been given clearly by Reder. Under conditions of disequilibrium, there is no reason that there should be a single market price, and we may very well expect that each firm will charge a different price [17]. The law that there is only one price on a competitive market (Jevons' Law of Indifference) is derived on the basis of profit- or utility-maximizing behavior on the part of both sides of the market; but there is no reason for such behavior to lead to unique price except in equilibrium, or possibly under conditions of perfect knowledge.

Let us consider in somewhat more detail the case in which demand exceeds supply. Assume that no firm can increase supply in a very short period. Then any individual entrepreneur knows that he can raise the price, even if his competitors do not raise theirs, because they cannot satisfy any more of the demand than they do already. The entrepreneur is faced with a sloping demand curve and raises his price in accordance with the profit-maximizing tactics of a monopolist, as sketched in the previous section. If none of the other sellers do in fact raise their prices, the entrepreneur will gradually approach his point of maximum profit, where the market will be cleared. But, under the conditions specified, it is equally to the profit of all other entrepreneurs to raise their prices also, although, if not subject to the same cost conditions, not necessarily by the same amount. The demand curve for the particular entrepreneur under consideration is thus shifting upward at the same time that he is exploring it. Thus supply will still not be in balance with demand, and the process continues.

It must also be stressed that the amount of uncertainty during this process is apt to be very considerable. Any estimate of the demand curve to a single entrepreneur involves a guess as to both the supply conditions and the prices of other sellers, as well as some idea of the demand curve to the industry as a whole. Under competitive conditions none of these is likely to be known very well. Thus the whole adjustment process is apt to be very irregular. Although the broad tendency will be for prices to rise when demand exceed supply, there can easily be a considerable dispersion of prices among different sellers of the same commodity, as well as considerable variability over time in the rate of change of prices.

The uncertainty, in turn, puts a premium on information. Traditional economic theory stresses the sufficiency of the price system as a source of information for guiding economic behavior, and this is correct enough at equilibrium. But the monopolist in general has stricter informational requirements than the competitor, since he needs to know his whole demand curve, not merely a single price. In conditions of disequilibrium, the demand curve is shifting as a result of forces outside the private market of the monopolist, and a premium is placed on the acquisition of information from sources other than the prices and quantities of the firm's own sales.

So far, our detailed analysis has covered the case of a firm acting as a monopolist because demand exceeds supply for the industry of which the firm is a part. We have already seen that, on a market where supply exceeds demand, each firm can also be regarded as a monopolist, though for different reasons. By a parallel argument each buyer on a market with an inequality between supply and demand can be regarded as a monopsonist. The behavior of each firm as a buyer can be described in the same manner as that of the seller, and we forebear from detailed repetition.

However, this further remark requires some revision of our previous picture of the market. In disequilibrium, the market consists of a number of monopolists facing a number of monopsonists. The most general picture is that of a shifting set of bilateral monopolies. The range of indeterminacy in each bargaining situation is limited but not completely eliminated by the possibilities of other bargains. In general, though, it is reasonable to suppose that if the selling side of the market is much more concentrated than the buying side, the main force in changing prices will be the monopolistic behavior of the sellers. The buyers would find little possibility of exerting their individual monopsonistic powers because there are so many of them for each seller. Similarly, if the buying side of the market is the more concentrated, as in nonunionized labor markets, the dynamics will come from that side. It is perhaps for reasons such as these that the immediate location of price decisions is usually vested in the more concentrated side of the market, in sellers in the case of most commodities, in buyers in the case of unorganized labor. (In organized labor markets, bilateral monopoly prevails.) Thus the dynamics of prices may be affected by the structure of the market even in cases where there are sufficient numbers in the market to insure reasonably competitive behavior at equilibrium.

Implications for the speed of adjustment

The preceding shows, of course, that the difference between supply and demand is a major factor in explaining the movement of prices, so that the Law of Supply and Demand, as expressed in equations (3) and (4), can be thought of as a useful approximation. However, the "price" whose movements are explained by the Law must be thought of as the average price. The model presented in this paper has some implications for the speed of adjustment in different markets, as represented by the function h.

Consider, as before, the case where demand exceeds supply and sellers are led to behave as monopolists. The existence of this excess both for the particular seller under consideration and for his competitors enters into the determination of the seller's anticipated demand curve. Given this, he sets his price so as to equate anticipated marginal revenue (possibly discounted in some form for uncertainty) to marginal cost. The price increase will thus depend on the shape of the marginal cost curve. It will be greater if the marginal cost is rising sharply than if it is flat. In particular, then, the speed of adjustment will be greater during a period of full utilization of capacity than in a situation of excess capacity.

A second consideration affecting the speed of adjustment, already remarked in passing, is the possibility of accumulating and decumulating inventories. An accumulation of inventories is both a signal to revise downward the anticipated demand curve and a cause of a downward shift in the marginal cost curve in the next period. A decumulation of inventories has the opposite effects. Hence, price adjustment will be more rapid in industries where inventories play a significant role.

A third factor suggested by the preceding analysis is the degree of information available to the individual entrepreneur. Relative absence of information about the behavior of others in the market increases the degree of uncertainty. Even in the absence of an aversion to risk-bearing, the chances that the entrepreneur will misread the signals are greater than if more information were available; we would therefore expect on the average that the responsiveness of prices to supply–demand differences would be less in the absence of information. An aversion to risk-bearing would increase the entrepreneur's unwillingness to venture on price changes in the absence of information. We would expect, therefore, that well-organized exchanges would display the greatest degree of price flexibility.

One special case in which information would be expected to be relatively scarce is that where the products are poorly standardized. Then knowledge of prices and availabilities of supply for other firms will not have a clear meaning for a particular firm, since its product may not be a perfect substitute, and therefore an excess of demand over supply elsewhere in the market may not be due to an upward shift in demand for all products on the market but to a shift away from its product to that of its competitors.

The competitiveness of the economy

In any state of disequilibrium, i.e., any situation in which supply does not equal demand, it follows from the above model that the economy will show evidences of monopoly and monopsony. These evidences will be the more intense, the greater the disequilibrium. We can understand from this point of view the feeling of the businessman that, contrary to economic theory, sales are by no means unlimited at the current market price. The demand for advertising and other forms of nonprice competition thus makes more sense than under the model of perfect competition at all times.

The model casts some light on the much-discussed problem of administered prices.[9] It was brought out by Gardiner Means and others in the 1930's that the quoted prices of some commodities produced by industries in which there was a high degree of concentration tended to be rigid, that is, insensitive to inequalities of demand and supply. Against this point of view it has been objected that the prices at which transactions actually take place differ from the quoted prices and are, for example, lower in conditions of excess capacity. Thus, the actual prices would be more nearly consistent with those of the competitive model. But it remains to be explained why the sellers resort to a fictitious price and secret undercutting instead of openly reducing prices. Explanations, such as Bailey's [18], which run in terms of informal social pressures within the industry, do not seem very satisfactory and, in any case, merely push the problem back one step.

If, however, it is accepted that an inequality of supply and demand leads to a condition of partial monopoly, then the most likely explanation for a divergence between quoted and actual prices is that it is a cloak for price discrimination. Not all buyers receive equal discounts, because they are not informed as to the prices actually paid. Such discrimination, if it can be shown to exist, would, of course, be incompatible with a purely competitive model.

The present model also suggests that the measurement of competitiveness by the concentration ratio has to be interpreted carefully. A degree of concentration which would be perfectly compatible with a reasonable degree of competition if the market were in equilibrium might easily fail to be so compatible in the event of serious inequality between supply and demand. There has been a position strongly held in recent years that the American economy is basically competitive, in that neither firms nor labor unions have, in fact, much control over prices, despite superficial appearances.[10] The present model suggests that the evidence, to the extent that it is valid, relates only to equilibrium and, therefore, to long-run situations. Such long-run competitiveness is not incompatible, on the present view, with considerable short-run monopoly powers in transitory situations.

The incomplete competitiveness of the economy under disequilibrium conditions implies a departure from the maximum of possible efficiency in the use of resources. To be sure, it does not necessarily follow that greater efficiency is necessarily achievable under feasible alternative rules. Any method of resource allocation requires a process for equating supply and demand (or some equivalent), and such a process may be in itself costly, though such costs are not considered in the usual formal analysis of welfare economics. Thus, a completely centralized system will incur high computational and informational costs. The monopolistic and monopsonistic misallocations implied by the model of the present paper may be thought of as costs alternative to those associated with centralization.

In particular, one would expect considerable departures from maximum efficiency in conditions of severe disequilibrium, such as inflations and depressions, despite Keynes's well-known remark to the contrary.[11] Under conditions of unemployment, the mobility of resources in response to price differences is seriously impaired. Thus, in a depression workers will not move from the farm to the city, despite considerable wage differences, because they are aware of the difficulty of getting a job; the individual worker faces a falling demand curve.

A remark on inflation

The above model casts some light on the concept of cost inflation. Such a doctrine requires that there be important elements of unregulated monopoly in the economy. There is at least some doubt that such elements are significant in the long run. However, the model of this paper suggests that in a certain sense all inflationary processes are cost inflations in that it is the monopoly power resulting from excess demand which is their proximate cause. This may explain why acute observers differ so sharply in their evaluation of the same phenomenon. Those who see cost inflation may be looking at an immediate causal factor, while those who speak of demand inflation have their eye on a more ultimate stimulus.

In view of this, this paper would suggest caution in treating cost inflations by direct regulation.[12] They may be transitory phenomena which are necessary to achieve equilibrium, in which case regulation may simply lead to the replacement of overt by suppressed inflation.

Notes

1   See, e.g., Klein ([1] page 118): "Instead of studying the behavior of individuals, Marx studied the behavior of classes directly."
2   K. Marx [2]: Chap. I, and especially the discussion of surplus value in Chaps. VI, VII, VIII, and IX.
3   See especially pp. 347–53.
4   The same view has been expressed by at least one Soviet textbook, Lapidus and Ostrovityanov, *Outlines of Political Economy*, referred to by H. Smith in "Marx and the Trade Cycle" [6].

5   An alternative interpretation sometimes adopted is that there is a basic contradiction between the two price theories. This position has been adopted by numerous critics of Marxism, following E. Böhm von Bawerk, *Karl Marx and the Close of His System* [7]. The same view has been taken by the ultra-Marxist, Daniel de Leon, who rejected Volume III as Engels' misinterpretation.

6   This problem has not gone unnoticed in the literature; thus T. Scitovsky observes, "The difficulty lies in visualizing a price that everybody on both sides of the market regards as given and that is determined by the "impersonal forces of the market'" [13].

7   If the total cost of producing x units is $C(x)$, the carrying cost is c per unit, and the amount carried forward is x_0, the cost associated with delivering x units in the next period is $C(x - x_0) + cx_0$. For low values of c, this cost will be less than $C(x)$, so that the cost curve for the next period has shifted downward.

8   Such models are closely related to those which have been developed in inventory theory over the last twelve years. See, for example, Arrow, Karlin, and Scarf [15].

9   See M. J. Bailey, "Administered Prices in the American Economy," pp. 89–106, and earlier references cited there [18].

10 For firms, this view has been held by Stigler [19], Nutter [20], and Harberger [21]. For trade unions, see Friedman [22].

11 "I see no reason to suppose that the existing system seriously misemploys the factors of production which are in use. . . . When 9,000,000 men are employed out of 10,000,000 willing and able to work, there is no evidence that the labor of the 9,000,000 men is misdirected" [23].

12 See the proposals of Lerner [24].

References

[1]   L. R. Klein, "Theories of Effective Demand and Employment," *Journal of Political Economy*, LV (April 1947), 108–31.

[2]   K. Marx, *Capital.* Charles H. Kerr, Chicago, 1906, Vol. I.

[3]   M. Dobb, *Marx as an Economist.* International Publishers, New York, 1945, pp. 19–20.

[4]   P. M. Sweezy, *The Theory of Capitalist Development.* Oxford, New York, 1942, Chap. VII.

[5]   O. Lange, "Marxian Economics and Modern Economic Theory," *Review of Economic Studies*, II (1934–35), 189–201; especially pp. 194, 195.

[6]   H. Smith, "Marx and the Trade Cycle," *Review of Economic Studies*, IV (June 1937), 197.

[7]   E. Böhm von Bawerk, *Karl Marx and the Close of His System.* Unwin, London, 1898.

[8]   T. Veblen, "Limitations of Marginal Utility" and "Professor Clark's Economics," reprinted in *The Place of Science in Modern Civilization and Other Essays.* Huebsch, New York, 1919, pp. 180–251.

[9] T. Veblen, *The Theory of Business Enterprise*. Scribner's, New York, 1904.

[10] W. C. Mitchell, *Business Cycles: The Problem and Its Setting*. National Bureau of Economic Research, New York, 1927, pp. 105-7.

[11] P. A. Samuelson, *Foundations of Economic Analysis*. Harvard University Press, Cambridge, 1947, Chap. IX.

[12] K. J. Arrow and L. Hurwicz, "On the Stability of the Competitive Equilibrium, I," this volume, III.1, pp. 199-228.

[13] T. Scitovsky, *Welfare and Competition*. Allen and Unwin, London, 1952, p. 16.

[14] O. Lange, *Price Flexibility and Employment*. Cowles Commission Monograph No. 8. Principia Press, Bloomington, Indiana, 1944, pp. 35-37, 107-9.

[15] K. J. Arrow, S. Karlin, and H. Scarf, *Studies in the Mathematical Theory of Inventory and Production*. Stanford University Press, Stanford, California, 1958.

[16] R. M. Triffin, *Monopolistic Competition and General Equilibrium Theory*. Harvard University Press, Cambridge, 1940, pp. 137-41.

[17] M. W. Reder, *Studies in the Theory of Welfare Economics:* Columbia University Press, New York, 1947, pp. 126-51.

[18] M. J. Bailey, "Administered Prices in the American Economy," in *The Relationship of Prices to Economic Stability and Growth*. Joint Economic Committee, U.S. Congress, Washington, D.C., 1958, pp. 89-106.

[19] G. J. Stigler, *Five Lectures on Economic Problems*. Longmans, Green, New York, London, and Toronto, 1949. Lecture 5, pp. 44-65.

[20] G. Warren Nutter, *The Extent of Enterprise Monopoly in the United States, 1899-1939*. University of Chicago Press, Chicago, 1951.

[21] A. C. Harberger, "Monopoly and Resource Allocation," *American Economic Review*, XLIV, No. 2 (May 1954), 77-87.

[22] M. Friedman, "Some Comments on the Significance of Labor Unions for Economic Policy," in D. M. Wright (ed.), *The Impact of the Union*. Harcourt, Brace, New York, 1951, Chap. X, pp. 204-34.

[23] J. M. Keynes, *The General Theory of Employment, Interest and Money*. Harcourt, Brace, New York, 1936, p. 379.

[24] A. P. Lerner, "Inflationary Depression and the Regulation of Administered Prices," in *The Relationship of Prices to Economic Stability and Growth*. Joint Economic Committee, U.S. Congress, Washington, D.C., 1958, pp. 267-68.

PART IV

General characterizations
of allocation processes

Optimality and informational efficiency in resource allocation processes[1]

LEONID HURWICZ

1. Introduction

This paper is primarily devoted to a study of the (static) optimality properties (e.g., Pareto-optimality of the equilibria) of certain resource allocation mechanisms. It is shown that one such mechanism (the "greed process") is optimal in a class of economic environments much broader than the class for which perfect competition is optimal. More specifically, the greed process has the desired optimality properties for all environments from which so-called external economies or diseconomies are absent; unlike perfect competition, the greed process does not presuppose the absence of indivisible goods, of discontinuities, or of increasing returns. However, the greed process lacks the dynamic (stability) properties known to hold for perfect competition, at least in certain special cases.

That the greed process does have certain optimality properties would be of little interest, were it not for the fact that it belongs to a class of *informationally decentralized* processes and hence shares with perfect competition a feature that has been extolled as one of the main virtues of the classical market mechanism. Still, just because it is designed to cover a broader class of environments, the greed process calls for more information (is informationally less efficient) than the competitive mechanism. To illustrate this, a variant of the latter (called "quasi-competitive") is constructed and is shown to have the desired optimality properties when the environment satisfies the usual divisibility and convexity assumptions, while requiring less information than does the greed process.

Even apart from its dynamic defects, the greed process is completely impractical because it calls for behavior on the part of the economic units that is in conflict with their self-interest. But it must be remembered that this weakness is shared by the competitive mechanism unless, roughly speaking, the environment is *atomistic* (i.e., all units are infinitesimal compared with the whole economy).

In a broader perspective, these findings suggest the possibility of a more systematic study of resource allocation mechanisms. In such a study, unlike in the more traditional approach, the mechanism becomes the unknown of the problem, rather than a datum.[2] Of course, to make the problem meaningful, we must define some domain of variation for this unknown. For instance, in the present paper, this domain is given as a certain class of difference equation systems ("adjustment processes"), but other choices could easily be made. The members of such a domain can then be appraised in terms of their various "performance characteristics," and, in particular, of their (static and dynamic) optimality properties, their informational efficiency, and the compatibility of their postulated behavior with self-interest (or other motivational variables).

One naturally finds that better performance can be obtained at the expense of coverage with respect to the nature of the economic environment, and vice versa. Thus the perfectly competitive mechanism, high on the scale of informational efficiency, has the other performance characteristics (optimality properties and incentive-compatibility) for the rather narrow class of atomistic environments possessing the various divisibility and convexity properties and free from external (dis-)economies. But a conflict with self-interest may arise if the environment is non-atomistic, and the optimality properties may fail when the convexity conditions are not satisfied. The greed process, on the other hand, scores relatively well (although less well than the perfectly competitive process) on the informational scale and is shown to have the static optimality properties, even without atomicity, divisibility, or convexity, for environments from which external (dis-)economies are absent, i.e., for a fairly broad class of environments; however, the greed process has poor dynamic characteristics and is in obvious conflict with individual self-interest.

These facts suggest a host of questions. For instance, for the class of environments free of external (dis-)economies, are there mechanisms whose performance characteristics are strictly better than those of the greed process, say with regard to either dynamic stability or informational efficiency, or compatibility with self-interest? Or, on the other hand, how much can we broaden the class of permissible environments and still expect to find mechanisms whose performance is at least as good as that of the greed process (i.e., informationally decentralized mechanisms possessing the static optimality properties)? So far, only fragmentary answers are available, indicating that the possibilities either of improving performance for the given classes of environments, or of broadening the coverage of environments without loss of performance, are rather limited.

Thus the choice of a resource allocation mechanism must be made with reference to the class of environments to be covered and in the light of some comparative valuation of the different dimensions of the performance characteristics. Given these data (environment class and performance valuation), the choice becomes a standard problem in optimization. But even when these data are either nonexistent or extremely vague (as they typically are in practice), a systematic analysis of the interrelationship between the environment coverage and the performance characteristics of a resource allocation mechanism should be of interest to those concerned with problems of economic organization, the comparative analysis of economic systems,[3] and the study of various institutional aspects of the economic system, whether it be a nation, a firm, or a government agency. Since the economist is at times called upon to express opinions on policy matters before the institutional framework is selected (e.g., within a firm or a young country), the matter is not altogether academic.

2. The economic environment and resource flows

The economic environment

We distinguish between the economic *environment*, to be considered as given, and the resource allocation mechanism (*adjustment process*), regarded as a variable (unknown) of the problem. There is, of course, some arbitrariness with respect to classifying certain aspects of the economic system under one of these two headings.

The economic environment is described with the help of the following notation and terminology:

$I = \{1, 2, \ldots, n\}$: the set of economic units (households, plants, government agencies, etc.);

$\mathcal{X}$: the commodity space (algebraically, an additive group);

0_x: the identity element of addition in $\mathcal{X}$ (i.e., $x + 0_x = x$);

$\mathcal{X}^{(n)} = \mathcal{X} \times \mathcal{X} \times \cdots \times \mathcal{X}$ (n times): the n-fold Cartesian product of $\mathcal{X}$.

X: the *admissible* consumption (holdings) set,[4] $X \subseteq \mathcal{X}^{(n)}$; the elements of X are called (admissible) *distributions*;

X^i: the ith projection of X;

$w_0{}^i$: the initial resource endowment of the ith unit; $w_0{}^i \in X^i \subseteq \mathcal{X}$;

$w_0 = (w_0{}^1, w_0{}^2, \ldots, w_0{}^n) \in X$;

R^i (also written as $\geq_i$):[5] the preference relation of the ith unit (R^i is a transitive, reflexive, connected relation on X);

$R = (R^1, R^2, \ldots, R^n)$;

Z: the *feasible* production set; $Z \subseteq \mathcal{X}^{(n)}$;

Z^i: the ith projection of Z;

$e = (I, \mathcal{X}; X, w_0, R, Z)$: the economic environment;

$e^i = (X^i, w_0{}^i, R^i, Z^i)$: the "characteristic" of the ith unit.

Resource-flow matrices

We find it convenient here to use the device of treating production in a manner formally analogous to exchange. To this end we introduce a fictitious unit ("nature"), referred to as the 0th unit. Now for $r, s = 0, 1, \ldots, n$, the expression $a_{rs} \in \mathcal{X}$ will represent the net flow of goods from unit s to unit r, with goods received by r counted as positive and goods given up by r as negative. Hence a_{s0} represents the input-output vector[6] of the sth economic unit, with output counted as positive, input as negative. From the definition, since a_{rs} represents *net* flow, it is natural to impose the skew-symmetry condition $a_{rs} + a_{sr} = 0_x$ ($r, s = 0, 1, \ldots, n$).

An $(n + 1) \times (n + 1)$ matrix a with entries from $\mathfrak{X}$, satisfying the skew-symmetry relation, i.e.,

$$a = \begin{pmatrix} a_{00} & a_{01} & \cdots & a_{0n} \\ a_{10} & a_{11} & \cdots & a_{1n} \\ \cdot & \cdot & & \cdot \\ \cdot & \cdot & & \cdot \\ \cdot & \cdot & & \cdot \\ a_{n0} & a_{n1} & \cdots & a_{nn} \end{pmatrix}$$

(where $a_{rs} \in \mathfrak{X}$, $a_{rs} + a_{sr} = 0_x$) is called a *resource-flow matrix* (of order n). The set of all resource-flow matrices of order n is denoted by $\mathfrak{A}$.

Given a resource-flow matrix a (of order n), we write

$$a_{.0} = (a_{10}, a_{20}, \ldots, a_{n0}), \qquad \sigma^i(a) = \Sigma_{s=0}^n a_{is},$$

$$\sigma(a) = [\sigma^1(a), \sigma^2(a), \ldots, \sigma^n(a)] ;$$

so that $a_{.0} \in \mathfrak{X}^{(n)}$, $\sigma^i(a) \in \mathfrak{X}$, and $\sigma(a) \in \mathfrak{X}^{(n)}$.

Clearly, if w_0 was the resource endowment n-tuple before the resource flow represented by a occurred, then the resource endowment n-tuple after the flow is given by $w_0 + \sigma(a)$. The n-tuple $a_{.0}$ represents the production activities of the n units.

Definition 1. A resource-flow matrix $a \in \mathfrak{A}$ is said to be *possible* (in e) if it is admissible (i.e., $w_0 + \sigma(a) \in X$) and feasible (i.e., $a_{.0} \in Z$).

Definition 2.

(a) We write $a' \geq_i a''$ if and only if $w_0 + \sigma(a') \geq_i w_0 + \sigma(a'')$.

(b) a' is said to be *(Pareto-)superior* (in e) *to* a'' if $a' \geq_i a''$ for all $i \in I$ and $a' >_k a''$ for some $k \in I$.

(c) a is said to be *(Pareto-)optimal* (in e) if (c_1), a is possible (in e), and, (c_2) no possible a' is Pareto-superior (in e) to a.

(d) We write $\hat{A}_e = \{a \in \mathfrak{A}: \hat{a}$ is Pareto-optimal in $e\}$; $\hat{w} \in \mathfrak{X}^{(n)}$ is said to be *(Pareto-)optimal* (in e) if $\hat{w} = w_0 + \sigma(\hat{a})$ for some $\hat{a} \in \hat{A}_e$.

3. Adjustment process

Given a set ("language") $\mathfrak{M}$, n functions ("response rules") f^i ($i = 1, 2, \ldots, n$), and an "outcome rule" φ, we define an ("abstract") adjustment process as $\pi \equiv (f, \varphi, \mathfrak{M})$, where $f = (f^1, f^2, \ldots, f^n)$. The "response rules" determine the nature of the difference equation system

(1) $m_{t+1}{}^i = f^i(m_t{}^1, m_t{}^2, \ldots, m_t{}^n; e)$ ($i = 1, 2, \ldots, n$),

where $m_\tau{}^i \in \mathfrak{M}$ represents the message formed by the ith unit at time τ. This equation system may be written more compactly as

(2) $m_{t+1} = f(m_t; e)$,

with $m_\tau = (m_\tau^1, m_\tau^2, \ldots, m_\tau^n) \in \mathfrak{M}^{(n)}$. ($\mathfrak{M}^{(n)} = \mathfrak{M} \times \mathfrak{M} \times \cdots \times \mathfrak{M}$ = the n-fold Cartesian product of $\mathfrak{M}$.)

The *process is in equilibrium at* $\overline{m} = (\overline{m}^1, \overline{m}^2, \ldots, \overline{m}^n) \in \mathfrak{M}^{(n)}$ if

(3) $\overline{m} = f(\overline{m}; e)$.

We write $\overline{M}_{e,f} = \{\overline{m} \in \mathfrak{M}^{(n)}: \overline{m} = f(\overline{m}; e)\}$, and the elements of this set are called the *equilibrium values* of the process.

With each equilibrium value $\overline{m}$ of the process the outcome rule φ (a function not depending on e) associates a (possibly empty) *outcome* set $\overline{A}$ of resource-flow matrices, i.e.,

(4) $\overline{A} = \varphi(\overline{m})$, $\overline{m} \in \overline{M}_{e,f}$, $\overline{A} \subseteq \mathfrak{a}$.

The elements of $\overline{A}$ are called *solutions*.

Given an adjustment process $\pi = (f, \varphi, \mathfrak{M})$ and an environment e, we write

$$\overline{A}_{e,\pi} = \bigcup_{\overline{m} \in M_{e,f}} \varphi(\overline{m}),$$

i.e., the union of outcomes.

Definition 3.   An adjustment process $\pi = (f, \varphi, \mathfrak{M})$ is said to be:

(a) *decisive* (in e), if $\hat{A}_e \neq \phi$ implies $\overline{A}_{e,\pi} \neq \phi$, i.e., if, when there are Pareto-optimal resource flows, there are also solutions;

(b) *essentially single-valued* (in e), if $\overline{m} \in \overline{M}_{e,f}, \overline{a}' \in \varphi(\overline{m}), \overline{a}'' \in \varphi(\overline{m})$ imply $\overline{a}' \sim_i \overline{a}''$ for each $i \in I$, i.e., if two solutions contained in the same outcome must be indifferent to all units;

(c) *non-wasteful* (in e), if $\overline{A}_{e,\pi} \subseteq \hat{A}_e$, i.e., if every solution is Pareto-optimal;

(d) *unbiased* (in e), if, given the environment $e = (I, \mathfrak{X}; X, w_0, R, Z)$ and any optimal $\hat{a} \in \hat{A}_e$, there exists a distribution $w_0^* \in X$ and an optimal $\hat{a}^* \in \hat{A}_e$ such that

$\Sigma_{i \in I} w_0^{*i} = \Sigma_{i \in I} w_0^i$, $w_0^* + \sigma(\hat{a}^*) = w_0 + \sigma(\hat{a})$.

$\hat{a}_{.0}^* = \hat{a}_{.0}$, $\hat{a}^* \in \overline{A}_{e^*,\pi}$,

where[7] $e^* = (I, \mathfrak{X}; X, w_0^*, R, Z)$; roughly speaking, this means that any optimal resource distribution can be reached as a solution of the given adjustment process following, if necessary, a redistribution of the initially available resource endowment;

(e) *Pareto-satisfactory* (in e), if it is essentially single-valued, unbiased, and non-wasteful (in e).

Remark A.   Each of the preceding properties is static in character, since only the equilibrium properties of the process are involved.

Remark B.   Under the classical assumptions of divisibility (of goods), convexity, continuity, etc., perfect competition has each of the preceding properties. Essential single-valuedness is evident. Decisiveness follows from the existence theorems,[8] while unbiasedness and non-wastefulness are the chief concerns of ("classical") welfare economics.[9]

It is well known that under monopoly (especially of the non-discriminating variety), non-optimal solutions may occur; hence such processes are not Pareto-satisfactory.

Definition 4.   An adjustment process is said to be *external* if the ith response function depends on the environment e only through the ith characteristic e^i, i.e., if, for each $i \in I$ and each $m \in \mathbb{m}^{(n)}$, $e*^i = e**^i$ implies $f^i(m; e^*) = f^i(m; e^{**})$.

Remark C.   If the process is external, we may write the response function as $f^i(m; e^i)$.

Remark D.   Externality is used in Definition 10 below as part of the concept of informational decentralization. Under externality, an economic unit, apart from the messages received, needs no information concerning (for example) the characteristics of the other units. Externality is among the informational features of the market mechanism stressed by Hayek [4].

4. Decomposable environments

Since an external process uses no properties of the environment except the n characteristics, it is intuitively clear that the process is not likely to be Pareto-satisfactory in environments whose Pareto-optimal sets are not determined by the various projections. Thus it is natural to focus the study of informationally decentralized processes on a class of environments free of external (dis-)economies; such environments will be called decomposable.[10] Formally, we have

Definition 5.   An economic environment e is said to be *decomposable* if:

(a)   the units are independent with regard to admissibility, i.e., $X = X^1 \times X^2 \times \cdots \times X^n$;

(b)   the units are *technologically independent*,[11] i.e., $Z = Z^1 \times Z^2 \times \cdots \times Z^n$;

(c)   each unit is *selfish* (individualistic),[12] i.e., for each $i \in I$, given the admissible distributions $w^*, w^{**}, w^*), w^{**})$, with their ith components denoted respectively by $w^{*i}, w^{**i}, w^*)^i, w^{**})^i$, we have $w^*) \geq_i w^{**})$ if

$$w^* \geq_i w^{**}, \qquad w^{*i} = w^*)^i, \qquad w^{**i} = w^{**})^i.$$

(if the ith unit is selfish, we write $w^{*i} \geq_i w^{**i}$ to mean $w^* \geq_i w^{**}$.)

5. Informationally decentralized adjustment processes

We start by defining the "concrete"[13] adjustment process as a special class of what we have called ("abstract") adjustment processes, obtained by imposing the following two conditions: (a) the "language" $\mathbb{m}$ consists of sets of resource-flow matrices, i.e.,[14]

$$\mathbb{m} \subseteq \{A: A \subseteq \mathfrak{a}\} \equiv 2^{\mathfrak{a}},$$

and (b) the outcome is determined by consensus in the sense that

$$\varphi(\overline{m}^1, \overline{m}^2, \ldots, \overline{m}^n) \equiv \varphi(\overline{A}^1, \overline{A}^2, \ldots, \overline{A}^n) = \bigcap_{i \in I} \overline{A}^i.$$

The equations of a concrete process may, therefore, be written as

$$A_{t+1}^{\ i} = f^i(A_t^1, A_t^2, \ldots, A_t^n; e) \qquad (i = 1, 2, \ldots, n),$$

or $A_{t+1} = f(A_t; e)$, where $A_\tau = (A_\tau^1, A_\tau^2, \ldots, A_\tau^n)$. The equilibrium condition then becomes $\overline{A} = f(\overline{A}; e)$, where $\overline{A} = (\overline{A}^1, \overline{A}^2, \ldots, \overline{A}^n)$, and the *outcome* is given by

$$\overline{A} = \bigcap_{i \in I} \overline{A}^i.$$

Note that a concrete adjustment process is completely specified by $(\mathfrak{A}, f)$, where $\mathfrak{M} \subseteq 2^{\mathfrak{A}}$ and $f = (f^1, f^2, \ldots, f^n)$, with $f^i(., e)$ a function on $\mathfrak{M}^{(n)}$ into $\mathfrak{M}$.

We may think of A_τ^i as a collection of alternative plans a_τ^i formulated by the ith unit at time τ. At one extreme, A_τ^i might be a one-element set, or even empty; at the other, it might be that $A_\tau^i = \mathfrak{A}$. In a completely centrally planned economy, with $i = 1$ representing the planning agency, a one-element $A_\tau^1 = \{a^1\}$ might represent the flow of goods prescribed by the central plan. If the other units ($j = 2, 3, \ldots, n$) had no say whatever in determining the direction of flow, this could be represented by specifying $A_\tau^j = \mathfrak{A}$ for each j. In such a case, of course, the "consensus" solution is obtained at a^1.

We are here primarily interested in processes whose informational properties correspond to the intuitive concept of decentralization, e.g., to the sort of decentralization implied by the assertion that the (perfectly competitive) market mechanism is informationally decentralized.

There are those who would simply identify (informational) decentralization with the market and price mechanisms, but this seems too narrow a viewpoint.

The basic idea inherent in the intuitive concept of decentralization seems to be that each unit is permitted to concern itself only with the effects of its actions (or the actions of others) on itself and that it has no direct information about the internal structure of the other units. The latter property has already been introduced under the name of externality (Definition 4 above). The former will now be stated. To begin with, if the ith unit formulates a plan $a = (a_{rs})$, it is permitted to specify only properties of a that determine the actions (production, exchange) to be undertaken by i; this amounts to specifying, in a, the entities $\Sigma_{j \in I} a_{ij}$ and a_{i0}, i.e., the ordered pair $s \equiv (d, z)$, where $d \equiv d^i(a) = \Sigma_{j \in I} a_{ij}$, and $z \equiv z^i(a) = a_{i0}$. Since in our model the ith unit must express itself by selecting a set $A \subseteq \mathfrak{A}$, the requirement that i be entitled to specify only $\Sigma_{j \in I} a_{ij}$ and a_{i0} can be formalized by stating that the process must be *self-relevant* in the sense of

Definition 6. A set A of resource-flow matrices is said to be *i-relevant* if given $a' \in \mathfrak{A}$ and $a'' \in \mathfrak{A}$, with $\Sigma_{j \in I} a_{ij}'' = \Sigma_{j \in I} a_{ij}'$ and $a_{i0}'' = a_{i0}'$, $a' \in A$ if and only if $a'' \in A$. An adjustment process in which, for each $i \in I$, the ith unit uses only i-relevant messages is called *self-relevant*.

Let A be self-relevant for i. Then it may be partitioned into subsets of the form

$$A_s \equiv A_{(d,z)} = \{a \in \mathcal{C}: \ \Sigma_{j \in I} a_{ij} = d, a_{i0} = z\},$$

where $s \equiv (d, z)$ is a point of $\mathcal{X} \times \mathcal{X}$. Hence we have

$$A = \cup_{s \in S} A_s,$$

where S is some subset of $\mathcal{X} \times \mathcal{X}$; thus it is seen that there is a one-to-one correspondence between self-relevant A's and the S sets. This enables us to write such processes in the form

$$S_{t+1}{}^i = f^i(S_t{}^1, S_t{}^2, \ldots, S_t{}^n; e) \qquad (i = 1, 2, \ldots, n),$$

where $S_\tau{}^i \subseteq \mathcal{X} \times \mathcal{X}$ is the image of a self-relevant $A_\tau{}^i \subseteq \mathcal{C}$, and consists of elements written as $(d_\tau{}^i, z_\tau{}^i), d_\tau{}^i \in \mathcal{X}, z_\tau{}^i \in \mathcal{X}$, with $d_\tau{}^i$ representing the exchange activities and $z_\tau{}^i$ the production activities of the ith unit.

We refer to $S_\tau{}^i$ as the *plan* of the ith unit at time τ, and its members $s_\tau{}^i$ as its (alternative) *simple plans*. An n-tuple

$$s = [s^1, s^2, \ldots, s^n] \qquad [s^i = (d^i, z^i), i \in I],$$

of simple plans is called a *program*.

If the program s were to be put in operation, the ith unit would be engaging in production activities yielding an input-output vector z^i, and in exchange activities from which it would emerge with a net increment in holdings given by d^i. Clearly, in a closed economy, this could be done only if the program is *consistent*, i.e., if $\Sigma_{i \in I} d^i = 0_x$.

A self-relevant process is *in equilibrium at* $S = (\bar{S}^1, \bar{S}^2, \ldots, \bar{S}^n)$ if

$$\bar{S}^i = f^i(\bar{S}^1, \bar{S}^2, \ldots, \bar{S}^n; e) \qquad (i = 1, 2, \ldots, n).$$

Definition 7. If the process is in equilibrium at $(\bar{S}^1, \bar{S}^2, \ldots, \bar{S}^n)$, a program $\bar{s} = [\bar{s}^1, \bar{s}^2, \ldots, \bar{s}^n]$ is called a *solution* (*program*), provided $\bar{s}^i \in \bar{S}^i$ for each $i \in I$ and $\bar{s}$ is consistent, i.e., provided $\Sigma_{i \in I} \bar{d}^i = 0_x$ and $\bar{s}^i = (\bar{d}^i, \bar{z}^i)$.

For a program to be *possible*, it must, of course, be consistent, and furthermore, the conditions of admissibility and feasibility must be satisfied.

Definition 8.[15] A program $s = [s^1, s^2, \ldots, s^n]$, where $s^i = (d^i, z^i), i \in I$, is called *achievable* if it is both *feasible* [i.e., $(z^1, z^2, \ldots, z^n) \in Z$] and *admissible* [i.e., $(w_0{}^1 + d^1 + z^1, w_0{}^2 + d^2 + z^2, \ldots, w_0{}^n + d^n + z^n) \in X$]. A program s is called *possible* if it is achievable and consistent (i.e., $\Sigma_{i \in I} d^i = 0_x$). A program s^* is said to be *Pareto-superior* to s^{**} if $w_0{}^i + d^{*i} + z^{*i} + \geq {}_i w_0{}^i + d^{**i} + z^{**i}$ for each $i \in I$ and $w_0{}^k + d^{*k} + z^{*k} >_k w_0{}^k + d^{***k} + z^{***k}$ for some $k \in I$. A program s is said to be *Pareto-optimal* if it is possible and if no possible s' is Pareto-superior to s.

Given the plans $S^1, S^2, \ldots, S^{i-1}, S^{i+1}, \ldots, S^n$, one can form $(n-1)$-tuples of the form

$$(s^1, s^2, \ldots, s^{i-1}, s^{i+1}, \ldots, s^n) \equiv s^{)i(},$$

where $s^k = (d^k, z^k)$, with $s^k \in S^k$, $k \in)i($.[16] As far as the ith unit is concerned, if $s^{)i(}$ were to be put into effect, consistency would require that $d^i = -\Sigma_{k \in)i(} d^k$. Hence the set of all d^i compatible with the plans $S^1, S^2, \ldots, S^{i-1}$, $S^{i+1}, \ldots, S^n$ is given by

$$\{x \in \mathfrak{X}: \ x = -\Sigma_{k \in)i(} d^k, (d^k, z^k) \in S^k \text{ for some } z^k\} = -\Sigma_{k \in)i(} D(S^k),$$

where $D(S) = \{d \in \mathfrak{X}: (d, z) \in S \text{ for some } z \in S\}$, i.e., $D(S)$ is the "*trade projection*" of S. Thus it is clearly in the spirit of information decentralization to require the ith response rule f^i to depend on the S^k, where $k \in)i($, through $\Sigma_{k \in)i(} D(S^k)$ only.[17] We introduce

Definition 9.   A self-relevant adjustment process

$$S_{t+1}^i = f^i(S_t^1, S_t^2, \ldots, S_t^n; e) \qquad (i = 1, 2, \ldots, n)$$

is called *aggregative* if, for each $i \in I$,

$$f^i(S^{*1}, S^{*2}, \ldots, S^{*n}; e) = f^i(S^{**1}, S^{**2}, \ldots, S^{**n}; e)$$

whenever $\Sigma_{k \in)i(} D(S^{*k}) = \Sigma_{k \in)i(} D(S^{**k})$.

We now have all the concepts needed to formulate

Definition 10.   A (concrete) adjustment process is said to be *informationally decentralized* if it is external, self-relevant, and aggregative.

Hence an informationally decentralized process can be written in the form

$$(5) \quad S_{t+1}^i = f^i(S_t^i, \Sigma_{k \in)i(} D(S_i^k); e^1) \qquad (i = 1, 2, \ldots, n).$$

Of particular interest are *impersonal* processes in which the response rule is the same for all units. This can be expressed formally by

Definition 11.   An informationally decentralized process f is said to be *impersonal* if for any $S \subseteq \mathfrak{X} \times \mathfrak{X}$, $D \subseteq \mathfrak{X}$, and $e^i = e^j$, we have $f^i(S, D; e^i) = f^j(S, D; e^j)$.

Such a process may be written as

$$S_{t+1}^i = f^*(S_t^i, \Sigma_{k \in)i(} D(S_t^k); e^i) \qquad (i = 1, 2, \ldots, n).$$

6. The "greed process"

Intuitively, it is fairly clear that there is no informationally decentralized process that is Pareto-satisfactory for all conceivable economic environments, and there are examples to confirm this. But even within the class of decomposable environments, the existence of such a process may not be self-evident. The purpose of the present section is to show that there does exist an informationally decentralized process [viz., the "greed process" defined by (6) below] that is Pareto-satisfactory for all decomposable environments.

The basic idea of this process is that the response $S_{t+1}{}^i$ of the ith unit at time $t + 1$ consists of all the (simple) i-achievable[18] plans $s_{t+1}{}^i$ that are at least as desirable for i as any (simple) i-achievable plan consistent with the aggregate trade projection of the other units' plans at time t. Because $S_{i+1}{}^i$ consists of plans no less desirable than the best previously offered by others, the process has been labeled the "greed process."

Formally, the *greed process* is defined by the following relations[19,20] [which are clearly a special case of (5) and hence informationally decentralized]:

$$
(6) \quad
\begin{cases}
\quad S_{t+1}{}^i = \{ s_{t+1}{}^i \in \mathcal{S}^i \colon s_{t+1}{}^i \geq {}_i s^{*i} \quad \text{for all } s^{*i} \in S_t{}^{*i} \}, \\[2mm]
\text{where} \\[2mm]
\quad S_t{}^{*i} = \{ s^{*i} = (d^{*i}, z^{*i}) \in \mathcal{S}^i \colon d^{*i} \in - \Sigma_{j \in)i(} D(S_t{}^j) \} \\[2mm]
\text{and} \\[2mm]
\quad D(S) = \{ d \in \mathfrak{X} \colon (d, z) \in S \quad \text{for some } z \in \mathfrak{X} \}.
\end{cases}
$$

At equilibrium, therefore,

$$
(7) \quad
\begin{cases}
\quad \bar{S}^i = \{ \bar{s}^i \in \mathcal{S}^i \colon \bar{s}^i \geq {}_i s^{*i} \quad \text{for all } s^{*i} \in \bar{S}^{*i} \}, \\[2mm]
\text{where} \\[2mm]
\quad \bar{S}^{*i} = \{ s^{*i} = (d^{*i}, z^{*i}) \in \mathcal{S}^i \colon d^* \in - \Sigma_{j \in)i(} D(\bar{S}^i) \} \\[2mm]
\text{and} \\[2mm]
\quad D(\bar{S}^j) = \{ \bar{d} \in \mathfrak{X} \colon (\bar{d}, \bar{z}) \in \bar{S}^j \quad \text{for some } \bar{z} \in \mathfrak{X} \}.
\end{cases}
$$

Pareto-satisfactoriness of the greed process in decomposable environments

It is seen from (7) that the greed process is essentially single-valued in the sense of Definition 3(b). To prove Pareto-satisfactoriness, therefore, we must show that it is non-wasteful and unbiased, provided the environment is decomposable.[21]

Theorem 1.   The greed process is non-wasteful in a decomposable environment.

. *Proof.*   It must be shown that every solution program is Pareto-optimal. Suppose not. Then there exists a non-optimal solution program $\bar{s} = [\bar{s}^1, \bar{s}^2, \ldots, \bar{s}^n]$. By Definition 7, $\bar{s}$ is consistent; (7) states that $\bar{s}^i$ is i-achievable for each $i \in I$. Hence (see note 18), $\bar{s}$ is possible.[22] Therefore, there must exist a possible program $\tilde{s} = [\tilde{s}^1, \tilde{s}^2, \ldots, \tilde{s}^n]$ that is Pareto-superior to $\bar{s}$, i.e.,

$$(8) \quad \tilde{s}^i \geq {}_i \bar{s}^i \quad \text{for all } i \in I,$$

and, say,

(9) $\tilde{s}^1 > {}_1\tilde{s}^1$.

Using (7), (8), and the fact that $\tilde{s}^i$ is i-achievable (since $\tilde{s}$ is possible), we have

(10) $\tilde{s}^i \in \bar{S}^i$ for all $i \in I$.

Furthermore, since $\tilde{s}$ is consistent,

(11) $\tilde{\tilde{s}}^1 \equiv (-\Sigma_{k \in)i(} \tilde{d}^k, \tilde{z}^1) = (\tilde{d}^1, \tilde{z}^1) \equiv \tilde{s}^1$,

so that $\tilde{\tilde{s}}^1$ is i-achievable. Hence, by (7) and (10), $\bar{s}^1 \geq {}_1\tilde{\tilde{s}}^1$, which, in view of (11), contradicts (9).

Theorem 2.   The greed process is unbiased in a decomposable environment.

Proof.   Let $\hat{s} = [\hat{s}^1, \hat{s}^2, \ldots, \hat{s}^n]$, where $\hat{s}^i = (\hat{d}^i, \hat{z}^i)$ be a Pareto-optimal program. We wish to show that it is a solution program. To this end, suppose that at the time t_0, the ith individual ($i \in I$) adopts the plan $S_0{}^i$ defined by

(12) $S_0{}^i = \{s_0{}^i = (d_0{}^i, z_0{}^i) \in \S^i: s_0{}^i \geq {}_1\hat{s}^i\}$.

According to the rules of the greed process (6), the plan $S_1{}^i$ of the ith unit at time $t_0 + 1$ will then be

(13) $\begin{cases} & S_1{}^i = \{s_1{}^i = (d_1{}^i, z_1{}^i) \in \S^i: s_1{}^i \geq {}_iS^{*i} \quad \text{for all } s^{*i} \in S_0{}^{*i}\}, \\ \text{where} \\ & S_0{}^{*i} = \{s^{*i} = (d^{*i}, z^{*i}) \in \S^i: d^{*i} \in -\Sigma_{j \in)i(} D(S_0{}^j)\} \\ \text{and} \\ & D(S_0{}^j) = \{d \in \mathfrak{X}: (d, z) \in S_0{}^j \quad \text{for some } z \in \mathfrak{X}\}. \end{cases}$

Now if we can show that

(14) $S_1{}^i = S_0{}^i$ for each $i \in I$,

it will follow that the process is in equilibrium at $(S_0{}^1, S_0{}^2, \ldots, S_0{}^n)$. But then $\hat{s}$ is a solution program since (by its Pareto-optimality) it is consistent and, by (12), $\hat{s}^i \in S_0{}^i$ for each $i \in I$. It therefore remains only to establish (14), which is accomplished by showing that

(15) $S_1{}^i \subseteq S_0{}^i$ for each $i \in I$

and

(16) $S_0{}^i \subseteq S_1{}^i$ for each $i \in I$.

To prove (15), it is sufficient to show that, for any $s_1{}^i \in S_1{}^i$, we have $s^i \geq {}_i\hat{s}^i$. By (13), this will be so, provided $\hat{s}^i \in S^{*i}$. Since $\hat{s}^i$ is i-achievable (by Pareto-optimality), it is enough to show that $\hat{d}^i \in -\Sigma_{j \in)i(} D(S_0{}^j)$, which is true since $\hat{d}^i = -\Sigma_{j \in)i(} \hat{d}^j$ (by consistency due to Pareto-optimality) and $\hat{d}^j \in D(S_0{}^j)$ for all j. Hence (15) holds.

Now suppose (16) false. Then, for some $i \in I$ and some $s_0{}^i \in S_0{}^i$, the requirements of (13) are violated. That is, there exists a consistent program $\tilde{s} = [\tilde{s}^1, \tilde{s}^2, \ldots, \tilde{s}^n]$, with $\tilde{s}^j = (\tilde{d}^j, \tilde{z}^j)$, such that $\tilde{s}^k \in S_0{}^k$ for all $k \in)i($, $\tilde{s}^i = (-\Sigma_{k \in)i(} \tilde{d}^k, \tilde{z}^i)$ is i-achievable, and the strict preference inequality

$\tilde{s}^i >_i s_0{}^i$ is satisfied. Then, since $s_0{}^i \geq_i \hat{s}^i$ holds by (12), it follows that

(17) $\tilde{s}^i >_i \hat{s}^i$.

On the other hand, since (by the construction above) $\tilde{s}^k \in S_0{}^k$ for all $k \in)i($, we have from (12)

(18) $\tilde{s}^k \geq_k \hat{s}^k$ for all $k \in)i($.

Now $\tilde{s}$ is possible since it is consistent, $\tilde{s}^j$ is j-achievable for each $j \in I$, and the environment is decomposable. In view of (17) and (18), $\tilde{s}$ is Pareto-superior to the Pareto-optimal program $\hat{s}$, which yields a contradiction.

7. The "quasi-competitive" process

It is natural to raise the question whether one could not find an informationally decentralized process that is Pareto-satisfactory[23] for all decomposable environments but (in some well-defined sense) simpler than the greed process. This question is not yet completely resolved. But it is of interest to see that a "simpler" process with the desired properties may be found if we are willing to restrict ourselves to a narrower class of "convex" Euclidean environments.[24] This "simpler" process is closely related to the competitive process (especially with respect to equilibrium properties) and is therefore labeled "quasi-competitive." This process is obtained from the greed process in the following manner. Whenever a certain trade d^* is compatible with the "offers" made to i by the other units, i responds (according to the rules of the greed process) as if all non-negative scalar multiples λd^* ($\lambda \geq 0$) had also been offered to it.[25] This seems to be in the spirit of the general concept of perfect competition, although it differs from the currently more usual interpretations.[26] Formally, the *quasi-competitive process* is defined,[27] for each $i \in I$, by[28]

(19) $S_{t+1}{}^i = \{s_{t+1}{}^i \in \mathcal{S}^i : s_{t+1}{}^i \geq_i \lambda s^{*i} \text{ for all } s^{*i} \in S_t{}^{*i} \text{ and all } \lambda \geq 0\}$,

with $S_t{}^{*i}$ defined as in (6); at equilibrium, therefore, for each $i \in I$,

(20) $\bar{S}^i = \{\bar{s}^i \in \mathcal{S}^i : \bar{s}^i \geq_i \lambda s^{*i} \text{ for all } s^{*i} \in \bar{S}^i \text{ and all } \lambda \geq 0\}$,

with $\bar{S}^{*i}$ defined as in (7).

The relationship of the greed and quasi-competitive processes can be made evident as follows. Write the greed process as

$S_{t+1}{}^i = g[\Sigma_{j \in)i(} D(S_t{}^j); e^i]$ $(i = 1, 2, \ldots, n)$.

Then the quasi-competitive process may be written as

$S_{t+1}{}^i = g[\lambda \Sigma_{j \in)i(} D(S_t{}^j); e^i]$ $(i = 1, 2, \ldots, n)$.

In the preceding formulas, g is the specific function characterizing the greed response and λD denotes the set $\{\lambda d : d \in D, \lambda \geq 0\}$, i.e., a cone through D

with vertex at 0_x. More explicitly, for any $D^* \subseteq \mathfrak{X}$ and any "characteristic" ϵ, we have

$$g(D^*; \epsilon) = \{(d, z) \in \mathcal{S}_\epsilon : w_0 + d + z \geqq w_0 - d^* + z^*,$$

$$\text{provided } d^* \in D^* \text{ and } (-d^*, z^*) \in \mathcal{S}_\epsilon\},$$

with $\mathcal{S}_\epsilon = \{d, z\}: w_0 + d + z \in X', z \in Z'\}$, $\epsilon = (X', w_0', \geqq, Z')$, $X' \subseteq \mathfrak{X}$. $w_0 \in \mathfrak{X}$, $Z' \subseteq \mathfrak{X}$.

We refer to the quasi-competitive process as *informationally more efficient* than the greed process in the sense that, for a given e^i, the response in the latter is based on the knowledge of the set $D_t \equiv \Sigma_{j \in)i(} D(S_t{}^j)$, while for the quasi-competitive response it is sufficient to know the smallest cone λD_t through D_t.[29]

In what follows, we shall show that the quasi-competitive process is nonwasteful for every decomposable environment (Theorem 3) and that it is unbiased for every "convex" environment (Theorem 4). Since essential single-valuedness is evident, it follows that the quasi-competitive process is Pareto-satisfactory. As to other properties, the quasi-competitive process is clearly impersonal (Definition 11). Its decisiveness, expressed in Definition 3(a), could be established, in a manner analogous to the existence of competitive equilibrium, but (as with competitive equilibrium) one would have to make additional restrictions on the nature of the environment.

8. Pareto-satisfactoriness of the quasi-competitive process in convex environments

The quasi-competitive process is seen to be essentially single-valued. An examination of the proof of Theorem 1 above shows that, without any additional assumptions on the environment (in particular, without using any convexity properties), the proof goes through *a fortiori* since $\lambda = 1$ is among the values for which the inequality $s^i \geq {}_i\lambda s^{*i}$ must hold. Hence we have

Theorem 3.   The quasi-competitive process is non-wasteful for every decomposable environment.

The counterpart of Theorem 2, on the other hand, does not hold without additional assumptions. We find it convenient to introduce

Definition 12.   A decomposable environment is called *convex* if:
(a) $\mathfrak{X}$ (the commodity space) is a (real) vector space;
(b)   for each $i \in I$, the sets X^i and Z^i are convex;
(c)   for each $i \in I$, and for each $x^* \in X^i$, the contour set $\{x \in X^i: x \geq {}_i x^*\}$ is convex;
(d)   ("steepness") from $x' >{}_i x''$ and $1 \geq \alpha > 0$, it follows that $\alpha x' + (1 - \alpha)x'' >{}_i x''$.

Remark E.   Property (c) in Definition 12 corresponds to the condition of quasi-concavity of the utility indicator. Property (d), together with continuity of the utility indicator, implies (c). The properties (a)–(d) of Definition 12 are essentially those usually assumed in welfare economics in connection with competitive equilibrium. They are in some respects slightly weaker than those made by Debreu in [3], except that he merely assumed $\Sigma_{i \in I} Z^i$, rather than each Z^i, to be convex. One should bear in mind, however, that "quasi-competitive" equilibrium is different from competitive equilibrium. For instance, in a situation such as that depicted by Arrow [1, fig. 3], there is no competitive equilibrium but there does exist a quasi-competitive equilibrium.

This may be seen with the help of the Edgeworth box diagram (Figure 1). In the figure, the holdings of unit 1 increase upwards and to the right, and those of unit 2 downwards and to the left. AB is an indifference curve for unit 1, whose contour set S_0^1, corresponding to the point A, consists of all points on and to the right of AB and on and above AE (as indicated by the line-shading); thus, for instance, unit 1 prefers G' and G'' to A. CAD is an indifference curve for unit 2, whose contour set S_0^2, corresponding to the point A, consists of points on or below CAD (as indicated by the dot-shading); thus, for instance, unit 2 prefers H to A. Now, with vertex at A, the admissible part $C(S_0^1)$ of the cone through S_0^1 consists of A and all points on and above KE but to the right of AF and KN, while the admissible part $C(S_0^2)$ of the cone through S_0^2 consists

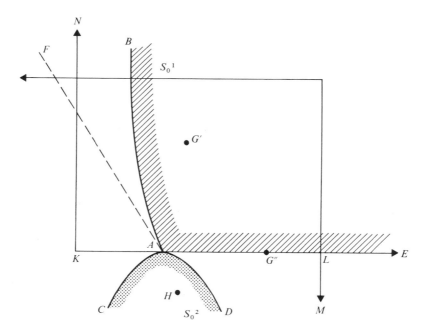

Figure 1

of A and all points on or to the left of LM but below KL. Hence A is the best (in fact, the only admissible) point for unit 1 from among points of $C(S_0{}^2)$, and also the best for unit 2 from among points of $C(S_0{}^1)$; hence quasi-competitive equilibrium prevails at A.

On the other hand, there is no competitive equilibrium at A: a negatively inclined price line through A would encourage unit 2 to move away from A to the interior of $S_0{}^2$, while a horizontal price line through A would encourage unit 1 to move away from A toward E.

Theorem 4. The quasi-competitive process is unbiased for every convex environment.

Proof. In view of Definition 3(d), it is enough to consider any "translate" of the given environment.[30] Hence, without loss of generality, we may take a Pareto-optimal program $\hat{s} = [\hat{s}^1, \hat{s}^2, \ldots, \hat{s}^n]$, where $\hat{s}^j = (\hat{d}^j, \hat{z}^j)$, such that

(21) $\quad \hat{d}^j = 0_x \quad$ for all $j \in I$,

and the theorem will be proved if it is shown that such a program is a solution of the quasi-competitive process.

As in the proof of Theorem 2, we define the sets

(22) $\quad S_0{}^i = \{s_0{}^i = (d_0{}^i, z_0{}^i) \in \mathcal{S}^i \colon s_0{}^i \geq_i \hat{s}^i\}$

and

(23) $\quad S_1{}^i = \{s_1{}^i = (d_1{}^i, z_1{}^i) \in \mathcal{S}^i \colon s^i \geq_i \lambda s^{*i} \quad$ for all $s^{*i} \in S_0{}^{*i}, \lambda \geq 0\}$,

with $S_0{}^{*i}$ defined as in (13).

It must again be shown that

(24) $\quad S_1{}^i \subseteq S_0{}^i \quad$ for each $i \in I$

and

(25) $\quad S_0{}^i \subseteq S_1{}^i \quad$ for each $i \in I$.

Since the inequality in (23) holds for $\lambda = 1$, (24) follows by the argument used to establish (15) in the proof of Theorem 2.

It remains to establish (25). Suppose (25) is false. Then, for some $i \in I$ and $s_0{}^i \in S_0{}^i$, we have $s_0{}^i \notin S_1{}^i$. Since $s_0{}^i \in \mathcal{S}^i$, there must exist a program $\tilde{s} = [\tilde{s}^1, \tilde{s}^2, \ldots, \tilde{s}^n]$, with $\tilde{s}^j = (\tilde{d}^j, \tilde{z}^j)$, and some $0 \leq \lambda < \infty$ such that

(26) $\quad \tilde{s}^i \in \mathcal{S}^i, \quad \tilde{d}^i = -\lambda \sum_{k \in)i(} \tilde{d}^k, \quad \tilde{s}^k \in S_0{}^k$ for $k \in)i(, \quad \tilde{s}^i >_i s_0{}^i$.

To show that this supposition leads to a contradiction, we find it convenient to consider first the case $\lambda \geq 1$, and then the case $0 \leq \lambda < 1$.

Case 1: $\lambda \geq 1$. We define a program $\tilde{\tilde{s}} = [\tilde{\tilde{s}}^1, \tilde{\tilde{s}}^2, \ldots, \tilde{\tilde{s}}^n]$ by the conditions

$$\tilde{\tilde{s}}^i = \left(1 - \frac{1}{\lambda}\right) \hat{s}^i + \frac{1}{\lambda} \tilde{s}^i, \quad \tilde{\tilde{s}}^k = \tilde{s}^k \text{ for each } k \in)i(.$$

Then

$$\Sigma_{j\in I}\,\widetilde{\widetilde{d}}^{\,j} = \widetilde{\widetilde{d}}^{\,i} + \Sigma_{k\in)i(}\,\widetilde{\widetilde{d}}^{\,k} = \frac{1}{\lambda}\,\widetilde{d}^{\,i} + \Sigma_{k\in)i(}\,\widetilde{d}^{\,k} = \frac{1}{\lambda}\left(-\lambda\,\Sigma_{k\in)i(}\,\widetilde{d}^{\,k}\right)$$

$$+ \Sigma_{k\in)i(}\,\widetilde{d}^{\,k} = 0_x,$$

so that $\widetilde{\widetilde{s}}$ is consistent.

Also, in view of the convexity of X^i,

$$\widetilde{\widetilde{w}}^{\,i} \equiv w_0^{\,i} + \widetilde{\widetilde{d}}^{\,i} + \widetilde{\widetilde{z}}^{\,i} = \left(1 - \frac{1}{\lambda}\right)\hat{w}^i + \frac{1}{\lambda}\,\widetilde{w}^i \in X^i,$$

since both $\hat{w}^i \equiv w_0^{\,i} + \hat{d}^{\,i} + \hat{z}^{\,i} \in X^i$ and $\widetilde{w}^i \equiv \widetilde{d}^{\,i} + \widetilde{z}^{\,i} \in X^i$. Similarly,

$$\widetilde{\widetilde{z}}^{\,i} = \left(1 - \frac{1}{\lambda}\right)\hat{z}^{\,i} + \frac{1}{\lambda}\,\widetilde{z}^{\,i} \in Z^i,$$

because of the convexity of Z^i.

Hence, $\widetilde{\widetilde{s}}^{\,i} \in \mathcal{S}^i$. On the other hand, for each $k \in)i($, we have $\widetilde{\widetilde{s}}^{\,k} \in \mathcal{S}^k$ by construction, since $\widetilde{\widetilde{s}}^{\,k} = \widetilde{s}^{\,k} \in S_0^{\,k} \subseteq \mathcal{S}^k$. Thus it has been shown that $\widetilde{\widetilde{s}}^{\,j} \in \mathcal{I}^j$ for each $j \in I$ and also that $\widetilde{\widetilde{s}}$ is consistent, which (in a decomposable environment) means that $\widetilde{\widetilde{s}}$ is possible.

Now, since $\widetilde{\widetilde{w}}^{\,i}$ is a convex mixture of $\hat{w}^i$ and $\widetilde{w}^i$, both of which belong to the convex contour set $\{x\colon\ x \geq {}_i\hat{w}^i\}$, it follows that $\widetilde{\widetilde{w}}^{\,i} \geq {}_i\hat{w}^i$, i.e., equivalently, $\widetilde{\widetilde{s}}^{\,i} \geq \hat{s}^{\,i}$. Also, for each $k \in)i($, we have $\widetilde{\widetilde{s}}^{\,k} \geq {}_k\hat{s}^{\,k}$, since $\widetilde{\widetilde{s}}^{\,k} = \widetilde{s}^{\,k} \in S_0^{\,k}$. Hence $\widetilde{\widetilde{s}}^{\,j} \geq {}_j\hat{s}^{\,j}$ for each $j \in I$. But $\widetilde{\widetilde{s}}$ is possible and $\hat{s}$ Pareto-optimal. Hence it must be that $\widetilde{\widetilde{s}}^{\,j} \sim {}_j\hat{s}^{\,j}$ for each $j \in I$; in particular, $\widetilde{\widetilde{s}}^{\,i} \sim {}_i\hat{s}^{\,i}$, i.e., equivalently, $\widetilde{\widetilde{w}}^{\,i} \sim {}_i\hat{w}^i$.

On the other hand, $\widetilde{s}^{\,i} > {}_is_0^{\,i} \geq {}_i\hat{s}^{\,i}$, so that $\widetilde{w}^i > {}_i\hat{w}^i$. It then follows from the "steepness" assumption [Definition 12(d)] that $\widetilde{\widetilde{w}}^{\,i} > {}_i\hat{w}^i$, since $\widetilde{\widetilde{w}}^{\,i}$ is a convex mixture of $\hat{w}^i$ and $\widetilde{w}^i$. This contradiction completes the proof for the case $\lambda \geq 1$.

Case 2: $0 \leq \lambda < 1$.   For this case, define $s^* = [s^{*1}, s^{*2}, \ldots, s^{*n}]$ by $s^{*k} = (1 - \lambda)\hat{s}^{\,k} + \lambda\widetilde{s}^{\,k}$ for each $k \in)i($ and $s^{*i} = \widetilde{s}^{\,i}$, with $\widetilde{s}$ given by (26) above.

By the convexity assumption, for each $k \in)i($ we have $s^{*k} \in \mathcal{S}^k$ and $s^{*k} \geq \hat{s}^{\,k}$. On the other hand, since $\hat{d}^{\,k} = 0_x$ by hypothesis, (26) yields

$$d^{*i} = \widetilde{d}^{\,i} = -\lambda\,\Sigma_{k\in)i(}\,\widetilde{d}^{\,k} = -\lambda\,\Sigma_{k\in)i(}\left(\frac{1}{\lambda}\,d^{*k}\right) = -\Sigma_{k\in)i(}\,d^{*k}.$$

Thus we see that s^* has all the properties given in (26) for $\widetilde{s}$, with $\lambda = 1$. Thus Case 2 ($0 \leq \lambda < 1$) has been reduced to Case 1 ($\lambda \geq 1$), which has already been disposed of. This completes the proof of the theorem.

9. Informational efficiency

It was noted in Section 7 that in "convex" Euclidean environments the quasi-competitive process is informationally more efficient than the greed process. In the present section, we give a more rigorous definition of the concept and a proof of the statement.

Consider an adjustment process $\pi = (f, \varphi, \mathfrak{M})$. The ith response function f^i has as its domain the set $\mathfrak{M}^{(n)} \times E$, where E is a class of economic environments. Define, for any economic environment e, the function f_e^i on $\mathfrak{M}^{(n)}$, given by $f_e^i(m) = f^i(m; e)$ for all $m \in \mathfrak{M}^{(n)}$. Now, for a given class E, the family of functions $f_e^i(e \in E, i \in I)$ induces a partitioning $\mathscr{P}_{f, E}$ on the space $\mathfrak{M}^{(n)}$, with m', $m'' \in \mathfrak{M}^{(n)}$ belonging to the same equivalence class if, for each $i \in I$, we have $f_e^i(m') = f_e^i(m'')$ for all $e \in E$. We adopt

Definition 13. The adjustment process $\pi^* = (f^*, \varphi, \mathfrak{M})$ is said to be *informationally at least as efficient as* $\pi^{**} = (f^{**}, \varphi, \mathfrak{M})$ *over the class of environments* E if the partitioning $\mathscr{P}_{f^{**}, E}$ is no less fine than the partitioning $\mathscr{P}_{f^*, E}$. That is, $f^{**i}(m'; e) = f^{**i}(m''; e)$ for all $e \in E$ and each $i \in I$ implies $f^{*i}(m'; e) = f^{*i}(m''; e)$ for all $e \in E$ and each $i \in I$, given any $m', m'' \in \mathfrak{M}^{(n)}$.[31]

If π^* is informationally at least as efficient over E as π^{**}, while π^{**} is not (is) informationally at least as efficient over E as π^{**}, we say that π^* is informationally more efficient over E than π^{**} (as efficient over E as π^{**}).

We shall now show that the quasi-competitive process is informationally more efficient over the class of (Euclidean space) convex environments than the greed process.

We recall that the ith response function for the greed function is of the form $g(D, \epsilon)$, where $D \subseteq \mathfrak{X}$ and $\epsilon = e^i$ is an individual "characteristic," while the quasi-competitive process has a response function of the form $g(\lambda D, \epsilon)$, where $\lambda D = \{x \in \mathfrak{X} : x = \lambda d, \lambda \geq 0, d \in D\}$, and g is the function defined in Section 7. Since the two processes are certainly not informationally equally efficient, it will suffice to show that if, for some $D', D'' \subseteq \mathfrak{X}$, we have $g(D', \epsilon) = g(D'', \epsilon)$ for all convex characteristics ϵ, then $g(\lambda D', \epsilon) = g(\lambda D'', \epsilon)$ for all convex characteristics ϵ.

Since, obviously, $g(\lambda D', \epsilon) = g(\lambda D'', \epsilon)$ if $\lambda D' = \lambda D''$, it is enough to consider the case $\lambda D' \neq \lambda D''$. It will therefore suffice to show that, given D' and D'' such that $\lambda D' \neq \lambda D''$, there exists a convex characteristic ϵ_0 such that $g(D', \epsilon_0) \neq g(D'', \epsilon_0)$. Without loss of generality we confine ourselves to the case of pure trade, so that ϵ_0 is given by the admissible set $X_0 \subseteq \mathfrak{X}$, initial holdings $w_0 \in \mathfrak{X}$, and a preference relation ρ_0.

Write $X_0^* = X_0 - \omega_0$, and

$$X' = g(D', \epsilon_0) = \{x \in X_0^* : x \geq d' \text{ for every } d' \in D' \cap X_0^*\},$$

with similar definition for X''. (The inequality $x \geq d'$ is in the sense of ρ_0.)

Thus we must find such values ρ_0 (together with X_0 and ω_0) that given any D' and D'' such that $\lambda D' \neq \lambda D''$, it follows that $X' \neq X''$.

Without loss of generality, we may now assume that there is an element $d_0 \in D''$ such that $d_0 \neq 0_x$ and $\lambda d_0 \notin D'$ for all $\lambda \geq 0$, for otherwise (taking into account the possibility of interchanging the labels D' and D'') it would follow that $\lambda D' = \lambda D''$.

Now suppose we can find a "convex" ordering ρ_0 (in the sense of Definition 12) and $x_0 \in X_0{}^*$ such that (for $d' \in X_0{}^*$) $d_0 > x_0 \geq d'$ for all $d' \in D'$ (with inequalities in the sense of ρ_0). Then $x_0 \in X'$, but $x_0 \notin X''$, and the proof is complete. To define the required ordering ρ_0, we find it convenient to rotate the axes in such a way that each point x can be written in the form $x = (y, z)$, where z is scalar, $d_0 = (0_g, \delta_0)$, and we may take $\delta_0 > 0$ since $d_0 \neq 0_x$.

We shall pick an ordering ρ_0 (related to the lexicographic ordering) defined by what follows. Given $x' = (y', z')$ and $x'' = (y'', z'')$, then:

(a) $x' > x''$ (i.e., x' is strictly preferred to x'' in the sense of ρ_0) if and only if $\|y'\| < \|y''\|$, or $\|y'\| = \|y''\|$ and $z' > z''$;

(b) $x' \sim x''$ (i.e., x' is indifferent to x'' in the sense of ρ_0) if and only if $\|y'\| = \|y''\|$ and $z' = z''$. [The symbol $\|y\|$ denotes the norm (length) of the vector y.]

It may be verified that the contour sets of ρ_0 are convex and that if $x' > x''$, then $\alpha x' + (1 - \alpha) x'' > x''$ for $0 < \alpha < 1$ (with the preference inequality in the sense of ρ_0).

Clearly, $d_0 > d'$ for all $d' \in D'$, since $\lambda d_0 \notin D'$ for all $\lambda \geq 0$. Now take $x_0 = (0_g, \frac{1}{2} \delta_0)$. Then $x_0 < d_0$, since both have zero as the norm of the first component; on the other hand, $x_0 > d_1'$ for all $d_1 = (0_g, \delta) \in D'$, since it must be that $\delta < 0$; also, $x_0 > d_2' = (y, z)$ for $y \neq 0_g$, since then $\|y\| > 0$. This completes the proof.

Notes

1   This paper is dedicated to Jacob Marschak on the occasion of his sixtieth birthday.

In an earlier version of a part of this paper [5], I expressed my indebtedness for stimulation and comments to a number of colleagues from the Cowles Commission and the University of Minnesota. I am particularly grateful to Kenneth J. Arrow and Hirofumi Uzawa for valuable suggestions resulting in the simplification of some of the proofs.

The paper is partly based on work done during my tenure of a fellowship at the Center for Advanced Study in the Behavioral Sciences; its completion was facilitated by grants (at the University of Minnesota and Stanford University) from the Office of Naval Research (Tasks NR-042-200 and NR-047-004) and (at Stanford University) from the Rockefeller Foundation.

2   The work of J. Marschak and R. Radner (e.g., [6], [9]) is carried on in this spirit. See also T. Marschak [7].

3   The relationship of the present work to the Hotelling-Lange-Lerner theory of marginal cost pricing and the socialist "competitive solution" will be discussed elsewhere.

4   For instance, it is often postulated that $X = (X^+)^{(n)}$ = the n-fold Cartesian product of the non-negative orthant X^+ of $\mathfrak{X}$.

5 For $w' \in \mathfrak{X}, w'' \in \mathfrak{X}$, we write $w' >_i w''$ to mean $w' \geq_i w''$ but not $w'' \geq_i w'$; $w' \sim_i w''$ means $w' \geq_i w''$ and $w'' \geq_i w'$.

6 Even though $\mathfrak{X}$ need not be a vector space (linear system) in the algebraic sense of the term, we find it convenient to call the elements of $\mathfrak{X}$ vectors.

7 We sometimes refer to e^* as a *translate* of e.

8 E.g., Arrow and Debreu [2], McKenzie [8].

9 See Arrow [1, Theorem 5 (non-wastefulness), Theorem 4 (unbiasedness)] and Debreu [3, Theorem 1 (non-wastefulness), Theorem 2 (unbiasedness)].

10 A term suggested by Jacob Marschak.

11 This is slightly stronger than the more familiar *additivity* condition (with ΣZ^i denoting the algebraic sum, not union):

$$\{x \in \mathfrak{X}: \ x = \Sigma_{i \in I} z^i \text{ for some } (z^1, z^2, \ldots, z^n) \in Z\} = \Sigma_{i \in I} Z_i.$$

12 In the sense that it cares only about its own share (component) of a distribution.

13 The adjective "concrete" is usually omitted where the context makes the nature of the process clear.

14 The expression $2^{\mathfrak{A}}$ denotes the power set of $\mathfrak{A}$.

15 All concepts are relative to an environment e.

16 We write $)i(= \{1, 2, \ldots, i - 1, i + 1, \ldots, n\} = I \sim \{i\}$; here $\sim$ represents the set-theoretic difference.

17 A somewhat milder condition on f^i, of interest in some contexts, is that f^i be symmetric in $S^1, S^2, \ldots, S^{i-1}, S^{i+1}, \ldots, S^n$. Such symmetry creates *anonymity* for units other than i in their offers to i.

18 A plan $s = (d, z)$ is called i-achievable if $w_0^i + d + z \in X^i$ and $z \in Z^i$. The set of all i-achievable (simple) plans is denoted by $\mathcal{S}^i$. In a decomposable environment, a program $s = \{s^1, s^2, \ldots, s^n\}$ is achievable if it is i-achievable for each $i \in I$; hence it is possible if it is consistent and i-achievable for each $i \in I$.

19 We write $s \geq_i s^*$, $s = (d, z)$, $s^* = (d^*, z^*)$ if and only if $w_0^i + d + z \geq_i w_0^i + d^* + z^*$. $\mathcal{S}^i$ is defined in note 18.

20 It may be helpful to give an equivalent but more detailed formulation of the greed process: $S_{t+1}^i = \{s_{t+1}^i = (d_{t+1}^i, z_{t+1}^i): w_0^i + d_{t+1}^i + z_{t+1}^i \in X^i; z_{t+1}^i \in Z^i; w_0^i + d_{t+1}^i + z_{t+1}^i \geq_i w_0^i - \Sigma_{k \in)i(} d_t^k + z^{*i}$ whenever $w_0^i - \Sigma_{k \in)i(} d_t^k + z^{*i} \in X^i$ and $z^{*i} \in Z^i$; and for some $z_t^k [k \in)i( ]$, $(d_t^k, z_t^k) \in S_t^k$ for each $k \in)i(\}$.

21 The greed process is also decisive and impersonal in the sense of Definitions 3(a) and 11.

22 It is at this point that use is made of the assumption of technological independence.

23 And preferably also decisive and impersonal.

24 See Definition 12.

25 Provided, of course, that $\lambda d^* \in \mathfrak{X}$. When $\mathfrak{X}$ is a vector space (as we shall assume), this condition is always satisfied.

26 Geometrically, in the quasi-competitive process each unit maximizes over the admissible part of the smallest *cone* (with vertex at 0_x) containing the others' offers, while in the usual interpretation of the competitive mecha-

nism there is maximization over the admissible part of the smallest *closed half-space* containing the others' offers and 0_x.

Unlike the process in the usual dynamic models of perfect competition, the quasi-competitive process does not presuppose the existence of a common price vector for the whole market while the adjustments are taking place (i.e., away from equilibrium). However, if the customary assumptions are made (strictly convex and "smooth" indifference surfaces), the cones of the quasi-competitive process turn out to be (non-closed) half-spaces (plus the vertex) and, *at equilibrium*, a unique price vector prevailing in the whole market may be defined.

(For an illustrative example of the difference between the two processes, see Remark E. In this case, the cone through $S_0{}^2$, apart from the vertex A, is an open half-space.)

27   With $\mathfrak{X}$ assumed to be a vector space ("perfect divisibility" of commodities).

28   S^i is defined in note 18.

29   A more rigorous formulation of the informational efficiency concept is found in Section 9.

30   See note 7 for definition of the translate.

31   In other contexts, other partitionings induced by f (in particular, that on E) serve as a natural basis for alternative concepts of informational efficiency.

References

[1]   Arrow, K. J. "An Extension of the Basic Theorems of Classical Welfare Economics," in J. Neyman, ed., *Proceedings of the Second Berkeley Symposium on Mathematical Statistics and Probability*, Berkeley and Los Angeles: University of California Press, 1951, pp. 507–32.

[2]   Arrow, K. J., and G. Debreu. "Existence of an Equilibrium for a Competitive Economy," *Econometrica*, Vol. 22 (1954), 265–90.

[3]   Debreu, G. "Valuation Equilibrium and Pareto Optimum," *Proceedings of the National Academy of Sciences*, Vol. 40 (1954), 588–92.

[4]   Hayek, F. A. "The Use of Knowledge in Society," *American Economic Review*, 35 (1945), 519–30.

[5]   Hurwicz, L. "Decentralized Resource Allocation," *Cowles Commission Discussion Paper: Economics No. 2112*, May, 1955.

[6]   Marschak, J. "Elements for a Theory of Teams," *Management Science*, Vol. 1 (1955), 127–37.

[7]   Marschak, T. "Centralization and Decentralization in Economic Organizations," Technical Report No. 42, Office of Naval Research Contract N6onr-25133, April 1957, Department of Economics, Stanford University.

[8]   McKenzie, L. "On the Existence of General Equilibrium for a Competitive Market," *Econometrica*, Vol. 27 (1959), 54–71.

[9]   Radner, R. "The Application of Linear Programming to Team Decision Problems," *Management Science*, Vol. 5 (1959), 143–50.

On the dimensional requirements of informationally decentralized Pareto-satisfactory processes [1]

LEONID HURWICZ

This note deals with the minimal dimensionality of the message space of informationally decentralized Pareto-satisfactory processes.[2] The results to be presented constitute fragments and may at best throw light on the shape of a general theory which is yet to be developed.[3] In Part I, we deal with "point-valued" processes, in which messages are points in finite-dimensional vector spaces; this case follows up the treatment in [3], Sec. 2 of Ch. 14. In Part II, the messages are "set-valued," and the processes are of the more general type considered in [2].

Point-valued processes may be regarded as a subclass of set-valued processes. In the present note, perfectly competitive processes are treated as point-valued, but a closely related "quasi-competitive" process [2] is of the set-valued variety.

Part I. Point-valued processes

1,0. Two results are given in Part I: (a) There are no informationally decentralized processes that are Pareto-satisfactory for classical environments and have lower dimensional requirements than the competitive processes.[4] (b) a finite-dimensional space is insufficient for an informationally decentralized process that is Pareto-satisfactory for all decomposable[5] environments.

Without being completely rigorous, let me indicate the approach used. First, although I refer to Pareto-satisfactory *processes*, I only study the static aspects of the optimality conditions for specific categories of environments. Informational decentralization always requires "privacy"[6] plus possibly smoothness, self-relevance, and anonymity properties. In the proof of Part I, the environment is represented parametrically, but conclusions hold for nonparametric families of environments. We shall only study the case of two-persons pure exchange, but again the analysis may easily be extended to multiperson situations involving production.

One more specialization of the mechanism model: Instead of considering a general multidimensional message complex m, we shall take it to be of the form

$$m = (x, \nu),$$

where x represents the proposed action vector (here the proposed trade vector), and ν is a vector of auxiliary parameters. (In the competitive process, prices play the role of such auxiliary parameters.) When $m = x$ (so that ν is absent), we have a *proposed action process* as a special case.

We denote by G^i relations appearing in the decentralized (privacy-satisfying) form of the optimality conditions. We may think of G^i as a verification sentence: If a message $m = (x, \nu)$ satisfies (does not satisfy) the relation G^i with respect to θ^i, the i-th agent states that the message is (is not) compatible with his characteristic parameter θ^i. These relations may be written

$$G^i(x, \nu; \theta^i) \quad (i = 1, \ldots, N),$$

where θ^i is the i-th (out of N) individual's parameter vector. Thus G^i is a ternary relation on the spaces of x, V, and θ^i. In the usual situations these relations are expressed as systems of equalities, say

$$g^i(x, \nu; \theta^i) = 0 \quad (i = 1, \ldots, N)$$

or

$$g^i(x, \nu; \theta^i) \geq 0 \quad (i = 1, \ldots, N),$$

where g^i is vector-valued.

1.1. Dimensional requirements in classical environments

In this context, "classical" means such that the first-order marginal equalities are necessary and sufficient for optimality; this involves convexity of preferences and conditions ruling outcorner optima. Actually, we consider a much narrower class (a subset of quadratic utility functions) because a wider class of environments cannot have lower dimensional requirements. Specifically, considering the case of two traders and three goods, we assume that the i-th individual's utility function is of the form

$$u_i = -\tfrac{1}{2} X_{i1}^2 + b_{i1} X_{i1} - \tfrac{1}{2} X_{i2}^2 + b_{i2} X_{i2} + X_{i3} \quad (i = 1, 2),$$

where X_{ij} represents the holdings (not the trade) of the j-th good by the i-th agent. Hence the usual optimality relations require that there exist auxiliary parameters μ_1, μ_2 such that

$$-x_{ij} + (b_{ij} - \omega_{ij}) = \mu_j \quad (i = 1, 2; j = 1, 2),$$

$$\Sigma_{i=1}^2 x_{ij} = 0 \quad (j = 1, 2, 3),$$

where ω_{ij} is the initial endowment and x_{ij} the *trade* in the j-th good for the i-th individual. $(x_{ij} = X_{ij} + \omega_{ij}$ for all i, j.)

Thus we see that two auxiliary parameters μ_j (or $M - 1$ parameters when there are M goods) are sufficient to specify the optimality conditions, and these optimality conditions are in a decentralized form:

$$g^i(x, \mu; \theta^i) = 0 \quad (i = 1, 2),$$

where

$$x = \|x_{ij}\|,$$

$$g^i \equiv \begin{pmatrix} g_1{}^i \\ g_1{}^i \end{pmatrix}, \qquad g_j{}^i \equiv -x_{ij} + (b_{ij} - \omega_{ij}) - \mu_j$$

$$\theta^i \equiv \begin{pmatrix} \theta_1{}^i \\ \theta_2{}^i \end{pmatrix}, \qquad \theta_j{}^i \equiv b_{ij} - \omega_{ij}$$

Since an analogous situation holds for classical environments in general, we conclude that this set of environments requires no more than $M - 1$ auxiliary parameters (when there are M goods and N traders).

The question is whether one could get by with fewer than $M - 1$ parameters.

We illustrate the technique of analysis on the $M = 3$ case, but its more general applicability will be apparent. We follow the approach used in [3], Sec. 2 of Ch. 14, where a crucial role is played by the *single-valuedness lemma* which asserts that, for a privacy-preserving process Pareto-satisfactory[7] over a class of environments E having the "uniqueness property" (to be defined in the following) with respect to a subclass E^*, the parameter vector from this subclass E^* is uniquely determined by (a single-valued function of) the message complex. We then examine the dimensionality of the space of variation of the parameter vector, and this imposes a minimum requirement on the message dimensions if the relevant[8] mapping is postulated to be "smooth"[9] (for example, to have a Lipschitzian selection[10]).

Definition. A class of environments E is said to possess the *uniqueness property* with respect to the parameter space Θ^* if and only if E has a subset E^* parametrized by a subset Θ^* such that, for any $\tilde{\theta} \in \Theta^*$, $\tilde{\tilde{\theta}} \in \Theta^*$, (i) $(\tilde{\theta}^1, \tilde{\theta}^2) \in \Theta$ and $(\tilde{\tilde{\theta}}^1, \tilde{\tilde{\theta}}^2) \in \Theta$ (that is, $\Theta \supseteq \mathrm{Pr}_1\Theta^* \times \mathrm{Pr}_2\Theta^*$) and (ii) if x is optimal for $(\tilde{\theta}^1, \tilde{\theta}^2)$, $(\tilde{\theta}^1, \tilde{\tilde{\theta}}^2)$, $(\tilde{\tilde{\theta}}^1, \tilde{\theta}^2)$, $(\tilde{\tilde{\theta}}^1, \tilde{\tilde{\theta}}^2)$, then

$$\tilde{\theta} = \tilde{\tilde{\theta}}.$$

The single-valuedness lemma. If a privacy-preserving process specified by the equilibrium relations G^i, $i = 1, 2$, and the outcome relation H, is Pareto-nonwasteful over the class of environments E parametrized by Θ which has the uniqueness property with respect to a subset Θ^* of Θ, and equilibria exist for all θ in $\mathrm{Pr}_1\Theta^* \times \mathrm{Pr}^2\Theta^*$, then the relations $\tilde{\theta} \in \Theta^*$, $\tilde{\tilde{\theta}} \in \Theta^*$, $G^i(m, \tilde{\theta}^i)$, $G^i(m, \tilde{\tilde{\theta}}^i)$, $i = 1, 2$, imply $\tilde{\theta} = \tilde{\tilde{\theta}}$.

Proof. The single-valuedness lemma is established by noting that if, for some message complex m, and $(\tilde{\theta}^1, \tilde{\theta}^2) \in \Theta^*$, $(\tilde{\tilde{\theta}}^1, \tilde{\tilde{\theta}}^2) \in \Theta^*$,

(1) $\quad G^i(m, \tilde{\theta}^i)$ and $G^i(m, \tilde{\tilde{\theta}}^i)$ $\quad (i = 1, 2)$

and $H(x, m)$ is the outcome relation [that is, $H(x, m)$ means that x is an action to be taken when m is an equilibrium message complex], then (by nonwastefulness) x is optimal for both $(\tilde{\theta}^1, \tilde{\theta}^2)$ and for $(\tilde{\tilde{\theta}}^1, \tilde{\tilde{\theta}}^2)$.

But since (1) implies that $G^1(m, \tilde{\theta}^1)$ and $G^2(m, \tilde{\tilde{\theta}}^2)$ also hold, nonwastefulness of the process over Θ also implies that x is optimal for $(\tilde{\theta}^1, \tilde{\tilde{\theta}}^2)$, and similarly for $(\tilde{\tilde{\theta}}^1, \tilde{\theta}^2)$.

Now the hypothesis of the uniqueness property is satisfied, and it follows that

$$\tilde{\theta} = \tilde{\tilde{\theta}},$$

that is, θ is a single-valued function of m.   Q.E.D.

Returning to the Edgeworth box quadratic case, it remains to be shown that the uniqueness property holds.

Using the fact that, at an optimum, $x_{1j} + x_{2j} = 0$, and writing

$$x_{1j} \equiv x_j, \qquad x = \begin{pmatrix} x_1 \\ x_2 \end{pmatrix},$$

we may restate the optimality relations for this case as

$$-x + \theta^1 = x + \theta^2.$$

Now suppose that, for a fixed x,

$$-x + \tilde{\theta}^1 = x + \tilde{\theta}^2$$
$$-x + \tilde{\theta}^1 = x + \tilde{\tilde{\theta}}^2$$
$$-x + \tilde{\tilde{\theta}}^1 = x + \tilde{\theta}^2$$
$$-x + \tilde{\tilde{\theta}}^1 = x + \tilde{\tilde{\theta}}^2.$$

Clearly, $\tilde{\theta} = \tilde{\tilde{\theta}}$ follows, and so the uniqueness property holds. Thus, by the single-valuedness lemma, we conclude that for any privacy-satisfying Pareto-satisfactory process, to be written as

$$G^i(x, v, \theta^i) \qquad (i = 1, 2),$$

$m = (x, v)$ uniquely determines $\theta = (\theta^1, \theta^2)$. Since θ can vary over, say, a four-dimensional unit cube, m must be four-dimensional if $G = (G^1, G^2)$ is quasi-Lipschitzian [that is, if its graph contains a Lipschitzian single-valued function $\theta = f(x, v)$].[11]

But $m = (x, v)$ and x is two-dimensional, hence v must be two-dimensional. The proof for $M \geqslant 2$ goes through in the same way.

As pointed out by David Starrett, and analogously to the case examined in [2], Sec. 2 of Ch. 14, a *proposed action* process is ruled out even *without the smoothness* assumption. This is so because here v is absent and we have

$$G^i(x, \theta^i) \qquad (i = 1, 2)$$

as our decentralized optimality relations. Now the "cross-fertilization" procedure implies that if x is optimal for $\tilde{\theta}$ and for $\tilde{\tilde{\theta}}$, then it is also optimal for $\tilde{\theta}^1$, $\tilde{\tilde{\theta}}^2$, but the optimality relations $-x + \theta^1 = x + \theta^2$ show that this is not so when

$\tilde{\theta} \neq \tilde{\tilde{\theta}}$. Thus even a nonsmooth proposed action privacy-satisfying Pareto-satisfactory process cannot exist.[12] (But, of course perfect competition is *not* a proposed action process[13]; it has $M - 1$ prices as auxiliary parameters.)

1.2. Dimensional requirements in decomposable nonconvex environments[14]

1.2.1. In this section it is shown that there are decomposable nonconvex environments that cannot be served by a finite-dimensional message space.[15]

The example considered in this section involves two goods: a primary good, denoted by t and a consumer good, denoted by y. The total initial supply of the good t is T. We will suppose (although it is shown later how this assumption can be removed) that t is indivisible, that is, it can only assume integer values; 0, 1, ..., T. If the total initial supply is so distributed that agent 1 has t and agent 2 has $T - t$, then their respective outputs of y will be denoted by

$$a_t^{\,1} \text{ and } a_t^{\,2} \qquad (0 \leqslant t \leqslant T),$$

so that the total output is $a_t^{\,1} + a_t^{\,2}$. Now we shall assume that the two agents are also consumers and that their utilities are strictly monotone in y.[16]

We note that under these assumptions an allocation of the primary good is optimal if and only if the total output is maximized; that is, an allocation $\bar{t}$ (in which agent 1 gets $\bar{t}$ of the primary good and agent 2 gets $T - \bar{t}$) is optimal if and only if[17]

$$a_{\bar{t}}^{\,1} + a_{\bar{t}}^{\,2} \geq a_t^{\,1} + a_t^{\,2} \qquad \text{for all } t.$$

To relate this economy to our general notation, we write (for a fixed $T \geq 1$)

$$\theta^{iT} = (a_0^{\,i}, a_1^{\,i}, \ldots, a_T^{\,i}) \qquad (i = 1, 2),$$

$$\Theta_T^{\,i} = \{\theta^{iT} : a_t^{\,i} \geq 0 \quad \text{for all } t\},$$

and

$$\Theta_T = \Theta_T^{\,1} \times \Theta_T^{\,2} = \{\theta_T : \theta_T = (\theta^{1T}, \theta^{2T}), \theta^{1T} \in \Theta_T^{\,1}, \theta^{2T} \in \Theta_T^{\,2}\}.$$

We now define a subset Θ_T^* of Θ_T by

$$\Theta_T^* = \{\theta_T \in \Theta_T : \Sigma_{t=0}^T a_t^{\,1} = \alpha_1, \Sigma_{t=0}^T a_t^{\,2} = \alpha_2, \text{ for some fixed } \alpha_1 > 0,$$

$$\alpha_2 > 0; a_t^{\,1} + a_t^{\,2} = a_0^{\,1} + a_0^{\,2} \text{ for all } t\}.$$

It follows from this definition that, for $\theta \in \Theta_T^*, \theta = (\theta^1, \theta^2), \theta^i = (a_0^{\,i}, a_1^{\,i}, \ldots, a_T^{\,i}), i = 1, 2$, we have

$$a_0^{\,1} = \alpha_1 - \Sigma_{t=1}^T a_t,$$

$$a_0^{\,2} = \frac{\alpha_1 + \alpha_2}{T + 1} - a_0^{\,1},$$

and

$$a_t^{\,2} = a_0^{\,1} + a_0^{\,2} - a_t^{\,1} \qquad \text{for all } t.$$

Hence $a_0{}^1, a_0{}^2, a_1{}^2, \ldots, a_T{}^2$ can be determined once $a_1{}^1, a_2{}^1, \ldots, a_T{}^1$ are given and, therefore,

$$\dim \Theta_T{}^* = T.$$

We shall now show that Θ_T possesses the uniqueness property with regard to $\Theta_T{}^*$, so that (by the single-valuedness lemma of Section 1.1) the message space must be at least of dimension T. By considering the sequence of environments parametrized by Θ_T, $T \to \infty$, we see the class of environments containing all environments of this sequence cannot be served by a finite-dimensional message space.

It remains to show that $\Theta_T{}^*$ does possess the uniqueness property, that is, if

(1) $\bar{t} \in \{0, 1, \ldots, T\}$,

(2) $(\tilde{\theta}^1, \tilde{\theta}^2) \equiv \tilde{\theta} \in \Theta_T{}^*$, $(\tilde{\tilde{\theta}}^1, \tilde{\tilde{\theta}}^2) \equiv \tilde{\tilde{\theta}} \in \Theta_T{}^*$,

(3) $\bar{t}$ is optimal for $(\tilde{\theta}^1, \tilde{\theta}^2), (\tilde{\theta}^1, \tilde{\tilde{\theta}}^2), (\tilde{\tilde{\theta}}^1, \tilde{\theta}^2), (\tilde{\tilde{\theta}}^1, \tilde{\tilde{\theta}}^2)$,

then

$$\tilde{\theta} = \tilde{\tilde{\theta}}.$$

To prove this implication, consider some $\bar{t}, \tilde{\theta}, \tilde{\tilde{\theta}}$ for which these hypotheses hold.

Since $\tilde{\theta} \in \Theta_T{}^*, \tilde{\tilde{\theta}} \in \Theta_T{}^*$, it follows that, for any $t' \in \{0, 1, \ldots, T\}$,

(1.1) $\tilde{a}_{t'}{}^1 + \tilde{a}_{t'}{}^2 = \tilde{a}_t{}^1 + \tilde{a}_t{}^2$ for all t

so that $0, 1, \ldots, T$ are optimal for $\tilde{\theta}$.

Similarly, $0, 1, \ldots, T$ are optimal for $\tilde{\tilde{\theta}}$, since, for any $t' \in \{0, 1, \ldots, T\}$,

(1.2) $\tilde{\tilde{a}}_{t'}{}^1 + \tilde{\tilde{a}}_{t'}{}^2 = \tilde{\tilde{a}}_t{}^1 + \tilde{\tilde{a}}_t{}^2$ for all t.

We pick an arbitrary $\bar{t} \in \{0, 1, \ldots, T\}$ and suppose that $\bar{t}$ is optimal not only for $\tilde{\theta}$ and $\tilde{\tilde{\theta}}$ but also for $(\tilde{\theta}^1, \tilde{\tilde{\theta}}^2)$ and for $(\tilde{\tilde{\theta}}^1, \tilde{\theta}^2)$.

It follows that

(2.1) $\tilde{a}_{\bar{t}}{}^1 + \tilde{\tilde{a}}_{\bar{t}}{}^2 \geq \tilde{a}_t{}^1 + \tilde{\tilde{a}}_t{}^2$ for all t,

(2.2) $\tilde{\tilde{a}}_{\bar{t}}{}^1 + \tilde{a}_{\bar{t}}{}^2 \geq \tilde{\tilde{a}}_t{}^1 + \tilde{a}_t{}^2$ for all t.

It is convenient to rewrite the preceding formulas in difference form (with $t' = \bar{t}$):

(1.1′) $\tilde{a}_{\bar{t}}{}^2 - \tilde{a}_t{}^2 = -(\tilde{a}_{\bar{t}}{}^1 - \tilde{a}_t{}^1)$

(1.2′) $\tilde{\tilde{a}}_{\bar{t}}{}^2 - \tilde{\tilde{a}}_t{}^2 = -(\tilde{\tilde{a}}_{\bar{t}}{}^1 - \tilde{\tilde{a}}_t{}^1)$ for all t.

(2.1′) $\tilde{a}_{\bar{t}}{}^1 - \tilde{a}_t{}^1 + (\tilde{\tilde{a}}_{\bar{t}}{}^2 - \tilde{\tilde{a}}_t{}^2) \geq 0$

(2.2′) $\tilde{\tilde{a}}_{\bar{t}}{}^1 - \tilde{\tilde{a}}_t{}^1 + (\tilde{a}_{\bar{t}}{}^2 - \tilde{a}_t{}^2) \geq 0$

Then, substituting from (1.2′) into (2.1′), we get

(3.1) $(\tilde{a}_{\bar{t}}{}^1 - \tilde{a}_t{}^1) - (\tilde{\tilde{a}}_{\bar{t}}{}^1 - \tilde{\tilde{a}}_t{}^1) \geq 0$ for all t, and substituting from $(1.1')$ into $(2.2')$, we get

(3.2) $(\tilde{\tilde{a}}_{\bar{t}}^{1} - \tilde{\tilde{a}}_{t}^{1}) - (\tilde{a}_{\bar{t}}^{1} - \tilde{a}_{t}^{1}) \geq 0$ for all t.

But (3.1) and (3.2) together imply

$(\tilde{\tilde{a}}_{\bar{t}}^{1} - \tilde{\tilde{a}}_{t}^{1}) - (\tilde{a}_{\bar{t}}^{1} - \tilde{a}_{t}^{1}) = 0$ for all t,

that is,

(4) $\tilde{\tilde{a}}_{t}^{1} = \tilde{a}_{t}^{1} + (\tilde{\tilde{a}}_{\bar{t}}^{1} - \tilde{a}_{\bar{t}}^{1})$ for all t.

Hence

(5) $\Sigma_{t=0}^{T} \tilde{\tilde{a}}_{t}^{1} = \Sigma_{t=0}^{T} \tilde{a}_{t}^{1} + (T+1)(\tilde{\tilde{a}}_{\bar{t}}^{1} - \tilde{a}_{\bar{t}}^{1})$.

But, by definition of $\Theta_T{}^*$,

(6) $\Sigma_{t=0}^{T} \tilde{\tilde{a}}_{t}^{1} = \Sigma_{t=0}^{T} \tilde{a}_{t}^{1} = \alpha_1$,

and so

$\tilde{\tilde{a}}_{\bar{t}}^{1} - \tilde{a}_{\bar{t}}^{1} = 0$.

Therefore, by (4), $\tilde{\tilde{a}}_{t}^{1} = \tilde{a}_{t}^{1}$, for all t, that is, $\tilde{\tilde{\theta}}^1 = \tilde{\theta}^1$. Similarly, $\tilde{\tilde{\theta}}^2 = \tilde{\theta}^2$, hence $\tilde{\theta} = \tilde{\tilde{\theta}}$. Thus $\Theta_T{}^*$ has the uniqueness property.

1.2.2. For a given T, the following is an example of a parametric mechanism (that is, with auxiliary parameters) which is privacy-satisfying. (We merely state the optimality conditions for t.)

The value t is optimal if and only if there exist auxiliary parameters ρ_t for $t \in \{0, 1, \ldots, T\}\backslash\{\bar{t}\}$ such that

$b_t^1 \geq \rho_t, \quad b_t^2 \geq -\rho_t$ for all $t \in \{0, 1, \ldots, T\}\backslash\{\bar{t}\}$,

where $b_t^i = a_{\bar{t}}^i - a_t^i$.

Here the number of parameters is one more than the lower bound following from the foregoing calculations. I do not know whether there exists a mechanism attaining that bound.

1.2.3. The example can be modified for a divisible t by defining α_t^i, t any real number such that $0 \leqslant t \leqslant T$, as the value obtained by linear interpolation between the values of α_t^i for *integral* t. The resulting utility function is Lipschitzian and could probably be smoothed further without affecting the optimality conditions.

Part II. Informational decentralization of set-valued processes in nondecomposable environments

2.0. In this section we illustrate the fact, also known from [3], that, in the absence of smoothness requirements, it is possible to construct mechanisms with low-dimensional message spaces, even in the presence of externalities.

Since it was shown in [2] that there exists a (set-valued) informationally decentralized process that is Pareto-satisfactory for all decomposable environments (the "greed process"), it is natural to ask whether an informationally decentralized could be constructed that is Pareto-satisfactory even for nondecomposable environments, that is, in the presence of externalities.

In this note it is shown that the answer is in the affirmative, at least in a two-person pure exchange economy with nonselfish preferences, provided no smoothness requirements are imposed. In fact, we are able to construct for this economy a very nonsmooth process using a one-dimensional message space. Such a process, using the Cantor mapping, is not even approximately feasible from a practical operational point of view. What our construction shows, as did that in Sec. 2 of [3], is that the problem should be investigated subject to some smoothness conditions. The construction given below is also of interest because it is applicable under much broader conditions than those postulated in [3].

2.1. More specifically, we shall construct an adjustment process where the message of the i-th person at time t is a set of proposed trades $X_t{}^i$ (a subset of the commodity space). The difference equations governing the process are

$$X_{t+1}{}^i = f^i(X_t{}^1, X_t{}^2; e^i) \qquad (i = 1, 2).$$

Therefore, the equilibrium conditions are

$$X^i = f^i(X^1, X^2; e^i) \qquad (i = 1, 2),$$

and the outcome is given by

$$X = \{x: \ x \in X^1, \ -x \in X^2\},$$

where X^1, X^2 are the equilibrium messages, $e^i = (\omega^i, R^i)$, R^i is the i-th preference relation, and ω^i is the i-th initial endowment. As stressed above, the response functions f^i need not be smooth.

As for the environment, each agent has an initial endowment $\omega^i \geqq 0$ and the admissible consumption set $E_M{}^+$ (the nonnegative orthant of the M-dimensional commodity space). His preferences are, in general, nonselfish; that is, they are relations R^i on the ordered pairs of commodity vectors allocated to the two agents and can be identified with subsets of the $4M$-dimensional space E_{4M}.[18]

The question of existence of a decentralized process is resolved in the affirmative if it is shown that the e^i can be "harmlessly" encoded in the X^i. The encoding results from the following response rules.

Following the familiar Cantor procedure, let φ be a one-to-one mapping from E_{4M} into the unit cube $[(0, \ldots, 0) \ (1, \ldots, 1)]$ of E_M, and let $S^i = \varphi(R^i)$ by the image (in E_M) of $R^i \subset E_{4M}$. Then, since φ is one-to-one, $R^i = \varphi^{-1}(S^i)$, that is, we can "decode" R^i from S^i.

To simplify exposition, we will describe the response rules for $M = 1$. The same procedure, however, can be carried out for any finite M, so that the conclusions are also valid for $M > 1$.

Now for $M = 1$ the commodity space is (a subset of) the real line, and so the proposals $X_t{}^i$ are subsets of the real line.

To define the response functions, we first describe the structure of the messages. Take the message X_t^1 emitted by the first agent at time t. This message consists of two disjoint parts X_t^{1*}, X_t^{1**} with

$$X_t^1 = X_t^{1*} \cup X_t^{1**},$$

where X_t^{1*} represents the "genuine" trade proposal, X_t^{1**} the encoding of information concerning ω^1 and R^1. Since no trade x is feasible for agent 1 unless $x \geq -\omega^1$, it follows that $X_t^{1*} \subseteq [-\omega^1, \infty)$. Hence the open interval $(-\infty, -\omega^1)$ is available for encoding the information about ω^1 and R^1. This will be accomplished by making X_t^{1**} consist of two parts: the point $-4 - \omega^1$ and the image $\varphi(R^1)$ translated to the left by $3 + \omega^1$ units; that is,

$$X_t^{1**} = \{-4 - \omega^1\} \cup T^1,$$

where

$$T^1 = S^1 - \{3 + \omega^1\}, \qquad S^1 = \varphi(R^1).$$

An example is shown in Figure 1 for the case where $0 < \omega^1 < 1$.

It is easy to see how agent 2, knowing the rules of encoding, could decode any X_t^1 to determine ω^1 and R^1.

First, he would obtain the value of ω^1 by taking the leftmost element of X_t^1, translating it to the right by 4 units and reversing the sign. Formally,

$$\omega^1(X_t^1) = -(4 + \min X_t^1).$$

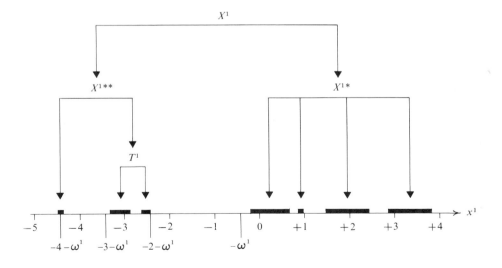

Figure 1

Knowing ω^1, agent 2 finds T^1 as that part of $X_t{}^1$ which is contained in the interval $[-3 - \omega^1, -2 - \omega^1]$, namely,

$$T^1(X_t{}^1) = X_t{}^1 \cap [-3 - \omega^1, -2 - \omega^1].$$

This is then translated to the right by $3 + \omega^1$ units to obtain the image S^1 in the unit interval, that is,

$$S^1(X_t{}^1) = T^1(X_t{}^1) + \{3 + \omega^1\}$$

and R^1 is obtained as the inverse image of S^1 by the Cantor function,

$$R^1(X_t{}^1) = \varphi^{-1}(S^1(X_t{}^1)).$$

We shall write $e^1(X_t{}^1) \equiv \langle \omega^1(X_t{}^1), R^1(X_t{}^1) \rangle$.

Finally, since ω^1 has already had decoded, agent 2 can determine the "genuine" part $X_t{}^{1*}$ of the first trader's proposal, using the formula

$$X_t{}^{1*} = X_t{}^1 \cap [-\omega^1, \infty).$$

Formally,

$$X_t{}^{1*}(X_t{}^1) = X_t{}^1 \cap [-\omega^1(X_t{}^1), \infty),$$

Agent 2 encodes his information in an analogous way, and so agent 1 can decode it by the corresponding procedures, thus obtaining

$$e^2(X_t{}^2) \equiv \langle \omega^2(X_t{}^2), R^2(X_t{}^2) \rangle,$$

as well as $X_t{}^{2*}(X_t{}^2)$.

Now each agent knows both e^1 and e^2, as well as $X_t{}^{1*}$ and $X_t{}^{2*}$. We shall suppose that each determines the set $X_t{}^*$ of trades compatible with both $X_t{}^{1*}$ and $X_t{}^{2*}$, that is,

$$X_t{}^* = \{x : x \in X_t{}^{1*}, -x \in X_t{}^{2*}\}.$$

Now agent 1 must inspect $X_t{}^*$ to see whether
(1) all elements of $X_t{}^*$ are Pareto-optimal for $\langle e^1, e^2(X_t{}^2) \rangle$,
(2) all elements of $X_t{}^*$ are Pareto-equivalent for $\langle e^1, e^2(X_t{}^2) \rangle$,
(3) $X_t{}^*$ is maximal with respect to properties (1) and (2).
If $X_t{}^*$ satisfies the preceding requirements, the response rule of agent 1 requires that his message remain unchanged, namely,

$$X_{t+1}{}^1 = X_t{}^1;$$

otherwise, he must change his message, that is,

$$X_{t+1}{}^1 \neq X_t{}^1.$$

(Since our analysis is static, it does not matter what the value of $X_{t+1}{}^1$ is in this case.)

The response rules for agent 2 are analogous.

2.2. It is clear, then, that (1) the equilibrium outcomes will be Pareto-optimal (nonwastefulness), (2) that for any Pareto-optimal trade there is an equilibrium outcome (unbiasedness), and (3) that any two outcomes generated by the same equilibrium (essential single-valuedness) are Pareto-equivalent. Hence our process is Pareto-satisfactory.

Finally, the response rules are of the form

$$X_{t+1}{}^i = f^i(X_t{}^1, X_t{}^2, e^i) \qquad (i = 1, 2,)$$

so that the process is informationally decentralized: given the knowledge of the two messages $X_t{}^1, X_t{}^2$, agent 1 need not know e^2 and vice versa.[19] Of course, $X_t{}^2$ "smuggles in" the information concerning e^2.

Thus we have constructed an informationally decentralized adjustment process despite the presence of nonselfish preferences. The ease with which we can smuggle through the information about e^i even in nondecomposable environments suggests that additional restrictions on information processing should be imposed to guarantee that there is informational decentralization.

"Smoothness" in some sense is one such restriction. Prohibition of individually infeasible proposals might be another.

Notes

1   The present version of this note owes a great deal to suggestions and criticism by Kenneth J. Arrow. Marcel K. Richter provided important insights related to Part II of this note. The author has not attempted to develop the results beyond those presented at the Conference Seminar on Decentralization, Northwestern University, February 1972, but some details and explanations have been added for the sake of clarity and completeness.

2   For terminology, see [2], except that I have replaced the term "externality" as used in [2] by "privacy."

3   A general theory has been developed by Mount and Reiter in [4]. Their (independently obtained) results overlap some of those in the present note.

4   "Competitive" means "perfectly competitive." We sometimes speak of *the* competitive process (in singular) because the leeway with respect to dynamizations is irrelevant to our static analysis.

5   Here "decomposable" means "free of externalities," both on production and consumption sides. The class of decomposable environments includes those characterized by indivisibilities, discontinuities, and nonconvexities.

6   Called "externality" in [2].

7   Actually, nonwastefulness is sufficient.

8   Using the notation of the single-valuedness lemma in the following, the relevant mapping is the inverse $\Psi_*{}^{-1}$ of Ψ_* which is defined $\Psi_*(\theta) = \{m: G^i(m, \theta^i), i = 1, 2, \theta \in \Theta^*\}$. We may, for instance, postulate that $\Psi_*{}^{-1}$ has a Lipschitzian selection for all Θ^* such that $\Theta^* = \{\theta \in \Theta: \theta = \varphi(\xi), \xi \in \Xi\}$ where Ξ is a Euclidean space of dimension not exceeding that of Θ and φ a smooth function.

9   The importance of smoothness considerations was first brought to my attention by Lloyd Shapley.

10   A *correspondence* Ψ: $A \to B$ is said to have a Lipschitzian selection if there exists a Lipschitzian *function* f: $A \to B$ such that $f(a) \in \Psi(a)$ for all $a \in A$.

11   More generally, the relevant property is that G be "non-Peano," i.e., not containing the multidimensional counterpart of the Peano space-filling curve.

12   It is easily seen that the preceding statement is valid not only for proposed action processes, but of any processes with a one-to-one outcome function.

13   Nor does it have a one-to-one outcome function.

14   "Decomposable" is defined in note 5.

15   For later results along these lines, see Xavier Calsamiglia [1].

16   Alternatively, one could assume a single consumer who gets the whole output.

17   Here and in the following, "for all t" means "for all $t \in \{0, 1, \ldots, T\}$."

18   This formulation, as well as other insights, owe much to discussions with Ket Richter; previously I had been using utility function representations (in the nonlexicographic case, sets in a space of $2M + 1$ dimensions).

19   Strictly speaking, we have verified only the "privacy" (externality in the terminology of [2]) requirement of the definition of informational decentralization. But of the other two requirements, anonymity is vacuous for an economy of two agents and "self-relevance" is satisfied when each message is a subset of the commodity space (hence of the same dimensionality!), as is the case here.

References

[1]   X. Calsamiglia, "On the Possibility of Informational Decentralization in Nonconvex Environments," University of Minnesota, Ph.D. Thesis, 1975.

[2]   L. Hurwicz, "Optimality and Informational Efficiency in Resource Allocation Processes," this volume, IV, pp. 393–412.

[3]   L. Hurwicz, "On Informationally Decentralized Systems," this volume, IV, pp. 425–459.

[4]   K. Mount, and S. Reiter, "Informational Size of Message Spaces," Discussion Paper 3, Center for Math. Studies in Econ. and Mgt. Sc., Northwestern University, 1972.

On informationally decentralized systems

LEONID HURWICZ[1]

1. Introduction

The purpose of the present paper is to discuss some of the problems that arise in laying the foundations of a theory of economic systems. The study of economic systems can be approached either in the spirit of "positive" science ("what is") or "normative" science ("what should be"). In either case, if the approach is analytical, the essential first step is a formalization of the concept of an economic system.

Informally, we think of an economic system as defined by a set of institutional or behavioral rules that enable us to distinguish, for example, capitalism from socialism, pure laissez-faire from mixed economy, or perhaps, perfect competition from oligopoly. On the other hand, resource endowment, technology, and individual preferences are viewed as given parameters with which the system must cope; the totality of such parameters will be referred to as the *environment*.[2] The symbol e will be used to denote a complete description of an environment; thus to know e means to know completely the initial endowment, the technology, and the preferences. A class of environments will be denoted by E. Thus partial (incomplete) knowledge of the environment is represented by the specification of a class E containing more than one element.

At a given point in time, an observer of an economy can characterize it as being in a certain *state s*. The state can be described in terms of various "real" activities such as consuming, producing, storing, and also in terms of "informational" activities such as making bids, presenting economic plans, performing calculations, etc. We could imagine giving this observer a specification so complete of all participants' behavior patterns that, given the knowledge of the environment and of the initial state, he could predict all the future states of the economy. (To simplify discussion, we presuppose for the moment a nonstochastic model, both with respect to environment and to behavior patterns.) The totality of these behavior patterns (as distinct from environment and state descriptions) may be called the economic *mechanism*, and we shall apply the same term even if the behavior patterns have stochastic aspects. We shall use the term *adjustment process* to label a mechanism belonging to a class to be described below.

Among examples of analytical formulations of economic mechanisms one can cite the various dynamic models of market processes (e.g., perfect competition), decentralized planning models (e.g., [23, 25]), and also models of processes designed to cope with indivisibilities, increasing returns, public goods, etc. [1, 2, 4, 9, 26, 27] .

An economic mechanism can be studied with regard to its *performance* in terms of some *welfare* criterion (e.g., Pareto-optimality or some social welfare function) in relation to the environments in which the mechanism operates. In fact, a major part of modern welfare economics deals with a special study of this type, viz., that of the performance of a particular mechanism (perfect competition) in terms of a particular performance (welfare) criterion (Pareto-optimality), depending on whether the environment is "classical" (no externalities, no indivisibilities, technology and preferences convex). Similarly, performance in terms of Pareto or related criteria has been studied for certain mechanisms capable of operating in nonclassical environments (e.g., the "greed process" in [13] or the process of Hurwicz, Radner, and Reiter [17].

Some models of mechanisms have been formulated for purposes of "positive" science, i.e., in the belief that they provide a useful instrument for the study of observed phenomena. This has, in particular, been the case with regard to both perfectly competitive and monopolistic (including oligopolistic) models. Other mechanisms have been proposed in a normative spirit, a classic example being the Lange model of a decentralized socialist economy. Many have been put forward as objects for study rather than proposals for adoption, but with an ultimate normative objective in mind.

To see whether a mechanism is worthy of serious study, one is led to examine its informational and incentive *feasibility*. On the informational side, the question is whether the mechanism allows for the dispersion of information and limitations on the capacity of various units to process information. On the incentive side, there is the problem whether the rules prescribed by the mechanism are compatible with either individual or group incentives.

Given the feasibility of a mechanism, the issue of its *efficiency* arises. Processing of information uses resources (both capital and operating) and alternative mechanisms may be more or less demanding in this respect.[3] Similarly, incentive-compatibility may involve a system of (positive and negative) rewards and resources to administer them (the enforcement system). To calculate the "net" welfare generated by a mechanism, given the environment e, one must take into account the drain on resources by the informational activities (the cost of information processing) and the incentive-inducing activities (the cost of enforcement).

Thus there are two types of "givens" in our problem: those pertaining to the feasibility and cost structure of alternative organizational structures (whether in the informational or incentival sphere) and those pertaining to the economic environment in the narrow sense of the term. In fact, these two types of givens are interrelated, if only because resources used to operate the organization cannot be used for "substantive" purposes.

In simplified form, this can be expressed by defining a function $h(x, q/e)$ which associates the resulting state s with the resources x used for substantive (as distinct from organizational) purposes when mechanism q prevails, given the environment e, and another function $b(q/e)$ defining the resource vector required to operate the mechanism q. A welfare ordering or function can then be defined on the space of the resulting states. We shall denote by $w = W(s)$ the measure (possibly vectorial) of welfare associated with the state s. Thus $w = W[h(x, q/e)]$. (The symbol "$/e$" means "given e".)

The fact that, for a given e, the resulting welfare w depends on q, as well as on the substantively utilized resources x, expresses the phenomenon of differential performance of different mechanisms, quite aside from what it costs to operate them. But in fact the operational costs (in resource terms) do differ, so that if the given initial resources are denoted by ω_e, the welfare w generated by the mechanism q in the environment e is given by

(1.1) $w = W[h(\omega_e - b(q/e), q/e)]$.

(This formulation ignores additional psychological and ideological welfare aspects of the mechanism.) The symbol for initial resources has the subscript e because initial resources constitute part of the specification of e. We refer to $\omega_e - b(q/e)$ as the resources available for substantive purposes.

Even aside from resource requirements, the *feasibility* of a mechanism is dependent on the environment, due to both technological and behavioral (preference) considerations. Thus with each environment e one may associate the class $Q(e)$ of mechanisms that are feasible, given e. For formula (1.1) to be meaningful, the mechanism q in it should be taken from this class.

Now the normative problem involves selecting a mechanism with only partial knowledge of the environment in which it will have to operate. Such knowledge might, for instance, be expressed (in the Bayesian spirit) as a probability measure on the space of conceivable environments. For the sake of simplicity, however, we shall suppose at this point that the "organizer" only has an *a priori* admissible class of environments E_0, without any probabilistic information within this class. We shall further assume that he knows the functions h, b, and $Q(.)$, i.e., of the dependence of mechanism feasibility on the prevailing environment. He can then find the class of mechanisms feasible over all of the *a priori* class E_0, viz., the intersection

$Q[E_0] = \cap_{e \in E_0} Q(e)$.

For any q in this feasible class $Q[E_0]$, and any environment e in E_0, he can determine the organizational cost $b(q/e)$, the initial resources ω_e implicit in e, and hence the welfare outcome w as given by (1.1). Thus the normative organizational problem acquires the form that is formally analogous to a statistical decision problem, since the organizer presumably wishes to maximize, for fixed e in E_0,

(1.2) $w = g(q, e), \quad q \in Q[E_0]$,

where the right-hand side is the same as the right-hand side of (1.1) expressed as a function of q and e. If a probability measure on E_0 were available to the organizer, he might maximize with respect to q the corresponding expected value

$\mathcal{E}_e g(q, e) \equiv G(q).$[4] In the absence of such "prior" probabilities, the organizer might adopt some principle of decision making under uncertainty, say maximin, over E_0 (see [12]).

It is not yet practical to carry out a complete analysis along the above lines, although the formalization given may be helpful in clarifying various informal arguments concerning the comparative merits of alternative economic systems. At the very least, however, our attention is focused on the main concepts that appear in this analysis, namely, those of the environment and mechanism. Clearly, a prerequisite for progress is the formalization of these two concepts. Both were introduced by Hurwicz [13], although not in as general a form as to encompass all cases of interest.

In particular, the environment e was defined as the ordered triple of initial resource endowment, preferences, and technology, $e = \langle \omega, R, Z \rangle$. The mechanism was characterized as an adjustment process, $\pi = \langle f, \phi, \mathfrak{M} \rangle$ with a given language $\mathfrak{M}$, set of response rules f, and an outcome rule ϕ. Somewhat more general adjustment processes were considered by Hurwicz in [16, 19].

The approach used in [13] is nowhere near the optimization problem formulated in (1.2). Rather, a subclass of all adjustment processes is defined as *informationally decentralized* if it satisfies certain restrictions with regard to the language and the nature of the response and outcome functions. These restrictions are satisfied by the "usual" (say Walrasian tâtonnement) models of the perfectly competitive process, so that the latter qualifies as informationally decentralized. The intent was to isolate those processes whose *informational* requirements were no greater, and if anything less, than those of the perfectly competitive process, regardless of the *behavioral* nature of these processes. Such a definition could be interpreted in the spirit of informational feasibility, in the sense that an informationally decentralized process is informationally feasible whenever the perfectly competitive process is. (The latter statement presupposes that the feasibility of the computations required by the process, as distinct from possession, transmission, or perception of information, is ignored.) There are two basic notions underlying the restrictions inherent in such a concept of informational decentralization. First, that there is *initial dispersion of information*, with each economic unit processing only partial knowledge of the environment e, viz., that of its own component e^i of e. Second, that it is impossible to transfer this information to other units in such a way that at some stage of the process some one unit would be, through messages received from others, in possession of complete information concerning e or concerning the proposed actions of all the other units; this can be expressed by saying that it is impossible through communication to centralize dispersed information, i.e., that there is *limited communication*.[5] Thus our concept of informational decentralization takes into account the initial dispersion of information together with the limitations of communication. Both of the latter concepts can be rigorously defined as certain properties of the response functions and of the language used in communication.[6]

Supposing that only informationally decentralized processes are feasible, one could still attempt to attack the problem of optimal mechanism selection stated in (1.2) by restricting the feasible class $Q[E_0]$ to processes that are informationally decentralized. Unfortunately, we run into difficulties. For one thing, little is known in a general way concerning the resource requirements $b(q/e)$ of the various processes. In fact, in traditional economic analysis, e.g., in comparisons of, say, perfect competition with monopoly or oligopoly, these requirements are not analyzed, and only substantive performance is compared. In terms of the notation used in (1.1), the comparison is between $h(x, q'/e)$ and $h(x, q''/e)$, rather than between $h[\omega_e - b(q'/e), q'/e]$ and $h[\omega_e - b(q''/e), q''/e]$, where q' and q'' are two alternative mechanisms, and x the resources available for *substantive* utilization (i.e., not needed to operate the mechanism).

To deal with the question of the welfare index w, we shall simplify this phase of exposition by postulating that preferences are expressible through numerical utility functions $U^1(s), \ldots, U^n(s)$ of the n individuals in the economy, each defined on the economy's alternative states s. Furthermore, let us at this point postulate complete determinacy of the process q in the sense that, given $e = \langle \omega, R, Z \rangle$ (which includes the specification of the initial distribution of resources, as well as the respective technologies and preferences of the various units), there is a unique outcome in terms of actions (production, resource flow), resource distributions, and, consequently, utilities. One may then define $W(s)$ as the n-tuple of utilities, say

$$W(s) = \langle U^1(s), \ldots, U^n(s) \rangle,$$

so that the explicit form of (1.1) would be

$$(1.3) \quad w = \langle U^1[h(\omega_e, q/e)], \ldots, U^n[h(\omega_e, q/e)] \rangle$$

where, in effect, we are setting $b(q/e) = 0$.

As an example, in an environment corresponding to the Edgeworth Box (pure exchange) case, and with q as perfect competition q^C, we might consider the outcome to be the competitive equilibrium allocation (assumed unique), say,

$$h(\omega_e, q/e) = c,$$

with

$$c = \langle c^1, \ldots, c^n \rangle,$$

and

$$w = \langle U^1(c^1), \ldots, U^n(c^n) \rangle,$$

where U^i is the utility function representing the (selfish) preferences of the i-th unit.

As a further step, for any mechanism q^*, one might adopt a scalar (Bergson-Samuelson Welfare) function, say,

$$\psi(u^{*1}, \ldots, u^{*n})$$

as the measure of the system's performance, so that

(1.4) $W[h(\omega_e, q/e)] = \psi(u^{*1}, \ldots, u^{*n})$

where the u^{*1} is again the utility of the final outcome for the i-th unit.

But, perhaps because of known paradoxes in the field of welfare functions, as well as lack of consensus as to a "reasonable" choice of the function ψ, the customary approach is in terms of the Pareto optimality of outcomes. Thus, let $Y(e)$ denote the set of allocations that are achievable, given the environment e, and $\hat{Y}(e)$ its Pareto-optimal subset. (It is important to note that both the feasible and the achievable sets are defined in terms of e, independently of q. This corresponds to ignoring the resource and psychological costs associated with the operation of the mechanism.) A basic question asked in welfare economics then is whether the utility image of the outcome defined by (1.3) is maximal, i.e., whether it corresponds to an element of the Pareto-optimal set $\hat{Y}(e)$. If it is, the process is called (Pareto-) *nonwasteful*. One of the main results of welfare economics is that, in the absence of externalities and of local saturation, competitive equilibrium is necessarily Pareto-optimal (see, e.g., Koopmans [22], Prop. 4), i.e., that the perfectly competitive process is nonwasteful. On the other hand, examples have been constructed to show that in similar environments, processes involving monopoly may yield nonoptimal outcomes, i.e., that such a process is wasteful in the sense just defined.

Although, other things being equal, nonwastefulness is an attractive normative postulate, it is by itself inadequate because it does not rule out the possibility that the mechanism would yield outcomes consistently favoring some units at the expense of others. Thus in an Edgeworth Box-type situation, a mechanism that would always place a given trader at his origin (i.e., allocate all goods to the other trader) would be nonwasteful when the preferences are assumed strictly monotone! The competitive equilibrium of a private ownership economy (see Debreu [8], pp. 78–80) yields a final allocation that is Pareto-noninferior to the initial one, and hence – despite its Pareto-optimality – may not appeal to those whose initial endowments are low.

It is therefore natural to seek a feature of the mechanism that would in some sense equalize the chances of the participants, regardless of their initial endowments. An obvious way to seek such equalization is to admit the possibility of redistribution of the initial endowment (and ownership shares), for instance, by a system of taxes and subsidies (see [22], p. 54). Now, with regard to a mechanism characterized by the admissibility of all feasible redistributions, one may ask whether every Pareto-optimal allocation can be attained as an outcome (equilibrium) following some feasible redistribution. (If so, we call the mechanism (Pareto-) *unbiased*.) Again, welfare economics answers this question in the affirmative (see [22], Prop. 5, pp. 50–51) for the competitive process with redistributions, provided that the environment is free of externalities and of local saturation, and has a convex technology and convex continuous preferences. (We omit an additional qualification stated in the last sentence of Koopmans' Prop. 5, pp. 50–51.) We shall refer to environments satisfying the assumptions of Koopmans' Prop. 5 (and hence, also 4) as *classical* and denote the set of classical environments by E_{CL}. Thus, in our terminology, the competitive mechanism (including redistributions) is unbiased for classical environments.

A further postulate to be considered has to do with the determinacy of the outcomes that result from the operation of the mechanism. It is appealing to demand single-valuedness, but even the competitive process operating in a classical environment may fail to yield it. An example is an Edgeworth Box situation where the indifference curves of the trader have linear stretches and there is a linear segment located simultaneously on the indifference curves of both traders, so that all points of the segment are Pareto-optimal and belong to the equilibrium set for the same price. However, such indeterminacy is not too worrisome because all points of the segment have the same utility, even though representing different physical allocations. Presumably, the participants would be willing to randomize the choice amount points of the segment. We shall refer to mechanisms in which the utility outcome is uniquely determined, even though the physical allocations may not be, as *essentially single-valued*. We shall not try to rule out the indeterminacy of allocations as long as utilities are determinate.

On the other hand, there is reason to regard as incomplete processes where the "outcome" is indeterminate even in utility terms, since a further mechanism would be required to resolve the remaining conflict. An example of such an incomplete process would be one yielding as its "outcome" the set of all Pareto-optimal allocations; here both the requirements of nonwastefulness and unbiasedness are satisfied, yet the remaining indeterminacy is clearly excessive.

We shall find it convenient to refer to mechanisms possessing the three attributes just introduced (nonwastefulness, unbiasedness, and essential single-valuedness) as (Pareto-) *satisfactory*. (Note that satisfactoriness is a property of a mechanism, while optimality is a property of an allocation; in our terminology, it would be incorrect to refer to a mechanism as Pareto-optimal.) The two results of welfare economics referred to above (Koopmans' props. 4 and 5) essentially assert that the perfectly competitive mechanism with redistributions is satisfactory for classical environments. On the other hand, many examples are available to show that this mechanism, generally speaking, fails to be satisfactory in nonclassical environments. (We are not saying that the environment must be classical for, say, unbiasedness, but rather that in Koopmans' Prop. 5 the various environmental assumptions cannot be dispensed with.) Also, as mentioned earlier, mechanisms such as those involving monopoly lack satisfactoriness even for classical environments.

With these well-known propositions of welfare economics as a point of departure, those interested in the normative theory of mechanisms have many options. Some will question whether (Pareto-) satisfactoriness is an acceptable normative postulate, but despite the validity of some objections, we shall not pursue this path. Our purpose will be to see to what extent, with satisfactoriness as the welfare criterion, it is possible to overcome the limitations of the competitive process. In particular, we shall be concerned with two such limitations.

We have already referred to one limitation, namely, the lack of Pareto-satisfactoriness of the competitive process in nonclassical environments. The question then arises as to whether one could design alternative informationally decentralized mechanisms that would be satisfactory even in nonclassical environments. The problem will be discussed in Section 2. Briefly, it appears that it is possible to design such mechanisms for broad classes of environments including those characterized by indivisibilities and nonconvexities, provided externalities are absent. On the other hand, examples are given to show that there may fail to exist informationally decentralized mechanisms guaranteeing satisfactoriness in the presence of externalities.

Another limitation of decentralized processes, including perfect competition, was noted in the presence of public goods – the incentive to misrepresent one's preferences, or perhaps resources and technology. Similarly, incentival difficulties have been pointed out with regard to rules proposed under the Lange-Lerner socialist competitive solution, perhaps because of the nature of the reward structure. Certain aspects of these problems will be examined in Section 3. It will be argued that the incentive toward misrepresentation is also present in a private goods economy except in the "atomistic" case. An example is constructed to show that (in an Edgeworth Box, pure exchange classical environment) not only is there an incentive toward misrepresentation when the competitive mechanism prevails, but that such incentive will appear for a broad class of informationally decentralized Pareto-satisfactory mechanisms. This suggests that there is a fundamental incentival difficulty in reconciling the two objectives of informational decentralization and unbiased welfare maximization.

2. Informational decentralization in nonclassical environments

In this section, we adopt Pareto-satisfactoriness as the performance criterion and abstract from incentival difficulties. We are interested in the performance of informationally decentralized mechanisms in nonclassical environments. Using the concept of informational decentralization of Hurwicz [13], we find that the competitive process qualifies as informationally decentralized, but is not Pareto-satisfactory for nonclassical environments. What are the alternatives?

It turns out that the situation is fundamentally different depending on whether externalities are absent ("decomposable" environments) or present ("nondecomposable" environments). For decomposable environments, a number of informationally decentralized mechanisms have been proposed. These include the "greed" process which is Pareto-satisfactory for all decomposable environments but does not in general converge; the stochastic adjustment process in [17] which is Pareto-satisfactory for two important categories of nonclassical environments (discrete and nonconvex continuous and converges in a probabilistic sense); Kanemitsu's "inertia-greed" process [20], which is Pareto-satisfactory and convergent for nonconvex continuous processes; the Arrow-Hurwicz [4] modified Lagrangean gradient process, which converges locally for certain nonconvex (increasing returns) environments. There are also recent contributions listed in the references [2, 9, 11, 26] which are in somewhat the same spirit.

With regard to processes in this category, given that they are informationally decentralized and Pareto-satisfactory for the specified class of nonclassical environments, there still remains the question whether they are informationally as efficient as possible without sacrificing these attributes. The answer depends, of course, on the concept of informational efficiency. In the definition proposed by Hurwicz [13], one process is informationally more efficient than another if the formation of messages at each step requires less information (in the sense of a strictly coarser partitioning) about the messages sent at the preceding step. Using this definition, Kanemitsu [21] showed that the greed process is not as informationally efficient a Pareto-satisfactory process as can be constructed for the class of decomposable environments, although the more efficient K-process he constructed differs only slightly from the greed process. It would be interesting, perhaps after introducing other definitions of informational efficiency, to find processes that are maximally informationally efficient with regard to a given class of environments; results of this type do not as yet seem to have been obtained.

When externalities are present (nondecomposable environments), neither perfect competition nor greed and similar processes can claim Pareto-satisfactoriness. In fact, when externalities are of the "nonseparable" type (see [7]), there may be difficulties in defining such processes without violating the requirements of informational decentralization. Thus one is led to ask whether informational decentralization is compatible with Pareto-satisfactoriness in nondecomposable environments.

What follows is not a general answer to this question, but rather an examination of a suggestive example. The example owes a great deal to the work on quadratic teams by J. Marschak [29] and Radner [30] and also to stimulating suggestions from T. Marschak [28]. Essentially, the result obtained is that, within the class of environments considered, informational decentralization is, in general, incompatible with Pareto-satisfactoriness. However, two points should be noted. On what might by some be considered the negative side of the ledger, the result is very dependent on the precise definition of informational decentralization. To the extent that the definition is controversial, so is the result. On the positive side, however, the result obtained is of interest even in the absence of agreement on the concept of informational decentralization. For what it shows is that the appearance of externalities increases the informational needs of the system, in the sense that, for certain states of information-processing capacity, Pareto-satisfactoriness can be promised if externalities are absent but not otherwise.

The model

There are n production units, each characterized by an activity variable a_i, ranging over a nondegenerate interval (e.g., all nonnegative reals), a parameter vector

θ_i, and an output relation

$$y_i = Y^i(a_1, \ldots, a_n; \theta_i) \qquad (i = 1, 2, \ldots, n).$$

The total output of the economy is the sum $y_1 + \ldots + y_n$. In the examples, we shall confine ourselves to the case where output is one-dimensional and so is each activity variable a_i; however, the parameter vector θ_i will still in general be multi-dimensional. Furthermore, we shall only treat the case of two production units ($n = 2$), and the output relations will be assumed quadratic in the a's. Without an explicit introduction of the consumers, we shall postulate that optimality is equivalent to the maximization of total output.

Externalities are said to be present if, for some i, Y^i depends on at least one $j (j \neq i)$; they are *unilateral* if Y^i depends on a_j but not vice versa, otherwise, *bilateral*; they are *separable* if

$$Y^i(a_1, \ldots, a_n; \theta_i) = Y_{i1}(a_1; \theta_{i1}) + \cdots + Y_{in}(a_n; \theta_{in}) \qquad (i = 1, \ldots, n).$$

The model can be related to our earlier terminology by noting that it defines a class of environments. The i-th unit's environment component e^i is defined by the function Y^i and its parameter θ_i; when the Y^i are required to be quadratic, e^i is completely defined by θ_i. Dispersion of information is postulated in the sense that θ_i is assumed known to the i-th unit and to no other units. For $j \neq i$, the only information available to the j-th unit about θ_i is derived from the exchange of messages specified by the adjustment process to be described below.

The message emitted by the i-th unit at time t is denoted by $m_i(t)$. (Since the adjustment process is a form of tâtonnement, "time" is to be interpreted as "computational," not historical.) The response functions are defined by the difference equation system

$$m_i(t + 1) - m_i(t) = g^i[m_1(t), \ldots, m_n(t); \theta] \qquad (i = 1, \ldots, n)$$

where $\theta = \langle \theta_1, \ldots, \theta_n \rangle$. (Thus the response functions are given by

$$f^i[m; \theta] = m_i + g^i[m; \theta],$$

where $m = \langle m_1, \ldots, m_n \rangle$.)

The process is in equilibrium at a message n-tuple $\overline{m} = \langle \overline{m}_1, \ldots, \overline{m}_n \rangle$ if

$$g^i(\overline{m}; \theta) = 0 \qquad (i = 1, \ldots, n),$$

which is written vectorially as

$$g(\overline{m}; \theta) = 0.$$

Given that the process is in equilibrium at $\overline{m}$, one must specify the outcome function to determine which actions a_i are to be taken. In their most general form, we shall consider ("parametric") outcome functions

$$\overline{a}_i = h^i(\overline{m}; \theta) \qquad (i = 1, \ldots, n),$$

written vectorially as

$$\bar{a} = h(\bar{m}; \theta),$$

with $a = \langle a_1, \ldots, a_n \rangle$.

Outcome functions are called *nonparametric* when h^i is independent of θ. (In Hurwicz [13, 14], only nonparametric outcome functions were considered.) Now, for the process to be informationally decentralized, it is required that θ_i replace the n-tuple $\theta = \langle \theta_1, \ldots, \theta_n \rangle$ as argument in g^i and h^i. Thus, under informational decentralization, the equilibrium and outcome conditions become (omitting the bars over m_i and a_i)

$$\left. \begin{array}{l} g^i(m; \theta_i) = 0 \\ a_i = h^i(m; \theta_i) \end{array} \right\} \quad (i = 1, \ldots, n).$$

(This is the "privacy" aspect of informational decentralization.) A particularly simple and natural outcome function is one that identifies messages as *proposed-action* levels, i.e.,

$$h^i(m; \theta) = m_i \quad (i = 1, \ldots, n).$$

(The so-called *concrete* process in [13] is of the proposed-action type, the action being trade and/or production.) The proposed-action outcome function is, of course, nonparametric since here $h^i(m; \theta) \equiv m_i$ and so does not depend on the parameter vector θ.

In considering the possibility of devising an informationally decentralized mechanism, we shall examine the possibility of doing this through a proposed-action process; should this be impossible, by a more general nonparametric process; and, finally, by parametric processes. Thus, a hierarchy of "impossibility" results may be obtained. If someone feels, for instance, that parametric processes are too general to be of interest, he may confine his attention to results relevant in the context of the narrower class of outcome functions.

We shall be dealing with quadratic output functions characterized by parameter values which make them strictly concave, so that first-order differential conditions yield unique optima. These conditions may be written as

$$\sum_{i=1}^{n} Y_k^i(a; \theta_i) = \quad (k = 1, \ldots, n)$$

where Y_k^i denotes the partial derivative $\partial Y^i / \partial a_k$. When solved for the a_i, the first-order optimality conditions will be written as

$$a_i = w^i(\theta) \quad (i = 1, \ldots, n),$$

or, vectorially,

$$a = w(\theta).$$

A process (defined by the functions g and h) is said to be *satisfactory* if and only if the following two conditions are satisfied:

(1) Given (a, θ) satisfying the optimality relation $a = w(\theta)$, there exists a message m (an n-tuple of reals) such that $g(m, \theta) = 0$ and $a = h(m, \theta)$;

(2) given (a, θ, m) satisfying the relations $g(m, \theta) = 0$ and $a = h(m, \theta)$, it follows that $a = w(\theta)$.

It will be noted that (2) is nonwastefulness while (1) is unbiasedness. Thus the concept just defined is a specialization of Pareto-satisfactoriness to the model at hand. Of course, the Pareto aspect is trivial, since there is no conflict of preferences.

The problem to be investigated is the following. For specified output functions, does there exist a satisfactory informationally decentralized process; i.e., are the functions g^i and h^i (both depending on θ through θ_i only), $(i = 1, \ldots, n)$, such that the above conditions (1) and (2) of satisfactoriness hold for all members of a specified class of output functions Y^i? It turns out that answers depend crucially on the class of output functions, even among the quadratics. This will be illustrated by considering three examples, always quadratic and always with $n = 2$.

Example A.   Output functions are given by

$$y_1 = \alpha_1 a_1 + \gamma_1 a_2 - (1/2)a_1^2$$

$$y_2 = \alpha_2 a_2 - (1/2)a_2^2,$$

with the parameter vectors

$$\theta_1 = (\alpha_1, \gamma_1)$$

$$\theta_2 = \alpha_2.$$

(This definition of parameter vectors means that the coefficient γ_1 indicating the impact of the second unit's activities on the first unit's productivity is known to unit 1 but not to unit 2.) In this instance, we have a unilateral separable externality. It is easily seen that the total output $y_1 + y_2$ will be maximized when

$$a_1 = \alpha_1$$

$$a_2 = \alpha_2 + \gamma_1,$$

so that these are the optimality relations $a = w(\theta)$.

Now the class of environments represented by Example A can be shown to be informationally decentralizable (*while preserving satisfactoriness*) or nondecentralizable depending on the additional requirements that one may wish to impose on the response and outcome functions. With proofs relegated to the Appendix below, the following results are obtained for environments and optimality relations of Example A.

(i) Decentralization is impossible with a one-to-one outcome function of the nonparametric type $a = h(m)$; hence, in particular, it is impossible to decentralize through a proposed-action-type process where $a = m$; this result has been gen-

eralized by T. Marschak to a wider class of environments and optimality relations than those of Example A (see Appendix).

(ii) Decentralization is impossible for a nonparametric outcome function
$a = h(m)$ (where $m = \langle m_1, m_2 \rangle$ and m_1, m_2 are real numbers), when h is required
to be Lipschitzian and g "quasi-Lipschitzian".[7]

(iii) Decentralization is possible through parametric Lipschitzian outcome
functions, with quasi-Lipschitzian response functions, namely, by the following
process:

$$g^1 \equiv \gamma_1 - m_1, \qquad h^1 \equiv \alpha_1$$
$$g^2 \equiv 0, \qquad h^2 \equiv \alpha_2 + m_1$$

(the process is parametric because the outcome functions contain the parameters
α_i, and it is informationally decentralized because g^1, h^1 do not depend on α_2,
while g^2, h^2 do not depend on α_1, γ_1).

(iv) Decentralization is possible through the following nonparametric, but
also non-Lipschitzian, process [where the symbols $p_1(\cdot)$ and $p_2(\cdot)$ represent the
two components of Peano's "space-filling curve" (see [3], p. 396)]:

$$g^1 \equiv [\alpha_1 - p_1(m_1)]^2 + [\gamma_1 - p_2(m_1)]^2, \qquad h^1 \equiv p^1(m_1);$$
$$g^2 \equiv \alpha_2 - m_2, \qquad\qquad\qquad\qquad h^2 \equiv m_2 + p_2(m_1)$$

[This process is nonparametric, since no parameters enter as arguments of the
outcome functions h^i; it is informationally decentralized because g^1 does not depend on α_2, while g^2 does not depend on α_1, γ_1; it is not Lipschitzian, in fact
not of bounded variation, because the Peano functions $p_i(\cdot)$ lack these
properties.]

This example is instructive for several reasons. First, consider result (i) as applied to proposed-action-type processes. Since communication of this type,
with bids, offers, etc., as distinct from some more abstract signals, is often most
natural (as in market processes), it is interesting to see that with communication
restricted to proposed actions, informational decentralization is incompatible
with satisfactoriness. The incompatibility arises from the presence of externality, i.e., the term $\gamma_1 a_2$ in Y^1; there would be no difficulty if this term were absent and known to be absent. Furthermore, the incompatibility arises even
though the externality is of the very "mild" unilateral and separable type!

Once we know that it is impossible to decentralize through a proposed-action
process, it is not surprising that the same is true for any outcome function h
which constitutes a one-to-one correspondence between actions and messages;
for by relabeling actions, we get back to a proposed-action-type process. Suppose
then that we are willing to adopt a signaling system that is not in a one-to-one relationship to actions, but where the process is still required to be nonparametric.
(The latter requirement amounts to specifying that, given the equilibrium message n-tuple, an outside agency with no knowledge of the environment could determine the corresponding actions.) Results (ii) and (iv) taken together tell us

that decentralization (in the sense of "privacy," i.e., g^i being independent of θ_j for $j \neq i$) is compatible with satisfactoriness, provided we are willing to use non-Lipschitzian functions.

Now, instead of using non-Lipschitzian functions, one could accomplish the same by the use of a two-dimensional message m_1, which would convey to unit 2 the values of the parameters α_1 and γ_1. Thus the Lipschitzian requirement has the effect of making certain that a single real number m_1 cannot be used to convey information about two numbers simultaneously. (A simple device, due to Cantor, for performing such a "trick" is to use, say, odd-numbered decimal digits of m_1 for the consecutive digits of α_1, and the even-numbered ones for those of γ_1.) If by "genuine dimensionality" of a message we mean the number of numbers it can convey without "tricks," the Lipschitzian requirement simply enforces "genuine" one-dimensional nature of the messages.

It is, of course, legitimate to question whether the requirement of "genuine" one-dimensionality is appropriate as a part of the definition of informational decentralization. But, for our purposes, this requirement is merely an example of the fact that the requirement of "privacy" (g_i depending on θ_i, not on θ_j, for $j \neq i$) is meaningless if there is no accompanying restriction on the process of conveying information between units. In any case, the result (ii) shows that the presence of externalities calls for less restricted information transfers than would otherwise be the case.

It is worth noting that there is a digital counterpart to the Lipschitzian requirement. Thus if we think of a communication process where the accuracy of, say, k digits is required, and communication is by means of k-digit messages, it is not possible to transmit two numbers in one message, except by cutting in half the obtainable accuracy (by $k/2$ digits of the message to convey one number and the other $k/2$ for the other number).

The limitation implicit in restricting the "genuine dimensionality" of messages is highly relevent to the original notion of informational decentralization (Hayek, Lange) where the consensus was that it is difficult to transfer the complex information concerning, for example, a firm's production function or a consumer's preference map. On the other hand, the market process generally envisaged involves price and quantity messages, usually interpreted as having the dimensionality of the commodity space. Thus it was, in effect, postulated that messages of lower dimensionality could be conveyed, but those of higher (possibly infinite) dimensionality could not. The above restriction on the dimensionality of the message m_1 is in the same spirit, although, admittedly, in a much simpler setting.

Finally, from the point of view of resource cost of communication, it might be reasonable to postulate that the cost of transmission increases with the "genuine dimensionality" of the message. If so, it is again of interest to know that externalities call for increased cost of communication. The alternatives, in situations such as that of Example A, are either sacrificing "privacy" (which might also entail additional costs) or giving up satisfactoriness (i.e., the optimization performance properties).

Since Example A is quite special (a separable unilateral externality), it is natural to inquire whether the phenomena there observed are also encountered in more general situations. In particular, one wishes to know whether, as in Example A (iii), a decentralization using Lipschitzian functions is always possible if one is willing to use parametric outcome functions $h^i(m; \theta_i)$. The answer depends on whether the externality is unilateral. Example B below exhibits such a Lipschitzian decentralized parametric outcome process for the general quadratic unilateral externality. Example C, on the other hand, where the externality is bilateral (though separable), cannot be decentralized even by parametric Lipschitzian functions.

Example B.   The output functions are given by

$$y_1 = \alpha_1 a_1 + \gamma_1 a_2 - (1/2)\beta_1 a_1^2 - (1/2)\eta_1 a_2^2 - \delta_1 a_1 a_2,$$

$$y_2 = \alpha_2 a_2 - (1/2)\beta_2 a_2^2,$$

which is a *unilateral* externality, separable if $\delta_1 = 0$ but not otherwise; it is the most general (except for constants) unilateral quadratic externality. It is assumed that unit i knows the parameters whose subscript is i, as in Example A. That is,

$$\theta_1 = (\alpha_1, \gamma_1, \beta_1, \eta_1, \delta_1)$$

$$\theta_2 = (\alpha_2, \beta_2).$$

Now the functions to be used by unit 1 have different appearance depending on whether the externality is separable or not (i.e., whether $\delta_1 = 0$). This causes complexity, but does not violate the requirements of informational decentralization, since δ_1 is one of the components of θ_1, i.e., known to unit 1. The functions for unit 2, on the other hand, are the same regardless of separability. We have

$$g^1 \equiv \begin{cases} m_1 - (\gamma_1 - \eta_1 m_2), & \text{if } \delta_1 = 0, \\ \alpha_1 - \dfrac{\beta_1}{\delta_1}(\gamma_1 - \eta_1 m_2 - m_1) - \delta_1 m_2, & \text{if } \delta_1 \neq 0; \end{cases}$$

$$h^1 \equiv \begin{cases} \dfrac{\alpha_1}{\beta_1}, & \text{if } \delta_1 = 0, \\ \dfrac{1}{\delta_1}(\gamma_1 - \eta_1 m_2 - m_1), & \text{if } \delta_1 \neq 0; \end{cases}$$

$$g^2 \equiv m_1 + \alpha_2 - \beta_2 m_2;$$

$$h^2 \equiv m_2.$$

Clearly, h^1 is parametric and all four functions are Lipschitzian; informational decentralization ("privacy") is satisfied since each g^i, h^i is independent of θ_j for $j \neq i$. The proof of Pareto-satisfactoriness will be omitted.

The next example has a separable *bilateral* externality, i.e., a bilateral externality of a relatively simple structure. Nevertheless, it can be shown that it is impossible to decentralize it, even with parametric functions, without violating the Lipschitzian conditions. On the other hand, if one is willing to use non-Lipschitzian functions (i.e., violate the "genuine dimensionality" limit on messages), decentralization even through nonparametric outcome functions becomes possible. The proofs are analogous to those of Example A but much more complex, and will not be given here.

Example C. The output functions are given by

$$y_1 = \alpha_1 a_1 + \gamma_1 a_2 - (1/2)\eta_1 a_2{}^2,$$

$$y_2 = \alpha_2 a_2 + \gamma_2 a_1 - (1/2)\eta_2 a_1{}^2,$$

with unit i knowing parameters whose subscript is i, i.e.,

$$\theta_1 = (\alpha_1, \gamma_1, \eta_1),$$

$$\theta_2 = (\alpha_2, \gamma_2, \eta_2).$$

Appendix

(i) Example A is not decentralizable through a proposed-action process.

Proof. Here $a = m$, hence $g(m, \theta) = 0$ becomes $g(a, \theta) = 0$. It will be shown below that if this process were decentralizable, the latter relation would define a single-valued function, say, $\theta = f(a)$, onto a neighborhood in the θ-space. But this contradicts the optimality relations $a_1 = \alpha_1, a_2 = \alpha_2 + \gamma_1$ which show that $\theta = (\alpha_1, \gamma_1, \alpha_2)$ is not uniquely determined by $\langle a_1, a_2 \rangle = a$.

The single-valuedness of f is established as follows. Let θ', θ'' be two, possibly distinct, parameter vector values compatible with a given value of a. Since g is assumed decentralized, θ enters each g^i only through θ^i, with $\theta^1 = (\alpha_1, \gamma_1)$ and $\theta^2 = \alpha_2$. We thus have

(1) $g^1(a, \theta_1') = 0, \quad g^2(a, \theta_2') = 0,$

(2) $g^1(a, \theta_1'') = 0, \quad g^2(a, \theta_2'') = 0,$

hence also,

(3) $g^1(a, \theta_1') = 0, \quad g^2(a, \theta_2'') = 0$

and

(4) $g^1(a, \theta_1'') = 0, \quad g^2(a, \theta_2') = 0.$

Since g is satisfactory, we have, respectively (by equivalence with the optimality relations),

(1*) $a_1 = \alpha_1', \quad a_2 = \alpha_2' + \gamma_1',$

(2*) $a_1 = \alpha_1'', \quad a_2 = \alpha_2'' + \gamma_2'',$

(3*) $a_1 = \alpha_1'$, $a_2 = \alpha_2'' + \gamma_1'$,

(4*) $a_1 = \alpha_1''$, $a_2 = \alpha_2' + \gamma_1''$.

Hence

$$\alpha_1' = \alpha_1'', \quad \alpha_2' = \alpha_2'', \quad \gamma_1' = \gamma_1''$$

so that $(\alpha_1, \gamma_1, \alpha_2)$ is uniquely determined by a.

The following generalization of this result to a wider class of situations than the quadratic two-person output-maximizing team has been provided by T. Marschak. Consider first a two-person organization. Mr. i $(i = 1, 2)$ observes an environment e_i in a set E_i and takes actions a_i. The optimality relations

$$a_1 = \hat{a}_1(e_1, e_2), \quad a_2 = \hat{a}_2(e_1, e_2)$$

are to be satisfied. If $\langle g^1, g^2 \rangle$ is a decentralized satisfactory proposed-action process, then $g^1(a_1, a_2, e_1) = g^2(a_1, a_2, e_2) = 0$ if and only if the quadruple (a_1, a_2, e_1, e_2) satisfies the optimality relations. Now if there exist $\overline{e}_1$ and $\overline{\overline{e}}_1$ in $E_1, \overline{e}_2$ and $\overline{\overline{e}}_2$ in E_2 and actions a_1^*, a_2^* such that (1) $\hat{a}_1(\overline{e}_1, \overline{e}_2) = \hat{a}_1(\overline{\overline{e}}_1, \overline{\overline{e}}_2) = a_1^*$, (2) $\hat{a}_2(\overline{e}_1, \overline{e}_2) = \hat{a}_2(\overline{\overline{e}}, \overline{\overline{e}}_2) = a_2^* \neq \hat{a}_2(\overline{e}_1, \overline{\overline{e}}_2)$, then there does not exist a decentralized satisfactory proposed-action process.

Proof. The following two quadruples (among others) satisfy the optimality relations: $(a_1^*, a_2^*, \overline{e}_1, \overline{e}_2)$ and $(a_1^*, a_2^*, \overline{\overline{e}}_1, \overline{\overline{e}}_2)$. If a decentralized proposed-action process $\langle g^1, g^2 \rangle$ were satisfactory, we would have

$$0 = g^1(a_1^*, a_2^*, \overline{e}_1) = g^2(a_1^*, a_2^*, \overline{\overline{e}}_2).$$

But that would, in turn, imply that the quadruple $(a_1^*, a_2^*, \overline{e}_1, \overline{\overline{e}}_2)$ satisfies the optimality relations, contrary to assumption (2).

[It is easily checked that Example A satisfies conditions (1) and (2) with $e_1 = (\alpha_1, \gamma_1), e_2 = \alpha_2, \hat{a}_1 = \alpha_1, \hat{a}_2 = \alpha_2 + \gamma_1$, and, for example, $\overline{e}_1 = (5, 4)$, $\overline{\overline{e}}_1 = (5, 7), \overline{e}_2 = 4, \overline{\overline{e}}_2 = 1, a_1^* = 5, a_2^* = 8$.]

The result extends to n-person organizations: if the conditions (1) and (2) are satisfied for some pair of persons and some fixed value of the environments of the other $n - 2$ persons, then a decentralized satisfactory proposed-action process does not exist.

Note however that *not every* externality in which one person's optimal action depends on another's environment as well as his own implies nonexistence of a satisfactory decentralized proposed-action process. Thus, e.g., if E_1 and E_2 are the reals and $\hat{a}_1(e_1, e_2) = e_1 + e_2, \hat{a}_2(e_1, e_2) = e_2$, then the process $g^1(a_1, a_2, e_1) = a_1 - a_2 - e_1, g^2(a_1, a_2, e_2) = a_2 - e_2$ has the required properties despite the presence of externalities.

(ii) Returning to Example A, we next show that the class of environments cannot be decentralized through a Lipschitzian process with a nonparametric outcome function. The essential step in the proof is the following.

Lemma.   In a decentralized satisfactory process, the parameter vector $\theta =$

$(\alpha_1, \gamma_2, \alpha_1)$ is a single-valued function, say, $\theta = f(m)$ from the two-dimensional message space of $m = \langle m_1, m_2 \rangle$ *onto* a neighborhood in the three-dimensional θ-space.

Proof. Let θ', θ'' be two, possibly distinct, parameter vector values compatible with a given value of m (at equilibrium). Since g is decentralized and the outcome functions nonparametric, we have

(1) (1.1) $\quad g^i(m, \theta_i') = 0, \quad a_i' = h^i(m)$

$\qquad$ (1.2) $\quad g^i(m, \theta_i'') = 0, \quad a_i'' = h^i(m) \quad \Big\} \quad (i = 1, 2);$

hence also

(2) (2.1) $\quad g^1(m, \theta_1') = 0, \quad g^2(m, \theta_2'') = 0, \quad a_1^* = h^1(m),$

$$a_2^* = h^2(m)$$

$\qquad$ (2.2) $\quad g^1(m, \theta_1'') = 0, \quad g^2(m, \theta_2') = 0, \quad a_1^{**} = h^1(m),$

$$a_2^{**} = h^2(m).$$

Since the process is satisfactory, it follows from the optimality relations that

(3) (3.1) $\quad a_1' \ = \alpha_1', \quad a_2' \ = \alpha_2' + \gamma_1'$

$\qquad$ (3.2) $\quad a_1'' = \alpha_1'', \quad a_2'' = \alpha_2'' + \gamma_1''$

$\qquad$ (3.3) $\quad a_1^* = \alpha_1', \quad a_2^* = \alpha_2'' + \gamma_1'$

$\qquad$ (3.4) $\quad a_1^{**} = \alpha_1'', \quad a_2^{**} = \alpha_2' + \gamma_1''.$

[Eqs. (3.1)–(3.4) are obtained respectively from (1.1), (1.2), (2.1), (2.2).] On the other hand, by (1) and (2),

$$a_1' = h^1(m) = a_1'',$$

so that

$$\alpha_1' = \alpha_1'',$$

and

$$a_2' = h^2(m) = a_2'' = a_2^* = a_2^{**},$$

which yields

$$\alpha_2' + \gamma_1' = \alpha_2'' + \gamma_1' = \alpha_2'' + \gamma_1' = \alpha_2' + \gamma_1''.$$

Therefore,

$$\alpha_2' = \alpha_2'' \quad \text{and} \quad \gamma_1' = \gamma_1''.$$

Thus $\theta' = \theta''$ and the single-valuedness assertion is proved. The range of the parameter vector θ has not been restricted in our example. But it is enough to suppose that it varies over some (three-dimensional) neighborhood. Then the satisfactoriness of the process requires that $g(m, \theta) = 0$ have a solution m for every value of θ in the neighborhood. This establishes the "onto" property of the mapping $f(\cdot)$ in the lemma.

The lemma having been established, it remains to show that the mapping f cannot be Lipschitzian. But this follows from the fact that a Lipschitzian mapping into a space of higher dimension yields an image of Jordan content zero (in the dimensionality of the range space); see Apostol [3], Theorem 10-8, p. 257.

3. Incentive-compatibility

A mechanism that is informationally feasible may be criticized on grounds of incompatibility with "natural" incentives. That is, participants in the process may find it advantageous to violate the rules of the process. Such violations might involve two or more units ("collusion") or single individuals. In what follows, we shall concentrate on the latter case, i.e., on the problem of *individual incentive-compatibility*.

Analytically, we think of the participants as taking part in an n-person non-cooperative game, with the response function of the i-th individual as his strategy and the utility to him of the outcome as the payoff. A process is defined as individually incentive-compatible if and only if the response functions it prescribes constitute a Nash equilibrium point for this game.[8] The use of utility, as distinct from merely postulating a complete ordering, is not essential, but is adopted for the sake of expository convenience. Also, we shall identify the outcome with the equilibrium allocation generated by the process.

Let the equilibrium of the process q^* be given by the usual relations

$$\overline{m}^i = f^{*i}(\overline{m}^i, \ldots, \overline{m}^n; e^i) \quad (i = 1, \ldots, n),$$

where f^{*i} is the response function prescribed by the prevailing mechanism q^*, and the process is *privacy-respecting* (satisfies the "privacy" requirement) in that f^{*i} depends on e through e^i only. Further, we define the i-th *strategy* as the function g^{*i} of the message n-tuple $m = \langle m^1, \ldots, m^n \rangle$ given by

$$(3.1) \quad g^{*i}(m^1, \ldots, m^n) = f^{*i}(m^1, \ldots, m^n; e^i) \quad \text{for all } m,$$

so that g^{*i} is determined by f^{*i} and e^i.

Now the *outcome* is a state (say, the equilibrium distributions) $\overline{s}$ given as a function of the equilibrium message n-tuple $\overline{m}$,

$$\overline{s} = \phi(\overline{m}).$$

In game theory language, the "payoff" to the i-th participant is, therefore,

$$u^{*i} = U^i(\overline{s}),$$

where U^i is the utility function of the i-th participant. Indirectly, u^{*i} depends on the strategy functions g^{*1}, which may be expressed by the relations

$$u^{*i} = u^i(g^{*1}, \ldots, g^{*n}), \quad i = 1, \ldots, n.$$

Let us write $g^* = \langle g^{*1}, \ldots, g^{*n} \rangle$ and denote by $g^{*)i(}$ the $(n-1)$-tuple obtained from g^* by deleting its i-th component g^{*i}. Then g^* constitutes a Nash equilibrium over some specified admissible strategy domains $G^1, \ldots, G^n$ if, for each $i = 1, \ldots, n$, the inequality

$$(3.2) \quad u^i(g^i, g^{*)i(}) \leq u^i(g^*)$$

holds for all g^i in G^i.

A mechanism is said to be individually incentive-compatible when the strategies implied by the response rules it prescribes constitute such a Nash equilibrium. It is clear, however, that the Nash equilibrium property of a strategy n-tuple g^* depends on the admissible strategy domains G^i. Since these domains consist of alternatives to the prescribed rules of behavior, they cannot be regarded as part of the "official" adjustment process. Rather, they are the "natural" alternatives to which participants might resort if it were to their advantage. Are there then any limits to how broad these domains of alternative strategies might be?

To find an answer to this question, let us consider the standard pure exchange (Edgeworth Box) case as the environment, and perfect competition q^C as the mechanism. Thus e^i specifies the initial endowment ω^i, the admissible consumption set X^i, and the (selfish) preference relation R^i (represented by the utility function U^i). The outcome is the competitive equilibrium allocation $c = \langle c^1, \ldots, c^n \rangle$, together with the corresponding competitive price p^C; for the sake of simplicity, this equilibrium will be assumed unique. By g^{Ci} we shall denote the competitive strategy function of the i-th participant, given his environmental characteristics e^i, i.e.,

$$g^{Ci}(m) = f^{Ci}(m; \mathring{e}^i) \qquad \text{for all } m,$$

with $\mathring{e}^i$ the true environmental characteristic, and f^{Ci} the response function prescribed by the competitive process when the i-th characteristic is $\mathring{e}^i$.

The n-tuple $g^C = \langle g^{C1}, \ldots, g^{Cn} \rangle$ is therefore incentive-compatible if, on the assumption that all others will abide by their g^{Cj} strategies, no participant i can profit by departing from his g^{Ci} and adopting some other strategy g^i within the permissible domain G^i.

We know, of course, that the opposite situation is the typical one. That is, with a finite number of participants, on the assumption that others will act as price-takers, it will pay a participant to behave monopolistically. If, for instance, traders $2, \ldots, n$ are assumed to behave as price-takers, there will usually exist a price $p^M \neq p^C$ at which $z^2, \ldots, z^n$ will be demanded by $2, \ldots, n$, respectively, acting as utility-maximizing price-takers, and such that $U^1(z^1) > U^1(c^1)$, $z^1 + z^2 + \cdots + z^n = \omega^1 + \omega + \cdots + \omega^n$, so that $z = \langle z^1, \ldots, z^n \rangle$ is feasible. [Note that p^M is not assumed to maximize $U^1(z^1)$, although such maximization is not ruled out.]

If we denote by the $g^{M,1}$ the monopolistic behavior strategy of the first trader, the case where p^M places the first trader at a higher utility level than would p^C is expressed by the inequality

$$u^1(g^{M,1}, g^{C)1}()) > u^1(g^{C1}, g^{C)1}()),$$

so that the perfectly competitive mechanism is not a Nash equilibrium (not individually incentive-compatible) if monopolistic behavior $g^{M,1}$ is in the admissible domain G^1.

Suppose, however, that there is a legal requirement to abide by the competitive rules which is enforced insofar as that can be done without violating the participant's "privacy." That is, the enforcement agency has no direct knowledge of the individual environmental components e^i, but each trader must be able to justify his observable behavior (bids) as a pricetaker's utility maximization.

Since the enforcement agency does not know the first trader's true e^1 (to be denoted by $\mathring{e}^1$), he will be able to use a strategy g^1 different from that dictated by the response function f^{C1} provided that there exists some (fictitious) $\tilde{e}^i$ such that, for each message n-tuple m,

$$g^1(m) = f^{C1}(m; \tilde{e}^1).$$

This simply means that the alternative (to price-taking) behavior g^1 can be "rationalized" as price-taking behavior for some fictitious specification of the first trader's initial endowment, consumption set, and preferences.

Some fictitious values for e^1 might be outside the class of environments for which the process was designed and would not "pass"; we may therefore suppose that the choice of fictitious values for the e^i is restricted to an *a priori* specified "plausible" class E^i. In our example, it seems reasonable to select the E^i so that their Cartesian product will yield the class of what we have called "classical" environments. (In the case of pure exchange, "classical" means absence of externalities, convexity, and continuity of preferences, and the convexity and closedness of the consumption set.)

In effect, our concept of incentive-compatibility merely requires that no one should find it profitable to "cheat," where cheating is defined as behavior that can be made to look "legal" by a misrepresentation of the participant's preferences or endowment, with the proviso that the fictitious preferences should be within certain "plausible" limits.

It is this notion of incentive-compatibility that seems to underlie the discussion of allocation mechanisms for public goods, as is seen in Samuelson's ([33], pp. 388-9) comment in connection with the Lindahl solution, to the effect that ". . . it is in the selfish interest of each person to give *false* signals, to pretend to have less interest in a given collective consumption activity than he really has . . . ." Similarly, Drèze and de la Vallée Poussin [9] refer to incentives for correct or incorrect revelation of preferences; thus the question is not whether the participants would at all refuse to "play the game," but rather whether they would behave in a way ostensibly consistent with the rules of the process but for a false set of preferences.

We shall see that even when departures from prescribed rules are confined to "plausible cheating" behavior, an important class of mechanisms, including perfect competition in nonatomistic[9] economies, turns out to lack individual incentive-compatibility. In such cases, one need not worry whether it is realistic to confine oneself to the (relatively) narrow class of "plausible cheating" alternatives as strategies, since the conclusion of incentive-incompatibility would follow *a fortiori* for a wider class of alternatives.

To summarize then, a privacy-respecting mechanism q^* is *individually incentive-compatible* with regard to individual environment classes $E^1, E^2, \ldots, E^n$ if the strategy n-tuple g^* defined by (3.1), where the f^{*i} are prescribed by the mechanism and the e^i are true (equal $\tilde{e}^i$), satisfies the inequalities (3.2) for $i = 1, \ldots, n$ for all g^i, such that

$$(3.4) \quad g^i(m) = f^{*i}(m; \tilde{e}^i),$$

with $\tilde{e}^i$ in E^i.

Samuelson's above-quoted comment thus implies that the Lindahl solution is not individually incentive-compatible.[10] The question is whether the failure of the various proposed mechanisms for the allocation of public goods to be individually incentive-compatible (in terms of the utility of final allocation as payoff) is peculiar to public goods, or whether it has a counterpart in economies where all goods are private.

In answering this question the crucial distinction is whether the economy is atomistic or not. If it is (i.e., if all traders are infinitesimal), we can agrėe with Samuelson ([33], p. 389) that the competitive process makes it unprofitable to depart from the rules of perfectly competitive behavior when everyone else continues to abide by these rules. But in the nonatomistic case, of which the standard Edgeworth Box situation for a finite number of traders is an instance, the situation is different. We have already noted the well-known fact that in "typical" situations, with the initial endowment not Pareto-optimal, it will be advantageous for a trader to behave monopolistically when others act as price-takers. But this is not sufficient to establish individual incentive-incompatibility according to our definition. To prove absence of incentive-compatibility we must show that when everyone else follows the rules of perfect competition (using their true preferences in utility maximization), it pays the remaining trader to behave in a way that is ostensibly price-taking, but with regard to a "plausible" false e^i (that is, false preferences or endowment or consumption set).[11] To be "plausible," this false set e^i must satisfy the classical requirements.

Although we shall not provide a rigorous proof, Figure 1 suggests that such a false preference map can easily be found. To construct it for $n = 2$ and two goods, it is enough to locate a monopoly allocation $z = \langle z^1, z^2 \rangle$, $z^i = (z_1{}^i), z_2{}^i)$, obtained at a monopoly price p^M, and to construct for trader 1 a false indifference curve (downward sloping, convex to the origin) tangent to the monopoly price line at z^1; this will make z into a (false) competitive allocation with regard to p^M, which now becomes a (false) competitive price. It remains to complete the false preference map for trader 1 by a family of indifference curves which

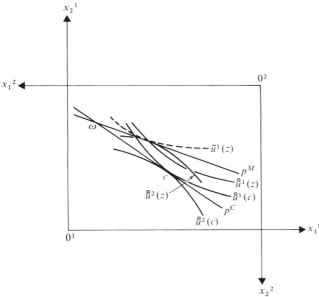

Figure 1

would not yield another false competitive equilibrium. That such a completion is possible in a particular case is shown in the Example D below. More generally, to make $[z, p^M]$ into a false competitive equilibrium, it would be sufficient for trader 1 to behave as a price-taker with regard to the (false) utility function given by

$$v = x_1^{\alpha} x_2$$

with

$$\alpha = (z_1^{\,1} p^M)/z_2^{\,1}.$$

(In the formula for v, x_1 and x_2 are the respective quantities of the two commodities obtained by trader 1.) This false utility function has not, however, been checked for uniqueness of equilibria.

Thus in a nonatomistic world, perfect competition is not guaranteed to be individually incentive-compatible even for classical environments and with all goods private.

At this point one may be inclined to look for mechanisms other than perfect competition in order to find one that would be individually incentive-compatible, at least for classical (but nonatomistic) environments free of public goods. However, we want the mechanism to be not merely individually incentive-compatible, but also Pareto-satisfactory and informationally decentralized. Some known processes satisfying the latter two requirements (e.g., the greed process [13]), the inertia-greed process [20], the stochastic adjustment process [17], can all be shown to lack incentive-compatibility. On the other hand, no process combining the three attributes (Pareto-satisfactoriness, informational decentralization, individual incentive-compatibility) has come to our attention. It becomes, therefore, natural to inquire whether such a combination is at all possible. We shall now give an informal argument in support of the conjecture of impossibility, formulated in the author's 1971 paper.

The requirement of informational decentralization enters through the postulate of "privacy," which means that no participant, including an enforcement agency if any, has any direct knowledge of others' preferences, endowments, technologies, etc., except possibly the restriction to the *a priori* given classes E^i. This makes it possible for any participant to act as if his endowment or preferences were different from what they are, provided that his observable behavior can be rationalized in terms of *some* plausible endowment or preferences. ("Plausible" here means belonging to the specified class E^i.) Now Pareto-satisfactoriness requires that the final outcome be feasible, hence within each participant's (survival) consumption set X^i. Consider an arbitrary Pareto-satisfactory privacy-respecting mechanism and suppose that corresponding to the true environment e the outcome is s. Let the first participant's utility associated with s be $u^1 = U^1(s)$ and suppose that there is an alternative feasible state $s\#$ which is preferred by participant 1, i.e., $U^1(s\#) > U^1(s)$. This participant then has the incentive to act as if his consumption set were not the true $\overset{\circ}{X}{}^1$ (which includes s) but a smaller false $\widetilde{X}^1$ containing only states whose utility for participant 1 is higher than $U^1(s)$. For, if the process is Pareto-satisfactory and privacy-respecting, it will then produce an outcome s'' which is feasible with respect to the false consumption set $\widetilde{X}^1$, hence more advantageous to participant 1 than the correct outcome s corresponding to the true $\overset{\circ}{X}{}^1$.

(This calculation is predicated on the assumption, implicit in the definition of incentive-compatibility, that other participants continue to follow the prescribed rules of the prevailing mechanism in terms of their true consumption sets, preferences, etc.) The preceding argument would constitute a proof of incentive-incompatibility in all Pareto-satisfactory informationally decentralized (privacy-respecting) processes, if one were willing to accept as "plausible" arbitrary consumption sets X^i, even though this implies that the initial endowment ω^i is far below the survival minimum.

What is particularly interesting about our problem is that a similar impossibility result can be obtained even when participants' falsifications are confined to classical environments, including the convexity of indifference curves, etc. To show this, we shall now confine ourselves to a somewhat narrower class of mechanisms by requiring (in addition to Pareto-satisfactoriness and respect for privacy) that the process always permits each participant to remain at a specified[12] endowment θ; this property, to be called the *no-trade option* is present in the perfectly competitive process; it implies that one can postulate the outcomes to have utility no less than that of the specified endowment θ, since otherwise the process lacks individual incentive-compatibility.

From this point on, we shall carry on the argument in terms of the two-person two-good pure exchange (Edgeworth Box) case. (Because of the negative nature of our claim, this approach is at the very least suggestive of the line of argument for the general case.) Now consider a situation where the specified endowment $\langle \theta^1, \theta^2 \rangle$ is not Pareto-optimal and suppose that the allocation $y^* = \langle y^{*1}, y^{*2} \rangle$ generated by a given process has no higher utility for trader 1 than the (unique) competitive[13] allocation $\langle c^1, c^2 \rangle$ would have; i.e., $U^1(y^{*1}) \leq U^1(c^1)$.[14] Assume, furthermore again, that there is a potential monopolistic advantage for trader 1; i.e., there is a feasible allocation $\langle z^1, z^2 \rangle$ and a price vector p^M such that trader 2 would demand z^2 if he were a price-taker and p^M were the given price, while $U^1(z^1) > U^1(c^1)$.

Let us note that for the class of processes now considered, the outcome must be Pareto-optimal and not below the initial utilities; hence for the case now considered the outcome must be a point of the "core," i.e., of the "contract curve" (that part of the Pareto-optimal curve which is within the lens-shaped area formed by the two indifference curves passing through the initial endowment point). Because the process respects privacy, the relevant contract curve will be the false one if, say, trader 1 plausibly falsifies his preferences, while trader 2 behaves correctly. Hence trader 1 will have an incentive to falsify his preferences if by so doing he can generate a false contract curve all points of which have a higher true utility to him than z^1. For the process will then produce an outcome on the false contract curve and trader 1 will necessarily profit, regardless of the particular point chosen on the false contract curve.

To illustrate the possibility of such falsification in a "classical" world, we have constructed the very simple Example D below, in which a false utility function results in a false contract curve all of whose points have a higher true utility for trader 1 than does his competitive allocation. It follows that there are classical environments in which no privacy-respecting Pareto-satisfactory process permitting the no-trade option is individually incentive-compatible. (We are implicitly assuming that communication is limited so as not to nullify the privacy.) Following the example, a somewhat more general result of similar nature is obtained.

Example D. (See Figure 2.) Pure exchange: two traders (identified by superscripts) and two goods (identified by subscripts). Each trader's true consumption set X^i is the nonnegative quadrant of the x_1, x_2-plane. The true utility function of each trader i is the same Cobb-Douglas function

$$u^i = x_1{}^i x_2{}^i \quad (i = 1, 2),$$

where the superscript i attached to x_j is not an exponent but merely refers to the i-th trader! The specified endowment is in the "northwest" corner of the Edgeworth Box, i.e.,

$$\theta^1 = (0, 1), \quad \theta^2 = (1, 0).$$

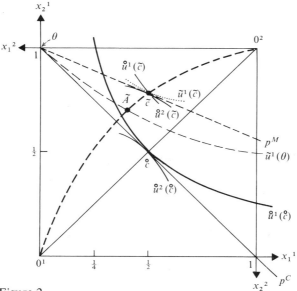

Figure 2

From the symmetry, the Pareto-optimal set is the diagonal of the (here square) box; the competitive price line[15] is the negative diagonal, and the competitive allocation is the center of the square, so $c^i = (1/2, 1/2)$ for $i = 1, 2$.

Since the true contract curve happens also to be the positive diagonal, all that can be said about the outcome is that it will be somewhere on that diagonal, since nothing more has been specified about the process. Without loss of generality, suppose that this point is either at the competitive point (the center) or closer to the origin of trader 1, i.e., in the lower half of the positive diagonal. Then, assuming that trader 2 will abide by the rules of the process, trader 1 will find it advantageous to use a fictitious utility function

$$v^1 = \begin{cases} x_2{}^1 - 1/(1 + x_1{}^1), & \text{for } x_2{}^1 > 0, \text{ or } x_2{}^1 = 0 \text{ with } x_1{}^1 \leq 1; \\ -(1/2), & \text{for } x_2{}^1 = 0 \text{ and } x_1{}^1 \geq 1. \end{cases}$$

It may be noted that, for $v^1 = 0$, the false indifference curve goes through the specified endowment point θ and is otherwise above the competitive price line.

It remains to be proved that this false utility function generates a (false) contract curve whose utility is always higher than the true utility of the competitive allocation c^1 which is given by $u^1(c^1) = (1/2) \cdot (1/2) = 1/4$. Now the lower endpoint $\tilde{A}$ of the false contract curve is obtained from the condition that the false indifference curve for $v^1 = 0$ whose equation is $x_2{}^1 = 1/(1 + x_1{}^1)$ is tangent to an indifference curve of trader 2. The coordinates of $\tilde{A}$ turn out to be $(-1 + \sqrt{2}, 1/\sqrt{2})$ and hence $u^1(\tilde{A}) = .29$, which exceeds $1/4$. Furthermore, the locus of false tangency points (i.e., the contract curve) has a positive slope, so the other points of the contract curve have both coordinates higher than those of $\tilde{A}$. It follows that their true utility u^1 always exceeds $1/4$ and hence is superior to the competitive allocation from the point of view of trader 1.

It follows that *no mechanism* of the class under consideration (Pareto-satisfactory, privacy-respecting, and permitting the no-trade option) is individually incentive-compatible for the environment assumed in our example, even if overt behavior is required to be consistent with some (false) classical environment. In particular, this reasoning and its conclusion is valid for the competitive mechanism which has the three postulated attributes. But in the competitive case we can also verify this conclusion directly by noting that, for the above false utility function v, the (false) competitive equilibrium allocation for trader 1 is the commodity bundle $\tilde{c}^1 = (1/2, 7/9)$ with the (false) competitive price $p = 4/9$. Since the true utility $u^1(\tilde{c}^1)$ of the false competitive allocation $\tilde{c}^1$ equals $(1/2) \cdot (7/9)$, and so exceeds the true utility $u^1(c^1) = (1/4)$ of the true competitive allocation c^1, it is seen directly that the competitive mechanism is not individually compatible for the environment of our example. Thus the direct proof is in accord with the general one.

A generalization

The preceding example is helpful because one can give an explicit construction of the various points and curves, but it is natural to inquire to what extent it represents a typical situation. Although the problem has not as yet been fully studied, the following generalization of the situation seen in the example is of some interest. We shall assume that the preferences (at least of trader 2) are such that neither good is inferior, and, furthermore, that preferences are monotone (at least for trader 1).[16] The environment is classical with regard to convexity and continuity, so that competitive equilibrium is guaranteed to exist. It is again assumed that there is a monopoly solution $[\langle z^1, z^2 \rangle, p^M]$ which is favorable to trader 1, in the sense that $u^1(z^1) > u^1(c^1)$; at p^M, trader 2, when acting as a price-taker, would demand z^2. Finally, we also assume that the monopoly point is an interior tangency point, i.e., a point where the price line p^M through θ is tangent to some indifference curve of trader 2. This indifference curve may have the equation

$$x_2{}^2 = G(x_1{}^2);$$

using the fact that

$$x_j{}^1 + x_j{}^2 = \theta_j{}^1 + \theta_j{}^2 \quad (j = 1, 2),$$

this equation may be rewritten as, say,

$$x_2{}^1 = g(x_1{}^1).$$

Since z^1 is the assumed point of tangency, we have

$$g'(z_1{}^1) = -p^M,$$

and since the p^M price line goes through θ,

$$z_2{}^1 - \theta_1{}^1 = -p^M(z_1{}^1 - \theta_1{}^1).$$

As a first candidate for a false indifference map of trader 1, we may consider the family of straight lines parallel to the price line p^M; the corresponding false utility function can be written as

$$v^1 = x_2{}^1 + p^M x_1{}^1 + \beta.$$

Clearly, z is now a point on the false (v^1) contract curve; furthermore, because both goods are noninferior for trader 2, all other points of this contract curve have coordinates that are respectively at least as great as those of z^1; since preferences of trader 1 are monotone, all points of the (false) contract curve are superior in terms of the true utility function u^1 to c^1, hence to the allocation prescribed by the process. Thus trader 1 would find it advantageous to pretend that his utility function is v^1 rather than u^1.

However, it would be more in the classical spirit to endow him with indifference curves that are strictly convex (to the origin), i.e., a strictly quasi-concave utility function. This can be accomplished by a slight deformation of the straight indifference lines of v^1 above. It can be done by slightly "bending" the line going through θ and z, so that the resulting curve is still tangent to the g-indifference curve of trader 2, with the point of tangency, say, $w = (w_1, w_2)$, $w_2 = g(w_1)$, such that $w_1 = z_1{}^1 - \epsilon$, where ϵ is a positive number chosen sufficiently small so that $u^1(w) > u^1(c^1)$, which is possible because of continuity of u^1. The new false utility function $v^{1\#}$ will be defined by

$$v^{1\#} = x_2{}^1 + p^M(x_1{}^1)^\alpha + \beta, \qquad 0 < \alpha < 1,$$

where α is obtained from the equation

$$-\alpha p^M w_1{}^{\alpha-1} = g'(w_1)$$

and β from

$$\theta_2{}^1 = -p^M(\theta_1{}^1)^\alpha - \beta.$$

By choosing ϵ small enough one can make certain that (at least for a continuously differentiable marginal rate of substitution $u_1{}^2/u_2{}^2$ of the second trader) the contract curve of the strictly convex map given by $v^{1\#}$ is arbitrarily close to the contract curve for the linear map given by v^1, hence (by continuity of preferences) truly superior to c^1 for trader 1. Thus, for the environments and mechanisms under consideration, false "plausible" revelation of preferences is both feasible and profitable, hence individual incentive-compatibility is absent.

One is thus faced with the dilemma of accepting mechanisms that are either not Pareto-satisfactory (with the no-trade option) or not privacy-respecting. If one does not wish to sacrifice Pareto-satisfactoriness, one is forced into making concessions on the side of informational decentralization, specifically with regard to privacy. These concessions will involve the diversion of some resources from substantive uses to the operation of the mechanism – to obtain more information concerning the characteristics e^i of the various individuals, and perhaps, to induce behavior prescribed by the mechanism. In terms of the notation of Eq. (1.1), the resource costs $b(q/e)$ of operating the mechanism[17] are (vectorially) higher than would have been the case if an incentive-compatible informationally decentralized mechanism were possible with the loss of Pareto-satisfactoriness. Consequently, the resources $\omega_e - b(q/e)_1$ available for substantive purposes are lower and hence the welfare possibilities, as measured by the indicator w in (1.1) are (vectorially) less than would otherwise have been the case.

To illustrate, suppose that the mechanism initially under consideration is perfect competition, and the environment classical but not atomistic. We know that perfect competition will be Pareto-satisfactory but not incentive-compatible. We may then modify the mechanism by creating an agency whose task will be to acquire information about the individual characteristics e^i of the participants and to enforce price-taking behavior. (This may seem somewhat less fantastic in the context of a Lange-Lerner economy, with the e^i being the technological characteristics of the various producing units.) Assuming that enforcement is successful, the modified system is again Pareto-satisfactory with respect to $\omega_e - b(q/e)$ where q is the modified mechanism and $b(q/e)$ represents the resource cost of operating the agency. Since perfect competition without the agency is incentive-incompatible, hence behaviorally infeasible, it cannot be considered as a realistic alternative to q. One could, on the other hand, suppose that there is some imperfectly competitive mechanism q' which is informationally decentralized but not Pareto-satisfactory with regard to resources used for substantive purposes. Supposing for a moment that $b(q'/e) = 0$ we could then compare, in terms of an appropriate welfare indicator W, the two expressions $W[h(\omega_e - b(q/e), q/e)]$ and $W[h(\omega_e, q'/e)]$. It is not *a priori* obvious which will be the higher, even though – according to our assumptions – $W[h(x, q/e)]$ would be higher than $W[h(x, q'/e)]$ for any given x. In other words, even though q' may be less efficient (in maximizing W) in utilizing the resources available for substantive purposes, it may make up for it by not requiring resources to operate the mechanism.

In a more realistic discussion one would recognize that all mechanisms require resources to operate, but the nature of the comparison might be somewhat similar.

The logic of informational assumptions underlying the concept of individual incentive-compatibility may well be questioned. Where do our results concerning the conflict between informational decentralization and incentives depend on the fact that the process is assumed to be privacy-respecting? A partial answer, at least, is obtained by imagining that the n-trader economy is enlarged by adding an $(n + 1)$-st unit, an enforcement agency whose privacy-respecting response function may be written as $f^{*n+1}(m^1, \ldots, m^{n+1}; e^{n+1})$. This means that the agency's knowledge concerning $e^1, \ldots, e^n$ would only be derived from the messages $m_t{}^i$, $i = 1, \ldots, n$, and of the prescribed response functions f^{*i}; thus if any of the traders uses a false e^i as an argument in his prescribed response function, there is no way for the enforcement agency to detect this. The same difficulty would arise if the traders themselves were entitled to enforce the prescribed rules of the process, say, by suing in court. For here again, by the "privacy" postulate trader j only knows about e^i through the messages m^i, and hence cannot prove that violation exists as long as a false e^i is drawn from the "plausible" class E^i.[18]

In the light of the fact that j does not know the true value of e^i, it might seem incongruous that the inequalities (3.2) implicitly contain the true values of e^i in their right-hand members. But this objection loses some of its force if one notes that the functions g^{*i} may be considered as observable in the course of the process, even though f^i and e^i separately are not. Hence, from the Nash solution point of view, the g^{*i} functions seem to be the proper ones to enter the definition of an equilibrium point in a noncooperative game. On the other hand, in view of the known difficulties with this approach to the theory of games, alternative lines of attack should certainly be explored.[19]

Notes

1   This work was carried on with the aid of National Science Foundation Grant GS-2077.

2   We are here thinking of technology and preferences as completely exogenous. Otherwise, only the exogenous components would be treated as environment.

3   In a more complete analysis, one would also take into account (either on the "cost" or "performance" side) the speed and accuracy of alternative information-processing systems.

4   The $\mathcal{E}_e$ denotes the mathematical expectation with respect to the given probability measure on E_0.

5   Both dispersion of information and limitation on communication may be regarded as extreme cases of imperfections in the distribution and flow of information. One way of formalizing such imperfections (see [19]) is by introducing error variables in connection with both environmental and message arguments of the response functions characterizing the adjustment process. Thus, instead of writing the adjustment equations as, say,

$$m_{t+1}{}^i = F_t{}^i(m_t{}^1, \ldots, m_t{}^n; e^1, \ldots, e^n) \qquad (i = 1, \ldots, n),$$

we may postulate similar relations but with $m_k{}^t$ and e^k replaced, respectively, by, say, $m_t{}^k + {}_m{}^i v_t{}^k$ and $e^k + {}_e{}^i v^k$, where the v's are random variables representing the errors of perception with regard to the messages received and the environmental characteristics. Dispersion of (environmental) information would then correspond to postulating that the variance of ${}_e{}^i v^i$ is zero, while the variance of ${}_e{}^i v^i$, $j \neq i$, is infinite. Similar postulates concerning the joint distribution of the ${}_m v$'s would reflect the limitations on communication. (In the above formula for the adjustment process, the environment e is conceived as described in terms of the n-tuple $e = \langle e^1, \ldots, e^n \rangle$, where e^i is the description of the environmental characteristics of the i-th unit.)

A further degree of realism can be introduced into the model by making the joint distribution of the error variables dependent on informational activities, associated with different cost levels.

6   The dispersion of information is reflected in the definition of informational decentralization by a property of the response function which, for want of a better term, is referred to as *privacy-respecting*, viz., that a response function, say, $F_t^i(m_t; e)$ depends on e through e^i only, so that it can be written as $f^i(m_t; e^i)$. (The earlier, even less fortunate, term for this property was "externality"; see [13].) The function F_t^i tells participant i at time t how to form his next message m_{t+1}^i, given the n-tuple $m_t = \langle m_t^1, \ldots, m_t^n \rangle$ of messages from the previous period and given the environment e. When dispersion prevails, a response function F_t^i, which depended on some e^j, $j \neq i$, would not be informationally feasible.

As for limitation on the nature of communication, the earlier version [13] required self-relevance of messages and aggregativeness of the response functions. The latter property is trivially satisfied in the examples of the present paper, since these examples refer to cases where the number of participants n equals 2.

In examples of Section 2, self-relevance would correspond to what are there defined as proposed-action processes. However, in Section 2, we consider a somewhat broader concept of decentralization in which the meaning of messages is unrestricted (so that self-relevance is not required), but the dimensionality of the messages must be what it would have been under self-relevance, i.e., the same as that of the action space. Furthermore, mathematical regularity (Lipschitzian) properties are imposed to make the dimensionality "genuine."

In both Sections 2 and 3, processes are required to be privacy-respecting. But, in 3, the limitations on the nature of communication are not spelled out explicitly; Section 2, on the other hand, deals with these limitations explicitly.

It is worth noting that by confining ourselves to first-order processes (i.e., first-order difference equation adjustment), we are in fact imposing a limitation on memory, hence, on communication. Even severe restrictions on the nature of communication at any given point in time could be largely circumvented by permitting an accumulation of information over many time periods. Hence some restriction on memory (i.e., order of the process) seems an essential feature of informational decentralization.

7   We call g "quasi-Lipschitzian" if and only if there exists a positive constant K such that, given m, m'', there exist θ', θ'' satisfying the relations $g(m', \theta') = 0$, $g(m'', \theta'') = 0$, such that the inequality $\| \theta' - \theta'' \| \leq K \cdot \| m' - m'' \|$ holds. (The symbol $\| x \|$ denotes the norm of x.) It may be noted that in this example, but not in similar situations involving more parameters, the Lipschitzian property may be softened to the requirement that the functions be of bounded variation.

8   See Drèze and de la Vallée Poussin [9], as well as Hurwicz [19]; the latter contains a somewhat modified version of suggestions initially presented at the Ann Arbor 1968 conference on the comparison of economic systems.

9   We use the term "atomistic" in the old-fashioned sense, meaning that every participant is infinitesimal as compared with the total market or economy. (In modern measure-theoretic language this case is called "nonatomic.")

10   On the other hand, Drèze and de la Vallée Poussin ([9], pp. 28–30) find their mechanism for the allocation of public goods to be individually incentive-compatible. The contrast seems to be due to the local and instantaneous nature of the Drèze-Poussin payoff function, since their criterion is whether $du^i/dt < 0$ for a participant departing from the prescribed strategy, while Samuelson implicitly considers the relevant payoff to be the utility of the final (equilibrium) allocation. We adopt the Samuelson payoff assumption in what follows.

11   One version of the game we imagine the traders to be playing is as follows: each trader picks an indifference map, a price-adjustment mechanism of Lange type is operated until market-clearing equilibrium prices are found, and then each trader collects the value his true utility function takes for the bundle which he obtains at the equilibrium.

12   $\theta = \langle\theta^1, \ldots, \theta^n\rangle$ is some redistribution of the initial endowment $\omega = \langle\omega^1, \ldots, \omega^n\rangle$, such that

$$\Sigma_{i=1}^n \, \theta^i = \Sigma_{i=1}^n \, \omega^i.$$

(The symbol θ used here is unrelated to that of Section 2.)

The interpretation of θ is that it may arise from some scheme of lump payments and subsidies preceding the tâtonnement phase of the process. By introducing the possibility of a redistribution from the initial ω to θ, we safeguard the requirement of having an unbiased, hence Pareto-satisfactory process. However, in what follows, θ plays the usual role of ω; in particular, the various price lines are assumed to go through θ and the competitive allocation is determined with reference to θ.

13   Because the environment is assumed classical, a competitive equilibrium necessarily exists.

14   Postulating this inequality involves no loss of generality, since it necessarily holds for at least one trader.

15   The competitive equilibrium is taken with respect to θ, hence the price line goes through θ.

16   Trader 1 is distinguished by the fact that the utility to him of the prescribed allocation is no higher than that of the competitive allocation would have been. As in the example, "competitive" means from θ as the initial allocation.

17   We are again ignoring the psychological cost associated with the loss of privacy and with the enforcement measures designed to compensate for the absence of incentive-compatibility.

18   It may be well to recall that, implicitly, we are assuming restrictions on communication that will make it impossible to "smuggle through" environmental information despite the privacy requirement.

19 Drèze and de la Vallée Poussin ([9], p. 26), for instance, show that, in their public goods model, minimaxing calls for honest relevation of preferences.

References

[1] M. Aoki, "The problem of Incentives in the Theory of Planning," paper presented at the Second World Congress of the Econometric Society, Cambridge, England, 1970 (unpublished).

[2] M. Aoki, "Two Planning Algorithms for an Economy with Public Goods," Discussion Paper No. 029, Kyoto Institute of Economic Research, Kyoto University, 1970.

[3] T. M. Apostol, *Mathematical Analysis*, Addison-Wesley, Reading, Mass., 1957.

[4] K. J. Arrow and L. Hurwicz, "Decentralization and Computation in Resource Allocation," this volume, II.1, pp. 41–95.

[5] A. Camacho, "Externalities, Optimality, and Informationally Decentralized Resource Allocation Processes," *International Economic Review*, *11*, 318–327 (1970).

[6] A. Camacho, "Centralization and Decentralization of Decision-making Mechanisms: a General Model," paper presented at the Second World Congress of the Econometric Society, Cambridge, England, 1970 (unpublished).

[7] O. A. Davis and A. Whinston, "Externalities Welfare and the Theory of Games," *Journal of Political Economy*, *70*, 241–262 (1962).

[8] G. Debreu, *Theory of Value*, Wiley, New York, 1959.

[9] J. H. Drèze and D. de la Vallée Poussin, "A Tâtonnement Process for Guiding and Financing an Efficient Production of Public Goods," Discussion Paper No. 6922, CORE, Univ. Cath. de Louvain, Belgium, 1969.

[10] T. Groves, "Incentives in a Team," paper presented at the Second World Congress of the Econometric Society, Cambridge, England, 1970 (unpublished).

[11] G. M. Heal, "Planning without Prices," *Review of Economic Studies*, *36*, 346–362 (1969).

[12] L. Hurwicz, "Theory of Economic Organization" (abstract), *Econometrica*, *19*, 54 (1951).

[13] L. Hurwicz, "Optimality and Informational Efficiency in Resource Allocation Processes," this volume, IV, pp. 393–412.

[14] L. Hurwicz, "Conditions for Economic Efficiency of Centralized and Decentralized Structures," in G. Grossman (ed.), *Value and Plan*, University of California Press, Berkeley, 1960, pp. 162–183.

[15] L. Hurwicz, "On Decentralizability in the Presence of Externalities," paper presented at the San Francisco meeting of the Econometric Society, 1966 (unpublished).

[16]   L. Hurwicz, "On the Concept and Possibility of Informational Decentralization," *American Economic Review*, *59*, 513–534 (1969).

[17]   L. Hurwicz, R. Radner, and S. Reiter (1970), "A Stochastic Decentralized Resource Allocation Process," 1970 (unpublished).

[18]   L. Hurwicz, "Organizational Structures for Joint Decision Making: a Designer's Point of View," in M. Tuite, R. Chisholm, and M. Radnor (eds.), *Interorganizational Decision-Making*, Aldine Press, Chicago (forthcoming).

[19]   L. Hurwicz, "Centralization and Decentralization in Economic Processes," Chapter 3 in A. Eckstein (ed.), *Comparison of Economic Systems: Theoretical and Methodological Approaches*, University of California Press, Berkeley (forthcoming).

[20]   H. Kanemitsu, "On the Stability of an Adjustment Process in Nonconvex Environments – a Case of the Commodity Space (Strong) Inertia-Greed Process," paper presented at the Second World Congress of the Econometric Society, Cambridge, England, 1970 (unpublished).

[21]   H. Kanemitsu, "Informational Efficiency and Decentralization in Optimal Resource Allocation," *The Economic Studies Quarterly*, *16*, 22–40 (1966).

[22]   T. C. Koopmans, *Three Essays on the State of Economic Science*, McGraw-Hill, New York, 1957.

[23]   J. Kornai and T. Lipták, "Two-level Planning," *Econometrica*, *33*, 141–169 (1965).

[24]   J. O. Ledyard, "Resource Allocation in Unselfish Environments," *American Economic Review*, *58*, 227–237 (1968).

[25]   E. Malinvaud, "Decentralized Procedures for Planning," Chapter 7 in Bacharach and Malinvaud (eds.), *Activity Analysis in the Theory of Growth and Planning*, Macmillan, London, 1967, pp. 170–208.

[26]   E. Malinvaud, "The Theory of Planning for Individual and Collective Consumption," outline of a paper to be presented at the *Symposium on the Problem of the National Economy Modeling*, Novosibirsk (Siberian Branch of the Acad. of Science of the USSR).

[27]   S. A. Marglin, "Information in Price and Command Systems of Planning," in J. Margolis and H. Guitton (eds.), *Public Economics*, Macmillan, London, 1969, pp. 54–77.

[28]   T. Marschak, "Centralization and Decentralization in Economic Organizations," *Econometrica*, *27*, 399–430 (1959).

[29]   J. Marschak, "Elements for a Theory of Teams," *Management Science*, *1*, 127–137 (1955).

[30]   R. Radner, "The Evaluation of Information in Organizations," in *Proceedings of the Fourth Berkeley Symposium on Mathematical Statistics and Probability*, University of California, Berkeley, vol. I, 1961, pp. 491–530.

[31]   S. Reiter, "A Market-adjustment Mechanism," Institute Paper No. 1, Institute for Quantitative Research in Economics and Management, School of Industrial Management, Purdue University, Lafayette, Indiana, 1960.

[32] S. Reiter, "Informational Efficiency of Resource Allocation Processes," abstract of a paper presented at the Second World Congress of the Econometric Society, Cambridge, England, 1970 (unpublished).

[33] P. A. Samuelson, "The Pure Theory of Public Expenditure," *The Review of Economics and Statistics*, *36*, 387–389 (1954).

Appendix

An optimality criterion for decision-making under ignorance

KENNETH J. ARROW
LEONID HURWICZ [1]

1. Introduction

It is intended here to offer a possible characterization of the concept of complete ignorance. Like other formulations, the problem is taken to be that of choice of an action from a given set when the consequences of any action are functions of an unknown state of nature. However, the properties regarded as defining an optimal choice are designed to reflect completely the idea that there is no *a priori* information available which gives any state of nature a distinguished position. Most importantly, the optimality criterion differs from those in the now more standard subjective probability framework by not presupposing a fixed list of states of nature. As we note shortly, the arguments and conclusions are much closer to Shackle's [8] than to those of Ramsey [5], de Finetti [3], and Savage [7].

The axiom systems of these last authors imply the existence of subjective probabilities as weights to be assigned to the different possible states of nature. These authors thus provide a foundation for the centuries-old use of probability as a guide to action. The concept of complete ignorance can be expressed in this subjective probability framework only by the assignment of equal probabilities to all the states of nature, which is the principle of indifference or insufficient reason implicit in the earliest combinatorial probability calculations of Pascal and Fermat and explicit in Jacob Bernoulli, Bayes, and Laplace. But it may be questioned whether the ignorance expressed by this concept is complete enough. A state of nature is a complete description of the world. But how we describe the world is a matter of language, not of fact. Any description can be made finer by introducing more elements to be described; hence, any state of nature can be expressed as a union of more elementary states of nature. Suppose, for example, there are two coins, but coin two is flipped only if coin one shows tails. There are then three states of nature. But if the betting was solely on the outcome of coin one, one would be loth to base a decision on the assumption that the three states of nature were equally probable, even if there was no *a priori* knowledge about the possible biases in the two coins.

Shackle's [8] formulation permits a different outlook. In this case, complete ignorance is to be interpreted as meaning that all states of nature have zero potential surprise. Then dividing a state of nature into two would have no effect on the action chosen if the reward to an action is the same under either substate. Indeed, more specifically, the standardized focus-gain and focus-loss become simply the maximum and minimum payoff to a given action, and the final decision among possible actions is made on the basis of the gambler indifference map, which, in this case of complete ignorance, simply orders these pairs.[2] In the present paper, we demonstrate that a plausible set of desirable properties for a rational criterion of choice under complete ignorance in fact leads to this special case of Shackle's theory.

The properties here are essentially drawn from a set developed by Chernoff [2].[3] However, though Chernoff presents the crucial condition referred to below as Property C in Section 4 (optimality of an action is unaffected by deletion of repetitious states), he does not in the final published version make use of it.

Milnor [4] presented some ten desirable properties for decision-making under ignorance; they are shown to be inconsistent as a whole, and he investigated the implications of various subsets. The conclusion of one of his results (Lemma 3) is implied by that of our theorem below, but the assumptions differ somewhat. Most importantly, he assumes that the choice is a continuous function of the payoffs, an assumption which we avoid.[4]

2. Notation and basic concepts

In accordance with the von Neumann–Morgenstern utility theorem, the consequences of an action under any particular state of nature can be represented by a real number. An action may be regarded as defined by its consequences under each alternative state of nature. Formally, an *action a* is a real-valued function over some set Ω of states of nature. The letter a will stand for the function, while $a(\omega)$ is the value taken on by the function for a given $\omega \in \Omega$.

A *decision problem A* is a set of actions, all of which have the same domain, denoted by $\Omega(A)$. Note that different decision problems may correspond not merely to different sets of available actions but also to different sets of possible states of nature. All of the studies mentioned in Section 1, other than that of Chernoff, consider only a fixed set of possible states of nature.

The problem of decision-making under ignorance is to assign to a decision problem A a subset $\hat{A}$, known as the *optimal set* for A. It is not assumed that every decision problem has an optimal set. We consider a fixed class $\tilde{P}$ of decision problems, each of which is supposed to have a non-null optimal set. If $a_1, a_2 \in A$, and either $a_1, a_2 \in \hat{A}$ or $a_1, a_2 \in A - \hat{A}$, we will say that a_1 and a_2 are *optimally equivalent* with respect to A, symbolized by

$$a_1 \; \tilde{o} \; a_2 \, [A].$$

The relation of optimal equivalence with respect to a fixed set A is clearly transitive, symmetric, and reflexive, and therefore properly an equivalence relation. If $a_1, a_2 \in A$ and $a_1 \in \hat{A}$, we shall say that a_1 is *revealed preferred* or *indifferent*[5] to a_2 with respect to A, and symbolize it by

$$a_1 (\geqq) a_2 [A].$$

Similarly, if $a_1, a_2 \in A, a_1 \in \hat{A}$, and $a_2 \in A - \hat{A}$, a_1 is said to be *revealed preferred* to a_2 with respect to A; the relation is symbolized by

$$a_1 (>) a_2 [A].$$

In particular, we will be concerned with decision problems containing just the actions a_1, a_2 (which are assumed to have the same domain) and denoted by (a_1, a_2). Define

$$a_1 \tilde{o} a_2 \quad \text{if } a_1 \tilde{o} a_2 [(a_1, a_2)],$$

$$a_1 (\geqq) a_2 \quad \text{if } a_1 (\geqq) a_2 [(a_1, a_2)],$$

$$a_1 (>) a_2 \quad \text{if } a_1 (>) a_2 [(a_1, a_2)].$$

Two decision problems A_1 and A_2 are said to be *isomorphic* if there exists a one-one mapping f of A_1 onto A_2 and a one-one mapping g of $\Omega(A_1)$ onto $\Omega(A_2)$ such that $f(a) \, o \, g = a$ for all a in A_1.[6] In effect, two decision problems are isomorphic if they can be obtained from each other by relabeling actions and states of nature.

If A_1 and A_2 are two decision problems, we shall say that A_2 is *derived from* A_1 *by deletion of repetitious states* if (1) $\Omega(A_2) \subset \Omega(A_1)$; (2) there is a one-one mapping f of A_1 onto A_2 such that $f(a)$ coincides with a on $\Omega(A_2)$; (3) for each ω in $\Omega(A_1) - \Omega(A_2)$, there is an ω' in $\Omega(A_2)$ such that $a(\omega) = a(\omega')$ for all a in A_1. In symbols

$$A_1 \to A_2.$$

3. Assumptions on the class of decision problems

The class $\tilde{P}$ of decision problems which have non-null optimal sets will be assumed to satisfy certain assumptions.

Assumption 1. If A is a decision problem with a finite number of actions, for each of which $\min_\omega a(\omega)$ and $\max_\omega a(\omega)$ exist, then $A \in \tilde{P}$.

Assumption 2. If $A_1 \to A_2$ and $A_1 \in \tilde{P}$, then $A_2 \in \tilde{P}$.

Assumption 3. If $a \in A$, where $A \in \tilde{P}$, then $\min_\omega a(\omega)$ and $\max_\omega a(\omega)$ exist.

Assumption 1 may be disputable if it is held that with every set of actions the set of probability distributions over those actions (the mixed strategies) must also be regarded as available. Assumption 3 is restrictive; however, it is automatically satisfied when $\Omega(A)$ is finite. A relaxation of this assumption is undoubtedly possible if some additional continuity properties are postulated for the optimality criterion.

4. Properties of the optimality criterion

By the *optimality criterion* is meant the rule defining $\hat{A}$ for every A in P. Certain properties of this criterion will be postulated, and the form of the criterion then deduced.

Property A. If $A_1 \subset A_2$ and $A_1 \cap \hat{A}_2$ is non-null, then $\hat{A}_1 = A_1 \cap \hat{A}_2$; that is, if an action is deemed optimal in a certain set of alternatives and if subsequently the range of alternative actions available is contracted but the optimal action is still available, then the optimal action for the larger problem is still optimal.[7]

Property B. If A_1 is isomorphic to A_2 and a is optimal in A_1, then $f(a)$ is optimal in A_2; that is, relabeling actions and states of nature is of no fundamental importance.[8]

Property C. If $A_1 \rightarrow A_2$, then $f(a)$ is optimal in A_2 if and only if a is optimal in A_1. If $a(\omega) = a(\omega')$ for all a in A_1, then, in effect, for that problem ω and ω' are the same state of nature, and deleting one of them from consideration should lead to no change in the optimal set.[9]

Property D. (1) If a is optimal in A, $a' \in A$, and $a'(\omega) \geq a(\omega)$ for all ω, then a' is optimal in A. (2) If a is not optimal in A, $a' \in A$, and $a'(\omega) \leq a(\omega)$ for all ω, then a' is not optimal in A.

5. Some lemmas

Lemma 1.

(1)   If $a_1 \tilde{o} a_2$, then $a_1 \tilde{o} a_2 [A]$ for all A for which $a_1, a_2 \in A$.
(2)   If $a_1 (\geq) a_2 [A]$ for some A, then $a_1 (\geq) a_2$.
(3)   If $a_1 (>) a_2 [A]$ for some A, then $a_1 (>) a_2$.

Proof. (1) If a_1, a_2 are not optimally equivalent with respect to A, suppose $a_1 \in \hat{A}, a_2 \in A - \hat{A}$. Since (a_1, a_2) intersects A, the optimal set for (a_1, a_2) consists of the one element a_1, by Property A, contradicting the hypothesis. (2) and (3) follow by similar applications of Property A.

Lemma 2. Suppose a_1 and a_2 have the same domain, $a_1(\omega_1) = a_2(\omega_2)$, $a_1(\omega_2) = a_2(\omega_1)$, $a_1(\omega) = a_2(\omega)$ for all $\omega \neq \omega_1, \omega_2$. Then $a_1 \tilde{o} a_2$.

Proof. Let g be defined by $g(\omega_1) = \omega_2, g(\omega_2) = \omega_1, g(\omega) = \omega$ for $\omega \neq \omega_1, \omega_2$. Let $b_i = a_i \circ g (i = 1, 2)$, and define a function f by $f(a_i) = b_i (i = 1, 2)$. It is easy to verify that (a_1, a_2) and (b_1, b_2) are isomorphic. Hence, if a_1 is optimal in (a_1, a_2), then b_1 is optimal in (b_1, b_2). But $b_2 = a_1, b_1 = a_2$, so that (a_1, a_2) and (b_1, b_2) are the same decision problem. That is, if a_1 is optimal in (a_1, a_2), then so is a_2. We can also interchange a_1 and a_2 in this statement, so that a_1 $\tilde{o} \, a_2$.

Lemma 3. Suppose m, M are real numbers with $m \leq M$, and a_1, a_2 take on the values m, M and no others. Then $a_1 \, \tilde{o} \, a_2$ if a_1 and a_2 have the same domain.

Proof. If $m = M$, then $a_1 = a_2$, and the result is trivial. Suppose $m < M$. Let Ω, the domain of a_1 and a_2, be broken up into four subsets:

$$\Omega_1 = \{\omega | a_1(\omega) = a_2(\omega) = m\},$$

$$\Omega_2 = \{\omega | a_1(\omega) = a_2(\omega) = M\},$$

$$\Omega_3 = \{\omega | a_1(\omega) = m, a_2(\omega) = M\},$$

$$\Omega_4 = \{\omega | a_1(\omega) = M, a_2(\omega) = m\}.$$

First suppose that Ω_3 and Ω_4 are both non-null. Let $\omega_3 \in \Omega_3, \omega_4 \in \Omega_4$. Let Ω', be formed from Ω by deleting all elements of Ω_3 and Ω_4 except ω_3 and ω_4, and define f by letting $f(a_i)$ coincide with a_i over Ω' and be undefined elsewhere. Since $a_i(\omega) = a_i(\omega_3)$ for $\omega \in \Omega_3 - (\omega_3), a_i(\omega) = a_i(\omega_4)$ for $\omega \in \Omega_4 - (\omega_4)$,

(1) $\quad (a_1, a_2) \to (f(a_1), f(a_2))$.

By construction $f(a_1)$ coincides with $f(a_2)$ for all $\omega \in \Omega'$ other than ω_3, ω_4; $f(a_1)(\omega_3) = m = f(a_2)(\omega_4), f(a_1)(\omega_4) = M = f(a_2)(\omega_3)$. By Lemma 2, $f(a_1)$ $\tilde{o} f(a_2)$. Since the optimal set for $(f(a_1), f(a_2))$ is non-null, both $f(a_1)$ and $f(a_2)$ must be optimal in $(f(a_1), f(a_2))$. By Property C, a_1 and a_2 are both optimal in (a_1, a_2) and therefore $a_1 \, \tilde{o} \, a_2$.

Now suppose Ω_4 is null, Ω_3 non-null. Since a_1 and a_2 must both take on both values, m and M, neither Ω_1 nor Ω_2 can be null. Let ω_j be any element of $\Omega_j (j = 1, 2, 3)$. Let $f_1(a_i)$ coincide with a_i for $\omega = \omega_j (i = 1, 2; j = 1, 2, 3)$, and be undefined elsewhere. Since $a_i(\omega) = a_i(\omega_j)$ for $\omega \in \Omega_j - (\omega_j)$ for each i and j,

(2) $\quad (a_1, a_2) \to (f_1(a_1), f_1(a_2))$.

Define a_3 as follows: $a_3(\omega_1) = M, a_3(\omega_2) = m, a_3(\omega_3) = M$. Then $f_1(a_2)(\omega_1) = a_2(\omega_1) = m = a_3(\omega_2); f_1(a_2)(\omega_2) = a_2(\omega_2) = M = a_3(\omega_1); f_1(a_2)(\omega_3) = a_2(\omega_3) = M = a_3(\omega_3)$. From Lemma 2,

(3) $\quad f_1(a_2) \, \tilde{o} \, a_3$.

Let A be the decision problem with elements $f_1(a_1), f_1(a_2), a_3$. Note that, since $a_1(\omega_1) = m = a_1(\omega_3)$,

(4) $\quad f_1(a_1)(\omega_1) = f_1(a_1)(\omega_3), \quad a_3(\omega_1) = a_3(\omega_3)$.

Let f_2 map the actions $f_1(a_1)$ and a_3 into actions having the same values for ω_1 and ω_2 and undefined for ω_3. Then, by (4),

(5) $\quad (f_1(a_1), a_3) \to (f_2 o f_1(a_1), f_2(a_3))$.

In the last decision problem, the first action has the values m and M for ω_1 and ω_2, respectively, while the second action has the values M and m for ω_1 and ω_2, respectively. By Lemma 2, $f_2 \, of_1(a_1) \, \tilde{o} \, f_2(a_3)$, and hence both must be optimal in $(f_2 \, o \, f_1(a_1), f_2(a_3))$. By Property C and (5), $f_1(a_1)$ and a_3 are both optimal in $(f_1(a_1), a_3)$ and hence $f_1(a_1) \, \tilde{o} \, a_3$. In conjunction with (3), it follows easily that all the elements of A are optimal, and therefore $f_1(a_1) \, \tilde{o} \, f_1(a_2)$, by Property A. From (2) and Property C, $a_1 \, \tilde{o} \, a_2$, which was to be proven.

The case where Ω_3, is null but Ω_4 is non-null follows by merely interchanging a_1 and a_2. The case where Ω_3 and Ω_4 are both null is trivial, since then $a_1 = a_2$.

Lemma 4.   For any given action a, let a' be an action with the same domain, where $a'(\omega_0) = \min_\omega a(\omega)$, $a'(\omega) = \max_\omega a(\omega)$ for $\omega \neq \omega_0$. Then $a \, \tilde{o} \, a'$.

Proof.   Let ω_1 be any state of nature for which a attains its minimum, ω_2 a state of nature for which a attains its maximum. Define a_1 as follows:

$$a_1(\omega_2) = \max_\omega a(\omega) = M(\text{say}), \qquad a_1(\omega) = \min_\omega a(\omega) = m$$

(say) for $\omega \neq \omega_2$. Define a_2 as follows:

$$a_2(\omega_1) = m, \qquad a_2(\omega) = M \qquad \text{for } \omega \neq \omega_1.$$

Let A be the decision problem with the four elements a, a', a_1, a_2. Suppose a is not optimal in A; since $a_1(\omega) \leq a(\omega)$ for all ω, a_1 is not optimal by Property D (2). But $a_2 \, \tilde{o} \, a_1$ by Lemma 3, and therefore $a_2 \, \tilde{o} \, a_1 \, [A]$ by Lemma 1, so that a_2 is not optimal in A. By the same argument, a' is not optimal in A, so that $\hat{A}$ is null, which is impossible. Therefore, a is optimal in A. Since $a_2(\omega) \geq a(\omega)$ for all ω, a_2 is optimal by Property D (1). Since $a' \, \tilde{o} \, a_2 \, [A]$, a' is optimal in A. By Property A, the optimal set for (a, a') consists of both those elements, so that $a \, \tilde{o} \, a'$.

6. Characterization of the optimality criterion

Theorem.   Under Assumptions 1–3, a necessary and sufficient condition that an optimality criterion possess Properties A–D is that there exist a weak ordering $\geq$ in the space of ordered pairs of real numbers (m, M) with $m \leq M$ possessing the following properties: (1) if $m_1 \geq M_2, M_1 \geq m_2$, then $(m_1, M_1) \geq (m_2, M_2)$; (2) for any $A \in \hat{P}$, $\hat{A} = \{a \mid (\min_\omega a(\omega), \max_\omega a(\omega)) \geq (\min_\omega a'(\omega), \max_\omega a'(\omega))$ for all $a \in A$.

Proof.   To prove necessity, we assume the existence of an optimality criterion satisfying Properties A–D. We first define the ordering over the half-space of ordered pairs of real numbers (m, M). Let ω' and ω'' be any two given states of nature; let $b(m, M)$ be the action defined by $b(m, M)(\omega') = m$, $b(m, M)(\omega'') = M$. (The function $b(m, M)$ maps each ordered pair into an action defined for two states of nature.) We will say

$$(m_1, M_1) \geq (m_2, M_2) \qquad \text{if and only if } b(m_1, M_1)(\geq)b(m_2, M_2).$$

It should be noted that varying ω' and ω'' changes the decision problem $(b(m_1, M_1), b(m_2, M_2))$ into another decision problem isomorphic to the first. The relation $\geqq$ is therefore, by Property B, independent of the choice of ω', ω''.

It must first be shown that the relation $\geqq$ is in fact an ordering. Suppose $(m_1, M_1) \geqq (m_2, M_2)$ and $(m_2, M_2) \geqq (m_3, M_3)$. Let A be the decision problem with elements $b(m_1, M_1)$, $b(m_2, M_2)$, $b(m_3, M_3)$. There is at least one optimal action. Suppose $b(m_3, M_3)$ is the only optimal action; then $b(m_3, M_3)(>)b(m_2, M_2)[A]$. By Lemma 1, $b(m_3, M_3)(>)b(m_2, M_2)$, which contradicts the hypothesis that $(m_2, M_2) \geqq (m_3, M_3)$. Suppose now that $b(m_2, M_2) \in \hat{A}$ but not $b(m_1, M_1)$. This also leads to a contradiction since $(m_1, M_1) \geqq (m_2, M_2)$. Hence, we must conclude that $b(m_1, M_1) \in \hat{A}$, so that $b(m_1, M_1)(\geqq)b(m_3, M_3)$ $[A]$, and therefore $b(m_1, M_1)(\geqq)b(m_3, M_3)$, or, by definition, $(m_1, M_1) \geqq (m_3, M_3)$.

The relation $\geqq$ is therefore transitive. Since any decision problem $(b(m_1, M_1), b(m_2, M_2))$ has at least one optimal element, either $(m_1, M_1) \geqq (m_2, M_2)$ or $(m_2, M_2) \geqq (m_1, M_1)$, so that the relation $\geqq$ is a weak ordering.

Suppose now $m_1 \geqq m_2, M_1 \geqq M_2$. If $(m_2, M_2) > (m_1, M_1)$, then $b(m_2, M_2)$ is the only optimal action in $(b(m_1, M_1), b(m_2, M_2))$. But $b(m_1, M_1)(\omega) \geqq b(m_2, M_2)(\omega)$ for both values of ω, so that $b(m_1, M_1)$ is also optimal, a contradiction. Hence, $(m_1, M_1) \geqq (m_2, M_2)$, which is conclusion (1) of the necessity part of the theorem.

Suppose $a \in \hat{A}$. Then $a(\geqq)a'[A]$ for all $a' \in A$, and therefore $a(\geqq)a'$ for all $a' \in A$. For some fixed ω', define

$$a_1(\omega') = \min_\omega a(\omega), \qquad a_1(\omega) = \max_\omega a(\omega) \qquad \text{for } \omega \neq \omega';$$

$$a_2(\omega') = \min_\omega a'(\omega), \qquad a_2(\omega) = \max_\omega a'(\omega) \qquad \text{for } \omega \neq \omega'.$$

By Lemma 4,

(1) $a_1 \tilde{o} a, \qquad a_2 \tilde{o} a'$.

Let A_1 be the decision problem with elements a, a', a_1, a_2. If a is not optimal in A_1, then neither is a_1 by (1). Hence, either a_2 or a' is optimal in A_1, and therefore both are by (1). Since $a'(>)a [A_1]$, $a'(>)a$, which is impossible since $a(\geqq)a'$. Hence $a \in \hat{A}_1$; by (1) $a_1 \in \hat{A}_1$, so that $a_1(\geqq)a_2 [A_1]$ and $a_1(\geqq)a_2$.

Let ω'' be any element of Ω other than ω'. For $\omega \neq \omega', \omega'', a_i(\omega) = a_i(\omega'')$ $(i = 1, 2)$. Let $f(a_i)$ coincide with a_i for $\omega = \omega', \omega''$ and be undefined elsewhere. Then

$$(a_1, a_2) \rightarrow (f(a_1), f(a_2)).$$

By Property C, $f(a_1)(\geqq)f(a_2)$. But $f(a_1) = b(\min_\omega a(\omega), \max_\omega a(\omega))$, $f(a_2) = b(\min_\omega a'(\omega), \max_\omega a'(\omega))$. Therefore, if $a \in \hat{A}$,

(2) $(\min_\omega a(\omega), \max_\omega a(\omega)) \geqq (\min_\omega a'(\omega), \max_\omega a'(\omega))$ $\qquad$ for all $a' \in A$.

Suppose now that $a \in A - \hat{A}$. Let a' be any element of $\hat{A}$, so that $a'(>)a$. By a repetition of the preceding argument, with the symbols $(\geqq)$ and $\geqq$ replaced by $(>)$ and $>$, respectively, and a and a' interchanged, it can be concluded that if $a \in A - \hat{A}$,

(3) $(\min_\omega a'(\omega), \max_\omega a'(\omega)) > (\min_\omega a(\omega), \max_\omega a(\omega))$

for some $a' \in A$.

Equations (2) and (3) together are equivalent to part (2) of the conclusion of the necessity part of the theorem. The sufficiency part of the theorem is very easily verified.

Remark.   The dominance property D is very weak; it is not excluded, for example, that one action may strictly dominate another, $a(\omega) > a'(\omega)$ for all ω, and yet a' may be optimal; it is only required that a must also be optimal in that case. There would be no difficulty in introducing an additional condition that an action strictly dominated by another not be optimal; in that case property (1) of the Theorem would be supplemented by the condition that if $m_1 > m_2, M_1 > M_2$, then $(m_1, M_1) > (m_2, M_2)$, where $>$ is the strict preference relation generated by the weak ordering $\geq$. It would not, however, be possible to require that an action semi-strictly dominated by another (i.e., an action a' for which there exists a such that $a(\omega) \geq a'(\omega)$ for all ω, $a(\omega) > a'(\omega)$ for at least one value of ω is not optimal. For clearly one action might semi-strictly dominate another and yet both have the same maximum and minimum payoffs.

Notes

1   The basic result of this paper was established by Hurwicz and circulated in a hectographed form, "Optimality Criteria for Decision-Making Under Ignorance," Cowles Commission Discussion Paper: Statistics, No. 370, 11 December 1951. The proof was considerably simplified by Arrow and circulated in mimeographed form, "Hurwicz's Optimality Criterion for Decision-Making Under Ignorance," Technical Report No. 6, Office of Naval Research Contract N6onr-25133 (NR-047-004), Stanford University, 1 February 1953, on which the text of the present paper is largely based. Neither report has been published previously.

2   It has been noted elsewhere that the statistical decision theory of Neyman and Pearson and especially the minimax theory of Wald can be interpreted as special cases of Shackle's theory; see Arrow [1; sections 3.2.4, 4.2.4.]

3   Hurwicz's original manuscript (see note 1) drew upon a series of hectographed reports. See H. Chernoff, "Remarks on a Rational Selection of a Decision Function," Cowles Commission Discussion Papers: Statistics, Nos. 326, 326A, 346, and 346A, January 1949, and April 1950.

4   Milnor drew upon an earlier unpublished paper by Hurwicz, among others.

5   This is closely related to the concept of revealed preference introduced in consumers' demand theory by Samuelson [6; pp. 151-2.]

6   The symbol $h_1 \ o \ h_2$ denotes the *composition* of the functions h_1 and h_2, i.e., h_1 is a function whose domain includes the range of h_2, and, if x is any value in the domain of h_2, the function $h_1 \ o \ h_2$ is also defined for x and

takes on the value $h_1[h_2(x)]$. Thus, in this case if the function f maps the action a into the action a', and the function g maps the state of nature ω into the state of nature ω', then $a'(\omega') = a(\omega)$, for all actions a and states of nature ω.

7 Property A is closely related to several of Chernoff's [2] requirements, postulates 4, 5, and 6, though stronger than these even taken together.

8 Property B is Chernoff's [2] postulate 3.

9 Property C is Chernoff's [2] postulate 9.

References

[1] K. J. Arrow, Alternative approaches to the theory of choice in risk-taking situations. *Econometrica* 19 (1951): 404–437. Reprinted in K. J. Arrow, *Essays in the Theory of Risk-Bearing.* Chicago: Markham, 1971, chapter 1.

[2] H. Chernoff, Rational selection of decision functions. *Econometrica* 22 (1954): 422–443.

[3] B. de Finetti, La prévision: ses lois logiques, ses sources subjectives. *Annales de l'Institut Henri Poincaré* (1937): 71–68. Translated by H. E. Kyburg in H. E. Kyburg, Jr., and H. E. Smookler (eds.), *Studies in Subjective Probability.* New York: Wiley, 1964, pp. 95–158.

[4] J. Milnor, Games against nature. In R. M. Thrall, C. H. Coombs, and R. L. Davis (eds.), *Decision Processes.* New York and London: Wiley and Chapman & Hall, 1954, chapter IV.

[5] F. P. Ramsey, Truth and probability. In F. P. Ramsey, *The Foundations of Mathematics and Other Logical Essays.* London: K. Paul, Trench, Trubner, and Company, 1931, pp. 156–198.

[6] P. A. Samuelson, *Foundations of Economic Analysis.* Cambridge, Mass.: Harvard University Press, 1947.

[7] L. J. Savage, *The Foundations of Statistics.* New York: Wiley, 1954.

[8] G. L. S. Shackle, *Expectation in Economics.* Cambridge, U.K.: Cambridge University Press, 1949.

Indexes

AUTHOR INDEX

Numerals in italics indicate citation of work.

SUBJECT INDEX

Numerals in italics indicate (formal or informal) definitions. Brackets indicate locations where the notion, but not necessarily the exact term, is mentioned.

acceptable (vector), 159
activity analysis, 6
adjustment function, 333
adjustment process, 8, *21*, 394, 395, 428: abstract, *396;* aggregative, *401;* anonymous, *411;* concrete, *398-9;* decisive, *397;* essentially single-valued, 23, *397*, 431; external (privacy preserving), *398*, 455; impersonal, *401;* informationally decentralized, *401;* instantaneous, 201; lagged, 201, 209; in the market, 356; non-wasteful, *22*, *397*, 430; Pareto-satisfactory, *23*, *397*, 425, 430, 435-6; privacy-preserving, (privacy-satisfying) 413, 414, 423, 424, *435*, 455; proposed action, 413, *435*, 436, 455; satisfactory, *see* adjustment process, Pareto-satisfactory; self-relevant, *399*, 413, 424, 455, 456; unbiased, *22*, *397*, 430, 456
adjustment speed, 50, 332, *333; see also* reaction speed
agents, economic, 19, [395]
anonymity, *see* adjustment process, anonymous
approximations, successive, 41, 58, 139
a priori class (environments): admissible, 427; plausible, 445
a priori information, 463
Arrow-Hurwicz gradient process, 13
asymptotic average production possibility set, *185*
atomistic (economy, environment), 393, *446*, 456
auctioneer, 21
authority (delegation), 29
autonomy, 29
auxiliary, *see* parameters

(*C'*), *256*
Cantor: function, 422; mapping, 420; procedure, 420
capitalism, 5, 43, 380, 425
capitalist, *see* capitalism
characteristic (individual, unit), [24], *395*
cheating, 28, 31; plausible, 446
classicist, 380
coefficient: insensitivity of prices, 313; of expectations (Metzler), 313; price reaction, 313
command (mechanism, system), 10, 21
commodities: desired, 46; primary (factor), 44, 46; produced, 44; *see also* goods

communication process: costs, 137; limited, 428, 454
competition: imperfect, 82, 140; perfect, 28, 30, [42]
competitive solution, socialist, 410, 432
competitiveness (of the economy), 387
complementarity, 184, 215, 221; gross 330, *331*
composite commodity (Hicks), 323
computation, [7], 8, 41, 42, 178-9
concentration ratio, 387
connected: family, *340;* set, *339*
constraint: locally convex, 104; transformed, 61
constraint qualification, *96-100*, 113, 120, 154, 159; *see also* Kuhn-Tucker, Slater
consumption function, 324
contained path, *97*, *120*
corners, 33, 230, 261-2, 263
cost, 69, 307, 309: marginal (pricing), 5, 11, 45, 64, 80-2, 94, 410; minimization, 45, 81
Cournot: duopoly, 309; oligopoly theory, 297, 306, 309
critical point (of an optimization problem), *17*
cross-fertilization procedure, 416
cusp, 121, 176
custodian, *see* resource custodian
cycling, 63, [74], 92

decentralization, viii, 23, 41, 42, 69, 72, 88, 94, 134, 136, 142
decentralization, informational, 12, 13, *24*, 393, *401*, 413, 426, 428, 435
decision problem, 464
decomposition (Dantzig-Wolfe) method, 9
deletion, *see* repetitious states
demand elasticity, *308*
demand function, excess: aggregate, 202; individual, 202
design (of resource allocation mechanisms), 3
desired commodities, 46
diagonal, dominant, 229, *249;* weighted, *349*
dimensional requirements, 413, 414, [415], 417, [418], [438]
direction: attainable, 97; locally constrained, 98; weakly attainable, 98
discrete (time parameter), 12

INDEX OF EXAMPLES